ALPHA - ANYBODY CAN CODE

OPTIMUM

PYTHON POWER

SERIES IV

UNLEASHING THE POTENTIAL OF DATA SCIENCE

WITH MACHINE LEARNING TECHNIQUES

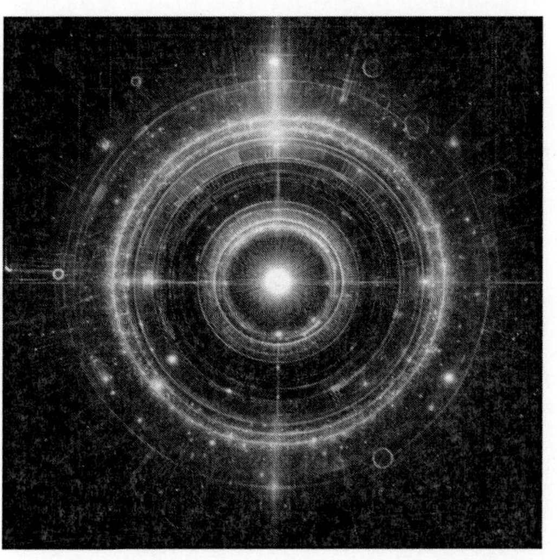

Unlocking the Power of Data Science:

Mastering Models, Algorithms, and Core Intuition!

SHREE SHAMBAV

OPTIMUM – PYTHON POWER – Series IV

UNLEASHING THE POTENTIAL OF DATA SCIENCE

WITH MACHINE LEARNING TECHNIQUES

Shree Shambav

Published by Shree Shambav, Tamil Nadu, India
Shree Shambav Ink & Imagination "Where Words Breathe and Imagination Soars"

First Edition, 2025

ISBN: 978-93-343-0069-7

Email:shreeshambav@gmail.com

Web:www.shambav.org

DEDICATION

"Isavasyam idam sarvam yat kim ca jagatyam jagat, tena tyaktena bhunjitha, ma gridhah kasyasvid dhanam"

To the Almighty,

the Divine Masters,

the family who listens,

and my parents who see –

your presence shapes the pages of my life's journey.

"Isavasyam idam sarvam yat kim ca jagatyam jagat"

Meaning: "God encompasses everything you perceive, see, or touch with your sense organs."

DISCLAIMER

The content presented in this book is intended for educational and informational purposes only. While every effort has been made to ensure the accuracy and relevance of the material, the author and publisher make no warranties, express or implied, about the completeness, reliability, or effectiveness of the methods, examples, or code provided.

This book is best suited for readers who have a foundational understanding of Python and basic programming concepts. Familiarity with data analysis, statistics, and introductory machine learning will enhance the reader's experience and comprehension.

The techniques and frameworks discussed are meant to serve as guidance and inspiration for data science and machine learning projects. However, individual results may vary based on the implementation context, tools used, and evolving technologies.

The author and publisher are not liable for any damages or losses, whether direct or indirect, that may result from the application of the content in this book. All trademarks, service marks, product names, or brand names mentioned are the property of their respective owners and are used for identification purposes only. This publication is independent and not affiliated with or endorsed by any of the referenced entities or platforms.

Readers are encouraged to consult official documentation, continue learning through reliable sources, and adapt solutions responsibly to suit their specific use cases.

Note - If any part of the book, in any sequence, hurts the reader's sentiments, it would be just out of a sheer accident, not intentional

EPIGRAM

"Data science is the voyage of exploration into the uncharted realms of information, where libraries serve as the compass, steering us through the complexities of data landscapes. More than mere tools, they are the architects of understanding, shaping narratives from the cacophony of data, and revealing the latent potential that lies within the algorithms, beckoning us to unlock the secrets of our digital universe."

– Shree Shambav

Suggested Reads

FROM BEST-SELLING AUTHOR

Endorsements

Optimum - Python Power Series IV is a must-read for anyone serious about learning data science with Python. This book's detailed roadmap and practical examples make it an invaluable resource for both new and experienced professionals. "A must-have in your data science library!

This book is a game changer!" The comprehensive explanations and hands-on activities improved my understanding and implementation of data science techniques. "'Optimum - Python Power Series IV' has become my go-to guide for dealing with complex data challenges.

As an educator, I strongly recommend 'Optimum - Python Power Series IV' to my pupils. It bridges the gap between theory and practice, offering a solid foundation in data science while also delving into advanced issues. The step-by-step instructions and real-world examples make learning more interesting and effective.

In a world dominated by data, 'Optimum - Python Power Series IV' stands out as a beacon of knowledge and competence. This book teaches readers how to use Python to its full potential in data science projects, making it an essential tool for driving innovation and success in any business.

About the Author

Shree Shambhav's remarkable journey spans the roles of author, speaker, artist, philanthropist, life coach, and entrepreneur. A world record holder, his deep passion for music led him to create soul-stirring albums, drawing inspiration from his celebrated poetry collection, Whispers of Eternity. With a rare blend of grace, wisdom, and purpose, he has touched countless lives, guiding individuals toward self-discovery, transformation, and excellence through his profound teachings, insightful counselling, and impactful literary contributions.

☐ LITERARY EXCELLENCE

Shree Shambav is a 33x best-selling author celebrated for his groundbreaking works across multiple genres, including Non-Fiction, Self-Help, Technology, Short Stories, Anthologies, and Poetry. His thought-provoking articles have also graced the pages of prominent magazines, solidifying his influence as a literary force.

His journey as an author took flight with the acclaimed "Journey of Soul – Karma", a masterpiece that explores the profound interplay of human experience, karma, and spiritual evolution. This seminal work earned him recognition and accolades in the literary world, marking the beginning of a legacy that continues to inspire.

☐ TECHNOLOGY AND INNOVATION

Shree Shambav's contributions extend beyond the realm of literature. A graduate of the prestigious Indian Institute of Management (IIM) and the National Institute of Technology

(NIT), he combines academic brilliance with real-world expertise. Throughout his illustrious career, he has held leadership positions in renowned multinational corporations, excelling in strategy, performance improvement, change management, and human capital development.

His technical acumen shines through his acclaimed "Optimum – Python Power Series", a comprehensive collection of books that serve as an invaluable resource for aspiring and seasoned technologists.

- Optimum - Python Series I: Ultimate Guide for Beginners laid the foundation for mastering Python.
- Optimum - Python Series II: Exploring Data Structures and Algorithms elevated readers' understanding of coding efficiency and problem-solving.
- Optimum – Python Power Series III: Unleashing the Potential of Data Science with Libraries stands as a crowning achievement, delving deep into essential libraries for data science and equipping readers with tools to thrive in this ever-evolving domain.

His latest endeavour, "OPTIMUM - Python Power Series IV" aims to be a comprehensive, practical, and up-to-date resource, empowering readers to harness the full potential of Python libraries in their data science endeavours. Unlock the Power of Data Science: Master Models, Algorithms, and Core Intuition. Shree Shambav's writing is enriched by his extensive consulting background and a profound comprehension of diverse industries, providing readers with invaluable insights and practical knowledge.

Each book is a testament to Shree Shambav's deep understanding of technology and his ability to make complex concepts accessible, actionable, and transformative.

☐ DRIVING INNOVATION ACROSS INDUSTRIES

Beyond his literary works, Shree Shambav's professional expertise has left an indelible mark across diverse industries, including banking, insurance, retail, and hospitality. He has architected and developed systems that are not only robust and resilient but also revolutionary:

Forecasting Engines and Predictive Models: For pricing, customer churn prediction, and risk portfolio management.

Data-Driven Systems: Web-based architectures, rule engines, ETL frameworks, and BI systems that streamline data flow, enhance accessibility, and support strategic decision-making.

Analytical Dashboards: Insightful tools that deliver powerful visualizations, enabling businesses to navigate challenges and optimize performance.

His work also extends to creating structured practice intellectual properties (IPs), KPI frameworks, and maturity models, empowering organizations to achieve sustainable growth and innovation.

☐ A PHILANTHROPIC SPIRIT AND ADVOCATE FOR CHANGE

Shree Shambav's vision transcends personal success. As a philanthropist and life coach, he remains deeply committed to societal well-being, working to uplift individuals and communities. Through the Ayur Rakshita Foundation (www.shambav-ayurrakshita.org), he leads initiatives that promote health, education, and holistic living, reflecting his belief in creating a harmonious and purposeful world.

☐ A LIFE DEDICATED TO LEARNING AND TRANSFORMATION

Shree Shambav's journey is a testament to his unwavering pursuit of knowledge, innovation, and service. Whether through his books, technical expertise, or philanthropic efforts, he continues to empower others to unlock their potential and live with greater meaning.

During his leisure time, he remains devoted to innovation, channelling his expertise into developing prediction models and exploring emerging fields—an embodiment of lifelong learning and curiosity.

☐ CONNECT WITH SHREE SHAMBAV

Shree Shambav extends his heartfelt gratitude to all those who have shown interest in his works. To explore his books, teachings, and initiatives:

Website: www.shambav.org

Foundation: www.shambav-ayurrakshita.org

Follow Him on Social Media: @shreeshambav

Technical Support and Reviewer

Apeksha Prabhu is a talented technology graduate who specialises in Computer Science and Technology. She has gained extensive experience in the field through her work as a full-stack developer and currently holds a position at Nokia.

Apeksha has completed many outstanding projects during her academic and professional careers. Her outstanding academic achievements match her outstanding practical experience. She has published research papers in prestigious technical journals such as IJERT and IJSCE. Her contributions to different publications show a deep understanding of complex technical concepts, meticulous attention to detail, and a dedication to the advancement of open-source Python.

Apeksha's work is filled with passion and an unwavering dedication to pushing the boundaries of what is possible in her field. She constantly strives to innovate and expand her knowledge, ensuring her work is always at the cutting edge of technological advancement.

Author's Note

As someone deeply passionate about the convergence of logic and creativity, I believe Python is more than just a programming language—it's a bridge between data and discovery. In this book, I've distilled years of exploration, experimentation, and learning into a structured guide that aims to make the vast world of machine learning accessible, practical, and empowering.

My hope is that this book not only teaches you how to code smarter but also inspires you to think deeper—to ask the why behind every algorithm, to see the elegance in models, and to explore solutions that create real-world impact.

Thank you for allowing me to be a part of your learning journey. May your pursuit of knowledge be as fulfilling as the insights you uncover.

With curiosity and conviction,

Shree Shambav

PREFACE

Welcome to "Optimum - Python Power Series IV: Unleashing the Potential of Data Science with Machine Learning Techniques." This book is the culmination of our dedication to providing a comprehensive and practical guide for anyone eager to delve into the world of data science. Whether you are a beginner, taking your first steps into this exciting field, or an experienced practitioner looking to enhance your skills, this book is designed to be your trusted companion on your data science journey.

Data science has revolutionised the way we understand and interact with data. From predicting trends and making informed decisions to uncovering hidden patterns and insights, data science has become an indispensable tool in various industries. Python, with its vast array of libraries and tools, has emerged as a powerful language for data scientists, enabling them to tackle complex data challenges with ease and efficiency.

In this book, we have meticulously curated a comprehensive roadmap that will guide you through the intricacies of approaching data science projects. We believe that Python is not just a programming language but a gateway to a multitude of tools and resources that empower you to address real-world challenges effectively. Our aim is to provide you with a profound understanding of how to approach data science projects, from handling data and performing complex computations to visualising trends, implementing machine learning algorithms, and extracting valuable insights.

Each chapter of this book is thoughtfully crafted to provide clear explanations, practical examples, and hands-on exercises. We have included a wide range of topics, from the fundamentals of data science and the Python Standard Library to advanced machine learning techniques and real-world case studies. Our goal is to ensure that you grasp the concepts thoroughly and can apply them confidently to real-world scenarios.

Throughout this journey, we will emphasize not only the technical aspects of data science but also the core intuition behind the models and algorithms. By the time you reach the end of this book, you will have the skills and knowledge required to tackle data science projects with confidence and creativity.

We invite you to embark on this exhilarating journey with us. Let "Optimum - Python Power Series IV" be your guide as you unlock the immense power and potential of Python in the field of data science. Open your mind to the endless possibilities, and get ready to transform into a proficient data scientist equipped to excel in this ever-evolving field.

Happy coding and exploring!

Sincerely,

Shree Shambav

INTRODUCTION

OPTIMUM Python Power Series IV: Unleashing the Potential of Data Science with Machine Learning Techniques

Unlocking the Power of Data Science: Mastering Models, Algorithms, and Core Intuition!

Welcome to the "OPTIMUM Python Power Series IV," where we embark on an exciting exploration of the vast potential of data science through the mastery of models, algorithms, and core intuition. In this book, we will delve into the world of data science, uncovering the remarkable capabilities that enable us to analyse, visualise, and derive insights from data.

Python has revolutionised the landscape of data science, providing an extensive array of tools and functionalities that streamline intricate tasks and empower data scientists to address real-world challenges. From data manipulation and preprocessing to statistical analysis, machine learning, and data visualisation, Python offers the building blocks that form the foundation of modern data science workflows.

"OPTIMUM Python Power Series IV" serves as your comprehensive guidebook to mastering machine learning and harnessing its full potential. Get ready to embark on an exhilarating journey as we delve into the world of data science, mastering models, algorithms, and core intuition. This book is your ultimate guide to unlocking the immense power and potential of Python in the field of data science.

Comprehensive Roadmap

In this book, we have meticulously curated a comprehensive roadmap that will take you through the intricacies of approaching data science projects using various models. We believe that Python is not just a programming language but a gateway to a multitude of tools and resources that empower you to tackle complex data challenges with ease and efficiency.

With "OPTIMUM Python Power Series IV" as your trusted companion, you will navigate through the vast landscape of data science. By the time you reach the end of this journey, you will possess a profound understanding of how to approach data science projects. You will gain the skills and knowledge required to efficiently handle data, perform complex computations, visualize trends and patterns, implement machine learning algorithms, and extract valuable insights from various data sources.

Journey Overview

We will begin our journey by understanding the fundamentals of data science and exploring the Python Standard Library, which provides a solid starting point for your data-driven projects. Throughout this book, we will provide clear explanations, practical examples, and hands-on exercises to reinforce your comprehension of each library. Our goal is not only to teach you how to use these libraries effectively but also to nurture your ability to think critically and solve real-world data challenges.

Target Audience

Whether you are a beginner, taking your first steps into the world of data science or an experienced practitioner looking to expand your toolkit, "OPTIMUM Python Power Series IV" aims to be a comprehensive, practical, and up-to-date resource, empowering readers to harness the full potential of Python libraries, models, and algorithms in their data science endeavours.

Why This Book?

Targeted Audience and Focus: Beginners, intermediate developers, and domain-specific professionals will find this book useful. It focuses on specific libraries or library combinations, offering in-depth coverage and practical examples for those specific areas of interest.

Pedagogical Approach: This book creates a classroom-like environment with effective learning strategies, step-by-step tutorials, practical exercises, and real-world examples to ensure that readers understand and can apply the concepts.

Book Coverage

Let's take a closer look at what this book covers:

- Fundamentals of Data Science and Python Standard Library
- Data manipulation and preprocessing techniques
- Statistical analysis and visualization methods
- Machine learning algorithms and their applications
- Advanced topics and real-world case studies

PART ONE: In this part, we have covered the fundamental concepts of machine learning, providing a comprehensive overview of its various aspects. We began by exploring the three main types: supervised, unsupervised, and reinforcement learning. Essential terminologies like features, labels, training data, testing data, and model evaluation metrics were introduced. Core categories and tasks, including classification, regression, clustering, dimensionality reduction, and association rule mining, were discussed along with a range of algorithms from traditional to advanced techniques. We examined the stages of the machine learning pipeline, including data collection, feature identification, exploratory data analysis, feature engineering, model training, and evaluation. Finally, we covered deploying models for predictions, offering insights and driving decision-making processes.

PART TWO: Machine Learning Basics - In this unit, we covered essential mathematics for data science. We started with linear algebra, focusing on matrices, matrix operations, and vectors. We discussed data dispersion, covering measures of central tendency and dispersion. Basic calculus, including integration and differentiation, was explored for its applications in data science. Probability theory was thoroughly examined, including marginal, conditional, and joint probabilities, along with Bayes' theorem and hypothesis testing. We introduced time series analysis and various probability distributions like exponential, binomial, Poisson, and normal distributions. Feature reduction techniques such as Recursive Feature Elimination were discussed. Loss functions, particularly binary cross-entropy, were explained. Sampling techniques, both probability and non-probability, were covered. Lastly, we delved into statistical regression, including linear regression, R-squared, and cross-validation, emphasizing model evaluation and the importance of addressing overfitting and underfitting.

PART THREE: This section provides a comprehensive overview of various aspects of data processing, starting with an introduction to data types, properties, and common issues encountered. It covers the creation of test datasets for classification and regression tasks, emphasising data quality and balance. A unit focuses on data cleaning, discussing techniques such as imputing missing values, handling categorical data, outliers, and data formatting, along with encoding methods like one-hot encoding and addressing the dummy variable trap.

Exploratory Data Analysis (EDA) is thoroughly explored, including univariate, bivariate, and multivariate analysis techniques to uncover patterns and relationships within the data, with practical examples illustrating the application of these techniques. Feature scaling and engineering are discussed in detail, covering normalization, standardization, encoding, and handling categorical variables, emphasising the importance of preprocessing features for machine learning tasks.

Finally, the section delves into handling imbalanced datasets, discussing resampling techniques like random under-sampling, over-sampling, and more advanced methods like SMOTE and NearMiss. It also highlights the importance of choosing appropriate performance metrics for evaluating models trained on imbalanced data, with practical examples demonstrating the application of these techniques in real-world scenarios. This provides learners with a comprehensive understanding of effective strategies for handling imbalanced datasets and evaluating model performance.

PART FOUR: In this comprehensive section, we covered a range of supervised and unsupervised learning techniques, including linear regression, logistic regression, and the fundamentals of clustering. We delved into various methods like Ordinary Least Squares (OLS), multiple linear regression, and advanced approaches such as Bayesian regression and regularization. Our exploration extended to essential concepts like loss functions and gradient descent, pivotal for optimizing regression models and enhancing their accuracy. Moreover, we delved into logistic regression, addressing sigmoid functions, different types, and activation functions like sigmoid, ReLU, and softmax. We also compared multiclass and multilabel classification, along with strategies like One-vs-All and One-vs-One. Additionally, we examined evaluation metrics like confusion matrices, accuracy, precision, recall, and F1 score, as well as advanced techniques such as the AUC-ROC curve and precision-recall curve, indispensable for evaluating model performance and facilitating data-driven decisions.

PART FIVE: This section of the book delved into four major machine learning techniques: K-Nearest Neighbors (KNN), Support Vector Machines (SVM), Decision Trees, and Naive Bayes. KNN was explained for its reliance on distance metrics and intuitive "nearest neighbor" approach, establishing a foundation for classification and regression tasks. SVM's adaptability in addressing diverse problems via various kernels and decision boundaries was emphasised, offering a thorough grasp of its capabilities. Decision trees were examined for their construction, optimal split determination, and methods to alleviate overfitting, underscoring the significance of cross-validation techniques. Naive Bayes' straightforwardness and effectiveness in classification tasks, grounded in Bayes' theorem, were elaborated upon alongside its tailored variants for different data types, providing insights into probabilistic approaches in machine learning.

PART SIX: In this unit, we explored various unsupervised learning techniques, focusing on clustering algorithms and dimensionality reduction methods. We began with clustering, covering algorithms like K-Means, the elbow method for determining the optimal number of clusters, and Mini-batch K-Means for large datasets. We also delved into hierarchical clustering, discussing types like Hierarchical Agglomerative Clustering and BIRCH. Dimensionality reduction techniques were another key focus, including Principal Component Analysis (PCA), its variants, and Singular Value Decomposition (SVD). We explored advanced methods, such as Incremental PCA and Randomized Singular Value Decomposition. Additionally, we examined t-SNE for visualization, DBSCAN for density-based clustering, and evaluation metrics like the Silhouette Score and Adjusted Rand Index (ARI), as well as advanced clustering methods like OPTICS, Spectral Clustering, Gaussian Mixture Models (GMM), and Mean-shift clustering.

PART SEVEN: In this unit, we explored essential data mining techniques, focusing on association rule learning and matrix factorization. We covered association rule learning, which identifies relationships and patterns within datasets using metrics like support, confidence, and lift. We detailed the Apriori algorithm, which finds frequent itemsets iteratively, and discussed various types of association rules. Also, compared association rule learning with clustering, highlighting their different focuses. The unit then covered the ECLAT algorithm as an alternative to Apriori, and addressed the limitations of Apriori by introducing the FP-Growth algorithm. Additionally, we provide an overview of matrix factorization techniques for uncovering latent features in data, and introduce recommender systems, explaining collaborative filtering, content-based filtering, and hybrid methods. Finally, we focused on using matrix factorization techniques as SVD and NMF in recommender systems to enhance recommendation accuracy.

PART EIGHT: In this unit, we covered ensemble methods and their various techniques and applications. We explored the differences between stacking, bagging, and boosting. Bagging, exemplified by models like Random Forest, reduces variance by combining predictions from multiple models trained on different data subsets. Boosting, including AdaBoost and Gradient Boosting, sequentially trains models to correct previous errors. We detailed Gradient Boosting, focusing on its optimization via the loss function, and examined XGBoost for its enhancements. Additionally, we discussed CatBoost for handling categorical features and LightGBM for its speed and efficiency. Lastly, we covered sampling techniques, evaluation metrics, and stacked generalization (stacking) for improved predictive accuracy.

In this book, we have meticulously curated a comprehensive roadmap to guide you through the intricacies of approaching data science projects. We believe that Python is not just a programming language but a gateway to a multitude of tools and resources that empower you to tackle complex data challenges with ease and efficiency.

With "Optimum - Python Power Series IV" as your trusted companion, you will navigate the vast landscape of data science, learning how to harness the full potential of libraries, models, and algorithms specifically designed for this purpose. By the end of this journey, you will possess a profound understanding of how to approach data science projects. You will gain the skills and knowledge required to efficiently handle data, perform complex computations, visualise trends and patterns, implement machine learning algorithms, and extract valuable insights from various data sources.

Whether you are a beginner looking to enter the exciting world of data science or an experienced practitioner seeking to enhance your skills, "Optimum - Python Power Series IV" offers something for everyone. Each chapter is thoughtfully crafted to provide clear explanations, practical examples, and hands-on exercises, ensuring that you grasp the concepts and can apply them to real-world scenarios.

So, fasten your seatbelts, open your mind to the endless possibilities of data science, and let "Optimum - Python Power Series IV" be your guide. Get ready to embark on an exciting journey that will transform you into a proficient data scientist equipped with the tools to excel in this ever-evolving field.

Happy coding and exploring!

☐ PROGRAMS

The table presents a detailed distribution of the programs included in this book, categorised by units within each part.

Part	Unit	Lessons covered	Program	Total Program
One	1	Getting started	1	**1**
Two	2	Basic Math and Statistics	12	**13**
Three	3	Data Processing	34	**34**
Four	4	Classification and Regression	25	**25**
Five	5	Machine Learning Models	10	**10**
Six	6	Clustering	18	**18**
Seven	7	Association	5	**5**
Eight	8	Ensemble	8	**8**
Appendix	A	Online Resources		
	B	Practice Question		**162**
	C	Assignments		**3**
	D	Quiz		**130**
	E	Projects		**2**
		Total Programs		**114**

☐ PRACTICE QUESTIONS

The table provides a comprehensive breakdown of the practice questions featured in this book, sorted by units within each part.

Part	Practice Question	Total
One	20	**20**
Two	22	**22**
Three	25	**25**
Four	20	**20**
Five	30	**30**
Six	15	**15**
Seven	15	**15**
Eight	15	**15**
Total Questions	**162**	**162**

☐ ASSIGNMENT AND QUIZ

The table provides a comprehensive breakdown of the assignment featured in this book, sorted by units within each part.

Part	Unit	Assignment	Quiz
1	1		15
2	2		
3	3	1	25
4	4	1	20
5	5	1	25
6	6		15
7	7		15
8	8		15
Total		**3**	**130**

☐ TABLES AND ILLUSTRATIONS

Part	Tables	Illustration	Flowchart
Getting started	1	2	0
One	6	12	0
Two	3	28	0
Three	14	36	0
Four	1	29	0
Five	1	18	0
Six	0	44	0
Seven	3	5	0
Eight	2	29	0
Total	**31**	**203**	0

CONTENTS

Getting Started

Data Science is an interdisciplinary field that amalgamates a diverse array of techniques, tools, and methodologies to glean insights and knowledge from data. It encompasses the application of scientific methods, statistical analysis, data visualisation, and machine learning algorithms to unearth patterns, formulate predictions, and inform decision-making processes.

☐ Machine learning, AI and Data Science are related fields but have distinct differences

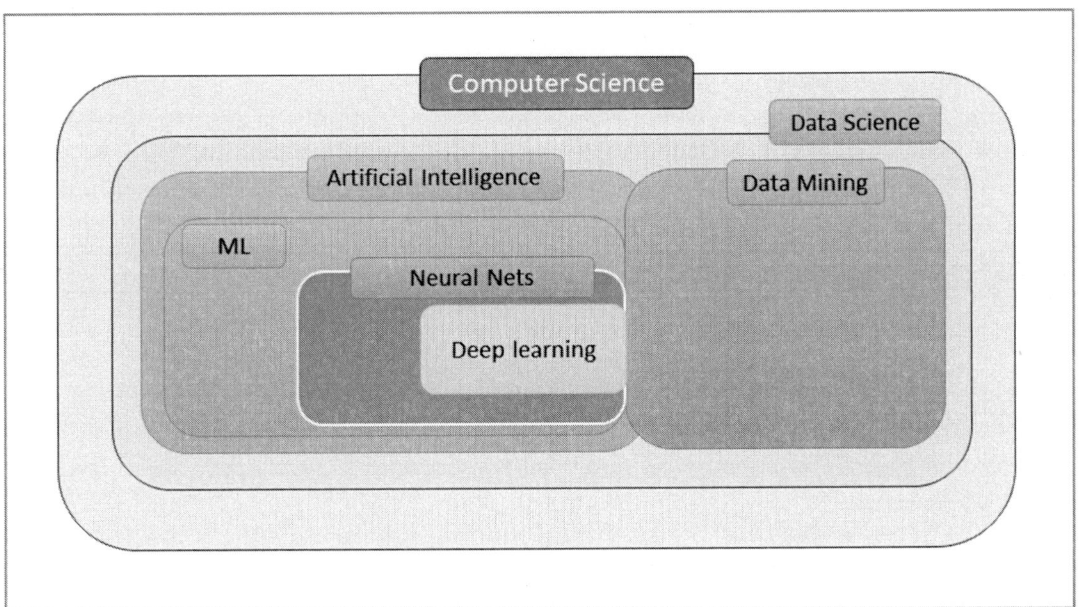

Data Science: Data science is a multifaceted discipline that harnesses scientific methodologies, algorithms, and systems to distil knowledge and insights from both structured and unstructured data. This interdisciplinary field employs an array of techniques, including data cleaning, exploration, visualisation, statistical analysis, and predictive modelling. Data scientists navigate large and intricate datasets to discern patterns, trends, and actionable insights, thereby aiding businesses in making informed decisions and addressing challenges. This expansive field encompasses a diverse array of tools and methodologies, spanning statistical analysis, data mining, machine learning, and data visualisation.

Artificial Intelligence (AI): Artificial Intelligence (AI) denotes the creation of intelligent systems capable of executing tasks typically associated with human intelligence. AI endeavours to replicate human cognitive functions, such as learning, reasoning, problem-solving, and decision-making. This expansive domain encompasses diverse subfields including natural language processing, computer vision, expert systems, and robotics. AI techniques span a spectrum from rule-based systems and symbolic reasoning to machine learning, deep learning, and neural networks.

Machine Learning: Machine learning constitutes a subset of artificial intelligence dedicated to crafting algorithms and models that empower computers to learn from data and autonomously make predictions or decisions devoid of explicit programming. This entails training a model on historical data and subsequently leveraging it to generate predictions or decisions concerning new data. Machine learning algorithms are segmented into supervised learning, unsupervised learning, and reinforcement learning contingent upon the presence of labelled training data and the learning objective. Widely employed across diverse domains, machine learning is instrumental in addressing intricate challenges and facilitating predictions in areas such as image and speech recognition, natural language processing, recommendation systems, and fraud detection.

In summary, data science represents a comprehensive domain encompassing diverse methodologies for extracting insights from data. Conversely, machine learning constitutes a subset of data science, concentrating primarily on crafting algorithms and models geared towards making predictions or decisions derived from data. While machine learning serves as a pivotal tool within data science, the latter encompasses a broader spectrum of skills and techniques extending beyond solely machine learning.

Data Science is a multidisciplinary field

Data Science is an interdisciplinary domain dedicated to extracting insights and knowledge from data through a multitude of techniques and tools. Within this realm, Machine Learning, Deep Learning, and Neural Networks stand as pivotal components. Here's a succinct overview of their respective roles:

Machine Learning: Machine Learning, a subset of Artificial Intelligence (AI), is dedicated to crafting algorithms and models that empower computers to learn from data and facilitate predictions or decisions. This entails training models on labelled or unlabelled data to discern patterns and relationships. Machine Learning algorithms find application across a vast array of tasks, including classification, regression, clustering, and recommendation systems. Crucially, it assumes a pivotal role in data analysis and predictive modelling within the realm of Data Science.

Deep Learning: Deep Learning, a subfield of Machine Learning, underscores the deployment of deep neural networks comprising multiple layers of interconnected artificial neurons. These networks have the capacity to learn hierarchical representations of data autonomously. The burgeoning popularity of Deep Learning stems from its triumphs in diverse tasks, including image and speech recognition, natural language processing, and autonomous driving. Its efficacy shines particularly bright when confronted with copious amounts of labelled data and intricate problem landscapes.

Neural Networks: Neural Networks serve as foundational elements within Deep Learning, drawing inspiration from the structural and functional dynamics of biological neural networks in the human brain. Comprising interconnected artificial neurons organised in layers, Neural Networks execute a sequence of operations. Each neuron receives input signals, undergoes activation through a specific function, and generates an output signal. The inter-neuron connections are characterised by weights, dictating the intensity of their relationships. Through iterative adjustment of these weights during the training phase, Neural Networks can discern intricate patterns and relationships inherent in the data.

In Data Science, Machine Learning serves as a powerful tool to analyse and make predictions from data, while Deep Learning and Neural Networks enable the creation of sophisticated models capable of learning complex patterns and representations. These techniques have revolutionised fields such as natural language processing, computer vision, and data-driven decision-making. Understanding and applying these concepts is essential for leveraging the full potential of Data Science in solving real-world problems.

☐ HERE ARE SOME KEY FEATURES OF DATA SCIENCE

Data Collection: Data Science starts with the collection of relevant data from an array of sources including databases, files, APIs, or through web scraping. This data may manifest in structured, semi-structured, or unstructured formats.

Data Cleaning and Preprocessing: Raw data often contains inconsistencies, missing values, outliers, and noise. To address these issues, data cleaning and preprocessing techniques are employed. These techniques serve to rectify discrepancies, fill in missing values, mitigate outliers, and filter out noise, thereby ensuring that the data is accurate, comprehensive, and primed for analysis.

Exploratory Data Analysis (EDA): EDA involves examining and understanding the data through summary statistics, data visualisation, and statistical techniques. It helps identify patterns, relationships, and trends in the data and guides the selection of appropriate modelling techniques.

Statistical Analysis: Data Science relies on statistical methods to quantify uncertainty, test hypotheses, and draw inferences from data. Descriptive statistics, hypothesis testing, inferential statistics, and regression analysis are commonly used to analyse and interpret data.

Feature Engineering: Feature engineering entails the strategic selection, transformation, and creation of new features derived from raw data to enhance the performance of machine learning models. This process demands domain expertise and ingenuity to extract pertinent information and encapsulate relevant patterns.

Model Evaluation and Validation: Data Science involves evaluating the performance of predictive models using appropriate evaluation metrics and validation techniques. Cross-validation, hold-out validation, and performance measures such as precision, accuracy, recall, and F1 score are used to assess model effectiveness.

Machine Learning: Machine Learning algorithms play a vital role in Data Science. These algorithms are trained on historical data to learn patterns and make predictions or classifications on new, unseen data. Supervised learning, unsupervised learning, and reinforcement learning are common types of machine learning techniques used in Data Science.

Data Visualization: Data visualization techniques are used to represent data visually, enabling easier comprehension and interpretation of complex patterns and relationships. Visualization tools and libraries help create charts, graphs, plots, and interactive dashboards to communicate insights effectively.

Deployment and Productionization: Data Science projects often involve deploying models into production environments, where they can generate real-time predictions or recommendations. This requires integrating models into applications, setting up infrastructure, and ensuring scalability, reliability, and security.

Continuous Learning and Improvement: Data Science is an iterative process that involves continuous learning, experimentation, and improvement. Data Scientists constantly refine their models, update their analyses, and adapt to changing data and business requirements.

By leveraging these features, Data Science enables organisations to make data-driven decisions, gain actionable insights, optimise processes, and drive innovation in various domains such as marketing, healthcare, finance, and more.

□ PROGRAMING LANGUAGES:

Various programming languages are utilised for AI and related tasks. Here are some examples:

Python: Known for its simplicity and vast ecosystem of libraries like TensorFlow, PyTorch, and scikit-learn, Python is one of the most popular languages for AI development.

R: Particularly prominent in statistical analysis and data visualisation, R is frequently used for tasks like exploratory data analysis and statistical modelling in AI applications.

Java: Although not as commonly associated with AI as Python or R, Java is still utilised for AI development, particularly in large-scale enterprise systems where performance and scalability are crucial.

Lisp: Lisp, particularly its dialects like Common Lisp and Clojure, has a rich history in AI research and development. It is known for its powerful meta-programming capabilities and is used in various AI applications.

SWI Prolog: Prolog is a logic programming language commonly used in fields like natural language processing and expert systems. SWI Prolog, in particular, is popular in medical projects and other domains where logical reasoning is essential.

Matlab: Widely used in engineering and scientific computing, Matlab provides extensive tools for numerical computing, simulation, and data analysis, making it suitable for certain AI tasks.

Julia: Julia is gaining popularity in scientific computing and AI due to its high performance and easy interoperability with other languages like Python and R. It is particularly well-suited for tasks involving numerical computation and optimisation.

These languages offer diverse capabilities and are chosen based on factors like the nature of the AI problem, existing infrastructure, performance requirements, and developer expertise.

☐ THE GROWTH OF AI UPTO 2023

1950: Alan Turing publishes "Computing Machinery and Intelligence," proposing the Turing Test as a measure of machine intelligence.

1951: Marvin Minsky and Dean Edmonds build the first neural network simulator, SNARC, at Princeton University.

1956: The term "artificial intelligence" is coined at the Dartmouth Summer Research Project on Artificial Intelligence, marking the official birth of AI as a field.

1959: Herbert Simon and Allen Newell develop the Logic Theorist, the first AI program capable of proving mathematical theorems.

1960: John McCarthy introduces the LISP programming language, which becomes a prominent language for AI research and development.

1961: The first industrial robot, the Unimate, is installed at General Motors, marking the beginning of AI applications in manufacturing.

1997: IBM's Deep Blue defeats world chess champion Garry Kasparov in a six-game match, showcasing the power of AI in strategic decision-making.

2005: Stanley, an autonomous vehicle developed by Stanford University, wins the DARPA Grand Challenge, demonstrating significant progress in AI and robotics for autonomous navigation.

2011: IBM's Watson defeats human champions on the quiz show Jeopardy!, demonstrating AI's ability to understand natural language and answer complex questions.

2012: The deep learning revolution accelerates with the success of AlexNet, a deep convolutional neural network, in the ImageNet Large Scale Visual Recognition Challenge.

2015: DeepMind's AlphaGo defeats world champion Go player Lee Sedol, marking a significant milestone in AI by mastering the complex game of Go, previously thought to be beyond the capabilities of AI.

2018: OpenAI's GPT (Generative Pre-trained Transformer) model demonstrates remarkable natural language understanding and generation capabilities, heralding advancements in language AI.

2019: The release of BERT (Bidirectional Encoder Representations from Transformers) by Google further advances natural language processing tasks, achieving state-of-the-art performance on various language understanding benchmarks.

2020: AI applications continue to proliferate across industries, with widespread adoption in healthcare, finance, transportation, and other sectors, driving innovation and efficiency improvements.

2023: AI continues to evolve rapidly, with advancements in areas such as reinforcement learning, autonomous systems, and AI ethics shaping the future of technology and society.

☐ AI SPECTRUM:

Artificial intelligence (AI) encompasses a spectrum of capabilities and goals. Here's an improved breakdown of the different types of AI:

Artificial Narrow Intelligence (ANI): ANI, also known as weak AI, refers to AI systems that are designed and trained for specific tasks or narrow domains. These systems excel at performing well-defined tasks within limited contexts. Examples include virtual personal assistants like Siri or Alexa, recommendation systems, and image recognition algorithms.

Artificial General Intelligence (AGI): AGI, often referred to as strong AI, represents a hypothetical AI system with human-level cognitive abilities across a broad range of domains. AGI would possess the ability to understand, learn, and apply knowledge in a manner similar to human intelligence. AGI remains a theoretical concept, and creating such a system is a major goal of AI research.

Artificial Super Intelligence (ASI): ASI goes beyond AGI and describes an AI system that surpasses human intelligence in every aspect, including creativity, problem-solving, and social skills. ASI represents the upper limit of AI capabilities and is often associated with speculative scenarios of AI surpassing human control and comprehension.

Each type of AI represents a different level of intelligence and capability, with ANI being the most prevalent and AGI and ASI representing increasingly advanced and theoretical stages of AI development. Understanding these distinctions is crucial for discussions about the potential impact and ethical considerations surrounding AI technology.

☐ ADVANCEMENT OF AI KEY FACTORS:

More Data: The proliferation of digital technologies has led to an exponential increase in the volume, variety, and velocity of data generated globally. This abundance of data provides a rich resource for AI systems to learn from and make predictions or decisions.

More Computational Power: Advances in hardware, such as GPUs (Graphics Processing Units) and specialised AI accelerators, have significantly increased computational power. This increased computational power enables the training and deployment of more complex AI models capable of processing vast amounts of data efficiently.

Better Algorithms: Ongoing research in machine learning and AI has led to the development of more sophisticated algorithms and techniques. These advancements have improved the performance and capabilities of AI systems, enabling them to tackle a wider range of tasks with greater accuracy and efficiency.

Broad Investment: There has been a surge in investment in AI research and development across various sectors, including technology, healthcare, finance, manufacturing, and transportation. This broad investment reflects the growing recognition of AI's potential to drive innovation, enhance productivity, and address complex challenges across industries.

Overall, the convergence of these factors has fuelled the rapid advancement and adoption of AI technologies, making it a central topic of discussion and a transformative force in shaping the future of society, economy, and technology.

What are Python libraries and why?

Python libraries are collections of pre-written code that provide a wide range of functionalities and tools to enhance Python programming. These libraries are developed by the Python community and serve as valuable resources for developers.

Python libraries address common programming challenges, such as data manipulation, scientific computing, machine learning, web development, and more. They offer ready-made solutions and functionalities that can be easily incorporated into projects, saving time and effort.

How Python libraries are useful in Data science?

Python libraries are incredibly useful in data science due to their extensive functionality and ease of use. Here are some key Python libraries and their specific contributions to data science:

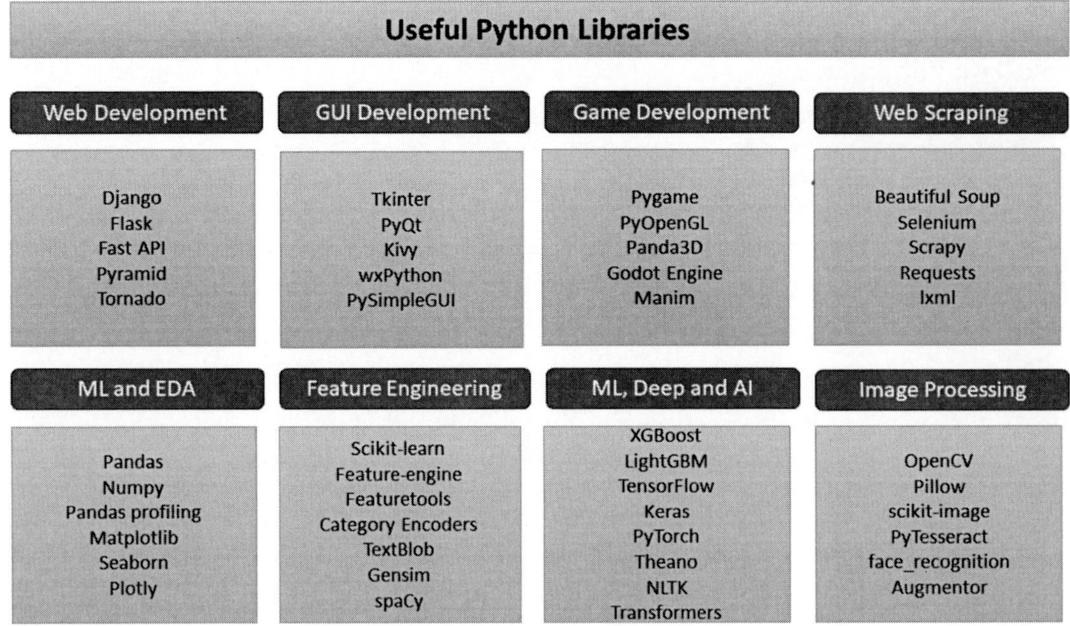

☐ HOW TO APPROACH DATA SCIENCE USING PYTHON LIBRARIES?

To approach Data Science using Python libraries, you can follow a systematic process that typically involves the following steps:

Define the problem: Begin by articulating the problem you aim to address or the question you seek to answer through data analysis. Gain a comprehensive understanding of the goals and objectives underlying your analysis to ensure alignment with overarching objectives.

Gather data: Proceed to collect pertinent data from diverse sources, including databases, files, APIs, or through web scraping methodologies. Prioritise the acquisition of clean, comprehensive datasets that accurately reflect the nuances of the problem at hand, laying a solid foundation for subsequent analysis and insights extraction.

Explore and preprocess the data: Use libraries like pandas and NumPy to explore the data, understand its structure, and identify any missing values or outliers. Preprocess the data by handling missing values, performing data cleaning, normalization, or feature engineering as necessary.

Perform data analysis: Utilize libraries like pandas, NumPy, and SciPy to perform various statistical analyses, data transformations, and calculations. Apply descriptive statistics, inferential statistics, and exploratory data analysis techniques to gain insights and understanding of the data.

Visualize the data: Use visualization libraries such as Matplotlib and Seaborn to create informative and visually appealing charts, plots, and graphs. Visualizations can help in understanding patterns, relationships, and trends in the data.

Build predictive models: Employ machine learning libraries like Scikit-learn or deep learning libraries like TensorFlow and Keras to build predictive models. Choose appropriate algorithms based on the problem type (regression, classification, clustering) and train the models using the prepared data.

Evaluate and validate models: Assess the performance of your models using evaluation metrics, cross-validation techniques, or train-test splits. Optimize the models by fine-tuning hyperparameters and adjusting the model architecture.

Communicate results: Present your findings and insights clearly and concisely using visualisations, reports, or interactive dashboards. Use libraries like Jupyter Notebook or data storytelling tools to effectively communicate your data analysis process and results.

Iterate and refine: Continuously iterate on your analysis, models, and visualisations based on feedback, new data, or changing requirements. Refine your approach and improve the accuracy and relevance of your analysis.

Throughout this process, make use of the extensive documentation and community support available for the Python libraries you are using. Experiment with different techniques, algorithms, and parameters to find the most suitable approach for your specific problem.

☐ WHAT DO YOU HOPE TO GAIN FROM THIS BOOK?

By delving into "Optimum - Python Power Series IV," you can expect to gain a comprehensive understanding of data science, equipped with practical skills and knowledge to tackle complex data challenges. This book is designed to:

Enhance Your Data Science Skills: Learn how to efficiently handle, manipulate, and preprocess data, and gain insights into performing complex computations and visualizations.

Master Machine Learning Techniques: Understand and implement various machine learning algorithms to solve real-world problems.

Develop Core Intuition: Build a solid foundation in the underlying principles of data science and machine learning, allowing you to think critically and creatively when approaching data-driven projects.

Practical Experience: Through hands-on exercises and real-world examples, you will be able to apply the concepts learned and develop practical solutions to data science challenges.

Boost Your Career: Whether you are a beginner or an experienced professional, this book will provide you with the tools and knowledge to advance in the rapidly evolving field of data science.

☐ How to Use This Book

Start with the Foundations

If you're new to machine learning, begin with the introductory chapters that explain core concepts, key terminologies, and the role of Python in the data science ecosystem.

Recommended Reference:

Optimum – Python Series I: Ultimate Guide for Beginners lays the groundwork for Python mastery.

Explore Hands-On Examples

Every concept is accompanied by real code snippets and practical use cases. Run them, tweak them, and observe how small changes influence outcomes—because the best way to learn is by doing.

Recommended Reference:

Optimum – Python Series II: Exploring Data Structures and Algorithms enhances understanding of efficient problem-solving.

Use as a Modular Reference

The book is designed to be modular. Feel free to navigate directly to chapters that align with your current goals. Each section is self-contained for ease of use.

Bridge Theory and Practice

We don't just show you how to write the code—we explain why it works. This book bridges the gap between conceptual clarity and real-world application.

Engage with the Evolving Field

Machine learning is fast-evolving. Use this book as a launchpad to explore emerging trends, libraries, and research areas once you've mastered the essentials.

Apply to Your Projects

Reinforce your learning by applying techniques to your own datasets and real-world problems. Experimentation leads to mastery.

Introduction to Generative AI & Reinforcement Learning

You'll also find a gateway to emerging domains like Generative AI and Reinforcement Learning—providing a glimpse into the future of intelligent systems.

☐ Who Is This Book Aimed At?

"Optimum - Python Power Series IV" is aimed at a wide range of readers, including:

- Beginners: Individuals new to data science who are looking to build a strong foundation in Python and data science concepts.
- Intermediate Practitioners: Those with some experience in data science who wish to deepen their understanding and enhance their skill set with more advanced techniques and practical applications.
- Experienced Professionals: Seasoned data scientists and analysts seeking to stay up-to-date with the latest tools, libraries, and methodologies in the field.
- Students and Educators: University students studying data science, computer science, or related fields, as well as educators looking for a comprehensive resource to support their teaching.
- Domain-Specific Professionals: Professionals in various industries who use data science in their work and wish to improve their ability to analyze and interpret data for better decision-making.

Recommended Reading: The Optimum Series by Shree Shambav

To deepen your understanding of fundamental concepts in data structures and algorithms, consider reading the book "Python OPTIMUM Series II: Exploring Data Structures and Algorithms" by Shree Shambav. This comprehensive guide delves into various topics essential for mastering algorithms and data structures.

In Part Four of the book, the focus is on tree data structures. You'll explore different types of binary trees, including full binary trees, perfect binary trees, complete binary trees, balanced binary trees, AVL trees, and B-trees. The book covers tree traversal techniques and operations such as insertion and deletion in B-trees and B+ trees. By studying these topics, you'll gain insight into the organisation and manipulation of hierarchical data structures.

Part Five of the book delves into graph-based data structures, which are fundamental for representing relationships between objects. You'll learn about spanning trees, strongly connected components, adjacency matrices, and adjacency lists. Additionally, the book covers essential graph traversal algorithms like depth-first search (DFS) and breadth-first search (BFS). These algorithms are crucial for exploring and analysing graph structures efficiently.

By reading this book, you'll develop a solid understanding of key concepts in data structures and algorithms, enabling you to tackle a wide range of problems and challenges in Data Science and programming.

☐ Environment Setup

Installing and managing libraries in Python is an essential skill for any developer. Here is an explanation of the general process:

Package Managers: Python utilises package managers, such as pip (preferred for Python 2 and 3) and conda (commonly used for data science projects), to install and manage libraries. These package managers simplify the process by handling dependencies and ensuring smooth installation.

Installing Libraries: To install a library using pip, open a command prompt or terminal and use the following command:

```
pip install library_name
```

Replace library_name with the name of the library you want to install. If you're using conda, the command is:

```
conda install library_name
```

Version Control: You can specify a particular version of a library during installation. For example, to install version 2.0 of a library:

```
pip install library_name==2.0
```

Requirements Files: In larger projects, it's common to maintain a requirements file that lists all the libraries required by the project. To install all the libraries listed in a requirements file, use the command:

```
pip install -r requirements.txt
```

Replace requirements.txt with the path to your requirements file.

Virtual Environments: Virtual environments allow you to create isolated Python environments for different projects, ensuring that library installations and versions remain separate. To create a virtual environment, use the following command:

```
python -m venv myenv
```

Replace myenv with the name you want to give to your virtual environment. Activate the virtual environment before installing libraries:

- On Windows: myenv\Scripts\activate
- On macOS/Linux: source myenv/bin/activate

Listing Installed Libraries: To view the libraries installed in your Python environment, you can use the following command:

```
pip list
```

```
pip install --upgrade library_name
```

Upgrading and Uninstalling Libraries: To upgrade a library to its latest version, use the command:

To uninstall a library, use:

```
pip uninstall library_name
```

Some libraries may require additional dependencies, such as external software or system-level packages. In such cases, the library's documentation will provide instructions for fulfilling those requirements.

Managing libraries effectively is crucial for maintaining a stable and efficient development environment. By leveraging package managers and best practices, you can easily install, upgrade, and uninstall libraries while keeping your project dependencies organised and controlled.

Reader Responses:

We highly value the feedback from our readers. It helps us improve and create titles that cater to your interests. Please share your thoughts about this book, what you found helpful or could be improved. You can send your general feedback to shreeshambav.optimum@gmail.com, and kindly include the book's title on the subject line. If you have knowledge or expertise on a particular subject and are interested in contributing to a book, please send your inquiries to the same email address mentioned above.

☐ ONLINE RESOURCES

The supplementary materials for the book can be accessed online at: www.shambav.org

Setup Instructions

The setup instructions provided here are the same as those in the book but include clickable links to all the components. If you encounter any difficulties during the setup process, please consult this resource.

Updates

Python, like any other language, undergoes continuous updates and changes. We maintain a comprehensive collection of updates, so if you encounter any issues, please check this resource to see if the instructions have been changed.

Data

The book provides some sample raw data for running the programs, but you can also create your samples using various file formats such as Excel, CSV, or JSON.

Practice Questions

You are encouraged to allocate ample time to work on the exercises independently. If you encounter any challenges and cannot proceed, consult this reference link.

Exercises and Assignments

While it's important to try the exercises on your own, you might encounter difficulties that prevent you from making progress. If that happens, you can find solutions to most of the exercises online. We encourage you to dedicate sufficient time to working on the exercises independently before seeking help.

Cheat Sheets

You can also find a wide range of cheat sheets online covering major concepts, which you can download and use for quick reference.

Errata

Despite our efforts to ensure the accuracy of our content, errors may still occur. If you come across any errors in the book, whether in the text or the code, please report them to us. Your feedback will not only help us improve future editions of this book but also assist other readers in avoiding any frustrations.

Advance Material

Advance material for those who want to learn more about the subject. Beginners can skip the advanced section at the start.

Reference Links

Activities	Sheets	Links
Login	Signup/Login page	https://www.shambav.org/artifacts/signup.php
Practice Question	With answer sheet	https://www.shambav.org/artifacts/optimum-python-series-4
Exercises, Assignments	With answers	
Quiz	Quiz answers	
Data	Data Sheet	
Supplementary	Advanced material	
Instruction	Setup instruction	
Advance materials	Programs, tricks, assignments, mini projects, issues	
Cheat sheets	Major concepts	

What Next:

In this part, we will cover the fundamental concepts of machine learning, providing a comprehensive overview of its various aspects. We will begin by exploring the three main types: supervised, unsupervised, and reinforcement learning. Essential terminologies like features, labels, training data, testing data, and model evaluation metrics were introduced. Core categories and tasks, including classification, regression, clustering, dimensionality reduction, and association rule mining, will be discussed along with a range of algorithms from traditional to advanced techniques. We will examine the stages of the machine learning pipeline, including data collection, feature identification, exploratory data analysis, feature engineering, model training, and evaluation. Finally, we covered deploying models for predictions, offering insights and driving decision-making processes.

To truly harness the power of data science and its essential libraries, delve into "OPTIMUM Python Power Series III: Unleashing the Potential of Data Science with Libraries" by Shree Shambav. This comprehensive guide will empower you with the knowledge and skills needed to leverage the full potential of essential Python libraries.

This book goes beyond mere familiarity with libraries like Numpy, Pandas, Matplotlib, Seaborn, Scikit-learn, and Sklearn. It delves into the depths of their capabilities, enabling you to unlock their full potential in your data science projects.

Explore Numpy's powerful array of manipulation capabilities, Pandas' flexible data handling functionalities, and Matplotlib's robust visualization tools. Dive into Seaborn's advanced statistical plotting capabilities and Sklearn's extensive machine learning algorithms and utilities.

By immersing yourself in this book, you'll gain a deep understanding of how to effectively utilise these libraries to tackle a wide range of data science tasks. Whether you're performing data analysis, visualization, or machine learning, this book will equip you with the knowledge and techniques to excel in your data science endeavours.

PART ONE

Getting Started

Machine Learning Basics

"Data is the ink of intelligence, and machine learning is the quill that writes the future—each algorithm, a brushstroke shaping the canvas of tomorrow."

– Shree Shambav

PART ONE

DAY ONE

Unit 1 - Lesson One

Introduction Machine Learning

☐ Introduction to Machine Learning:

Master said, "Arthur Samuel, an early American leader in computer gaming and artificial intelligence, introduced the term "Machine Learning" in 1959 during his tenure at IBM. He described machine learning as 'the field of study that gives computers the ability to learn without being explicitly programmed.'"

However, there is no single, universally accepted definition of machine learning. Different authors offer varied interpretations.

- Machine learning involves programming computers to optimise a performance criterion using example data or past experiences. It entails defining a model with parameters and employing a computer program to adjust these parameters based on training data or past experiences. The model may be predictive, making forecasts for the future, or descriptive, extracting insights from data.
- The field of study referred to as machine learning deals with constructing computer programs that enhance their performance with experience.

> "Machine learning is the art of empowering machines to learn and evolve from data, transforming algorithms into powerful tools that uncover patterns, make predictions, and shape the future." – Shree Shambav

Machine learning is a subset of artificial intelligence dedicated to developing algorithms and statistical models that enable computers to enhance their performance in tasks through experience. These algorithms and models are crafted to learn from data and make predictions or decisions without explicit instructions. There are various types of machine learning, including supervised learning, unsupervised learning, and reinforcement learning. Supervised learning entails training a model on labelled data, whereas unsupervised learning involves training on unlabelled data. Reinforcement learning involves training through trial and error. Machine learning finds application in diverse areas, including image and speech recognition, natural language processing, and recommender systems.

Definition of learning:

A computer program is considered to learn from experience E concerning a class of tasks T and a performance measure P if its performance at tasks T, as evaluated by P, improves with experience E.

Examples:

Handwriting recognition learning problem:

Task T: Recognizing and classifying handwritten words within images.

Performance P: Percentage of words correctly classified.

Training experience E: A dataset of handwritten words with corresponding classifications.

Definition: A computer program that learns from experience is commonly referred to as a machine learning program or simply a learning program.

☐ **Classification of Machine Learning**

Master explained that the Machine learning implementations can be categorised into four major types based on the nature of the learning signal or response available to a learning system:

Supervised learning:

Supervised learning involves learning a function that maps input to output based on labelled input-output pairs. The data provided for training is labelled, and both classification and regression problems fall into this category.

Learning Algorithms

- Linear Regression
- Logistic Regression
- Decision Trees
- Random Forests

- Naïve Bayes
- KNN
- Support Vector Machines (SVM)
- Gradient Boosting

Purpose: Used for tasks with labelled examples, aiming to learn the mapping between input features and output labels.

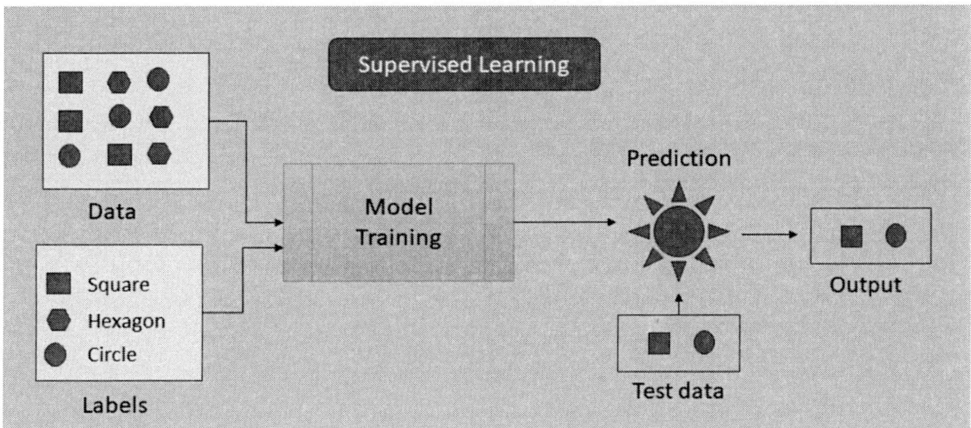

Example — Consider a dataset of patients entering a clinic, where each patient's gender, age, and health status (labelled as "healthy" or "sick") are recorded.

Gender	Age	Label
Male	69	sick
Male	48	healthy
Female	56	sick
Female	50	healthy

Unsupervised learning:

Unsupervised learning algorithms draw inferences from datasets consisting of input data without labelled responses. In this type, the data lacks explicit classification or categorisation. Example: A dataset of patients entering a clinic containing only gender and age information.

This learning method mirrors human observation-based classification, where objects or events are grouped based on similarity. Many recommendation systems and marketing automation tools use unsupervised learning.

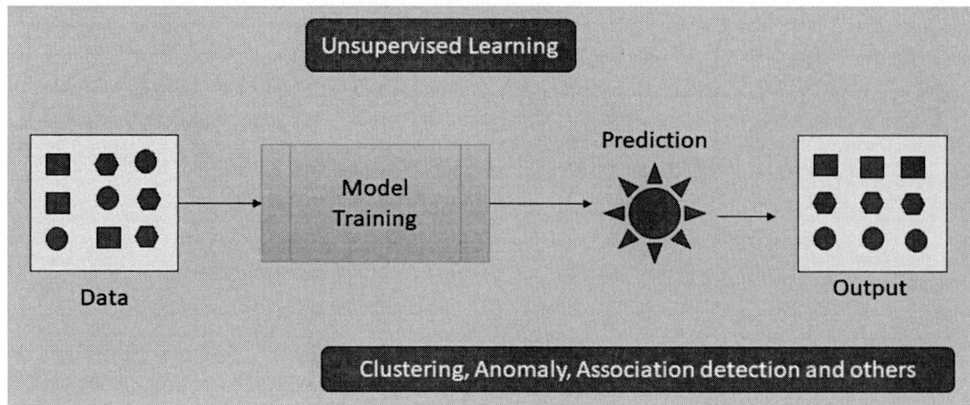

Learning Algorithm:

- K-means Clustering
- DBSCAN
- Gaussian Mixture Models (GMM)
- Principal Component Analysis (PCA)
- Independent Component Analysis (ICA)

Purpose: Applied to tasks such as clustering, dimensionality reduction, and feature extraction when labelled examples are absent or the goal is to discover patterns in data.

Gender	**Age**
Male	69
Male	48
Female	56
Female	50

Reinforcement learning:

Reinforcement learning focuses on teaching an agent to act in a way that maximises its rewards within a given environment. Unlike supervised learning, the agent is not provided with specific instructions but discovers the most rewarding actions through trial and error. For instance, teaching a dog a new trick involves rewarding or punishing it based on its actions.

Semi-supervised learning:

Semi-supervised learning occurs when a training set contains incomplete target outputs, with some target labels missing. This approach combines a small labelled dataset with a larger unlabelled dataset during training, bridging the gap between supervised and unsupervised learning.

☐ Another categorisation

Another categorisation of machine learning tasks is based on the desired output:

Classification: Involves dividing inputs into two or more classes, with the model assigning unseen inputs to one or more predefined classes. This is typically accomplished through supervised learning. An example is spam filtering, where emails are classified as "spam" or "not spam."

Regression: Addresses cases where the outputs are continuous rather than discrete. Also, in a supervised problem, regression predicts numerical values based on input data.

Clustering: Involves dividing a set of inputs into groups, with the groups not known beforehand. This is typically an unsupervised task.

Learning algorithm for clustering:

- K-means
- Agglomerative Clustering
- Spectral Clustering
- DBSCAN

Purpose: Groups unlabelled data into clusters, identifying inherent structures or relationships without labelled examples.

Machine learning enables the resolution of problems that cannot be addressed using traditional approaches. By leveraging ML algorithms and modern computing technologies, scalability and efficiency can be improved. Modern ML models have applications ranging from predicting disease outbreaks to analysing stock market trends.

Need

Master explained that the need for machine learning (ML) arises from the proliferation of data sources such as cloud data, the Internet of Things (IoT), and social media. ML enables the analysis, processing, and predictive modelling of vast datasets, leveraging the abundance of data available. With ML, organisations can harness data to generate insights, improve decision-making processes, uncover patterns and trends, and solve complex problems effectively. The applications of ML span various domains, including healthcare, finance, marketing, and cybersecurity, where it plays a crucial role in optimising processes, enhancing efficiency, and driving innovation.

Terminologies of ML

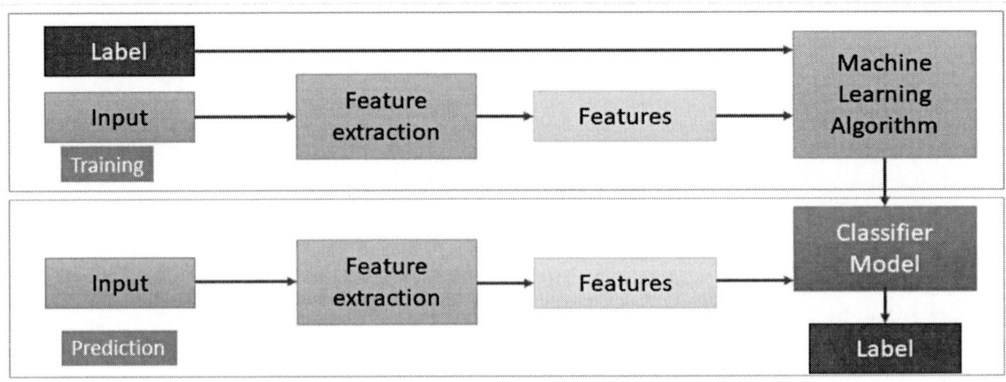

Model: A model, also known as a hypothesis, is a representation learned from data using machine learning algorithms. It encapsulates the learned patterns and relationships within the data, enabling predictions or classifications for new, unseen instances.

Feature: A feature refers to an individual measurable property or characteristic of the data. Features provide the input information to the model and are typically represented as a feature vector. These vectors encapsulate multiple features, such as colour, smell, or taste, which are essential for making predictions or classifications. Selecting informative, discriminating, and independent features is crucial for the effectiveness of machine learning algorithms. Feature extraction techniques are often employed to extract relevant features from raw data.

Target (Label): The target variable, also known as the label, is the value that the model aims to predict. In the context of the fruit example discussed earlier, the label corresponds to the name of the fruit, such as apple, orange, or banana. During training, the model learns to associate input features with the corresponding target labels.

Training: Training involves providing the model with a dataset containing input features, along with their corresponding target labels. The model learns from this labelled data to generate predictions or classifications for new instances. Through iterative optimisation processes, the model adjusts its parameters to minimise prediction errors and improve performance on the training data.

Prediction: Once trained, the model can make predictions or classifications for new input instances. Given a set of input features, the model outputs a predicted label or value. It is essential to evaluate the model's performance on unseen data to ensure its generalisation ability. A well-performing model should demonstrate robust performance in unseen instances, indicating its effectiveness in making accurate predictions.

Enhanced Machine Learning Process:

Define Objective: Clearly articulate the problem or goal that the machine learning model aims to address or achieve.

Data Gathering: Collect relevant data sources that contain information necessary for training and testing the model.

Data Preparation: Cleanse, preprocess, and format the data to ensure it is suitable for analysis and model training.

Data Exploration: Explore and analyse the data to gain insights into its characteristics, distributions, and relationships.

Building Model: Develop and train machine learning models using appropriate algorithms and techniques tailored to the defined objective.

Model Evaluation: Assess the performance of the trained models using evaluation metrics and techniques to ensure they meet the defined criteria and objectives.

Predictions: Deploy the trained models to make predictions or decisions on new or unseen data, leveraging the insights gained from the model evaluation process.

Steps to Get Started with Machine Learning:

- Define the Problem: Identify the problem you want to solve and determine if machine learning can be used to solve it.

- Collect Data: Gather and clean the data that you will use to train your model. The quality of your model will depend on the quality of your data.

- Explore the Data: Use data visualization and statistical methods to understand the structure and relationships within your data.

- Pre-process the Data: Prepare the data for modeling by normalizing, transforming, and cleaning it as necessary.

- Split the Data: Divide the data into training and test datasets to validate your model.

- Choose a Model: Select a machine learning model that is appropriate for your problem and the data you have collected.
- Train the Model: Use the training data to train the model, adjusting its parameters to fit the data as accurately as possible.
- Evaluate the Model: Use the test data to evaluate the performance of the model and determine its accuracy.
- Fine-tune the Model: Based on the results of the evaluation, fine-tune the model by adjusting its parameters and repeating the training process until the desired level of accuracy is achieved.
- Deploy the Model: Integrate the model into your application or system, making it available for use by others.
- Monitor the Model: Continuously monitor the performance of the model to ensure that it continues to provide accurate results over time.

Approach for Weather Forecast Example:

Step 1: Define Objective

- Identify the prediction target: Will it rain? (Yes/No)
- Determine relevant input features: Humidity level, precipitation, wind speed, etc.
- Classify the problem: Binary classification

Step 2: Data Gathering

- Assess data availability and sources
- Utilise sampling techniques or access datasets from platforms like Kaggle

Step 3: Prepare Data

- Transform data into a desired format for analysis
- Perform data cleaning: Handle missing values, remove corrupted or unnecessary data

Step 4: Data Exploration

- Analyse patterns and trends in the data

- Extract insights and observe correlations between variables

Step 5: Build ML Model

- Select appropriate predictive model
- Split data into training and testing sets
- Train the model to predict the likelihood of rain (Yes/No)
- Choose classification algorithms such as Logistic Regression, SVM, Naïve Bayes, based on problem requirements

Step 6: Model Evaluation and Optimisation

- Assess model efficiency and accuracy
- Optimise model performance using techniques like parameter tuning and hyperparameter optimisation

Step 7: Prediction

- Use the trained model to make predictions
- Output categorical predictions: e.g., "Raining: Yes" or "Raining: No"

This refined approach provides a structured framework for developing a weather forecasting model, ensuring thorough data preparation, model selection, evaluation, and prediction.

Master said, "Akshaya, here is a simple machine learning example in Python that illustrates how to train a model to predict the species of iris flowers based on their sepal and petal measurements. We'll use the popular Iris dataset for this task."

Example P1 – U1 – D1	
ML - simple machine learning	**Output**
# Importing necessary libraries import pandas as pd from sklearn.datasets import load_iris from sklearn.model_selection import train_test_split from sklearn.linear_model import LogisticRegression from sklearn.metrics import accuracy_score	Accuracy: 1.0

```
# Load the Iris dataset
iris = load_iris()
# Creating a DataFrame from the dataset
df = pd.DataFrame(data=iris.data, columns=iris.feature_names)
df['target'] = iris.target
# Splitting the data into features and target
X = df.drop('target', axis=1)
y = df['target']
# Splitting the data into training and testing sets
X_train, X_test, y_train, y_test = train_test_split(X, y, test_size=0.2, random_state=42)
# Training the Logistic Regression model
model = LogisticRegression(max_iter=1000)
model.fit(X_train, y_train)
# Making predictions on the test data
y_pred = model.predict(X_test)
# Calculating the accuracy of the model
accuracy = accuracy_score(y_test, y_pred)
print("Accuracy:", accuracy)
```

This Python code demonstrates a simple machine learning example using the Iris dataset. The goal is to train a model to predict the species of iris flowers based on their sepal and petal measurements. Here's a breakdown of the code:

- **Importing Libraries:** Necessary libraries such as pandas for data manipulation, load_iris to load the Iris dataset, train_test_split for splitting the dataset, LogisticRegression for creating the model, and accuracy_score for evaluating the model's accuracy are imported.
- **Loading the Dataset:** The Iris dataset is loaded using the load_iris function from

sklearn.datasets.

- **Creating DataFrame:** The dataset is converted into a DataFrame for easier manipulation and analysis.
- **Splitting Data:** The data is split into features (X) and target variable (y), where X contains the sepal and petal measurements, and y contains the target variable (species).
- **Splitting into Training and Testing Sets:** The dataset is further split into training and testing sets using train_test_split, with 80% of the data used for training and 20% for testing.
- **Training the Model:** A logistic regression model is instantiated and trained on the training data using the fit method.
- **Making Predictions:** Predictions are made on the test data using the trained model's predict method.
- **Evaluating Model Accuracy:** The accuracy of the model is calculated by comparing the predicted values with the actual values from the test set using the accuracy_score function.
- **Printing Accuracy:** Finally, the accuracy of the model is printed to assess its performance in predicting the species of iris flowers based on their measurements.

This code provides a concise demonstration of a typical machine learning workflow, including data loading, preprocessing, model training, prediction, and evaluation.

Summary

In this unit, we covered the fundamental concepts of machine learning, providing a comprehensive overview of its various aspects. We began by exploring the three main types of machine learning: supervised, unsupervised, and reinforcement learning.

Additionally, we introduced essential terminologies in machine learning, such as features, labels, training data, testing data, and model evaluation metrics. Understanding these terms is crucial for building and evaluating machine learning models effectively.

PART ONE

DAY TWO

Unit 2 - Lesson TWO

Introduction Machine Learning

Basics of ML

☐ Types of Machine Learning (ML)

Master said, "Classical machine learning techniques emerged from the foundation of pure statistics, solving formal mathematical tasks such as pattern recognition, clustering, and vector calculations. These methods have stood the test of time and remain integral components of modern data analysis and decision-making processes."

In today's digital landscape, classical machine learning algorithms are omnipresent, quietly powering numerous aspects of our online experiences. From the recommendations you see on e-commerce websites to the fraud detection mechanisms safeguarding your financial transactions, these algorithms work tirelessly in the background, analysing data and making predictions in real-time.

While big tech companies heavily invest in cutting-edge neural networks to gain even a fraction of a percentage improvement in accuracy, smaller businesses often find solace in the simplicity and reliability of classical approaches. Spending resources on complex algorithms may not always be feasible or necessary, especially when simpler methods can yield satisfactory results.

Despite their ubiquity, classical machine learning techniques remain accessible and intuitive, akin to basic arithmetic. Their straightforward nature allows them to be easily understood and applied, making them invaluable tools for analysts, researchers, and practitioners across various industries. Just like basic arithmetic, classical machine learning methods quietly power countless everyday tasks, enriching our digital experiences without us even realizing it.

☐ Different types of Searches

Uninformed Search Algorithms: Uninformed search algorithms operate without any additional information beyond the problem definition. These include:

- Depth-First Search (DFS): Explores as far as possible along each branch before backtracking.
- Breadth-First Search (BFS): Explores all neighbour nodes at the present depth before moving to the next level.
- Dijkstra's Algorithm: Finds the shortest path between nodes in a weighted graph.
- Bidirectional Search: Simultaneously explores the search space from the start and goal nodes.

Informed Search Algorithms: Informed search algorithms utilize domain-specific knowledge to guide the search process efficiently. Examples include:

- Greedy Best-First Search: Expands the node that appears to be the closest to the goal, based on a heuristic function.
- Memory-Bounded Search: Limits the memory usage during search, often by prioritizing promising nodes.
- Bidirectional Heuristic Search: Utilizes heuristic functions to guide the search process in both directions simultaneously.

Adversarial Search Algorithms: Adversarial search algorithms are employed in game-playing scenarios, where agents aim to outsmart each other. Examples include:

- Basics of Game Theory: Provides a framework for decision-making in competitive environments.
- MiniMax: A decision rule used for minimizing the possible loss for a worst-case scenario.
- Monte Carlo Tree Search (MCTS): Utilizes random sampling and tree exploration to determine the best move in games with large search spaces.

Multi-Agent Search Algorithms: Multi-agent search algorithms involve multiple agents coordinating to achieve common or conflicting objectives. Examples include:

- Cooperative Search: Agents collaborate to achieve shared goals.
- Distributed Search: Tasks are distributed among multiple agents to improve efficiency.
- Competitive Search: Agents compete against each other to achieve individual objectives.

To further explore data structures and algorithms, consider reading "Optimum - Exploring Data Structures and Algorithms - Series 2" by Shree Shambav. This comprehensive resource delves deeper into various concepts and techniques, providing valuable insights into data structures and algorithms.

☐ Different Types

Master said, "Machine learning encompasses various algorithms, each tailored to different tasks and scenarios."

Here are some of the primary types:

- Supervised Machine Learning
- Unsupervised Machine Learning
- Semi-Supervised Machine Learning
- Reinforcement Learning

☐ Supervised Learning:

"In the realm of machine learning, supervised learning is the art of mentorship, where labelled data serves as the guiding beacon, nurturing the growth of intelligent systems." – Shree Shambav.

Machine learning models learn more efficiently with labelled data, making it a cornerstone in real-life applications. These applications often fall into two main categories: classification, which involves predicting the category of an object, and regression, which entails predicting a specific point on a numeric axis.

Classification:

For instance, imagine sorting socks by colour, categorising documents by language, or organising music by genre. These tasks illustrate the fundamental concept of splitting objects based on known attributes.

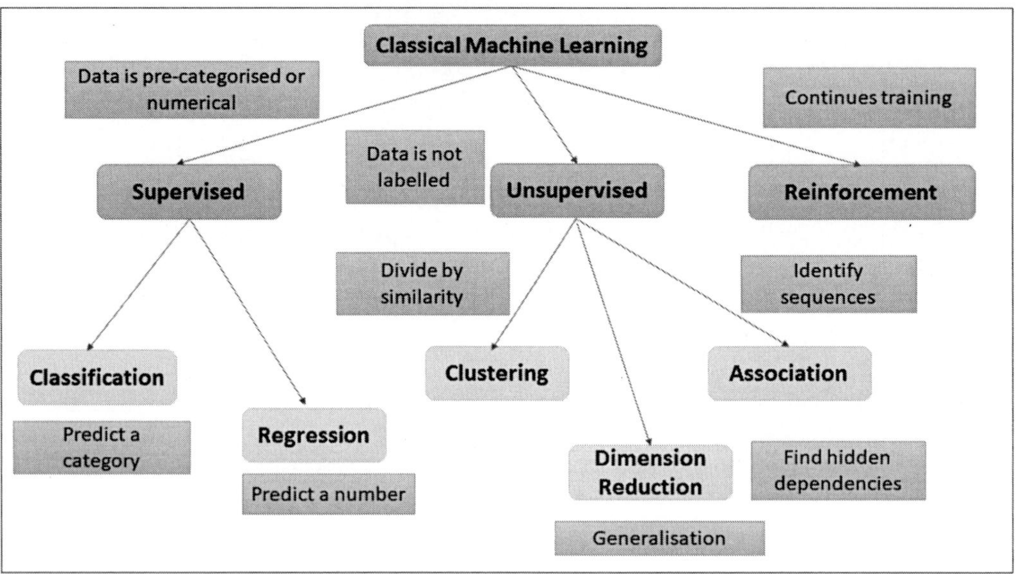

Applications of labelled data span a wide range of domains, including:

- Spam Filtering
- Language Detection
- Search of Similar Documents
- Sentiment Analysis
- Recognition of Handwritten Characters and Numbers
- Fraud Detection

Several popular algorithms excel in handling labelled data, including Logistic Regression, Support Vector Machines, Random Forest, Decision Trees, K-Nearest Neighbours (KNN), and Naïve Bayes

Supervised learning in machine learning refers to a paradigm where the algorithm learns patterns and relationships in data by being trained on labelled examples. In supervised learning, each training example consists of input data and its corresponding correct output label. The algorithm uses these labelled examples to learn the mapping between the input data and the output labels, enabling it to make predictions or decisions when presented with new, unseen data.

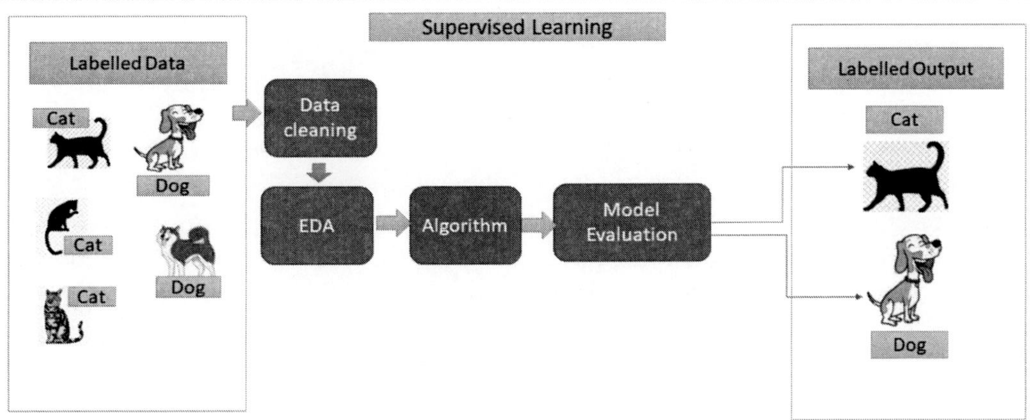

To illustrate supervised learning with a cat and dog image example:

Training Data Preparation: We collect a dataset of images containing both cats and dogs. Each image is labelled with the corresponding class label, indicating whether it depicts a cat or a dog. These labels serve as the ground truth for the training process.

Training the Model: We feed these labelled images into a supervised learning algorithm. The algorithm learns to recognise patterns and features in the images that distinguish cats from dogs.

Model Training: During the training process, the algorithm adjusts its internal parameters based on the input-output pairs provided in the training data. It learns to generalise from these examples and improve its ability to accurately classify images.

Evaluation: After training, we evaluate the trained model's performance using a separate dataset called the validation set. This set contains images that the model has not seen during training. We compare the model's predictions with the accurate labels to assess its accuracy and generalisation ability.

Prediction: Once the model is trained and evaluated, we can use it to make predictions on new, unseen images. When presented with a new image of either a cat or a dog, the model predicts the corresponding label based on the learned patterns and features.

In summary, supervised learning in machine learning involves training a model on labelled data to learn the underlying patterns and relationships, enabling it to make accurate predictions or classifications on unseen data. In the context of a cat and dog image example, the algorithm learns to distinguish between cats and dogs based on labelled examples of images containing both animals.

Regression:

Master explained that Regression deals with predicting continuous target variables, representing numerical values. It's akin to classification but focuses on forecasting numeric outcomes. For instance, predicting house prices or forecasting sales. It's widely used in finance and data analysis due to its adaptability and is even integrated into tools like Excel. The process involves algorithmically fitting a line or curve to data points, indicating the average correlation.

Regression comes in various forms. Linear regression fits a straight line, while polynomial regression fits a curve. Other types exist for specialised applications. Popular algorithms include Linear Regression, Polynomial Regression, Ridge Regression, Lasso Regression, Decision Trees, and Random Forests. Each offers unique capabilities, allowing practitioners to model and predict continuous variables effectively, from simple to complex patterns. Choosing the right algorithm depends on data characteristics and desired outcomes.

Advantages:

- High accuracy: Supervised learning models trained on labelled data often achieve high accuracy in predictions.
- Interpretable decision-making: The decision-making process in supervised learning models is often interpretable, providing insights into how predictions are made.
- Utilisation of pre-trained models: Supervised learning models can leverage pre-trained models, saving time and resources in developing new models from scratch.

Disadvantages:

- Limited pattern recognition: Supervised learning may struggle with unseen or unexpected patterns not present in the training data, limiting its ability to generalise to new data.
- Dependence on labelled data: Supervised learning relies solely on labelled data, which can be time-consuming and costly to acquire.
- Risk of poor generalisation: Poor generalisation may occur when supervised learning models fail to perform well on new or unseen data.

Applications of Supervised Learning

- Image Classification: Identifying objects, faces, and features in images.
- Natural Language Processing: Extracting information from text, such as sentiment analysis and entity recognition.

- Speech Recognition: Converting spoken language into text.
- Recommendation Systems: Providing personalised recommendations to users.
- Predictive Analytics: Forecasting outcomes like sales, customer churn, and stock prices.
- Medical Diagnosis: Detecting diseases and medical conditions.
- Fraud Detection: Identifying fraudulent transactions.
- Autonomous Vehicles: Recognising and responding to objects in the environment.
- Email Spam Detection: Classifying emails as spam or not spam.
- Quality Control in Manufacturing: Inspecting products for defects.
- Credit Scoring: Assessing the risk of borrower default.
- Customer Support: Automating customer support tasks.
- Weather Forecasting: Making predictions for meteorological parameters.
- Sports Analytics: Analysing player performance, making game predictions, and optimising strategies.

☐ Unsupervised Learning

> "Unsupervised learning is the art of discovery, where algorithms venture into the depths of unlabelled data, illuminating hidden patterns and relationships without the need for external guidance or supervision." – Shree Shambav

Master said, "Unsupervised learning in machine learning is a paradigm where the algorithm learns from unlabelled data, seeking to uncover hidden patterns, structures, or relationships within the data without explicit guidance or supervision. Unlike supervised learning, there are no predefined output labels provided during the training process."

Clustering: Clustering is the process of grouping similar data points into clusters, enabling insights into the inherent structure of the dataset. This technique is fundamental in various domains, including research and science, where it aids in uncovering patterns, identifying relationships, and segmenting data for further analysis.

High-Dimension Visualisation: In many real-world scenarios, data exists in high-dimensional spaces, making it challenging to visualise and comprehend. By leveraging computational tools, such as dimensionality reduction techniques and advanced visualisation algorithms, computers assist in rendering high-dimensional data into lower-dimensional representations that are easier to interpret and analyse.

Generative Models: Generative models learn the underlying probability distribution of the input data and can subsequently generate new samples that resemble the original data. This capability is invaluable for enhancing the robustness of classifiers and other machine learning models. By synthesising additional data points, generative models augment the training dataset, leading to improved model performance and generalisation of unseen data.

To explain unsupervised learning with a cat and dog image example:

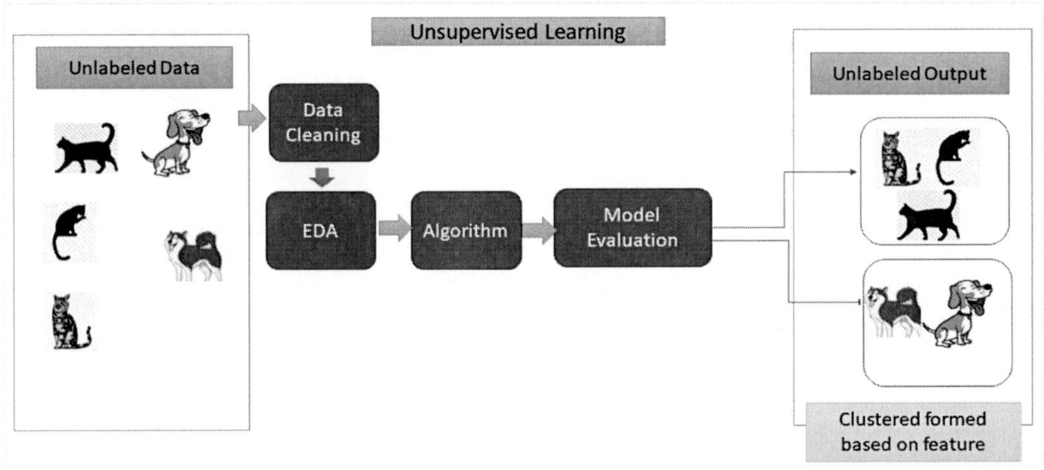

Dataset Preparation: We gather a dataset containing images of cats and dogs, but this time, the images are not labelled with their corresponding class (i.e., whether it's a cat or a dog).

Training the Model: We feed these unlabelled images into an unsupervised learning algorithm, such as clustering or dimensionality reduction techniques. The algorithm explores the data and tries to identify inherent structures or patterns without being explicitly told which images belong to which class.

Learning Hidden Structures: The unsupervised learning algorithm may discover clusters of similar images based on visual similarities, without knowledge of the specific classes. For example, it might find clusters of images that predominantly contain cats or dogs, even though it doesn't know what they represent.

Model Evaluation: Unlike supervised learning, there are no ground truth labels to evaluate the performance of the model. Instead, evaluation of unsupervised learning often involves a qualitative assessment by human experts or domain knowledge validation.

Discovering Insights: Once trained, the model can be used to uncover insights or patterns within the data. For example, it might reveal that certain features or characteristics are common among a group of images, leading to discoveries about the visual similarities between cats and dogs.

In summary, unsupervised learning in machine learning involves extracting meaningful information from unlabelled data without explicit guidance. In the context of a cat and dog image example, the unsupervised learning algorithm seeks to identify inherent structures or patterns within the dataset, potentially revealing insights about the visual characteristics of cats and dogs without prior knowledge of their classes.

Case 1 - Clustering:

Clustering, also known as cluster analysis, is a machine learning technique used to group unlabelled data points into clusters containing similar data points. Essentially, it seeks to identify patterns in the data based on similarities in features such as shape, size, colour, and behaviour, and then partition the data accordingly. As an unsupervised learning method, clustering does not require labelled data for training, making it suitable for exploring unstructured datasets.

After clustering, each cluster is assigned a unique identifier, which can be used to streamline the analysis of large and complex datasets. This technique finds applications in various domains, including statistical data analysis, market segmentation, social network analysis, image segmentation, and anomaly detection.

For example, consider a shopping mall where similar items are grouped together for easy access. T-shirts are placed in one section, trousers in another, and fruits in yet another. Similarly, clustering algorithms group data points based on similarities, facilitating organisation and analysis. Other applications include document clustering based on topic and recommendation systems in e-commerce and entertainment platforms.

Overall, clustering is a versatile technique with widespread applications across industries, contributing to tasks such as targeted marketing, data-driven decision-making, and personalised recommendations on digital platforms.

- Clustering methods categorise into Hard clustering, where each datapoint belongs to only one group, and Soft Clustering, allowing data points to belong to multiple groups. Here are the main types of clustering methods:

- Partitioning Clustering: Divides data into distinct non-hierarchical groups, typically centroid-based. K-Means is a common example where the dataset is divided into K groups based on minimising the distance between data points and cluster centroids.

- Density-Based Clustering: Connects areas of high density into clusters, allowing for arbitrary shapes. Algorithms like DBSCAN identify clusters by connecting dense areas in the dataset, separating them from sparser regions.
- Distribution Model-Based Clustering: Divide data based on probability distributions. Expectation-Maximisation Clustering with GMM assumes data points are Gaussian distributed, grouping them based on probability.
- Hierarchical Clustering: Creates a hierarchy of clusters in a tree-like structure. Agglomerative Hierarchical Clustering successively merges data points or clusters, allowing for flexible selection of clusters by cutting the tree at the desired level.
- Fuzzy Clustering: Assigns membership coefficients to data points, allowing them to belong to multiple clusters with varying degrees of membership. Fuzzy C-means algorithm is an example where data objects may have partial membership to multiple clusters.

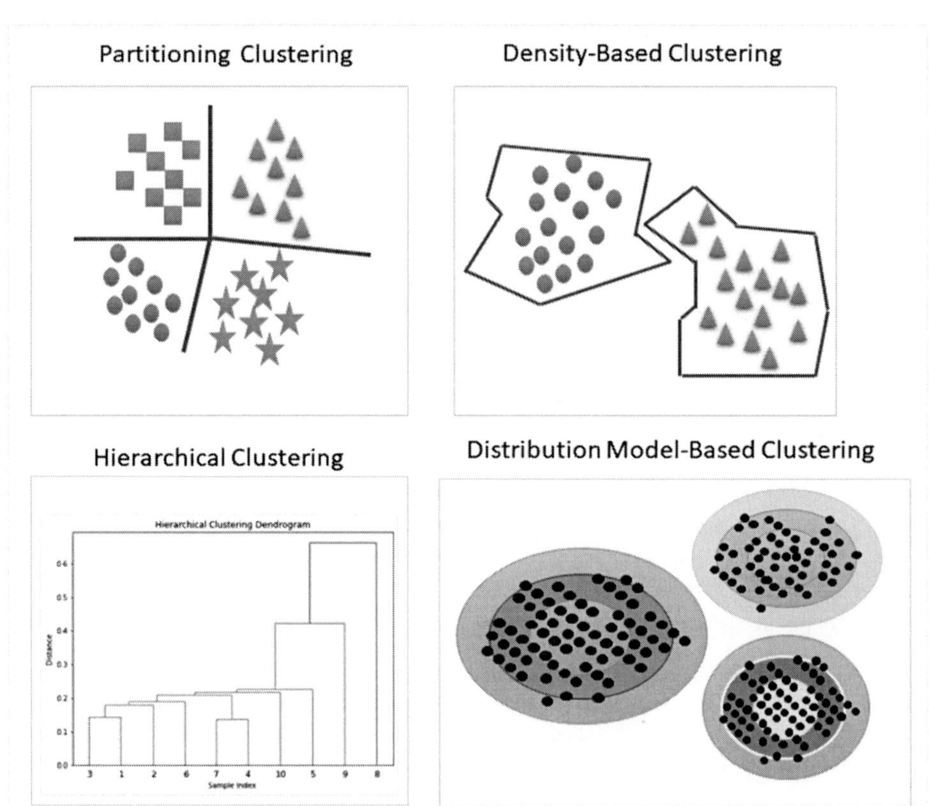

Popular Clustering Algorithms:

K-Means Algorithm:

- Divides data into clusters with equal variance.
- Requires specifying the number of clusters (K).
- Fast and computationally efficient with linear complexity O(n).

Mean-shift Algorithm:

- Identifies dense areas in data density distribution.
- Utilises a centroid-based approach to update centroids within a specified region.

DBSCAN Algorithm (Density-Based Spatial Clustering of Applications with Noise):

- Divides data into clusters based on density.
- Can identify clusters of arbitrary shapes and handles noise well.

Expectation-Maximisation Clustering using GMM (Gaussian Mixture Models):

- Suitable for data following Gaussian distributions.
- Assumes data points are generated from a mixture of Gaussian distributions.

Agglomerative Hierarchical Algorithm:

- Performs hierarchical clustering by merging individual data points or clusters.
- Represents cluster hierarchy using a dendrogram.

Affinity Propagation:

- Automatically determines the number of clusters.
- Utilises message passing between data points to find exemplars.
- Has a time complexity of O(N2T), which can be a drawback for large datasets.

BIRCH (Balanced Iterative Reducing and Clustering using Hierarchies):

- BIRCH is a hierarchical clustering algorithm that efficiently handles large datasets.
- It uses a tree-like data structure to represent the clustering hierarchy, allowing for

scalability to large datasets.

- Parameters such as the branching factor and threshold value control the granularity of clustering.
- BIRCH is suitable for applications where scalability, data reduction, and outlier detection are important considerations.

OPTICS (Ordering Points to Identify the Clustering Structure):

- OPTICS is a density-based clustering algorithm that does not require the specification of the number of clusters beforehand.
- It identifies clusters of varying densities and shapes, making it suitable for datasets with irregular geometries.
- OPTICS produces a reachability plot, which provides a visualization of the clustering structure and allows for flexible parameter tuning.
- It is effective for applications requiring outlier removal, variable cluster density, and transductive learning.

Spectral Clustering:

- Spectral clustering is a graph-based clustering method that uses the eigenvalues and eigenvectors of a similarity matrix to partition data.
- It is effective for datasets with non-linear separability and non-flat geometries.
- Spectral clustering can capture complex cluster structures and is suitable for applications requiring accurate delineation of clusters.
- It operates on the spectral domain and is advantageous for data represented in graph or network structures.

Applications of Clustering:

Identification of Cancer Cells:

Clustering algorithms are applied to identify cancerous cells by grouping them into distinct clusters from non-cancerous cells.

Search Engines:

Search engines utilise clustering to provide accurate search results by grouping similar data objects together. This improves the relevance of search queries.

Customer Segmentation:

Market research utilises clustering to segment customers based on their preferences and behaviours, aiding in targeted marketing strategies.

Biology:

Clustering is used in biology to classify species of plants and animals using image recognition techniques, facilitating biological research and conservation efforts.

Land Use Analysis:

In Geographic Information Systems (GIS), clustering helps identify areas of similar land use patterns. This information assists in urban planning and resource allocation by determining the most suitable land use for specific areas.

Case 2 - Dimensionality Reduction: Generalisation:

Apeksha asked, "What is Dimension Reduction (Generalisation)?"

Master said, "Dimension reduction, also known as generalisation, is a process in machine learning and data analysis aimed at reducing the number of features (or dimensions) in a dataset while preserving its essential characteristics. By representing data in a lower-dimensional space, dimension reduction techniques enable more efficient computation, visualisation, and interpretation of complex datasets."

Applications: Dimension reduction finds applications in various domains, including:

- Recommender Systems: Enhancing the performance and efficiency of recommendation engines by reducing the dimensionality of user-item interaction data, thereby improving recommendations.

- Beautiful Visualisations: Creating visually appealing and interpretable representations of high-dimensional data for exploration and analysis purposes.

- Topic Modelling and Document Similarity: Identifying latent topics and extracting semantic relationships between documents in large text corpora for tasks such as document clustering and similarity search.

- Fake Image Analysis: Detecting and analysing counterfeit or manipulated images by reducing the dimensionality of image features and identifying anomalies.

- Risk Management: Identifying and managing risks in financial and business applications by analysing high-dimensional datasets and extracting meaningful insights.

Popular Algorithms: Several algorithms are commonly used for dimension reduction, including:

- Principal Component Analysis (PCA): A linear technique that projects data onto orthogonal axes to maximise variance and reduce dimensionality.
- Singular Value Decomposition (SVD): A matrix factorisation technique that decomposes a matrix into its constituent parts to reduce dimensionality.
- Latent Dirichlet Allocation (LDA): A probabilistic generative model used for topic modelling and document clustering.
- Latent Semantic Analysis (LSA, pLSA, GLSA): Techniques for analysing relationships between documents and terms in large text corpora.
- t-Distributed Stochastic Neighbor Embedding (t-SNE): A nonlinear technique for visualising high-dimensional data in lower-dimensional space while preserving local structure.
- By leveraging these dimension reduction techniques and algorithms, practitioners can efficiently handle high-dimensional data and extract meaningful insights for various applications across different domains.

Case 3 - Association rule:

Sam asked, "What is an association rule?"

Master said, "Association rules are patterns or relationships discovered within datasets, typically consisting of a set of items that frequently occur together. They reveal correlations or dependencies among variables in transactional data, offering valuable insights into consumer behaviour, market trends, and product relationships."

Popular Algorithms: Several algorithms are commonly used for association rule mining, including:

- Apriori Algorithm: A classical algorithm that efficiently discovers frequent itemsets and generates association rules based on support and confidence measures.
- FP-Growth (Frequent Pattern Growth): Utilises a prefix-tree structure to mine frequent itemsets without generating candidate itemsets explicitly, offering improved efficiency over the Apriori algorithm.
- Eclat (Equivalence Class Transformation): Mines frequent itemsets by intersecting transaction identifiers, making it particularly efficient for datasets with a large number of transactions.

These algorithms empower organisations to uncover hidden relationships, extract actionable insights, and make informed decisions based on the discovered associations within their datasets.

Applications: Association rules find wide-ranging applications, including:

- Market Basket Analysis: Identifies frequently co-occurring items in retail transactions, enabling targeted marketing strategies and product recommendations.
- Customer Behaviour Analysis: Uncovers purchasing patterns and preferences among customers, facilitating personalised marketing campaigns and customer segmentation.
- Healthcare Data Mining: Identifies associations between medical conditions, symptoms, and treatments, aiding in disease diagnosis, treatment planning, and patient care.
- Web Usage Mining: Analyses user navigation patterns on websites to optimise content delivery, improve user experience, and enhance website design.
- Fraud Detection: Detects suspicious patterns or anomalies in financial transactions, helping to identify fraudulent activities and mitigate risks.

Advantages of Unsupervised:

- Discovery of hidden patterns: Unsupervised learning helps uncover hidden patterns and relationships within data that may not be apparent through manual inspection.
- Versatile applications: Widely used for tasks such as customer segmentation, anomaly detection, and data exploration across various industries.
- Elimination of data labelling effort: Since unsupervised learning does not require labelled data, it reduces the effort and cost associated with data labelling.

Disadvantages of Unsupervised:

- Lack of label guidance: Without labelled data, it can be challenging to assess the quality of the model's output or predictions.
- Interpretability challenges: Cluster interpretations may not always be clear, and meaningful interpretations may be lacking.
- Feature extraction techniques: While unsupervised learning offers techniques like

autoencoders and dimensionality reduction for feature extraction, interpreting the extracted features may not always be straightforward.

Applications of Unsupervised Learning:

- Clustering: Grouping similar data points into clusters based on their intrinsic properties.
- Anomaly Detection: Identifying outliers or anomalies in data that deviate from the norm.
- Dimensionality Reduction: Reducing the dimensionality of data while preserving its essential information to facilitate visualization and analysis.
- Recommendation Systems: Suggesting products, movies, or content to users based on their historical behaviour or preferences.
- Topic Modelling: Discovering latent topics within a collection of documents or text data.
- Density Estimation: Estimating the probability density function of data to understand its distribution.
- Image and Video Compression: Reducing the storage requirements of multimedia content while maintaining quality.
- Data Preprocessing: Assisting with data preprocessing tasks such as cleaning, imputation of missing values, and scaling.
- Market Basket Analysis: Uncovering associations between products in transactional data.
- Genomic Data Analysis: Identifying patterns or grouping genes with similar expression profiles in genomics research.
- Image Segmentation: Segmenting images into meaningful regions for analysis and processing.
- Community Detection in Social Networks: Identifying communities or groups of individuals with similar interests or connections in social network analysis.
- Customer Behaviour Analysis: Uncovering patterns and insights from customer data to improve marketing strategies and product recommendations.
- Content Recommendation: Classifying and tagging content to enhance content recommendation systems.

- Exploratory Data Analysis (EDA): Exploring data to gain insights and understanding before defining specific tasks or analyses.

Semi-Supervised:

> "Semi-supervised learning embraces the synergy between guidance and exploration, harmonising the power of labelled data to steer learning pathways, while harnessing the latent insights hidden within unlabelled data, driving towards enhanced model performance and understanding." – Shree Shambav.

Master said, "Semi-supervised learning in machine learning is a hybrid approach that combines elements of both supervised and unsupervised learning. In semi-supervised learning, the algorithm is trained on a dataset that contains both labelled and unlabelled data. The goal is to leverage the labelled data to guide the learning process while also benefiting from the additional information provided by the unlabelled data."

To explain semi-supervised learning with a cat and dog image example:

Dataset Preparation: We start with a dataset containing images of cats and dogs. However,

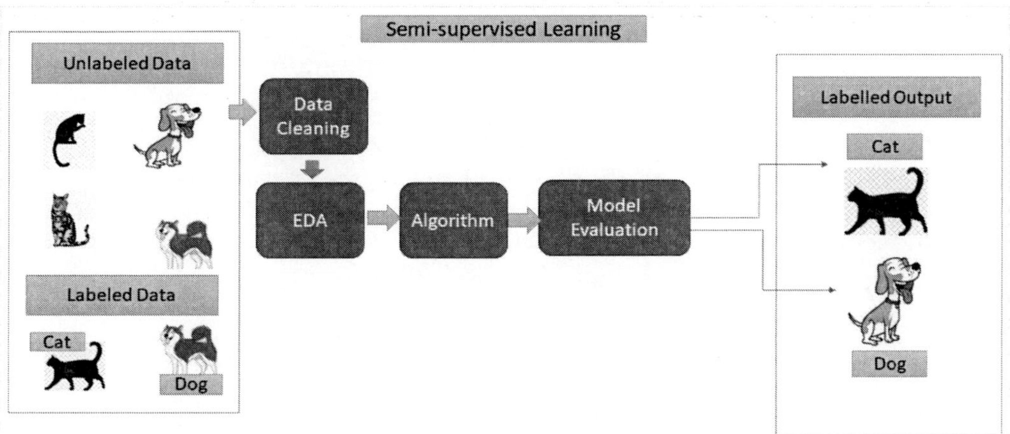

unlike traditional supervised learning, where all images are labelled with their corresponding class (cat or dog), only a subset of the images is labelled, while the majority remain unlabelled.

Training Process: During the training process, the algorithm learns from both the labelled and unlabelled data. It uses the labelled examples to guide its learning and make predictions based on the provided labels. At the same time, it also analyses the unlabelled examples to uncover patterns and structures within the data.

Leveraging Labelled Data: The labelled examples serve as anchor points for the algorithm, providing explicit guidance on how to classify similar images. The algorithm uses these labelled examples to refine its decision boundaries and improve its predictive accuracy.

Utilising Unlabelled Data: The unlabelled examples contribute to the learning process by providing additional information about the underlying distribution of the data. The algorithm uses this unlabelled information to generalise better and capture the inherent structure of the data more effectively.

Balancing Supervision and Exploration: Semi-supervised learning strikes a balance between the supervision provided by the labelled data and the exploration enabled by the unlabelled data. It leverages the strengths of both approaches to achieve improved performance compared to using only labelled or unlabelled data alone.

In summary, semi-supervised learning in machine learning combines labelled and unlabelled data to train models, leveraging the labelled data for guidance while also benefiting from the additional information provided by the unlabelled data. In the context of a cat and dog image example, semi-supervised learning would involve training a model using a combination of labelled images (e.g., with explicit labels indicating cats or dogs) and unlabelled images (e.g., without explicit labels), enabling the algorithm to learn more effectively from the available data.

Types of Semi-Supervised Learning Methods

Semi-supervised learning techniques leverage both labelled and unlabelled data to improve model performance and generalisation. Here are some common methods:

Graph-Based Semi-Supervised Learning: This method represents data points as nodes in a graph, where edges denote similarities between points. Labels from labelled data points are propagated through the graph to unlabelled points based on their relationships.

Label Propagation: In label propagation, labels from labelled instances are iteratively propagated to neighbouring unlabelled instances based on their similarity. This process continues until convergence, refining the labels of unlabelled data.

Co-Training: Co-training involves training multiple models on different subsets of unlabelled data. These models then label each other's predictions, enabling them to learn from different perspectives and improve overall performance.

Self-Training: Self-training begins by training a model on the labelled data. The trained model is then used to predict labels for unlabelled instances, which are added to the labelled set. The model is retrained on this expanded dataset, refining its predictions iteratively.

Generative Adversarial Networks (GANs): GANs consist of two neural networks - a generator and a discriminator - that compete against each other. The generator creates synthetic data samples, while the discriminator distinguishes between real and synthetic samples. GANs can generate unlabelled data for semi-supervised learning, enhancing the dataset and improving model performance.

These semi-supervised learning methods offer diverse approaches to leverage unlabelled data effectively, contributing to more robust and accurate models in various applications.

Advantages of Semi-Supervised Machine Learning

- Enhanced Generalisation: Semi-supervised learning combines both labelled and unlabelled data, leading to improved model generalisation and performance on unseen data.
- Versatility: Semi-supervised methods can be applied to a wide range of data types and domains, making them suitable for various real-world applications.
- Cost-Efficiency: Leveraging unlabelled data reduces the need for extensive manual labelling, resulting in cost savings and faster model development.

Disadvantages of Semi-Supervised Machine Learning

- Complexity: Implementing semi-supervised methods can be more complex compared to supervised or unsupervised approaches, requiring specialised algorithms and techniques.
- Label Dependency: Semi-supervised learning still relies on a portion of labelled data, which may not always be readily available or easy to obtain, limiting its applicability in some scenarios.
- Impact of Unlabelled Data: The quality and characteristics of unlabelled data can significantly influence model performance, requiring careful consideration and preprocessing.

Applications of Semi-Supervised Learning

- Natural Language Processing (NLP): Improve language models and classifiers by incorporating a small set of labelled text data with a larger pool of unlabelled text.
- Speech Recognition: Boost the accuracy of speech recognition systems by utilising a limited amount of transcribed speech data along with a larger set of unlabelled audio.

- Recommendation Systems: Enhance personalised recommendations by supplementing sparse labelled user-item interactions with extensive unlabelled user behaviour data.
- Healthcare and Medical Imaging: Improve medical image analysis by integrating labelled medical images with a larger set of unlabelled images, facilitating better diagnosis and treatment planning.

Reinforcement Learning:

Master said, "Reinforcement learning (RL) in machine learning is a type of learning paradigm where an agent learns to make decisions by interacting with an environment. The agent takes actions in the environment and receives feedback in the form of rewards or penalties based on its actions. The goal of the agent is to maximise cumulative rewards over time by learning a policy—a mapping from states to actions—that guides its decision-making process."

> "Reinforcement learning embodies the essence of adaptability, as agents navigate the dynamic landscape of environments, driven by the pursuit of optimising rewards over time through learned decision-making strategies." – Shree Shambav

To explain reinforcement learning with a cat and dog image example:

Environment Setup: Imagine an environment where there are two rooms, one containing images of cats and the other containing images of dogs. The agent (e.g., an AI model) can observe the images in each room and take actions.

Agent Interaction: At each time step, the agent selects an action to perform. For example, it might choose to move from one room to another, or it might decide to observe an image in the current room.

Feedback and Rewards: After taking an action, the agent receives feedback from the environment. If the agent observes an image of a cat and receives a positive reward, it learns that being in the cat room is beneficial. Conversely, if it observes an image of a dog and receives a negative reward, it learns that being in the dog room is disadvantageous.

Learning and Policy Improvement: The agent learns from its interactions with the environment and updates its policy based on the received rewards. Over time, it learns which actions lead to higher rewards and refines its decision-making strategy accordingly.

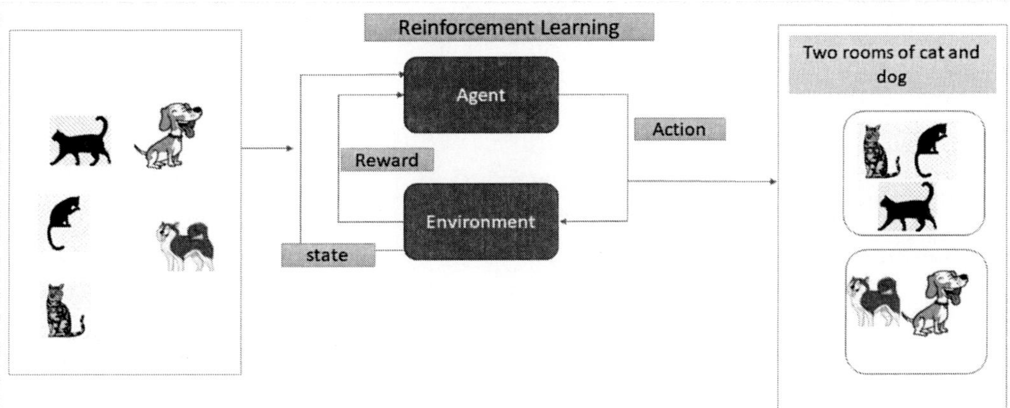

Goal Achievement: The ultimate goal of the agent is to maximise cumulative rewards over time. It learns to navigate the environment effectively, choosing actions that lead to desirable outcomes, such as spending more time in the cat room (if the objective is to maximise rewards associated with cat images) and avoiding the dog room.

In summary, reinforcement learning in machine learning involves an agent learning to make decisions by interacting with an environment, receiving feedback in the form of rewards or penalties, and adjusting its behaviour to maximise cumulative rewards over time. In the context of a cat and dog image example, the agent learns to navigate between rooms to observe images that result in positive rewards (e.g., cat images) while avoiding actions that lead to negative rewards (e.g., dog images).

Here are some of the most common reinforcements learning algorithms:

Q-learning: Q-learning is a model-free reinforcement learning algorithm that learns a Q-function, which maps states to actions. The Q-function estimates the expected reward of taking a particular action in a given state.

SARSA (State-Action-Reward-State-Action): SARSA is another model-free reinforcement learning algorithm that learns a Q-function. Unlike Q-learning, SARSA updates the Q-function for the action that was actually taken, rather than the optimal action.

Deep Q-learning: Deep Q-learning is a combination of Q-learning and deep learning. It employs a neural network to represent the Q-function, allowing it to learn complex relationships between states and actions.

These algorithms form the foundation of reinforcement learning and are widely used in various applications, including robotics, gaming, and autonomous systems. Each algorithm has its unique characteristics and is suited for different types of environments and tasks.

Example: Imagine training an AI agent to play chess. As the agent explores various moves, it receives feedback, either positive or negative, based on the outcome. Reinforcement Learning finds applications where agents learn tasks by interacting with their environment.

Types of Reinforcement Learning:

Positive Reinforcement:

- Rewards the agent for desired actions.
- Encourages the repetition of favourable behaviours.

Examples: Giving a treat to a dog for sitting, awarding points in a game for a correct answer.

Negative Reinforcement:

- Removes undesirable stimuli to promote desired behaviour.
- Discourages the repetition of unfavourable actions.

Examples: Turning off a loud buzzer when a lever is pressed, avoiding a penalty by completing a task.

Advantages of Reinforcement Learning:

- Enables autonomous decision-making suitable for tasks requiring sequential decisions, such as robotics and game-playing.
- Preferred for achieving long-term results that are challenging to attain.
- Applicable to solving complex problems resistant to conventional techniques.

Disadvantages of Reinforcement Learning:

- Training RL agents can be computationally intensive and time-consuming.
- Not ideal for solving straightforward problems.
- Requires substantial data and computational resources, making it impractical and

costly.

Applications of Reinforcement Learning:

- Game Playing: Reinforcement Learning (RL) can train agents to master various games, including complex ones like chess.
- Robotics: RL enables robots to learn autonomously, performing tasks such as grasping objects or navigating through environments.
- Autonomous Vehicles: RL plays a crucial role in training self-driving cars to make decisions and navigate safely on roads.
- Recommendation Systems: RL enhances recommendation algorithms by learning user preferences and providing personalised suggestions.
- Healthcare: RL aids in optimising treatment plans, drug discovery, and personalised medicine.
- Natural Language Processing (NLP): RL powers dialogue systems and chatbots, enabling more natural and responsive interactions.
- Finance and Trading: RL is applied in algorithmic trading, where agents learn to make profitable decisions in dynamic market conditions.
- Supply Chain and Inventory Management: RL optimises supply chain operations by managing inventory levels and distribution networks efficiently.
- Energy Management: RL optimises energy consumption in various domains, including smart grids and building automation.
- Adaptive Personal Assistants: RL improves personal assistants by learning user preferences and adapting to individual needs.
- Virtual Reality (VR) and Augmented Reality (AR): RL algorithms create immersive and interactive experiences in VR and AR applications.
- Industrial Control: RL optimises industrial processes by learning control policies that maximise efficiency and productivity.
- Education: RL is used to develop adaptive learning systems that personalise educational content and pace to individual students.
- Agriculture: RL optimises agricultural operations, such as crop management and yield

prediction, to enhance productivity and sustainability.

Supervised vs Unsupervised vs Reinforcement:

	Supervised	Unsupervised	Reinforcement
Definition	The machine learns by using labelled data.	The machine learns by using unlabelled data.	An agent interacts with its environment by producing actions, discovering errors or rewards.
Types of problems	Regression and classification	Association and Clustering	Reward based
Types of data	Labelled	Unlabelled	No pre-defined
Training	External supervision	No supervision	No supervision
Algorithm	Linear, Logistic, SVM, KNN etc	K-Means, C-Means etc	Q-Learning, SARSA, etc

Types of problem solved using Machine Learning:

Regression	Classification	Clustering
Supervised	Supervised	Unsupervised
Output is a continuous quantity. Example: 10.01, 1000.01	Output is a categorical quantity. Example: Gender Male/Female, Yes/No	Assign data points in cluster. Example: Netflix group based on age, gender, interest, geography
Main aim to forecast and predict	Main aim to compute category of the data	Main aim is to group similar items into cluster
Example: Predict stock market price	Example: Classify email as spam or non-spam	Example: Find all transaction fraudulent in nature
Algorithm: Linear Regression	Algorithm: Logistic Regression, Naïve Bayes, K nearest neighbour, SVM	Algorithm: K Means

General Steps to follow: ML Problem

Master said, "Machine learning (ML) is a technique used to automate analytical model building, enabling machines to learn from data without explicit programming. It encompasses various traditional disciplines and operates as a subset of artificial intelligence (AI)."

An ML pipeline represents a systematic workflow guiding the development of machine learning models. By automating the process, ML pipelines streamline model creation, making it systematic and efficient. The pipeline consists of several sequential steps, ensuring a structured approach to building ML models.

In the context of customer care services for a hypothetical company, such as an online bookshop, an ML pipeline would guide the development of a model to enhance customer support. Here's a breakdown of the pipeline's steps using this example:

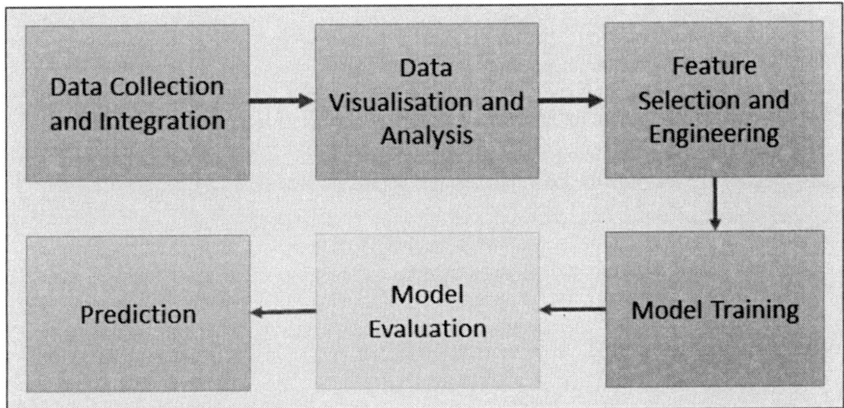

Step 1: Data Collection and Integration

The initial step of the ML pipeline involves collecting and integrating data essential for model development. Here's an in-depth look at this pivotal phase:

Data Collection:

This phase entails gathering diverse data from various sources pertinent to the problem at hand.

In our example of optimising customer care services for an online bookstore, collected data might include customer purchase history, past orders, prime membership status, Kindle ownership, and complaint records.

The quantity and quality of collected data significantly influence model performance, with a larger, more diverse dataset generally leading to better outcomes.

Data Integration:

After collecting data, it's crucial to integrate disparate datasets into a unified format.

Integration involves combining related data points and organising them cohesively for subsequent analysis.

This phase ensures that all relevant data is readily accessible for further processing and modelling.

Feature Identification:

Each piece of information within the collected data represents a potential feature that could influence the model's predictions.

Features, also known as inputs, play a vital role in shaping the model's learning process and predictive accuracy.

Identifying pertinent features is essential for building an effective model that captures relevant patterns and relationships within the data.

Step 2: Exploratory Data Analysis and Visualisation:

Once the data is collected and integrated, developers proceed to explore and visualize the dataset to gain deeper insights:

Data Visualisation:

Visualisation techniques such as histograms, scatter plots, and heatmaps are employed to elucidate patterns and relationships within the dataset.

Visual exploration facilitates the identification of hidden insights and outliers that may impact model performance.

Developers can visually assess data distribution, identify trends, and detect anomalies, aiding in informed decision-making for subsequent model development.

Data Analysis:

Visualised data is analysed to discern underlying patterns and correlations, guiding the selection of appropriate machine learning techniques.

In our example, unsupervised learning methods might be utilised to uncover customer purchasing habits and segmentation.

Step 3: Feature Selection and Engineering:

Feature selection and engineering involve shaping the dataset to optimise model performance:

Feature Selection:

Developers choose relevant features that have the most significant impact on the model's predictive capabilities.

Selected features should exhibit minimal correlation among themselves while maximising correlation with the target variable.

Careful feature selection ensures that the model focuses on the most informative attributes, enhancing its predictive accuracy.

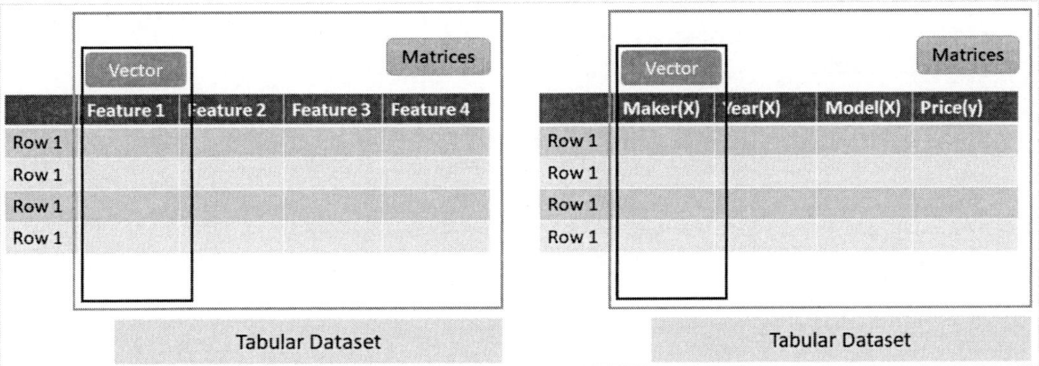

Feature Engineering:

Feature engineering encompasses transforming raw data into more meaningful and predictive features.

Techniques such as scaling, normalisation, and creating interaction terms are employed to extract additional insights from the dataset.

This phase is critical for refining the dataset and extracting maximum predictive power from the available features.

Step 4: Model Training:

With the dataset prepared and features engineered, the model training phase begins:

Data Splitting:

The dataset is partitioned into three subsets: training data, validation data, and test data.

Typically, 70% to 80% of the data is allocated to the training set, which is used to train the model.

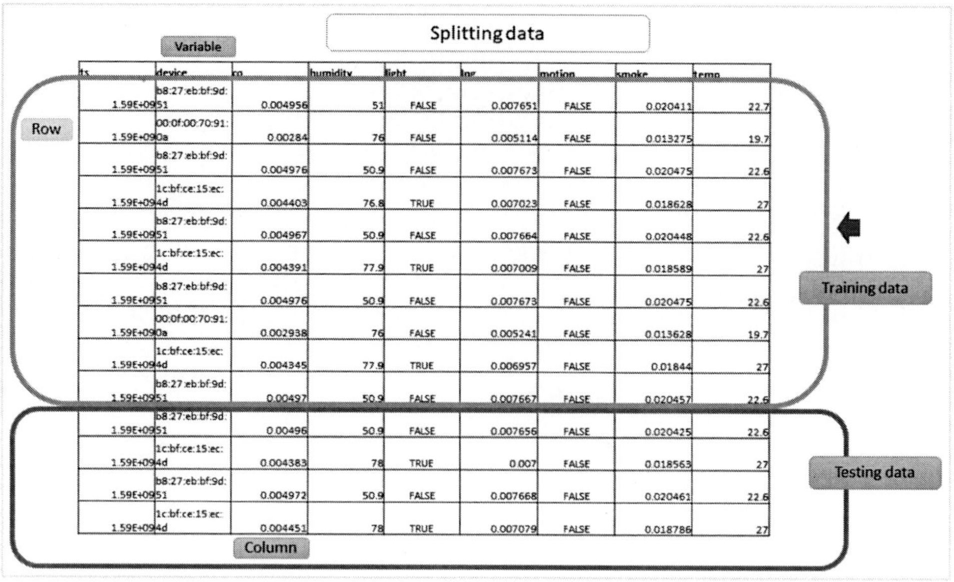

ts	device	co	humidity	light	lpg	motion	smoke	temp
1.59E+09	b8:27:eb:bf:9d:51	0.004956	51	FALSE	0.007651	FALSE	0.020411	22.7
1.59E+09	00:0f:00:70:91:0a	0.00284	76	FALSE	0.005114	FALSE	0.013275	19.7
1.59E+09	b8:27:eb:bf:9d:51	0.004976	50.9	FALSE	0.007673	FALSE	0.020475	22.6
1.59E+09	1c:bf:ce:15:ec:4d	0.004403	76.8	TRUE	0.007023	FALSE	0.018628	27
1.59E+09	b8:27:eb:bf:9d:51	0.004967	50.9	FALSE	0.007664	FALSE	0.020448	22.6
1.59E+09	1c:bf:ce:15:ec:4d	0.004391	77.9	TRUE	0.007009	FALSE	0.018589	27
1.59E+09	b8:27:eb:bf:9d:51	0.004976	50.9	FALSE	0.007673	FALSE	0.020475	22.6
1.59E+09	00:0f:00:70:91:0a	0.002938	76	FALSE	0.005241	FALSE	0.013628	19.7
1.59E+09	1c:bf:ce:15:ec:4d	0.004345	77.9	TRUE	0.006957	FALSE	0.01844	27
1.59E+09	b8:27:eb:bf:9d:51	0.00497	50.9	FALSE	0.007667	FALSE	0.020457	22.6
1.59E+09	b8:27:eb:bf:9d:51	0.00496	50.9	FALSE	0.007656	FALSE	0.020425	22.6
1.59E+09	1c:bf:ce:15:ec:4d	0.004383	78	TRUE	0.007	FALSE	0.018563	27
1.59E+09	b8:27:eb:bf:9d:51	0.004972	50.9	FALSE	0.007668	FALSE	0.020461	22.6
1.59E+09	1c:bf:ce:15:ec:4d	0.004451	78	TRUE	0.007079	FALSE	0.018786	27

The validation set, comprising around 10% to 15% of the data, is used for hyperparameter tuning to prevent overfitting or underfitting.

The remaining portion, also 10% to 15%, constitutes the test set, utilised to evaluate the model's performance after training.

Model Training:

Using the training data, the model is trained to learn patterns and relationships within the data.

Various machine learning algorithms, such as regression, classification, or clustering, may be employed based on the nature of the problem and dataset characteristics.

The model iteratively adjusts its parameters to minimise the difference between predicted and actual outcomes, optimising its predictive capabilities.

Step 5: Model Evaluation:

Following model training, the performance of the trained model is evaluated:

Evaluation Data Usage:

The validation or development dataset is utilised to assess the model's performance and fine-tune hyperparameters.

To ensure robustness, the test dataset is employed for final model evaluation, providing an unbiased assessment of its predictive accuracy.

Metrics Calculation:

Evaluation metrics, such as accuracy, precision, recall, F1-score, and confusion matrix, are computed to quantify the model's performance.

This metrics provide insights into the model's ability to make accurate predictions and handle various classes or categories within the dataset.

Step 6: Prediction:

In the prediction phase, the trained model is deployed to make predictions on new or unseen data.

Model Deployment:

The model is deployed in production environments where it can make real-time predictions or provide insights.

Deployment involves integrating the model into existing systems or applications, ensuring seamless integration and functionality.

Prediction Generation:

With the model deployed, it is ready to generate predictions based on input data.

Predictions are made on both training and test datasets to assess the model's performance and validate its predictive capabilities.

Overall, the ML pipeline provides a structured framework for systematically developing, training, evaluating, and deploying machine learning models, ensuring efficiency, reliability, and effectiveness throughout the model development lifecycle.

Summary

In this unit, we delved into the foundational principles of machine learning, offering a holistic understanding of its diverse facets. We embarked on our journey by elucidating the core categories of machine learning: supervised, unsupervised, semi-supervised, and reinforcement learning.

Within each category, we explored various types of learning tasks, including Classification, Regression, Clustering, Dimensionality Reduction, and Association Rule Mining. For each task, we uncovered a spectrum of algorithms tailored to meet specific objectives, ranging from traditional methods like decision trees and logistic regression to advanced techniques such as deep learning and ensemble methods.

Moreover, we navigated through the essential stages of the machine learning pipeline, starting with Data Collection and Integration, where raw data is gathered and harmonised from disparate sources. We then proceeded to Feature Identification, where relevant attributes are identified to inform subsequent analysis. Subsequently, we engaged in Exploratory Data Analysis and Visualisation, employing statistical techniques and graphical methods to glean insights from the data.

Following data exploration, we ventured into Feature Selection and Engineering, refining our dataset to enhance model performance. This phase was crucial in optimising the predictive power of our models by selecting pertinent features and crafting new ones.

Moving forward, we transitioned to Model Training, where algorithms are trained on labelled data to recognise patterns and make predictions. This was followed by Model Evaluation, where the performance of trained models was rigorously assessed using appropriate metrics.

Finally, we culminated our journey with Prediction, where well-trained models were deployed to make informed predictions on unseen data, thereby unlocking valuable insights and driving decision-making processes. Throughout this unit, we gained a comprehensive understanding of machine learning methodologies and their applications across diverse domains.

What Next

In this unit, we will cover essential mathematics for data science, starting with linear algebra and vectors. We will discuss data dispersion, basic calculus applications, and probability theory, including Bayes' theorem and hypothesis testing. Time series analysis and various probability distributions will be introduced. Feature reduction techniques, such as Recursive Feature Elimination, and loss functions, such as binary cross-entropy, will be explained. Sampling techniques, both probability and non-probability, will be covered. Lastly, we will delve into statistical regression, focusing on linear regression, R-squared, cross-validation, and addressing overfitting and underfitting.

P1-U1-L1-2 - Practice Question

1. What are the core categories of machine learning discussed in this unit?
2. Define supervised learning and provide an example.
3. Explain unsupervised learning and give an example.
4. What is semi-supervised learning, and when is it used?
5. Describe reinforcement learning and provide a real-world application.
6. What are the main types of learning tasks in machine learning?
7. Give an example of a classification task.
8. Explain Regression and provide a real-world scenario.
9. What is clustering, and when is it used?
10. Describe Dimensionality Reduction and its significance.
11. What is Association Rule Mining, and give an example?
12. Name some traditional machine learning algorithms.
13. Mention some advanced machine learning techniques.
14. Explain the Data Collection and Integration stage of the machine learning pipeline.
15. What is Feature Identification, and why is it important?
16. Describe Exploratory Data Analysis (EDA) and its role in machine learning.
17. What is Feature Selection, and how does it contribute to model performance?
18. Explain the Model Training phase of the machine learning pipeline.
19. What is Model Evaluation, and why is it necessary?
20. Define Prediction and its significance in machine learning.

PART TWO

INTRODUCTION

BASIC OF AI

"The true power of AI lies not in replacing human intelligence, but in amplifying it—making us more creative, efficient, and visionary than ever before."

– Shree Shambav

PART TWO

DAY THREE

Unit 2 - Lesson One

Role of Mathematics

□ Understanding the Role of Mathematics in Machine Learning

Whether you're starting your journey in machine learning or contemplating a career transition, grasping fundamental mathematical concepts is essential. Before delving into the intricate world of machine learning algorithms, it's crucial to lay a strong foundation in key mathematical areas such as:

Statistics: Statistical concepts form the backbone of machine learning, helping us understand data distributions, variability, and uncertainty. From descriptive statistics to inferential methods, statistical techniques enable us to glean insights from data and make informed decisions.

Probability Distribution: Probability theory underpins many machine learning algorithms, allowing us to model uncertainty and quantify the likelihood of events. Understanding probability distributions is pivotal for tasks such as parameter estimation, hypothesis testing, and generative modelling.

Linear Algebra and Matrix Operations: Linear algebra plays a central role in machine learning, facilitating operations on high-dimensional data and parameter spaces. Matrices and vectors are ubiquitous in tasks like feature representation, model optimization, and dimensionality reduction.

Regression and Optimization: Regression analysis provides a framework for modelling relationships between variables, enabling us to predict continuous outcomes and estimate parameters. Optimization techniques, rooted in calculus and numerical methods, empower us to fine-tune models and minimize prediction errors.

Geometry and Dimensionality Reduction: Geometric intuition aids in visualizing data structures and understanding manifold learning techniques. Dimensionality reduction methods leverage geometric concepts to compress data while preserving essential information, enhancing model interpretability and efficiency.

By mastering these mathematical concepts, you gain a deeper understanding of the underlying principles driving machine learning algorithms. This knowledge empowers you to:

- Develop intuition about algorithm behaviour and performance.
- Interpret model outputs and diagnose potential issues.
- Design robust experiments and validate model assumptions.
- Explore advanced topics such as deep learning and probabilistic modelling with confidence.

In essence, mathematics serves as the bedrock of machine learning, providing the analytical framework necessary to navigate complex data landscapes and unlock actionable insights. Embrace the journey of learning and applying mathematical principles in your pursuit of mastering machine learning.

Linear Algebra and Matrix Operations

Linear Algebra is a branch of mathematics that deals with vector spaces and linear transformations between them. It provides a powerful framework for representing and solving systems of linear equations and is fundamental to many areas of science and engineering, including machine learning and computer graphics.

Vectors and Matrices

In Linear Algebra, vectors represent quantities with both magnitude and direction, while matrices are rectangular arrays of numbers arranged in rows and columns. Vectors can be thought of as special cases of matrices, with one-dimensional arrays representing column or row vectors.

Matrix

Matrix Introduction:

Master said, "Matrices serve as a fundamental data structure in Linear Algebra, enabling the representation and manipulation of linear transformations and systems of linear equations. They are commonly used to encode data and perform mathematical operations in various applications."

Understanding Matrices

Matrices are fundamental mathematical structures used to represent and manipulate data in various fields, including mathematics, computer science, and engineering. They consist of rectangular arrays of numbers, symbols, or characters organised into rows and columns.

Structure of Matrices

A matrix is defined by its dimensions, which specify the number of rows and columns it contains. For example, a matrix with m rows and n columns is said to have an order of m x n. The elements of a matrix are the individual entries located at each row-column intersection.

Representation and Terminology

In practical terms, matrices can represent a wide range of data types and structures. For instance, in geometric applications, matrices can represent transformations of points or vectors in space. In statistical analysis, matrices are used to store data sets or model relationships between variables.

Example: Array of Points

Consider a scenario where points are arranged in space, each associated with specific coordinates. By organising these points into rows and columns, we create a matrix where each element corresponds to a point's coordinates. This array of points forms a matrix, with each row representing a point and each column representing a dimension (e.g., x-coordinate, y-coordinate).

Elements of a Matrix

The individual items within a matrix are referred to as elements. These elements can be numbers, symbols, or any other type of data. Each element occupies a specific position within the matrix, determined by its row and column indices.

Order of a Matrix

The order of a matrix is determined by the number of rows and columns it possesses. For example, a matrix with 3 rows and 2 columns has an order of 3×2. The order provides crucial information about the matrix's size and shape, facilitating operations such as addition, subtraction, and multiplication.

$$\begin{bmatrix} 1 & 2 \\ 3 & 4 \end{bmatrix}_{2x2} \quad \begin{bmatrix} 1 & 2 \\ 3 & 4 \\ 5 & 6 \end{bmatrix}_{3x3}$$

Matrix Addition

Matrix addition involves adding corresponding elements of two matrices of the same dimensions. This operation is performed element-wise, resulting in a new matrix with the same dimensions as the original matrices.

Addition

$$A = \begin{bmatrix} 1 & 2 \\ 3 & 4 \end{bmatrix} \quad B = \begin{bmatrix} 2 & 3 \\ 4 & 4 \end{bmatrix} \quad \Rightarrow \quad A + B = \begin{bmatrix} 1+2 & 2+3 \\ 3+4 & 4+4 \end{bmatrix} = \begin{bmatrix} 3 & 5 \\ 7 & 8 \end{bmatrix}$$

Matrix Subtraction

Subtraction of matrices is an operation performed between two matrices of the same dimensions. It involves subtracting the corresponding elements of one matrix from the corresponding elements of another matrix to produce a new matrix of the same dimensions.

Subtraction

$$A = \begin{bmatrix} 1 & 2 \\ 3 & 4 \end{bmatrix} \quad B = \begin{bmatrix} 2 & 3 \\ 4 & 4 \end{bmatrix} \quad \Rightarrow \quad A - B = \begin{bmatrix} 1-2 & 2-3 \\ 3-4 & 4-4 \end{bmatrix} = \begin{bmatrix} -1 & -1 \\ -1 & 0 \end{bmatrix}$$

Scalar Multiplication of Matrices

Master said, "Scalar multiplication of matrices involves multiplying each element of a matrix by a scalar (a single number). This operation is performed by multiplying every element of the matrix by the scalar to obtain a new matrix with the same dimensions."

When performing scalar multiplication on a matrix A with scalar k, denoted as k·A, each element aij in the resulting matrix B is given by:

$\mathbf{b_{ij} = k \cdot a_{ij}}$

Scalar

$$A = \begin{bmatrix} 1 & 2 \\ 3 & 4 \end{bmatrix} \quad 3A = \begin{bmatrix} 3x1 & 3x2 \\ 3x3 & 3x4 \end{bmatrix} = \begin{bmatrix} 3 & 6 \\ 9 & 12 \end{bmatrix}$$

Matrix Multiplication

Master explained that the Matrix multiplication is a more complex operation that combines rows and columns of matrices to produce a new matrix. The resulting matrix's dimensions are determined by the number of rows of the first matrix and the number of columns of the second matrix.

When a matrix A of size (I x j) is multiplied by a matrix B of size (j x k), the resulting product matrix AB has dimensions (I x k). Each element cij of the product matrix is obtained by taking the dot product of the ith row of matrix A and the jth column of matrix B.

Multiplication

$$A = \begin{bmatrix} 1 & 2 \\ 4 & 5 \end{bmatrix} \quad B = \begin{bmatrix} 2 & 3 \\ 6 & 7 \end{bmatrix} \Rightarrow AB = \begin{bmatrix} (1x2) + (2x6) & (1x3) + (2x7) \\ (4x2) + (5x6) & (4x3) + (5x7) \end{bmatrix} = \begin{bmatrix} 14 & 17 \\ 38 & 47 \end{bmatrix}$$

Transpose of a Matrix

The transpose of a matrix is a derived matrix achieved by exchanging its rows with columns, effectively transforming the original matrix where rows become columns and columns become rows. When you transpose an m x n matrix, it becomes an n x m matrix. In this process, each element originally found at position (i, j) in the original matrix now occupies the position (j, i) in the transposed matrix. It's important to note that the transpose operation doesn't alter the original matrix; it merely reorganises its elements.

Transpose

$$A = \begin{bmatrix} 1 & 2 \\ 4 & 5 \end{bmatrix} \quad A^T = \begin{bmatrix} 1 & 4 \\ 2 & 5 \end{bmatrix}$$

Properties of the Transpose of a Matrix

- Symmetry under Double Transposition: $(A^T)^T=A$ The transpose of a matrix, when transposed again, results in the original matrix.
- Addition Transpose Property: $(A+B)^T=A^T+B^T$ The transpose of the sum of two matrices is equal to the sum of their individual transposes.
- Multiplication Transpose Property: $(AB)^T=B^TA^T$ The transpose of the product of two matrices is equal to the product of their transposes in the reverse order.

Properties of Matrix addition and multiplication

The properties governing the operations of multiplication and addition of matrices are outlined below:

- Commutative Property of Addition: $A+B=B+A$ Matrices exhibit commutativity under addition, meaning the order in which matrices are added does not affect the result.
- Associative Property of Addition: $(A+B)+C=A+(B+C)$ The addition of matrices follows the associative property, allowing grouping without altering the sum.
- Non-Commutative Property of Multiplication: $AB \neq BA$ Unlike addition, multiplication of matrices is generally not commutative, meaning the order of multiplication matters.
- Associative Property of Multiplication: $(AB)C = A(BC)$ The associative property holds for matrix multiplication, enabling flexibility in grouping matrices for multiplication.
- Distributive Property: $A(B+C) = AB+AC$ Matrix multiplication distributes over addition, facilitating the expansion of expressions involving matrices.

Understanding these properties is fundamental in performing matrix operations and manipulating expressions involving matrices in a consistent and systematic manner.

Trace

The trace of a square matrix is the sum of its diagonal elements. It represents the sum of eigenvalues of the matrix and is often used in various mathematical and statistical computations.

Trace

$$A = \begin{bmatrix} 1 & 2 \\ 4 & 5 \end{bmatrix} \qquad \text{Trace } A = 1+5 = 6$$

Types of Matrices

- Row Matrix: A matrix with a single row and no columns is termed a Row Matrix.
- Column Matrix: A matrix with a single column and no rows is termed a Column Matrix.
- Horizontal Matrix: If the number of rows is less than the number of columns, it is known as a Horizontal Matrix.
- Vertical Matrix: If the number of columns is less than the number of rows, it is known as a Vertical Matrix.
- Rectangular Matrix: A matrix with unequal numbers of rows and columns is referred to as a Rectangular Matrix.
- Square Matrix: A matrix where the number of rows equals the number of columns is called a Square Matrix.
- Diagonal Matrix: A square matrix with zero non-diagonal elements is referred to as a Diagonal Matrix.
- Zero or Null Matrix: A matrix where all elements are zero is termed a Zero Matrix or Null Matrix.
- Unit or Identity Matrix: A diagonal matrix with all diagonal elements equal to 1 is termed a Unit Matrix or Identity Matrix (represented by I).
- Symmetric Matrix: A square matrix is considered symmetric if its transpose equals the original matrix ($A^T = A$).
- Skew-symmetric Matrix: A square matrix is skew-symmetric if its transpose equals the negative of the original matrix ($A^T = -A$).
- Orthogonal Matrix: An orthogonal matrix satisfies the condition $AA^T = A^TA = I$.
- Idempotent Matrix: A matrix is idempotent if the square of the matrix equals the matrix itself ($A^2 = A$).
- Involutory Matrix: An involutory matrix satisfies the condition $A^2 = I$.
- Upper Triangular Matrix: A square matrix with all elements below the diagonal being zero is an upper triangular matrix.
- Lower Triangular Matrix: A square matrix with all elements above the diagonal being zero is a lower triangular matrix.
- Singular Matrix: A square matrix with a determinant of zero ($|A| = 0$) is termed a Singular Matrix.

- Nonsingular Matrix: A square matrix with a nonzero determinant is termed a Nonsingular Matrix.

Determinant

The determinant of a square matrix is a scalar value that encodes information about the matrix's properties, such as invertibility and orientation change. It plays a crucial role in solving systems of linear equations and calculating the inverse of a matrix.

The determinant of a square matrix is a scalar value associated with that matrix, denoted as $|A|$, where A is the matrix. It serves as a measure of the matrix's properties, such as invertibility and volume scaling factor.

Key Properties:

- Square Matrix Requirement: The determinant can only be calculated for square matrices, where the number of rows is equal to the number of columns.
- Calculation: The determinant of a square matrix is computed by summing the products of the elements of the matrix with their respective cofactors.

Finding the Determinant of a Square Matrix

To calculate the determinant of a square matrix A, we follow these steps:

Base Case: For a 1×1 matrix (a single-element matrix), the determinant is simply the value of that element.

Recursive Approach: For larger square matrices A of size $n\times n$, we can use a recursive approach:

- Choose a row or column to expand along (usually the first row or column).
- For each element in the chosen row or column, calculate its cofactor by removing the row and column containing that element and finding the determinant of the resulting matrix.
- Multiply each element by its cofactor and sum the results.

Sign Convention: Apply the sign convention (+/-) to alternate terms based on their position in the matrix.

Example: For a 2×2 matrix A with elements a,b,c,d, the determinant is calculated as |A|=ad−bc.

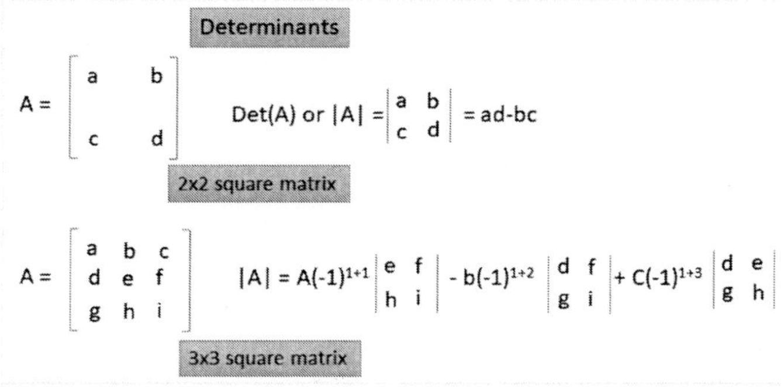

Determinants

$$A = \begin{bmatrix} a & b \\ c & d \end{bmatrix} \qquad \text{Det(A) or } |A| = \begin{vmatrix} a & b \\ c & d \end{vmatrix} = ad-bc$$

2x2 square matrix

$$A = \begin{bmatrix} a & b & c \\ d & e & f \\ g & h & i \end{bmatrix} \qquad |A| = A(-1)^{1+1}\begin{vmatrix} e & f \\ h & i \end{vmatrix} - b(-1)^{1+2}\begin{vmatrix} d & f \\ g & i \end{vmatrix} + C(-1)^{1+3}\begin{vmatrix} d & e \\ g & h \end{vmatrix}$$

3x3 square matrix

Minor and Cofactor of Matrix

Akshaya asked, "What is Minor and cofactor of matrix?"

Master said, "Minors and cofactors serve as fundamental components in matrix algebra, crucial for computing the adjoint and inverse of a matrix. A minor represents a reduced portion of the original matrix, obtained by removing the row and column associated with a specific element. On the other hand, a cofactor is derived from the minor by multiplying it with $(-1)_{i+j}$, where i and j represent the row and column indices of the element."

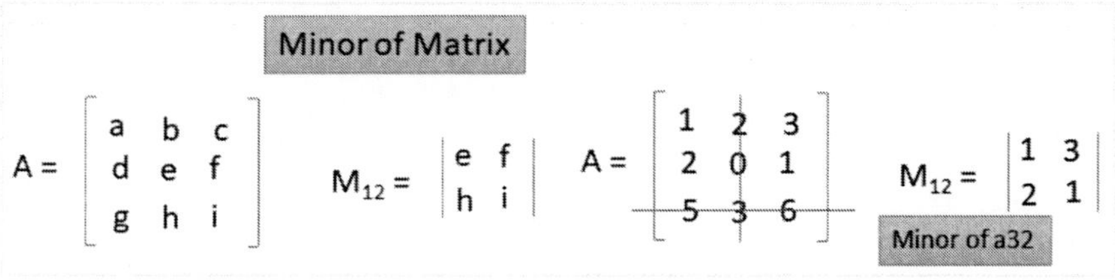

Minor of Matrix

$$A = \begin{bmatrix} a & b & c \\ d & e & f \\ g & h & i \end{bmatrix} \qquad M_{12} = \begin{vmatrix} e & f \\ h & i \end{vmatrix} \qquad A = \begin{bmatrix} 1 & 2 & 3 \\ 2 & 0 & 1 \\ 5 & 3 & 6 \end{bmatrix} \qquad M_{12} = \begin{vmatrix} 1 & 3 \\ 2 & 1 \end{vmatrix}$$

Minor of a32

These concepts are indispensable in Linear Algebra, playing pivotal roles in determinant calculations, as well as in determining the adjoint and inverse of matrices.

Key Properties:

- Representation: The minor of a matrix element aij is represented by M_{ij}.
- Calculation: To find the minor of an element a_{ij}, we remove the ith row and j^{th} column from the matrix and calculate the determinant of the resulting submatrix.

Cofactor:

The cofactor of an element aij in a determinant, denoted by Aij or Cij, is determined as follows:

Cij = $(-1)_{i+j}$ M_{ij}

Cofactors

Det(A) or |A| = $\begin{bmatrix} 5 & 3 & 1 \\ 2 & 0 & -1 \\ 1 & 2 & 3 \end{bmatrix}$ Cofactors of elements = $(-1)^{3+2} \begin{vmatrix} 5 & 1 \\ 2 & -1 \end{vmatrix}$ =(-1)((5*-1) – (2*1) =(-1)((-5) – (2) = 7

Cofactor of a32

Adjoint of Matrix:

To compute the adjoint of a matrix, follow these steps:

- Step 1: Calculate the cofactors of each element of the given matrix.
- Step 2: Form a new matrix using the cofactors obtained in Step 1.
- Step 3: Transpose the matrix obtained in Step 2.
- Step 4: The resulting transposed matrix is the adjoint of the given matrix.

Inverse of a Matrix

The inverse of a matrix is a matrix that, when multiplied by the original matrix, yields the identity matrix. Finding the inverse of a matrix is crucial for solving systems of linear equations and performing various mathematical transformations.

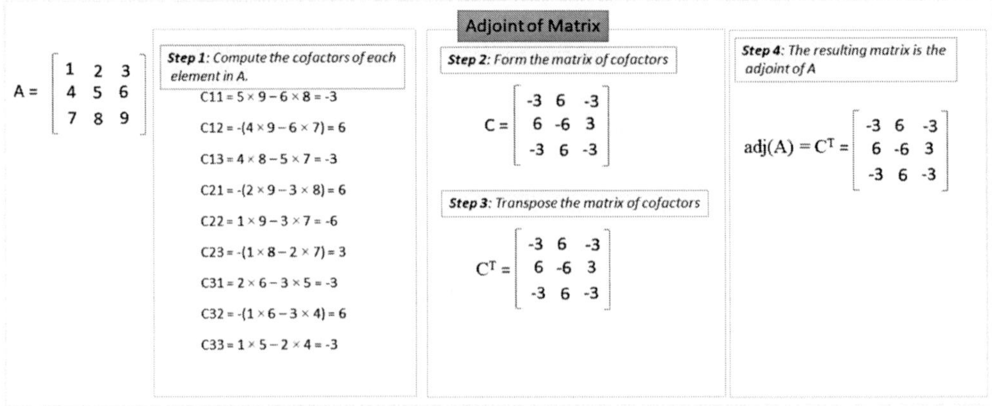

Example: Let's find the inverse of matrix A:

- Step 1: Calculate the determinant of matrix A.
- Step 2: If the determinant is non-zero, proceed to compute the adjoint of matrix A.
- Step 3: Apply the formula A−1= $\frac{(adj(A))}{|A|}$ to find the inverse of matrix A. If the determinant is zero, matrix A does not have an inverse.

PART TWO

DAY THREE

Unit 2 - Lesson Two

Dispersion of Data

☐ Measure of Central Tendency

Master said, "The measures of central tendency are statistical parameters used to summarise a set of data by identifying the central point within that dataset. The most commonly used measures of central tendency are the mean, median, and mode. These parameters are discussed below."

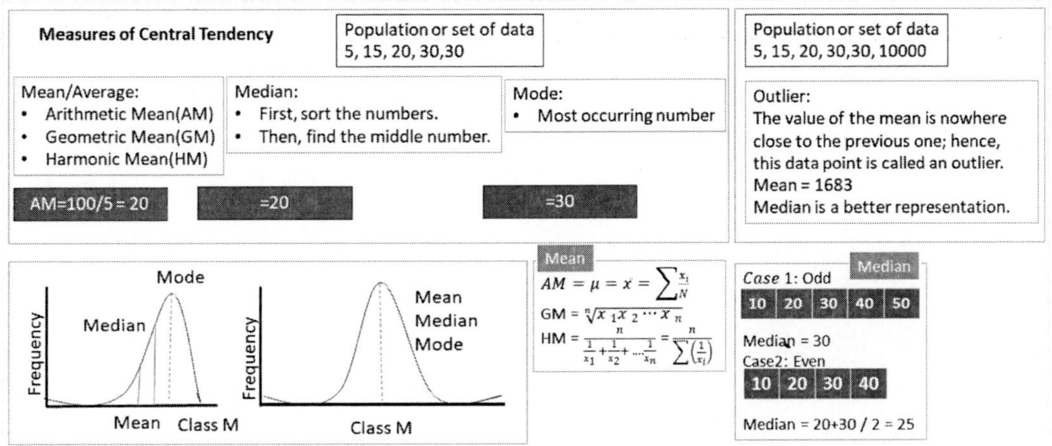

Akshaya asked "What is Mean?"

Master explained, the mean, often referred to as the average, is the most commonly used measure of central tendency. It represents the sum of all values in a dataset divided by the total number of values. It is applicable to both continuous and discrete data.

Suppose we have n values in a dataset denoted as x1, x2, x3, …, xn. The mean $\bar{x}$ is given by:

$$\bar{x} = x_1 + x_2 + x_3 + \cdots + x_n$$

Mean (Average): The mean is calculated by adding up all the values in a dataset and then dividing the sum by the total number of values in the dataset.

Mean(μ) $= \frac{\sum_{i=1}^{n} x_i}{n}$

For example, if we have the data set {1,2,3,4,5}, the mean is calculated as:

$\bar{x}$ = 1+2+3+4+55 = 15/5 = 3

Mean Using NumPy

The mean value of a NumPy array is derived by summing all its elements and dividing the total by the count of elements. This calculation is facilitated by the np.mean() function.

Example P2 – U2 – D1	
NumPy – Mean functions	**Output**

import numpy as np
# Create a numpy array. 	
s_Marks = np.array([89, 98, 97, 96, 99, 98])
# Calculate the mean of the marks. 	
marks_Mean = np.mean(s_Marks)
print(marks_Mean)
	96.16666666666667

Mean of NumPy N-d Array

Example P2 – U2 – D2	
NumPy – Mean	**Output**

import numpy as np
# Create a 2D array. 	
array_1 = np.array([[1, 2, 3],
[4, 5, 6],
[7, 8, 9]])
# Calculate the mean for the entire array. 	
result_1 = np.mean(array_1)
print("Compute the mean for the entire array:",result_1)
	Compute the mean for the entire array: 5.0
	Calculate the mean along the vertical axis: [4. 5. 6.]
	Calculate the mean along the horizontal axis: [2. 5. 8.]

# Calculate the mean along the vertical axis (axis=0). 	
result_2 = np.mean(array_1, axis=0)
print("Calculate the mean along the vertical axis:",result_2)
# Calculate the mean along the horizontal axis (axis=1). 	
result_3 = np.mean(array_1, axis=1)
print("Calculate the mean along the horizontal axis:",result_3)	

Apeksha asked "What is Median?"

Master said, "The median is the middle value of a dataset when the values are arranged in ascending or descending order. It is a useful measure of central tendency, especially for skewed distributions."

- If the number of values n is odd, the median is the $\frac{(n+1)}{2}$ observation.
- If the number of values n is even, the median is the average of the $\frac{(n)}{2}$th and $\frac{(n+1)}{2}$th observations.

> The median represents the middle value in a sorted dataset. In cases where there is an even number of observations, the median is calculated as the average of the two middle values.
>
> For an odd-sized dataset: **Median = Middle Value**
>
> For an even-sized: **Median = (Middle Value_1 + Middle Value_2)/2**

Median = Lower Boundary of Median Class+ (N/2 - (Frequency of Median Class) – Cumulative Frequency of Preceding Class) × Class Width

For example:

For the dataset {1,3,3,6,7,8,9} (odd number of values), the median is the 4th value: 6.

For the dataset {1,2,3,4,5,6,8,9} (even number of values), the median is the average of the 4th and 5th values: (4+5)/2 = 4.5.

Find Median

The median in a NumPy array is the value at the centre, effectively dividing the sorted array into two equal halves.

```
11, 15, 17, 18, 19, 21, 24
```

Calculating the median involves arranging the elements in ascending order:

Example P2 – U2 – D3	
NumPy – Statistical functions	**Output**

import numpy as np
# Create a one-dimensional array containing seven elements. 	
array_1 = np.array([11, 15, 17, 18, 19, 21, 24])
# Compute the median for arrays with an odd number of elements. 	
odd_Median = np.median(array_1)
print(odd_Median)
# Create a one-dimensional array containing eight elements. 	
array_2 = np.array([11, 15, 17, 18, 19, 21, 24, 26])
# Determine the median for arrays with an even number of elements. 	
even_Median = np.median(array_2)
print(even_Median)
	18.0
	18.5

In this case, the median is the centre value, which is 18. It's worth noting that when you have:

- An odd number of elements, the median is the middle element.
- An even number of elements, the median is the average of the two middle elements.

Now, we will delve into the process of calculating the median using NumPy for arrays with both odd and even numbers of elements.

Median of NumPy 2D Array

Master said, "The process of calculating the median isn't limited to 1D arrays; it's applicable to 2D arrays as well. When working with a 2D array, we have the flexibility to compute the median either vertically or horizontally, individually or across the entire array."

To find the median of a 2D array, we use the np.median() function with the axis parameter, which allows us to specify the axis along which to perform the calculation. If we set:

- axis = 0, it calculates the median along the vertical axis.
- axis = 1, it calculates the median along the horizontal axis.

Where we don't specify the axis parameter, the median is computed over the entire array.

Example P2 – U2 – D4	
NumPy – Median for 2D array	**Output**

import numpy as np
# Create a 2D array. 	
array_1 = np.array([[1, 2, 3],
[11,12,13],
[21, 22, 23]])
# Calculate the median along the horizontal axis. 	
result_1 = np.median(array_1, axis=1)
print("Calculate the median along the horizontal axis:", result_1)
# Calculate the median along the vertical axis. 	
result_2 = np.median(array_1, axis=0)
print("Calculate the median along the vertical axis:", result_2)
# Calculate the median of the entire array. 	
result_3 = np.median(array_1)
print("Compute the median for the entire array:", result_3)
	Calculate the median along the horizontal axis: [2. 12. 22.]
	Calculate the median along the vertical axis: [11. 12. 13.]
	Compute the median for the entire array: 12.0

Akanksh asked, "What is Mode?"

Master said, "The mode is the value that occurs most frequently in a dataset. A dataset may have one mode, more than one mode, or no mode at all if no number repeats."

For example:

- For the dataset $\{1,2,2,3,4\}$, the mode is 2 because it appears most frequently.
- For the dataset $\{1,1,2,2,3\}$, the modes are 1 and 2 (bimodal).
- For the dataset $\{1,2,3,4\}$, there is no mode because no number repeats.

The mode for grouped data can be calculated using the following formula:

$$\text{Mode} = l + \frac{f_1 - f_0}{[2f_1 - f_0 - f_2]} h$$

Where:

- l is the lower-class limit of the modal class.

- h is the class size.
- f1 is the frequency of the modal class.
- f0 is the frequency of the class preceding the modal class.
- f2 is the frequency of the class succeeding in the modal class.

We have the following class intervals and frequencies:

Class Interval	Frequency
10 - 20	5
20 - 30	15
30 - 40	25
40 - 50	10
50 - 60	5

Here, the modal class is 30 - 40 with a frequency f1=25. The class size h=10. The frequency of the preceding class (20 - 30) is f0 = 15, and the frequency of the succeeding class (40 - 50) is f2 = 10.

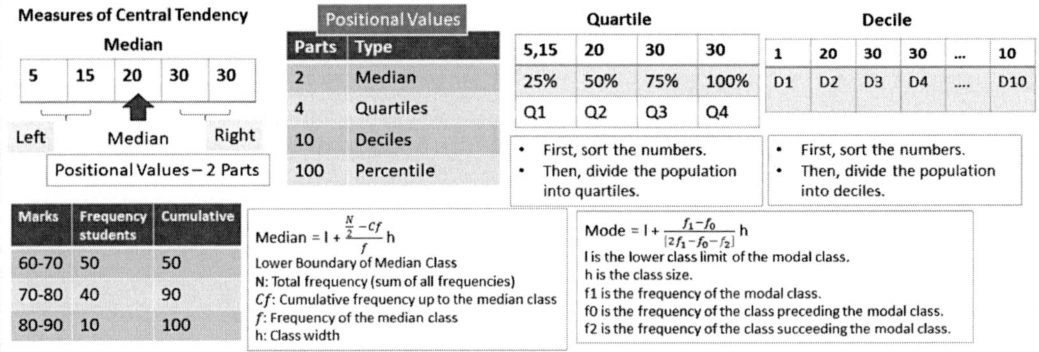

Plugging these values into the formula:

Mode = 30 + [((25−15) / ((25−15) + (25−10))] × 10

Mode = 30 + [(10) / (10+15)] × 10 = 34

This approach ensures a more accurate estimation of the mode in a grouped frequency distribution, reflecting the influence of adjacent frequencies.

Understanding these measures of central tendency allows for better summarisation and analysis of data, providing valuable insights into the dataset's characteristics.

Measures of Dispersion

Master said, "Dispersion refers to the extent to which data points in a statistical distribution or data set are spread out or scattered. Statistical dispersion indicates how much the values in a data set differ from the average value, providing insight into the variability of the data."

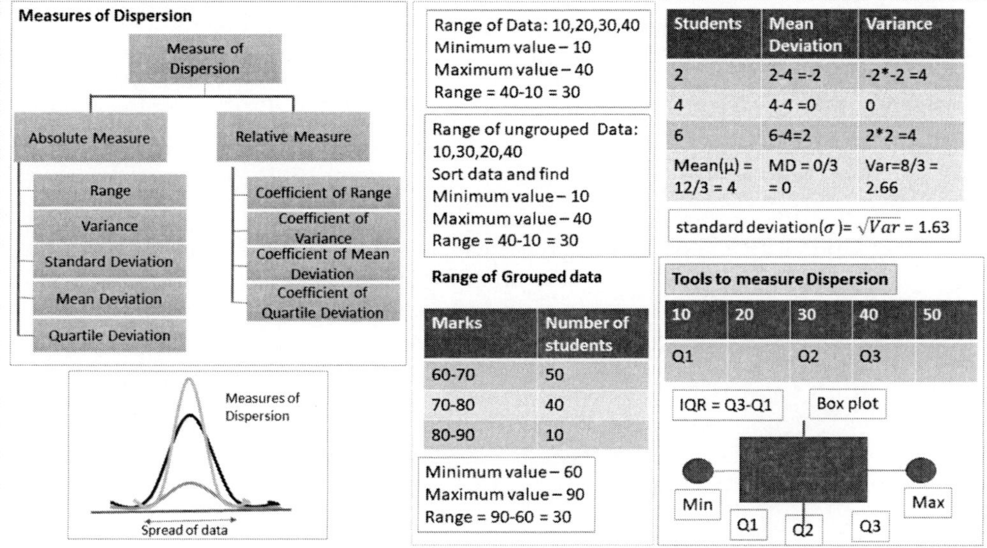

Measures of Dispersion

In statistics, measures of dispersion quantify the variability or spread of data points. These measures help determine how homogeneous or heterogeneous the data is, revealing whether the data points are closely clustered or widely spread out.

Types of Measures of Dispersion

There are two main categories of dispersion measures in statistics:

- Absolute Measures of Dispersion
- Relative Measures of Dispersion

Absolute Measures of Dispersion

Master explained, Absolute measures of dispersion are expressed in the same units as the data set. These measures quantify variations in terms of average deviations of observations, such as the range, standard deviation, and quartile deviation.

Types of Absolute Measures of Dispersion:

Range: The difference between the maximum and minimum values in a data set.

Range = Maximum value − Minimum value

Example: For the data set {1, 3, 5, 6, 7}, the range is 7 - 1 = 6.

Variance: The average of the squared differences from the mean. Variance quantifies the extent of dispersion of data points around the mean.

Variance: Variance(σ^2) $= \frac{\sum_{i=1}^{n}(x_i-\mu)^2}{n}$

Here, xi represents individual data points, μ is the mean, and n is the number of observations.

Standard Deviation: The standard deviation, denoted by σ (sigma), is the square root of the variance. It provides a measure of the extent to which the values in a dataset deviate from the mean.

Standard Deviation(σ)= $\sqrt{\boldsymbol{Variance}}$

Quartiles and Quartile Deviation: Quartiles divide the data into quarters, and the quartile deviation is half the difference between the third and first quartile.

Quartile Deviation $= \frac{Q3-Q1}{2}$

Mean and Mean Deviation: The mean is the average of the numbers, and the mean deviation (or mean absolute deviation) is the arithmetic mean of the absolute deviations from a central tendency measure.

Mean Deviation = $\sum\frac{|x-mean|}{N}$

Relative Measures of Dispersion

Relative measures of dispersion are used to compare the variability of two or more data sets without the influence of units. These measures provide a dimensionless comparison of variability.

Common Relative Measures of Dispersion:

Coefficient of Range:

```
Coefficient of Range = (Xmax−Xmin) / (Xmax+Xmin)
```

Coefficient of Variation:

```
Coefficient of Variation = Standard Deviation / Mean
```

Coefficient of Standard Deviation:

```
Coefficient of Standard Deviation=Standard Deviation/Mean
```

Coefficient of Quartile Deviation:

```
Coefficient of Quartile Deviation = (Q3−Q1)/(Q3+Q1)
```

Coefficient of Mean Deviation:

```
Coefficient of Mean Deviation = Mean Deviation/Mean
```

Coefficient of Dispersion: This is generally used when comparing two series with different units or averages.

In summary, measures of dispersion provide critical insights into the spread and variability of data, allowing statisticians to understand the distribution and compare different data sets effectively.

Example:

Case 1:

Find the Variance and Standard Deviation of the Following Numbers: 1, 3, 5, 5, 6, 7, 9, 10.

Solution:

Calculate the Mean:

Mean = (1+3+5+5+6+7+9+10) = 46/8 = 5.75

Subtract the Mean from Each Individual Value:

(1–5.75), (3–5.75), (5–5.75), (5–5.75), (6–5.75), (7–5.75), (9–5.75), (10–5.75)

= −4.75, −2.75, −0.75, −0.75, 0.25, 1.25, 3.25, 4.25

Square Each of the Differences:

$(-4.75)^2$, $(-2.75)^2$, $(-0.75)^2$, $(-0.75)^2$, $(0.25)^2$, $(1.25)^2$, $(3.25)^2$, $(4.25)^2$

= 22.5625, 7.5625, 0.5625, 0.5625, 0.0625, 1.5625, 10.5625, 18.0625

Sum the Squared Differences:

61.49922.5625+7.5625+0.5625+0.5625+0.0625+1.5625+10.5625+18.0625

= 61.499

Calculate the Variance:

Variance(σ2) = 61.499/8 = 7.687375

Calculate the Standard Deviation:

Standard Deviation(σ) = 7.687375 ≈ 2.77

Case 2:

Calculate the Range and Coefficient of Range for the Following Data Values: 45, 55, 63, 76, 67, 84, 75, 48, 62, 65

Solution:

Identify the Data Values:

X_i: 45,55,63,76,67,84,75,48,62,65

Determine the Maximum and Minimum Values:

Maximum value (Xmax) = 84

Minimum value (Xmin) = 45

Calculate the Range:

Range = Xmax−Xmin = 84−45 = 39

Calculate the Coefficient of Range:

Coefficient of Range = (Xmax−Xmin) / (Xmax + Xmin)

= (84−45)/ (84+45) = 39/129 ≈ 0.302

Standard Deviation

Master explained, the standard deviation serves as a measure of the dispersion of data within an array, revealing the extent to which data points diverge from the mean. A smaller standard deviation suggests data points are closely clustered around the mean, indicating less variability. Conversely, a larger standard deviation indicates data points are more widely scattered, reflecting greater variability. In NumPy, the np.std() function is employed to calculate the standard deviation of an array.

Example P1 – U2 – D5	
Standard functions	**Output**

import numpy as np
# Create a numpy array. 	
s_Marks = np.array([89, 98, 97, 96, 99, 98])
# Calculate the standard deviation of the scores. 	
marks_Std = np.std(s_Marks)
print("Standard deviation of marks:",marks_Std)
	Standard deviation of marks:
	3.337497399083464

Compute Percentile

Master explained, to ascertain the nth percentile of an array using NumPy, we utilise the percentile() function.

Example P1 – U2 – D6	
Percentile	**Output**

import numpy as np
# Create an array. 	
array_1 = np.array([11, 15, 17, 18, 19, 21, 24, 26, 28, 30])
# Calculate the 25th percentile of the array. 	
result_1 = np.percentile(array_1, 25)
print("The 25th percentile value:",result_1)
# Calculate the 75th percentile of the array. 	
result_2 = np.percentile(array_1, 75)
print("The 75th percentile value:",result_2)
	The 25th percentile value: 17.25
	The 75th percentile value: 25.5

Basics of Calculus:

Master said, "Let's delve into the basics of calculus and explore its applications in machine learning and deep learning."

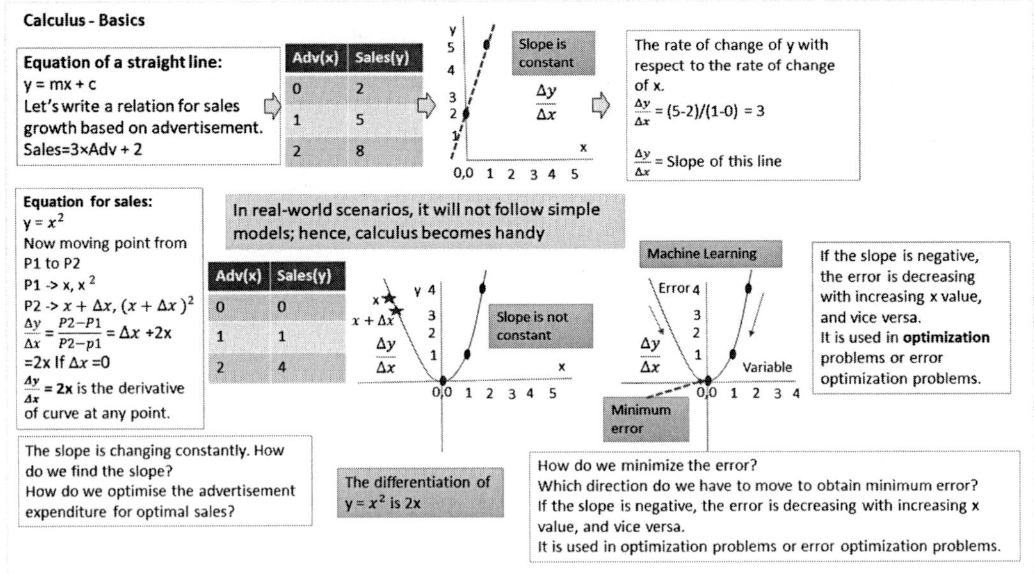

Equation of a Straight Line:

$$y = mx + c$$

Let's write a relation to sales growth based on the advertisement:

Sales = 3 × Adv

The Rate of Change of y with Respect to x:

$$\frac{\Delta y}{\Delta x} = (5\text{-}2)/(1\text{-}0) = 3$$

$$\frac{\Delta y}{\Delta x} = \text{Slope of this line}$$

> **Note:** In real-world scenarios, it will not follow simple models; hence, calculus becomes handy.

Equation for Sales:

$y = x^2$

Moving a Point from P1 to P2:

P1 to P2

P1 -> x, x^2

P2 -> $x + \Delta x, (x + \Delta x)^2$

$\frac{\Delta y}{\Delta x} = \frac{P2-P1}{P2-p1} = \Delta x + 2x = 2x$ If $\Delta x = 0$

This is the derivative of the curve at any point. The differentiation of $y = x^2$ is 2x

Sam asked, "For the slope is changing constantly. How Do We Find the Slope?"

Master said, "When the slope is changing constantly, we find the slope by using the derivative of the function. The derivative gives us the rate of change at any point on the curve."

Sam asked, "How Do We Optimise the Advertisement Expenditure for Optimal Sales?"

Master said, "To optimise advertisement expenditure for optimal sales, we need to determine the point where the marginal cost of advertising equals the marginal benefit. This involves using calculus to find the maximum point on the sales function curve, where the derivative (slope) is zero."

John asked, "How Do We Minimise the Error?"

Master said, "To minimise the error, we need to determine the direction in which to move. If the slope is negative, the error is decreasing with increasing x values, and if the slope is positive, the error is decreasing with decreasing x values. This concept is crucial in optimisation problems or error minimisation problems."

Why Integration?

We have predefined formulas to find the area of shapes like squares, circles, and rhombuses. However, in real-world scenarios, we often encounter shapes that do not fit these predefined categories.

Calculus - Basics

Why Integration?
We have predefined formulas to find the area of shapes like squares, circles, and rhombuses. However, in real-world scenarios, we often encounter shapes that do not fit these predefined categories.

Consider the equation:
Y = x^2

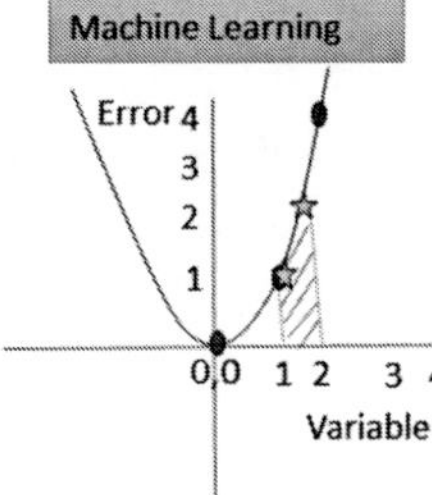

To find the area of a shaded portion:
$\int_{x=1}^{x=2} x^2 = \frac{x^3}{3} = \frac{2^3}{3} - \frac{1^3}{3} = \frac{8-1}{3} = \frac{7}{3}$

Integration is also used in probability distribution functions, such as the Bernoulli distribution, to find the area under the curve.

Consider the equation:

y = x2

To find the area of a shaded portion under this curve, we use integration.

$$\int_{x=1}^{x=2} x^2 = \frac{x^3}{3} = \frac{2^3}{3} - \frac{1^3}{3} = \frac{8-1}{3} = \frac{7}{3}$$

Integration is also used in probability distribution functions, such as the Bernoulli distribution, to find the area under the curve.

PART TWO

DAY THREE

Unit 2 - Lesson THREE

Law of Probability I

Probability theory studies random events and helps us understand the likelihood of their occurrence. There are two main approaches to studying probability theory:

- Theoretical Probability
- Experimental Probability

☐ Theoretical Probability

Theoretical probability is based on the assumption of equally likely outcomes. It is calculated using the formula:

P(A) = Number of favourable outcomes / Total number of possible outcomes

This approach relies on reasoning and mathematical calculations, rather than actual experiments.

Example: The probability of rolling a 3 on a fair six-sided die is:

P(rolling a 3) = 1/6

Experimental Probability

Experimental probability, also known as empirical probability, is based on the actual results of an experiment. It is calculated using the formula:

P(A) = Number of times event A occurs / Total number of trials

This approach relies on collecting data from experiments and observations.

Example: If a six-sided die is rolled 60 times and the number 3 appears 10 times, the experimental probability of rolling a 3 is:

P(rolling a 3) = 10/60 = **1/6**

By understanding both theoretical and experimental probability, we can gain a comprehensive understanding of random events and their likelihood of occurrence.

Akshaya asked, "Master probability is a numerical measure?"

Master said, "Probability is a measure of the likelihood of a particular event occurring. It is numerically represented between 0 and 1, where 0 indicates that the event will not occur, and 1 indicates that the event will certainly occur."

Let us understand:

- Numerical representation of likelihood of an event: 0 <= P <= 1: Probability P always falls within this range.
- Likelihood: Low when nearing to zero high when nearing to one: A probability closer to 0 means the event is less likely, whereas a probability closer to 1 means the event is more likely.
- Event: 0.1
    - Less chance of occurring in random experiment?
    - If an event has a probability of 0.1 (or 10%), it means there is a low chance of this event occurring in a random experiment.
- Random experiment is unbiased experiment: A random experiment refers to a process where all outcomes are equally likely to occur, which is the basis for calculating probabilities in many cases.

Master said, "Yes, probability is indeed a numerical measure that describes the likelihood of an event occurring, with 0.1 (or 10%) indicating a relatively low chance of occurrence in a random experiment."

☐ Various statistical methods:

Master explained, Probability theory has numerous applications in statistics, playing a crucial role in various statistical methods and analyses.

Key applications include:

Descriptive Statistics:

Probability theory aids in understanding and interpreting data summaries, measures of central tendency, variability, and data distributions.

Inferential Statistics:

It forms the basis for making inferences about populations from sample data. This includes hypothesis testing, the construction of confidence intervals, and the estimation of population parameters.

Regression Analysis:

Probability distributions of errors are used to model and estimate the relationships between variables, helping to understand how changes in one variable affect another.

Bayesian Statistics:

Bayesian methods use probability to represent uncertainty about the parameters of interest. These probabilities are updated as more data becomes available, allowing for more dynamic and iterative analysis.

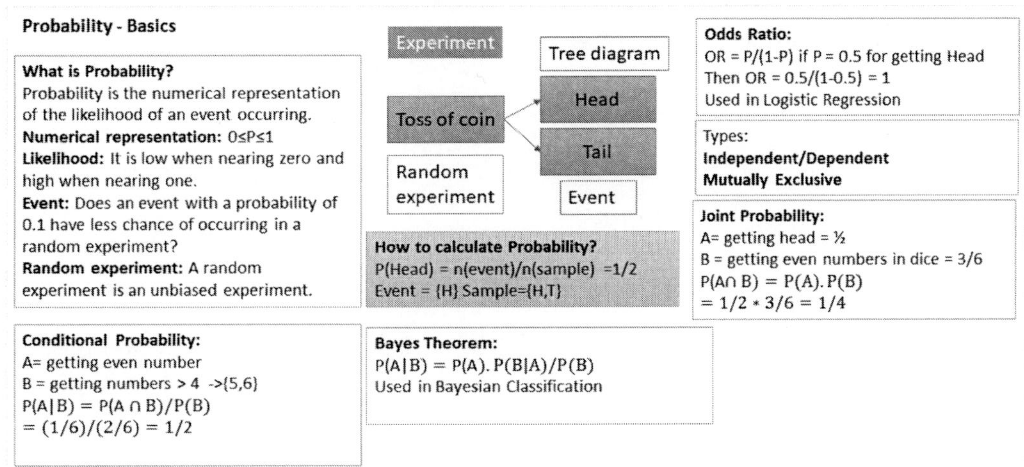

By integrating probability theory, statisticians can effectively summarize data, draw conclusions about populations, model relationships between variables, and update beliefs based on new information.

□ Types of Events in Probability

Master explained, understanding the various types of events that can occur during random experiments is essential in probability theory. The different types of events include:

Impossible and Sure Events

- Impossible Event: An event that cannot occur.
- Sure Event: An event that is certain to occur.

Simple Event and Compound Event

- Simple Event: An event that consists of a single outcome.
- Compound Event: An event that consists of more than one outcome.

Dependent and Independent Events

- Dependent Events: Events whose outcomes affect each other.
- Independent Events: Events whose outcomes do not affect each other.

Mutually Exclusive Events

- Events that cannot occur simultaneously.

Exhaustive Events

- Events that cover all possible outcomes of an experiment.

Equally Likely Events

- Events where each outcome is equally likely to occur.

Understanding these distinctions helps in accurately calculating probabilities and analysing outcomes in various scenarios.

Union and Intersection of Events in Probability

Master explained, in probability theory, events are defined as subsets of a sample space. The union and intersection of events are fundamental operations that help analyse probabilities.

Union of Events: The union of two events A and B, denoted as AUB, includes all outcomes that belong to either event A, event B, or both. In other words, AUB consists of outcomes that occur in at least one of the events.

Intersection of Events: The intersection of two events A and B, denoted as A∩B, includes outcomes that belong to both event A and event B. In other words, A∩B consists of outcomes that occur in both events simultaneously.

Example:

Consider a standard deck of 52 playing cards.

Let A be the event of drawing a red card.

Let B be the event of drawing a face card (jack, queen, or king).

- **Union (AUB):** Includes outcomes that are either red cards, face cards, or both. So, AUB includes all red cards (26 cards), all face cards (12 cards), and the red face cards (6 cards: two red jacks, two red queens, and two red kings).
- **Intersection (A∩B):** Includes outcomes that are both red cards and face cards. In this case, the red face cards (6 cards: two red jacks, two red queens, and two red kings).

Understanding the union and intersection of events helps in analysing probabilities and determining relationships between different outcomes in probability experiments.

Algebra of Events

Master said, "Events in probability theory can be manipulated using set operations, much like sets in mathematics. Understanding these operations is crucial for analysing probabilities and outcomes in various scenarios."

Two or more events can be combined using four primary operations: union, intersection, complement, and difference. Events are subsets of the sample space S, representing possible outcomes of an experiment.

Let's consider three events A, B, and C defined over the sample space S:

Union of Events (AUBUC): Includes outcomes that belong to at least one of the events A, B, or C.

Intersection of Events (A∩B∩C): Includes outcomes that belong to all three events A, B, and C.

Complement of an Event (Ac): Includes outcomes that do not belong to event A.

Difference of Events (A−B): Includes outcomes that belong to event AAA but do not belong to event B.

Example:

Consider rolling a fair six-sided die.

Let A be the event of rolling an even number: A = {2,4,6}.

Let B be the event of rolling a number greater than 3: B = {4,5,6}.

Let C be the event of rolling a prime number: C = {2,3,5}.

- **Union (AUBUC):** Includes outcomes that are even numbers, greater than 3, or prime. So, AUBUC = {2,3,4,5,6}.
- **Intersection (A∩B∩C):** Includes outcomes that are even numbers, greater than 3, and prime. In this case, A∩B∩C = {2}.
- **Complement (A^c):** Includes outcomes that are not even numbers. So, A^c = {1,3,5}.
- **Difference (A−B):** Includes outcomes that are even numbers but not greater than 3. Therefore, A−B = {2}

Understanding the algebra of events helps in manipulating and combining different sets of outcomes, thereby facilitating the computation of probabilities, and making informed decisions in probability theory.

Sample Problems on Events in Probability

Consider a die thrown in the game of Ludo, where:

- E1 denotes the event of getting even numbers.
- E2 represents the event of getting a number more than 3.

Find the sets for the following events:

E1 or E2

E1 and E2

Solution:

The sample space for the die is: S = {1,2,3,4,5,6}

Events defined:

- E1 (even numbers) = {2, 4, 6}

- E2 (numbers more than 3) = {4, 5, 6}

E1 or E2

This represents the union of E1 and E2, which includes outcomes that belong to either E1, E2, or both:

$E1 \cup E2 = \{2,4,5,6\}$

E1 and E2

This represents the intersection of E1 and E2, which includes outcomes that belong to both E1 and E2:

$E1 \cap E2 = \{4,6\}$

Understanding these sets helps in calculating probabilities and determining the occurrence of specific outcomes in probability experiments involving dice rolls or similar random events.

Random Variable

In probability theory, a random variable is a variable that can assume any of the possible outcomes of a random experiment. There are two types of random variables:

Discrete Random Variable:

A discrete random variable can take on a countable number of distinct values, such as 0, 1, 2, and so on.

Example: The number of heads obtained in three-coin tosses.

Continuous Random Variable

A continuous random variable can take an infinite number of values within a given range.

Example: The time taken for a computer to complete a specific task.

By distinguishing between these types, we can apply appropriate probability distributions and statistical methods to analyse random phenomena accurately.

Conditional Probability:

Conditional probability, expressed as P(A|B), signifies the probability of event A transpiring, provided that event B has already occurred. This concept is pivotal in probability theory and is computed utilising the following formula:

$$P(A|B) = \frac{P(A \cap B)}{P(B)}$$

Here:

P(A|B) is the conditional probability of A given B.

P(A∩B) is the probability of both A and B occurring.

P(B) is the probability of event B.

Interpretation:

Conditional probability provides insights into the likelihood of an event A happening in the context of the occurrence of another event B. It helps us refine probabilities when additional information about the situation is known.

Example:

Let's consider two events:

- Event A: Drawing a red card from a deck.
- Event B: Drawing a face card from the same deck.

The conditional probability P(A|B) represents the probability of drawing a red card given that a face card has already been drawn.

Properties:

- P(A|A) = 1: The probability of A given A is always 1.
- P(A|B) = 0 if P(A∩B) = 0: If events A and B are mutually exclusive, the conditional probability is zero.
- P(A|B)P(B) = P(B|A)P(A): This is known as Bayes' Theorem.

A profound comprehension of conditional probability is indispensable for making accurate predictions and informed decisions across many domains, spanning from statistics and machine learning to real-world applications where events exhibit interconnectedness and dependencies.

Probability Theory Formulas

Master said, "Probability theory involves various formulas to calculate and understand the likelihood of different events. Some key formulas are discussed below."

Theoretical Probability Formula:

$$P(A) = \text{Number of Favourable Outcomes} / \text{Number of Total Outcomes}$$

Empirical Probability Formula:

$$P(A) = \text{Number of Times Event A Occurs} / \text{Total Number of Trials}$$

Addition Rule of Probability:

$$P(A \cup B) = P(A) + P(B) - P(A \cap B)$$

This rule calculates the probability of either event A or event B occurring, accounting for their overlap.

Complementary Rule of Probability:

$$P(A') = 1 - P(A)$$

This rule calculates the probability of event A not occurring.

Independent Events:

$$P(A \cap B) = P(A) \cdot P(B)$$

For two independent events, the probability of both events occurring is the product of their individual probabilities.

Example: Tossing one coin is not affected by the tossing of another coin.

Dependent Events:

P(A∩B) = P(A)·P(B | A)

Example: The probability of drawing a red ball from a box containing 4 red balls and 3 green balls changes if two balls have already been taken out of the box.

Mutually Exclusive Events:

Two events A and B are said to be mutually exclusive if they cannot occur simultaneously.

P(A∪B) = P(A) or P(B) = P(A) + P(B)

Conditional Probability:

P(A|B) = P(A∩B) / P(B)

This rule calculates the probability of event A occurring, given that event B has occurred.

Bayes' Theorem:

P(A|B) = P(B | A)·P(A) / P(B)

Bayes' Theorem relates the conditional and marginal probabilities of random events, allowing us to update probabilities based on new information.

These formulas form the foundation of probability theory, enabling us to analyse and predict the likelihood of various events.

PART TWO

DAY THREE

Unit 2 - Lesson FOUR

Law of Probability II

☐ Law of Total Probability

Master said, "The law of total probability is a fundamental principle in probability theory that helps in calculating the probability of an event by considering all possible ways that event can occur. It is particularly useful in scenarios where events are interconnected and conditional probabilities are involved."

Key Concepts:

- Certain Event: An event that is sure to happen has a probability of 1.
- Impossible Event: An event that cannot happen has a probability of 0.
- Marginal Probability: The probability of an event occurring without any conditions.
- Conditional Probability: The probability of an event occurring given that another event has occurred.

The law of total probability bridges the gap between marginal probability and conditional probability. It states that if we have a partition of the sample space into mutually exclusive events B1, B2, …, Bn, then the probability of any event A can be found by considering all the ways A can occur through the events in the partition.

For events $B_1, B_2,\ldots,B_n$ forming a partition of the sample space S (i.e., $B_i \cap B_j = \emptyset$ for $i \neq \boldsymbol{j}$ and $\bigcup_{i=1}^{n} \boldsymbol{B_i} = \boldsymbol{s}$), the law of total probability is expressed as:

$$\mathbf{P(A)} = \Sigma_{i=1}^{n} \mathbf{P(Bi) \cdot P(A|B_i)}$$

Where:

- P(A) is the probability of event A.
- P(A|Bi) is the conditional probability of A given Bi.
- P(Bi) is the probability of Bi.

Case 1:

Suppose we have two types of boxes, each containing a mix of red and blue balls:

- Box 1 contains 3 red balls and 2 blue balls.
- Box 2 contains 1 red ball and 4 blue balls.

We randomly choose a box and then randomly draw a ball from the chosen box. Let:

- A be the event that a red ball is drawn.
- B1 be the event that Box 1 is chosen.
- B2 be the event that Box 2 is chosen.

Probabilities:

P(B1) = 0.5 (since we are equally likely to choose either box).

P(B2) = 0.5

P(A|B1) = 3/5 (probability of drawing a red ball from Box 1).

P(A|B2) = 1/5 (probability of drawing a red ball from Box 2).

Applying the Law of Total Probability:

$P(A) = P(A|B1) \cdot P(B1) + P(A|B2) \cdot P(B2)$

$P(A) = (3/5) * 0.5 + (1/5) * 0.5 = 0.4$

So, the probability of drawing a red ball is 0.4.

Probability of Complementary Events

Nikash asked, "What is complementary events?"

Master said, "Complementary events are pairs of events where one event's occurrence means the other does not occur. If A is an event, the complement of A is ¬A (not A)."

Probability of Complementary Event:

$P(\neg A) = 1 - P(A)$

Probability Space:

A probability space is a mathematical framework for describing random experiments. It consists of three components:

- **Sample Space (S):** The set of all possible outcomes.
- **Events:** Subsets of the sample space.
- **Probability Measure (P):** A function assigning probabilities to events.

$S = \{1,2,3,4,5,6\}$

$A = \{1,2,3,4\}$ $B=\{3,4,5\}$ $A \cap B = \{3,4\}$ $(A \cup B) = \{1,2,3,4,5\}$ $A' = \{5,6\}$

$P(A \text{ and } B) = (A \cap B) / S = 2/6 = 0.33 = 33\%$

$P(A \text{ or } B) = (A \cup B) = 5/6 = 0.833 = 83.3\%$

$P(A') = 2/6 = 1/3$ $P(A) = 4/6 = 2/3$

Note:

$P(A) + P(A') = 2/3 + 1/3 = 1$

$P(A) = 1 - P(A')$

A' or (¬A) complementary or event not occurring.

Case 2: Example Using the Law of Total Probability

Consider a factory producing two types of products: Type 1 and Type 2. The probabilities of producing each type are:

- P(Type 1) = 0.6
- P(Type 2) = 0.4

The probabilities of a product being defective given its type are:

- P(Defective|Type 1) = 0.02
- P(Defective|Type 2) = 0.05

Using the law of total probability, we can calculate the overall probability of a product being defective:

$$P(\text{Defective}) = P(\text{Defective}|\text{Type 1}) \cdot P(\text{Type 1}) + P(\text{Defective}|\text{Type 2}) \cdot P(\text{Type 2})$$

$$P(\text{Defective}) = (0.02 \cdot 0.6) + (0.05 \cdot 0.4) = 0.012 + 0.02 = 0.032$$

Thus, the overall probability of a product being defective is 0.032, or 3.2%.

Bayes Theorem

Master said, "Bayes Theorem provides a way to update the probability estimate for an event based on new evidence."

Definitions:

Conditional Probability: The probability of an event occurring given that another event has occurred.

$$P(A|B)$$

Marginal Probability: The probability of an event occurring regardless of other events.

$$P(A)$$

Joint Probability: The probability of two events occurring together.

$$P(A \cap B)$$

Master said, "Let's use an example to understand conditional, marginal, and joint probabilities through the following illustration."

Case 1: Two-way tables

Bayes Theorem

S	Education	Selection
1	Grad	Y
2	Grad	N
3	PG	Y
4	PG	Y
5	Grad	N
6	Grad	Y
7	PG	N

What is the probability of a Graduate getting selected for the job ?

S	Education	Selected
1	Grad	Y
6	Grad	Y

Conditional Probability: P(S|G)

Education	Selected	Rejected	Total
Grad	2	2	4
PG	2	1	3
Total	4	3	7

Probability that a randomly chosen candidate is a PG.
=3/7 (Outcome of interest/Total possibilities) **Marginal Probability**

Probability that a randomly chosen candidate is Graduate and is selected.
=2/7 Joint Probability

Probability that a randomly chosen candidate is a PG and when he is known to have been selected.
=2/4 (Conditional Probability)

Case 2:

Master said, "Suppose we have a medical test for a disease. We want to find the probability that a person has the disease given that they tested positive."

Given Data:

P(Disease): The probability that a randomly chosen person has the disease.

$P(D) = 0.01$

P(No Disease): The probability that a randomly chosen person does not have the disease.

$P(\neg D) = 0.99$

P(Positive Test | Disease): The probability that a person tests positive given that they have the disease.

$P(T^{+}|D) = 0.99$

P(Positive Test | No Disease): The probability that a person tests positive given that they do not have the disease.

$P(T^{+}|\neg D) = 0.05$

Objective:

Calculate $P(D|T^+)$, the probability that a person has the disease given that they tested positive.

Steps to Calculate Using Bayes Theorem:

Calculate the Joint Probabilities:

$P(D \cap T^+) = P(T^+|D) \cdot P(D) = 0.99 \cdot 0.01 = 0.0099$

$P(\neg D \cap T^+) = P(T^+|\neg D) \cdot P(\neg D) = 0.05 \cdot 0.99 = 0.04$

Calculate the Marginal Probability of Testing Positive:

$P(T^+) = P(D \cap T^+) + P(\neg D \cap T^+) = 0.0099 + 0.0495$

Apply Bayes Theorem:

$P(D|T^+) = P(D \cap T^+)/P(T^+) = 0.0099/0.0594 \approx 0.1667$

Summary:

Using Bayes Theorem, we have calculated that the probability of having the disease given a positive test result is approximately 16.67%.

Conditional Probability

Sam asked, "What is conditional probability?"

Master said, "Conditional probability, expressed as P(A|B), signifies the probability of event A transpiring, provided that event B has already occurred."

This concept is pivotal in probability theory and is computed utilising the following formula:

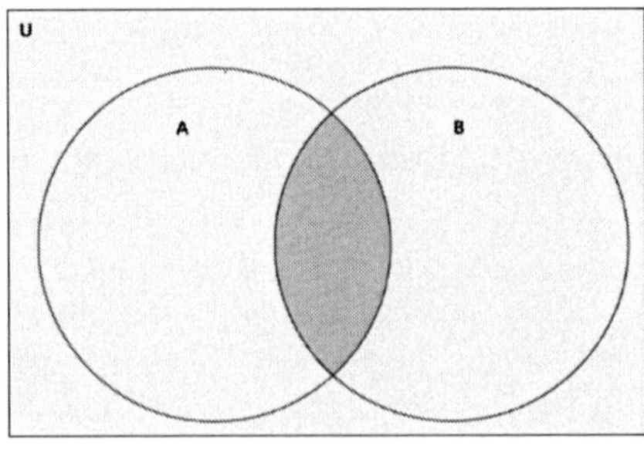

$$P(A|B) = \frac{P(A \cap B)}{P(B)}$$

Here:

- $P(A|B)$ is the conditional probability of A given B.
- $P(A \cap B)$ is the probability of both A and B occurring.
- $P(B)$ is the probability of event B.

Interpretation:

Conditional probability provides insights into the likelihood of an event A happening in the context of the occurrence of another event B. It helps us refine probabilities when additional information about the situation is known.

Example:

Let's consider two events:

- Event A: Drawing a red card from a deck.
- Event B: Drawing a face card from the same deck.

The conditional probability $P(A|B)$ represents the probability of drawing a red card given that a face card has already been drawn.

Properties:

- $P(A|A) = 1$: The probability of A given A is always 1.
- $P(A|B) = 0$ if $P(A \cap B) = 0$: If events A and B are mutually exclusive, the conditional probability is zero.
- $P(A|B)\ P(B) = P(B|A)\ P(A)$: This is known as Bayes' Theorem.

A profound comprehension of conditional probability is indispensable for making accurate predictions and informed decisions across many domains, spanning from statistics and machine learning to real-world applications where events exhibit interconnectedness and dependencies.

Marginal Probability:

John asked, "What is Marginal probability?"

Master said, "Marginal probability refers to the probability of a single event occurring without considering the occurrence of any other events. It is obtained by summing or integrating probabilities over all possible values of the other events. The term 'marginal' implies that we are focusing on the margins, considering only one variable while ignoring the others."

$$P(A) = \Sigma_{i=1}^{n} P(A \cap B_i)$$

For a discrete random variable:

$$P(X = x) = \sum P\,(X = x, Y = y_i)$$

For a continuous random variable:

$$P(X = x) = \int P\,(X = x, Y = y)dy$$

Here:

- $P(X = x)$ is the marginal probability of X.
- $P(X = x, Y = y_i)$ is the joint probability of X and Y.

Interpretation:

Marginal probability helps in understanding the likelihood of individual events, irrespective of the occurrence of other events. It is often used when dealing with joint probabilities in the context of two or more variables.

Example:

Let's consider two events:

- Event X: Tossing a fair coin and obtaining a Head.
- Event Y: Rolling a fair six-sided die and obtaining a 4.

The marginal probability, denoted as P(X), represents the probability of obtaining a Head from the coin toss, regardless of the outcome of the die roll.

Properties:

- $\sum P(X=x) = 1$ (for discrete variables): The sum of all marginal probabilities for each value of X is equal to 1.
- $\int P\,(X = x)dx = 1$ (for continuous variables): The integral of all marginal probabilities over the entire range is equal to 1.

Marginal probability is a fundamental concept, especially when dealing with multivariate probability distributions, and is essential for simplifying complex probability models.

Bayes' Theorem

$$P(B_i|A) = \frac{P(B_i)\cdot P(A|B_i)}{\sum_{j=1}^{n} P(B_j)\cdot P(B)\cdot P(A|B_j)}$$

These formulas provide the foundation for calculating probabilities, considering both independent and interconnected events, enabling a comprehensive understanding of the likelihood of various outcomes.

P-Value and Hypothesis

P-Value and Hypothesis Testing

Sam asked, "What is P-Value?"

Master replied, "The p-value is a measure used in statistical hypothesis testing to determine the significance of the observed data. It indicates the probability of obtaining a test result at least as extreme as the one observed, assuming that the null hypothesis H_0 is true."

Sam asked, "What is Hypothesis Testing?"

Master explained, Hypothesis testing is a statistical method used to make decisions about the population based on sample data. It involves testing an assumption (the null hypothesis) against an alternative hypothesis to determine whether there is enough evidence to reject the null hypothesis.

Steps to Follow with Example:

Collect Data

- Gather the necessary data through experiments or observations.

Define Significance Level (α)

- Choose a significance level (commonly 0.05) to determine the threshold for rejecting the null hypothesis.

Conduct a Test to Obtain the P-Value

- Perform a statistical test, such as a t-test, chi-square test, ANOVA, or z-test, to calculate the p-value.

Make a Decision Based on the P-Value

- Compare the p-value to the significance level to decide whether to accept or reject the null hypothesis.

Example:

Master said, "Let's say we want to test whether a new drug is effective in lowering blood pressure. We collect data from a sample of patients."

Step 1: Collect Data

- Measure the blood pressure of patients before and after taking the drug.

Step 2: Define Significance Level

- Set the significance level at $\alpha=0.05$.

Step 3: Conduct a Test

- Perform a t-test to compare the mean blood pressure before and after taking the drug, resulting in a p-value.

Step 4: Make a Decision

- If the p-value ≤ 0.05, reject the null hypothesis (conclude that the drug is effective).
- If the p-value > 0.05, fail to reject the null hypothesis (conclude that there is not enough evidence to say the drug is effective).

Interpreting P-Value

- If $P \leq 0.01$: Very strong evidence against the null hypothesis.
- If $0.01 < P \leq 0.05$: Strong evidence against the null hypothesis.
- If $0.05 < P \leq 0.1$: Mild evidence against the null hypothesis.
- If $P > 0.1$: No evidence against the null hypothesis.

P Value and Hypothesis Testing

Steps:
Collect Data
Define Significance level $\propto$
Conduct a test
Make a decision

Gender	Marks	Subject
M	95	M
F	84	S
M	85	M
F	90	M

One sample vs Two sample test

	Categorical	Continuous
Categorical	Chi square	Two sample T test Anova
Continuous	Logistic regression	Correlation

Hypotheses:

- Null Hypothesis (H_0): The assumption that there is no effect or difference.
- Alternative Hypothesis (H_A): The assumption that there is an effect or difference.

By following these steps and interpreting the p-value correctly, we can make informed decisions about our hypotheses.

One-Sample vs. Two-Sample Test

Master explained, when to use each test and why, especially in the context of calculating the p-value?

Using the T-Test

Statement: "Male students' average marks are higher than female students' average marks."

One-Sample Test: A one-sample test is used when you are examining one variable or feature, either categorical or continuous, and comparing its mean to a known value or target.

Example: You want to test if the average marks of a class are different from a passing mark of 50.

Two-Sample Test: A two-sample test is used when comparing two variables or features. Both variables can be continuous, or one can be categorical and the other continuous.

Example: Comparing the average marks of male students and female students.

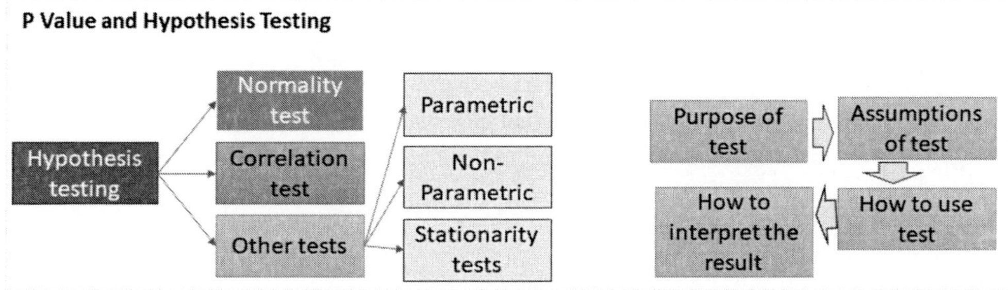

Master explained, when to Use the T-Test?

- When you have one categorical variable (Gender) and one continuous variable (Marks).
- If the categorical variable has only two classes (Male and Female), you use the t-test.

Example Scenario:

- Null Hypothesis (H_0): There is no difference in average marks between male and female students.
- Alternative Hypothesis (H_A): Male students' average marks are higher than female students' average marks.

If there are more than two classes in the categorical feature (e.g., adding a third class category), you would use an ANOVA (Analysis of Variance).

Using the Chi-Square Test: If you want to analyse the relationship between two categorical features, such as Gender and Subject, you would use the Chi-square test.

Example Scenario:

You want to determine if the distribution of students across different subjects (Math, Science, etc.) is independent of their gender.

- Null Hypothesis (H_0): The distribution of students across subjects is independent of gender.
- Alternative Hypothesis (H_A): The distribution of students across subjects is not independent of gender.

Summary

One-Sample Test: Used for comparing the mean of one variable to a known value.

Two-Sample Test: Used for comparing the means of two variables.

- Use the t-test when you have one categorical variable with two classes and one continuous variable.
- Use ANOVA when you have a categorical variable with more than two classes.

Chi-Square Test: Used for analysing the relationship between two categorical variables.

Understanding these tests and when to use them helps in accurately determining relationships and differences in your data.

In the given code:

Normality Tests:

- Shapiro-Wilk Test: Prints whether 'volatile acidity' is normally distributed based on the p-value.
- D'Agostino and Pearson's K² Test: Prints whether 'volatile acidity' is normally distributed based on the p-value.

Correlation Tests:

- Pearson Correlation: Prints whether 'volatile acidity' and 'pH' are independent or dependent based on the p-value.
- Spearman Correlation: Prints whether 'volatile acidity' and 'pH' are independent or dependent based on the p-value.

Exercise P2-U2 – D7

Hypothesis and Testing

```
import pandas as pd
from scipy.stats import shapiro, normaltest, pearsonr, spearmanr, chi2_contingency
# Load the dataset with semicolon as the separator
path = r'C:\Users\User\mraj4\Documents\Optimum\Py-lib\scikit\wine_quality\winequality-red.csv'
data = pd.read_csv(path, sep=';', quotechar='"')
# Print the column names to verify the correct names
print("Column names in the dataset:", data.columns)

# Extract the features
volatile_acidity = data['volatile acidity']
pH = data['pH']

# Normality tests for 'volatile acidity'
# Shapiro-Wilk test
shapiro_test_stat, shapiro_p_value = shapiro(volatile_acidity)
print(f"Shapiro-Wilk Test: Test Statistic = {shapiro_test_stat}, P-Value = {shapiro_p_value}")
if shapiro_p_value > 0.05:
    print("The feature 'volatile acidity' is normally distributed (Shapiro-Wilk Test).")
else:
    print("The feature 'volatile acidity' is not normally distributed (Shapiro-Wilk Test).")

# D'Agostino and Pearson's K^2 Normality test
k2_test_stat, k2_p_value = normaltest(volatile_acidity)
print(f"D'Agostino and Pearson's K^2 Test: Test Statistic = {k2_test_stat}, P-Value = {k2_p_value}")
if k2_p_value > 0.05:
    print("The feature 'volatile acidity' is normally distributed (D'Agostino and Pearson's K^2 Test).")
```

```
else:
    print("The feature 'volatile acidity' is not normally distributed (D'Agostino and Pearson's K^2 Test).")

# Correlation between 'volatile acidity' and 'pH'
# Pearson correlation
pearson_corr, pearson_p_value = pearsonr(volatile_acidity, pH)
print(f"Pearson Correlation: Correlation Coefficient = {pearson_corr}, P-Value = {pearson_p_value}")
if pearson_p_value > 0.05:
    print("The features 'volatile acidity' and 'pH' are independent (Pearson Correlation).")
else:
    print("The features 'volatile acidity' and 'pH' are dependent (Pearson Correlation).")

# Spearman correlation
spearman_corr, spearman_p_value = spearmanr(volatile_acidity, pH)
print(f"Spearman Correlation: Correlation Coefficient = {spearman_corr}, P-Value = {spearman_p_value}")
if spearman_p_value > 0.05:
    print("The features 'volatile acidity' and 'pH' are independent (Spearman Correlation).")
else:
    print("The features 'volatile acidity' and 'pH' are dependent (Spearman Correlation).")

# Create categorical features for Chi-square test
# Binning 'volatile acidity' into categories
data['volatile_acidity_cat'] = pd.qcut(data['volatile acidity'], q=4, labels=['Low', 'Medium-Low', 'Medium-High', 'High'])

# Binning 'pH' into categories
data['pH_cat'] = pd.qcut(data['pH'], q=4, labels=['Low', 'Medium-Low', 'Medium-High', 'High'])

# Contingency table for Chi-square test
contingency_table = pd.crosstab(data['volatile_acidity_cat'], data['pH_cat'])

# Chi-square test of independence
chi2_stat, p_value, dof, expected = chi2_contingency(contingency_table)
print(f"Chi-square Test: Chi2 Statistic = {chi2_stat}, P-Value = {p_value}")
if p_value > 0.05:
    print("The features 'volatile acidity' and 'pH' are independent (Chi-square Test).")
else:
    print("The features 'volatile acidity' and 'pH' are dependent (Chi-square Test).")
```

Chi-square Test of Independence:

- Categorical Binning: 'volatile acidity' and 'pH' are binned into categories for the Chi-square test.
- Contingency Table: A contingency table is created for the categorical features.
- Chi-square Test: Prints whether 'volatile acidity' and 'pH' are independent or dependent based on the p-value.

Output:

Shapiro-Wilk Test: Test Statistic = 0.9743338823318481, P-Value = 2.686385373947307e-16

The feature 'volatile acidity' is not normally distributed (Shapiro-Wilk Test).

D'Agostino and Pearson's K^2 Test: Test Statistic = 143.4193435598286, P-Value = 7.192589039756692e-32

The feature 'volatile acidity' is not normally distributed (D'Agostino and Pearson's K^2 Test).

Pearson Correlation: Correlation Coefficient = 0.23493729440739328, P-Value = 1.7189939570061834e-21

The features 'volatile acidity' and 'pH' are dependent (Pearson Correlation).

Spearman Correlation: Correlation Coefficient = 0.2335715187440911, P-Value = 2.968485979060143e-21

The features 'volatile acidity' and 'pH' are dependent (Spearman Correlation).

Chi-square Test: Chi2 Statistic = 77.97096952358629, P-Value = 4.083663363888954e-13

The features 'volatile acidity' and 'pH' are dependent (Chi-square Test).

Parametric and Non-Parametric Tests

Parametric Tests

Sam asked, "Master explain Parametric test?"

Master said, "Let us try to understand using Parametric Test Assumptions."

- The data is normally distributed.
- The variances are equal (homoscedasticity).
- The data is measured on an interval or ratio scale.

T-Test:

Master said, "T-Test is used to determine if there is a significant difference between the means of two groups."

Types of T-Tests:

- One-Sample T-Test: Compares the mean of a single sample to a known value or population mean.
- Independent Samples T-Test: Compares the means of two independent groups.
- Paired Samples T-Test: Compares means from the same group at different times (e.g., before and after a treatment).

ANOVA (Analysis of Variance):

Tests whether the means of two or more independent samples are significantly different.

Assumptions:

- The samples are from populations that follow a normal distribution.
- The variances of populations are equal (homogeneity of variance).
- The observations are independent.

Non-Parametric Tests

Master said, "Let us now try to understand the non-parametric tests?"

Mann-Whitney U Test:

- Tests whether the distribution of two independent samples is equal or not.
- Does not assume a normal distribution.

Wilcoxon Signed-Rank Test:

- A non-parametric test for comparing two paired samples to assess whether their population mean ranks differ.
- Used as an alternative to the paired samples t-test when the population cannot be assumed to be normally distributed.

Kruskal-Wallis Test:

- A non-parametric version of ANOVA.
- Used to test whether samples originate from the same distribution.
- Does not assume normal distribution and is used for comparing more than two independent groups.

Time Series Analysis

John asked, "What is stationarity?"

Master said, "Stationarity is a key concept in time series analysis and statistics. A time series is said to be stationary if its statistical properties, such as mean, variance, and autocorrelation, do not change over time. In other words, the series looks similar at any point in time, making it easier to model and predict."

There are two main types of stationarity:

Strict Stationarity (Strong Stationarity):

A time series is strictly stationary if the joint distribution of any set of observations is the same, regardless of the time at which they are taken.

Weak Stationarity (Second-Order Stationarity or Wide-Sense Stationarity):

A time series is weakly stationary if its mean and variance are constant over time, and the covariance between two time points depends only on the time lag between them, not on the actual time at which the covariance is computed.

Master explained, why is Stationarity Important?

- Model Simplicity: Stationary time series are easier to model and predict because their properties do not change over time.
- Statistical Inference: Many statistical methods and models, like ARIMA (AutoRegressive Integrated Moving Average), assume that the underlying time series is stationary.
- Predictability: Stationary processes tend to revert to a mean, making future values more predictable compared to non-stationary processes, which may exhibit trends or seasonal patterns.

Examples of Non-Stationarity:

- Trends: A time series with a clear upward or downward trend over time is non-stationary.

- Seasonality: A time series that shows regular patterns or cycles over time (like monthly sales figures) is non-stationary.
- Changing Variance: If the variance of a time series increases or decreases over time, it is non-stationary.

Making a Time Series Stationary:

- Differencing: Subtracting the previous observation from the current observation to remove trends.
- De-trending: Removing a fitted trend line from the data.
- De-seasonalizing: Removing seasonal effects by, for example, subtracting the seasonal mean.

Understanding and ensuring stationarity is often a crucial first step in time series analysis and modelling.

Let us understand the Test of Stationarity:

Dickey-Fuller Test:

- Tests the null hypothesis that a time series is non-stationary.
- Stationarity implies that the statistical properties of the series do not change over time.

KPSS Test (Kwiatkowski-Phillips-Schmidt-Shin):

- Tests the null hypothesis that a time series is stationary.
- Complements the Dickey-Fuller test by providing a test for stationarity.

Here's a brief breakdown of what each part of the code does:

Imports:

- numpy (np) for numerical operations.
- pandas (pd) for data manipulation.
- scipy.stats for statistical tests (ttest_1samp, ttest_ind, ttest_rel, f_oneway, mannwhitneyu, wilcoxon, kruskal).
- statsmodels.tsa.stattools for time series analysis (adfuller, kpss).

Data Generation:

- Several datasets (data1, data2, data3, data4, data5, time_series) are generated:

- data1, data2, data3: Normally distributed data with different means.
- data4, data5: Non-normally distributed data (exponential distribution).
- time_series: A cumulative sum of normally distributed random numbers, representing time series data.

Exercise P2-U2 – D8

Parametric and Non-parametric

```
import numpy as np
import pandas as pd
from scipy.stats import ttest_1samp, ttest_ind, ttest_rel, f_oneway
from scipy.stats import mannwhitneyu, wilcoxon, kruskal
from statsmodels.tsa.stattools import adfuller, kpss

# Generate random data
np.random.seed(0)
# Parametric tests
data1 = np.random.normal(loc=50, scale=10, size=100)  # Normally distributed data
data2 = np.random.normal(loc=55, scale=10, size=100)  # Normally distributed data with
different mean
data3 = np.random.normal(loc=60, scale=10, size=100)  # Another sample

# Non-parametric test data
data4 = np.random.exponential(scale=1, size=100)  # Non-normally distributed data
data5 = np.random.exponential(scale=2, size=100)  # Another sample

# Time series data
time_series = np.cumsum(np.random.normal(loc=0, scale=1, size=100))

# One-sample T-test
t_stat, p_val = ttest_1samp(data1, 50)
print(f"One-Sample T-Test: T-Statistic = {t_stat}, P-Value = {p_val}")

# Independent samples T-test
t_stat, p_val = ttest_ind(data1, data2)
print(f"Independent Samples T-Test: T-Statistic = {t_stat}, P-Value = {p_val}")

# Paired samples T-test
t_stat, p_val = ttest_rel(data1, data1 + np.random.normal(loc=0, scale=5, size=100))
print(f"Paired Samples T-Test: T-Statistic = {t_stat}, P-Value = {p_val}")

# ANOVA
f_stat, p_val = f_oneway(data1, data2, data3)
print(f"ANOVA: F-Statistic = {f_stat}, P-Value = {p_val}")

# Mann-Whitney U Test
```

```
u_stat, p_val = mannwhitneyu(data4, data5)
print(f"Mann-Whitney U Test: U-Statistic = {u_stat}, P-Value = {p_val}")

# Wilcoxon Signed-Rank Test
w_stat, p_val = wilcoxon(data1, data1 + np.random.normal(loc=0, scale=5, size=100))
print(f"Wilcoxon Signed-Rank Test: W-Statistic = {w_stat}, P-Value = {p_val}")

# Kruskal-Wallis Test
h_stat, p_val = kruskal(data1, data2, data3)
print(f"Kruskal-Wallis Test: H-Statistic = {h_stat}, P-Value = {p_val}")

# Dickey-Fuller Test
adf_stat, adf_p_val, used_lag, n_obs, crit_values, icbest = adfuller(time_series)
print(f"Dickey-Fuller Test: ADF Statistic = {adf_stat}, P-Value = {adf_p_val}")

# KPSS Test
kpss_stat, kpss_p_val, lags, crit_values = kpss(time_series, regression='c')
print(f"KPSS Test: KPSS Statistic = {kpss_stat}, P-Value = {kpss_p_val}")

# Interpret the results
print("\nInterpretation:")
if p_val < 0.05:
    print("For parametric and non-parametric tests, the null hypothesis is rejected (significant difference).")
else:
    print("For parametric and non-parametric tests, the null hypothesis is not rejected (no significant difference).")

if adf_p_val < 0.05:
    print("Dickey-Fuller Test: The time series is stationary.")
else:
    print("Dickey-Fuller Test: The time series is non-stationary.")

if kpss_p_val > 0.05:
    print("KPSS Test: The time series is stationary.")
else:
    print("KPSS Test: The time series is non-stationary.")
```

Statistical Tests

Parametric Tests:

- One-Sample T-test (ttest_1samp): Compares the mean of data1 against a known mean of 50.
- Independent Samples T-test (ttest_ind): Compares data1 and data2.
- Paired Samples T-test (ttest_rel): Compares data1 and data1 with added noise.

- ANOVA (f_oneway): Tests if there is a significant difference between the means of data1, data2, and data3.

Non-parametric Tests:

- Mann-Whitney U Test (mannwhitneyu): Compares data4 and data5.
- Wilcoxon Signed-Rank Test (wilcoxon): Compares data1 and data1 with added noise.
- Kruskal-Wallis Test (kruskal): Tests if there is a significant difference between the distributions of data1, data2, and data3.

Time Series Tests:

- Dickey-Fuller Test (adfuller): Tests if time_series is stationary.
- KPSS Test (kpss): Tests if time_series is stationary.

Interpreting Results:

- Prints whether each test rejects or fails to reject the null hypothesis based on a significance level of 0.05.
- Specifically mentions the stationarity of time_series using both Dickey-Fuller and KPSS tests.

Output:

- Displays the statistics and p-values for each test.
- Provides interpretation statements based on the p-values obtained from each test.

Output:

One-Sample T-Test: T-Statistic = 0.5904283402851587, P-Value = 0.5562489158694748

Independent Samples T-Test: T-Statistic = -3.5971927597496247, P-Value = 0.00040627960203623494

Paired Samples T-Test: T-Statistic = 1.9245734659128422, P-Value = 0.05715372751439706

ANOVA: F-Statistic = 19.476212850706954, P-Value = 1.1274108620248522e-08

Mann-Whitney U Test: U-Statistic = 3402.0, P-Value = 9.488457341012419e-05

Wilcoxon Signed-Rank Test: W-Statistic = 2127.0, P-Value = 0.17117023411272703

Kruskal-Wallis Test: H-Statistic = 33.55982192691033, P-Value = 5.159139388955764e-08

Dickey-Fuller Test: ADF Statistic = -1.0292951766776126, P-Value = 0.7424301932863581

KPSS Test: KPSS Statistic = 0.9295802605609097, P-Value = 0.01

Interpretation:

For parametric and non-parametric tests, the null hypothesis is rejected (significant difference).

Dickey-Fuller Test: The time series is non-stationary.

KPSS Test: The time series is non-stationary.

This code snippet serves as a comprehensive example of how to perform and interpret various statistical tests in Python, covering both parametric and non-parametric tests, as well as tests for time series data.

Summary

Parametric tests, such as the T-test and ANOVA, require assumptions about the data's distribution and variance. Non-parametric tests, like the Mann-Whitney U test and Kruskal-Wallis test, do not require these assumptions and are useful for ordinal data or when parametric test assumptions are violated. For time series analysis, tests like the Dickey-Fuller and KPSS are used to determine if a series is stationary.

By understanding the assumptions and applications of these tests, researchers can choose the appropriate method for their data analysis needs.

Probability Distribution

Sam asked, "What is probability distribution?"

Master said, "A probability distribution entails the allocation of probabilities to potential outcomes of a random variable, delineating the dispersion of probabilities across the various values that the random variable can assume. Probability distributions play a fundamental role in probability theory and statistics, serving as vital tools to encapsulate and model uncertainty and randomness."

Variable Types

Traditional Type:

- Example: X+5 = 6

Random Type:

Example: Using a random experiment like tossing a coin

$$X = \begin{Bmatrix} 0 & H \\ 1 & T \end{Bmatrix}$$

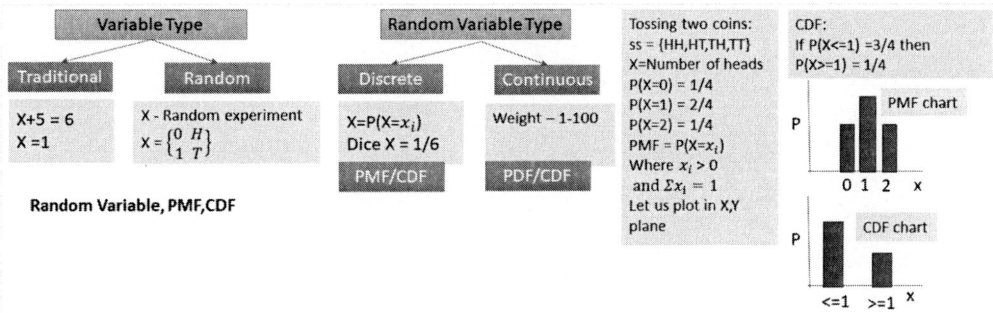

Discrete and Continuous Types

Master said, "Let us understand discrete and continuous type?"

Discrete:

Definition: A variable that uses Probability Mass Function (PMF) and Cumulative Distribution Function (CDF).

> Formula: $X = P(X=x_i)$

Example: Rolling a dice, where each face (1 through 6) has a probability

P(X)=Pi

- P >= 0
- $\sum P_i = 1$

PMF:

> Formula: PMF= $P(X=x_i)$
>
> Where $x_i \geq 0$ and $\sum x_i=1$

Plot: Plot the PMF on an X-Y plane

Plotting PMF using an Experiment of Tossing Two Coins:

Experiment:

Sample Space: ss = {HH, HT, TH, TT}

Random Variable X: Number of heads

- P(X=0) =1/4
- P(X=1) = 2/4
- P(X=2) = 1/4

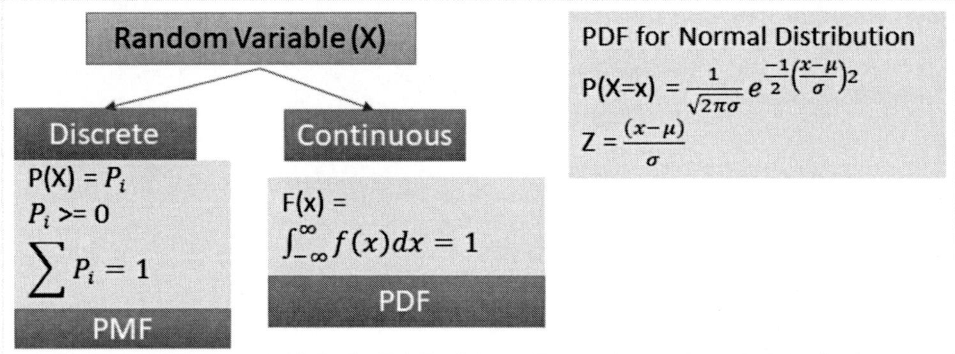

Continuous:

Definition: A variable that uses Probability Density Function (PDF) and Cumulative Distribution Function (CDF).

Example: Weight from 1 to 100

Finding PDF:

F(x) = $\int_{-\infty}^{\infty} f(x)dx = 1$

Finding CDF:

CDF:

Definition: The cumulative probability up to a certain value.

Example: If P(X≤1) = 3/4, then P(X≥1) = 1/4

PDF for Normal Distribution:

Formula:

PDF: f(x) = P(X=x) = $\frac{1}{\sigma\sqrt{2\Pi}} e^{-\frac{1}{2}\left(\frac{x\text{-}\mu}{\sigma}\right)^2}$

Mean: μ

Variance: σ^2

Standard Score Z:

$Z = \frac{(x-\mu)}{\sigma}$

Types of Probability Distributions

Discrete Probability Distribution	Continuous Probability Distribution
Examples: Binomial, Poisson distributions.	Examples: Normal, Uniform distributions.
Probability Mass Function (PMF): $P(X=x_i)$	Probability Density Function (PDF): $P(a \le X \le b) = \int_a^b f(x)\, dx$
Mean: $\mu = \sum_i x_i \cdot P(X=xi)$	Mean: $\mu = \int_{-\infty}^{\infty} x. f(x)\, dx$
Variance: $\sigma^2 = \sum_i (x_i - \mu)^2 \cdot P(X=x_i)$	Variance: $\sigma 2 = \int_{-\infty}^{\infty} x. f(x-\mu)^2\, dx$

Uniform Distribution:

Master said, "The uniform distribution, sometimes referred to as the rectangular distribution, is a probability distribution wherein all outcomes possess an equal likelihood of occurrence. In this distribution, every value within a specified range carries an identical probability of happening."

For a continuous uniform distribution, the probability density function (PDF) is defined as follows:

$$f(x) = \frac{1}{b-a}$$

Here:

- f(x) is the probability density function.
- a and b are the parameters representing the interval [a, b].

Discrete uniform distribution:

Master explained, for a discrete uniform distribution with outcomes $x_1, x_2 \dots, x^n$ the probability mass function (pmf) is given by:

$$P(X=x_i) = \frac{1}{n}$$

Here:

- $P(X = x_i)$ is the probability of the specific outcome x_i.
- n is the total number of possible outcomes.

Exponential Distribution:

Sam asked, "What is exponential distribution?"

Master said, "The exponential distribution characterises the time intervals between events in a Poisson process, where events unfold continuously and independently at a steady average rate."

The probability density function (PDF) for an exponential distribution is expressed as follows:

$$f(x;\lambda) = \lambda e^{-\lambda x}$$

Here:

- $f(x; \lambda)$ is the probability density function.
- λ is the rate parameter, representing the average number of events in a unit time.
- e is Euler's number.

The cumulative distribution function (cdf) for the exponential distribution is:

$F(x; \lambda) = 1 - e^{-\lambda x}$

Probability Distribution Function

Master explained, Probability Mass Function (PMF): Applicable to discrete random variables, it calculates the probability of a specific outcome X taking on a particular value xi, denoted as P(X=xi).

Probability Density Function (PDF): Utilised for continuous random variables, it represents the probability distribution of the variable X across its possible values. It is denoted as f(x).

Formulas

Binomial Distribution:

PMF: $P(X=k) = \binom{n}{k} p^k (1-p)^{n-k}$

Mean: $\mu = np$

Variance: $\sigma^2 = np(1-p)$

Poisson Distribution:

PMF: $P(X=k) = \frac{\lambda^k e^{-\lambda}}{k!}$

Mean: $\mu = \lambda$

Variance: $\sigma^2 = \lambda$

Normal Distribution:

PDF: $f(x) = \frac{1}{\sigma\sqrt{2\Pi}} e^{-\frac{1}{2}\left(\frac{x \cdot \mu}{\sigma}\right)^2}$

Mean: μ

Variance: σ^2

These are fundamental concepts and formulas for understanding probability distributions in statistics.

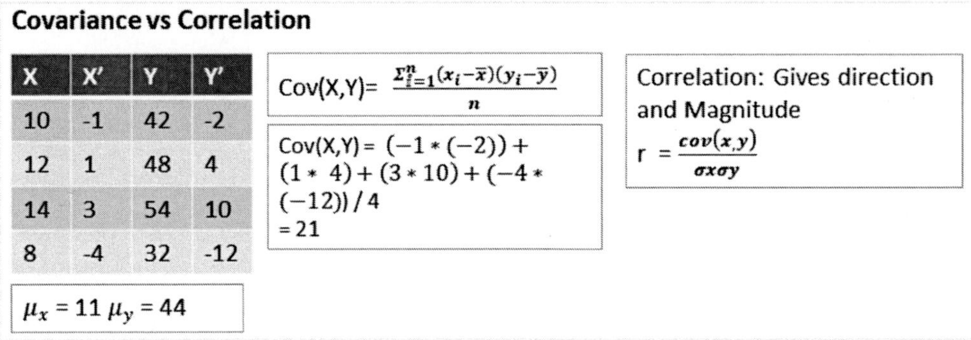

Covariance

John asked, "What is the difference between covariance and correlation?"

Master said, "Covariance serves as a metric indicating the degree to which two random variables vary in tandem. Essentially, it quantifies the extent to which deviations from the mean of one variable correlate with deviations from the mean of another variable."

The formula for computing the covariance between two random variables X and Y is expressed as follows:

$$\text{Cov(X,Y)} = \frac{\Sigma_{i=1}^{n}(x_i-\bar{x})(y_i-\bar{y})}{n}$$

Here:

- X_i and Y_i are individual data points.
- $\bar{x}$ and $\bar{y}$ are the means of X and Y, respectively.
- n is the number of data points.

Interpretation:

- If Cov(X,Y) > 0, it implies a positive relationship, indicating that above-average values of one variable tend to coincide with above-average values of the other.
- If Cov(X,Y) < 0, it indicates a negative relationship, signifying that above-average values of one variable tend to correspond with below-average values of the other.
- If Cov(X,Y) = 0, it suggests no linear relationship between the variables.

Correlation:

Correlation is a standardised metric indicating both the strength and direction of the linear relationship between the two variables. Derived from covariance, correlation is scaled to always fall within the range of -1 to 1. The correlation coefficient (denoted as r) is employed to quantify correlation.

The formula for calculating the correlation coefficient between variables X and Y is expressed as follows:

$$r = \frac{cov(x,y)}{\sigma x \sigma y}$$

Here:

- Cov(X,Y) is the covariance between X and Y.
- σ_X and σ_Y are the standard deviations of X and Y, respectively.

Properties of r:

- The correlation coefficient (r) ranges from -1 to 1.
- $r = 1$ indicates a perfect positive linear relationship.
- $r = -1$ indicates a perfect negative linear relationship.
- $r = 0$ indicates no linear relationship.
- The closer $|r|$ is to 1, the stronger the linear relationship between the variables.

Correlation is a unitless measure, making it easier to interpret compared to covariance, which is in the original units of the variables. It is widely used in statistics, finance, and various scientific fields to assess relationships between variables.

Recursive Feature Selection:

Akshaya asked, "When do we use Recursive feature selection?"

Master said, "This process Iteratively removes the least significant features and builds the model again until the optimal number of features is reached."

Purpose: To find the best subset of features for model training.

Reduction Techniques:

Correlation: Measures the statistical relationship between two variables.

PCA (Principal Component Analysis): Reduces the dimensionality of the data by transforming it into a new set of variables (principal components) that are uncorrelated.

VIF (Variance Inflation Factor): Detects multicollinearity in the features.

RFE (Recursive Feature Elimination):

Difference: Unlike simple reduction techniques, RFE is a wrapper method that uses a model to recursively remove features and train the model until the optimal set of features is left.

Usage: Can be used with various algorithms, such as decision trees, to identify the most significant features.

Training Data:

Example: Consists of 10 features and 1 target feature.

RFE with Decision Tree:

Example: An RFE process using a decision tree algorithm might select 4 out of 10 features as the most important ones.

RFECV (Recursive Feature Elimination with Cross-Validation):

Purpose: Combines RFE with cross-validation to automatically select the optimal number of features.

Benefit: More robust feature selection as it evaluates feature importance while considering the cross-validation score.

Loss Function and Cost Function

Optimisation: Regression

Loss Function

Definition: A loss function quantifies the error between the predicted value ($\hat{y}_i$) and the actual value (y) for a single data point.

- Purpose: It provides a measure of how well the model is performing for each individual example in the dataset.
- Example: For Mean Squared Error (MSE), the loss function for a single data point is $(y_i - \hat{y}_i)^2$.

Cost Function

Definition: A cost function is an aggregate of the loss functions over the entire training dataset. It provides a single scalar value that summarises the model's performance.

- Purpose: It helps in evaluating the overall performance of the model across all data points.
- Example: For MSE, the cost function is the average of the squared errors:

$$= \frac{1}{N}\sum_{i=1}^{N}(\varepsilon_i)^2 = \frac{1}{N}\sum_{i=1}^{N}(y_i - \hat{y}_i)^2$$

Given the provided linear regression coefficients $\beta_0 = 150$ and $\beta_1 = 0.5$, we will calculate the predicted heights for weights 70, 72, and 74. Then, we will find the loss using the Mean Absolute Error (MAE).

Step-by-Step Calculation:

Linear Regression Equation: The linear regression model is: $y = \beta_0 + \beta_1 x$

Given β_0=150 and β_1=0.5

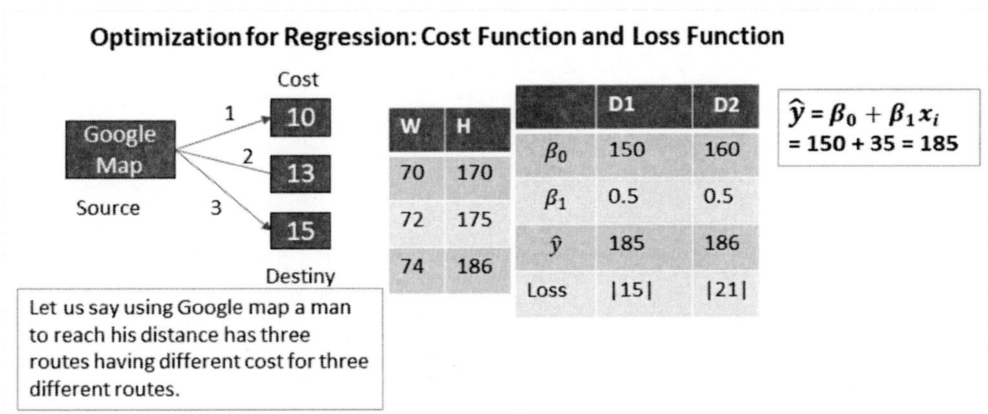

Predicted Heights: For the weights 70, 72, and 74, the predicted heights ($\hat{y}$) are calculated as follows:

$\hat{y}(70) = 150+0.5\cdot70=150+35=185$

$\hat{y}\ (72) = 150+0.5\cdot72=150+36=186$

$\hat{y}\ (74) = 150+0.5\cdot74=150+37=187$

Actual Heights: The actual heights (y) given in the problem are:

y(70) = 170	y(72) = 175	y(74) = 186

Mean Absolute Error (MAE):

The MAE is calculated as the average of the absolute differences between the actual and predicted heights.

$\text{MAE}= \frac{1}{N}\sum_{i=1}^{N}\lvert y_i - \hat{y}_i\rvert$

For our data:

MAE=1/3(|170−185|+|175−186|+|186−187|)

=1/3(15+11+1) = 1/3(27) = 9

Summary:

Predicted Heights:	Mean Absolute Error (MAE):
$\hat{y}$ (70) = 185 $\hat{y}$ (72) = 186 $\hat{y}$ (74) = 187	MAE = 9

Thus, the predicted heights for weights 70, 72, and 74 are 185, 186, and 187 respectively, and the Mean Absolute Error (MAE) is 9.

Binary Cross Entropy Loss Calculation:

Optimisation: Classification

Master said, "To calculate the Binary Cross Entropy Loss and compare the optimisation using Manhattan Distance (MD) and Euclidean Distance (ED), let's break down the process step by step."

Optimization for Classification: Binary Cross Entropy Loss

Using the formulae:

$L = \frac{1}{N} \sum_{i=1}^{N} \log P_i$

MD: |8-6| + |7-5|

ED: $\sqrt{2^2 + 2^2}$

Time/Viewer	x1	x2	x3
A	8	7	
B	6	5	

Binary Cross Entropy Loss Calculation:

Probabilities:

Assume we have predicted probabilities Pi and true labels Yi.

For binary classification, the true label Yi can be either 0 or 1.

Binary Cross Entropy Loss Formula:

$$L = \frac{1}{N} \sum_{i=1}^{N} \log P_i$$

$$L = -\frac{1}{N} \sum_{i=1}^{N} [\ y_i \log P_i + (1 - y_i)\log(1 - P_i)\ ]$$

In this case, let's consider an example where we have two probabilities and their corresponding true labels.

Example Calculation:

- Predicted Probabilities: $P_1 = 0.8$ $P_2 = 0.4$
- True Labels: $Y_1 = 1$, $Y_2 = 0$

Binary Cross Entropy Loss:

$L = -1/2\ [Y_1\log(P_1) + (1-Y_1)\log(1-P_1) + Y_2\log(P_2) + (1-Y_2)\log(1-P_2)]$

$= -1/2[1 \cdot \log(0.8) + (1-1) \cdot \log(1-0.8) + 0 \cdot \log(0.4) + (1-0) \cdot \log(1-0.4)]$

$= -1/2[\log(0.8)+\log(0.6)] = -1/2[-0.223+(-0.511)] = -1/2[-0.734] =$ **0.367**

Distance Measures Calculation:

Manhattan Distance (MD):

$$MD = |8-6| + |7-5| = 2+2 = 4$$

Euclidean Distance (ED):

$$ED = \sqrt{(8-6)^2 + (7-5)^2} = \sqrt{2^2 + 2^2} = \sqrt{8} = 2\sqrt{2} \approx 2.83$$

Summary:

Binary Cross Entropy Loss	Manhattan Distance	Euclidean Distance
L=0.367	MD=4	ED ≈ 2.83

These calculations provide a framework for evaluating classification loss using Binary Cross Entropy and comparing optimisation techniques using distance measures.

Probability and Likelihood

Akshaya asked, "What is the difference between probability and likelihood?"

Probability:

Master said, "In probability theory, when we say a person randomly selected will have a hike of 1% to 3%, we're considering the likelihood of this event under a specific distribution, in this case, a normal distribution with mean (μ) 0 and standard deviation (σ) 1."

Probability, $P(1 <= X <= 3 \mid \mu = 0, \sigma = 1)$: This represents the probability that a randomly selected value (X) from a normal distribution with mean 0 and standard deviation 1 falls between 1% and 3%.

Likelihood:

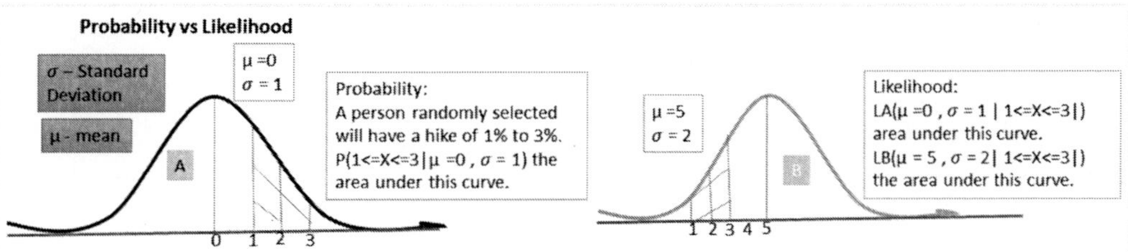

Likelihood in statistics refers to how probable the observed data are given a specific model parameter (μ, σ in this case).

- Likelihood $L_A(\mu = 0, \sigma = 1 \mid 1 <= X <= 3)$: This indicates the likelihood of observing the values between 1% and 3% hike, given that the distribution parameters are $\mu = 0$ and $\sigma = 1$.
- Likelihood $L_B(\mu = 5, \sigma = 2 \mid 1 <= X <= 3)$: Here, the likelihood represents the probability of observing the values between 1% and 3% hike, but under a different set of distribution parameters, $\mu = 5$ and $\sigma = 2$.

Key Differences:

- Probability focuses on the likelihood of an event occurring under a specific distribution (fixed distribution parameters).
- Likelihood assesses how likely it is to observe certain data given different parameter values of the distribution (varying distribution parameters).

In summary, probability deals with the likelihood of events happening under fixed conditions, while likelihood deals with how likely observed data are given different hypothetical conditions of the underlying distribution.

PART TWO

DAY THREE

Unit 2 - Lesson FIVE

SAMPLING

Master said, "Sampling is a technique used to select individual members or a subset of a population to make statistical inferences about the whole population. This method allows researchers to estimate population characteristics without studying the entire group, making it a time-efficient and cost-effective approach. Sampling is fundamental in research design, enabling actionable insights to be derived without the need for exhaustive data collection from the entire population."

For instance, consider a drug manufacturer aiming to study the adverse side effects of a drug on a country's population. Conducting a study involving the entire population is impractical. Instead, the researcher selects a representative sample from different demographics and studies them, providing indicative feedback on the drug's effects.

Akshaya asked, "What is a Population?"

Master said, "A population in research refers to the entire group of individuals or instances about whom the study aims to draw conclusions. This group shares a common characteristic or set of characteristics, making them the focus of the research. Populations can be large, such as the entire adult population of a country, or smaller, such as students in a particular school."

Roopa asked, "What is a Sampling Frame?"

Master said, "A sampling frame is a list or database from which a sample is drawn. It includes all the members of the population that the researcher intends to study. The sampling frame must be comprehensive and up-to-date to ensure that the sample accurately represents the population. For example, if a researcher is studying university students, the sampling frame could be a list of all enrolled students at the university. The quality and accuracy of the sampling frame are critical for the validity of the research findings."

☐ Types of Sampling: Sampling Methods

Sampling in market research is broadly categorised into two types: probability sampling and non-probability sampling. Each method has distinct characteristics and is suited for different types of research. Let's delve into these methods and their subtypes.

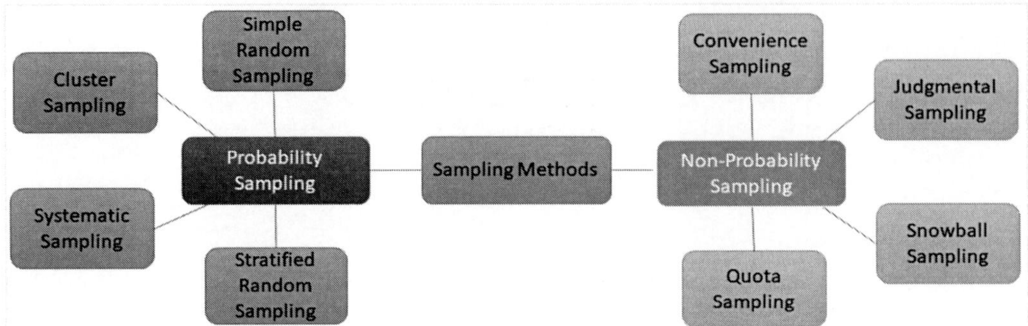

Probability Sampling

Master said, "Probability sampling is a technique where the researcher selects samples from a population based on specific criteria, ensuring that every member has an equal chance of being included. This method is systematic and aims to create a representative sample."

Types of probability sampling include:

Simple Random Sampling:

Every member of the population has an equal chance of being selected, often using random number generators or drawing lots. This method is ideal for small populations and when each member's selection can be completely random.

Example: In a company with 500 employees, the HR department wants to select participants for a new training program. They place the names of all 500 employees into a bowl and draw names at random. Each employee has an equal chance of being selected.

Systematic Sampling: Systematic sampling involves selecting sample members from a population at regular intervals. The process begins with choosing a starting point and then selecting every nth member of the population. Selection follows a fixed, periodic interval (e.g., every 10th person on a list), starting from a random point.

Example: A researcher wants to select a systematic sample of 500 people from a population of 5000. They assign a number to each person from 1 to 5000 and then select every 10th person (since 5000/500 = 10) to be part of the sample.

Stratified Sampling: The population is divided into subgroups (strata) based on a characteristic (e.g., age, income), and random samples are taken from each stratum.

Example: A researcher wants to study the spending habits of people in different income brackets. They divide the population into strata based on annual family income (e.g., less than $25,000, $26,000 – $30,000, $31,000 – $35,000, etc.). They then randomly select individuals from each income bracket to ensure that each income group is represented in the sample. This approach helps marketers determine which income groups to target for a particular product.

Cluster or Multistage Sampling: The population is divided into clusters, often geographically. Random clusters are selected, and then members within these clusters are randomly sampled.

Example: To estimate the number of immigrants in the United States, the government divides the country into clusters based on states such as California, Texas, and Florida. They then randomly select a few states and survey all immigrants within those states to draw conclusions about the entire population.

Probability Proportional to Size Sampling: Larger groups in the population have a higher chance of being selected. The probability of selection is proportional to the size of the group.

Uses of Probability Sampling

Probability sampling has several critical applications that enhance the quality and reliability of research findings:

Reduce Sample Bias

Probability sampling significantly minimises sample bias, ensuring that the selection process is random and impartial. This method allows each member of the population an equal chance of being selected, which results in a sample that accurately represents the population. Consequently, the data collected is of higher quality and more reliable for drawing conclusions.

Example: In a study aiming to understand the average screen time among teenagers, using probability sampling ensures that the sample includes teenagers from different backgrounds, schools, and regions, providing a comprehensive overview of screen time habits.

Represent a Diverse Population

When dealing with a vast and diverse population, it is crucial to have a sample that represents all subgroups within the population adequately. Probability sampling ensures that every subgroup, regardless of size, has a chance to be included in the sample, preventing skewed data that might overrepresent or underrepresent certain demographics.

Example: Suppose a company like Square wants to understand potential users of their point-of-sale devices. Conducting a survey using probability sampling across the US, including individuals from various industries and socio-economic backgrounds, will provide a well-rounded understanding of their target market.

Create an Accurate Sample

Probability sampling enables researchers to design and create a sample that is an accurate reflection of the population. By using a systematic approach to select participants, researchers can gather well-defined data that is crucial for making informed decisions and generalizations about the entire population.

Example: In medical research, where it is essential to study the effects of a new drug, probability sampling can help ensure that the sample includes participants from different age groups, genders, and health backgrounds. This results in comprehensive data that accurately reflects the drug's effects across the entire population.

By utilising probability sampling, researchers can achieve a more accurate and unbiased representation of the population, leading to more valid and generalizable research findings.

Non-Probability Sampling

Non-probability sampling is a technique where the samples are gathered in a process that does not give all the individuals in the population equal chances of being selected. This method relies on the judgment of the researcher or statistician to choose the members of the population to be included in the sample. It is particularly useful in situations where time, cost constraints, or the preliminary stages of research make it impractical to use probability sampling methods. Types of non-probability sampling include:

Convenience Sampling:

Convenience sampling involves selecting samples based on their ease of access and proximity to the researcher. This method is often used when time and resources are limited, making it impractical to collect a sample that accurately represents the entire population.

Example: A startup company might distribute flyers at a local mall to promote an event or product launch. The people approached are selected based on their immediate availability and proximity, not because they represent a larger population.

Judgmental or Purposive Sampling:

Judgmental or purposive sampling involves selecting a sample based on the researcher's knowledge and judgment about the population. The researcher selects individuals who are most beneficial to the study based on specific characteristics or criteria.

Example: If researchers want to study the motivations of individuals pursuing a master's degree, they might ask a screening question, "Are you interested in doing your master's degree in ...?" Only those who respond affirmatively are included in the sample.

Snowball Sampling

Snowball sampling is used when the population is hard to reach or identify. This method relies on existing study subjects to recruit future subjects from among their acquaintances. It is particularly useful for studying sensitive topics or hard-to-reach populations.

Example: To gather data on illegal immigrants, a researcher might start with a few known individuals and ask them to refer others. Similarly, for sensitive issues like HIV/AIDS, researchers might contact a few individuals and ask them to refer others who might be willing to participate.

Quota Sampling:

Quota sampling involves dividing the population into mutually exclusive subgroups and then selecting samples from each group based on a pre-set quota. This method ensures that the sample has the same proportions of individuals as the entire population concerning specific characteristics.

Example: If a researcher wants to study the buying habits of different age groups, they might set quotas to include a certain number of individuals from each age group (e.g., 18-25, 26-35, etc.) to ensure that all age groups are adequately represented.

Uses of Non-Probability Sampling

Non-probability sampling is particularly useful in several scenarios:

Hypothesis Creation: When researchers have limited or no prior information, they use non-probability sampling to quickly gather preliminary data and form hypotheses. This method helps generate initial insights and build a foundation for more detailed research.

Exploratory Research: Non-probability sampling is widely used in qualitative research, pilot studies, or exploratory research. It allows researchers to explore new areas of interest without the constraints of a rigid sampling framework.

Budget and Time Constraints: When facing budget and time limitations, non-probability sampling is often the preferred method. It allows for quicker data collection and flexibility in respondent selection, making it easier to gather preliminary data without extensive resources.

Difference between probability sampling and non-probability sampling methods

Aspect	Probability Sampling Methods	Non-Probability Sampling Methods
Definition	Sampling based on probability theory	Sampling based on subjective judgment
Alternatively Known as	Random sampling method	Non-random sampling method
Population Selection	Random selection from the population	Arbitrary selection from the population
Nature	Conclusive research	Exploratory research
Sample	Methodical representation of population demographics	Potential skew in population demographics representation
Time Taken	Longer time due to predefined selection parameters	Quicker due to undefined sample and selection criteria
Results	Unbiased results contributing to research conclusiveness	Results may be biased, rendering research speculative
Hypothesis	Guided by an underlying hypothesis	Hypothesis often emerges after the study

Deciding on the Type of Sampling to Use

Choosing the appropriate sampling method is crucial for the success of any research study. Here are steps that expert researchers follow to determine the best sampling method:

Define Research Goals: Clearly outline the objectives of your study. These goals typically revolve around cost, precision, and accuracy.

Identify Potential Sampling Techniques: Consider various sampling methods that might help achieve your research goals. Evaluate the strengths and weaknesses of each method.

Test Sampling Methods: Conduct small-scale tests using different sampling techniques to see which one aligns best with your research objectives. Analyse the effectiveness of each method.

Select the Optimal Method: Based on your tests and evaluations, choose the sampling method that best meets the goals of your research, ensuring it balances cost, precision, and accuracy.

John asked, "What is a true distribution?"

Master said, "'True distribution' refers to the actual distribution of a variable or phenomenon within a population. It represents the complete set of possible values and their respective probabilities within the entire population. In statistical analysis, researchers often seek to estimate or infer this true distribution based on samples taken from the population."

Akshatha asked "What is good confidence?"

Master said, "'Good confidence' typically refers to a high level of confidence in the results or conclusions drawn from a statistical analysis. This confidence is often expressed through confidence intervals or confidence levels. A good confidence level indicates a high degree of certainty that the findings accurately reflect the true characteristics of the population being studied. This level of confidence is usually determined based on the sample size, variability within the data, and the chosen level of significance."

Sam asked, "How to figure out ideal sample size?"

Example:

Master said, "To introduce a new healthy drink product in the market, we aim to compare its average rating against that of another product. However, we must determine an optimal sample size that ensures good confidence in our conclusions while avoiding resource wastage."

To address this, we'll undertake two trials:

Trail	**True Distribution**	**Average Rating**	**Sample size**
1	1 star – 15% 2 Star – 65% 3 Star – 20%	2.05	10,100,1000
2	1 star – 5% 2 Star – 50% 3 Star – 45%	2.4	10,100,1000

Objective: Determine the sample size required to confidently assert that the new drink is better.

Through these trials, we'll assess various true distributions and their corresponding sample sizes to pinpoint the minimum sampling required.

Exercise P2-U2 – D9

Sampling

```
import numpy as np
import matplotlib.pyplot as plt
import seaborn as sns
def generate_ratings(rating_distr, n):
   # Generate n ratings from the given ratings distribution
   randvals = np.random.random(n).reshape(-1, 1)
   ratings = np.argmax(randvals < rating_distr.cumsum(), axis=1) + 1
   return ratings

def simulate_runs(rating_distr, n, runs=10000):
   # Simulate many runs with that sample size
   avg_ratings = []

   for _ in range(runs):
      curr_ratings = generate_ratings(rating_distr, n)
      avg_ratings.append(curr_ratings.mean())

   return np.array(avg_ratings)

def plot_distribution(n, avg_ratings, avg, sd, pct, plot=True):
   if plot:
      plt.figure(figsize=(10,4))
      sns.histplot(avg_ratings, kde=True)
      plt.title('n=%s\nAvg: %.3f  |  SD: %.3f\nPct Distr: %.3f'%(n, avg, sd, pct),
fontsize=20)
      plt.axvline(2, color='r')
      plt.xlabel('Avg Rating', fontsize=16)
      plt.ylabel('Density', fontsize=16)
      plt.show()

def calculate_sample_sizes(rating_distributions):
   required_sample_sizes = []
   for rating_distribution in rating_distributions:
      req_samp_size = -1
      for n in [5, 10, 25, 50, 100, 250, 500, 1000]:
         avg_ratings = simulate_runs(rating_distribution, n)
         pct = np.mean(avg_ratings > 2) if np.mean(avg_ratings > 2) > 0.95 else
np.mean(avg_ratings < 2)
         if pct > 0.95:
            req_samp_size = n
            break
      required_sample_sizes.append(req_samp_size)
```

```
    return required_sample_sizes

# Trail One
RATING_DISTR_1 = np.array([0.15, 0.65, 0.2])
n_values = [10, 100, 1000]
for n in n_values:
    avg_ratings = simulate_runs(RATING_DISTR_1, n)
    avg, sd = avg_ratings.mean(), avg_ratings.std()
    pct = np.mean(avg_ratings > 2)
    plot_distribution(n, avg_ratings, avg, sd, pct)

# Trail Two
RATING_DISTR_2 = np.array([0.05, 0.5, 0.45])
rating_distributions = [np.array([p1,p2,1-p1-p2]) for p1 in np.arange(0,1.1,.1) for p2 in np.arange(0, 1-p1, 0.1)]
required_sample_sizes = calculate_sample_sizes(rating_distributions)

p1_vals = np.array([item[0] for item in rating_distributions])
p2_vals = np.array([item[1] for item in rating_distributions])

plt.figure(figsize=(7,7))
plt.scatter(p1_vals, p2_vals, s=required_sample_sizes, alpha=0.5)
plt.xticks(np.arange(0,1,.1), fontsize=14)
plt.yticks(np.arange(0,1,.1), fontsize=14)
plt.xlabel('p1 Fraction', fontsize=18)
plt.ylabel('p2 Fraction', fontsize=18)
for i,r in enumerate(required_sample_sizes):
    plt.annotate(r, (p1_vals[i]-.01*len(str(r)), p2_vals[i]-.01), fontsize=20, fontweight=2)
plt.plot(p1_vals, -2*p1_vals+1)
plt.xlim(-.05,1)
plt.ylim(-.05,1)
plt.show()
```

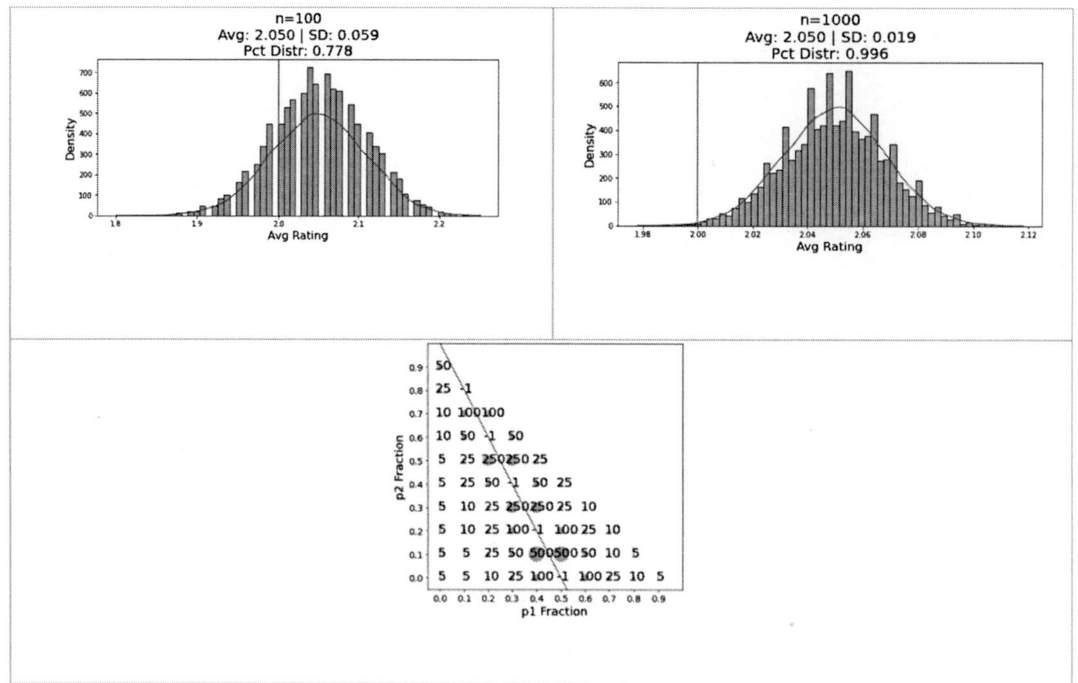

Rejection Sampling

Accept- Reject:

Master explained that the Rejection sampling is a fundamental technique used in statistics, computer science, and various other fields to generate samples from a target distribution. It is particularly useful when direct sampling from the target distribution is challenging or infeasible.

Understanding Rejection Sampling:

The core concept of rejection sampling involves generating samples from a desired probability distribution function (PDF) p(s). The basic idea is to sample from a simpler distribution, known as the proposal distribution g(s), and then accept or reject these samples based on whether they fall under the desired distribution p(s).

The target distribution p(s) can be expressed as:

$$p(s) = f(s)/NC$$

Here:

- f(s) is a function proportional to the target distribution.

- NC is the normalising constant, which is often difficult to compute.

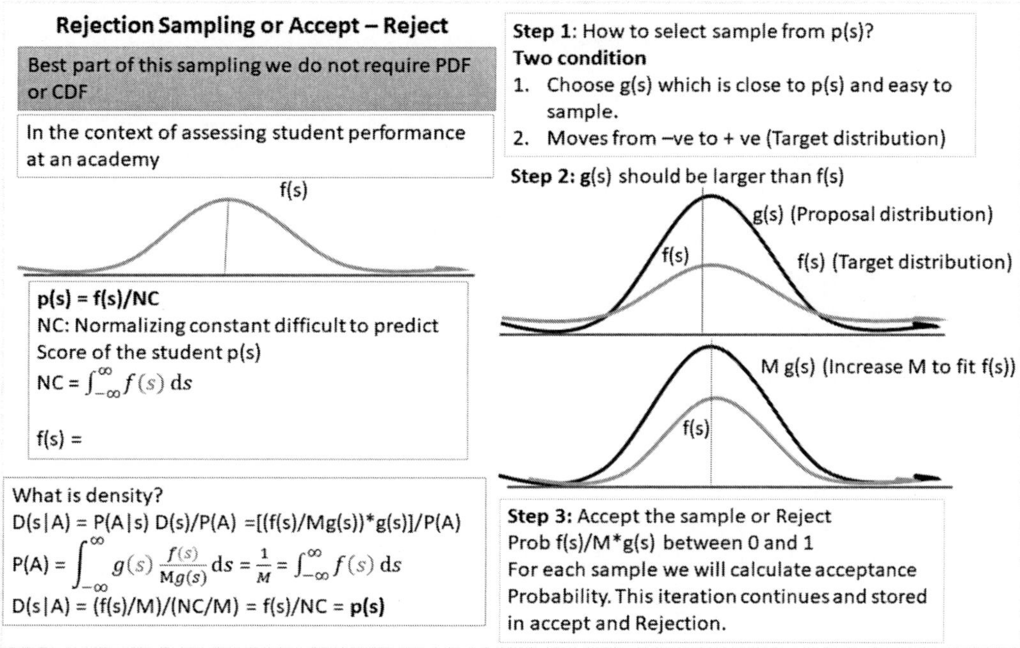

Example: Score of a Student p(s)

Steps in Rejection Sampling

Step 1: How to Select Samples from p(s)?

Choose g(s) (Proposal Distribution):

- g(s) should be close to p(s) and easy to sample from.
- g(s) should cover the entire range of p(s), typically from $-\infty$- to $+\infty$.

Step 2: Ensure g(s) is larger than f(s)

- Scale the proposal distribution g(s) using a constant M such that: $g(s) \geq f(s)$

Step 3: Accept or Reject the Sample

- For each sample, calculate the acceptance probability: Acceptance Probability = $f(s)/M \cdot g(s)$. This probability is between 0 and 1.
- Generate a uniform random number u in the range [0, 1]. Accept the sample if $u \leq f(s)/M \cdot g(s)$; otherwise, reject it.

Density Calculation

The density of accepted samples can be expressed as:

D(s | A) = P(A | s) D(s)/P(A) =[(f(s)/Mg(s))*g(s)]/P(A)

Where:

P(A) is the probability of accepting a sample:

$$P(A) = \int_{-\infty}^{\infty} g(s) \frac{f(s)}{Mg(s)} ds = \frac{1}{M} = \int_{-\infty}^{\infty} f(s)\, ds$$

Thus:

D(s | A) = (f(s)/M)/(NC/M) = f(s)/NC = **p(s)**

Rejection sampling allows us to generate samples from a complex target distribution by using a simpler proposal distribution and an acceptance-rejection mechanism. This method ensures that the generated samples follow the desired distribution p(s), despite the challenges in directly sampling from it.

Example:

The code demonstrates the use of the rejection sampling algorithm to generate samples from a target probability distribution when direct sampling is challenging. In this example, the target distribution is a double gamma distribution, and the envelope distribution is a normal distribution.

Exercise P2-U2 – D10

Rejection Sampling

```
import numpy as np
import pandas as pd
import matplotlib.pyplot as plt
import scipy.stats as stats
# Define the target distribution (double gamma distribution)
target_dist = stats.dgamma(a=1)

# Define the envelope distribution (normal distribution)
envelope_dist = stats.norm(loc=0, scale=2)

# Generate samples for the PDF
x = np.linspace(
   min(target_dist.ppf(0.001), envelope_dist.ppf(0.001)),
```

```
    max(target_dist.ppf(0.999), envelope_dist.ppf(0.999)),
    1000
)
target_samples = target_dist.pdf(x)
envelope_samples = envelope_dist.pdf(x)

# Find the scaling constant for the envelope distribution
M = max(target_samples / envelope_samples)

# Plot the target and envelope distributions
df = pd.DataFrame({'Target': target_samples, 'Envelope': M * envelope_samples},
index=x)
ax = df.plot(style=['--', '-'], color=['black', 'blue'], figsize=(8, 6), linewidth=2.0)

# Highlight a specific point for illustration
highlight_x = 2
ax.plot((highlight_x, highlight_x), (0, target_dist.pdf(highlight_x)), 'g--', linewidth=2.0)
ax.plot((highlight_x, highlight_x), (target_dist.pdf(highlight_x), M *
envelope_dist.pdf(highlight_x)), 'r--', linewidth=2.0)
ax.text(1.0, 0.20, 'Reject', color='red')
ax.text(1.0, 0.03, 'Accept', color='green')

# Define the rejection sampling function
def rejection_sampling():
    while True:
        sample = np.random.normal(0, 2)
        envelope = M * envelope_dist.pdf(sample)
        random_prob = np.random.uniform(0, envelope)
        if random_prob < target_dist.pdf(sample):
            return sample

# Generate samples using the rejection sampling algorithm
samples = [rejection_sampling() for _ in range(10000)]

# Plot histogram of the samples vs. the target PDF
fig, ax = plt.subplots(figsize=(8, 6))
df['Target'].plot(ax=ax, color='blue', style='--', linewidth=2.0)
pd.Series(samples).plot.hist(bins=300, density=True, color='green', alpha=0.3,
linewidth=0.0, ax=ax)
ax.legend(['Target PDF', 'Rejection Sampling'])
plt.show()
```

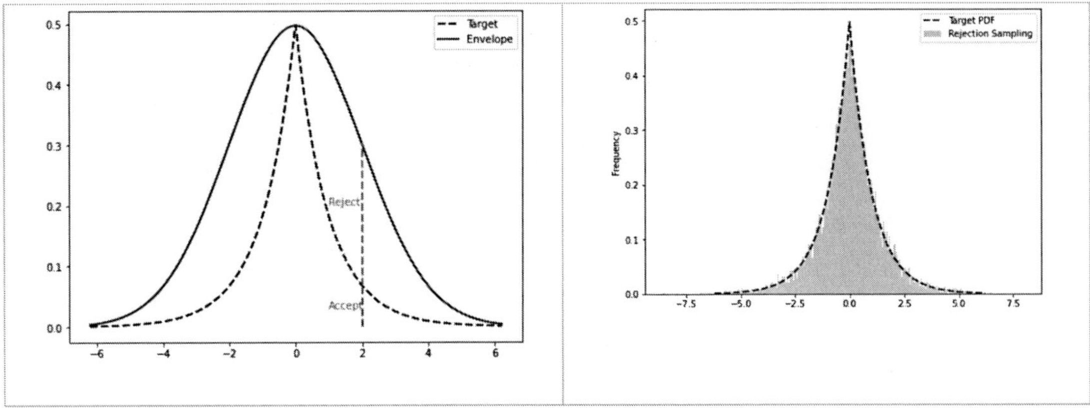

Key Steps and Components:

Define Distributions:

- target_dist is defined as a double gamma distribution.
- envelope_dist is defined as a normal distribution with a mean of 0 and a standard deviation of 2.

Generate Samples for PDF:

Samples for the probability density functions (PDFs) of both distributions are generated over a specified range using numpy.linspace.

Scaling Constant (M):

The scaling constant M is calculated as the maximum ratio of the target distribution's PDF to the envelope distribution's PDF. This ensures that the envelope distribution sufficiently covers the target distribution.

Plot Target and Envelope Distributions:

- The target and scaled envelope distributions are plotted for visualization.
- A specific point (x = 2) is highlighted to illustrate the acceptance and rejection regions.

Rejection Sampling Function:

rejection_sampling() is a function that implements the rejection sampling algorithm:

- Sample from the envelope distribution.
- Calculate the acceptance probability.
- Accept or reject the sample based on the calculated probability.
- Return the accepted sample.

Generate Samples:

A list comprehension is used to generate 10,000 samples from the target distribution using the rejection sampling algorithm.

Plot Histogram of Samples:

The histogram of the generated samples is plotted alongside the target PDF to compare the distribution of the samples to the target distribution.

This code provides a clear and practical example of rejection sampling, illustrating how to sample from a complex target distribution using a simpler, easier-to-sample envelope distribution. The visualizations help in understanding the acceptance and rejection process within the sampling algorithm.

PART TWO

DAY THREE

Unit 2 - Lesson SIX

Statistical Regression

Akshaya asked, "What is sampling?"

☐ Linear Regression

Master said, "Linear regression serves as a fundamental statistical model for understanding the relationship between a dependent variable and one or more independent variables, achieved by fitting a linear equation to observed data. The objective is to pinpoint the optimal linear equation that accurately predicts the dependent variable's value based on the independent variables."

Math equation:

$$Y = \beta_0 + \beta_1 X^1 + \beta_2 X^2 + \ldots + \beta_n X^n + \epsilon$$

where $\beta 0$ is the intercept, $\beta 1, \beta 2, \ldots, \beta n$ are the coefficients representing the effect of each independent variable on the dependent variable, $X1, X2, \ldots, Xn$, and ϵ is the error term accounting for unexplained variability.

Problem statement: What is the expected duration of a patient's hospital stay after a minor surgery?

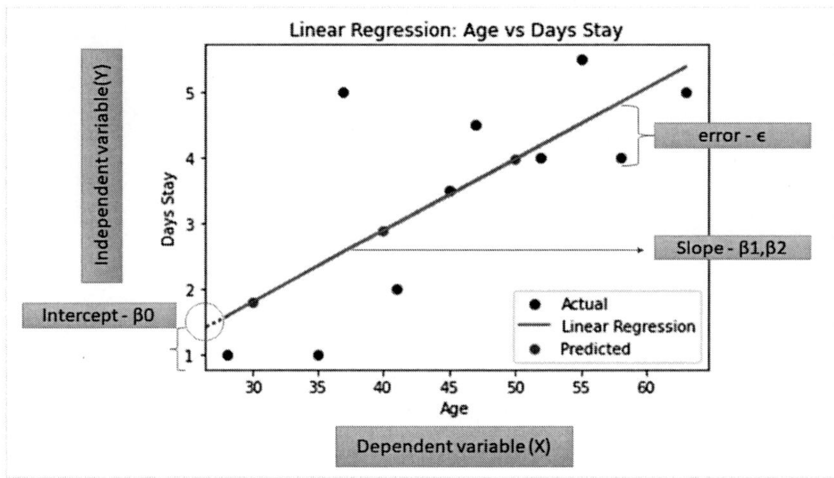

Main Assumptions of Linear Regression

Linearity:

- **Assumption:** The relationship between the independent variables and the dependent variable is linear.
- **Check:** Plot the observed vs. predicted values. The plot should show a linear trend.

Independence:

- **Assumption:** The residuals (errors) are independent of each other.
- **Check:** Use the Durbin-Watson statistic or plot residuals vs. time to check for autocorrelation.

Homoscedasticity:

- **Assumption:** The residuals have constant variance at every level of the independent variables.
- **Check:** Plot the residuals vs. the predicted values. The spread should be consistent across all levels.

Normality of Residuals:

- **Assumption:** The residuals are normally distributed.
- **Check:** Use a Q-Q plot or a histogram of the residuals to assess normality.

No Multicollinearity:

- **Assumption:** The independent variables are not too highly correlated with each other.
- **Check:** Calculate the Variance Inflation Factor (VIF). VIF values greater than 10 indicate significant multicollinearity.

By ensuring these assumptions are met, the linear regression model will provide reliable and accurate predictions.

R Squared

Apeksha asked, "What is R Squared?"

Master said, "R squared (R^2) is a statistical measure that represents the proportion of the variance in the dependent variable (in this case, the quantity of carrots) that is predictable from the independent variable (fertiliser used)." In other words, it shows how well the independent variable explains the variation in the dependent variable.

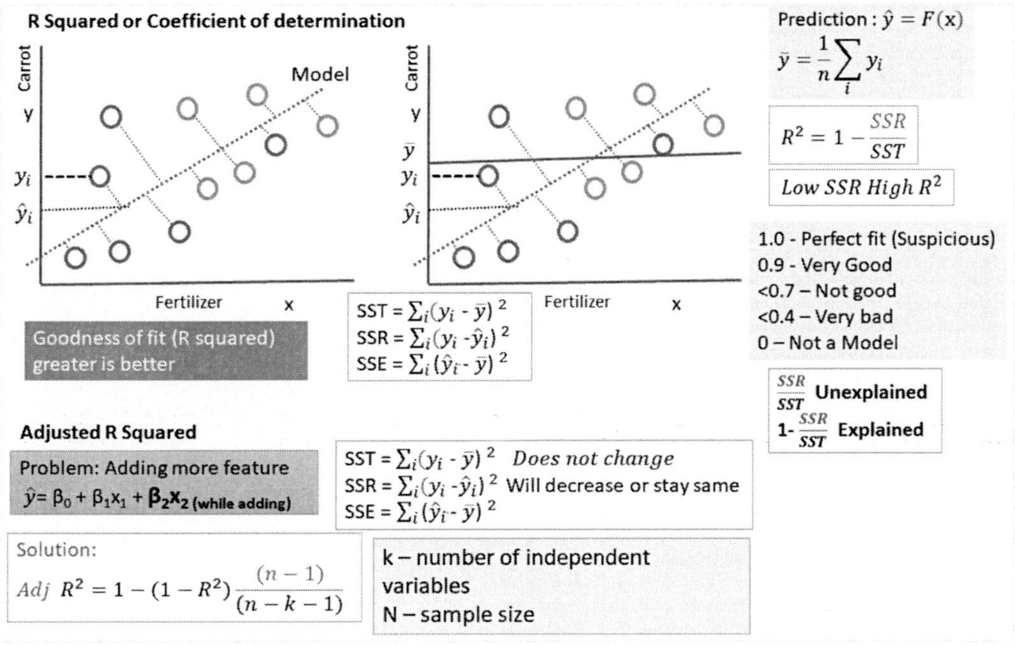

Key Components:

SST (Total Sum of Squares): Measures the total variance in the dependent variable. It is calculated as:

$$SST = \sum_i (y_i - \bar{y})^2$$

Here, y_i is the actual value, and $\bar{y}$ is the mean of the actual values. SST does not change.

SSR (Residual Sum of Squares): Measures the variance that the model cannot explain. It is calculated as:

$$SSR = \sum_i (y_i - \hat{y}_i)^2$$

Here, y_i is the actual value, and $\hat{y}_i$ is the predicted value. SSR will decrease or stay the same as the model improves.

SSE (Explained Sum of Squares): Measures the variance that the model can explain. It is calculated as:

$$SSE = \sum_i (\hat{y}_i - \bar{y})^2$$

Here, $\hat{y}_i$ is the predicted value, and $\bar{y}$ is the mean of the actual values.

Relationships:

SST is the sum of SSR and SSE:

$$SST=SSR+SSE$$

R Squared Calculation:

R^2 is calculated as:

$$R^2 = 1 - \frac{SSR}{SST}$$

Interpretation:

High R^2: A high R^2 indicates a good fit, meaning the independent variable explains a large portion of the variance in the dependent variable.

1.0: Perfect fit (but could be suspicious if too high)

0.9: Very good fit

Low R2: Indicates a poor fit, meaning the independent variable does not explain much of the variance.

< 0.7: Not good

< 0.4: Very bad

0: The model does not explain any variance

Example:

If we use fertiliser (independent variable) to predict the quantity of carrots (dependent variable):

Prediction Model: $\hat{y} = F(x)$

Mean of Actual Values = $\bar{y} = \frac{1}{n}\sum_i y_i$

Summary:

SSR/SST: Represents the unexplained variance.

1 - SSR/SST: Represents the explained variance.

In essence, R^2 provides a metric to gauge the effectiveness of the model in explaining the variation in the dependent variable.

Adjusted R Squared:

Akanksh asked, "What is Adjusted R Squared?"

Master said, "Adjusted R squared (R^2_{adj}) is a modified version of R squared (R^2) that adjusts for the number of predictors (independent variables) in a model. It provides a more accurate measure of the goodness-of-fit, especially when multiple independent variables are included. Adjusted R2 accounts for the possibility of overfitting that can occur when more predictors are added to a model."

Problem: Adding More Features

When adding more features (independent variables) to a regression model, the standard R^2 will typically increase regardless of whether those features are actually useful. This can lead to overfitting, where the model performs well on the training data but poorly on new data.

For example, if you start with a simple model:

$\hat{y} = \beta_0 + \beta_1 x_1$

and then add another feature:

$$\hat{y} = \beta_0 + \beta_1 x_1 + \beta_2 x_2$$

the R^2 value will generally increase, even if x_2 doesn't actually contribute meaningful predictive power.

Solution: Adjusted R Squared

Adjusted R^2 adjusts the R^2 value based on the number of predictors and the sample size, providing a more accurate measure of model performance. The formula for adjusted R^2 is:

Where:

- R^2 is the coefficient of determination.
- n is the sample size.
- k is the number of independent variables (predictors).

Interpretation:

- Adjusted R^2 increases only if the new predictor improves the model more than would be expected by chance.
- Adjusted R^2 decreases when a predictor improves the model less than expected by chance.
- Adjusted R^2 can be lower than R^2 when adding variables that do not improve the model.

Example Calculation:

Assume you have a dataset with n=100 samples and you are adding predictors to your model. Suppose your initial R^2 value is 0.8 with 2 predictors (k=2).

Calculate the adjustment factor:

$$Adj\ R^2 = 1 - (1 - R^2)\frac{(n-1)}{(n-k-1)}$$

(n-1)/(n-k-1) = (100−1) / (100−2−1) = 9997 ≈ 1.0206

Calculate the adjusted R^2:

Adjusted R^2 = 1−(1−0.8)×1.0206 = 1 – (0.2×1.0206) ≈ 1

In this example, the adjusted R^2 is slightly lower than the R^2, indicating that the adjustment for the number of predictors has been taken into account.

Adjusted R^2 is a better metric for evaluating the goodness-of-fit for regression models, especially when comparing models with different numbers of predictors.

Overfitting and Underfitting:

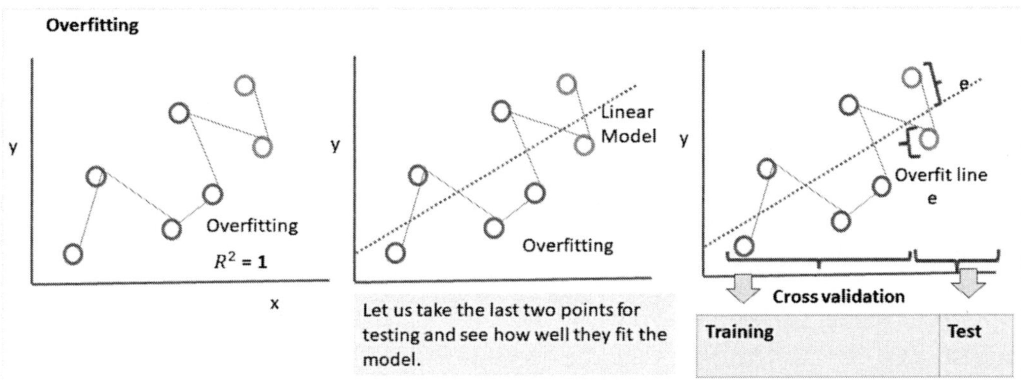

Sam asked, "What is Overfitting and Underfitting in Linear Regression?"

Master said, "In the context of linear regression, overfitting and underfitting refer to how well a model generalizes to unseen data."

Overfitting occurs when a model learns the training data too well, capturing noise and fluctuations that do not generalize to new data. An overfitted model has high accuracy on training data but performs poorly on test data.

- Symptoms: Complex models, many features, high variance.
- Example: A polynomial regression model with a high degree that fits the training data perfectly but fails to predict new data accurately.

Underfitting occurs when a model is too simple to capture the underlying patterns in the data. An underfitted model performs poorly on both training and test data.

- Symptoms: Simple models, few features, high bias.
- Example: A linear regression model trying to fit data that has a non-linear relationship.

Sam asked, "Why we should not have Overfitting in training dataset?"

Master explained that the Overfitting should be avoided because it leads to a model that performs well on the training data but poorly on new, unseen data. This lack of generalization can result in:

- Poor Predictive Performance: The model does not accurately predict outcomes on new data.
- Misleading Metrics: High accuracy on training data may give a false sense of confidence in the model's performance.
- Overcomplexity: The model becomes unnecessarily complicated, making it harder to interpret and more prone to errors.

Roopa asked, "What is a Linear Model?"

Master explained that a linear model is a type of statistical model where the relationship between the independent variables (features) and the dependent variable (target) is assumed to be linear. The general form of a linear regression model is:

$$\hat{y} = \beta_0 + \beta_1 x_1 + \beta_2 x_2 + \ldots + \beta_n x_n$$

Let Us Take the Last Two Points for Testing and See How Well They Fit the Model

In practice, to evaluate how well a model fits new data, you can use a portion of your dataset as a test set. For example, if you have a dataset with 100 points, you might use the first 90 points for training and the last 10 points for testing.

Comparing Overfitting and Underfitting

Overfitting:

- High variance for testing data and low variance for training data.
- The model performs well on the training data but poorly on unseen test data.
- Both Ridge and Lasso can help mitigate overfitting by adding regularization.

Underfitting:

- High bias for both training and testing data.
- The model is too simple to capture the underlying structure of the data.
- Increasing the complexity of the model (e.g., by adding more features or using a less

regularized model) can help reduce underfitting.

Objective: Minimize the Cost Function

The objective of both Ridge and Lasso regression is to minimize the cost function, which is a combination of the residual sum of squares and a regularization term. This helps in achieving a balance between bias and variance, thereby improving the generalizability of the model.

By understanding the specific purposes and effects of Ridge and Lasso regression, you can choose the appropriate technique based on your specific problem and dataset characteristics.

Cross-Validation

Nikash asked, "What is Cross-Validation?"

Master said, "Cross-validation is a technique for assessing how well a model generalizes to an independent dataset. It involves partitioning the data into subsets, training the model on some subsets, and testing it on the remaining subsets."

The most common types of cross-validation are:

K-Fold Cross-Validation: The data is divided into k equally sized folds. The model is trained k times, each time using a different fold as the test set and the remaining folds as the training set. The performance metric is averaged over the k trials.

Example: 5-fold cross-validation involves splitting the data into 5 parts, training on 4 parts, and testing on the 5th part, repeating this process 5 times.

Leave-One-Out Cross-Validation (LOOCV): A special case of k-fold cross-validation where k is equal to the number of data points. Each data point is used once as a test set while the remaining data points form the training set.

Benefits of Cross-Validation

Better Model Evaluation: Provides a more accurate estimate of model performance on unseen data.

Model Selection: Helps in comparing different models or hyperparameters to select the best one.

Reduced Overfitting: Ensures that the model's performance is evaluated on multiple splits, reducing the likelihood of overfitting to a particular training set.

Example of Cross-Validation in Python

Here's a simple example using scikit-learn's KFold cross-validation:

Example P2 – U2 – D11	

KFold cross-validation	Output

from sklearn.model_selection import cross_val_score, KFold
from sklearn.linear_model import LinearRegression
import numpy as np
# Example data 	
X = np.random.rand(100, 2) # 100 samples, 2 features
y = np.random.rand(100)   # 100 target values
 	
# Linear Regression model 	
model = LinearRegression()
# KFold cross-validation 	
kf = KFold(n_splits=5)
scores = cross_val_score(model, X, y, cv=kf, scoring='r2')
 	
# Output the R^2 scores for each fold 	
print("R^2 scores for each fold:", scores)
print("Average R^2 score:", np.mean(scores))
	R^2 scores for each fold: [0.00911414 -0.12103126 -0.14164467 -0.05827198 -0.22336518]
	Average R^2 score:
	-
	0.10703978948838133

This example demonstrates how to perform 5-fold cross-validation and print the R^2 scores for each fold as well as the average R^2 score.

Vector Norms

Akshaya asked, "What are Vector Norms?"

Master said, "Vector norms are functions that assign a non-negative scalar value to a vector, which provides a measure of the vector's magnitude or length. Different norms capture different notions of vector length."

L2 Norm (Euclidean Norm)

The L2 norm, also known as the Euclidean norm, is the most commonly used vector norm. It represents the straight-line distance from the origin to the point defined by the vector in Euclidean space. The L2 norm of a vector β is defined as:

$$\|\vec{\beta}\|_2 = \sqrt{\beta_0^2 + \beta_1^2 + \cdots + \beta_n^2}$$

For a 2-dimensional vector $\vec{\beta} = \begin{bmatrix}\beta_0 \\ \beta_1\end{bmatrix}$, the L2 norm is:

$$\|\vec{\beta}\|_2 = \sqrt{\beta_0^2 + \beta_1^2}$$

This norm is analogous to the Cartesian distance.

L1 Norm (Manhattan Norm)

The L1 norm, also known as the Manhattan norm, is the sum of the absolute values of the vector's components. It captures the total "travel distance" in each dimension. The L1 norm of a vector β is defined as:

$$\|\vec{\beta}\|_1 = |\beta_0| + |\beta_1^2| + .. + |\beta_n^2|$$

For a 2-dimensional vector $\vec{\beta} = \begin{bmatrix} \beta_0 \\ \beta_1 \end{bmatrix}$, the L1 norm is:

$$\|\vec{\beta}\|_1 = |\beta_0| + |\beta_1^2|$$

This norm captures the magnitude of the vector.

General Definitions

For a vector $\beta = \begin{bmatrix} \beta_0 \\ \beta_1 \\ \dots \\ \beta_n \end{bmatrix}$

L2 Norm (Euclidean Norm) and L1 Norm (Manhattan Norm):

$$\|\vec{\beta}\|_2 = \sqrt{\beta_0^2 + \beta_1^2 + \cdots + \beta_n^2}$$

$$\|\vec{\beta}\|_1 = |\beta_0| + |\beta_1^2| + .. + |\beta_n^2|$$

Example:

For $\beta = \begin{bmatrix} 1 \\ 1 \end{bmatrix}$

L2 Norm: $\|\beta\|_2 = \sqrt{1^2 + 1^2} = \sqrt{2} \approx 1.41$

L1 Norm: $\|\beta\|_1 = |1|+|1| = 2$

For $\beta = \begin{bmatrix} 3 \\ 4 \end{bmatrix}$

L2 Norm: $\|\beta\|_2 = \sqrt{3^2 + 4^2} = \sqrt{25} \approx 5$

L1 Norm: $\|\beta\|_1 = |3|+|4| = 7$

Summary of L2 and L1 Norms

- L2 Norm ($\|\beta\|_2$) is useful for measuring straight-line distances and is sensitive to large components.
- L1 Norm ($\|\beta\|_1$) is useful for measuring the sum of absolute values, often used in sparse modelling techniques where many components may be zero or near zero.

OLS (Ordinary Least Square)

John asked, "Why do we need OLS?"

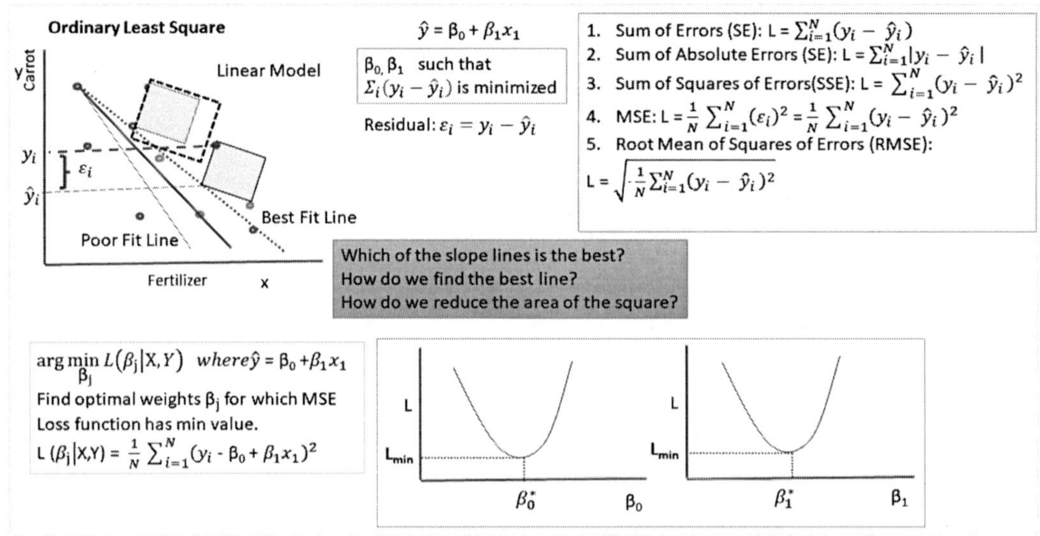

Master said, "Ordinary Least Squares (OLS) is a fundamental technique in regression analysis used to estimate the parameters of a linear model. The goal of OLS is to find the line (or hyperplane in higher dimensions) that best fits the data by minimising the sum of the squared differences between the observed values and the values predicted by the model."

Roopa asked, "Which slope line is the best?"

Master said, "The best slope line in the context of OLS is the one that minimises the sum of squared residuals (differences between observed and predicted values). This line is known as the 'best fit' line or the regression line."

Roopa asked, "How do we find the best line?"

Master said, "To find the best line, we use the OLS method, which involves solving for the coefficients (β0 and β1) that minimise the sum of squared errors (SSE) between the observed values (y_i) and the predicted values ($\hat{y}$)."

Roopa asked, "How do we reduce the area of the square?"

Master explained that in the context of regression analysis, reducing the "area of the square" refers to minimising the sum of squared errors (SSE). This is achieved through the following loss functions:

Sum of Errors (SE):

$$L = \sum_{i=1}^{N} (y_i - \hat{y}_i)$$

However, this is not commonly used because positive and negative errors can cancel out.

Sum of Absolute Errors (SAE):

$$L = \sum_{i=1}^{N} |y_i - \hat{y}_i|$$

This loss function measures the total absolute difference between predicted and observed values.

Sum of Squares of Errors (SSE):

$$L = \sum_{i=1}^{N} (y_i - \hat{y}_i)^2$$

This is the most common loss function used in OLS. It squares the errors to ensure all are positive and penalizes larger errors more heavily.

Mean Squared Error (MSE):

$$L = \frac{1}{N}\sum_{i=1}^{N}(\varepsilon_i)^2 = \frac{1}{N}\sum_{i=1}^{N}(y_i - \hat{y}_i)^2$$

This is the average of the SSE and provides a measure of the average squared difference between predicted and observed values.

Root Mean Squared Error (RMSE):

$$L = \sqrt{\frac{1}{N}\sum_{i=1}^{N}(y_i - \hat{y}_i)^2}$$

This is the square root of MSE and gives an error metric in the same units as the original data, making it more interpretable.

Finding Optimal Weights

The optimal weights (β_j) are found by minimising the MSE:

$$\arg\min_{\beta_j} L(\beta_j|X, Y) \quad where \hat{y} = \beta_0 + \beta_1 x_1$$

The goal is to find the values of β_j that minimize the loss function:

$$L(\beta_j|X, Y) = \frac{1}{N}\sum_{i=1}^{N}(y_i - \beta_0 + \beta_1 x_1)^2$$

This involves solving the normal equations:

$$X^T X\beta = X^T y$$

where X is the design matrix containing the input variables, and y is the vector of the observed values.

OLS in Scalar Form

Step 1: Calculate the Gradient of the Loss Function with Respect to All Variables (Partial Derivative)

To find the optimal coefficients β_0 and β_1 in a simple linear regression model, we first need to calculate the gradient of the loss function. The loss function we use is the Sum of Squares of Errors (SSE):

$$L = \sum_{i=1}^{N} (y_i - \hat{y}_i)^2 \text{ Given Model } \hat{y} = \beta_0 + \beta_1 x_i$$

The gradients (partial derivatives) of the loss function with respect to β_0 and β_1 are:

$$\frac{dL}{d\beta_0} = \frac{2}{N} \sum_{i=1}^{N} (y_i - \hat{y}_i) * 1 = \frac{2}{N} \sum_{i=1}^{N} (y_i - \beta_0 + \beta_1 x_i)$$

$$\frac{dL}{d\beta_1} = \frac{2}{N} \sum_{i=1}^{N} (y_i - \hat{y}_i)\, x_i * 1 = \frac{2}{N} \sum_{i=1}^{N} (y_i - \beta_0 + \beta_1 x_i) * x_i$$

Step 2: Equate These Gradients to Zero and Solve for the Optimal Values of the Model Coefficients β_j

To find the optimal values of β_0 and β_1, we set the gradients to zero and solve the resulting equations:

$$\frac{dL}{d\beta_0} = \frac{2}{N} \sum_{i=1}^{N} (y_i - \hat{y}_i) * 1 = \frac{2}{N} \sum_{i=1}^{N} (y_i - \beta_0 + \beta_1 x_i) = 0$$

$$\frac{dL}{d\beta_1} = \frac{2}{N} \sum_{i=1}^{N} (y_i - \hat{y}_i)\, x_i * 1 = \frac{2}{N} \sum_{i=1}^{N} (y_i - \beta_0 + \beta_1 x_i) * x_i = 0$$

$\underset{\beta_j}{arg\ min}\ L(\beta_j|X,Y)$ $where\ \hat{y} = \beta_0 + \beta_1 x_1$

Find optimal weights β_j for which MSE

Loss function has min value.

$L(\beta_j|X,Y) = \frac{1}{N} \sum_{i=1}^{N} (y_i - \beta_0 + \beta_1 x_1)^2$

OLS in Scaler Form:

Step 1: Calculate the Gradient of the Loss function respect to all variables. (Partial derivative)

Final Gradient

$\frac{dL}{d\beta_0} = \frac{2}{N} \Sigma(y - \hat{y}) \times 1$

$\frac{dL}{d\beta_1} = \frac{2}{N} \Sigma(y - \hat{y}) \times x_1$

Step 2: Equate these gradients to zero and solve for the optimal values of the model coefficients β_j

$\beta_1^* = \frac{\sum_{i=1}^{N} (\overline{x_1 y}) - (\bar{x}_1 \bar{y})}{\sum_{i=1}^{N} (\bar{x}_1^2 - (\bar{x}_1)^2)}$ and $\beta_0^* = \bar{y} - (\beta_1^*\ \bar{x})$

x_1	y	$(x_1)^2$	x_1y
1	5.1	1	5.1
3	12.2	9	36.6
5	10.2	25	51
Mean = 3	9.16	11.67	30.9

β_1^* = ((30.9) – (3*9.16)) / ((11.67) – (3*3))
= 3.42/2.67 = 1.275
β_0^* = (9.16) – (1.28 *3) = 5.34

Ordinary Least Square

These equations simplify to:

$$\sum_{i=1}^{N}(y_i - \beta_0 + \beta_1 x_i) = 0$$

$$\sum_{i=1}^{N}(y_i - \beta_0 + \beta_1 x_i) * x_i = 0$$

Solving these equations simultaneously, we get the following formulas for the optimal coefficients β_0^* and β_1^*:

$$\beta_1^* = \frac{\sum_{i=1}^{N} (\overline{x_1 y}) - (\bar{x}_1 \bar{y})}{\sum_{i=1}^{N} (\bar{x}_1^2 - (\bar{x}_1)^2)} \text{ and } \beta_0^* = \bar{y} - (\beta_1^* \; \bar{x})$$

where $\bar{x}$ and $\bar{y}$ are the means of x and y respectively.

Steps:

- Step 1: Calculate the gradients of the loss function with respect to β0 and β1.
- Step 2: Set these gradients to zero and solve the resulting system of equations to find the optimal values of β0 and β1.
- The optimal slope (β1*) and intercept (β0*) minimise the sum of squared errors, resulting in the best fit line for the data.

Example P2 – U2 – D12	
OLS – Scalar Form	**Output**

import numpy as np
# Input data 	
x = np.array([1, 3, 5])
Y = np.array([5.1, 12.2, 10.2])
 	
# Calculate means of x and Y 	
x_mean = np.mean(x)
Y_mean = np.mean(Y)
 	
# Calculate the numerator and denominator for beta_1 	
numerator = np.sum((x - x_mean) * (Y - Y_mean))
denominator = np.sum((x - x_mean) ** 2)
 	
# Calculate beta_1 	
beta_1 = numerator / denominator
# Calculate beta_0 	
beta_0 = Y_mean - beta_1 * x_mean
# Print the coefficients 	
print(f"Optimal coefficients: beta_0 = {beta_0}, beta_1 = {beta_1}")
	Optimal coefficients: beta_0 = 5.341666666666667, beta_1 = 1.275

OLS is essential for fitting a linear model to data by minimising the sum of squared errors. The best fit line is determined by finding the coefficients that minimise this error. Various loss functions, such as SSE, MSE, and RMSE, provide different ways to measure and minimise the prediction error, ensuring the model's accuracy and reliability.

Difference Between Loss Function, Cost Function, and Penalty Function

Loss Function

Definition: A loss function quantifies the error between the predicted value ($\hat{y}_i$) and the actual value (y) for a single data point.

- Purpose: It provides a measure of how well the model is performing for each individual example in the dataset.
- Example: For Mean Squared Error (MSE), the loss function for a single data point is $(y_i - \hat{y}_i)^2$.

Cost Function

Definition: A cost function is an aggregate of the loss functions over the entire training dataset. It provides a single scalar value that summarises the model's performance.

- Purpose: It helps in evaluating the overall performance of the model across all data points.
- Example: For MSE, the cost function is the average of the squared errors:

$$= \frac{1}{N} \sum_{i=1}^{N} (\varepsilon_i)^2 = \frac{1}{N} \sum_{i=1}^{N} (y_i - \hat{y}_i)^2$$

Penalty Function

Definition: A penalty function imposes a cost on certain aspects of the model, typically to discourage complexity and prevent overfitting. It is added to the loss or cost function.

Purpose: To regularise the model by penalising large coefficients and thereby encouraging simpler models.

Example: Regularisation terms such as L1 (Lasso) and L2 (Ridge) regularization:

L1 Regularization: $\lambda \sum_{J=1} |\beta_j|$

L2 Regularization: $\lambda \sum_{j=1}^{P} \beta_j^2$

where λ is the regularization parameter.

Loss Function vs Cost Function vs Objective Function:

Example:

MAE as the Loss function: L = $|y_i - \hat{y}_i|$

MAE as the cost function: J = $\frac{1}{N}\sum_{i=1}^{N} | y_i - \hat{y}_i |$

Note: For cost function author as used L at some places instead of J.

Objective Function:

Definition: The objective function is the function that is optimised during training. It often consists of the cost function plus any penalty (regularization) terms.

Example: If we add L2 regularization to our cost function, the objective function becomes:

$$= \frac{1}{N}\sum_{i=1}^{N} | y_i - \hat{y}_i | + \lambda \sum_{j=1}^{P} \beta_j^2$$

This aims to minimize both the prediction error and the model complexity.

Summary

- Loss Function: Measures the error for a single prediction.
- Cost Function: Aggregates the loss over the entire dataset.
- Penalty Function: Adds a penalty for model complexity.
- Objective Function: Combines the cost function and penalty function to form the function optimised during training.

These concepts are essential for understanding model training, evaluation, and regularization in machine learning.

Differences Between OLS, LASSO, RIDGE Regression, and Heteroskedasticity

Ordinary Least Squares (OLS) Regression

Definition: OLS is a linear regression method that estimates the coefficients by minimising the sum of the squared differences between the observed and predicted values.

Objective: Minimize the Residual Sum of Squares (RSS):

$$L = \sum_{i=1}^{N} (y_i - \hat{y}_i)^2$$

Use Case: Best used when there is no multicollinearity in the data and all variables are assumed to have equal importance.

LASSO (Least Absolute Shrinkage and Selection Operator) Regression

Definition: LASSO is a type of regression that includes a penalty equivalent to the absolute value of the magnitude of coefficients.

Objective: Minimize the cost function with an L1 penalty:

$$J = \sum_{i=1}^{N} (y_i - \hat{y}_i)^2 + \sum_{J=1} |\beta_j|$$

Use Case: Effective for feature selection, as it tends to shrink some coefficients to zero, effectively removing some features. Useful when there is multicollinearity among the predictors.

Ridge Regression

Definition: Ridge regression, also known as Tikhonov regularization, includes a penalty equivalent to the square of the magnitude of coefficients.

Objective: Minimize the cost function with an L2 penalty:

$$J = \sum_{i=1}^{N} (y_i - \hat{y}_i)^2 + \lambda \sum_{j=1}^{P} \beta_j^2$$

Use Case: Effective when dealing with multicollinearity. Unlike LASSO, Ridge regression does not set coefficients to zero but shrinks them towards zero.

Heteroskedasticity

Definition: Heteroskedasticity occurs when the variance of the errors (residuals) is not constant across all levels of the independent variables. In other words, the spread of residuals varies with the fitted values.

Problem: It violates one of the key assumptions of OLS regression (homoscedasticity), leading to inefficient estimates and biased standard errors, which can affect hypothesis tests.

Detection: Can be detected using plots of residuals versus fitted values or statistical tests like the Breusch-Pagan test.

Correction: Methods to correct heteroskedasticity include using robust standard errors, transforming variables, or applying weighted least squares regression.

Summary of Key Differences

Aspect	OLS	LASSO	Ridge	Heteroskedasticity
Coefficient Shrinkage	No	Yes, some coefficients may become zero	Yes, but all coefficients shrink	Not applicable
Feature Selection	No	Yes	No	Not applicable
Multicollinearity	Can be problematic	Handles multicollinearity	Handles multicollinearity	Increases standard errors, leading to inefficient estimates
Use Case	Simple linear regression	Sparse models, feature selection	Multicollinearity, shrinkage	Requires correction for accurate regression results

Let's consider a dataset where we want to predict house prices:

OLS Regression:

Model:

$$\hat{y} = \beta_0 + \beta_1 x_1 + \beta_2 x_2 + \cdots + \beta_n x_n$$

Objective: Minimize the sum of squared errors.

LASSO Regression:

- Model: Same as OLS, but with an L1 penalty.
- Objective: Minimize the sum of squared errors plus the sum of absolute values of coefficients.

Ridge Regression:

- Model: Same as OLS, but with an L2 penalty.
- Objective: Minimize the sum of squared errors plus the sum of squared values of coefficients.

Heteroskedasticity:

- Issue: Suppose the variance of errors increases with the size of the house. This could lead to inefficient estimates in our OLS model.
- Detection: Plot residuals vs. fitted values to check for patterns.
- Correction: Apply robust standard errors or transform variables to stabilise variance.

By understanding and addressing these concepts, we can create more accurate and robust regression models suitable for various types of data and conditions.

□ Understanding Regularization Techniques

Generalized Model: Low Bias, Low Variance

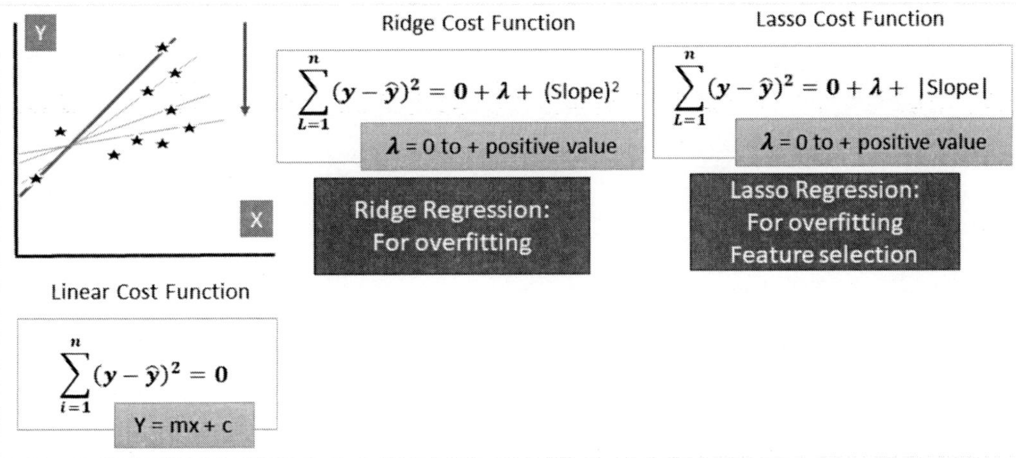

Master said, "In statistical modelling, the goal is often to find a balance between bias and variance to avoid overfitting or underfitting. Both Ridge and Lasso regression are techniques used to achieve this balance by adding a regularization term to the linear regression model."

Sam asked, "When do we use Ridge and Lasso regression?"

Ridge Regression

Purpose:

Master explained, Ridge regression is primarily used to reduce overfitting, especially in cases where the number of predictors is large or when predictors are highly correlated.

Mechanism:

It works by adding a penalty equal to the square of the magnitude of coefficients to the cost function.

This penalty term is controlled by a parameter, λ, which determines the amount of shrinkage. As λ increases, the magnitude of the coefficients decreases, which in turn reduces the model complexity.

Cost Function:

$$\sum_{L=1}^{n}(y - \hat{y})^2 = \mathbf{0} + \lambda \sum_{j=1}^{P} \beta_j^2$$

where:

- $\sum_{L=1}^{n}(y - \hat{y})^2 = \mathbf{0}$ is the sum of squared residuals (the standard loss function for linear regression),
- $\lambda \sum_{j=1}^{P} \beta_j^2$ is the regularization term, with λ being the regularization parameter and βj the coefficients of the model.

Effect:

- Ridge regression reduces the steepness (slope) of the best-fit line by shrinking the coefficients towards zero but never actually setting them to zero.
- It is particularly useful when all the predictors need to be retained, but their impact needs to be minimized to reduce overfitting.

Lasso Regression

Purpose:

Lasso regression is used to reduce overfitting and perform feature selection by enforcing sparsity in the model coefficients.

Mechanism:

It works by adding a penalty equal to the absolute value of the magnitude of coefficients to the cost function.

This penalty term is also controlled by a parameter, λ, which influences the degree of regularization. Unlike Ridge regression, Lasso can shrink some coefficients to exactly zero, effectively performing feature selection.

Cost Function:

$$\sum_{L=1}^{n}(y-\hat{y})^2 = \mathbf{0} + \lambda \sum_{J=1} |\beta_j|$$

where:

- $\sum_{L=1}^{n}(y-\hat{y})^2 = \mathbf{0}$ is the sum of squared residuals,
- $\lambda \sum_{J=1} |\beta_j|$ is the regularization term, with λ being the regularization parameter and β_j the coefficients of the model.

Effect:

- Lasso regression can shrink some coefficients to zero, effectively removing those predictors from the model. This makes it a useful tool for feature selection.
- It helps in reducing the model complexity by eliminating less important features, thereby preventing overfitting and improving the interpretability of the model.

Elastic Net Regression

Purpose

Elastic Net Regression is a type of linear regression that combines the penalties of both Ridge (L2) and Lasso (L1) regression techniques. Its primary purposes are:

- **To improve model prediction accuracy:** By combining the strengths of both L1 and L2 regularizations, Elastic Net can yield better prediction accuracy, especially when dealing with highly correlated predictors.
- **To handle multicollinearity:** When predictors are highly correlated, Elastic Net tends to select groups of correlated variables.
- **To perform variable selection:** Elastic Net can perform feature selection, identifying the most significant predictors by shrinking some coefficients exactly to zero, similar to Lasso regression.

Mechanism

The mechanism can be summarized as follows:

- **Combining L1 and L2 Penalties:** Elastic Net adds the absolute value of the magnitude of coefficients (L1) and the squared magnitude of coefficients (L2) to the loss function.
- **Balancing the Penalties:** It uses two hyperparameters, λ (lambda) and α (alpha), to control the mixing of L1 and L2 penalties. λ determines the overall strength of regularization, while αa controls the ratio between L1 and L2 penalties.

Cost Function

The cost function for Elastic Net Regression is a combination of the cost functions for Ridge and Lasso regressions. It can be expressed as:

$$\sum_{L=1}^{n}(y-\hat{y})^2 = \mathbf{0} + \lambda 1 \sum_{J=1} |\beta_j| + \lambda 2 \sum_{j=1}^{P} \beta_j^2$$

$$J(\beta) = \frac{1}{2n} \Sigma (y_i - \hat{y})^2 + \lambda \ (\frac{1-\alpha}{2} \sum_{j=1}^{P} \beta_j^2 + \alpha \sum_{J=1} |\beta_j|)$$

Where:

- $J(\beta)$ is the cost function.
- n is the number of observations.
- y_i is the actual value.
- $\hat{y}$ is the predicted value.
- βj is the coefficient for the j-th predictor.
- λ is the overall regularization strength.
- a is the mixing parameter ($0 \leq a \leq 1$).

Effect

The effect of using Elastic Net Regression includes:

- **Regularization:** By applying both L1 and L2 penalties, Elastic Net reduces the likelihood of overfitting by penalising large coefficients, thus promoting simpler models.

- **Feature Selection and Shrinkage:** Similar to Lasso, Elastic Net can shrink some coefficients to zero, effectively performing variable selection and reducing model complexity.

- **Handling Multicollinearity:** When predictors are correlated, Elastic Net tends to select groups of correlated variables together rather than arbitrarily selecting one, which improves the model's stability and interpretability.

- **Balance Between Ridge and Lasso:** By tuning α, Elastic Net can smoothly transition between Ridge (when α is close to 0) and Lasso (when α is close to 1), allowing for flexible modelling strategies based on the problem at hand.

Elastic Net Regression is a powerful regularization and variable selection method that combines the benefits of both Ridge and Lasso regressions. By tuning the hyperparameters λ and α, Elastic Net can handle multicollinearity, perform variable selection, and improve prediction accuracy, making it a versatile tool in the field of regression analysis.

Example P2 – U2 – D13	
Ridge, Lasso and Elastic Net, Regression	**Output**

# Step 1: Import Libraries 	
import pandas as pd
import numpy as np
import matplotlib.pyplot as plt
from sklearn.linear_model import LinearRegression, Ridge, Lasso, ElasticNet
from sklearn.model_selection import train_test_split
from sklearn.impute import SimpleImputer
from sklearn.metrics import mean_squared_error
 	
# Step 2: Loading and cleaning the Data 	
# Load the dataset 	
path = r'C:\Users\User\mraj4\Documents\Optimum\Py-lib\scikit\kc_house_data.csv'
data = pd.read_csv(path)
 	
# Dropping the numerically non-sensical variables 	
dropColumns = ['id', 'date', 'zipcode']
data = data.drop(dropColumns, axis=1)
 	
# Separating the dependent and independent variables 	
y = data['price']
X = data.drop('price', axis=1)
 	
# Impute missing values using mean strategy 	
imputer = SimpleImputer(strategy='mean')
X_imputed = imputer.fit_transform(X)
 	
# Dividing the data into training and testing set 	
X_train, X_test, y_train, y_test = train_test_split(X_imputed, y, test_size=0.25, random_state=42)
	Linear Regression Score: 0.6994769052085597
	Ridge Regression Score: 0.699409051249718
	Lasso Regression Score: 0.699746982918269
	
	Comparison of Regression Models
	Score
	Regression Models

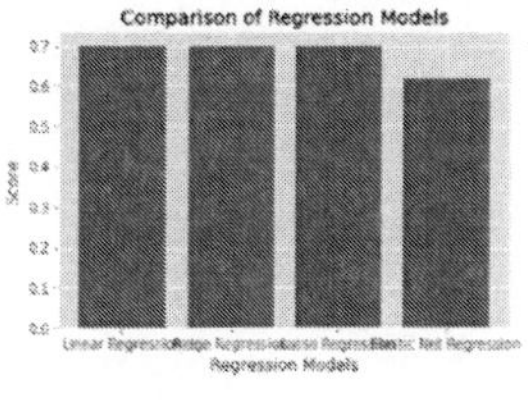

```
# Step 3: Building and evaluating the different models
# Building and fitting the Linear Regression model
linearModel = LinearRegression()
linearModel.fit(X_train, y_train)

# Evaluating the Linear Regression model
linear_score = linearModel.score(X_test, y_test)
print("Linear Regression Score:", linear_score)

# Building and fitting the Ridge Regression model
ridgeModel = Ridge(alpha=1)
ridgeModel.fit(X_train, y_train)

# Evaluating the Ridge Regression model
ridge_score = ridgeModel.score(X_test, y_test)
print("Ridge Regression Score:", ridge_score)

# Building and fitting the Lasso Regression model
lassoModel = Lasso(alpha=1)
lassoModel.fit(X_train, y_train)

# Evaluating the Lasso Regression model
lasso_score = lassoModel.score(X_test, y_test)
print("Lasso Regression Score:", lasso_score)

# Building and fitting the Elastic Net Regression model
elasticNetModel = ElasticNet(alpha=1, l1_ratio=0.5,
max_iter=100000)
elasticNetModel.fit(X_train, y_train)

# Evaluating the Elastic Net Regression model
elastic_score = elasticNetModel.score(X_test, y_test)
print("Elastic Net Regression Score:", elastic_score)

# Step 4: Comparing and Visualizing the results
models = ['Linear Regression', 'Ridge Regression', 'Lasso
Regression', 'Elastic Net Regression']
scores = [linear_score, ridge_score, lasso_score, elastic_score]

plt.bar(models, scores)
plt.xlabel('Regression Models')
plt.ylabel('Score')
plt.title('Comparison of Regression Models')
plt.show()
```

Summary:

In this unit, we covered all the fundamental mathematical foundations for learning data science. We started with a thorough examination of linear algebra, focussing on matrix structure, matrix operations, and vector applications. These ideas are crucial because they serve as the foundation for a variety of data science techniques and methodologies.

We then moved on to data dispersion, talking about measures of central tendency like the mean, median, and mode, as well as dispersion measures like range, variance, and standard deviation. Understanding these ideas is essential for effectively summarising and describing data sets.

Basic calculus was another critical area covered, highlighting the usage of integration and differentiation in data science applications. These mathematical tools are often employed in optimization problems and the development of machine learning models.

Probability theory was a major focus, where we explored the fundamental concepts of probability, including certain and uncertain events. We discussed marginal, conditional, and joint probabilities, and key probability rules such as the addition rule and Bayes' theorem. This section also covered hypothesis testing, including P-values, and the differences between one-sample and two-sample tests, as well as parametric and non-parametric tests.

Time series analysis was introduced to equip learners with techniques and methods for analyzing time-dependent data. Additionally, we examined various probability distributions, both discrete and continuous, such as exponential, binomial, Poisson, and normal distributions. These distributions are vital for modelling and understanding different types of data.

Feature reduction techniques like Recursive Feature Elimination (RFE) and RFECV were discussed to help in selecting significant features, which is essential for building efficient models. We also covered loss, penalty, and cost functions, focusing on the calculation and significance of binary cross-entropy loss.

Another important topic was sampling procedures, which included both probability and non-probability sampling methods, as well as rejection sampling methods. These strategies are critical for obtaining representative data samples.

Finally, we covered statistical regression, starting with the basics of linear regression and its key components, such as SST, SSR, and SSE. We discussed how to calculate and interpret R-squared and adjusted R-squared values, and the importance of addressing overfitting and underfitting in model development. Cross-validation techniques were also introduced to evaluate model performance.

By mastering these mathematical principles, learners will build a solid foundation for effective learning and applying data science techniques, enabling them to tackle complex data problems with confidence.

What Next:

The unit provides a comprehensive overview of various aspects of data processing, starting with an introduction to data, types, properties, and common issues encountered. It covers creating test datasets for classification and regression tasks, emphasising data quality and balance.

Another unit focuses on data cleaning, discussing techniques like imputing missing values, handling categorical data, outliers, and data formatting. Encoding methods such as one-hot encoding and handling the dummy variable trap are also covered.

Exploratory Data Analysis (EDA) is thoroughly explored, including univariate, bivariate, and multivariate analysis techniques, to uncover patterns and relationships within the data. Practical examples illustrate the application of EDA techniques.

Feature Scaling and Engineering are discussed in detail, covering techniques like normalization, standardization, encoding, and handling categorical variables. The unit emphasises the importance of preprocessing features for machine learning tasks.

Finally, the unit delves into handling imbalanced datasets, discussing resampling techniques like random under-sampling, over-sampling, and more advanced methods like SMOTE and NearMiss. It also highlights the importance of choosing appropriate performance metrics for evaluating models trained on imbalanced data. Practical examples demonstrate the application of these techniques in real-world scenarios, providing learners with a comprehensive understanding of effective strategies for handling imbalanced datasets and evaluating model performance.

P2-U2-L1-6 - Practice Question

1. What is the range of the dataset [1,3,5,7,9]?
2. How is the standard deviation different from variance?
3. What is the derivative of f(x)=x2?
4. Define conditional probability.
5. What does a P-value represent in hypothesis testing?
6. What is the main difference between parametric and non-parametric tests?
7. What is a moving average in time series analysis?
8. What is the key characteristic of a normal distribution?
9. Describe the binomial distribution.
10. What is the purpose of Recursive Feature Elimination (RFE)?
11. What does the binary cross-entropy loss measure?
12. What is the difference between probability and non-probability sampling?
13. What does the R-squared value indicate in linear regression?

14. What is a Type I error in hypothesis testing?
15. What is autocorrelation in a time series?
16. What is the difference between a stationary and a non-stationary time series?
17. How do you determine if a data set follows a normal distribution?
18. What is the purpose of Principal Component Analysis (PCA)?
19. What is stratified sampling?
20. What does multicollinearity refer to in regression analysis?
21. What is the purpose of cross-validation in model training?
22. How do you interpret an adjusted R-squared value?

PART THREE

INTRODUCTION

Data Processing

"In every dataset lies a question waiting to be answered. Through analysis, we turn curiosity into direction, and direction into discovery."

– Shree Shambav

PART THREE

DAY SIX

Unit 3 - Lesson One

Understanding Data

☐ Data Analysis

Mater said, "Data Analysis is the process of examining, cleaning, transforming, and interpreting data to discover meaningful insights, patterns, and trends. It involves extracting valuable information from raw data to facilitate informed decision-making and solve complex problems."

Analysis, at its core, aims to answer questions such as "How?" and "Why?" by examining past events or phenomena. For instance, it might explore how a company's growth evolved over the last quarter or why there was a drop in sales during a particular period. This process typically involves filtering and refining large datasets to extract relevant information, which becomes the focus of the analysis. Sometimes, analysts may also integrate multiple datasets to identify recurring patterns or correlations, such as comparing sales data over consecutive years to discern underlying trends.

Data analysis holds significant importance for businesses and organisations across various industries. For instance, consider a retail business faced with the challenge of managing inventory effectively. By leveraging data analytics, the business can predict customer demand and adjust stock levels accordingly, minimising the risk of overstocking or understocking. In essence, data analysis enables businesses to make data-driven decisions, optimise operations, and enhance performance.

In summary, data analysis empowers organisations to derive actionable insights from data, enabling them to make informed decisions, mitigate risks, and seize opportunities for growth and improvement.

Types of Data Analysis Methods

Descriptive Analysis:

Descriptive Analysis involves examining historical data to understand past events and performance. It aims to uncover patterns, trends, and insights from past data, providing a valuable context for decision-making. This method is commonly used in various business domains, such as sales, marketing, operations, and finance to gain insights into past performance.

Example: Analysing sales data from DMart to identify products with high demand trends, enabling informed decisions on inventory stocking.

Diagnostic Analysis:

Diagnostic Analysis complements Descriptive Analysis by delving deeper into the reasons behind past events or trends. It seeks to understand the root causes of observed patterns and behaviours, providing insights into why certain events occurred. By analysing historical data in detail, diagnostic analysis helps identify contributing factors and underlying dynamics.

Example: Investigating the factors driving the high demand for specific products at DMart, such as brand reputation or product quality.

Predictive Analysis:

Predictive Analysis utilises insights from descriptive and diagnostic analyses to forecast future trends and outcomes. By leveraging historical data and identifying patterns, predictive analysis generates predictive models to anticipate future events or behaviours. This method enables organisations to make proactive decisions and plan for future scenarios based on data-driven insights.

Example: Using past purchase behaviour data to predict customer preferences and provide personalised product recommendations on platforms like Amazon and Netflix.

Prescriptive Analysis:

Prescriptive Analysis represents the highest level of data analysis, focusing on recommending optimal actions or solutions based on predictive insights. It goes beyond predicting future outcomes by providing actionable recommendations to achieve desired outcomes. Prescriptive analysis helps organisations make informed decisions and take proactive steps to maximise desired outcomes.

Example: Google's self-driving car using predictive insights to make real-time decisions, such as when to turn or slow down, to ensure safe and efficient navigation.

Statistical Analysis:

Statistical Analysis involves using statistical techniques to analyse data sets and uncover key insights. It focuses on summarising data, identifying relationships between variables, and extracting meaningful information through visualisations. Statistical analysis helps researchers and analysts understand data distributions, relationships, and important variables, guiding decision-making processes.

In summary, these data analysis methods provide a systematic framework for extracting insights from data, enabling organisations to make informed decisions and drive business success.

Data Analysis Process

Nikash asked, "What is the Data Analysis Process?"

Master explained that the data analysis process is a systematic approach to transforming raw data into actionable insights for decision-making. While variations exist, most data analysis processes comprise six general steps:

Specify Data Requirements:

In this initial step, define the objectives and questions you seek to address through data analysis. Whether it's reducing production costs, understanding customer perceptions, or enhancing sales opportunities, clarity on data requirements is crucial.

Collect Data:

Identify and gather data from both internal and external sources relevant to your objectives. Organize data storage and maintain a standardized collection process to ensure consistency and accessibility.

Internal source	**External source**
Customer service data	Global finance data
Human resource data	Public government data
Marketing analytics	Google public data
Sales statistics	Social media APIs

Clean and Process the Data:

Before analysis, ensure data accuracy and usability by identifying and rectifying errors or inconsistencies. Scrub for duplicates, remove formatting, and maintain error logs to monitor trends.

Analyse the Data:

Utilize various data analysis techniques to uncover insights and patterns relevant to your objectives. This may include descriptive analysis to understand variables and inferential analysis to explore relationships and make predictions.

Descriptive Analysis	**Inferential Analysis**
Measures of tendency	Correlation
Measures of spread	Regression

Interpretation:

Interpret the analyzed data to derive actionable insights. Consider whether the data effectively addresses your questions, defends against objections, and explores all relevant angles. Acknowledge any limitations in the analysis.

Report:

Communicate the findings of the data analysis to relevant stakeholders, tailoring the presentation to different audiences' needs.

- Keep it Succinct: Organize data to facilitate easy navigation and comprehension.
- Make it Visual: Utilize data visualization techniques to enhance clarity and understanding.
- Include an Executive Summary: Provide a concise overview of key findings to inform decision-making efficiently.

By following these steps, organizations can harness the power of data analysis to inform strategic decisions and drive business success.

Top Data Analysis Tools

Master said, "Data analysis tools are essential for streamlining data processing, manipulation, and interpretation. They empower users to uncover relationships, correlations, patterns, and trends within datasets, facilitating informed decision-making and actionable insights. These tools offer a range of functionalities, including data cleaning, visualization, statistical analysis, and machine learning integration. By providing intuitive interfaces and powerful analytical capabilities, data analysis tools empower users across industries to derive value from data and drive business growth."

Some of the leading data analysis tools include:

Python: Python, with libraries such as Pandas, NumPy, and SciPy, is a versatile programming language widely used for data analysis, offering extensive data manipulation, statistical analysis, and machine learning capabilities.

R: is a programming language and environment specifically designed for statistical analysis and data visualization. It provides a rich ecosystem of packages for data exploration, modelling, and visualization.

SQL: Structured Query Language (SQL) is essential for querying, managing, and analysing structured data in relational databases. It enables users to extract valuable insights through data manipulation and aggregation functions.

Microsoft Excel: Excel is a widely used spreadsheet application that offers powerful data analysis tools, including pivot tables, charts, and functions for statistical analysis and modelling.

Tableau: Tableau is a leading data visualization tool that enables users to create interactive and insightful dashboards, reports, and visualizations from diverse datasets, fostering data-driven decision-making.

Power BI: Microsoft Power BI is a business analytics tool that provides self-service data visualization and business intelligence capabilities, allowing users to create interactive reports and dashboards for data analysis and sharing.

Jupyter Notebook: Jupyter Notebook is an open-source web application that allows users to create and share documents containing live code, equations, visualizations, and narrative text, making it ideal for data exploration, analysis, and collaboration.

MATLAB: MATLAB is a high-level programming language and environment primarily used for numerical computing and data analysis, offering a wide range of built-in functions and toolboxes for advanced analysis and modelling.

SAS: SAS (Statistical Analysis System) is a software suite widely used for advanced analytics, business intelligence, and data management, offering a comprehensive set of tools for data analysis, visualization, and predictive modelling.

SPSS: IBM SPSS Statistics is a statistical analysis software package that enables users to analyse data, generate descriptive statistics, and conduct advanced statistical analyses, making it suitable for both research and business applications.

These data analysis tools cater to diverse user needs and skill levels, empowering individuals, and organisations to derive valuable insights from data and drive informed decision-making.

Data Analytics

Master explained that Data analytics play a pivotal role in modern business operations, offering a systematic approach to extracting insights from vast volumes of data.

Here's an enhanced version:

What are Data Analytics?

Data analytics is a dynamic discipline centered around the collection, processing, and interpretation of data to uncover actionable insights and facilitate informed decision-making. It involves leveraging various techniques and tools to transform raw data into valuable knowledge, thereby driving strategic initiatives and organisational growth.

Understanding Data Analytics

In today's digitally-driven landscape, the proliferation of data presents unparalleled opportunities. With robust computing capabilities and extensive datasets at our disposal, organisations can harness the power of data analytics to drive data-driven decision-making. By analysing historical trends and patterns, businesses can derive meaningful insights to guide future strategies and initiatives.

Data analytics encompasses a diverse set of methodologies for analysing data and extracting actionable insights. By delving into data streams, businesses can identify trends, correlations, and performance metrics that drive operational efficiency and enhance overall effectiveness.

For example, in the manufacturing sector, organisations leverage data analytics to optimise production processes, streamline workflow management, and minimise downtime. By analysing machine performance metrics and production data, manufacturers can fine-tune operations to maximise productivity and minimise costs.

Beyond manufacturing, data analytics find applications across various industries. In the gaming sector, analytic-driven insights inform the design of engaging user experiences and personalised reward systems, fostering player retention and loyalty. Similarly, content providers utilise analytics to tailor content recommendations, enhance user engagement, and optimise advertising strategies.

In essence, data analytics serves as a cornerstone for strategic decision-making, empowering organisations to unlock hidden insights, capitalise on emerging trends, and drive sustainable growth in an increasingly competitive marketplace.

Types of Data Analytics

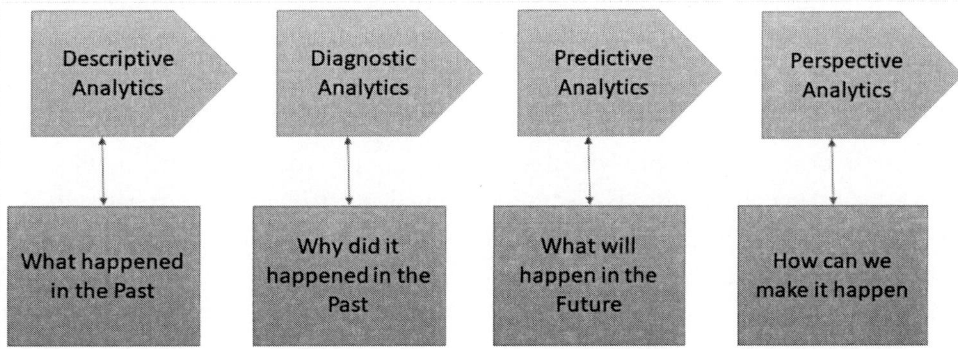

Data analytics encompasses a spectrum of methodologies aimed at extracting insights and driving informed decision-making. Here's an enhanced breakdown of the four major types:

Predictive Analytics

Predictive analytics transform data into actionable insights by forecasting future outcomes or likelihoods of events. Leveraging statistical techniques, machine learning algorithms, and historical data, predictive analytics enables organisations to make informed predictions about future events. Key techniques include:

- Linear Regression
- Time Series Analysis and Forecasting
- Data Mining

Predictive modelling, decision analysis, and transaction profiling are fundamental components of predictive analytics, empowering organisations to anticipate future trends and optimise strategic decision-making.

Descriptive Analytics

Descriptive analytics involves analysing past data to gain insights into historical performance and inform future strategies. By mining historical data, organisations can understand the factors contributing to past successes or failures, facilitating informed decision-making across various domains, such as sales, marketing, operations, and finance. Common methods include:

- Data Queries
- Reports
- Descriptive Statistics

- Data Dashboard

Descriptive analytics quantifies relationships within data to classify customers or prospects into groups, providing valuable insights into customer behaviour and product preferences.

Prescriptive Analytics

Prescriptive analytics go beyond predicting future outcomes by recommending optimal decision options to capitalise on predictions. By synthesising big data, mathematical science, and machine learning, prescriptive analytics suggest decision options and illustrate the implications of each option. Key features include:

- Automatic synthesis of big data
- Decision option suggestions
- Implication illustration

Prescriptive analytics enables organisations to leverage predictive insights and make informed decisions that maximise opportunities and mitigate risks.

Diagnostic Analytics

Diagnostic analytics utilises historical data to uncover dependencies and patterns, offering insights into past events or problems. By analysing historical data, organisations gain a deeper understanding of the underlying factors and potential solutions. Common techniques include:

- Data Discovery
- Data Mining
- Correlations

Diagnostic analytics provide valuable insights into problem-solving by leveraging historical data and identifying trends or patterns that inform decision-making processes.

Role of Data Analytics

Data analytics serves as a cornerstone for optimising operations, improving efficiency, and driving performance across diverse industries by unveiling invaluable patterns and insights. Here's an enhanced overview of its pivotal role and the key steps involved in the process.

Data Mining

Data mining initiates the process by collecting data from varied sources and transforming it into a standardised format for subsequent analysis. While this step can be time-intensive, it is critical to assemble a comprehensive dataset that forms the foundation of data analytics.

Data Management

Once collected, data must be efficiently stored, managed, and made accessible for analysis. Establishing a robust database infrastructure is paramount for managing the vast volumes of information garnered during the mining process. SQL (Structured Query Language) remains a prevalent tool for database management, facilitating streamlined querying and analysis of relational databases.

Statistical Analysis

In this phase, the collected data undergo rigorous statistical analysis to unearth trends and patterns. Statistical modelling techniques are employed to interpret the data and extrapolate predictions about future trends. Widely used programming languages like Python, along with specialised tools like R, are instrumental in conducting statistical analysis and graphical modelling.

Data Presentation

The insights gleaned from data analytics must be effectively communicated to stakeholders to drive informed decision-making. This final step entails presenting the results in a format that is accessible and comprehensible to diverse stakeholders, including decision-makers, analysts, and shareholders. Clear and concise data presentation is paramount for empowering stakeholders to leverage insights and steer business growth effectively.

To install the necessary libraries for Python data analysis and machine learning, you can use pip, Python's package installer. Open your command line or terminal and enter the following commands:

pip install numpy pandas matplotlib seaborn scipy scikit-learn tensorflow

This will install the following libraries:

- NumPy: for numerical computing and array manipulation.
- pandas: for data manipulation and analysis.
- Matplotlib: for data visualization.
- Seaborn: for statistical data visualization.
- SciPy: for scientific computing and advanced mathematics.
- scikit-learn: for machine learning algorithms and tools.
- TensorFlow: for machine learning and deep learning models.

After running these commands, you'll have all the necessary libraries installed and ready to use for your data analysis, data visualisation and machine learning projects.

By referring Shree Shambav "Optimum Python – Series III," you can enhance your knowledge and skills in utilizing Python libraries such as NumPy, pandas, Matplotlib, Seaborn, SciPy, scikit-learn.

PART THREE

DAY SIX

Unit 3 - Lesson Two

Data Pre-Processing

Data preprocessing encompasses the essential steps of transforming raw data into a refined dataset suitable for algorithmic analysis. Its primary goal is to enhance the quality and compatibility of the data for effective utilisation in various analytical processes. When data is initially gathered from diverse sources, it often exists in a raw, unstructured format, posing challenges for meaningful analysis.

□ The Need for Data Preprocessing

Master said, "In the realm of Machine Learning endeavours, the efficacy of applied models hinges greatly on the integrity and coherence of the input data. Different algorithms demand specific data formats to operate optimally; for instance, the Random Forest algorithm is incompatible with null values. Hence, preprocessing becomes imperative to handle such discrepancies and ensure seamless execution of algorithms like Random Forest."

Furthermore, data preprocessing facilitates the creation of a standardised format that accommodates multiple Machine Learning and Deep Learning algorithms within a single dataset. By refining the data in this manner, analysts can explore various algorithms and select the most suitable one based on performance metrics and the specific requirements of the task at hand.

Types of Data

Data is the bedrock of Machine Learning, serving as the foundation upon which models are trained and insights are derived. It encompasses a wide array of observations or measurements that are utilised to fuel machine learning algorithms. The quality and quantity of data are paramount in determining the efficacy of machine learning models, with both aspects significantly influencing model performance.

Data comes in diverse forms, including numerical, categorical, and time-series data, sourced from databases, spreadsheets, APIs, and other repositories. Machine learning algorithms leverage this data to discern patterns and relationships between input variables and target outputs, empowering them to perform tasks like prediction and classification.

Two fundamental types of data exist:

Labelled Data: This includes a designated label or target variable that the model endeavours to predict. Labelled data facilitates supervised learning tasks, aiding the model in understanding the relationship between input features and corresponding labels.

Unlabelled Data: In contrast, unlabelled data lacks predefined labels or target variables. This type of data is commonly utilised in unsupervised learning scenarios, where the model autonomously identifies patterns and structures within the data.

Data is often divided into training and testing sets, with the former employed to train the model and the latter utilised to assess its performance. Ensuring a random and representative split of the data is crucial to mitigate bias and enhance the model's generalisation capabilities.

Data preprocessing constitutes a pivotal phase in the machine learning pipeline, encompassing tasks such as data cleaning, normalisation, handling missing values, and feature selection or engineering. These preprocessing steps are indispensable for refining the raw data into a format conducive to effective model training and evaluation.

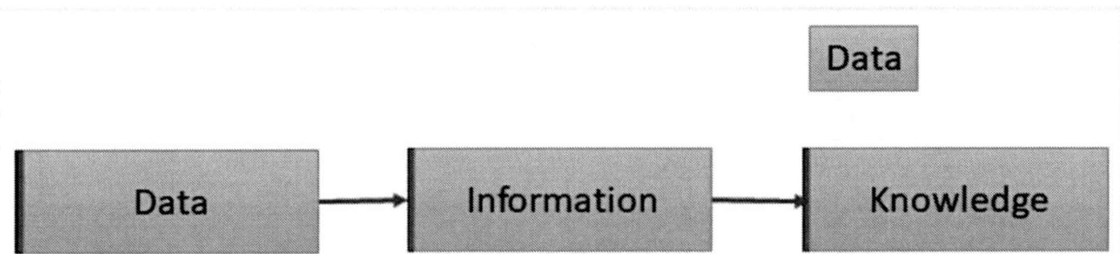

Beyond its raw form, data evolves into information and, eventually, knowledge through interpretation, manipulation, and synthesis. Information represents the processed and meaningful derivation from data, while knowledge encapsulates the amalgamation of inferred insights, experiences, and learnings, fostering awareness and understanding for individuals and organisations alike.

Splitting Data

Sam asked, "How do we split data in Machine Learning?"

Master said, "Splitting data in machine learning is a critical step that involves partitioning the available dataset into distinct subsets for training, validation, and testing purposes. Each subset serves a specific role in the model development and evaluation process, ensuring robustness and accuracy in model performance."

Training Data:

- The training data comprises a significant portion of the dataset and is utilized to train the machine learning model.
- This subset includes both input features and corresponding output labels or target variables.
- During the training phase, the model learns from the patterns and relationships present in the training data, adjusting its parameters to minimize errors and improve predictive performance.

Validation Data:

- The validation data is used for fine-tuning the model and optimizing hyperparameters, which are predefined parameters set before the model begins learning.
- This subset aids in monitoring the model's performance during training, enabling iterative adjustments to enhance its accuracy and generalization capabilities.
- By evaluating the model's performance on the validation data, developers can make informed decisions regarding model architecture, hyperparameter settings, and optimization strategies.

Testing Data:

- The testing data provides an unbiased assessment of the trained model's performance and generalization ability.
- Once the model training is complete, the testing data is fed into the trained model to generate predictions without revealing the actual output.
- The model's predictions are then compared against the ground truth values present in the testing data to evaluate its predictive accuracy and effectiveness.
- Testing data serves as a crucial benchmark for gauging the model's performance on unseen data and assessing its real-world applicability.

By dividing the dataset into these distinct subsets and allocating them specific roles, developers can systematically train, validate, and evaluate machine learning models, ensuring reliable and robust performance across diverse scenarios.

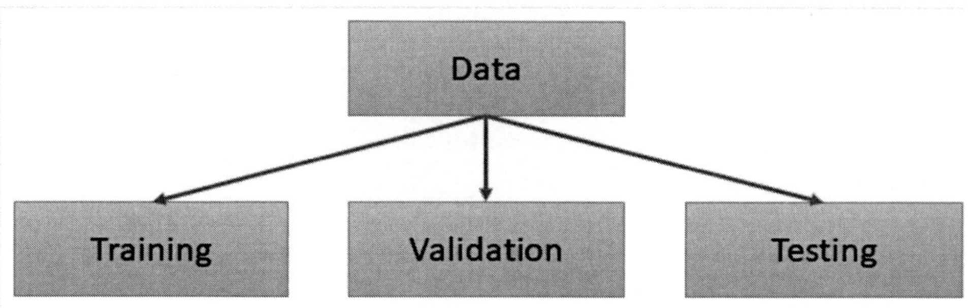

Master continued, "In a scenario where a Shopping Mart Owner conducts a survey, the collected list of questions and corresponding answers constitutes the raw data. However, sifting through this extensive dataset manually for insights is impractical and time-consuming. To streamline this process and extract meaningful insights efficiently, the data undergoes manipulation through software, calculations, and visualisation techniques, resulting in processed information."

Data serves as the foundation for deriving information, forming an indispensable precursor to meaningful insights. Through manipulation and analysis, data transforms into actionable information, facilitating informed decision-making and problem-solving.

Furthermore, knowledge transcends technical content, encompassing the cognitive processes that differentiate individuals' understanding and interpretation of information. It incorporates contextual understanding, insights, and expertise, shaping how information is perceived and utilised.

In the realm of data analysis, various forms of data play distinct roles:

Numeric Data:

- Numeric features represent measurable characteristics expressed in numerical values.
- Examples include quantitative data, such as age, income, or quantity.

Categorical Data:

- Categorical features represent attributes with a finite and often fixed set of possible values based on qualitative properties.
- Also known as nominal features, they categorise data into distinct groups or classes.
- Examples include gender, type of fruit, or product category.

Ordinal Data:

- Ordinal variables denote nominal features with categories arranged in an ordered sequence.
- These categories maintain a hierarchical order, allowing for relative comparisons.
- Examples include rankings, ratings, or ordered scales such as satisfaction levels ranging from “not at all happy” to “very happy.”

Understanding the nature and characteristics of different data types enables effective analysis and interpretation, guiding the selection of appropriate analytical techniques and methodologies. By leveraging these insights, businesses and organisations can derive actionable intelligence, driving informed decision-making and fostering innovation.

Properties of Data

Volume:

- Definition: Refers to the scale or size of the data, often measured in terms of its quantity or storage requirements.
- Significance: With the proliferation of technology and the digital landscape, data is generated at an unprecedented rate, encompassing vast amounts of information.

Variety:

- Definition: Denotes the diverse forms and types of data, including structured, unstructured, and semi-structured data across various domains.
- Significance: Different data sources such as healthcare records, images, videos, and audio recordings contribute to a rich and multifaceted data landscape, providing valuable insights into diverse domains.

Velocity:

- Definition: Represents the speed at which data is generated, processed, and analyzed, often in real-time or near real-time scenarios.
- Significance: With the advent of IoT, social media, and streaming services, data is streamed and processed rapidly, necessitating efficient data handling and analysis capabilities.

Value:

- Definition: Indicates the meaningfulness and utility of data in terms of the insights and information it provides to researchers, analysts, and decision-makers.
- Significance: Data holds value when it contributes to informed decision-making, innovation, and the creation of actionable insights, driving business growth and societal progress.

Veracity:

- Definition: Refers to the accuracy, reliability, and trustworthiness of the data, ensuring that it is free from errors, inconsistencies, or biases.
- Significance: High-quality and trustworthy data is essential for producing reliable analyses, predictions, and insights, mitigating the risk of erroneous conclusions and decisions.

Viability:

- Definition: Describes the suitability and adaptability of data for integration into various systems, processes, and applications.
- Significance: Data viability ensures that data can be effectively utilized across different platforms, applications, and analytical frameworks, enhancing its usability and value.

Security:

- Definition: Encompasses the measures and protocols implemented to safeguard data from unauthorized access, breaches, or malicious activities.
- Significance: Data security ensures the confidentiality, integrity, and availability of sensitive information, preserving trust and compliance with regulatory standards.

Accessibility:

- Definition: Refers to the ease and convenience of obtaining, retrieving, and utilizing data for analysis, decision-making, and research purposes.
- Significance: Accessible data fosters collaboration, transparency, and innovation, empowering stakeholders to leverage data-driven insights for strategic initiatives and problem-solving.

Integrity:

- Definition: Denotes the accuracy, consistency, and reliability of data throughout its lifecycle, from creation to storage, processing, and archiving.
- Significance: Data integrity ensures that information remains accurate, complete, and unaltered, maintaining its reliability and trustworthiness for analytical and decision-making purposes.

Usability:

- Definition: Reflects the ease of use, interpretability, and user-friendliness of data for end-users, analysts, and stakeholders.
- Significance: Usable data enables efficient analysis, visualization, and interpretation, empowering users to derive actionable insights and make informed decisions effectively.

Understanding and managing these properties of data are essential for organizations and researchers to harness the full potential of data assets, drive innovation, and achieve strategic objectives effectively.

Example:

Let's say you're part of a team at a car manufacturing company tasked with developing a model to predict the fuel efficiency of cars based on their weight and engine size. In this scenario, the fuel efficiency serves as the target variable (or label), while weight and engine size are the features (or input variables).

To build this model, you start by collecting data from various car models, recording their weight, engine size, and corresponding fuel efficiency. Each data point is represented as a tuple (weight, engine size, fuel efficiency).

Once you have a dataset, you split it into two sets: a training set and a testing set. The training set is used to train the model, teaching it to understand the relationships between weight, engine size, and fuel efficiency. The testing set is then used to evaluate how well the trained model performs on new, unseen data.

During preprocessing, you might need to address any missing values or handle outliers that could impact the accuracy of your model's predictions.

Example P3 – U3 – D1	
ML - Data	**Output**
# Import necessary modules from sklearn.linear_model import LogisticRegression # Example input data	Predicted fuel efficiency: 1

# Each data point consists of weight and engine size, and the corresponding fuel efficiency is the target variable 	
X = [[1, 2], [2, 3], [3, 4], [4, 5], [5, 6]] # Features: weight and engine size
y = [0, 0, 1, 1, 1] # Target variable: fuel efficiency
# Train a logistic regression model 	
model = LogisticRegression()
model.fit(X, y)
# Make a prediction for a new data point [6, 7] 	
new_data_point = [[6, 7]]
predicted_fuel_efficiency =
model.predict(new_data_point)[0]
# Output the prediction 	
print("Predicted fuel efficiency:",
predicted_fuel_efficiency)	

Advantages and Disadvantages

Advantages:

- Improved accuracy: With access to a large dataset, machine learning algorithms can learn intricate patterns and relationships, leading to more accurate predictions and classifications.
- Automation: Machine learning models automate decision-making processes, enabling businesses to streamline operations and increase efficiency.
- Personalisation: By analysing user data, machine learning algorithms can tailor experiences to individual preferences, enhancing user satisfaction and engagement.
- Cost savings: Automation through machine learning can reduce the need for manual labour, resulting in cost savings for businesses.

Disadvantages:

- Bias: Data used to train machine learning models may contain biases, leading to biased predictions and decisions.
- Privacy concerns: Collecting and storing large amounts of data can raise privacy concerns and pose security risks if not properly handled.
- Data quality: The quality of data used for training is crucial, as poor-quality data can result in inaccurate predictions and classifications.

- Lack of interpretability: Some machine learning models are complex and difficult to interpret, making it challenging to understand the reasoning behind their decisions.

Issues of Using Data in Machine Learning:

Data Quality: Ensuring the quality of data is paramount in machine learning. Low-quality data, such as data with missing values, outliers, or errors, can significantly impact the performance of machine learning models. For instance, in healthcare, inaccurate patient records or mislabelled medical images can lead to incorrect diagnoses or treatment recommendations.

Data Quantity: The amount of data available for training is crucial for the success of machine learning models. Insufficient data can hinder the model's ability to generalise well to unseen examples. For instance, in rare disease diagnosis, there may be limited patient data available, making it challenging to develop accurate predictive models.

Bias and Fairness: Bias in training data can propagate through machine learning models and result in unfair or discriminatory outcomes. For example, biased hiring data can lead to algorithms that favour certain demographics over others in job application screenings. Ensuring fairness and mitigating bias in machine learning models is essential for ethical and equitable decision-making.

Overfitting and Underfitting: Overfitting occurs when a model captures noise in the training data rather than underlying patterns, resulting in poor performance on new data. Underfitting, on the other hand, happens when a model is too simplistic to capture the complexity of the data. Both overfitting and underfitting can degrade the model's predictive accuracy and generalisation ability.

Privacy and Security: Machine learning models trained on sensitive data, such as personal or financial information, raise concerns about privacy and security. Unauthorised access to or misuse of these models can lead to privacy breaches and identity theft. Protecting data privacy and ensuring secure model deployment are critical considerations in machine learning applications.

Interpretability: The interpretability of machine learning models refers to the ease of understanding their decision-making processes. Complex models like deep neural networks may lack interpretability, making it challenging to explain why a particular prediction was made. In high-stakes domains such as healthcare or finance, interpretable models are preferred for transparency and accountability.

By addressing these issues and implementing best practices for data collection, preprocessing, and model training, machine learning practitioners can develop more reliable and ethical solutions across various domains.

Understanding Data Processing

Data processing is integral to the machine learning (ML) pipeline, pivotal in readying data for modelling. Its aim is to refine, structure, and format data for optimal utilisation in ML model construction.

Key steps in data processing typically encompass:

Data Collection: Gathering data from diverse sources, spanning sensors, databases, or other systems. This data may exhibit varied structures, ranging from structured to unstructured, and diverse formats like text, images, or audio.

Data Preprocessing: This phase involves data refinement, encompassing cleaning, filtering, and transformation to enhance its suitability for subsequent analysis. Tasks may include handling missing values, scaling, normalisation, or format conversion.

Data Analysis: Here, data undergoes scrutiny through statistical analysis, machine learning algorithms, or visualisation techniques. The objective is to glean insights or knowledge from the data.

Data Interpretation: This stage entails deciphering analysis outcomes and drawing informed conclusions. It may also involve articulating findings clearly, potentially through reports, dashboards, or visualisations.

Data Storage and Management: Post-processing and analysis, secure and accessible storage and management of data are imperative. This could involve database storage, cloud solutions, or other systems, with backup and recovery protocols for safeguarding against data loss.

Data Visualisation and Reporting: The culmination involves presenting analysis outcomes to stakeholders in an understandable and actionable format. This may entail crafting visualisations, reports, or dashboards, spotlighting critical insights and trends.

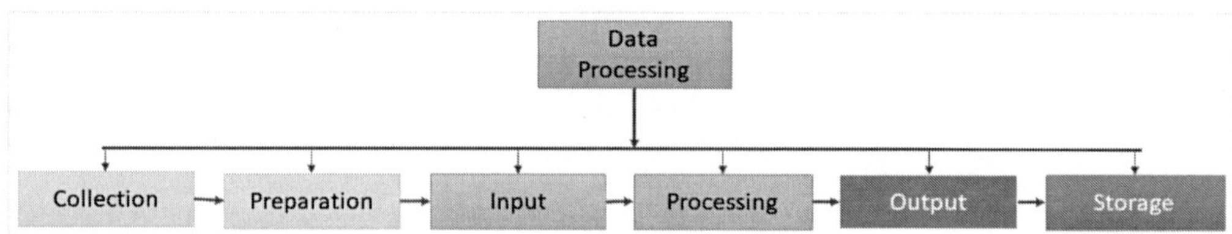

Various tools and libraries cater to data processing in ML, such as pandas for Python and RapidMiner's Data Transformation and Cleansing tool. Tool selection hinges on project-specific needs, including data size, complexity, and desired outcomes.

Data Collection: Initiating machine learning (ML) endeavours demands high-quality, accurate data sourced from authenticated repositories like data.gov.in, Kaggle, or the UCI dataset repository. Just as students seek the finest study materials for optimal results in competitive exams, quality data facilitates smoother model learning, enhancing its efficacy during testing. However, acquiring such data demands significant investments in capital, time, and resources. Organisations and researchers must meticulously delineate their data requirements to align with their tasks or research objectives. For instance, developing a Facial Expression Recogniser necessitates a diverse array of images portraying various human expressions, ensuring the model's credibility and reliability.

Preparation: Collected data often arrives in a raw format unsuitable for direct machine ingestion. Thus, preparation involves collating datasets from disparate sources, analysing them, and constructing a refined dataset for subsequent processing and exploration. This preparatory phase may be conducted manually or through automated procedures. Numeric representations of data expedite the model's learning process. For example, an image can be translated into an N x N matrix, with each cell denoting a pixel's value.

Input: Following preparation, data may require conversion into machine-readable formats. This entails employing conversion algorithms, necessitating high computational precision. Data can originate from diverse sources, such as MNIST Digit data (images), audio files, or video clips.

Processing: This pivotal stage entails executing algorithms and ML techniques to process instructions across vast data volumes with accuracy and efficiency.

Output: Here, the machine furnishes results in a comprehensible format, facilitating user inference. Outputs may manifest as reports, graphs, videos, or other media.

Storage: Concluding the process, this step entails preserving obtained outputs, data models, and pertinent information for future utilisation.

Advantages of Data Processing:

Improved Model Performance: Data processing enhances ML model performance by refining and transforming data into a modelling-friendly format, facilitating more accurate predictions.

Enhanced Data Representation: Through processing, data is moulded into a format that better reflects underlying relationships and patterns. This facilitates easier comprehension and learning for ML models, leading to more nuanced insights.

Increased Accuracy: Data processing ensures data accuracy, consistency, and error-free quality, thereby enhancing the precision of ML model outputs and predictions.

Disadvantages of Data Processing:

Time-Consuming Nature: Data processing, especially with large and intricate datasets, can consume considerable time and resources, potentially slowing down the ML development process.

Susceptibility to Errors: The transformation and cleaning involved in data processing can introduce errors or inadvertently discard crucial information, compromising the integrity and reliability of the ML model's outputs.

Limited Data Understanding: In some cases, data processing may obscure the original nuances and complexities of the dataset, leading to a diminished understanding of underlying relationships and patterns. This can hamper the model's ability to capture all relevant features during training.

Create Test Dataset Using Scikit:

Master said, "Scikit-learn (sklearn) stands out as a premier machine learning library for Python, offering an extensive array of functionalities, including data generation. One notable feature is its robust dataset generator, which empowers users to craft custom datasets swiftly and effortlessly. To leverage this functionality, you'll need to import sklearn.datasets.samples_generator. Among the diverse set of sample generators it provides, three prominent ones are make_blobs, make_moons, and make_circles."

Here's a brief overview of these sample generators:

- **make_blobs:** This generator creates clusters of points in a multi-dimensional space, ideal for testing clustering algorithms. It's particularly useful for scenarios where the clusters are well-separated.
- **make_moons:** This generator constructs a two-dimensional dataset shaped like two interleaving half circles, which is valuable for evaluating classification algorithms.
- **make_circles:** Similar to make_moons, this generator generates a two-dimensional dataset, but in this case, the data points form concentric circles. It's particularly useful for testing algorithms that deal with non-linearly separable data.

Utilising these generators from the sklearn.datasets.samples_generator module offers a seamless and efficient approach to creating custom datasets tailored to your specific needs.

Examples:

Example P3 – U3 – D2	
ML – Create Test Data	**Output**

# Importing necessary libraries 	
from sklearn.datasets import make_blobs
import matplotlib.pyplot as plt
import matplotlib.style as style
 	
# Setting plot style 	
style.use("fivethirtyeight")
# Generating test datasets using make_blobs 	
X, y = make_blobs(n_samples=100, centers=3, cluster_std=1, n_features=2)
# Plotting the generated data 	
plt.scatter(X[:, 0], X[:, 1], s=40, color='g')
plt.xlabel("X")
plt.ylabel("Y")
plt.title("Generated Data")
plt.show()
	Generated Data
	10 5 0 −5 −10 Y
	−5 0 5 10 X

This code snippet demonstrates how to use scikit-learn's make_blobs function to generate synthetic data for testing machine learning algorithms.

First, necessary libraries are imported: make_blobs from sklearn.datasets and pyplot from matplotlib. The style submodule from matplotlib is also imported to set a specific plot style ("fivethirtyeight").

Next, the make_blobs function is used to create a dataset with 100 samples, 3 centers (clusters), a standard deviation of 1 for each cluster (cluster_std=1), and 2 features (n_features=2).

The generated data points are then plotted using plt.scatter(). The x and y coordinates of the data points are extracted from X[:, 0] and X[:, 1], respectively. The 's' parameter sets the size of the data points to 40, and the color of the points is set to green ('g').

Labels for the x and y axes are added using plt.xlabel() and plt.ylabel() functions, respectively. Finally, the plot is displayed using plt.show().

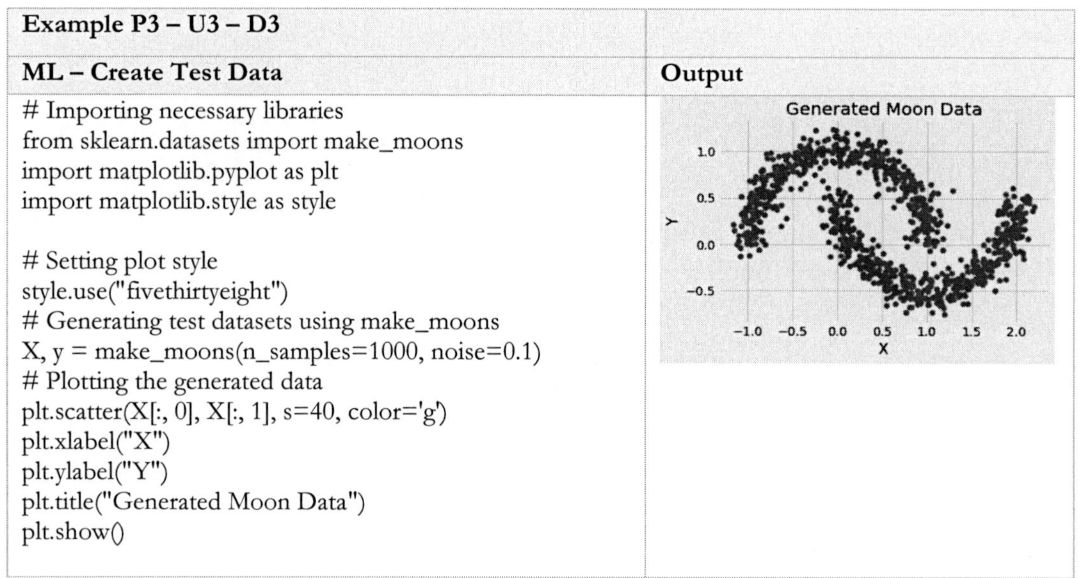

Example P3 – U3 – D3

ML – Create Test Data	Output
See code below	See chart labels below

```
# Importing necessary libraries
from sklearn.datasets import make_moons
import matplotlib.pyplot as plt
import matplotlib.style as style

# Setting plot style
style.use("fivethirtyeight")
# Generating test datasets using make_moons
X, y = make_moons(n_samples=1000, noise=0.1)
# Plotting the generated data
plt.scatter(X[:, 0], X[:, 1], s=40, color='g')
plt.xlabel("X")
plt.ylabel("Y")
plt.title("Generated Moon Data")
plt.show()
```


This code snippet demonstrates how to use scikit-learn's make_moons function to generate synthetic moon-shaped data for testing machine learning algorithms.

First, the necessary libraries are imported: make_moons from sklearn.datasets, and pyplot from matplotlib. The style submodule from matplotlib is also imported to set a specific plot style ("fivethirtyeight").

Next, the make_moons function is used to create a dataset with 1000 samples and a noise level of 0.1. This function generates a two-dimensional dataset with points arranged in the shape of two interleaving half circles representing moons.

The generated data points are then plotted using plt.scatter(). The x and y coordinates of the data points are extracted from X[:, 0] and X[:, 1], respectively. The s parameter sets the size of the data points to 40, and the color of the points is set to green ('g').

Labels for the x and y axes are added using plt.xlabel() and plt.ylabel() functions, respectively. Additionally, a title "Generated Moon Data" is added to the plot using plt.title(). Finally, the plot is displayed using plt.show().

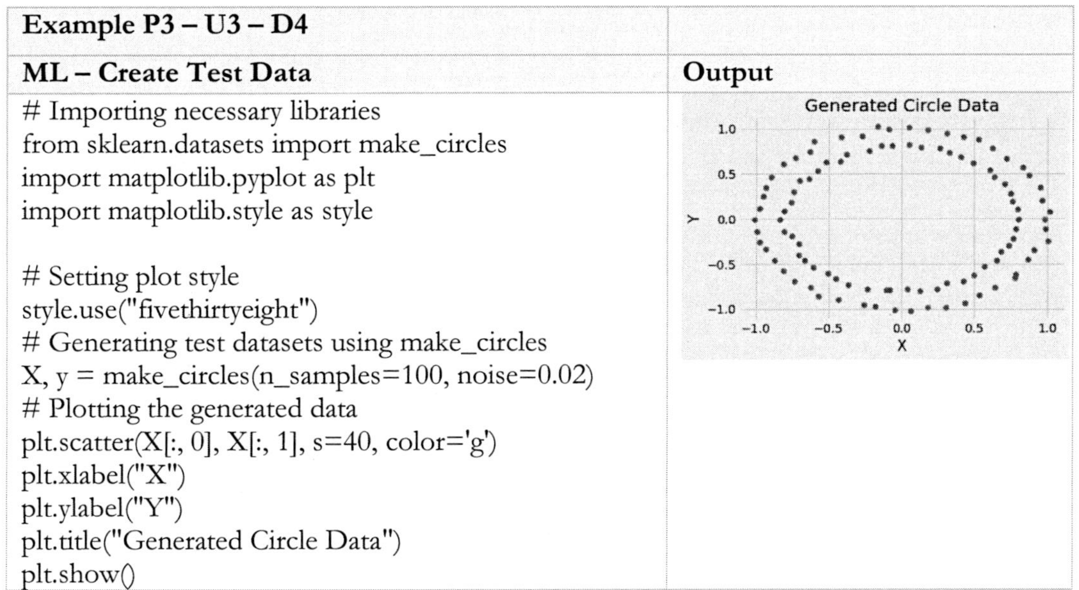

Example P3 – U3 – D4	
ML – Create Test Data	**Output**

```
# Importing necessary libraries
from sklearn.datasets import make_circles
import matplotlib.pyplot as plt
import matplotlib.style as style

# Setting plot style
style.use("fivethirtyeight")
# Generating test datasets using make_circles
X, y = make_circles(n_samples=100, noise=0.02)
# Plotting the generated data
plt.scatter(X[:, 0], X[:, 1], s=40, color='g')
plt.xlabel("X")
plt.ylabel("Y")
plt.title("Generated Circle Data")
plt.show()
```

☐ Advantages of Creating Test Datasets using Scikit-learn (Sklearn):

Time-saving: Sklearn offers a rapid and straightforward method to generate test datasets for machine learning tasks, significantly reducing the time required compared to manual dataset creation.

Consistency: The datasets generated by Sklearn are consistent and reproducible, fostering consistency in experiments and ensuring reliable results across different runs.

Flexibility: Sklearn provides a diverse array of functions for dataset generation, spanning classification, regression, clustering, and more. This versatility makes it adaptable for generating test datasets catering to various machine learning tasks.

Control over Dataset Parameters: With Sklearn, users can customise dataset generation by specifying parameters such as sample size, feature count, and noise level. This granular control empowers users to tailor test datasets to their specific requirements.

Disadvantages of Creating Test Datasets using Scikit-learn (Sklearn):

Limited Dataset Complexity: Sklearn datasets tend to be simplistic and may not capture the intricacies of real-world datasets. Consequently, they might not adequately test the performance of machine learning algorithms on complex data.

Lack of Diversity: Sklearn datasets may lack the diversity present in real-world datasets, potentially limiting the generalizability of machine learning models trained on them.

Overfitting Risk: Generating test datasets too similar to training datasets raises the risk of overfitting models, leading to poor performance on new, unseen data.

In summary, Sklearn offers a convenient means to swiftly generate test datasets, but it's essential to recognize the limitations and potential drawbacks. While synthetic datasets serve as valuable tools for testing, incorporating real-world datasets whenever feasible ensures a more accurate representation of the problem domain and enhances model performance evaluation.

Generate Test Dataset:

When delving into the realm of Machine Learning, datasets are often the first consideration. While numerous datasets are available on platforms like Kaggle, sometimes it's advantageous to extract and generate your dataset. This approach affords greater control over the data and enables tailored training of machine learning models. Let's explore the process of generating random datasets using the sklearn.datasets library in Python.

Generate Test Datasets for Classification:

Binary Classification:

Example 1: Utilize make_circles() to generate 2D binary classification data featuring a spherical decision boundary.

Example 2: Employ make_moons() to create two interlocking half circles, ideal for binary classification tasks.

Example 1:

Example P3 – U3 – D5	
ML – Create Test Data	**Output**

```
# Import necessary libraries
from sklearn.datasets import make_circles
import matplotlib.pyplot as plt

# Generate 2D classification dataset
X, y = make_circles(n_samples=200, shuffle=True,
              noise=0.1, random_state=42)
# Plot the generated dataset
plt.scatter(X[:, 0], X[:, 1], c=y, cmap='viridis',
edgecolors='k')
plt.xlabel("Feature 1")
plt.ylabel("Feature 2")
plt.title("Generated 2D Classification Dataset")
plt.colorbar(label='Class')
```

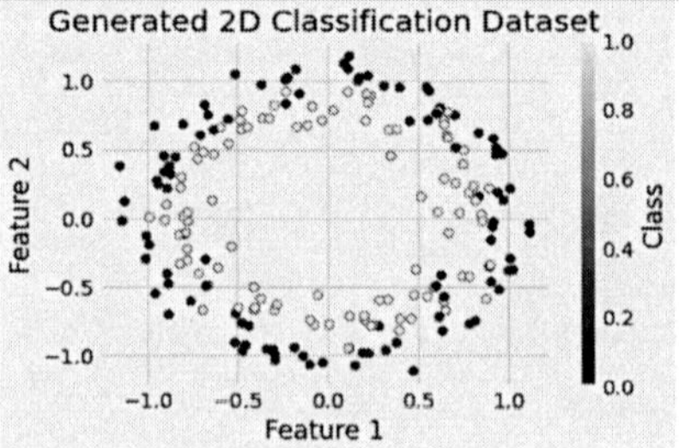

```
plt.show()
```

This code generates a 2D classification dataset using the make_circles function from scikit-learn. It creates 200 samples with noise, shuffles the data, and then plots the dataset using matplotlib's scatter plot. Each class is represented by a different color. Additionally, labels are added to the axes, a title is included, and a color bar is added to indicate the classes.

Example 2:

Example P3 – U3 – D6	
ML – Create Test Data	**Output**

```
# Import necessary libraries
from sklearn.datasets import make_moons
import matplotlib.pyplot as plt

# Generate 2D classification dataset
X, y = make_moons(n_samples=500, shuffle=True,
            noise=0.15, random_state=42)

# Plot the generated dataset
plt.figure(figsize=(8, 6))  # Adjust figure size for
better visualization
plt.scatter(X[:, 0], X[:, 1], c=y, cmap='viridis',
edgecolors='k')
plt.xlabel("Feature 1")
plt.ylabel("Feature 2")
plt.title("Generated 2D Classification Dataset")
plt.colorbar(label='Class')
plt.grid(True, linestyle='--', alpha=0.5)  # Add grid
lines for clarity
plt.show()
```

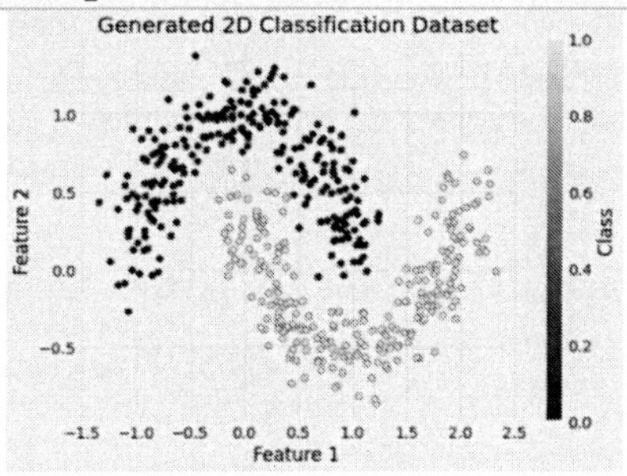

This code utilizes scikit-learn's make_moons function to generate a 2D classification dataset with 500 samples. The dataset is then plotted using matplotlib's scatter plot, where each class is represented by a different color. The code also adds labels to the axes, a title to the plot, a color bar to indicate the classes, and grid lines for better visualisation.

Multi-Class Classification:

Example 1: Generate blob-shaped data for clustering purposes using make_blobs().

Example 2: Employ make_classification() to produce multi-class classification data, balancing attributes like n_informative, n_redundant, and n_classes.

Example 3: Generate random multi-label classification data using make_multilabel_classification().

Example 1:

Example P3 – U3 – D7	
ML – Create Test Data	**Output**

# Import necessary libraries 	
from sklearn.datasets import make_blobs
import matplotlib.pyplot as plt
 	
# Generate 2D classification dataset 	
X, y = make_blobs(n_samples=500, centers=3, n_features=2, random_state=23)
# Plot the generated dataset 	
plt.figure(figsize=(8, 6)) # Adjust figure size for better visualization
plt.scatter(X[:, 0], X[:, 1], c=y, cmap='viridis', edgecolors='k')
plt.xlabel("Feature 1")
plt.ylabel("Feature 2")
plt.title("Generated 2D Classification Dataset")
plt.colorbar(label='Class')
plt.grid(True, linestyle='--', alpha=0.5) # Add grid lines for clarity
plt.show()
	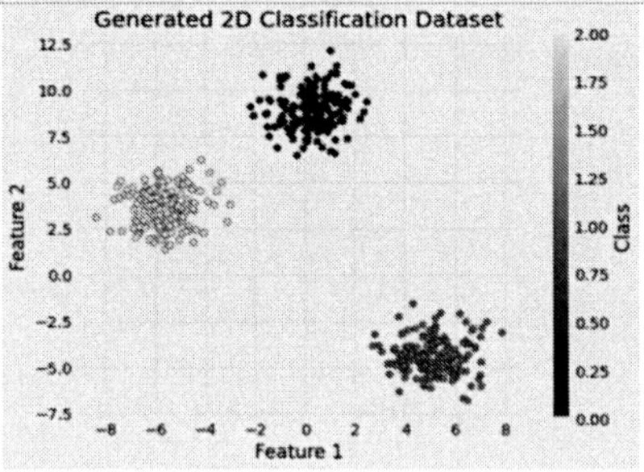 Generated 2D Classification Dataset

This code snippet generates a 2D classification dataset using scikit-learn's make_blobs function. It creates 500 samples with three centers and two features. The dataset is then plotted using matplotlib's scatter plot, where each class is represented by a different color. Additionally, labels are added to the axes, a title is included, a color bar indicates the classes, and grid lines are added for better visualisation.

Example 2:

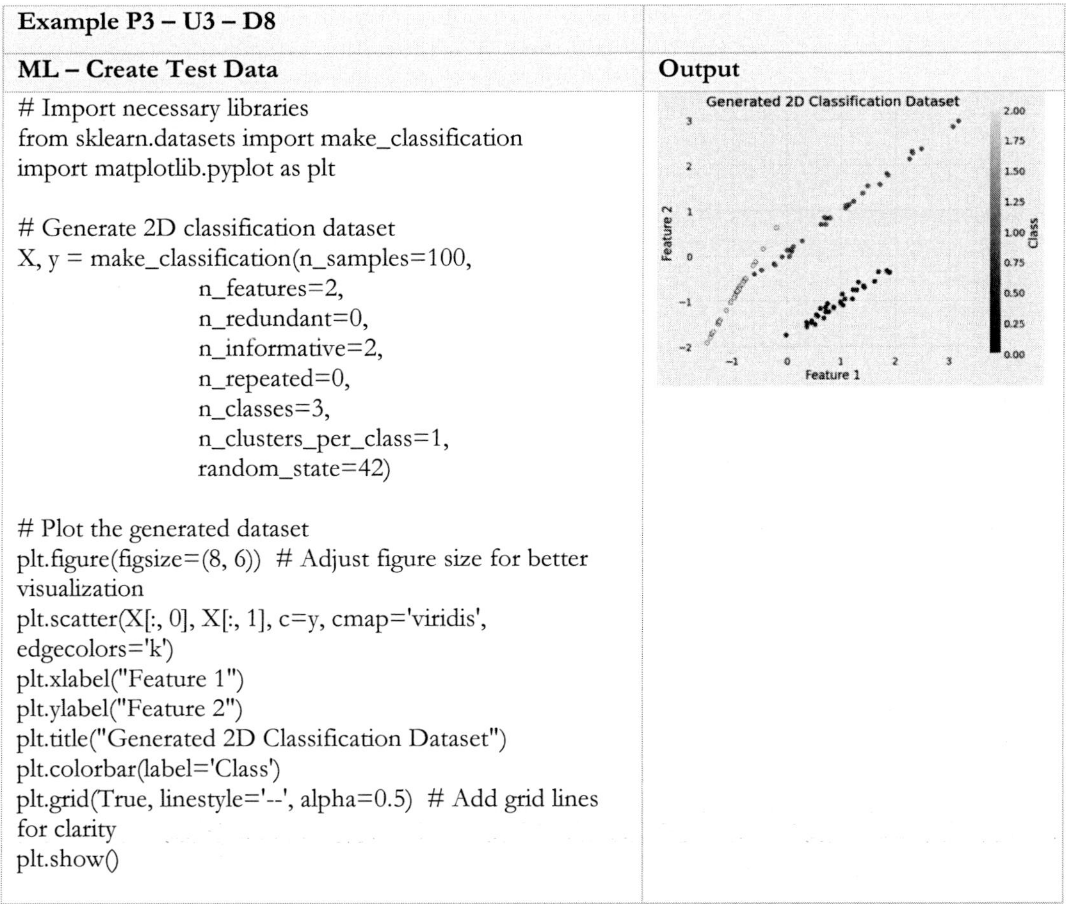

Example P3 – U3 – D8	
ML – Create Test Data	**Output**

```
# Import necessary libraries
from sklearn.datasets import make_classification
import matplotlib.pyplot as plt

# Generate 2D classification dataset
X, y = make_classification(n_samples=100,
                           n_features=2,
                           n_redundant=0,
                           n_informative=2,
                           n_repeated=0,
                           n_classes=3,
                           n_clusters_per_class=1,
                           random_state=42)

# Plot the generated dataset
plt.figure(figsize=(8, 6)) # Adjust figure size for better
visualization
plt.scatter(X[:, 0], X[:, 1], c=y, cmap='viridis',
edgecolors='k')
plt.xlabel("Feature 1")
plt.ylabel("Feature 2")
plt.title("Generated 2D Classification Dataset")
plt.colorbar(label='Class')
plt.grid(True, linestyle='--', alpha=0.5) # Add grid lines
for clarity
plt.show()
```


This code snippet generates a 2D classification dataset using scikit-learn's make_classification function. It creates 100 samples with two features and three classes. The dataset is then plotted using matplotlib's scatter plot, where each class is represented by a different color. Additionally, labels are added to the axes, a title is included, a color bar indicates the classes, and grid lines are added for better visualisation.

Example 3:

Example P3 – U3 – D9	
ML – Create Test Data	**Output**

```
# Import necessary libraries
from sklearn.datasets import
make_multilabel_classification
import pandas as pd
import matplotlib.pyplot as plt
```

```
     X1    X2  Label1  Label2
0  14.0  34.0       0       1
1  30.0  22.0       1       1
2  29.0  19.0       1       1
3  21.0  19.0       1       1
```

# Generate 2D classification dataset 	
X, y =
make_multilabel_classification(n_samples=500, n_features=2,
n_classes=2, n_labels=2,
allow_unlabeled=True,
random_state=23)
 	
# Create pandas DataFrame from generated dataset 	
df = pd.DataFrame(X, columns=['X1', 'X2'])
df['Label1'] = y[:, 0]
df['Label2'] = y[:, 1]
 	
# Display the first few rows of the DataFrame 	
print(df.head())
 	
# Plot the generated datasets 	
plt.scatter(df['X1'], df['X2'], c=df['Label1'], cmap='viridis', edgecolors='k')
plt.xlabel("Feature 1")
plt.ylabel("Feature 2")
plt.title("Generated 2D Classification Dataset")
plt.colorbar(label='Label 1')
plt.grid(True, linestyle='--', alpha=0.5) # Add grid lines for clarity
plt.show()
	4 16.0 32.0 0 1 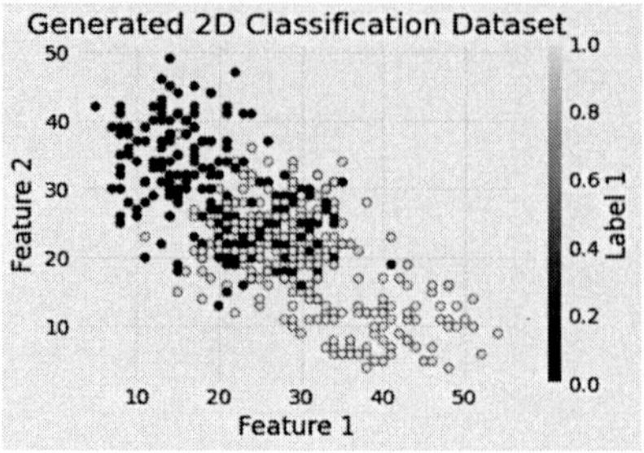
	
	Generated 2D Classification Dataset

This code snippet generates a 2D multi-label classification dataset using scikit-learn's make_multilabel_classification function. It creates 500 samples with two features and two labels per sample. The dataset is then converted into a Pandas DataFrame for easier handling and visualisation. The first few rows of the DataFrame are displayed to inspect the data structure. Finally, the dataset is plotted using matplotlib's scatter plot, where each class is represented by a different color. Labels are added to the axes, a title is included, a color bar indicates the classes, and grid lines are added for better visualisation.

Generate Test Datasets for Regression:

Example 1: Create a 1-dimensional feature and target for linear regression with make_regression(). Example 2: Generate multilabel feature data with minimal correlation using make_sparse_uncorrelated().

Example 3: Utilize make_friedman2() to produce multilabel feature data suitable for regression tasks.

Example 1:

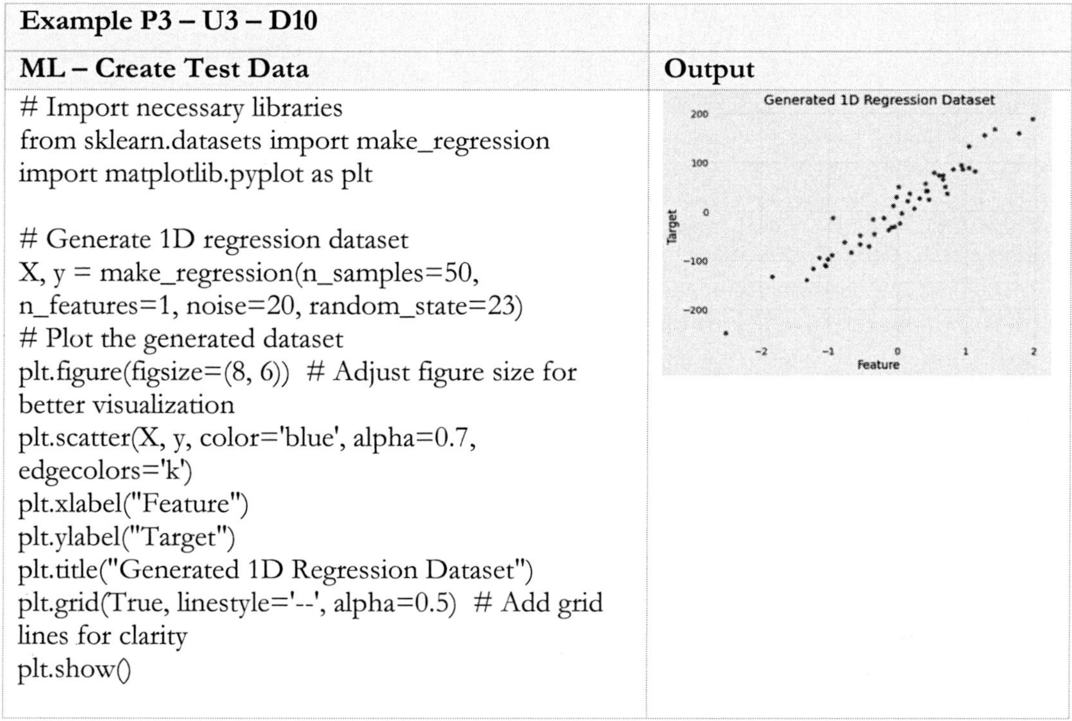

Example P3 – U3 – D10	
ML – Create Test Data	**Output**

```
# Import necessary libraries
from sklearn.datasets import make_regression
import matplotlib.pyplot as plt

# Generate 1D regression dataset
X, y = make_regression(n_samples=50,
n_features=1, noise=20, random_state=23)
# Plot the generated dataset
plt.figure(figsize=(8, 6))  # Adjust figure size for
better visualization
plt.scatter(X, y, color='blue', alpha=0.7,
edgecolors='k')
plt.xlabel("Feature")
plt.ylabel("Target")
plt.title("Generated 1D Regression Dataset")
plt.grid(True, linestyle='--', alpha=0.5)  # Add grid
lines for clarity
plt.show()
```


This code snippet generates a 1D regression dataset using scikit-learn's make_regression function. It creates 50 samples with one feature and noisy target values. The dataset is then plotted using matplotlib's scatter plot, where the feature is plotted against the target. Labels are added to the axes, a title is included, and grid lines are added for better visualisation.

Example 2:

Example P3 – U3 – D11	
ML – Create Test Data	**Output**

```
# Import necessary libraries
from sklearn.datasets import
make_sparse_uncorrelated
import matplotlib.pyplot as plt

# Generate 1D regression dataset
X, y = make_sparse_uncorrelated(n_samples=100,
n_features=4, random_state=23)
# Plot the generated datasets
plt.figure(figsize=(12, 10))
for i in range(4):
    plt.subplot(2, 2, i+1)
    plt.scatter(X[:, i], y)
```

```
    plt.xlabel('X{}'.format(i+1))
    plt.ylabel('Y')
plt.tight_layout()  # Adjust subplots for better spacing
plt.show()
```

This code generates a 1D regression dataset with four features using scikit-learn's make_sparse_uncorrelated function. It creates 100 samples with uncorrelated features and corresponding target values. The dataset is then plotted using matplotlib's subplot feature, with each subplot representing one feature against the target. Labels are added to the axes, and the subplots are arranged in a 2x2 grid for better visualisation. Finally, plt.tight_layout() is used to adjust the subplots for better spacing.

Example 3:

Example P3 – U3 – D12	
ML – Create Test Data	**Output**

```
# Import necessary libraries
from sklearn.datasets import make_friedman2
import matplotlib.pyplot as plt

# Generate 1D regression dataset
X, y = make_friedman2(n_samples=100, random_state=23)
# Plot the generated datasets
plt.figure(figsize=(12, 10))
for i in range(4):
    plt.subplot(2, 2, i+1)
    plt.scatter(X[:, i], y)
    plt.xlabel('X{}'.format(i+1))
    plt.ylabel('Y')
plt.tight_layout()  # Adjust subplots for better spacing
plt.show()
```

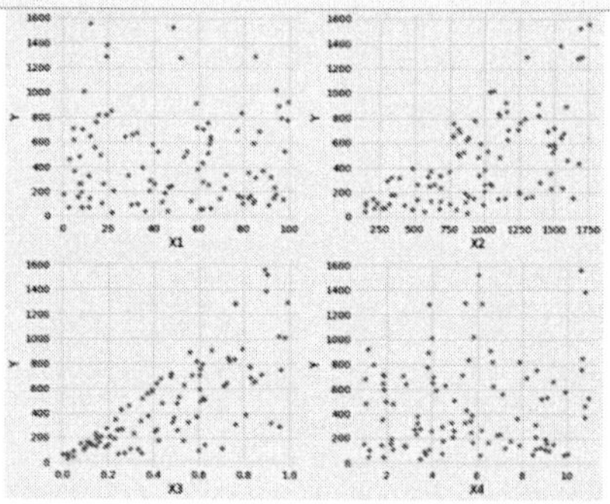

This code generates a 1D regression dataset with four features using scikit-learn's make_friedman2 function. It creates 100 samples with features and corresponding target values. The dataset is then plotted using matplotlib's subplot feature, with each subplot representing one feature against the target. Labels are added to the axes, and the subplots are arranged in a 2x2 grid for better visualisation. Finally, plt.tight_layout() is used to adjust the subplots for better spacing.

Summary:

This unit provided a comprehensive overview of understanding data processing and introduced the fundamentals of working with data. Beginning with an introduction to data, the unit covered various aspects including types of data, properties of data, and common issues encountered when dealing with data.

One of the key topics discussed was understanding data processing, which involves the transformation of raw data into a usable format for analysis. This process encompasses data cleaning, transformation, integration, and interpretation, all aimed at extracting meaningful insights from the data.

A significant part of the unit focused on creating test datasets for different types of machine learning tasks. For classification tasks, methods for generating test datasets for binary classification and multi-class classification were explored. This involved creating datasets with features and labels, balancing class distributions, and ensuring data quality.

Additionally, the unit delved into generating test datasets for regression tasks, where the goal is to predict continuous numerical values. Techniques for creating regression datasets, handling outliers, and ensuring data consistency were discussed.

Overall, this unit provided a foundational understanding of data processing and equipped learners with practical skills for generating test datasets for various machine learning tasks, laying the groundwork for further exploration in the field of data science and machine learning.

PART THREE

DAY SEVEN

Unit 3 - Lesson Three

Understanding Data Cleaning

Data Cleaning

> "Cleansing data is akin to polishing a gemstone; it entails not just identifying and rectifying errors, inconsistencies, and inaccuracies, but also sculpting a narrative of reliability and trustworthiness within the dataset. It's the meticulous art of refining raw information into a gleaming foundation, essential for yielding insights that illuminate pathways for informed decisions and transformative analyses."
> – Shree Shambav

John asked, "What is Data Cleaning?"

Master said, "Data cleaning, often referred to as data cleansing or preprocessing, is an essential step in the machine learning and data science pipeline. It involves identifying and rectifying errors, inconsistencies, and inaccuracies within a dataset to enhance its quality and usability. This process is critical because raw data is frequently noisy, incomplete, or inconsistent, potentially undermining the accuracy and reliability of subsequent analyses or models. Data scientists dedicate a significant amount of time to data cleaning, as it is believed that having high-quality data is more impactful than utilising sophisticated algorithms alone."

Sam asked, "Why is Data Cleaning Important?"

Master said, "Data cleaning is vital in the data preparation process as it significantly impacts the accuracy, reliability, and overall quality of a dataset."

Without proper data cleaning, inaccuracies, outliers, missing values, and inconsistencies can compromise the validity of analytical results, undermining decision-making. Clean data is essential for more effective modelling and pattern recognition, as algorithms perform optimally when fed high-quality, error-free input.

Moreover, clean datasets enhance the interpretability of findings, aiding in the formulation of actionable insights. This underscores the importance of data cleaning in ensuring the integrity of conclusions drawn from data-driven analyses.

Data Cleaning in Data Science

Data cleaning is a cornerstone of data science, essential for ensuring the accuracy and reliability of datasets. In the realm of data science, where insights and predictions hinge on vast and intricate datasets, the quality of input data profoundly shapes the credibility of analytical outcomes. Data cleaning encompasses the systematic identification and rectification of errors, inconsistencies, and inaccuracies within a dataset. This process involves tasks like handling missing values, eliminating duplicates, and addressing outliers. Such meticulous attention to detail is pivotal for bolstering the integrity of analyses, fostering more precise modelling, and ultimately enabling informed decision-making grounded in trustworthy and high-quality data.

Steps to Perform Data Cleanliness

Performing data cleaning involves a systematic process to identify and rectify errors, inconsistencies, and inaccuracies in a dataset. The following steps are essential for ensuring data cleanliness:

- Removal of Unwanted Observations: Identify and eliminate irrelevant or redundant observations from the dataset. This involves scrutinising data entries for duplicate records, irrelevant information, or data points that do not contribute meaningfully to the analysis. Removing unwanted observations streamlines the dataset, reducing noise and improving overall quality.

- Fixing Structural Errors: Address structural issues in the dataset, such as inconsistencies in data formats, naming conventions, or variable types. Standardise formats, correct naming discrepancies, and ensure uniformity in data representation. Fixing structural errors enhances data consistency and facilitates accurate analysis and interpretation.

- Managing Unwanted Outliers: Identify and manage outliers, which are data points significantly deviating from the norm. Depending on the context, decide whether to remove outliers or transform them to minimise their impact on analysis. Managing outliers is crucial for obtaining more accurate and reliable insights from the data.

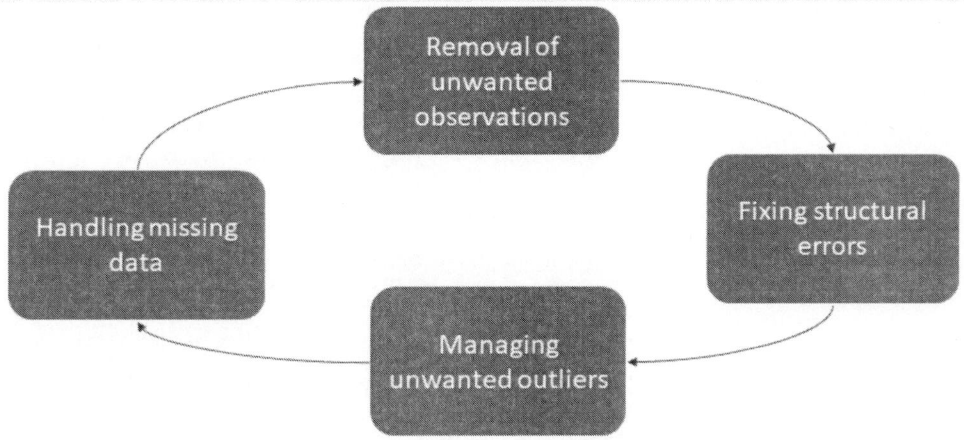

- Handling Missing Data: Devise strategies to handle missing data effectively. This may involve imputing missing values based on statistical methods, removing records with missing values, or employing advanced imputation techniques. Handling missing data ensures a more complete dataset, preventing biases and maintaining the integrity of analyses.

Imputing missing values

Master explained that imputing missing values is a critical step in data preprocessing, as missing data can significantly impact the accuracy and reliability of statistical analyses. There are various strategies for imputing missing values, ranging from simple methods like mean, median, or mode imputation to more advanced techniques such as k-nearest neighbors (KNN) imputation and regularization. However, the choice of imputation method depends on factors such as the nature of the data and the underlying business context.

In addressing missing data, we have two prominent strategies at our disposal: Mean imputation and Median imputation, each suited to different scenarios.

Mean imputation proves effective when the data adheres to a normal distribution and lacks significant outliers. By replacing missing values with the mean of the existing data points, we maintain the overall central tendency of the dataset, contributing to its coherence and statistical integrity.

Conversely, when the dataset exhibits skewness or contains outliers, Median imputation emerges as the preferred approach. By substituting missing values with the median—a robust measure of central tendency less influenced by outliers—we mitigate the impact of extreme values on the imputed data, thereby preserving its representativeness and accuracy.

While mean or median imputation is straightforward and commonly used, it may not always be appropriate, especially if the missing data pattern is non-random or if there are outliers in the data. In such cases, imputing missing values based on domain knowledge or common insights about the data can be more effective. Additionally, advanced imputation algorithms like KNN or regularization can provide more accurate imputations by considering the relationships between variables in the dataset.

It's essential to note that imputing missing values should be done cautiously, and decisions regarding imputation methods should be informed by a thorough understanding of the data and its context. Domain knowledge plays a crucial role in guiding imputation decisions and ensuring the validity of the imputed values. Ultimately, the goal of imputation is to preserve the integrity of the data while mitigating the impact of missing values on subsequent analyses.

Akshaya asked, "How to Perform Data Cleanliness?"

Master said, "Performing data cleanliness involves a systematic approach to enhance the quality and reliability of a dataset. The process begins with a comprehensive understanding of the data, inspecting its structure and identifying issues such as missing values, duplicates, and outliers. Addressing missing data involves strategic decisions on imputation or removal, while duplicates are systematically eliminated to reduce redundancy. Managing outliers ensures that extreme values do not unduly influence analysis. Structural errors are corrected to standardize formats and variable types, promoting consistency."

Throughout the process, documentation of changes is crucial for transparency and reproducibility. Iterative validation and testing confirm the effectiveness of the data cleanliness steps, ultimately resulting in a refined dataset ready for meaningful analysis and insights.

Example:

To understand each step for database cleaning using the Titanic dataset, we'll follow these necessary steps:

Example P3 – U3 – D13	
ML – Data Cleansing - Info	**Output**

import pandas as pd
# Load the dataset from a CSV file 	
path =
r'C:\Users\User\mraj4\Documents\Optimum\Py-lib\scikit\titanic.csv'
df = pd.read_csv(path)
# Display the first few rows of the dataset 	
print(df.head())
# Display the last few rows of the dataset 	
#print(df.tail())
	PassengerId Survived Pclass ...
	Fare Cabin Embarked
	0 1 0 3 ... 7.2500
	NaN S
	1 2 1 1 ...
	71.2833 C85 C
	2 3 1 3 ... 7.9250
	NaN S

Begin by exploring the dataset to understand its structure, features, and distributions. This involves examining summary statistics, visualisations, and correlations between variables to gain insights into the data.

Example P3 – U3 – D14	
ML- Data Cleansing	**Output**

# import pandas as pd 	
# # Load the dataset from a CSV file 	
# path = 	
r'C:\Users\User\mraj4\Documents\Optimum\Py-lib\scikit\titanic.csv'
# df = pd.read_csv(path) 	
# Inspect the structure of the dataset 	
print("Dataset Information:")
print(df.info())
 	
# Summary statistics for numerical columns 	
print("\nSummary Statistics for Numerical Columns:")
print(df.describe())
 	
# Check for missing values 	
print("\nMissing Values:")
print(df.isnull().sum())
 	
# Check for duplicate rows 	
duplicate_rows = df[df.duplicated()]
if not duplicate_rows.empty:
    print("\nDuplicate Rows:")
    print(duplicate_rows)
else:
    print("\nNo Duplicate Rows found.")
 	
# Check for outliers (this depends on the specific analysis) 	
# Further exploration and visualization may be required for outlier detection 		

The Python code provides a comprehensive overview of data inspection and exploration for the Titanic dataset:

- It loads the dataset from a CSV file and displays its structure using df.info().
- Summary statistics for numerical columns are generated with df.describe().

- The code checks for missing values in each column and prints the sum of null values using df.isnull().sum().
- Duplicate rows are identified using df.duplicated() and printed if found.

Output

```
Dataset Information:
<class 'pandas.core.frame.DataFrame'>
RangeIndex: 156 entries, 0 to 155
Data columns (total 13 columns):
 #   Column       Non-Null Count  Dtype
---  ------       --------------  -----
 0   PassengerId  156 non-null    int64
 1   Survived     156 non-null    int64
 2   Pclass       156 non-null    int64
 3   Lname        156 non-null    object
 4   Name         156 non-null    object
 5   Sex          156 non-null    object
 6   Age          126 non-null    float64
 7   SibSp        156 non-null    int64
 8   Parch        156 non-null    int64
 9   Ticket       156 non-null    object
 10  Fare         156 non-null    float64
 11  Cabin        31 non-null     object
 12  Embarked     155 non-null    object
dtypes: float64(2), int64(5), object(6)
memory usage: 16.0+ KB
None

Summary Statistics for Numerical Columns:
       PassengerId    Survived      Pclass  ...       SibSp       Parch        Fare
count   156.000000  156.000000  156.000000  ...  156.000000  156.000000  156.000000
mean     78.500000    0.346154    2.423077  ...    0.615385    0.397436   28.109587
std      45.177428    0.477275    0.795459  ...    1.056235    0.870146   39.401047
min       1.000000    0.000000    1.000000  ...    0.000000    0.000000    6.750000
25%      39.750000    0.000000    2.000000  ...    0.000000    0.000000    8.003150
50%      78.500000    0.000000    3.000000  ...    0.000000    0.000000   14.454200
75%     117.250000    1.000000    3.000000  ...    1.000000    0.000000   30.371850
max     156.000000    1.000000    3.000000  ...    5.000000    5.000000  263.000000

[8 rows x 7 columns]

Missing Values:
PassengerId    0
Survived       0
Pclass         0
Lname          0
```

```
Name          0
Sex           0
Age          30
SibSp         0
Parch         0
Ticket        0
Fare          0
Cabin       125
Embarked      1
dtype: int64
No Duplicate Rows found.
```

From the data info, it's evident that columns like Age and Cabin have unequal counts, indicating missing values. Moreover, some columns are categorical, denoted by the 'object' data type, while others are numerical, represented by 'integer' and 'float' data types. Let's delve deeper into the dataset by examining categorical and numerical columns. Additionally, we notice missing values in columns such as Age, Cabin, and Embarked, while no duplicate values are found. Furthermore, the provided code snippet furnishes statistics for numerical columns, offering valuable insights into their distribution and variability.

Example P3 – U3 – D15	
ML - Data Cleansing – Categorical/Numerical	**Output**

# import pandas as pd 	
# # Load the dataset from a CSV file 	
# path = 	
r'C:\Users\User\mraj4\Documents\Optimum\Py-lib\scikit\titanic.csv'
# df = pd.read_csv(path) 	
 	
# Check categorical columns 	
categorical_columns =
df.select_dtypes(include=['object']).columns.tolist()
print("Categorical Columns:")
print(categorical_columns)
 	
# Check numerical columns 	
numerical_columns = df.select_dtypes(include=['int', 'float']).columns.tolist()
print("\nNumerical Columns:")
print(numerical_columns)
	Categorical Columns:
	['Lname', 'Name', 'Sex', 'Ticket', 'Cabin', 'Embarked']
	
	Numerical Columns:
	['PassengerId', 'Survived', 'Pclass', 'Age', 'SibSp', 'Parch', 'Fare']

The Python code efficiently identifies categorical and numerical columns in the Titanic dataset:

The code utilizes the select_dtypes method to filter columns based on data types, isolating categorical columns with object data type and numerical columns with integer or float data types.

Categorical columns are printed first, followed by numerical columns, providing a clear and concise overview of the dataset's structure.

Example P3 – U3 – D16	
ML - Data Cleansing – Unique values	**Output**
# import pandas as pd # # Load the dataset from a CSV file # path = r'C:\Users\User\mraj4\Documents\Optimum\Py-lib\scikit\titanic.csv' # df = pd.read_csv(path) # Check the total number of unique values in categorical columns categorical_columns = df.select_dtypes(include=['object']).columns unique_values = df[categorical_columns].nunique() print("Total number of unique values in categorical columns:") print(unique_values)	Total number of unique values in categorical columns: Lname 141 Name 152 Sex 2 Ticket 145 Cabin 28 Embarked 3 dtype: int64

This Python code efficiently calculates and prints the total number of unique values in categorical columns of the Titanic dataset:

Utilizing the select_dtypes method with the include parameter, the code filters columns based on object data type, thereby isolating categorical columns.

The nunique() method is applied to the filtered categorical columns to calculate the total number of unique values in each.

The results are printed out, providing a succinct overview of the unique value counts for each categorical column in the dataset.

Steps to Perform Data Cleansing

Removal of Unwanted Observations:

This step involves eliminating duplicate, redundant, or irrelevant values from the dataset. Duplicate observations commonly occur during data collection, while irrelevant observations do not align with the specific problem being addressed.

- **Duplicate Observations:** Duplicate entries can skew results and affect efficiency. Identifying and removing duplicates helps maintain dataset integrity.

- **Redundant Observations:** Redundant data, which repeats across the dataset, can lead to inaccurate results. Eliminating redundancy ensures more faithful outcomes.

- **Irrelevant Observations:** Data points that hold no significance to the analysis should be removed. This streamlines the dataset and enhances clarity.

<table>
<tr><th>Example P3 – U3 – D17</th><th></th></tr>
<tr><th>ML - Data Cleansing – Removal</th><th>Output</th></tr>
<tr><td><pre>
import pandas as pd

Define the file path
path =
r'C:\Users\User\mraj4\Documents\Optimum\Py-
lib\scikit\titanic.csv'

Load the dataset
df = pd.read_csv(path)

# Step 1: Removal of Unwanted Observations
# Duplicate Observations
df_duplicates = df[df.duplicated()]
df = df.drop_duplicates()
# Redundant Observations
# Drop redundant columns
redundant_columns = ['redundant_column1',
'redundant_column2']
df = df.drop(columns=redundant_columns)
# Irrelevant Observations
# Define conditions to filter irrelevant observations
irrelevant_conditions = (df['irrelevant_column1'] ==
'irrelevant_condition1') | \
                    (df['irrelevant_column2'] ==
'irrelevant_condition2')
# Remove irrelevant observations
df = df[~irrelevant_conditions]
# Display cleaned dataset
print("Cleaned Dataset:")
print(df.head())
</pre></td><td><pre>
leaned Dataset:
   PassengerId Survived Pclass ...
Fare Cabin Embarked
0   1   0   3 ...   7.2500
NaN   S
1   2   1   1 ...
71.2833   C85   C
</pre></td></tr>
</table>

Replace 'redundant_column1', 'redundant_column2', 'irrelevant_column1', and 'irrelevant_column2' with the actual column names in your dataset that you consider redundant or irrelevant. Adjust the conditions in irrelevant_conditions to match the specific criteria for identifying irrelevant observations in your dataset.

Handling Categorical Data

Master said, "As machines cannot interpret text data, categorical column values need to be converted to numerical types. In this scenario, we choose to drop the 'Name' column due to its unique nature and minimal influence on target variables. For the 'Ticket' column, we first print 50 unique tickets to assess its significance."

Example P3 – U3 – D18	
ML - Data Cleansing	**Output**

# import pandas as pd 	
# # Define the file path 	
# path = 	
r'C:\Users\User\mraj4\Documents\Optimum\Py-lib\scikit\titanic.csv'
 	
# Load the dataset 	
# df = pd.read_csv(path) 	
# Display the first 50 unique values of the 'Ticket' column 	
print("First 50 unique values of the 'Ticket' column:")
print(df['Ticket'].unique()[:50])
	First 50 unique values of the 'Ticket' column:
	['A/5 21171' 'PC 17599'
	'STON/O2. 3101282' '113803'
	'373450' '330877' ….

The code efficiently prints the first 50 unique values of the 'Ticket' column from the Titanic dataset.

Example P3 – U3 – D19	
ML - Data Cleansing – Dropping column	**Output**

import pandas as pd
# Define the file path 	
path =
r'C:\Users\User\mraj4\Documents\Optimum\Py-lib\scikit\titanic.csv'
# Load the dataset 	
df = pd.read_csv(path)
# Dropping the 'Name' and 'Ticket' columns 	
df = df.drop(columns=['Name', 'Ticket'])
# Display the modified dataframe 	
print("DataFrame after dropping 'Name' and 'Ticket' columns:")
print(df.head())
print(df.shape)
	DataFrame after dropping 'Name' and 'Ticket' columns:
	PassengerId Survived Pclass Lname ... Parch Fare Cabin Embarked
	0 1 0 3 Braund ...
	0 7.2500 NaN S
	1 2 1 1 Cumings ...
	0 71.2833 C85 C
	
	[5 rows x 11 columns]
	(156, 11)

This code efficiently drops the 'Name' and 'Ticket' columns from the Titanic dataset and displays the modified dataframe.

Handling Missing Data

Missing data is a prevalent challenge encountered in real-world datasets, stemming from a variety of factors including human errors, system failures, or inconsistencies in data collection procedures. Addressing missing data is crucial for ensuring the integrity and reliability of analyses and predictions derived from the dataset. To manage missing data effectively, we employ a range of techniques such as imputation, deletion, or substitution. Each approach has its advantages and considerations, and the choice of method depends on the nature of the dataset and the specific requirements of the analysis.

Example P3 – U3 – D20	
ML - Data Cleansing – Percentage Missing value	**Output**

# import pandas as pd 	
# # Define the file path 	
# path = 	
r'C:\Users\User\mraj4\Documents\Optimum\Py-lib\scikit\titanic.csv'
# # Load the dataset 	
# df = pd.read_csv(path) 	
 	
# Check the percentage of missing values column-wise 	
missing_percentage = round((df1.isnull().sum() / df1.shape[0]) * 100, 2)
print("Percentage of missing values column-wise:")
print(missing_percentage)
	Percentage of missing values column-wise:
	PassengerId 0.00
	Survived 0.00
	Pclass 0.00
	Lname 0.00
	Name 0.00
	Sex 0.00
	Age 19.23
	SibSp 0.00
	Parch 0.00
	Ticket 0.00
	Fare 0.00
	Cabin 80.13
	Embarked 0.64

This code efficiently calculates the percentage of missing values column-wise in the Titanic dataset using the isnull() method to identify missing values, and sum() to count the total number of null values. It then computes the percentage by dividing the sum of null values by the total number of rows and multiplying by 100. Finally, it rounds the percentages to two decimal places for clarity.

Dropping Observations with missing values

Master said, "It's crucial not to disregard or eliminate missing observations outright, as they may carry valuable information. Addressing them requires careful consideration."

The two primary methods for managing missing data are:

- Dropping observations with missing values: While this approach is common, it's essential to acknowledge that the absence of a value can itself convey meaningful information.

- Imputation: In real-world scenarios, especially when making predictions on new data, it's often necessary to handle missing features.

Examining the data reveals that the 'Cabin' column has a substantial 80.13% of null values, while 'Age' has 19.23% and 'Embarked' has just 0.64% null values.

Given the high proportion of null values in the 'Cabin' column, it's impractical to impute them. Therefore, we opt to drop the entire 'Cabin' column. For 'Embarked,' with only 0.64% null values, we can safely remove the corresponding rows without significant data loss.

Example P3 – U3 – D21	
ML - Data Cleansing	**Output**

# import pandas as pd 	
# # Define the file path 	
# path = 	
r'C:\Users\User\mraj4\Documents\Optimum\Py-lib\scikit\titanic.csv'
 	
# # Load the dataset 	
# df = pd.read_csv(path) 	
 	
# Drop the 'Cabin' column 	
df1.drop(columns='Cabin', inplace=True)
# Drop rows with missing values in 'Embarked' column 	
df1.dropna(subset=['Embarked'], axis=0, inplace=True)
# Check the shape of the DataFrame 	
print(df1.shape)
	(155, 10)

The code efficiently handles missing data by dropping the 'Cabin' column entirely and removing rows with missing values in the 'Embarked' column, ensuring the dataset is clean and ready for further analysis or modelling.

Imputing missing values

Imputing missing values involves filling in those gaps based on existing data. It's crucial to recognise that the absence of a value often carries valuable information, and thus, informing the algorithm about missingness is essential.

When imputing values, it's important to note that we're not introducing new information, but rather reinforcing existing patterns observed in the data. This underscores the significance of choosing appropriate imputation methods.

Two common strategies for imputing missing values are Mean and Median imputation:

- Mean imputation is suitable when the data follows a normal distribution and lacks extreme outliers. It involves replacing missing values with the mean of the available data.

- Median imputation is preferred when the data contains outliers or exhibits skewness. By using the median value, which is less influenced by outliers, this method offers a robust approach to imputation.

Selecting the appropriate imputation method depends on the distribution and characteristics of the data, ensuring that the imputed values accurately represent the underlying patterns while maintaining the integrity of the dataset.

Example P3 – U3 – D22	
ML - Data Cleansing – Imputing Missing value	**Output**

# import pandas as pd 	
# # Define the file path 	
# path = 	
r'C:\Users\User\mraj4\Documents\Optimum\Py-lib\scikit\titanic.csv'
 	
# # Load the dataset 	
# df = pd.read_csv(path) 	
# Mean imputation for missing values in 'Age' column 	
df1['Age'].fillna(df1['Age'].mean(), inplace=True)
# Check for null values again 	
null_values_count = df1.isnull().sum()
print(null_values_count)
	PassengerId 0
	Survived 0
	Pclass 0
	Lname 0
	Sex 0
	Age 0
	SibSp 0
	Parch 0
	Fare 0
	Embarked 0

Handling Outliers

Outliers, those extreme values that significantly deviate from the majority of the data, pose challenges to analysis and model performance. Employing techniques like clustering, interpolation, or transformation can mitigate their impact.

To identify outliers, a commonly used tool is the box plot, also known as a box-and-whisker plot. This graphical representation illustrates the distribution of a dataset by displaying its median, quartiles, and potential outliers. Within the box plot, the line represents the median, while the box signifies the interquartile range (IQR). The whiskers extend to the most extreme non-outlier values within 1.5 times the IQR. Any individual points beyond these whiskers are flagged as potential outliers. By presenting a clear summary of the data's range, a box plot facilitates the detection of outliers or skewness in the distribution, aiding in informed decision-making during analysis.

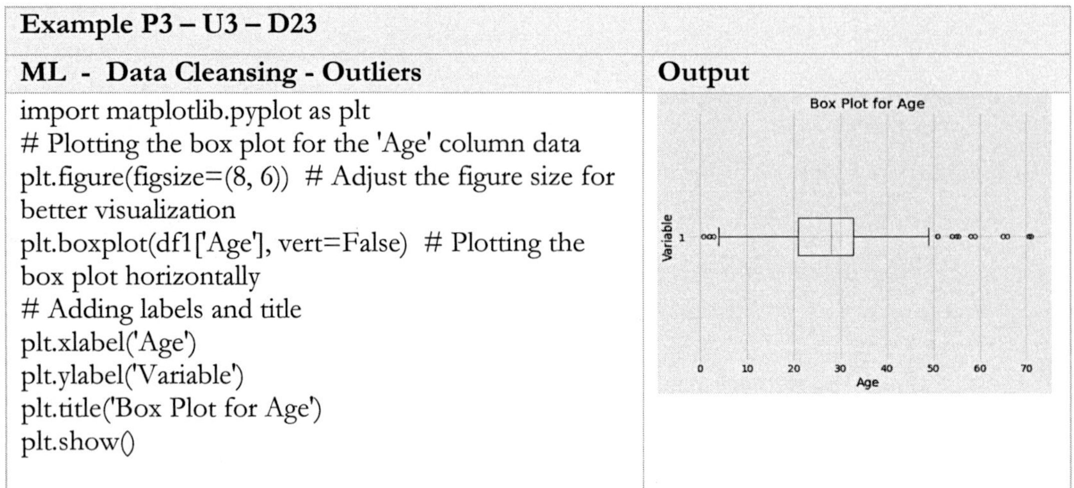

Example P3 – U3 – D23	
ML - Data Cleansing - Outliers	**Output**

import matplotlib.pyplot as plt
# Plotting the box plot for the 'Age' column data 	
plt.figure(figsize=(8, 6)) # Adjust the figure size for better visualization
plt.boxplot(df1['Age'], vert=False) # Plotting the box plot horizontally
# Adding labels and title 	
plt.xlabel('Age')
plt.ylabel('Variable')
plt.title('Box Plot for Age')
plt.show()
	Box Plot for Age
	Variable
	1
	0 10 20 30 40 50 60 70
	Age

The Box and Whisker plot above vividly illustrate outliers within our age dataset. Notably, values falling below 5 and above 55 are classified as outliers.

Calculate Statistics and Bounds:

Example P3 – U3 – D24	
ML - Data Cleansing	**Output**

# Calculate summary statistics 	
mean_age = df1['Age'].mean()
std_age = df1['Age'].std()
print('Mean Age:', mean_age)
print('Std Age:', std_age)
 	
# Calculate the lower and upper bounds 	
lower_bound = mean_age - 2 * std_age
upper_bound = mean_age + 2 * std_age
print('Lower Bound:', lower_bound)
print('Upper Bound:', upper_bound)
# Filter out the outliers 	
df_filtered = df1[(df1['Age'] >= lower_bound) & (df1['Age'] <= upper_bound)]
print('Filter:', df_filtered)
	Mean Age: 28.062639999999995
	Std Age: 13.142011160011627
	Lower Bound: 1.7786176799767404
	Upper Bound: 54.34666232002325
	
	Filter: PassengerId Survived Pclass ... Parch Fare Embarked
	0 1 0 3 ... 0 7.2500 S

PART THREE

DAY SEVEN

Unit 3 - Lesson Four

Understanding Data Transformation

Master said, "Data transformation is the process of converting data from one format to another, enhancing its suitability for analysis. Techniques such as normalisation, scaling, or encoding are employed to refine the data for analytical purposes."

Data Validation and Verification

Data validation and verification are crucial steps to ensure the accuracy and consistency of data by cross-referencing it with external sources or expert knowledge.

Machine Learning Prediction:

In preparing for machine learning predictions, we first segregate independent and target features. For our analysis, we consider only 'Sex', 'Age', 'SibSp', 'Parch', 'Fare', and 'Embarked' as independent features, with 'Survived' serving as the target variable. The exclusion of 'PassengerId' is justified by its negligible impact on survival rate.

```
X = df1[['Pclass','Sex','Age', 'SibSp','Parch','Fare','Embarked']]
Y = df1['Survived']
```

Data Formatting

Data formatting involves standardising data into a structured format suitable for algorithmic processing. Common techniques include Scaling and Normalisation, which optimises data for analysis and model application.

Scaling:

Scaling is a fundamental data preprocessing step that entails transforming feature values to a defined range while preserving the distribution's shape.

It proves especially valuable when features exhibit disparate scales, a scenario where certain algorithms may be unduly influenced by feature magnitudes.

Two widely used scaling techniques are Min-Max scaling and Standardization (Z-score scaling).

Min-Max Scaling: This method rescales feature values to a designated range, often between 0 and 1. It conserves the original distribution, ensuring that the minimum value maps to 0 and the maximum value to 1.

Example P3 – U3 – D25	
ML - Data Cleansing - MinMaxScaler	**Output**

from sklearn.preprocessing import MinMaxScaler
# Define features (X) and target (Y) 	
X = df1[['Pclass', 'Sex', 'Age', 'SibSp', 'Parch', 'Fare', 'Embarked']]
Y = df1['Survived']
# Initialize the MinMaxScaler with feature range (0, 1) 	
scaler = MinMaxScaler(feature_range=(0, 1))
# Select numerical columns 	
num_cols = X.select_dtypes(include='number').columns
# Create a copy of X 	
x1 = X.copy()
# Fit the scaler and transform the numerical columns 	
x1[num_cols] = scaler.fit_transform(x1[num_cols])
# Display the transformed data 	
print(x1.head())
	Pclass Sex Age SibSp
	Parch Fare Embarked
	0 1.0 male 0.301696 0.2
	0.0 0.001951 S
	1 0.0 female 0.529714 0.2
	0.0 0.251837 C

Standardization (Z-score scaling):

Master explained that the Standardization is a pivotal data transformation technique that aligns feature values to have a mean of 0 and a standard deviation of 1. By centering the data around its mean and scaling it in proportion to the standard deviation, standardization fosters uniformity in feature magnitudes.

This process imbues the data with compatibility for algorithms assuming a Gaussian distribution or those mandating features with zero mean and unit variance.

Consequently, it bolsters model resilience and efficacy across diverse machine learning frameworks.

The formula for Z-score scaling is expressed as:

$$Z = (X - \mu) / \sigma$$

Where,

X = Data

μ = Mean value of X

σ = Standard deviation of X

Example P3 – U3 – D26	
ML - Data Cleansing - Standardization	**Output**

from sklearn.preprocessing import StandardScaler
# Define features (X) and target (Y) 	
X = df1[['Pclass', 'Sex', 'Age', 'SibSp', 'Parch', 'Fare', 'Embarked']]
Y = df1['Survived']
# Initialize the StandardScaler 	
scaler = StandardScaler()
# Select numerical columns 	
num_cols = X.select_dtypes(include='number').columns
# Create a copy of X 	
x2 = X.copy()
# Fit the scaler and transform the numerical columns 	
x2[num_cols] = scaler.fit_transform(x2[num_cols])
# Display the transformed data 	
print("StandardScaler:")
print(x2.head())
	StandardScaler:
	Pclass Sex Age SibSp Parch Fare Embarked
	0 0.721263 male -0.462813 0.360777 -0.460004 -0.523879 S

Data Cleansing Tools:

Some notable data cleansing tools include:

- OpenRefine
- Trifacta Wrangler

- TIBCO Clarity
- Cloudingo
- IBM Infosphere Quality Stage

Advantages of Data Cleaning:

- Improved Model Performance: By eliminating errors, inconsistencies, and irrelevant data, data cleaning enhances the model's ability to learn effectively.
- Increased Accuracy: Ensuring data accuracy, consistency, and error-free quality leads to higher precision in analysis and predictions.
- Better Representation of Data: Data cleaning transforms raw data into a format that accurately reflects underlying relationships and patterns, enhancing interpretability.
- Enhanced Data Quality: Enhancing data reliability and accuracy through cleaning processes strengthens its overall quality.
- Improved Data Security: Identification and removal of sensitive or confidential information safeguard data integrity and security.

Disadvantages of Data Cleaning:

- Time-Consuming: Data cleaning can be laborious, particularly for extensive or intricate datasets.
- Error-Prone: Transformation and cleaning processes may inadvertently lead to the loss of crucial information or introduce new errors.
- Cost and Resource-Intensive: Data cleaning demands substantial time, effort, and expertise. It often requires specialised software tools, contributing to cost and complexity.
- Overfitting Risk: Excessive data removal during cleaning can potentially lead to overfitting, where the model performs well on training data but poorly on unseen data.

One Hot Encoding

Nikash asked, "what is one hot encoding?"

Master said, "In many real-world datasets used in data science projects, we encounter columns with mixed data types - both categorical and numerical. However, some machine learning models struggle to work directly with categorical data, necessitating its conversion into numerical form. For instance, consider a dataset containing a "Gender" column with categorical values like "Male" and "Female." These labels lack any inherent order, and since they're represented as strings, machine learning models may erroneously interpret them as having a hierarchical relationship."

One potential solution to this challenge is label encoding, where each label is assigned a numerical value. For example, "Male" and "Female" might be mapped to 0 and 1, respectively. However, this approach can introduce bias into the model, as it may erroneously attribute higher importance to the numerical values (e.g., 1 > 0), even though both labels hold equal significance in the dataset.

To address this issue, we turn to One Hot Encoding. This technique transforms categorical variables into a binary matrix representation, where each category becomes a separate binary column (or "dummy" variable). Each column indicates the presence or absence of a category, effectively removing any implicit ordering among the labels and ensuring equal importance for each category in the model.

One Hot Encoding

One-hot encoding is a fundamental technique used to represent categorical variables as numerical values in machine learning models.

Advantages:

- Enables the use of categorical variables in models that require numerical input, broadening the scope of applicable algorithms.
- Enhances model performance by providing comprehensive information about categorical variables, aiding in more informed decision-making.
- Mitigates the issue of ordinality, particularly beneficial when categorical variables exhibit natural ordering, preventing misinterpretation of ordinal relationships.

Disadvantages:

- Increased dimensionality: Each category in the variable generates a separate column, potentially complicating the model and prolonging training times.
- Sparse data: Most observations have a value of 0 in the majority of one-hot encoded columns, leading to sparse matrices.
- Overfitting risk: Particularly pronounced with numerous categories and limited sample sizes, potentially compromising model generalization.

One-hot encoding serves as a potent tool for handling categorical data, yet its implementation warrants caution due to potential challenges like increased dimensionality, sparsity, and overfitting. It's prudent to explore alternative encoding methods such as ordinal or binary encoding, considering the specific characteristics of the dataset and the goals of the analysis.

In One Hot Encoding, each categorical parameter generates separate columns for each label. For instance, in the case of gender, there will be distinct columns for "Male" and "Female." When a data point is associated with a specific label, the corresponding column value will be 1, while all other label columns will hold 0. This approach ensures a clear representation of categorical data without imposing any ordinal relationships.

Let's elucidate this with an example: Suppose we have a dataset containing information about fruits, their respective categories, and prices.

One Hot Encoding

Fruit	Categorical Value	Price
Mango	1	2
Apple	2	2.5
apple	2	4
Orange	3	1.5

Mango	Apple	Orange	Price
1	0	0	2
0	1	0	2.5
0	1	0	4
0	0	1	1.5

Output – After applying One-hot encoding

The provided code demonstrates the process of performing One-Hot Encoding on categorical data using Python's pandas library.

Data Preparation: First, a dummy dataset representing employee information is created using a Python dictionary. This dataset includes columns for employee ID, gender, and remarks. The data dictionary is then converted into a pandas DataFrame for further processing.

Exploratory Data Analysis: The code prints out the unique values present in the 'Gender' and 'Remarks' columns to understand the categorical variables' distinct categories. Additionally, it computes and prints the count of occurrences for each category within these columns.

Example P3 – U3 – D27	
ML - Data Cleansing	**Output**

import pandas as pd
# Building a dummy employee dataset for example 	
data = {'Employee id': [10, 20, 15, 25, 30],
'Gender': ['M', 'F', 'F', 'M', 'F'],
	['M' 'F']
	['Good' 'Nice' 'Great']
	Gender
	F 3

'Remarks': ['Good', 'Nice', 'Good', 'Great', 'Nice']
}
 	
# Convert dictionary to DataFrame 	
df = pd.DataFrame(data)
# Display unique values for 'Gender' and 'Remarks' 	
print(df['Gender'].unique())
print(df['Remarks'].unique())
# Count occurrences of each category in 'Gender' and 'Remarks' 	
gender_counts = df['Gender'].value_counts()
remarks_counts = df['Remarks'].value_counts()
print(gender_counts)
print(remarks_counts)
# Perform One-Hot Encoding 	
one_hot_encoded_data = pd.get_dummies(df, columns=['Remarks', 'Gender'])
# Display the one-hot encoded DataFrame 	
print(one_hot_encoded_data)
	M 2
	Name: count, dtype: int64
	Remarks
	Good 2
	Nice 2
	Great 1
	Name: count, dtype: int64
	
	Employee id Remarks_Good Remarks_Great Remarks_Nice Gender_F Gender_M
	0 10 True False False False True
	1 20 False False True True False

One-Hot Encoding: Using the pd.get_dummies() function from pandas, the code performs One-Hot Encoding on the DataFrame, specifically on the 'Remarks' and 'Gender' columns. This process creates new binary columns for each unique category within these columns, where a value of 1 indicates the presence of that category, and 0 indicates absence.

Displaying Results: Finally, the code prints the resulting DataFrame after One-Hot Encoding, showcasing the transformed dataset with the new binary columns representing the categorical variables' categories.

Overall, this code serves as a concise example illustrating the One-Hot Encoding technique for converting categorical variables into a format suitable for machine learning algorithms' consumption.

One Hot Encoding using Scikit:

Example P3 – U3 – D28	
ML - Data Cleansing	**Output**

import pandas as pd
from sklearn.preprocessing import OneHotEncoder
# Building a dummy employee dataset for example 	
data = {'Employee id': [10, 20, 15, 25, 30],
'Gender': ['M', 'F', 'F', 'M', 'F'],
'Remarks': ['Good', 'Nice', 'Good', 'Great', 'Nice'],
	Original Employee Data:
	Employee id Gender Remarks
	0 10 M Good
	1 20 F Nice
	2 15 F Good
	3 25 M Great
	4 30 F Nice

}
# Converting dictionary to a Pandas DataFrame 	
df = pd.DataFrame(data)
# Print the original dataframe 	
print("Original Employee Data:")
print(df)
# Extract categorical columns from the dataframe 	
categorical_columns =
df.select_dtypes(include=['object']).columns
# Initialize OneHotEncoder 	
encoder = OneHotEncoder(sparse=False)
# Apply one-hot encoding to the categorical columns 	
one_hot_encoded =
encoder.fit_transform(df[categorical_columns])
# Create a DataFrame with the one-hot encoded columns 	
one_hot_df = pd.DataFrame(one_hot_encoded,
columns=encoder.get_feature_names_out(categorica
l_columns))
# Concatenate the one-hot encoded dataframe with the original dataframe 	
df_encoded = pd.concat([df, one_hot_df], axis=1)
# Drop the original categorical columns 	
df_encoded.drop(categorical_columns, axis=1,
inplace=True)
# Display the resulting dataframe 	
print("\nEncoded Employee Data:")
print(df_encoded)
	Encoded Employee Data:
	Employee id Gender_F
	Gender_M Remarks_Good
	Remarks_Great Remarks_Nice
	0 10 0.0 1.0
	1.0 0.0 0.0
	1 20 1.0 0.0
	0.0 0.0 1.0

Dummy variable trap in Regression Models

Apeksha asked, "What is a Dummy Variable Trap?"

Master said, "In regression analysis, dealing with diverse data types is common, ranging from quantitative (numerical) to qualitative (categorical). While numerical data can be directly utilized, categorical data necessitates transformation."

One common method for transforming categorical attributes into numerical form is label encoding, which assigns a unique integer to each category. However, this approach alone may not suffice. Hence, one-hot encoding is often employed in regression models following label encoding. This technique generates new attributes, known as dummy variables, corresponding to each category in the original attribute. Dummy variables act as "proxy" variables for categorical data in regression models, with each variable indicating the presence or absence of a specific category.

The Dummy Variable Trap:

The dummy variable trap arises when the created dummy variables exhibit high correlation (multicollinearity), where one variable can be predicted from others. Using all dummy variables in regression models can lead to this trap, undermining the model's effectiveness. Therefore, it's crucial to design regression models to exclude one dummy variable to avoid redundancy and ensure model robustness.

In linear regression models, the dummy variable technique is employed to infer relationships between features (including categorical data) and outcomes. Dummy variables, also known as indicator variables, are artificially created to represent attributes with multiple distinct categories or levels.

Multicollinearity:

Akshaya asked, "What is Multicollinearity?"

Master explained that Multicollinearity occurs when independent variables are highly correlated, leading to redundancy in the model. In simple terms, it means the value of one variable can be predicted from the values of other variables. Identifying and addressing multicollinearity is essential for ensuring the accuracy and reliability of regression models.

Explanation:

To illustrate the concept of the dummy variable trap, let's use an example where wages are modeled as a function of gender in a linear regression setting.

In linear regression, the mathematical equation typically appears as:

$$Wages = \beta 0 + \beta 1 \times Gender$$

Suppose our dataset contains two possible gender values: "Male" and "Female". To incorporate gender into the regression model, we introduce two dummy variables:

- DM (Dummy variable for Male)
- DF (Dummy variable for Female)

The modified equation for linear regression becomes:

$$Wages = \beta 0 + \beta 1 \times DM + \beta 2 \times DF$$

Now, let's create a table with arbitrary values to visualize the dummy variable trap. For simplicity, let's assume all constant values are equal to 1.

Gender	**Male(DM)**	**Female(DF)**
Male	1	0
Female	0	1

In this table, if the gender is male, the value of the "Male" column (DM) will be 1, and the value of the "Female" column (DF) will be 0. Conversely, if the gender is female, the value of the "Male" column will be 0, and the value of the "Female" column will be 1.

This representation of dummy variables ensures that each observation is encoded accurately with respect to gender, facilitating regression analysis.

Wages	**β0 (Constant)**	**Male(β1*DM)**	**Female(β2*DF)**
W1	1	1	0
W2	1	0	1
W3	1	0	1
W4	1	0	1
W5	1	1	0

To better illustrate the dummy variable trap, let's introduce a new column by summing the values in the "Male" and "Female" columns and incorporate it into our dataset. This addition will provide a clearer view of the problem.

Wages	β0 (Constant)	Male(β1*DM)	Female(β2*DF)	Calc
W1	1	1	0	1
W2	1	0	1	1
W3	1	0	1	1
W4	1	0	1	1
W5	1	1	0	1

Observations have been made that the values in the "Constant" and "Calc" columns are identical. This violates the assumption of linear regression that observations should be independent of each other, which is what we refer to as the dummy variable trap. Including all dummy variables in the dataset compromises the accuracy of the regression model.

To prevent falling into the dummy variable trap, it's advisable to include one less (n-1) dummy variable than the total number of categories present in the categorical data (n). This is because the nth dummy variable is redundant, as it doesn't provide any new information.

By eliminating one dummy variable from our equation, the new equation becomes:

$$Wages = \beta 0 + \beta 1 \times DM$$

In this equation, if the value of "DM" is 1, it represents Male, and if it's 0, it represents Female. This adjustment ensures that we avoid redundancy in the regression model, maintaining its accuracy and reliability.

Wages	$\beta 0$ (Constant)	Male($\beta 1$*DM)
W1	1	1
W2	1	0
W3	1	0
W4	1	0
W5	1	1

Since we have only one dummy column, we don't need to introduce a new column. By observing that its value differs from the "Constant" column, we have effectively avoided falling into the dummy variable trap.

Dummy Variable Trap Test

To ascertain whether a dataset exhibits the dummy variable trap scenario, we perform a determinant test. This involves multiplying the transpose of the independent variable matrix (X') with the independent variable matrix (X), and then calculating its determinant.

If the determinant equals 0, it indicates the presence of the dummy variable trap scenario.

If the determinant does not equal 0, it suggests that the dataset does not exhibit the dummy variable trap scenario.

Conclusion

To prevent falling into the dummy variable trap, it's crucial to include one less (n-1) variable than the total number of categories present in the categorical data (n) when adding dummy variables.

Example P3 – U3 – D29	
ML – Dummy Variable Trap	**Output**

import numpy as np
 	
def check_dummy_variable_trap(X):
   """
   Check for the dummy variable trap scenario in a dataset.
   Parameters:
   - X: Independent variable matrix (numpy array)
 	
   Returns:
   - True if dummy variable trap scenario is detected, False otherwise
	Dummy Variable Trap Detected: False

```
    """
    # Calculate X transpose
    X_transpose = np.transpose(X)
    # Calculate the determinant of X transpose
multiplied by X
    determinant = np.linalg.det(np.dot(X_transpose,
X))
    # Check if determinant is zero
    if determinant == 0:
        return True  # Dummy variable trap scenario
detected
    else:
        return False  # No dummy variable trap
scenario detected

# Example usage:
# Define your independent variable matrix X
X = np.array([[1, 0, 1],
              [0, 1, 1],
              [1, 1, 1]])

# Check for dummy variable trap scenario
trap_detected = check_dummy_variable_trap(X)
print("Dummy Variable Trap Detected:",
trap_detected)
```

Sampling Distribution

Master said, "In the realm of statistics, various distributions hold sway, each offering unique insights into data behaviour. Among them, the normal (Gaussian), exponential, and binomial distributions stand as prominent."

Let us try to understand Sampling Distribution.

Imagine having a dataset at hand. By extracting a finite number of data points from it and repeatedly calculating certain statistical measures, we embark on the journey of Sampling Distribution. Plotting the distribution curve of these sample statistics unveils the essence of this distribution, offering a glimpse into the variability and tendencies encapsulated within the data.

When we delve deeper, we encounter a remarkable theorem: the Central Limit Theorem. This theorem asserts that regardless of the original data distribution's nature, when we draw samples and compute their means, the resulting distribution of these sample means tends towards normality. This phenomenon holds profound implications for statistical inference and modelling, underlining the robustness and universality of the normal distribution.

Example P3 – U3 – D30	
DS - Sample Distribution	**Output**

```
import numpy as np
import matplotlib.pyplot as plt
# Generate an array of numbers from 0 to 9
num = np.arange(10)
# Dictionary to store sample mean frequencies
sample_freq = {}

# Iterating through all possible pairs of numbers
from 0 to 3
for i in range(4):
    for j in range(4):
        # Calculate the mean of each pair
        mean_of_two = (num[i] + num[j]) / 2

        # Update the frequency count for the mean
        sample_freq[mean_of_two] =
sample_freq.get(mean_of_two, 0) + 1

# Scatter plot of sample mean frequencies
plt.scatter(sample_freq.keys(), sample_freq.values())
plt.show()

# Extracting all mean values and their frequencies
means = [key for key, value in sample_freq.items()
for _ in range(value)]
# Calculating the standard error
se = np.std(means) / np.sqrt(len(means))
print(f'Standard Error of the samples is {se}.')
```

Standard Error of the samples is 0.19764235376052372.

From the scatter plot, we discern a symmetrical distribution of the sample statistic. Extrapolating from this observation, as we hypothetically extend our sampling to an infinite number of random points, we anticipate witnessing the emergence of a normal (Gaussian) distribution.

Standard Error

Consider a sampling distribution derived from a set of sample statistics. The Standard Error (SE) of these statistics quantifies their variability. It is computed by dividing the standard deviation of the sample statistics by the square root of the sample size. This metric provides crucial insights into the precision and reliability of our estimations.

Summary:

This unit delves into the critical process of data cleaning, which is essential for ensuring the quality and reliability of data used in machine learning and data analysis tasks. Beginning with an exploration of understanding data cleaning, the unit covers various techniques and methodologies for improving data quality and consistency.

One of the key topics discussed is imputing missing values, where strategies for handling missing data are explored. The unit outlines the steps involved in performing data cleansing, which include identifying and handling categorical data, dealing with missing data, and addressing outliers. Strategies for handling categorical data, such as one-hot encoding and dummy variable creation, are explained in detail.

Additionally, the unit covers methods for handling outliers, which are data points that deviate significantly from the rest of the dataset. Techniques for identifying and addressing outliers, such as calculating statistics and setting bounds, are discussed.

Furthermore, the unit explores data formatting techniques, including scaling and standardization, which are used to ensure that features are on a similar scale and have comparable ranges. The concept of the dummy variable trap is also introduced, along with methods for avoiding it.

Overall, this unit equips learners with the knowledge and skills necessary to perform effective data cleaning, ensuring that datasets are accurate, reliable, and suitable for analysis in machine learning and data science applications.

PART THREE

DAY EIGHT

Unit 3 - Lesson Five

Exploratory Data Analysis (EDA)

Exploratory Data Analysis

Exploratory Data Analysis (EDA) is an indispensable phase in the data analysis process, employing statistical and visualization techniques to reveal crucial aspects of the dataset and illuminate patterns, relationships, and potential issues. This thorough examination enables a comprehensive understanding of the dataset from various perspectives, allowing for description and summarization without preemptive assumptions about its contents.

The significance of Exploratory Data Analysis lies in its role as a foundational step before delving into statistical modelling or machine learning. By scrutinizing the dataset, data scientists can ensure the integrity of the data, identify any anomalies, and address imperfections. EDA is an integral component of data science projects within any organization.

Roopa asked "Why Exploratory Data Analysis is Important?"

Master said, "Data Imperfections: Raw data often exhibits imperfections, such as skewness, outliers, or missing values. EDA serves as a means to identify and understand these imperfections, paving the way for informed decision-making."

Model Performance: Building a model on raw and unexplored data may lead to sub-optimal performance. EDA is essential for refining the dataset, addressing discrepancies, and enhancing the quality of subsequent models.

Avoiding Mistakes: Rushing into machine learning without a thorough EDA can result in critical mistakes, including inaccurate models, accurate models trained on flawed data, improper variable creation during data preparation, and inefficient resource utilization.

In essence, Exploratory Data Analysis is not a step to be overlooked or hastily executed. It is a meticulous process that ensures the data's reliability, uncovers hidden insights, and lays the groundwork for the success of subsequent data science endeavors.

Data Collection

Data collection is a fundamental phase within exploratory data analysis, encompassing the discovery and integration of data into our system. Obtaining high-quality, reliable data is crucial, and it can be sourced from diverse platforms, including public repositories such as Github, Kaggle, Machine Learning Repository, and others.

Data Cleaning

Data cleaning is the meticulous process of refining your dataset by eliminating unwanted variables and values, rectifying irregularities, and ensuring data integrity. Addressing anomalies is vital, as they can distort the dataset and compromise the accuracy of subsequent analyses. Key steps in data cleaning include:

- Handling Missing Values: Identifying and addressing missing values is pivotal for a comprehensive dataset. This involves strategies like imputation or removal of incomplete entries.
- Outlier Detection and Removal: Outliers can significantly impact statistical measures. Detecting and removing outliers contribute to a more robust dataset and accurate analysis.
- Trimming Unnecessary Rows/Columns: Streamlining the dataset by removing redundant rows or columns enhances its efficiency and reduces complexity.
- Re-Indexing and Reformatting: Adjusting the index and format of the data ensures uniformity, facilitating smoother analysis and interpretation.
- Data collection and cleaning lay the groundwork for meaningful exploratory data analysis, ensuring that subsequent insights and conclusions are based on a foundation of reliable, well-structured data.

Understand the Data

- Load the dataset into your environment.
- Examine the first few rows to get a sense of the data.

- Check basic statistics (mean, median, standard deviation) to understand the distribution of numerical features.

Handle Missing Data

- Identify missing values in the dataset.
- Decide on an appropriate strategy to handle missing data (imputation, removal, etc.).

Explore Data Types

- Check the data types of each feature (numerical, categorical, etc.).
- Ensure that data types are appropriate for each feature.

Univariate Analysis

- Analyze individual variables one at a time.
- For numerical features: plot histograms, box plots, and compute summary statistics.
- For categorical features: use bar charts to show the distribution of categories.

Bivariate Analysis

- Explore relationships between pairs of variables.
- For numerical features: use scatter plots, correlation matrices, and pair plots.
- For categorical features: use stacked bar charts, chi-square tests, etc.

Multivariate Analysis

- Explore relationships between more than two variables.
- Use techniques such as heatmaps, 3D plots, or advanced statistical methods.

Outlier Detection

- Identify and handle outliers that may affect the quality of the analysis.
- Use visualizations like box plots or statistical methods to detect outliers.

Feature Engineering

- Derive new features based on existing ones if needed.
- Transform existing features based on their distribution (e.g., log transformation).

- Encode categorical variables using techniques such as one-hot encoding.

Addressing Skewness and Transformation

- Examine the distribution of numerical features and apply transformations if necessary (e.g., log transformation).

Correlation Analysis

- Analyze correlations between features and the target variable.
- Identify multicollinearity between features (correlation between independent variables).

Explore Data Distributions

- Understand the distribution of the target variable in classification and regression problems.
- Ensure a balanced distribution for better model training.

Dimensionality Reduction

- Apply dimensionality reduction techniques (e.g., PCA) to visualize high-dimensional data.
- Identify the most relevant features.

Data Partitioning

- Split the dataset into training and testing sets for model evaluation.

Data Visualization

- Utilize various plots and charts to visualize patterns and trends.
- Matplotlib, Seaborn, and Plotly are popular libraries for data visualization.

Summary Statistics

- Compute additional summary statistics if needed.
- Use descriptive statistics to summarize key features.

Hypothesis Testing

- Formulate hypotheses about the data and test them using statistical methods.
- Identify statistically significant relationships.

Document Findings

- Document insights, patterns, and potential challenges discovered during EDA.
- Use comments, markdown, or a separate report to communicate findings.

Iterative Process

EDA is often an iterative process. As you gain insights and make decisions, you may need to revisit previous steps.

By following these steps, you can build a solid understanding of your dataset, which is crucial for making informed decisions during the subsequent stages of the machine learning pipeline.

Types of EDA

Exploratory Data Analysis (EDA) is a crucial step in data analysis, aiming to uncover patterns, identify relationships, and gain insights from datasets. Depending on the number of columns or variables we are analysing, EDA can be divided into several types.

Here are some common types of EDA techniques:

Univariate Analysis: This type of analysis focuses on examining individual variables within the dataset. It involves summarising and visualising a single variable at a time to understand its distribution, central tendency, spread, and other relevant statistics. Techniques like histograms, box plots, bar charts, and summary statistics are commonly used in univariate analysis.

Bivariate Analysis: Bivariate analysis explores the relationship between two variables. It helps discover associations, correlations, and dependencies between pairs of variables. Scatter plots, line plots, correlation matrices, and cross-tabulation are commonly used techniques in bivariate analysis.

Multivariate Analysis: Multivariate analysis extends bivariate analysis to include more than two variables. It aims to understand the complex interactions and dependencies among multiple variables in a dataset. Techniques such as heatmaps, parallel coordinates, factor analysis, and principal component analysis (PCA) are used for multivariate analysis.

Time Series Analysis: Time series analysis is applied to datasets with a temporal component. It involves analysing and modelling patterns, trends, and seasonality over time. Techniques like line plots, autocorrelation analysis, moving averages, and ARIMA models are commonly used in time series analysis.

Missing Data Analysis: Dealing with missing data is crucial in datasets, as it can affect the reliability of analysis. Missing data analysis involves identifying missing values, understanding the patterns of missingness, and employing suitable techniques to handle missing data. Techniques such as missing data patterns, imputation methods, and sensitivity analysis are employed in missing data analysis.

Outlier Analysis: Outliers are data points that significantly deviate from the general pattern of the data. Outlier analysis aims to identify and understand the presence of outliers, their potential causes, and their impact on the analysis. Techniques such as box plots, scatter plots, z-scores, and clustering algorithms are used for outlier analysis.

Data Visualisation: Data visualisation plays a vital role in EDA by creating visual representations of the data to aid understanding and exploration. Various visualisation techniques, including bar charts, histograms, scatter plots, line plots, heatmaps, and interactive dashboards, are used to represent different types of data.

These are just a few examples of the types of EDA techniques that can be employed during data analysis. The selection of methods depends on the data characteristics, research questions, and the insights sought from the analysis. EDA serves as a foundation for more advanced statistical analysis and modelling techniques.

Example P3 – U3 – D31

ML - EDA

```
# Step 1: Importing Required Libraries
import pandas as pd
import matplotlib.pyplot as plt
import seaborn as sns
import warnings
# Suppress warnings
warnings.filterwarnings('ignore')

# Step 2: Reading Dataset
# Define the file path
path = r'C:\Users\User\mraj4\Documents\Optimum\Py-lib\scikit\wine\winequality-red.csv'
# Load the dataset
df = pd.read_csv(path, sep=';')
# Replace whitespace in column names with underscores
df.columns = df.columns.str.replace(' ', '_')
print(df.head())
```

```
# Step 3: Analyzing the Data
## Data Information
print("Data Information:")
print(df.info())

## Descriptive Statistics
print("\nDescriptive Statistics:")
print(df.describe())

## Columns List
print("\nColumns List:")
print(df.columns.tolist())

## Check for Missing Values
print("\nMissing Values:")
print(df.isnull().sum())

## Check for Duplicate Values
print("\nDuplicate Values:")
print(df.duplicated().sum())

# # Step 4: Univariate Analysis
## Count Plot for Quality
quality_counts = df['quality'].value_counts()
plt.figure(figsize=(8, 6))
plt.bar(quality_counts.index, quality_counts, color='#FF1493') # Using hexadecimal
color code for dark pink
plt.title('Count Plot of Quality')
plt.xlabel('Quality')
plt.ylabel('Count')
plt.show()

# ## Kernel Density Plots
# # Set Seaborn style
sns.set_style("darkgrid")
# Identify numerical columns
numerical_columns = df.select_dtypes(include=["int64", "float64"]).columns
# Plot distribution of each numerical feature
plt.figure(figsize=(14, len(numerical_columns) * 3))
for idx, feature in enumerate(numerical_columns, 1):
    plt.subplot(len(numerical_columns), 2, idx)
    sns.histplot(df[feature], kde=True)
    plt.title(f"{feature} | Skewness: {round(df[feature].skew(), 2)}")
# Adjust layout and show plots
plt.tight_layout()
plt.show()

# ## Swarm Plot for Quality and Alcohol
```

```
plt.figure(figsize=(10, 8))
sns.swarmplot(x="quality", y="alcohol", data=df, palette='viridis')
plt.title('Swarm Plot for Quality and Alcohol')
plt.xlabel('Quality')
plt.ylabel('Alcohol')
plt.show()

# Step 5: Bivariate Analysis
# Pair Plot
plt.figure(figsize=(12, 10))
sns.pairplot(df)
plt.suptitle('Pair Plot for DataFrame', y=1.02)  # Adjust title position
plt.show()

# Violin Plot
df['quality'] = df['quality'].astype(str)  # Convert 'quality' to categorical
plt.figure(figsize=(10, 8))
sns.violinplot(x="quality", y="alcohol", data=df, palette='Pastel1', alpha=0.7)
plt.title('Violin Plot for Quality and Alcohol')
plt.xlabel('Quality')
plt.ylabel('Alcohol')
plt.show()

# Box Plot
plt.figure(figsize=(10, 8))
sns.boxplot(x='quality', y='alcohol', data=df, palette='Pastel1')
plt.title('Box Plot for Quality and Alcohol')
plt.xlabel('Quality')
plt.ylabel('Alcohol')
plt.show()

# Step 6: Multivariate Analysis
# Correlation Matrix
plt.figure(figsize=(15, 10))
# Using Seaborn to create a heatmap
sns.heatmap(df.corr(), annot=True, fmt='.2f', cmap='Pastel2', linewidths=2)
plt.title('Correlation Heatmap')
plt.show()
```

Analysing Data:

Shape: The shape attribute reveals the dimensions of the dataset, indicating the number of features (columns) and observations (rows).

Info(): The info() method provides a comprehensive insight into the dataset, including data types, the quantity of records in each column, null values, presence, data types, and memory usage.

Descriptive Statistics: Utilizing df.describe() generates statistical summaries for numerical columns. This includes count, mean, standard deviation, minimum, and quartiles, providing an overview of central tendencies and spread within the dataset.

Column Names: df.columns.tolist() converts the column names into a Python list, facilitating convenient access and manipulation of column names.

Missing Values: df.isnull().sum() checks each column for missing values and returns the sum of null values, highlighting potential data gaps.

Unique Values: The df.nunique() function calculates the number of unique values in each column, offering insights into the diversity of data within each feature.

Univariate Analysis

Apeksha asked, "What is Univariate analysis?"

Master said, "Univariate analysis involves examining individual variables to understand their distribution, central tendency, and spread. Data visualization plays a crucial role in univariate analysis as it helps in better understanding the data. The Matplotlib and Seaborn libraries are commonly used for data visualization in Python."

Matplotlib is a powerful 2D plotting library that enables the creation of basic charts to visualize data.

Seaborn is built on top of Matplotlib and provides a high-level interface for creating attractive and informative statistical graphics. It offers seamless integration with Pandas and NumPy, making it easy to work with data frames and arrays.

Univariate analysis can be performed on both numerical and categorical data.

In this example, we will use various types of plots such as swarm plots, violin plots, and count plots to visualize univariate data.

Univariate Plots

Count Plot: The count plot graph displays the distribution of wine quality ratings. It provides a visual representation of the frequency of each quality rating within the dataset.

Kernel Density Plot: The kernel density plot illustrates the skewness of each feature in the dataset. A skewness value of 0 indicates a symmetrical distribution, while values greater than 0 represent a positively skewed distribution. In a positively skewed distribution, the tail extends towards higher values, indicating the presence of outliers.

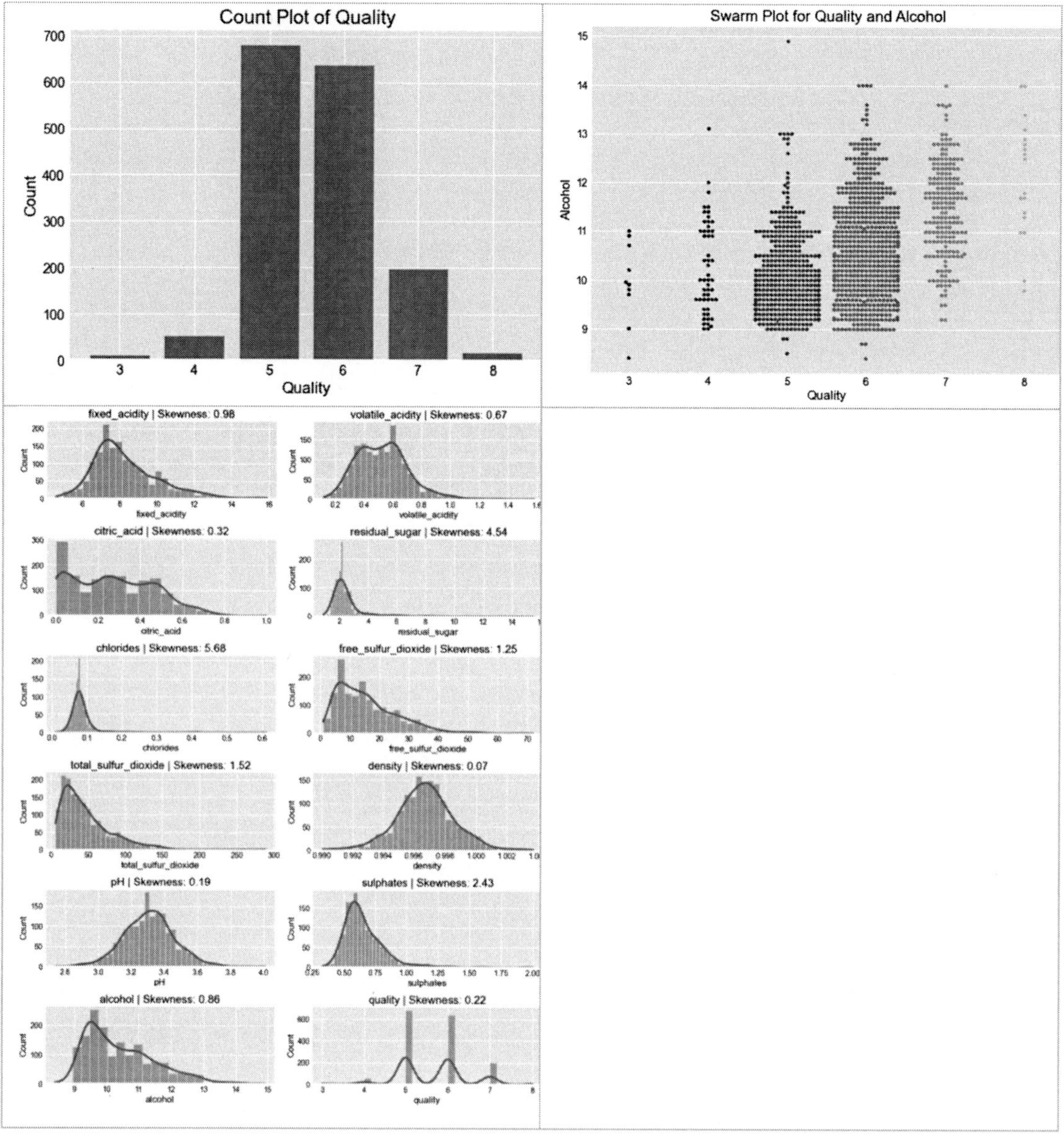

Swarm Plot: The swarm plot visualises the relationship between the 'Quality' and 'Alcohol' columns. It reveals the concentration of data points along the x-axis (Quality) and y-axis (Alcohol). Denser regions indicate where most data points cluster, while isolated points represent outliers that deviate significantly from the majority of observations.

Bivariate

Roopa asked, "What is Bivariate analysis?"

Master said, "Bivariate analysis involves examining two variables simultaneously to uncover patterns, dependencies, or interactions between them. This statistical method helps understand how changes in one variable correspond to changes in another, offering insights into their interdependence within a dataset. Various plots, such as Pair plots, violin plots, and Box plots, are commonly used for bivariate analysis."

Bivariate Plots

Pair Plot:

- Diagonal plots display histograms or kernel density plots, illustrating the distribution of individual variables.
- Scatter plots in the lower triangle exhibit the relationship between pairs of variables.
- Mirror-image scatter plots above and below the diagonal indicate symmetry.
- Centered histogram plots represent peak locations, while skewness is observed by assessing whether histograms are symmetrical or skewed.

Violin Plot Interpretation:

- Wider width implies higher density, suggesting more data points.
- Symmetrical plot indicates a balanced distribution.
- Peak or bulge signifies the most common value in the distribution.
- Longer tails indicate greater variability.
- The median line inside the violin plot represents central tendencies.

Box Plot Interpretation:

- The box represents the Interquartile Range (IQR), where a longer box indicates greater variability.
- The median line in the box indicates central tendency.
- Whiskers extend from the box to the smallest and largest values within a specified range.
- Individual points beyond the whiskers represent outliers.
- A compact box indicates low variability, while a stretched box indicates higher variability.

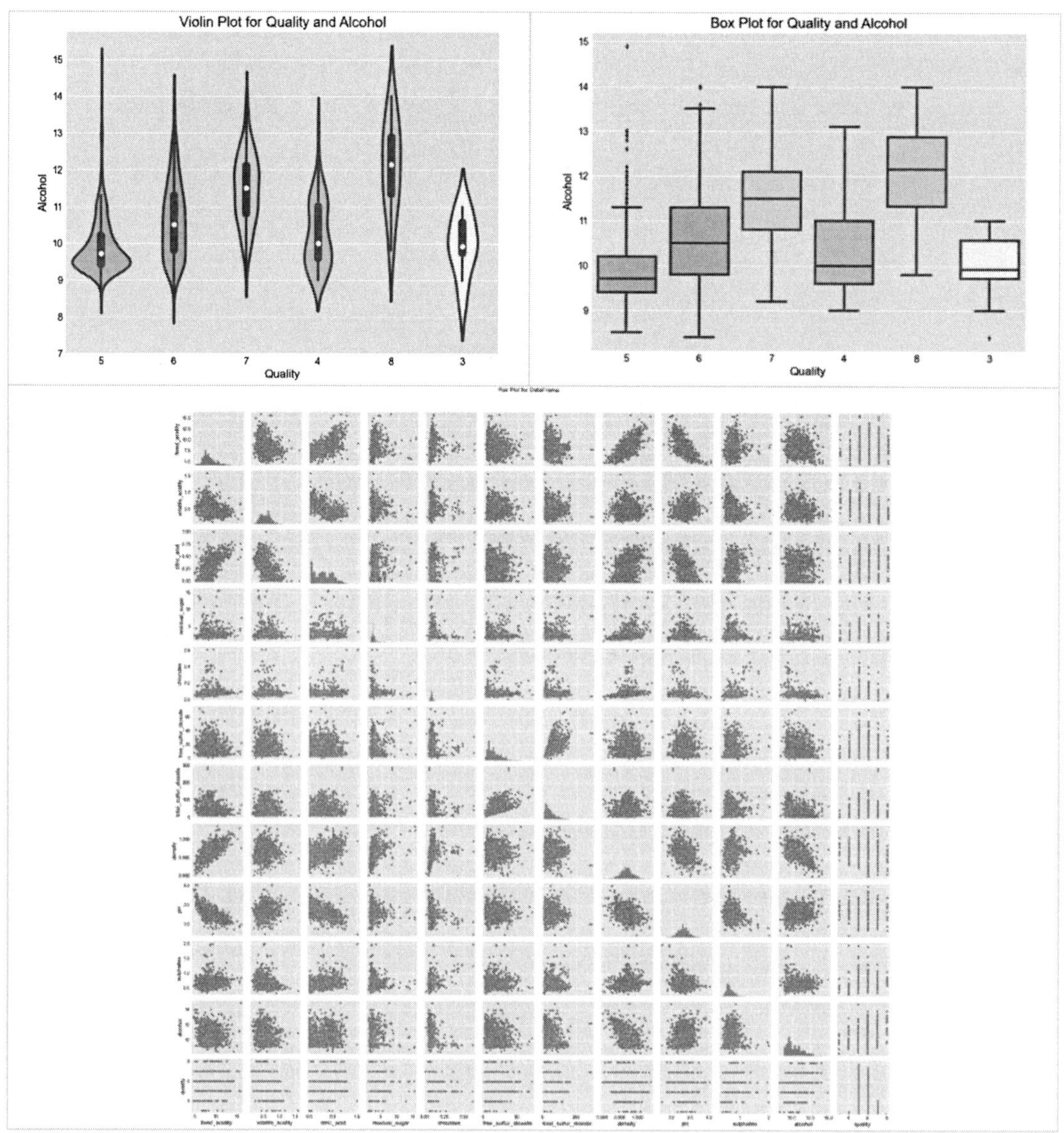

Multivariate Analysis

Master said, "Multivariate analysis delves into the interactions among three or more variables in a dataset simultaneously. It aims to offer a holistic understanding of how multiple variables collectively behave, revealing intricate patterns, relationships, and interactions between them."

Employing sophisticated statistical techniques like factor analysis, principal component analysis, and multivariate regression, multivariate analysis explores correlations and dependencies among numerous variables. This approach is instrumental in unravelling complex relationships present in multidimensional datasets.

Widely applied across diverse domains such as biology, economics, and marketing, multivariate analysis facilitates deep insights and empowers decision-makers to make well-informed judgments based on the nuanced relationships discovered in multidimensional datasets.

Multivariate Plot

For instance, a correlation matrix plot is a useful tool in multivariate analysis, allowing visual exploration of correlations between multiple variables simultaneously.

Correlation Heatmap

	fixed_acidity	volatile_acidity	citric_acid	residual_sugar	chlorides	free_sulfur_dioxide	total_sulfur_dioxide	density	pH	sulphates	alcohol	quality
fixed_acidity	1.00	-0.26	0.67	0.11	0.09	-0.15	-0.11	0.67	-0.68	0.18	-0.06	0.12
volatile_acidity	-0.26	1.00	-0.55	0.00	0.06	-0.01	0.08	0.02	0.23	-0.26	-0.20	-0.39
citric_acid	0.67	-0.55	1.00	0.14	0.20	-0.06	0.04	0.36	-0.54	0.31	0.11	0.23
residual_sugar	0.11	0.00	0.14	1.00	0.06	0.19	0.20	0.36	-0.09	0.01	0.04	0.01
chlorides	0.09	0.06	0.20	0.06	1.00	0.01	0.05	0.20	-0.27	0.37	-0.22	-0.13
free_sulfur_dioxide	-0.15	-0.01	-0.06	0.19	0.01	1.00	0.67	-0.02	0.07	0.05	-0.07	-0.05
total_sulfur_dioxide	-0.11	0.08	0.04	0.20	0.05	0.67	1.00	0.07	-0.07	0.04	-0.21	-0.19
density	0.67	0.02	0.36	0.36	0.20	-0.02	0.07	1.00	-0.34	0.15	-0.50	-0.17
pH	-0.68	0.23	-0.54	-0.09	-0.27	0.07	-0.07	-0.34	1.00	-0.20	0.21	-0.06
sulphates	0.18	-0.26	0.31	0.01	0.37	0.05	0.04	0.15	-0.20	1.00	0.09	0.25
alcohol	-0.06	-0.20	0.11	0.04	-0.22	-0.07	-0.21	-0.50	0.21	0.09	1.00	0.48
quality	0.12	-0.39	0.23	0.01	-0.13	-0.05	-0.19	-0.17	-0.06	0.25	0.48	1.00

Summary:

This unit delves deeply into Exploratory Data Analysis (EDA), a pivotal phase in the data analysis process designed to extract insights and comprehend the underlying patterns and connections within a dataset.

The module commences by elucidating the concept of EDA and its significance in unveiling crucial trends, patterns, and irregularities within the data. It covers an array of EDA techniques, encompassing graphical methods, statistical summaries, and hypothesis testing.

The first facet of EDA explored is univariate analysis, which scrutinizes the distribution and attributes of individual variables in isolation. Techniques such as count plots, Kernel density plots, Swarm plots, and summary statistics are employed to discern the central tendency, dispersion, and shape of the data.

Bivariate analysis broadens the exploration to examine relationships between pairs of variables, with the goal of revealing correlations, associations, and dependencies. Visualizations like Pair Plots, Violin Plots, and Box Plots are leveraged to visualize and analyse these relationships.

Multivariate analysis extends the analysis to investigate relationships among multiple variables concurrently. Techniques such as correlation matrix plots, factor analysis, and cluster analysis are utilised to detect patterns, clusters, and latent structures within the dataset.

Throughout the unit, practical examples and case studies are utilised to demonstrate the application of EDA techniques in real-world scenarios. By the conclusion of the module, learners acquire a comprehensive understanding of the diverse forms of EDA and the tools and methodologies available for proficiently analysing and interpreting data.

PART THREE

DAY EIGHT

Unit 3 - Lesson Six

Feature Scaling and Engineering

Feature Scaling and Engineering

Master said, "Feature engineering stands as a critical process in data science and machine learning, entailing the transformation of raw data into a format better suited for model training. The objective is to craft informative, pertinent, and efficient features that enhance the performance of machine learning models. Proficient feature engineering can yield superior model accuracy, interpretability, and generalization."

Below are the steps typically involved in feature engineering:

Understanding the Domain

- Gain a deep understanding of the problem domain and the context of the data.
- Identify the business or scientific goals to inform feature selection.

Handle Missing Values

- Address missing values in the dataset using techniques like imputation, deletion, or interpolation.
- Consider creating new features to capture information about missingness.

Encoding Categorical Variables

- Convert categorical variables into a numerical format using techniques like one-hot encoding or label encoding.

- Create binary or dummy variables to represent categorical information.

Creating Interaction Features

- Generate new features by combining or interacting existing features.
- For example, for a dataset with 'length' and 'width' columns, you could create a new feature 'area' by multiplying them.

Handle Outliers

- Identify and handle outliers in the dataset, either by removing them or transforming the feature distribution.
- Use robust statistics or transformations like log scaling to mitigate the impact of outliers.

Deal with Skewed Distributions

- Transform skewed distributions using mathematical transformations such as logarithmic or square root transformations.
- This helps in normalizing the distribution of the features.

Binning and Discretization

- Convert continuous variables into discrete categories by binning or discretization.
- This can help capture non-linear relationships and patterns.

Scale Features

- Standardize or normalize numerical features to ensure that they are on a similar scale.
- Scaling is important for algorithms sensitive to the magnitude of features, such as gradient-based optimization methods.

Create Interaction Terms

- Generate new features by combining or interacting existing features.
- For example, create product terms or ratios between features.

Polynomial Features

- Introduce polynomial features by squaring or cubing existing features.

- This is particularly useful when relationships are non-linear.

Time-Based Features

- Extract time-related information (e.g., day of the week, month, season) from timestamp features.
- Create lag features to capture temporal dependencies.

Domain-Specific Features

- Incorporate domain-specific knowledge to create features that are relevant to the problem at hand.
- Leverage external data sources to enhance feature sets.

Dimensionality Reduction

- Utilise dimensionality reduction techniques, such as Principal Component Analysis (PCA), to decrease the number of features while retaining pertinent information.

Feature Selection

- Use techniques like recursive feature elimination or feature importance scores to select the most relevant features.
- Remove redundant or irrelevant features that do not contribute significantly to the model's performance.

Check for Multicollinearity

- Assess multicollinearity between features to ensure that they are not highly correlated, as it can impact model interpretability.
- Use correlation matrices or variance inflation factor (VIF) analysis.

Iterate and Experiment

- Feature engineering is an iterative process. Experimenting with various transformations and combinations of features is essential.
- Evaluate the impact of feature engineering on model performance through cross-validation.

Transformations

- Apply mathematical transformations to the data, such as logarithmic or square root transformations.

- Transformation can help stabilize variance and make the data more suitable for certain models.

Scaling and Normalization

- Scale numerical features to a similar range to avoid biasing machine learning models toward features with larger magnitudes.
- Common techniques include Min-Max scaling or Z-score normalization.

Feature Extraction

- Extract relevant information from existing features to reduce dimensionality.
- Techniques like Principal Component Analysis (PCA) or Singular Value Decomposition (SVD) can be used for feature extraction.

Time-based Features

- If dealing with time-series data, extract features such as day of the week, month, or year.
- Create lag features to capture historical trends.

Text Data Processing

- For text data, perform text processing techniques such as tokenization, stemming, and vectorization.
- Convert text data into numerical format suitable for machine learning models.

Domain-specific Features

- Introduce features based on domain knowledge or external information that can enhance model performance.
- Incorporate relevant features that might impact the target variable.

Cross-validation

- Use cross-validation to assess the impact of feature engineering on model performance.
- Evaluate different feature sets and transformations to find the most effective combination.

Iterative Process

- Feature engineering is often an iterative process. As you build models and evaluate performance, you may discover the need for additional or different features.

Documentation and Communication

- Document the feature engineering process, including the rationale behind each transformation.

- Communicate findings and decisions to stakeholders and team members.

Keep in mind that the success of a machine learning model heavily relies on the quality of its features. Thoughtful and informed feature engineering can markedly enhance the overall performance of your models.

Feature Scaling and Engineering

Feature Engineering encompasses four essential components:

Feature Transformation: This involves refining features to prepare them for utilisation in machine learning algorithms. Feature transformation is further divided into:

- Feature Scaling: Normalising the scale of features to ensure uniform contribution to the model and mitigate dominance by those with larger values.

- Missing Value Imputation: Addressing missing data by filling in or estimating values.

- Encoding Categorical and Numerical Data: Converting categorical and numerical data into a format suitable for analysis and modelling.

- Outlier Handling: Managing outliers to prevent them from skewing the analysis or model results.

Feature Construction: This stage involves creating new features from existing ones or combining features to extract more relevant information for modelling.

Feature Selection: Selecting the most pertinent features to improve model performance, reduce dimensionality, and enhance interpretability.

Feature Extraction: Extracting essential information from raw features to represent data more effectively for modelling purposes.

In the realm of Feature Scaling, we apply preprocessing techniques to ensure uniformity across features. Commonly used methods include:

- Standardisation: Scaling features to have a mean of 0 and a standard deviation of 1, facilitating comparisons between features.

- Normalisation: Rescaling features to a common range, often between 0 and 1, preserving the relative relationships between feature values.

By comprehensively addressing each aspect of feature engineering, we enhance the quality and effectiveness of our machine learning models.

Feature Engineering Analogy

Master said, "Feature engineering is a crucial step in the machine learning pipeline, where we transform raw data into meaningful features that facilitate model learning and prediction."

Feature selection can be likened to selecting ingredients from a well-stocked kitchen to make a pizza. Just as we choose only the essential items like flour, yeast, and cheese, feature selection involves identifying and retaining only the most relevant features for model training and prediction.

Feature transformation is akin to preparing ingredients before cooking. For example, chopping onions and tomatoes makes them more manageable for cooking. Similarly, feature transformation involves modifying and scaling existing features to improve model performance. Techniques like log normalization and standard scaling are commonly used for this purpose.

Feature construction and extraction is comparable to creating a new sauce from various ingredients. By combining olive oil, garlic, tomatoes, and spices, we create something new and flavourful. Similarly, feature extraction involves generating new features from existing ones to capture additional information and improve model accuracy. Techniques like principal component analysis (PCA) and polynomial feature expansion are examples of feature extraction methods used in machine learning.

Overall, feature engineering plays a vital role in building accurate and robust machine learning models by transforming raw data into informative features that enhance model performance and predictive capabilities.

Feature scaling

Nikash asked, "What is feature scaling?"

Master said, "Feature scaling is a preprocessing technique used in machine learning to standardize or normalize the range of features in the dataset. It ensures that all features contribute equally to the analysis and prevents features with larger scales from dominating the model training process."

Example:

Imagine you have a dataset comprising 3000 individuals, each characterized by three independent features: Age, Salary, and the number of bedrooms in their apartment. Each data point is labelled as either "YES" or "NO," indicating whether the individual can buy a property based on these features.

The goal is to train a model capable of predicting whether someone can purchase a property given their feature values. Once trained, the model creates an N-dimensional graph, where N represents the number of features in the dataset. This graph visually represents how the model categorises data points.

In the graph, star data points denote individuals labelled as "YES" (indicating they can buy the property), while circles represent those labelled as "NO" (indicating they cannot). The model learns from these labelled data points during training.

Now, imagine a new data point, represented by a diamond in the graph, with different feature values for Age, Salary, and the number of bedrooms in their apartment. The model's task is to predict whether this data point belongs to the "YES" or "NO" class based on its feature values.

By training the model on labelled data and evaluating its performance, we enable it to make informed predictions on new, unseen data, helping individuals assess their likelihood of property ownership based on their unique circumstances.

When confronted with datasets featuring disparate ranges, units of measurement, or orders of magnitude across its features, employing feature scaling becomes indispensable. Failure to address such discrepancies can introduce biases into model performance or impede the learning process.

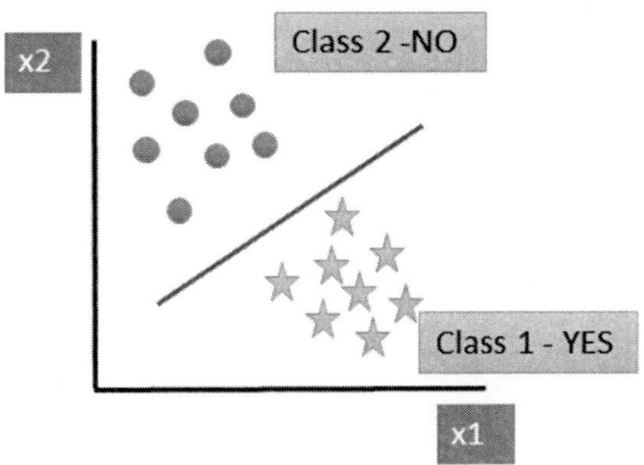

Commonly used techniques for feature scaling, including standardization, normalization, and min-max scaling, offer effective remedies. These methods adjust feature values while preserving their relative relationships and distributions.

Feature scaling plays a crucial role in transforming the dataset's features onto a more uniform scale. This transformation not only simplifies the task of building machine learning models but also ensures their accuracy and efficacy. By bringing features onto a consistent scale, scaling enables meaningful comparisons between them, aids model convergence, and prevents any single feature from unduly influencing model outcomes based solely on its magnitude.

In essence, feature scaling acts as a vital preparatory step in the machine learning pipeline, fostering robust and reliable model development by harmonising the disparate characteristics of dataset features.

Certain machine learning algorithms exhibit sensitivity to feature scaling, while others remain largely unaffected.

Gradient Descent-Based Algorithms:

Algorithms such as linear regression, logistic regression, neural networks, and PCA, which leverage gradient descent for optimisation, necessitate feature scaling. In gradient descent, the step size of the descent is influenced by the feature values. The varying ranges of features can result in disparate step sizes for each feature, potentially hindering the convergence of the optimisation process. To ensure smooth progress towards the minima and uniform updates across all features, it's essential to scale the data before feeding it into the model.

Distance-Based Algorithms:

Algorithms like KNN, K-means clustering, and SVM are profoundly influenced by the range of features. These algorithms rely on computing distances between data points to gauge their similarity. Variations in feature ranges can significantly impact distance computations, leading to skewed assessments of similarity and potentially undermining algorithm performance.

Tree-Based Algorithms:

Conversely, tree-based algorithms, such as decision trees and random forests, exhibit remarkable insensitivity to feature scaling. In a decision tree, each node's split is based on a single feature, aiming to enhance the node's homogeneity. Since decision trees focus solely on optimising splits based on individual features, the scale of other features has negligible impact on the splitting process. Consequently, tree-based algorithms remain invariant to the scale of features, simplifying the modelling process and offering robust performance across diverse datasets.

Understanding the impact of feature scaling on different algorithms aids in selecting appropriate preprocessing techniques, thereby optimising model performance and ensuring reliable outcomes across various machine learning tasks.

Distance-Based Algorithms

Feature scaling is particularly important for algorithms that rely on distance measures, such as K-nearest neighbors (KNN) and support vector machines (SVM).

When predicting the class of a new data point, the model employs distance calculations from the centroids of each class group. The data point is assigned to the class with the minimum centroid distance.

Distances between the centroid and data point can be computed using various methods:

Minkowski Distance: The Minkowski distance encompasses both Euclidean and Manhattan distances as special cases. When the parameter 'r' is set to 2, it mirrors the formula for Euclidean distance, while 'r' set to 1 yields the formula for Manhattan distance.

Minkowski Distance = $\left(\sum_{i=1}^{n}(|x_i - y_i|)^r\right)^{\frac{1}{r}}$

These distance measures enable the model to assess the similarity between the new data point and the centroids of each class, facilitating accurate classification. Choosing the appropriate distance measure depends on the dataset characteristics and the desired behaviour of the model.

Usage:

- K-Nearest Neighbors (KNN)
- K-Means Clustering
- Recommender Systems

In order to identify the nearest points or groups for a query point in the KNN algorithm, appropriate distance metrics are essential. Here are some commonly used distance metrics:

Euclidean Distance (L2 Norm): This metric calculates the Cartesian distance between two points in a plane or hyperplane. Visualised as the straight-line length joining the two points, it aids in measuring the net displacement between the two states of an object.

Euclidean Distance = $\left(\sum_{i=1}^{n}(|x_i - y_i|)^2\right)^{\frac{1}{2}} = \sqrt{(x_2 - x_1)^2 + (y_2 - y_1)^2}$

d(x,y) = $\sqrt[r]{\sum_{k=1}^{n}(x_k - y_k)^r}$

Here, x represents the data point's value, y represents the centroid's value, k signifies the number of feature values, and r denotes the chosen exponent. For instance, in a dataset with k=3 features, Euclidean distance can be computed.

Manhattan Distance (L1 Norm): Manhattan Distance is preferred when the focus is on the total distance travelled by an object rather than just its displacement. It is computed by summing the absolute differences between the coordinates of the points across multiple dimensions.

Manhattan Distance = $\left(\sum_{i=1}^{n}(|x_i - y_i|)^1\right)^{\frac{1}{1}}$ = |x2−x1|+|y2−y1|

d(x,y) = $\sum_{k=1}^{n} |x_k - y_k|$

In this formula, x and y represent the data point and centroid values, respectively, k denotes the number of features, and n represents the total number of features.

Cosine Similarity:

Measures the cosine of the angle between two vectors.

Formula:

$$\cos(\theta) = \frac{\sum_{i=1}^{N} P_i Q_i}{\sum_{i=1}^{N} P_i^2 \sum_{i=1}^{N} Q_i^2}$$

Cosine Distance:

Derived from cosine similarity.

Formula:

$1-\cos(\theta)$

Other Distance Measures

Chebyshev Distance:

Measures the maximum absolute difference between coordinates.

Formula:

$\max_i(|p_i - q_i|)$

Hamming Distance:

Measures the number of positions at which the corresponding symbols are different.

Commonly used for categorical data and binary strings.

Formula:

$\sum_{i=1}^{N} \mathbf{1}(p_i \neq q_i)$, where 1 is the indicator function.

Jaccard Distance:

Measures dissimilarity between two sets.

Formula:

$$1 - \frac{|A \cap B|}{|A \cup B|}$$

Mahalanobis Distance:

Measures the distance between a point and a distribution.

Accounts for correlations between variables.

Formula:

$D_M(p,q) = \sqrt{(p-q)^T S^{-1} (p-q)}$, where S is the covariance matrix.

In the given dataset, three independent features are present: age, salary, and the number of bedrooms in the apartment (BHK). Each feature operates within its respective range: age spans from 10 to 50, salary ranges from 40,000 to 100,000 dollars, and bedrooms vary from 1 to 5.

Example: Suppose the centroid of class 1, representing individuals who can buy the property, is [40, 60,000, 3]. Meanwhile, we have a data point to predict: [47, 65000, 2]. Employing the Manhattan distance method, we calculate the distance between this data point and the centroid:

Distance = (|40−47|+|60,000−65,000|+|3−2|)

We observe that the salary feature significantly influences the distance calculation, potentially overshadowing the impact of the other features. This dominance occurs because each feature operates on a different scale, and their magnitudes are not comparable. In essence, salary might exert undue influence on the prediction, overshadowing age and bedrooms.

This lack of uniformity among feature scales can lead to inaccurate predictions, as demonstrated in this scenario. Since features are independent, with no inherent relationship between age, salary, and bedrooms, a model that doesn't account for feature scaling may consistently predict incorrectly.

The straightforward remedy to this issue is Feature Scaling. By employing Feature Scaling algorithms, such as scaling features to a fixed range like [-1, 1] or [0, 1], we bring all features to a comparable scale. Consequently, no single feature can dominate others, ensuring a more balanced influence of each feature on the prediction of outcome. This approach enhances the model's accuracy and reliability, enabling it to make more precise predictions even when features operate on disparate scales.

Common Techniques for Feature scaling and Normalization

The significance of Feature Scaling and Normalisation lies in their pivotal roles in ensuring robust and unbiased machine learning outcomes.

Preventing Biased Learning: Certain machine learning algorithms are inherently sensitive to feature scales. When left unaddressed, features with larger magnitudes may unduly influence the learning process, potentially biasing the model towards those dominant features. By scaling features, we mitigate this bias, enabling the model to consider all features on an equal footing, thus fostering more balanced and accurate predictions.

Improving Convergence: Scaling plays a crucial role in expediting the convergence of gradient-based optimisation algorithms, such as gradient descent. By bringing features onto a comparable scale, scaling facilitates smoother and more efficient optimisation, reducing the likelihood of oscillations or slow convergence. This acceleration in convergence enhances the efficiency and effectiveness of the learning process, enabling models to reach optimal solutions more rapidly.

Ensuring Fair Comparisons: Scaling features enables fair and meaningful comparisons across different units or measurement scales present in the dataset. Without normalisation, variations in feature scales could lead to skewed interpretations of feature importance or misleading comparisons between features. By standardising feature scales, we ensure that each feature contributes proportionally to the model's learning process, preserving the integrity of comparisons and facilitating accurate assessments of feature relevance.

Min-Max Scaling (Normalization)

Min-max scaling is a popular normalization technique that rescales features to a predetermined range, usually between 0 and 1.

Formula:

```
Xscaled = ( X−Xmin) / (Xmax – Xmin)
```

where X represents the original feature value, Xscaled denotes the scaled feature value, Xmin is the minimum value of X, and Xmax is the maximum value of X.

This scaling method involves a simple two-step process:

- Find the minimum and maximum values within the column.
- Subtract the minimum value from each entry and divide the result by the difference between the maximum and minimum values.

Min-max scaling is particularly suitable for features with a bounded range and no significant outliers. It ensures that all feature values are transformed to a common scale, with the minimum value in the original dataset mapped to 0 and the maximum value mapped to 1. The remaining values are linearly scaled within this range, preserving their relative relationships while normalizing their magnitudes.

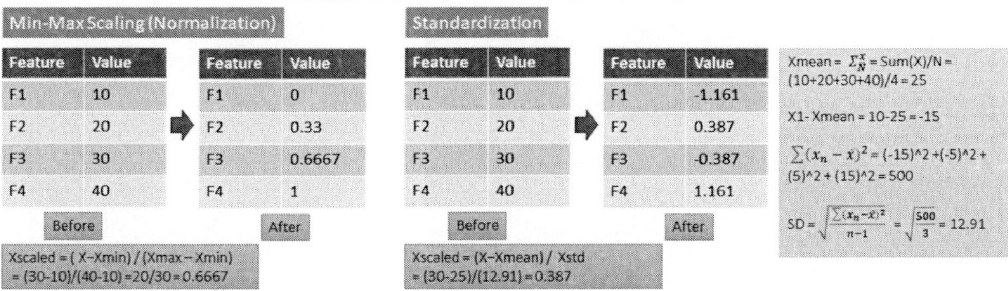

Mean Normalization:

Mean normalization, is indeed similar to the min-max scaling method. However, instead of subtracting each entry by the minimum value and dividing by the range (maximum - minimum), we subtract each entry by the mean value of the entire dataset and then divide by the range.

Formula:

Xscaled = (X−Xmean) / (Xmax – Xmin)

The steps for mean normalization are as follows:

- Calculate the mean (average) of the entire dataset.
- Subtract the mean from each entry in the dataset.
- Divide the result by the range, which is the difference between the maximum and

minimum values in the dataset.

This method ensures that the scaled values are centered around zero (since we subtract the mean) and rescaled based on the variability of the entire dataset (since we divide by the range).

In summary, mean normalization provides a way to scale features to a similar range as min-max scaling, but with the added benefit of centering the values around the mean of the dataset.

Standardization (Z-score Scaling)

Standardization, also known as Z-score scaling, is a widely used technique that transforms features to have a zero mean and unit variance.

Formula:

$$X\text{scaled} = (X - X\text{mean}) \ / \ X\text{std}$$

where X represents the original feature value, Xscaled denotes the scaled feature value, Xmean is the mean of X, and Xstd is the standard deviation of X.

This method is particularly suitable for features with unknown or non-normal distributions. It standardizes feature scales, making them comparable across different features and datasets, irrespective of their original distributions.

This scaling method relies on the statistical properties of the data, particularly its central tendencies and variance.

First, we calculate the mean and standard deviation of the data that we intend to normalize. Next, we subtract the mean value from each entry and divide the result by the standard deviation.

This process ensures that the distribution of the data conforms to a standard normal distribution, particularly beneficial if the original distribution is skewed. By subtracting the mean and dividing by the standard deviation, we centre the data around a mean of zero and scale it to have a standard deviation of 1.

Robust Scaling

Robust Scaling, also known as Median Scaling or IQR Scaling, offers a robust method for rescaling features by leveraging statistical measures that are less sensitive to outliers.

$$X\text{scaled} = (X - X\text{median}) \ / \ \text{IQR}$$

where X represents the original feature value, Xscaled denotes the scaled feature value, Xmedian is the median of X, and IQR is the interquartile range.

This scaling technique relies on two fundamental statistical measures:

- Median: The median represents the middle value of the dataset when arranged in ascending order. Unlike the mean, the median is less influenced by outliers, making it a robust measure of central tendency.
- Interquartile Range (IQR): The IQR is a measure of statistical dispersion, representing the range between the first quartile (25th percentile) and the third quartile (75th percentile) of the dataset. It provides insight into the spread of the middle 50% of the data, offering robustness against outliers.

To apply Robust Scaling, we subtract the median from each feature value and then divide the result by the interquartile range. This process ensures that the scaled feature values are centered around zero and scaled proportionally based on the variability within the middle 50% of the dataset.

By utilising robust statistical measures, Robust Scaling offers resilience against outliers while effectively standardising feature scales. This makes it particularly suitable for datasets containing skewed or heavily tailed distributions, where traditional scaling methods may yield biased results.

Robust Scaling

Before

Feature	Value
F1	10
F2	20
F3	30
F4	40

After

Feature	Value
F1	-0.75
F2	-0.25
F3	0.025
F4	0.75

*X*scaled = (*X*−*X*median) / IQR
*X*median = (20+30)/2 =25
IQR = Difference between 75th Percentile (Q3) and the 25th Percentile
Q1 = 15 and Q3 = 35
IQR = Q3−Q1 = 35-15 =20

Log Transformation

Before

Feature	Value
F1	10
F2	20
F3	30
F4	40

After

Feature	Value
F1	1
F2	1.301
F3	1.477
F4	1.602

With Base $\mathbf{Log_{10}}$ **(10)**

Log Transformation

Log Transformation is a powerful technique that applies the logarithm function to features, effectively normalizing skewed distributions and enhancing the interpretability of the data.

This method is particularly beneficial for features exhibiting highly skewed or long-tailed distributions, where traditional scaling techniques may not suffice. By taking the logarithm of each value in the dataset, typically with base 10, Log Transformation compresses large values and expands smaller ones, leading to a more symmetrical distribution.

The logarithmic scale produced by this transformation offers several advantages:

- Normalization of Skewed Distributions: Log Transformation helps mitigate the effects of skewness by spreading out extreme values and compressing the range of large values, resulting in a more symmetric distribution.
- Equalization of Variances: It stabilises the variance across different parts of the dataset, making the data more homoscedastic and suitable for linear modelling assumptions.
- Enhanced Interpretability: Log-transformed data often better aligns with human perception and intuition, facilitating easier interpretation and analysis.
- Reduction of Outlier Influence: Extreme values are compressed, reducing their impact on statistical analyses and model fitting.

By leveraging the logarithm function, Log Transformation offers a versatile approach to preprocessing skewed data, improving the performance and robustness of subsequent analyses and machine learning models.

Example P3 – U3 – D32	
ML	**Output**

import pandas as pd
import numpy as np
from sklearn.preprocessing import MinMaxScaler, Normalizer, StandardScaler, RobustScaler
 	
# Step 1: Reading Dataset 	
# Define the file path 	
path = r'C:\Users\User\mraj4\Documents\Optimum\Py-lib\scikit\feature.csv'
# Load the dataset 	
df = pd.read_csv(path)
print(df.head())
 	
# Log Transformation 	
log_transformed = np.log(df + 1) # Adding 1 to avoid log(0)
print("Log Transformation:", log_transformed.head())
 	
# Absolute Maximum Scaling 	
max_vals = np.max(np.abs(df))
scaled_max_abs = (df - max_vals) / max_vals
print("Absolute Maximum Scaling:", scaled_max_abs.head())
 	
# Min-Max Scaling 	
scaler = MinMaxScaler()
scaled_min_max = scaler.fit_transform(df)
scaled_df = pd.DataFrame(scaled_min_max, columns=df.columns)
print("Min-Max Scaling:", scaled_df.head())
 	
# Normalization 	
scaler = Normalizer()
scaled_normalization = scaler.fit_transform(df)
scaled_df = pd.DataFrame(scaled_normalization, columns=df.columns)
print("Normalization Scaling:", scaled_df.head())
 	
# Standardization 	
	Lot_area SubClass
	0 8450 60
	1 9600 20
	2 11250 60
	Log Transformation: Lot_area SubClass
	0 9.042040 4.110874
	1 9.169623 3.044522
	2 9.328212 4.110874
	Absolute Maximum Scaling:
	Lot_area SubClass
	0 -0.960742 -0.999721
	1 -0.955400 -0.999907
	2 -0.947734 -0.999721
	Min-Max Scaling: Lot_area SubClass
	0 0.033420 0.235294
	1 0.038795 0.000000
	2 0.046507 0.235294
	Normalization Scaling: Lot_area SubClass
	0 0.999975 0.007100
	1 0.999998 0.002083
	2 0.999986 0.005333
	Standardization Scaling:
	Lot_area SubClass
	0 -0.207142 0.073375
	1 -0.091886 -0.872563
	2 0.073480 0.073375
	Robust Scaler Scaling: Lot_area SubClass
	0 -0.254076 0.2
	1 0.030015 -0.6
	2 0.437624 0.2

```
scaler = StandardScaler()
scaled_standardization = scaler.fit_transform(df)
scaled_df = pd.DataFrame(scaled_standardization,
columns=df.columns)
print("Standardization Scaling:", scaled_df.head())

# Robust Scaler
scaler = RobustScaler()
scaled_robust = scaler.fit_transform(df)
scaled_df = pd.DataFrame(scaled_robust,
columns=df.columns)
print("Robust Scaler Scaling:", scaled_df.head())
```

Encoding:

In machine learning, encoding is the process of representing categorical data (data that can take on a limited, and usually fixed, number of values) in a numerical format. One-hot encoding is one of the popular techniques for this purpose, but there are other encoding methods as well. Here are some different types of encoding techniques used in machine learning:

One-Hot Encoding

Description: Converts categorical variables into binary vectors.

How it works: Each category is represented by a binary vector, and only the index corresponding to the category is marked as 1, while all others are 0.

Color	Red	Blue	Green
Red	1	0	0
Blue	o	1	0
Green	0	0	1

Label Encoding

Description: Assigns a unique numerical label to each category.

How it works: Categories are mapped to integers based on their order of appearance.

Color	Label
Red	0
Blue	1
Green	2

Ordinal Encoding

Description: Assigns numerical values to categories based on their ordinal relationship.

How it works: The order of categories is considered, and each category is assigned a corresponding numerical value.

Size	Ordinal Encoding
Small	1
Medium	2
Large	3

Binary Encoding

Description: Converts categories into binary code.

How it works: Categories are first converted to numerical values and then represented in binary.

Color	Binary Encoding
Red	001
Blue	010
Green	100

Frequency Encoding

Description: Assigns frequencies of categories as their numerical representation.

How it works: Categories are replaced with their respective frequencies in the dataset.

Color	Frequency Encoding
Red	2
Blue	3
Green	1

Dummy Variable

Master said, "In statistics and econometrics, a dummy variable (or indicator variable) is used to represent categorical data numerically. It is often employed to incorporate qualitative data, such as gender, region, or any other characteristic that can be categorized into distinct groups, into regression models."

For a binary categorical variable (taking values 0 or 1), a dummy variable is created to represent the two categories. For instance, if we have a variable X representing gender, we might create a dummy variable D such that:

- 1 if the individual is female
- 0 if the individual is male

This allows us to include gender as a factor in regression analysis.

Dummy Variable Trap

The dummy variable trap refers to a situation where two or more dummy variables are highly correlated. It occurs when one dummy variable can be accurately predicted from the others. This can lead to multicollinearity issues in regression analysis, where the independent variables are highly correlated.

The trap specifically arises when a set of dummy variables includes a constant term, and the summation of these dummy variables equals the constant term. For example, consider two dummy variables D_1 and D_2 representing gender:

$$D_1+D_2=1$$

Here, if $D_1=1$, then D_2 must be 0 (and vice versa) to satisfy the equation. This perfect multicollinearity can cause problems in regression analysis because the variables are perfectly correlated, making it impossible to uniquely determine the effect of each dummy variable.

To avoid the dummy variable trap, it's common to exclude one of the dummy variables. For instance, if you have 'k' categories, you might include only 'k−1' dummy variables. This is known as "dropping one level" and helps prevent multicollinearity while still capturing the necessary information about the categories.

Summary:

This unit delves into the realm of Feature Scaling and Engineering, a crucial aspect of data preprocessing aimed at optimising the performance of machine learning algorithms by transforming and selecting relevant features.

The module begins by elucidating the significance of Feature Scaling and Engineering in preparing data for machine learning tasks. It covers various techniques, such as Feature Transformation, Construction, Selection, and Extraction, which play a pivotal role in enhancing the quality and effectiveness of features used in predictive modelling.

Feature Scaling, a fundamental preprocessing step, is explored in detail. It encompasses Gradient Descent-Based, Distance-Based, and Tree-Based Algorithms, elucidating their role in scaling features to a uniform range to facilitate the convergence of optimisation algorithms and improve model performance.

The unit also covers common techniques for Feature Scaling and Normalization, including Min-Max Scaling (Normalization), Mean Normalization, Standardization (Z-score Scaling), Robust

Scaling, and Log Transformation. Each technique is explained in-depth, along with its applications and considerations.

Encoding, another critical aspect of Feature Engineering, is discussed extensively. Techniques such as One-Hot Encoding, Label Encoding, Binary Encoding, and Frequency Encoding are explored, shedding light on their usage for converting categorical variables into numerical representations suitable for machine learning algorithms.

Furthermore, the concept of Dummy Variables and the associated Dummy Variable Trap are elucidated to prevent multicollinearity issues arising from categorical variables with multiple levels.

Throughout the unit, practical examples and case studies are provided to illustrate the application of feature scaling, engineering, and encoding techniques in real-world scenarios. By the conclusion of the module, learners acquire a comprehensive understanding of feature preprocessing methods essential for building robust and efficient machine learning models.

PART THREE

DAY EIGHT

Unit 3 - Lesson Seven

IMBALANCED Dataset

Akanksh asked, "What is an Imbalanced Dataset?"

Master said, "An imbalanced dataset occurs when the distribution of classes within the dataset is skewed, meaning one class (typically the minority class) is significantly less represented than the other class (majority class). For instance, if you're predicting between Category-A and Category-B, and Category-A has a much larger number of instances compared to Category-B, you have an imbalanced dataset."

In an imbalanced dataset, machine learning models tend to be biased towards the majority class, leading to poor performance in predicting the minority class. For example, if Category-A constitutes 90% of the dataset and Category-B only 10%, a model might achieve high accuracy by simply predicting all instances as Category-A, yet fail to correctly predict instances of Category-B.

Akanksh asked, "How can we address this issue?"

SMOTE (Synthetic Minority Over-sampling Technique):

- SMOTE is an oversampling technique that addresses class imbalance by creating synthetic samples of the minority class.
- It works by generating synthetic instances that are similar to existing minority class instances, effectively balancing the class distribution.
- SMOTE helps prevent model bias towards the majority class by ensuring equal representation of both classes.

NearMiss:

- NearMiss is an undersampling technique used to balance class distribution by reducing the number of instances in the majority class.
- Unlike SMOTE, NearMiss selects instances from the majority class based on their proximity to minority class instances.
- By reducing the number of majority class instances, NearMiss aims to make the dataset more balanced, enabling the model to better capture patterns in the minority class.

In summary, addressing imbalanced datasets requires techniques like SMOTE for oversampling or NearMiss for undersampling to ensure that machine learning models can effectively learn from both classes without being biased towards the majority class.

Resampling Techniques

Master said, "Resampling is a widely adopted approach for addressing highly unbalanced datasets, where samples are either removed from the majority class (under-sampling) or added to the minority class (over-sampling) to achieve better class balance."

While resampling techniques offer the advantage of balancing classes, they also come with their drawbacks.

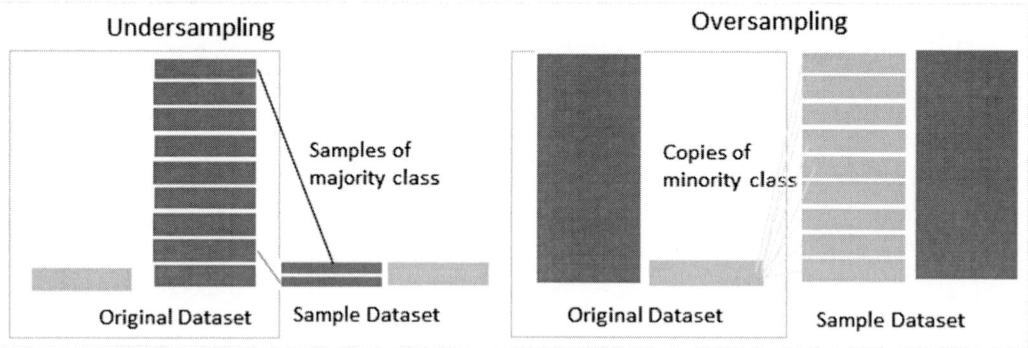

In over-sampling, the simplest method involves duplicating random records from the minority class, which can lead to overfitting. On the other hand, under-sampling involves removing random records from the majority class, which may result in information loss.

To mitigate these drawbacks, more sophisticated techniques can be employed. For example, in under-sampling, clustering the records of the majority class and removing records from each cluster can help preserve information. In over-sampling, instead of creating exact copies of minority class records, introducing small variations into those copies can create more diverse synthetic samples.

Let's explore some of these resampling techniques using the Python library imbalanced-learn, which is compatible with scikit-learn.

Random Under-Sampling With imblearn:

RandomUnderSampler is a straightforward method for balancing data by randomly selecting a subset of data for the targeted classes. It under-samples the majority class(es) by randomly picking samples with or without replacement.

Random Over-Sampling With imblearn:

Generating new samples in the minority classes can help address imbalanced data. A simple strategy is to generate new samples by random sampling with replacement from the existing samples. The RandomOverSampler is one such method for achieving this.

Under-Sampling: Tomek Links:

Tomek links refer to pairs of very close instances but of opposite classes. Removing instances of the majority class of each pair increases the separation between the two classes, making the classification process easier. Tomek's link is considered to exist if the two samples are the nearest neighbors to each other.

SMOTE Algorithm Working Procedure (Synthetic Minority Over-sampling Technique)

Objective: To balance the class distribution, synthetic samples are generated for the minority class.

Stage 1: Minority Class Selection: First, a minority class instance, denoted as set A, is chosen. For each instance in set A, its k-closest neighbors are identified by calculating the Euclidean distance between the instance and every example in set A.

Stage 2: Generating Synthetic Instances: The oversampling rate N is determined based on the imbalance ratio. For each instance in set A, N synthetic instances (x_1, x_2, … x_n) are randomly generated from its k-closest neighbors.

Stage 3: Synthetic Instance Generation: For each synthetic instance (k = 1, 2, 3, … N), the following equation is used to create a new instance:

$$xnew = x + rand(0,1) \times (xneighbor - x)$$

Where rand(0,1) represents a random number between 0 and 1, xneighbor is a randomly selected neighbor from the k-closest neighbors, and xnew is the newly generated synthetic instance.

```
from imblearn.over_sampling import SMOTE
X_resampled, y_resampled = SMOTE().fit_resample(X, y)
```

Advantages:

- Addresses class imbalance by creating synthetic samples.
- Reduces the risk of model overfitting on the majority class.

Drawbacks:

- May lead to overfitting if not used cautiously.
- Sensitivity to the choice of k.

NearMiss Algorithm

Objective: To balance the class distribution by removing samples from the majority class that are close to other majority class samples, thereby reducing redundancy.

NearMiss is an under-sampling method aimed at balancing class distribution by randomly removing majority class instances. It focuses on removing instances of the majority class when instances of different classes are very close to each other, thereby increasing the separation between the classes and improving classification accuracy.

Close neighbor techniques, such as NearMiss, are commonly used to address the issue of data loss in under-sampling methods.

The working procedure of NearMiss can be summarized as follows:

- Stage 1: Calculation of Distances: First, the algorithm calculates the distances between all instances of the majority class and instances of the minority class. Here, the majority class is the class to be under-sampled.
- Stage 2: Selection of Instances: Next, "n" instances of the majority class with the smallest distances to those in the minority class are selected.
- Stage 3: Expansion of Minority Class: If there are k instances in the minority class, the nearest technique will result in k*n instances of the majority class.

There are different variations of the NearMiss Algorithm for finding n nearest instances in the majority class, including:

- NearMiss - Version 1: Selects instances of the majority class for which the average distances to the k nearest instances of the minority class are smallest.
- NearMiss - Version 2: Selects instances of the majority class for which the average distances to the k farthest instances of the minority class are smallest.
- NearMiss - Version 3: Operates in 2 stages. Firstly, for each minority class instance, their M closest neighbors are stored. Then, the majority class instances are selected for which the average distance to the N nearest neighbors is the largest.SMOTE Algorithm Working Procedure.

```
from imblearn.under_sampling import NearMiss

X_resampled, y_resampled = NearMiss().fit_resample(X, y)
```

Advantages:

- Reduces the size of the majority class, balancing the class distribution.
- Helps in creating a more robust decision boundary by removing redundant majority class samples.

Drawbacks:

- May lead to information loss from the majority class.
- Sensitivity to parameter tuning.

Changing the Performance Metric

Accuracy may not provide the most reliable evaluation of imbalanced datasets due to its susceptibility to being misled.

To gain better insights into model performance, consider using alternative metrics, such as:

Confusion Matrix: A tabular representation showing correct predictions and types of incorrect predictions, including true positives, true negatives, false positives, and false negatives.

Precision: The number of true positives divided by all positive predictions. Also known as Positive Predictive Value, precision measures the exactness of a classifier. Low precision indicates a high number of false positives.

Recall: The number of true positives divided by the number of positive values in the test data. Also called Sensitivity or the True Positive Rate, recall measures the completeness of a classifier. Low recall indicates a high number of false negatives.

F1 Score: The weighted average of precision and recall, providing a balance between the two metrics.

Area Under ROC Curve (AUROC): AUROC represents the likelihood of your model distinguishing observations from two classes. It quantifies the model's ability to rank observations correctly when randomly selecting one observation from each class. A higher AUROC indicates better model performance.

Example 1:

Example P3 – U3 – D33	
ML	**Output**

# Step 1: Importing all libraries 	
# Data creation and processing 	
import pandas as pd
import numpy as np
from sklearn.datasets import make_classification
# Data visualization 	
import matplotlib.pyplot as plt
import seaborn as sns
# Model training and evaluation 	
from sklearn.model_selection import train_test_split
from sklearn.ensemble import RandomForestClassifier
from sklearn.metrics import classification_report, roc_auc_score, accuracy_score, f1_score, roc_curve
 	
# Sampling techniques 	
from imblearn.over_sampling import RandomOverSampler, SMOTE
from imblearn.under_sampling import RandomUnderSampler, NearMiss
from collections import Counter
 	
# Step 2: Create Imbalanced Dataset 	
X, y = make_classification(n_samples=100000, n_features=2, n_informative=2,
n_redundant=0, n_repeated=0, n_classes=2,
n_clusters_per_class=1,
weights=[0.995, 0.005],
class_sep=0.5, random_state=0)
df = pd.DataFrame({'feature1': X[:, 0], 'feature2': X[:, 1], 'target': y})
 	
# Check the target distribution 	
print(df['target'].value_counts(normalize=True))
	target
	0 0.9897
	1 0.0103
	
	Name: proportion, dtype: float64
	Training set size: 80000
	Test set size: 20000
	
	Number of records after Random Over Sampling: [(0, 79156), (1, 79156)]
	
	Number of records after SMOTE Oversampling: [(0, 79156), (1, 79156)]
	
	Number of records after Random Under Sampling: [(0, 844), (1, 844)]
	
	Number of records after NearMiss Undersampling: [(0, 844), (1, 844)]

```
# Step 3: Visualize the Dataset
plt.figure(figsize=(12, 8))
sns.scatterplot(x='feature1', y='feature2', hue='target',
data=df)

# Step 4: Train-Test Split
X_train, X_test, y_train, y_test = train_test_split(X, y,
test_size=0.2, random_state=101)
print('Training set size:', X_train.shape[0])
print('Test set size:', X_test.shape[0])

# Step 5: Baseline Model
rf = RandomForestClassifier()
baseline_model = rf.fit(X_train, y_train)
baseline_prediction = baseline_model.predict(X_test)
print('Baseline Model Performance:')
print(classification_report(y_test, baseline_prediction))
baseline_auc_roc = roc_auc_score(y_test,
baseline_prediction)
baseline_accuracy = accuracy_score(y_test,
baseline_prediction)
baseline_f1 = f1_score(y_test, baseline_prediction)

# Step 6: Random Over Sampling
ros = RandomOverSampler(random_state=101)
X_train_ros, y_train_ros = ros.fit_resample(X_train,
y_train)
print('Number of records after Random Over Sampling:',
sorted(Counter(y_train_ros).items()))
ros_model = rf.fit(X_train_ros, y_train_ros)
ros_prediction = ros_model.predict(X_test)
print('Random Over Sampling Model Performance:')
print(classification_report(y_test, ros_prediction))
ros_auc_roc = roc_auc_score(y_test, ros_prediction)
ros_accuracy = accuracy_score(y_test, ros_prediction)
ros_f1 = f1_score(y_test, ros_prediction)

# Step 7: SMOTE Oversampling
smote = SMOTE(random_state=42)
X_train_smote, y_train_smote =
smote.fit_resample(X_train, y_train)
print('Number of records after SMOTE Oversampling:',
sorted(Counter(y_train_smote).items()))
smote_model = rf.fit(X_train_smote, y_train_smote)
smote_prediction = smote_model.predict(X_test)
print('SMOTE Oversampling Model Performance:')
print(classification_report(y_test, smote_prediction))
smote_auc_roc = roc_auc_score(y_test, smote_prediction)
```

```
smote_accuracy = accuracy_score(y_test,
smote_prediction)
smote_f1 = f1_score(y_test, smote_prediction)

# Step 8: Random Under Sampling
rus = RandomUnderSampler(random_state=101)
X_train_rus, y_train_rus = rus.fit_resample(X_train,
y_train)
print('Number of records after Random Under Sampling:',
sorted(Counter(y_train_rus).items()))
rus_model = rf.fit(X_train_rus, y_train_rus)
rus_prediction = rus_model.predict(X_test)
print('Random Under Sampling Model Performance:')
print(classification_report(y_test, rus_prediction))
rus_auc_roc = roc_auc_score(y_test, rus_prediction)
rus_accuracy = accuracy_score(y_test, rus_prediction)
rus_f1 = f1_score(y_test, rus_prediction)

# Step 9: NearMiss Undersampling
nearmiss = NearMiss(version=3)
X_train_nearmiss, y_train_nearmiss =
nearmiss.fit_resample(X_train, y_train)
print('Number of records after NearMiss Undersampling:',
sorted(Counter(y_train_nearmiss).items()))
nearmiss_model = rf.fit(X_train_nearmiss,
y_train_nearmiss)
nearmiss_prediction = nearmiss_model.predict(X_test)
print('NearMiss Undersampling Model Performance:')
print(classification_report(y_test, nearmiss_prediction))
nearmiss_auc_roc = roc_auc_score(y_test,
nearmiss_prediction)
nearmiss_accuracy = accuracy_score(y_test,
nearmiss_prediction)
nearmiss_f1 = f1_score(y_test, nearmiss_prediction)

# Step 10: Plot ROC-AUC Curve
plt.figure(figsize=(10, 6))
fpr, tpr, _ = roc_curve(y_test, baseline_prediction)
plt.plot(fpr, tpr, label=f'Baseline (AUC-ROC =
{baseline_auc_roc:.2f})')

fpr, tpr, _ = roc_curve(y_test, ros_prediction)
plt.plot(fpr, tpr, label=f'Random Over Sampling (AUC-
ROC = {ros_auc_roc:.2f})')
fpr, tpr, _ = roc_curve(y_test, smote_prediction)
plt.plot(fpr, tpr, label=f'SMOTE (AUC-ROC =
{smote_auc_roc:.2f})')
fpr, tpr, _ = roc_curve(y_test, rus_prediction)
```

plt.plot(fpr, tpr, label=f'Random Under Sampling (AUC-ROC = {rus_auc_roc:.2f})') fpr, tpr, _ = roc_curve(y_test, nearmiss_prediction) plt.plot(fpr, tpr, label=f'NearMiss (AUC-ROC = {nearmiss_auc_roc:.2f})') plt.plot([0, 1], [0, 1], linestyle='--', label='No Skill') plt.xlabel('False Positive Rate') plt.ylabel('True Positive Rate') plt.title('ROC Curve') plt.legend() plt.show()	

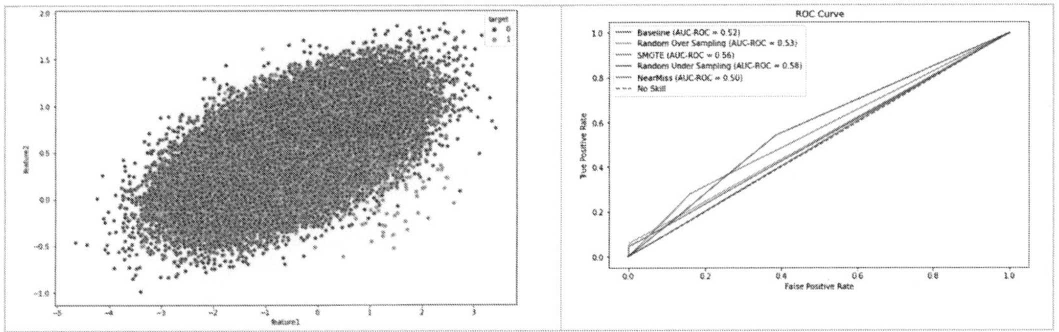

Example 2:

Example P1 – U1 – D34	
ML – Handling Imbalanced Data – SMOTE, NearMiss	**Output**
# Import necessary modules import pandas as pd import numpy as np import matplotlib.pyplot as plt from sklearn.linear_model import LogisticRegression from sklearn.preprocessing import StandardScaler from sklearn.metrics import confusion_matrix, classification_report from sklearn.model_selection import train_test_split from imblearn.over_sampling import SMOTE from imblearn.under_sampling import NearMiss from collections import Counter # Step 1: Reading Dataset	After OverSampling, counts of label "1": 199019 After OverSampling, counts of label "0": 199019 After Undersampling, counts of label "1": 345 After Undersampling, counts of label "0": 345

```
path =
r'C:\Users\User\mraj4\Documents\Optimum\Py-
lib\scikit\creditcard.csv'
df = pd.read_csv(path)
print(df.head())
print(df.info())

# Normalize the Amount column
df['normAmount'] =
StandardScaler().fit_transform(np.array(df['Amount']
).reshape(-1, 1))

# Drop Time and Amount columns as they are not
relevant for prediction purpose
df = df.drop(['Time', 'Amount'], axis=1)

# Split the data into features and target variable
X = df.drop('Class', axis=1)
y = df['Class']

# Split the data into training and testing sets
X_train, X_test, y_train, y_test = train_test_split(X,
y, test_size=0.3, random_state=0)

# Train the model without handling the imbalanced
class distribution
lr = LogisticRegression()
lr.fit(X_train, y_train.ravel())
predictions = lr.predict(X_test)
print(classification_report(y_test, predictions))

# Using SMOTE Algorithm
sm = SMOTE(random_state=2)
X_train_res, y_train_res = sm.fit_resample(X_train,
y_train.ravel())
print('After OverSampling, counts of label "1":',
sum(y_train_res == 1))
print('After OverSampling, counts of label "0":',
sum(y_train_res == 0))
lr1 = LogisticRegression()
lr1.fit(X_train_res, y_train_res.ravel())
predictions = lr1.predict(X_test)
print(classification_report(y_test, predictions))

# NearMiss Algorithm
nr = NearMiss()
X_train_miss, y_train_miss =
nr.fit_resample(X_train, y_train.ravel())
```

```
print('After Undersampling, counts of label "1":',
sum(y_train_miss == 1))
print('After Undersampling, counts of label "0":',
sum(y_train_miss == 0))
lr2 = LogisticRegression()
lr2.fit(X_train_miss, y_train_miss.ravel())
predictions = lr2.predict(X_test)
print(classification_report(y_test, predictions))
```

Advantages and Disadvantages of Under-Sampling

Advantages:

- Helps improve run time and storage problems by reducing the number of training data samples, particularly when dealing with large datasets.

Disadvantages:

- May discard potentially useful information crucial for building robust classifiers, leading to the loss of valuable insights.
- The random selection process in under-sampling may introduce bias, resulting in an inaccurate representation of the population and potentially skewed results when applied to the actual test dataset.

Advantages and Disadvantages of Over-Sampling

Advantages:

- Preserves all available data, eliminating the risk of information loss inherent in under-sampling techniques.
- Often outperforms under-sampling methods in terms of model performance and predictive accuracy.

Disadvantages:

- Increases the risk of overfitting since it duplicates minority class events, potentially leading to models that are overly tailored to the training data and perform poorly on unseen data.

Summary:

This unit delves into the challenges posed by imbalanced datasets and explores various resampling techniques aimed at addressing this imbalance to improve the performance of machine learning models.

The module begins by elucidating the concept of imbalanced datasets, where the distribution of classes is skewed, leading to biased models that prioritise the majority class. It highlights the implications of such imbalance on model training and evaluation and underscores the need for specialised techniques to mitigate its effects.

Resampling techniques, a key approach for handling imbalanced datasets, are discussed comprehensively. The unit covers Random Under-Sampling, which involves randomly removing instances from the majority class to balance the class distribution. Conversely, Random Over-Sampling duplicates instances from the minority class to increase its representation in the dataset.

Additionally, the unit explores more sophisticated techniques, such as Under-Sampling using Tomek Links, which identifies and removes pairs of instances from different classes that are in close proximity, thereby enhancing class separability. SMOTE (Synthetic Minority Over-sampling Technique) is introduced as an oversampling method that generates synthetic instances for the minority class based on feature interpolation.

NearMiss Algorithm, another under-sampling approach, selects instances from the majority class that are close to the minority class instances, thereby preserving important information while balancing the dataset.

Moreover, the unit discusses the importance of changing the performance metric when evaluating models trained on imbalanced datasets. It emphasises the limitations of accuracy and introduces alternative metrics such as precision, recall, F1 score, and area under the ROC curve (AUROC) that provide a more nuanced assessment of model performance in the context of class imbalance.

Throughout the unit, practical examples and case studies are used to illustrate the application of these resampling techniques and performance metrics in real-world scenarios. By the end of the module, learners gain a comprehensive understanding of strategies for effectively handling imbalanced datasets and evaluating model performance in such scenarios.

What Next:

In this unit, we will cover supervised and unsupervised learning techniques, including linear regression, logistic regression, and basics of clustering. We explore methods like OLS, multiple linear regression, and advanced techniques, such as Bayesian regression and regularization.

Additionally, we will discuss logistic regression extensively, covering sigmoid functions, types of logistic regression, and activation functions like sigmoid, relu, and softmax. We will also compare Multiclass vs Multilabel classification and strategies like One-vs-All and One-vs-One.

Furthermore, we delved into evaluation metrics such as confusion matrix, Accuracy, Precision, Recall, F1 score, and advanced techniques like AUC-ROC curve and Precision-Recall curve. Understanding these metrics is crucial for assessing model performance and making informed decisions.

P3-U3-L1-7 - Practice Question

1. What is data processing, and why is it essential in data analysis?
2. How can test datasets be created for binary classification tasks?
3. What techniques are used for handling missing values in data cleaning?
4. Explain the concept of one-hot encoding and its role in data preprocessing.
5. What is Exploratory Data Analysis (EDA), and why is it important in data analysis?
6. How can outliers be handled in data cleaning?
7. What are the common techniques for feature scaling and normalization?
8. What is the Dummy Variable Trap, and how can it be avoided?
9. What is Feature Engineering, and why is it important in machine learning?
10. What are some resampling techniques used for handling imbalanced datasets?
11. How does Random Over-Sampling address class imbalance in datasets?
12. What is the goal of Exploratory Data Analysis (EDA)?
13. What are some techniques used in multivariate analysis?
14. Why is it important to change the performance metric when evaluating models on imbalanced datasets?
15. How does Feature Scaling improve the performance of machine learning algorithms?
16. What are some techniques for handling outliers in data cleaning?
17. How can the Dummy Variable Trap be avoided?
18. What is the purpose of Feature Engineering?
19. How does SMOTE address class imbalance in datasets?
20. What is the significance of Exploratory Data Analysis (EDA) in data analysis?
21. Why is it important to handle missing values in data cleaning?
22. How can imbalanced datasets affect model training and evaluation?
23. What role does Feature Scaling play in machine learning?
24. What are some common techniques for encoding categorical variables?
25. How does Random Under-Sampling address the class imbalance in datasets?

Assignment: P3 – A1

Problem Statement: Exploratory Data Analysis of Used Car Dataset

Background: A company dealing with used cars wants to gain insights into the market trends and factors influencing car prices. They have collected data on various car models, including their specifications and prices.

Objective: The objective of this project is to perform Exploratory Data Analysis (EDA) to understand the dataset's characteristics, identify patterns, and explore relationships among different variables.

Data Description: The dataset contains information about used cars, including features such as:

- Name: Name of the car model
- Location: Location of sale
- Year: Year of manufacture
- Kilometers_Driven: Total kilometers driven
- Fuel_Type: Type of fuel used (e.g., Petrol, Diesel, CNG)
- Transmission: Type of transmission (e.g., Manual, Automatic)
- Owner_Type: Type of ownership (e.g., First Owner, Second Owner)
- Mileage: Mileage of the car (in kilometers per liter)
- Engine: Engine capacity (in CC)
- Power: Power of the engine (in bhp)
- Seats: Number of seats
- Price: Price of the car (in lakhs)

Tasks:

Data Cleaning and Preparation:

- Identify and handle missing values.
- Perform data reduction by removing unnecessary columns.

- Introduce new features like 'Car_Age', 'Brand', and 'Model' for better analysis.

Exploratory Data Analysis (EDA):

- Compute summary statistics and visualise distributions of numerical variables.
- Analyse the relationship between car prices and various features using scatter plots, box plots, and correlation analysis.
- Conduct univariate and bivariate analysis to understand the distributions and relationships of variables.
- Perform multivariate analysis to explore complex relationships among multiple variables simultaneously.

Insights and Recommendations:

- Summarise key findings and trends observed in the dataset.
- Provide actionable insights and recommendations based on the analysis to assist the company in pricing strategies and decision-making.

By conducting comprehensive exploratory data analysis, the company aims to gain valuable insights into the used car market, understand customer preferences, and optimise business operations.

PART FOUR

Machine Learning

Classification and Regression

"Machine learning is not about teaching computers to think—it's about teaching them to learn, adapt, and reveal patterns hidden beyond human perception."

– Shree Shambav

PART FOUR

DAY TEN

Unit 4 - Lesson One

Supervised Learning

Supervised Learning

Master said, "Within the realm of machine learning, numerous algorithms address specific tasks and challenges."

Here's an overview of some common machine learning models:

Case One: Linear Regression

Task: Regression

- Description: Models the relationship between a dependent variable and one or more independent variables by fitting a linear equation to the observed data.
- Algorithm: Linear regression is a supervised learning algorithm used for predicting a continuous outcome.
- Application: Predicting house prices, stock prices, or any other numeric value.

Problem Statement: Utilise the Boston House Prices Dataset to analyse house sales data and construct a machine learning model capable of predicting housing prices.

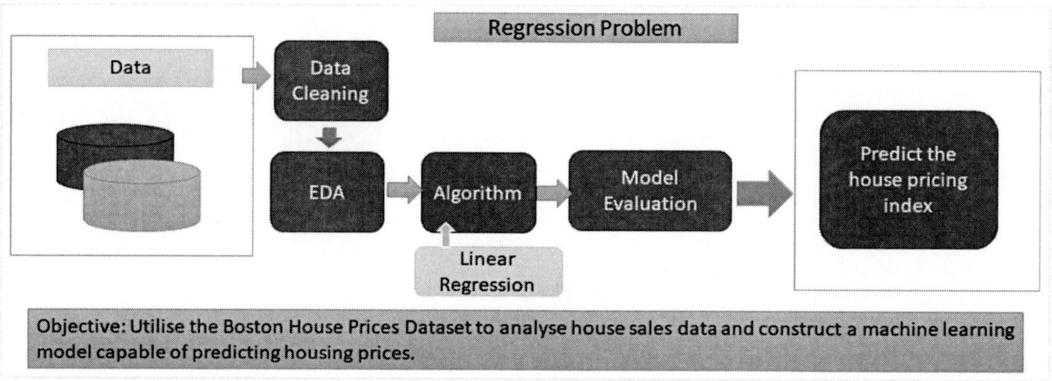

Case Two: Logistic Regression

Task: Classification

- Description: Used for binary classification problems; it estimates the probability that an instance belongs to a particular category.
- Algorithm: Logistic regression is used for binary classification problems.
- Application: Spam detection, disease prediction, and credit scoring.

Problem Statement: Analyse a bank credit dataset to determine loan approval decisions based on applicant profiles.

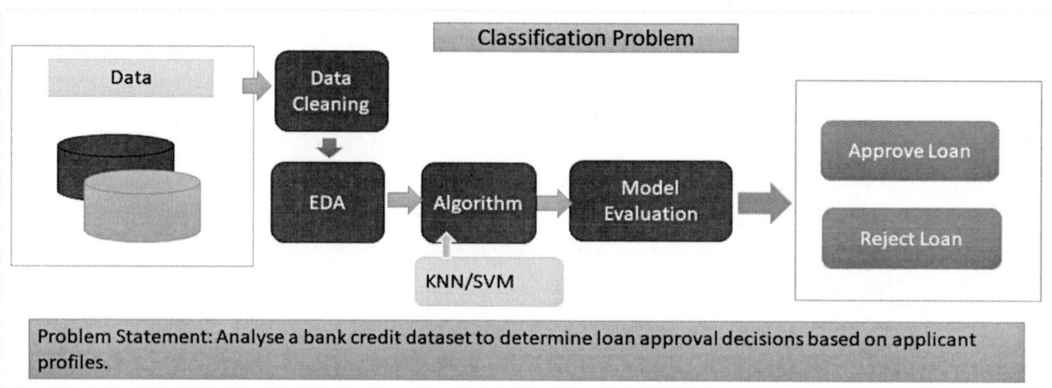

Case Three: Clustering Algorithms (e.g., K-Means, Hierarchical Clustering)

Task: Clustering

- Description: Grouping similar data points together based on certain criteria or features.

- Algorithm: K-Means is an unsupervised clustering algorithm that partitions data into clusters.
- Application: Image segmentation, customer segmentation, and anomaly detection.

Problem Statement: Cluster a set of movies into categories of either "good" or "average" based on their social media reach.

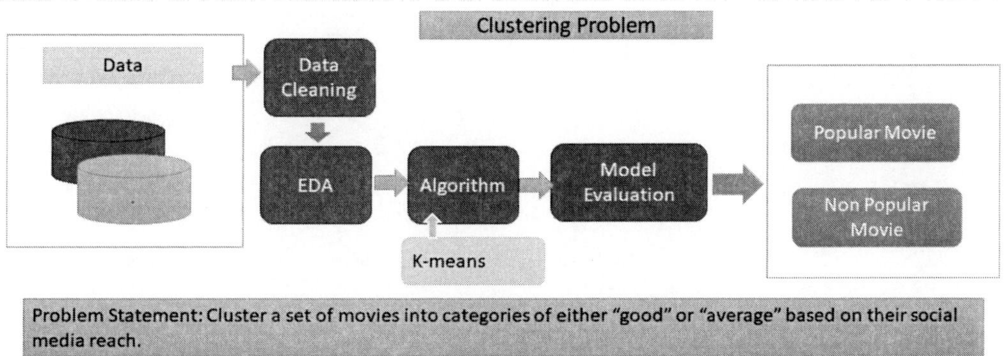

Machine learning algorithms

Now, let's explore various types of machine learning algorithms.

Linear Regression:

Linear regression serves as a fundamental statistical model for understanding the relationship between a dependent variable and one or more independent variables, achieved by fitting a linear equation to observed data. The objective is to pinpoint the optimal linear equation that accurately predicts the dependent variable's value based on the independent variables.

It's crucial to note that the dependent variable (Y) is always continuous, while the independent variable (X) can be either continuous or discrete.

For instance, consider analysing the price of a stock over a period of time. Here, the stock price represents the dependent variable, while time acts as the independent variable. By plotting these variables, assuming a linear relationship, we seek to find the best-fitting linear equation. This results in a depiction that resembles more of a straight line than a curve, reflecting the assumed linear variation between the variables.

Math equation:

$$Y = \beta_0 + \beta_1 X^1 + \beta_2 X^2 + \ldots + \beta_n X^n + \epsilon$$

where β0 is the intercept, β1,β2,…,βn are the coefficients representing the effect of each independent variable on the dependent variable, X1,X2,…,Xn, and ϵ is the error term accounting for unexplained variability.

Problem statement: What is the expected duration of a patient's hospital stay after a minor surgery?

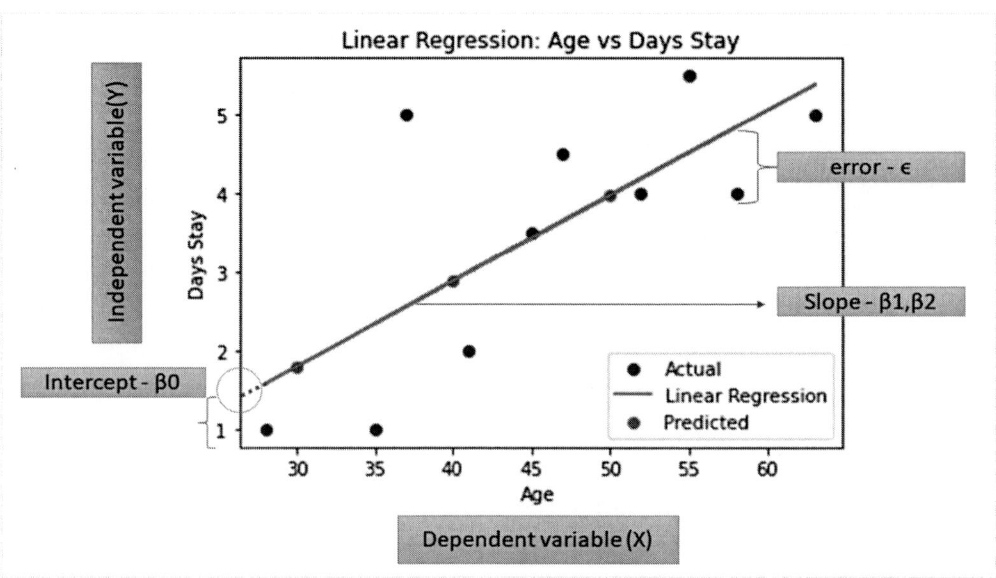

OLS (Ordinary Least Square)

Let us utilise Python's statsmodels module to execute the Ordinary Least Squares (OLS) method of linear regression. This method allows us to establish the relationship between a dependent variable (y) and at least one independent variable (x).

The provided code implements linear regression using the Ordinary Least Squares (OLS) method using Python's statsmodels library. Here's a breakdown of the code:

Example P4 – U4 – D1

Linear Regression - OLS

```
import statsmodels.api as sm
import pandas as pd
# Load the dataset from a CSV file.
path = r'C:\Users\User\mraj4\Documents\Optimum\Py-lib\scikit\Linear_Reg.csv'
df = pd.read_csv(path)

# Defining the variables
x = df['x']
y = df['y']
```

```
# Adding the constant term
x = sm.add_constant(x)
# Performing the regression and fitting the model
model = sm.OLS(y, x)
result = model.fit()
# Printing the summary table
print(result.summary())
```

The provided code implements linear regression using the Ordinary Least Squares (OLS) method using Python's statsmodels library. Here's a breakdown of the code:

```
Output:
OLS Regression Results
==============================================================================
Dep. Variable:                  y          R-squared:                  0.989
Model:                          OLS        Adj. R-squared:             0.989
Method:                         Least Squares  F-statistic:            2.709e+04
Date:              Sun, 12 May 2024        Prob (F-statistic):         1.33e-294
Time:                   16:17:45           Log-Likelihood:             -757.98
No. Observations:               300        AIC:                        1520.
Df Residuals:                   298        BIC:                        1527.
Df Model:                       1
Covariance Type:            nonrobust
==============================================================================
              coef     std err        t       P>|t|     [0.025     0.975]
------------------------------------------------------------------------------
const      -0.4618     0.360     -1.284     0.200     -1.169      0.246
x           1.0143     0.006    164.598     0.000      1.002      1.026
==============================================================================
Omnibus:                   1.034   Durbin-Watson:               2.006
Prob(Omnibus):             0.596   Jarque-Bera (JB):            0.825
Skew:                      0.117   Prob(JB):                    0.662
Kurtosis:                  3.104   Cond. No.                    120.
==============================================================================
Notes:
[1] Standard Errors assume that the covariance matrix of the errors is correctly specified.
Accuracy (One-vs-Rest): 0.855
Accuracy (One-vs-One): 0.855
```

Importing Libraries: The code begins by importing the necessary libraries: statsmodels.api for implementing linear regression and pandas for data manipulation.

Loading Dataset: It loads the dataset from a CSV file using pd.read_csv function from the pandas library.

Defining Variables: It defines the independent variable x and dependent variable y from the dataset.

Adding Constant Term: A constant term is added to the independent variable x using the sm.add_constant function. This is necessary for the intercept term in the linear regression equation.

Performing Regression: It performs the linear regression using the OLS method with the sm.OLS(y, x) function.

Fitting the Model: The regression model is fitted to the data using the fit method, which returns a result object containing information about the regression.

The R-squared value, also known as the coefficient of determination, represents the proportion of variance in the dependent variable that can be explained by the independent variables in the model. It ranges from 0 to 1, with higher values indicating a better fit of the model to the data.

Adjusted R-squared is a modified version of R-squared that adjusts for the number of independent variables in the model. It increases when additional variables are included in the model, provided they improve the model's performance.

The F-statistic is the ratio of the mean squared error of the model to the mean squared error of the residuals. It assesses the overall significance of the model, indicating whether the model is statistically significant in explaining the variance in the dependent variable.

The coefficients, denoted as "coef," represent the estimated values of the independent variables and the constant term in the regression equation. These coefficients indicate the direction and strength of the relationship between each independent variable and the dependent variable.

The t-statistic measures the significance of each coefficient by comparing the estimated value to the hypothesised value relative to the standard error. It helps determine whether the coefficients are statistically different from zero.

To predict values using the regression model, we use the coefficients obtained from the regression results. For example, if the coefficient of the independent variable (x) is 1.0143 and the constant term is -0.4618, we substitute these values into the original regression equation to obtain predicted values. These predicted values can then be used to plot the regression line using a visualisation library like Matplotlib.

Example P4 – U4 – D2

Linear Regression - OLS

```
import pandas as pd
import matplotlib.pyplot as plt
import numpy as np
# Load the dataset from a CSV file.
path =
r'C:\Users\User\mraj4\Documents\Optimum\Py-
lib\scikit\Linear_Reg.csv'
df = pd.read_csv(path)

# Extracting x and y values from the dataset
x = df['x']
y = df['y']

# Plotting the original data points
plt.scatter(x, y, label='Original Data')

# Calculating the range of x values for the regression
line
max_x = x.max()
min_x = x.min()

# Generating values for the regression line
x_range = np.arange(min_x, max_x, 1)
y_regression = 1.0143 * x_range - 0.4618

# Plotting the regression line
plt.plot(x_range, y_regression, color='red',
label='Regression Line')
# Adding labels and legend
plt.xlabel('x')
plt.ylabel('y')
plt.title('Linear Regression')
plt.legend()
# Displaying the plot
plt.show()
```

Output

Accuracy (One-vs-Rest): 0.855
Accuracy (One-vs-One): 0.855

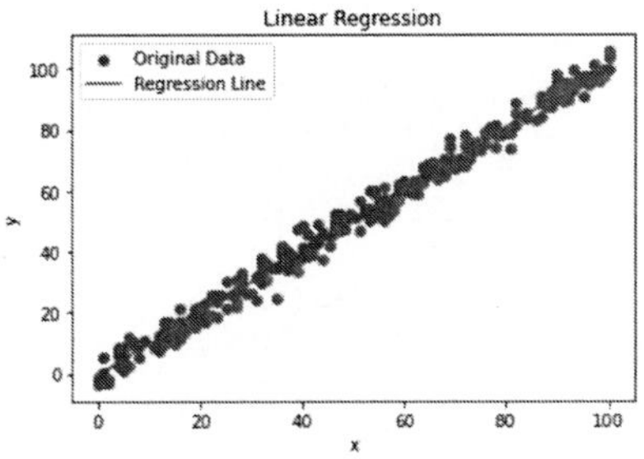

Using Scikit

Problem statement: What is the expected duration of a patient's hospital stay after a minor surgery?

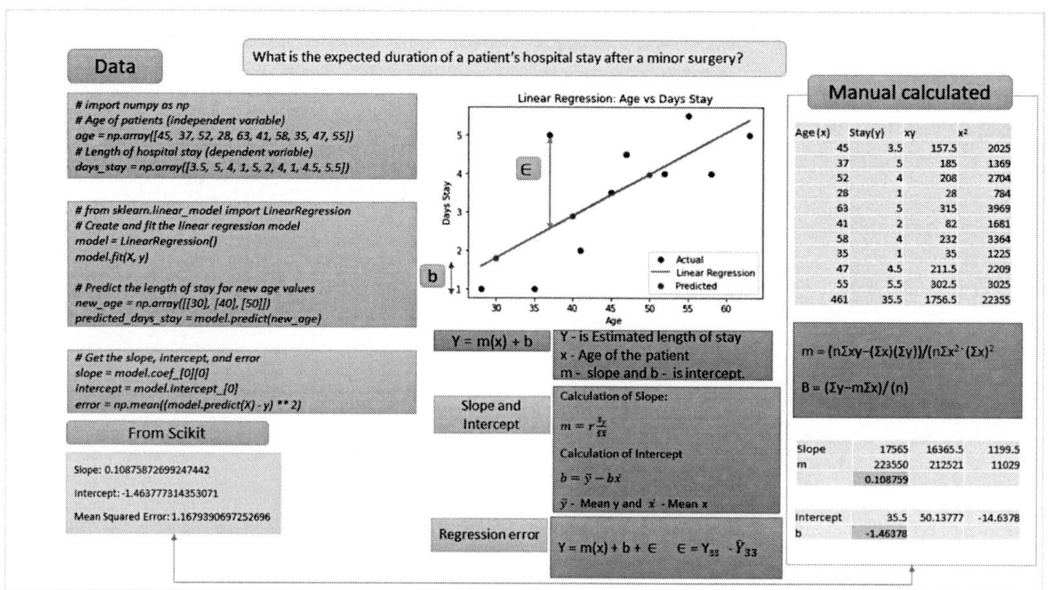

Multiple Linear Regression

These are two primary types of linear regression:

Simple Linear Regression: In simple linear regression, we model the relationship between a single independent variable (feature) and a dependent variable (response) by fitting a linear equation to the observed data points. The aim is to find the best-fit line that minimises the sum of squared differences between the observed and predicted values.

Multiple Linear Regression: Multiple linear regression extends simple linear regression to model the relationship between two or more independent variables and a dependent variable. It involves fitting a linear equation with multiple predictors to the observed data, aiming to capture the combined effect of these predictors on the response variable.

$$\mathbf{Y = \beta_0 + \beta_1X^1 + \beta_2X^2 + \ldots + \beta_nX^n + \epsilon}$$

The key steps to perform multiple linear regression are analogous to those of simple linear regression.

Assumptions of a regression model include:

Linearity: The relationship between the dependent and independent variables should be linear. This means that changes in the independent variables result in proportional changes in the dependent variable.

Homoscedasticity: The variance of the errors (residuals) should remain constant across all levels of the independent variables. In other words, the spread of the residuals should be consistent.

Multivariate Normality: Multiple regression assumes that the residuals (the differences between observed and predicted values) are normally distributed. This assumption is crucial for conducting statistical inference.

Lack of Multicollinearity: It is assumed that there is little or no multicollinearity among the independent variables. Multicollinearity occurs when two or more independent variables are highly correlated, which can lead to unstable parameter estimates.

Methods of Building Models

These are different strategies for building predictive models, each with its own approach to selecting and evaluating features. Let's break down each method:

All-in:

In this method, all available features are included in the model without any feature selection. It's a straightforward approach but may lead to overfitting if the dataset contains irrelevant or redundant features.

Backward Elimination:

Backward elimination is a feature selection technique where we start with all features and iteratively remove the least significant ones based on a chosen criterion, such as p-values in regression or feature importance scores. This process continues until no further improvement in the model's performance is observed.

Remove the predictor with the highest P-value (if P > SL), where SL represents the significance level, typically set at 0.05.

Forward Selection:

Unlike backward elimination, forward selection starts with an empty set of features and iteratively adds the most significant feature at each step. The process continues until no further improvement in performance is observed or until a predefined criterion is met.

If the P-value is less than the significance level (SL), add one extra predictor to the selected model. This step involves iteratively adding predictors to the model that demonstrates P-values below the predetermined significance threshold.

Bidirectional Elimination:

Bidirectional elimination, also known as stepwise selection, combines both forward and backward elimination. It starts with an empty set of features, then iteratively adds the most significant feature and removes the least significant one based on a predefined criterion. This process continues until no further improvement in performance is observed.

Score Comparison:

Score comparison involves building multiple models with different subsets of features and comparing their performance using a chosen evaluation metric. This method allows for a more comprehensive exploration of feature combinations, but can be computationally intensive.

Comparing different models based on performance metrics, such as R-squared, adjusted R-squared, AIC, BIC, etc. Models with higher scores or lower error metrics are preferred.

Each method has its advantages and disadvantages, and the choice depends on factors such as the dataset size, computational resources, and the desired balance between model complexity and performance. It's important to carefully consider the characteristics of the dataset and the goals of the analysis when selecting a method for building predictive models.

Example P4 – U4 – D3	
Linear Regression	**Output**
import numpy as np import matplotlib.pyplot as plt from mpl_toolkits.mplot3d import Axes3D # Function to generate synthetic dataset def generate_dataset(n): x = []	Accuracy (One-vs-Rest): 0.855 Accuracy (One-vs-One): 0.855

```
    y = []
    random_x1 = np.random.rand()
    random_x2 = np.random.rand()
    for i in range(n):
        x1 = i
        x2 = i/2 + np.random.rand()*n
        x.append([1, x1, x2])  # Adding bias term and features
        y.append(random_x1 * x1 + random_x2 * x2 + 1)  #
Generating labels using a linear function
    return np.array(x), np.array(y)

# Generating dataset
x, y = generate_dataset(200)

# Plotting the original data points
fig = plt.figure()
ax = fig.add_subplot(111, projection='3d')
ax.scatter(x[:, 1], x[:, 2], y, label='y', s=5)
ax.legend()
ax.view_init(45, 0)
plt.show()

# Function to calculate Mean Squared Error
def mse(coef, x, y):
    return np.mean((np.dot(x, coef) - y)**2)/2

# Function to calculate gradients
def gradients(coef, x, y):
    return np.mean(x.transpose()*(np.dot(x, coef) - y), axis=1)

# Function to perform multilinear regression using Adam
optimizer
def multilinear_regression(coef, x, y, lr, b1=0.9, b2=0.999,
epsilon=1e-8):
    prev_error = 0
    m_coef = np.zeros(coef.shape)
    v_coef = np.zeros(coef.shape)
    moment_m_coef = np.zeros(coef.shape)
    moment_v_coef = np.zeros(coef.shape)
    t = 0

    while True:
        # Calculate mean squared error
        error = mse(coef, x, y)
        if abs(error - prev_error) <= epsilon:  # Check
convergence
            break
        prev_error = error
```

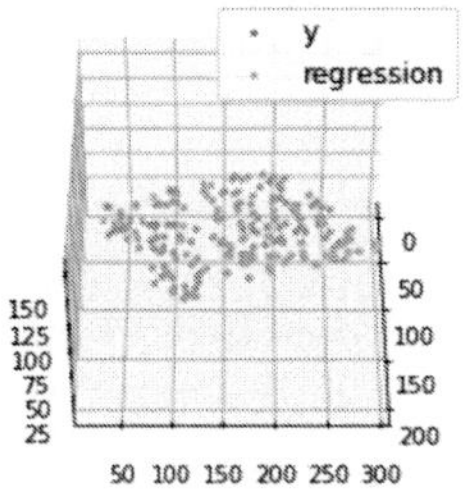

```
        grad = gradients(coef, x, y)
        t += 1
        m_coef = b1 * m_coef + (1-b1)*grad
        v_coef = b2 * v_coef + (1-b2)*grad**2
        moment_m_coef = m_coef / (1-b1**t)
        moment_v_coef = v_coef / (1-b2**t)

        # Update coefficients using Adam optimizer
        delta = ((lr / moment_v_coef**0.5 + 1e-8) *
                 (b1 * moment_m_coef + (1-b1)*grad/(1-b1**t)))

        coef = np.subtract(coef, delta)
    return coef

# Initialize coefficients
coef = np.array([0, 0, 0])

# Perform multilinear regression
c = multilinear_regression(coef, x, y, 1e-1)

# Plotting the regression line
fig = plt.figure()
ax = fig.add_subplot(111, projection='3d')

# Plotting original data points
ax.scatter(x[:, 1], x[:, 2], y, label='y', s=5, color="dodgerblue")

# Plotting the regression line
ax.scatter(x[:, 1], x[:, 2], c[0] + c[1]*x[:, 1] + c[2]*x[:, 2],
           label='regression', s=5, color="orange")

ax.view_init(45, 0)
ax.legend()
plt.show()
```

Problem Statement:

Utilising the provided weather dataset stored in a CSV file, this project aims to analyse the relationship between minimum and maximum temperatures. The dataset contains information regarding minimum temperature (MinTemp) and maximum temperature (MaxTemp) recorded over a period of time.

Tasks:

- Load the weather dataset from the CSV file.
- Visualise the relationship between minimum and maximum temperatures using a

scatter plot.

- Conduct exploratory data analysis (EDA) by visualising the distribution of maximum temperatures.
- Split the dataset into training and testing sets for model evaluation.
- Implement linear regression to model the relationship between minimum and maximum temperatures.
- Train the linear regression model on the training data.
- Print the intercept and coefficients of the linear regression model.
- Predict maximum temperatures (y_pred) for the test data (X_test).
- Visualize the comparison between actual and predicted maximum temperatures using a bar plot.
- Visualize the linear regression line fitted to the test data.

Example P4 – U4 – D4

Linear Regression

```
import pandas as pd
import numpy as np
import matplotlib.pyplot as plt
import seaborn
from sklearn.model_selection import train_test_split
from sklearn.linear_model import LinearRegression
from sklearn import metrics
from pandas import read_csv

# Load the dataset from a CSV file.
path = r'C:\Users\User\mraj4\Documents\Optimum\Py-lib\scikit\weather.csv'
df = read_csv(path)
# print(df.shape)
# print(df.describe())

df.plot(x='MinTemp', y='MaxTemp' , style='o')
plt.title('minimum vs maximum')
plt.xlabel('min_Temp')
plt.ylabel('max_Temp')
plt.show()

plt.figure(figsize=(15,10))
```

```
plt.tight_layout()
seaborn.distplot(df['MaxTemp'])
plt.show()

X= df['MinTemp'].values.reshape(-1,1)
y= df['MaxTemp'].values.reshape(-1,1)
X_train,X_test,y_train,y_test = train_test_split(X,y,test_size=0.2, random_state=0)

model =LinearRegression()
model.fit(X_train,y_train)

print('Intercept is :',model.intercept_)
print('Coefficient is :' ,model.coef_)

y_pred= model.predict(X_test)
df= pd.DataFrame({'Actual': y_test.flatten(), 'Predicted': y_pred.flatten()})
print(df)

df1= df.head(25)
df1.plot(kind='bar', figsize=(16,10))
plt.grid(which='major', linestyle='-',linewidth='0.5', color='red')
plt.grid(which='minor', linestyle=':',linewidth='0.5', color='black')
plt.show()

plt.scatter(X_test,y_test,color='gray')
plt.plot(X_test,y_pred,color='green',linewidth=2)
plt.show()

print('Mean abolute error:', metrics.mean_absolute_error(y_test,y_pred))
print('Mean squared error:', metrics.mean_squared_error(y_test,y_pred))
print('Root mean squared error:', np.sqrt(metrics.mean_squared_error(y_test,y_pred)))
```

Objective: Through the application of linear regression, ascertain the predictive relationship between minimum and maximum temperatures, enabling accurate forecasts of maximum temperatures based on minimum temperatures. Additionally, evaluate the performance of the linear regression model using various evaluation metrics such as mean absolute error, mean squared error, and root mean squared error.

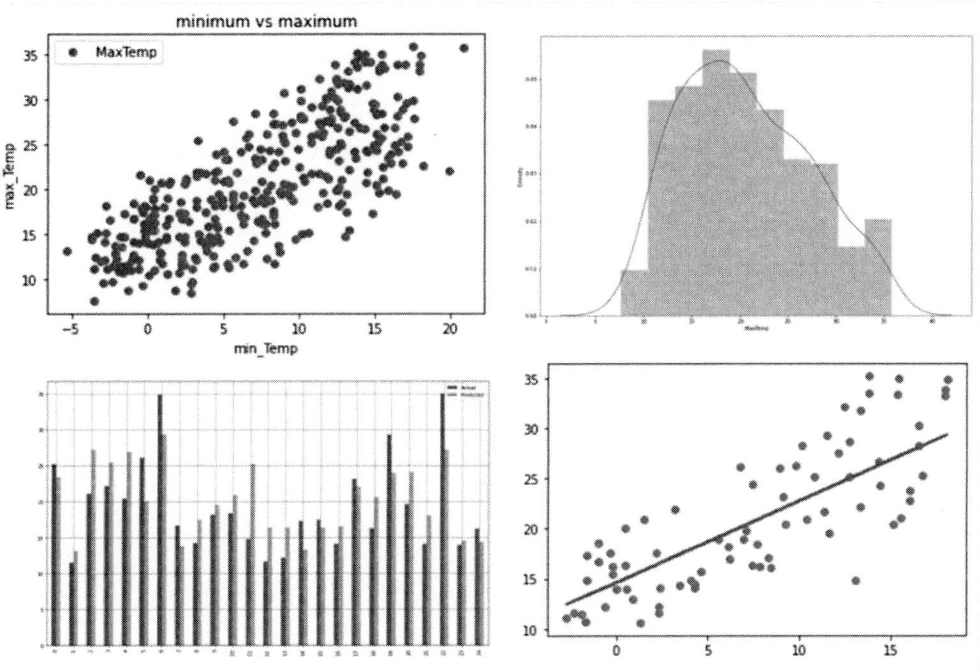

Intercept, Coefficient and Accuracy:

Intercept	Coefficient
14.56202411	0.81953755

	Actual	Predicted
0	25.2	23.413030
1	11.5	13.086857
2	21.1	27.264856
3	22.2	25.461874
4	20.4	26.937041
..	...	...
69	18.9	20.216833
70	22.8	27.674625
71	16.1	21.446140
72	25.1	24.970151
73	12.2	14.070302

Accuracy	
Mean abolute error	3.5094353112899594
Mean squared error	17.011877668640622
Root mean squared error	4.124545753006096

Note: The errors mentioned earlier will be comprehensively addressed in the forthcoming section dedicated to evaluating model accuracy. This example aimed to elucidate the workings of linear regression. Subsequent chapters will delve into various machine learning models using scikit-learn and explore different techniques for tuning these models.

Polynomial regression

Apeksha asked, "What is Polynomial regression?"

Master said, "Polynomial regression is a type of regression analysis used to model the relationship between the independent variable x and the dependent variable y as an n-degree polynomial function. Unlike linear regression, which assumes a linear relationship between variables, polynomial regression can capture more complex relationships by fitting a polynomial curve to the data."

Polynomial regression allows us to capture nonlinear relationships between variables by introducing higher-order polynomial terms. For example, a quadratic polynomial regression model (second-degree polynomial) has the form:

$$\mathbf{Y} = \beta_0 + \beta_1\mathbf{X}^1 + \beta_2\mathbf{X}^2 + \ldots + \beta_n\mathbf{X}^n + \epsilon$$

It is a powerful tool for modelling complex data patterns and can provide more accurate predictions when the relationship between variables is nonlinear. However, care should be taken to avoid overfitting, especially with higher-degree polynomial models, as they can be prone to capture noise in the data. Regularization techniques can be employed to mitigate overfitting in polynomial regression models.

Prerequisites for Polynomial Regression:

Understanding Linear Regression: Polynomial regression builds upon the principles of linear regression, which involves fitting a linear relationship between the independent and dependent variables. It's essential to grasp the concepts of linear regression before diving into polynomial regression.

Familiarity with Gradient Descent: Gradient descent is an optimization algorithm used to minimise the cost function and find the optimal parameters in regression models. Knowledge of gradient descent is beneficial for understanding how polynomial regression models are trained and optimized.

Let's begin by applying linear regression to non-linear data to illustrate the limitations of linear models and the necessity for polynomial regression.

Example P4 – U4 – D5

Linear Regression

```
# Importing libraries
import numpy as np
import pandas as pd
from sklearn.model_selection import train_test_split
import matplotlib.pyplot as plt
from sklearn.linear_model import LinearRegression

def main():
    # Create dataset
    X = np.array([[1], [2], [3], [4], [5], [6], [7]])
    Y = np.array([35000, 40000, 50000, 70000, 100000, 140000,
190000])

    # Model training
    model = LinearRegression()
    model.fit(X, Y)

    # Prediction
    Y_pred = model.predict(X)

    # Visualization
    plt.scatter(X, Y, color='red')
    plt.plot(X, Y_pred, color='black')
    plt.title('X vs Y')
    plt.xlabel('X')
    plt.ylabel('Y')
    plt.show()
if __name__ == "__main__":
    main()
```

Output

Accuracy (One-vs-Rest): 0.855

Accuracy (One-vs-One): 0.855

The given chart illustrates that Linear Regression struggles to adequately fit the training data, indicating a failure to discern the underlying pattern in Y relative to X. This failure arises from the linear nature of its hypothetical function, which is ill-suited to model the non-linear relationship between X and Y present in the data.

In univariate linear regression, the hypothesis function is represented as:

h(x) = w * x

Here, x is the feature vector, and w is the weight vector.

This issue, commonly known as underfitting, can be addressed by introducing new feature vectors derived from the original features. In univariate polynomial regression, the hypothesis function takes the form:

$$\mathbf{h(x) = w_1x + w_2x^2 + ... + w_nx^n}$$

Here, w is the weight vector, and x^2 represents the derived feature obtained by raising x to the power of 2.

After transforming the original X into their higher degree terms, it will make our hypothetical function able to fit the non-linear data. Here is the implementation of the Polynomial Regression model from scratch and validation of the model on a dummy dataset.

We also normalized the X before feeding into the model just to avoid gradient vanishing and exploding problems.

Example P4 – U4 – D6	
Polynomial Linear Regression	**Output**

```
import numpy as np
import matplotlib.pyplot as plt

class PolynomialRegression:
    def __init__(self, degree, learning_rate, iterations):
        self.degree = degree
        self.learning_rate = learning_rate
        self.iterations = iterations

    def transform(self, X):
        X_transform = np.ones((self.m, 1))
        for j in range(1, self.degree + 1):
            x_pow = np.power(X, j)
            X_transform = np.append(X_transform,
x_pow.reshape(-1, 1), axis=1)
        return X_transform

    def normalize(self, X):
        X[:, 1:] = (X[:, 1:] - np.mean(X[:, 1:], axis=0)) /
np.std(X[:, 1:], axis=0)
        return X

    def fit(self, X, Y):
        self.X = X
        self.Y = Y
```

Accuracy (One-vs-Rest): 0.855
Accuracy (One-vs-One): 0.855

```
        self.m, self.n = self.X.shape
        self.W = np.zeros(self.degree + 1)
        X_transform = self.transform(self.X)
        X_normalize = self.normalize(X_transform)
        for i in range(self.iterations):
            h = self.predict(self.X)
            error = h - self.Y
            self.W = self.W - self.learning_rate * (1 / self.m) *
np.dot(X_normalize.T, error)
        return self

    def predict(self, X):
        X_transform = self.transform(X)
        X_normalize = self.normalize(X_transform)
        return np.dot(X_transform, self.W)

def main():
    # Create dataset
    X = np.array([[1], [2], [3], [4], [5], [6], [7]])
    Y = np.array([35000, 40000, 50000, 70000, 100000, 140000,
190000])
    # Model training
    model = PolynomialRegression(degree=2,
learning_rate=0.01, iterations=500)
    model.fit(X, Y)
    # Prediction on training set
    Y_pred = model.predict(X)
    # Visualization
    plt.scatter(X, Y, color='red')
    plt.plot(X, Y_pred, color='black')
    plt.title('X vs Y')
    plt.xlabel('X')
    plt.ylabel('Y')
    plt.show()

if __name__ == "__main__":
    main()
```

Here's a brief overview of the code:

Importing Libraries: The code imports necessary libraries such as NumPy and Matplotlib for numerical operations and plotting.

PolynomialRegression Class: This class defines the Polynomial Regression model. It has methods for transforming input features into polynomial features, normalizing the features, fitting the model to the training data, and making predictions.

Transform Method: This method transforms input features to polynomial features up to a specified degree.

Normalize Method: This method normalizes polynomial features to have zero mean and unit variance.

Fit Method: This method trains the Polynomial Regression model using gradient descent optimization. It iteratively updates the model parameters to minimise the mean squared error between predicted and actual values.

Predict Method: This method makes predictions using the trained model.

Main Function: The main function creates a dataset, initialises and trains a Polynomial Regression model, makes predictions on the training set, and visualizes the results using Matplotlib.

The output visualization showcases Polynomial Regression fitting the non-linear data by generating a curve.

Loss Function:

Akshaya asked, "What is a loss function?"

Master said, "A **loss function** (or cost function) is a mathematical function that quantifies the difference between the predicted values (output of a model) and the actual values (ground truth). It measures how well or poorly a model performs. The goal of training a machine learning model is to minimize the loss function, thereby improving the accuracy of the model's predictions."

For example, in regression tasks, common loss functions include:

Mean Squared Error (MSE):

Commonly used for regression tasks. It calculates the average of the squares of the differences between predicted and actual values.

$$L(y, \hat{y}) = \frac{1}{n} \sum_{i=0}^{n} (\frac{1}{n} \left((y_i - \hat{y}_j)^2 \right))$$

Where:

- n is the number of observations in the dataset.
- y_i is the actual value of the target variable for the ith observation.
- $\hat{y}_j$ is the predicted value of the target variable for the ith observation.

Mean Absolute Error (MAE)

$$L(y, \hat{y}) = \frac{1}{n}\sum_{i=0}^{n}\frac{1}{n}\left|(y_i - \hat{y}_i)^2\right|$$

In classification tasks, common loss functions include:

Cross Entropy Loss:

Commonly used for classification tasks. It measures the performance of a classification model whose output is a probability value between 0 and 1.

$$L(y, \hat{y}) = \frac{1}{n}\sum_{i=0}^{n}(y_i\, log\hat{y}_i + (1 - \hat{y}_i)log(1 - \hat{y}_i))$$

To compute MSE:

- Calculate the squared difference between each actual (y_i) and predicted ($\hat{y}_j$) value.
- Sum up all the squared differences.
- Divide the sum by the total number of observations (*n*).

Example P4 – U4 – D7	
Loss Function - MSE	**Output**

import numpy as np
# Actual values 	
y_actual = np.array([3, -0.5, 2, 7])
# Predicted values 	
y_predicted = np.array([2.5, 0.0, 2, 8])
# Calculate MSE 	
mse = np.mean((y_actual - y_predicted) ** 2)
print(f'Mean Squared Error: {mse}')
	Mean Squared Error: 0.375

Nikash asked, "How Regular Loss Function Works?"

Master said, "A regular loss function works by assigning a penalty to the model based on how far the predicted values are from the actual values. The specific form of the penalty depends on the choice of the loss function."

- **Model Prediction:** The model takes an input and produces a predicted output. For example, in linear regression, the prediction is a linear combination of the input features.

- **Calculate Loss:** The loss function compares the predicted output to the actual output and calculates a loss value. For example, in MSE, it calculates the squared difference between predicted and actual values.

- **Backpropagation:** The loss value is propagated back through the model to adjust the model parameters (weights and biases) to minimize the loss.

Sam asked, "What is Gradient Descent?"

Master said, "Gradient Descent is an optimization algorithm used to minimize the loss function. It iteratively adjusts the model parameters to find the minimum value of the loss function."

How Gradient Descent Works?

1. Initialize Parameters: Start with initial guesses for the model parameters (weights and biases).

2. Compute the Gradient: Calculate the gradient of the loss function with respect to each parameter. The gradient is a vector of partial derivatives that points in the direction of the steepest ascent of the loss function.

3. Update Parameters: Update the parameters in the opposite direction of the gradient. The update rule is:

$$\Theta := \theta - \eta \nabla L(\theta)$$

   where θ represents the parameters, η is the learning rate (a small positive number), and $\nabla L(\theta)$ is the gradient of the loss function.

4. Iterate: Repeat steps 2 and 3 until the loss function converges to a minimum (or stops improving significantly).

Visual Representation:

Consider a simple quadratic loss function $L(w)=(w-2)^2$:

Initialize: Start with an initial guess, say $w=0$.

Compute Gradient: Compute the derivative of the loss function, $\frac{dL}{dw} = 2(w-2)$.

Update: Update the parameter using $w := w - \eta \times 2(w-2)$

Iterate: Repeat the update step until convergence.

Model: $\hat{y}$ = w (x +x²)

MSE = $\frac{1}{n}\sum_{i=1}^{n}\left((y_i - \hat{y}_i)^2\right)$

Loss Function:

$L(y, \hat{y}) = \frac{1}{n}\sum_{i=1}^{n}(y - \hat{y}_i)^2$

$L(y, x, w) = \frac{1}{n}\sum_{i=1}^{n}(wx_i + wx_i^2 - y_i)^2$

Thus, the derivative of the MSE loss function with respect to w is:

$\frac{dL}{dw} = \frac{2}{n}\sum_{i=1}^{n}(x_i + x_i^2)(wx_i + wx_i^2 - y_i)$

This gradient can then be used in optimization algorithms like gradient

The code has several key functionalities: generating data, calculating loss and gradient, performing gradient descent, and plotting the results.

Example P4 – U4 – D8

Gradient Descent

```
import numpy as np
import matplotlib.pyplot as plt
import pandas as pd

# Generate synthetic data
numvals = 50
true_w = 0.5
xvals = np.sort(5 * (np.random.random(numvals) - 0.5))
yvals = true_w * (xvals + xvals**2) + np.random.normal(0, 0.1, numvals)
yvals[int(numvals * 0.1):] += 2

# Plot the synthetic data
plt.figure(figsize=(7, 7))
plt.scatter(xvals, yvals)
plt.xlabel('x', fontsize=20)
plt.ylabel('y', fontsize=20)
plt.title('Data', fontsize=25)
plt.show()

# Define the loss function
def get_loss(w, xvals, yvals):
    return np.sum((w * xvals + w * xvals**2 - yvals) ** 2)
```

```
# Define the gradient of the loss function
def get_gradient(w, xvals, yvals):
    return np.sum(2 * (xvals + xvals**2) * (w * xvals + w * xvals**2 - yvals))

# Plot the loss function over a range of w values
wvals = np.arange(0, 1.5, 0.1)
lossvals = [get_loss(w, xvals, yvals) for w in wvals]

plt.figure(figsize=(10, 4))
plt.plot(wvals, lossvals)
plt.xlabel('w', fontsize=20)
plt.ylabel('Loss', fontsize=20)
plt.title('Loss Function', fontsize=25)
plt.show()

# Plot the gradient of the loss function over a range of w values
gradvals = [get_gradient(w, xvals, yvals) for w in wvals]

plt.figure(figsize=(10, 4))
plt.plot(wvals, gradvals)
plt.axhline(0, color='k')
plt.xlabel('w', fontsize=20)
plt.ylabel('Gradient', fontsize=20)
plt.title('Gradient', fontsize=25)
plt.show()

# Perform gradient descent
def perform_gradient_descent(init_w, eta, num_iters, get_gradient):
    w_vals = [init_w]
    for _ in range(num_iters):
        grad = get_gradient(w_vals[-1], xvals, yvals)
        w_vals.append(w_vals[-1] - eta * grad)
    return w_vals

# Perform gradient descent with initial parameters
w_vals = perform_gradient_descent(0, 0.0001, 50, get_gradient)

plt.figure(figsize=(10, 4))
plt.plot(w_vals)
plt.xlabel('Iteration', fontsize=20)
plt.ylabel('w', fontsize=20)
plt.title(f'Gradient Descent Progress\nFinal w: {round(w_vals[-1], 2)}', fontsize=25)
plt.show()

# Plot the fitted model
xrange = np.arange(xvals.min(), xvals.max(), 0.01)
pred_yvals_loss1 = w_vals[-1] * (xrange + xrange**2)
```

```
plt.figure(figsize=(7, 7))
plt.scatter(xvals, yvals)
plt.plot(xrange, pred_yvals_loss1)
plt.xlabel('x', fontsize=20)
plt.ylabel('y', fontsize=20)
plt.title('Fitted Model', fontsize=25)
plt.show()

# Redefine the loss and gradient functions with an exponential weight
def get_loss_exp(w, xvals, yvals):
    ivals = np.arange(1, len(xvals) + 1)
    return np.sum(np.exp(-ivals) * (w * xvals + w * xvals**2 - yvals) ** 2)

def get_gradient_exp(w, xvals, yvals):
    ivals = np.arange(1, len(xvals) + 1)
    return np.sum(2 * np.exp(-ivals) * (xvals + xvals**2) * (w * xvals + w * xvals**2 - yvals))

# Plot the new loss function
lossvals_exp = [get_loss_exp(w, xvals, yvals) for w in wvals]

plt.figure(figsize=(10, 4))
plt.plot(wvals, lossvals_exp)
plt.xlabel('w', fontsize=20)
plt.ylabel('Loss', fontsize=20)
plt.title('Exponential Loss Function', fontsize=25)
plt.show()

# Plot the new gradient function
gradvals_exp = [get_gradient_exp(w, xvals, yvals) for w in wvals]

plt.figure(figsize=(10, 4))
plt.plot(wvals, gradvals_exp)
plt.axhline(0, color='k')
plt.xlabel('w', fontsize=20)
plt.ylabel('Gradient', fontsize=20)
plt.title('Exponential Gradient', fontsize=25)
plt.show()

# Perform gradient descent with the new exponential gradient function
w_vals_exp = perform_gradient_descent(0, 0.01, 50, get_gradient_exp)

plt.figure(figsize=(10, 4))
plt.plot(w_vals_exp)
plt.xlabel('Iteration', fontsize=20)
plt.ylabel('w', fontsize=20)
plt.title(f'Exponential Gradient Descent Progress\nFinal w: {round(w_vals_exp[-1], 2)}',
fontsize=25)
plt.show()
```

```
# Plot the fitted model with the new exponential loss
pred_yvals_loss2 = w_vals_exp[-1] * (xrange + xrange**2)

plt.figure(figsize=(7, 7))
plt.scatter(xvals, yvals)
plt.plot(xrange, pred_yvals_loss2)
plt.xlabel('x', fontsize=20)
plt.ylabel('y', fontsize=20)
plt.title('Fitted Model with Exponential Loss', fontsize=25)
plt.show()

# Compare the results of the two models
plt.figure(figsize=(7, 7))
plt.scatter(xvals, yvals)
p1, = plt.plot(xrange, pred_yvals_loss1, label='Linear Loss')
p2, = plt.plot(xrange, pred_yvals_loss2, label='Exponential Loss')
plt.xlabel('x', fontsize=20)
plt.ylabel('y', fontsize=20)
plt.title('Comparison of Fitted Models', fontsize=25)
plt.legend(fontsize=20)
plt.show()
```

The purpose of this code is to demonstrate the application of gradient descent to fit a model to synthetic data. The code includes the following steps:

Data Generation:

Synthetic data is created based on a quadratic relationship with added noise to simulate real-world data.

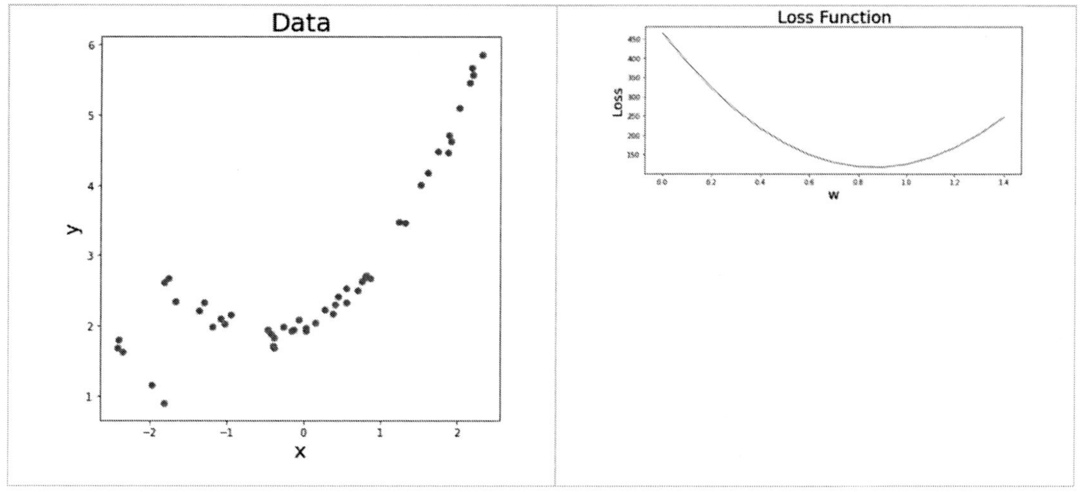

Loss Function and Gradient Computation:

The loss function calculates the difference between predicted and actual values.

The gradient of the loss function is computed to guide the updates during gradient descent.

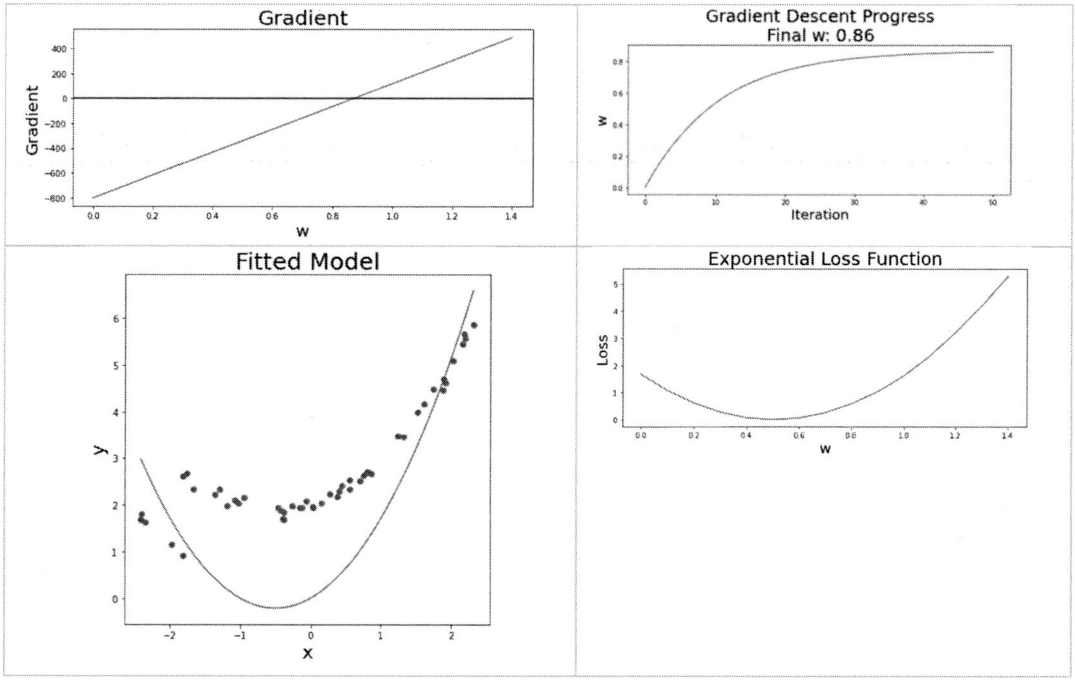

Gradient Descent:

An iterative optimization method is used to find the parameter w that minimizes the loss function.

Two types of loss functions are explored: linear and exponentially weighted.

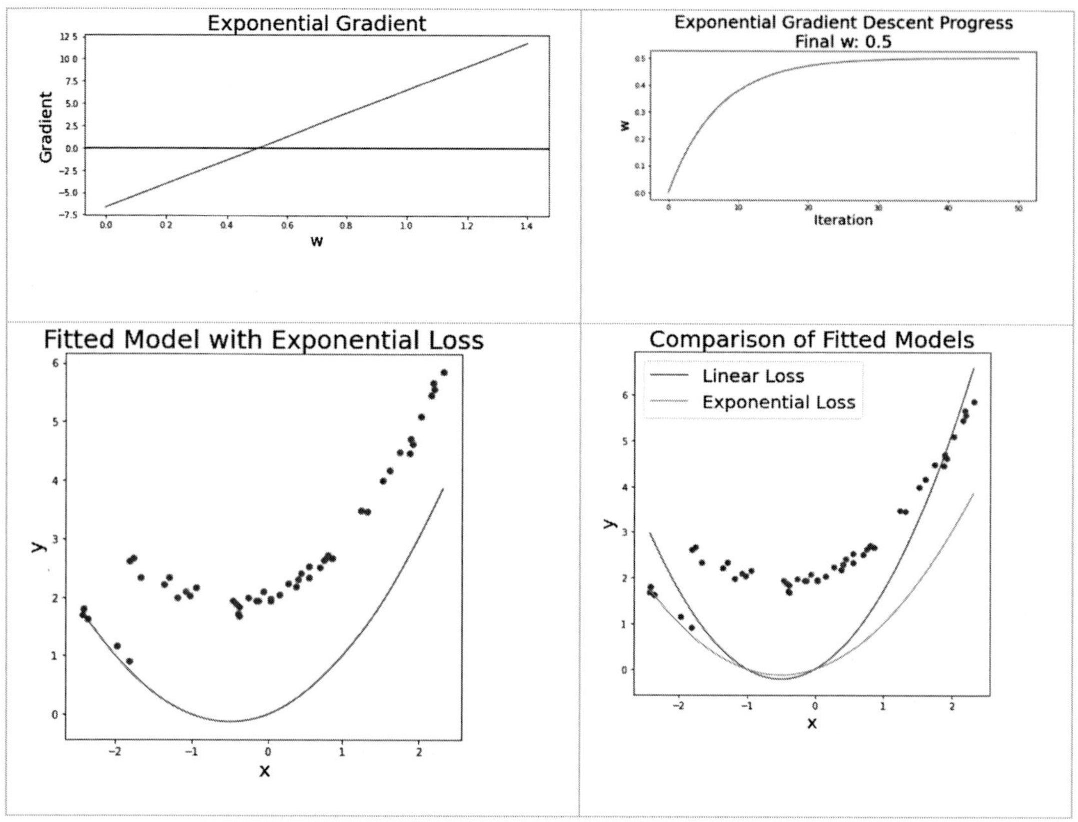

Visualization:

Various plots are created to visualise the data, the loss function, the gradient, the progress of gradient descent, and the fitted models.

A comparison of models fitted with different loss functions is provided.

Regularization in Loss Functions

Master explained that in addition to the regular loss terms, regularization terms can be added to the loss function to prevent overfitting. Common types of regularization include:

L1 Regularization (Lasso): Adds the sum of absolute values of weights to the loss function.

$$L = \text{Original Loss} + \lambda \sum_{J=1} |\beta_j|$$

L2 Regularization (Ridge): Adds the sum of squares of weights to the loss function.

$$L = \text{Original Loss} + \lambda \sum_{j} \beta_j^2$$

Elastic Net: A combination of L1 and L2 regularization.

Summary:

In this unit, we explored both supervised and unsupervised learning techniques. We delved into the fundamentals of linear regression, logistic regression, and clustering methods. Additionally, we discussed ordinary least squares (OLS) regression and multiple linear regression, highlighting their importance in modelling relationships between variables.

To refine our models, we examined various methods, such as backward elimination, forward selection, bidirectional elimination, and score comparison. These techniques aid in selecting the most relevant features and optimising model performance.

Additionally, we delved into polynomial regression, a robust advancement of linear regression, enabling us to effectively model nonlinear relationships among variables. This technique empowers us to capture intricate data patterns, thus enhancing the precision of our predictions. Moreover, we explored the concepts of loss function and gradient descent, fundamental tools essential for optimizing regression models and refining their performance.

PART FOUR

DAY ELEVEN

Unit 4 - Lesson Two

Regression

Bayesian Regression

Bayesian regression utilises Bayesian statistics to estimate parameters in a linear regression model, incorporating prior knowledge about the parameters. This approach often yields more accurate parameter estimates, provides uncertainty measures, and allows for stronger conclusions compared to ordinary least squares (OLS) regression. It can also be extended to tasks like model selection and outlier detection.

In Bayesian regression, Bayes' theorem is employed to estimate the likelihood of parameters given observed data. The objective is to find the optimal parameters for a linear model that describes the relationship between independent and dependent variables.

Compared to traditional linear regression, Bayesian regression differs in its assumption about the data-generating process. While linear regression assumes a Gaussian distribution, Bayesian regression imposes prior probability distributions on parameters, offering greater flexibility and enabling the incorporation of prior beliefs about the data. This allows for the construction of complex models reflecting prior knowledge.

Bayesian regression provides more accurate predictive measures with fewer data points and generates estimates of uncertainty around parameter estimates. However, traditional linear regression is simpler to implement and faster with simpler models, often yielding satisfactory results when data assumptions are met.

Bayesian regression is particularly valuable when data is limited or poorly distributed. Its output is derived from a probability distribution, unlike traditional regression, where output is a single value for each attribute. This probabilistic approach enhances the model's robustness and adaptability in diverse data scenarios.

The key concepts in Bayesian Regression are:

Bayes' Theorem: This theorem establishes the relationship between an event's prior probability and its posterior probability after considering evidence. It states that the conditional probability of an event is proportional to the probability of the event given certain conditions, multiplied by the prior probability of the event, divided by the probability of the conditions.

In probability theory, Bayes' theorem states:

$$P(A|B) = P(B|A) \cdot P(A) \;/\; P(B)$$

where:

- P(A|B) is the probability of event A occurring given that event B has already occurred,
- P(B|A) is the probability of event B occurring given that event A has already occurred,
- P(A) is the probability of event A occurring, and
- P(B) is the probability of event B occurring.

Maximum Likelihood Estimation (MLE): MLE is a method used to estimate the parameters of a statistical model by maximising the likelihood function. It determines parameter values that make the observed data most probable under the assumed model. MLE does not incorporate prior information or assumptions about the parameters, providing point estimates of the parameters.

Maximum A Posteriori (MAP) Estimation: MAP estimation combines prior information with the likelihood function to estimate parameters. It involves finding parameter values that maximise the posterior distribution, obtained by applying Bayes' theorem. MAP estimation specifies a prior distribution for the parameters, representing prior beliefs or knowledge. The likelihood function is multiplied by the prior distribution to obtain the joint distribution, and the parameter values maximising this joint distribution are chosen as the MAP estimates. MAP estimation provides point estimates of parameters, incorporating prior information.

Likelihood Function: The likelihood function represents the probability of observed data given parameter values in a statistical model. It quantifies how well the model explains the observed data.

Precision: Precision refers to the level of certainty or uncertainty associated with parameter estimates in Bayesian regression.

Negative Log-Likelihood: It is the negative logarithm of the likelihood function and is often used in optimization algorithms to find parameter estimates.

Prior: In Bayesian inference, the prior distribution represents existing knowledge or beliefs about parameters before observing data. It influences the posterior distribution.

Posterior Distribution: The posterior distribution is the updated probability distribution of parameters after observing data. It combines prior knowledge with observed data to provide updated estimates of parameters.

The posterior expression is given below:

Posterior = (Likelihood·Prior) / (Normalization)

where the expression parameters are explained as follows:

- Posterior: It represents the likelihood that an event, such as H, will occur given the occurrence of another event, such as E, denoted as P(H|E).
- Likelihood: This is a function that computes the likelihood of an event, typically involving a variable to be marginalised.
- Prior: It refers to the likelihood that event H occurred before event *A*A, denoted as P(H).

Types of Bayesian Regression

Bayesian regression encompasses various techniques that utilise Bayesian inference principles to estimate model parameters and make predictions. Some common types include:

Bayesian Ridge Regression: This approach applies L2 regularization to the model parameters, making it useful for handling multicollinearity issues and preventing overfitting. The posterior distribution of the coefficients is typically assumed to be normally distributed.

Bayesian Lasso Regression: Bayesian Lasso incorporates L1 regularization into the model parameters, similar to ridge regression. This regularization technique promotes sparsity in the model, potentially leading to variable selection by setting some coefficients to zero.

Bayesian Polynomial Regression: By introducing polynomial terms for the independent variables in the model, Bayesian regression can be extended to polynomial regression. This allows for modelling nonlinear relationships between variables, offering greater flexibility in capturing complex patterns in the data.

Generalized Linear Models (GLM): Bayesian regression methods can be adapted to fit generalized linear models (GLMs), which accommodate non-normal response variables and support various link functions. GLMs are particularly useful for modelling data with non-Gaussian distributions and handling response variables that exhibit non-constant variance or are not linearly related to the predictors.

Example P4 – U4 – D9

Bayesian Regression

```
import torch
import pyro
import pyro.distributions as dist
from pyro.infer import SVI, Trace_ELBO, Predictive
from pyro.optim import Adam
import matplotlib.pyplot as plt
import seaborn as sns

# Set random seed for reproducibility
torch.manual_seed(0)

# Generate sample data
X = torch.linspace(0, 10, 100)
true_slope, true_intercept = 2, 1
Y = true_intercept + true_slope * X + torch.randn(100)

# Bayesian regression model
def model(X, Y):
    slope = pyro.sample("slope", dist.Normal(0, 10))
    intercept = pyro.sample("intercept", dist.Normal(0, 10))
    sigma = pyro.sample("sigma", dist.HalfNormal(1))
    mu = intercept + slope * X
    with pyro.plate("data", len(X)):
        pyro.sample("obs", dist.Normal(mu, sigma), obs=Y)

# Guide for approximate posterior distributions
def guide(X, Y):
    slope_loc = pyro.param("slope_loc", torch.tensor(0.0))
    slope_scale = pyro.param("slope_scale", torch.tensor(1.0),
                             constraint=dist.constraints.positive)
    intercept_loc = pyro.param("intercept_loc", torch.tensor(0.0))
    intercept_scale = pyro.param("intercept_scale", torch.tensor(1.0),
                                 constraint=dist.constraints.positive)
    sigma_loc = pyro.param("sigma_loc", torch.tensor(1.0),
                           constraint=dist.constraints.positive)
    slope = pyro.sample("slope", dist.Normal(slope_loc, slope_scale))
    intercept = pyro.sample("intercept", dist.Normal(intercept_loc,
                                                     intercept_scale))
    sigma = pyro.sample("sigma", dist.HalfNormal(sigma_loc))
```

```
# Initialize SVI and optimizer
optim = Adam({"lr": 0.01})
svi = SVI(model, guide, optim, loss=Trace_ELBO())

# Inference loop
num_iterations = 1000
for i in range(num_iterations):
    loss = svi.step(X, Y)
    if (i + 1) % 100 == 0:
        print(f"Iteration {i + 1}/{num_iterations} - Loss: {loss}")

# Posterior samples using Predictive
predictive = Predictive(model, guide=guide, num_samples=1000)
posterior = predictive(X, Y)

# Extract parameter samples
slope_samples = posterior["slope"]
intercept_samples = posterior["intercept"]
sigma_samples = posterior["sigma"]

# Compute posterior means
slope_mean = slope_samples.mean()
intercept_mean = intercept_samples.mean()
sigma_mean = sigma_samples.mean()

# Print estimated parameters
print("Estimated Slope:", slope_mean.item())
print("Estimated Intercept:", intercept_mean.item())
print("Estimated Sigma:", sigma_mean.item())

# Plot posterior distributions
fig, axs = plt.subplots(1, 3, figsize=(15, 5))
titles = ["Posterior Distribution of Slope",
          "Posterior Distribution of Intercept",
          "Posterior Distribution of Sigma"]
params = [slope_samples, intercept_samples, sigma_samples]

for ax, title, param in zip(axs, titles, params):
    sns.kdeplot(param, shade=True, ax=ax)
    ax.set_title(title)
    ax.set_xlabel(title.split()[-1])
    ax.set_ylabel("Density")
plt.tight_layout()
plt.show()
```

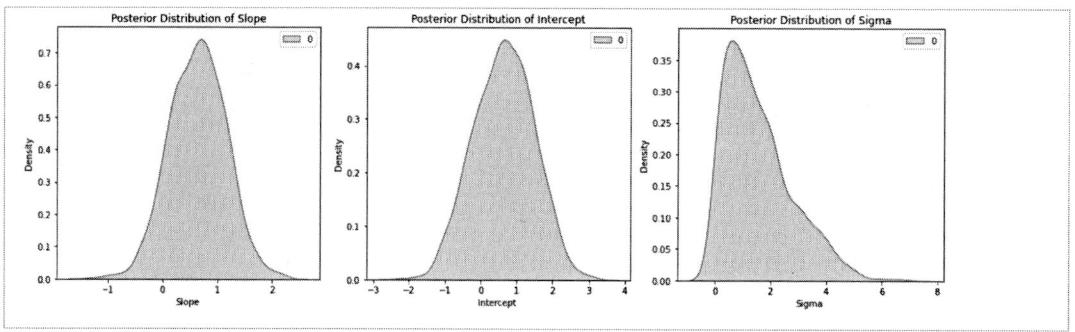

Advantages of Bayesian Regression:

- Effective with Small Datasets: Bayesian Regression performs well even when the dataset size is small, making it suitable for scenarios with limited data availability.
- Well-Suited for Online Learning: It excels in online learning settings where data is received in real-time. Unlike batch-based learning, Bayesian Regression doesn't require storing the entire dataset beforehand.
- Robust and Mathematically Sound: The Bayesian approach is robust and mathematically sound, making it a reliable method even without extensive prior knowledge of the dataset.
- Incorporation of Prior Information: Bayesian regression methods allow the incorporation of external information through skewed distributions, enhancing model flexibility and adaptability.

Disadvantages of Bayesian Regression:

- Time-Consuming Inference: The inference process in Bayesian Regression can be computationally intensive, particularly for complex models or large datasets, leading to longer training times.
- Inefficiency with Large Datasets: For datasets with a large volume of data points, the Bayesian approach may not be as efficient as traditional frequentist methods, such as ordinary least squares regression.
- Dependency and Installation Challenges: Implementing Bayesian Regression may pose challenges in environments with strict dependency controls or limited ability to install new packages.
- Vulnerable to Model Assumptions: Similar to frequentist regression models, Bayesian models are susceptible to basic mistakes, like assuming linearity between predictor variables and the outcome variable, highlighting the importance of careful model

specification and validation.

Quantile regression

Apeksha asked, "How to Perform Quantile Regression in Python?"

Master said, "Quantile regression extends the concept of linear regression by modelling the relationship between a set of variables (independent variables) and various quantiles (or percentiles) of the dependent variable."

For instance, consider a scenario where we have a dataset containing information about the total distance travelled and the total emission generated by 20 cars of different brands.

In this example, we aim to construct a quantile regression model with the following variables:

- Distance Travelled: This serves as the predictor variable.
- Emission Generated: This is our response variable.

Let's proceed to create and analyse our quantile regression model using Python.

Now, let's leverage this model to estimate the 70th percentile of emissions generated based on the total distance travelled by cars.

Example P4 – U4 – D10	
Quantile Regression	**Output**

# Importing libraries 	
import numpy as np
import pandas as pd
import statsmodels.api as sm
import statsmodels.formula.api as smf
import matplotlib.pyplot as plt
 	
# Set random seed for reproducibility 	
np.random.seed(0)
 	
# Number of rows 	
rows = 20
 	
# Constructing Distance column 	
Distance = np.random.uniform(1, 10, rows)
 	
# Constructing Emission column 	
	coef std err t
	P>|t| [0.025
	0.975]
	------------------------------- 	
	--- 	
	Intercept 39.5647
	2.276 17.386 0.000
	34.784 44.346
	Distance 1.3042
	0.343 3.806 0.001
	0.584 2.024

```
Emission = 40 + Distance + np.random.normal(loc=0,
scale=.25*Distance, size=20)

# Creating a dataset
df = pd.DataFrame({'Distance': Distance,
            'Emission': Emission})

# Fit the model
model = smf.quantreg('Emission ~ Distance', df).fit(q=0.7)

# View model summary
print(model.summary())

# Define figure and axis
fig, ax = plt.subplots(figsize=(10, 8))

# Define the line equation for the quantile regression
y_line = lambda a, b: a + Distance * b
y = y_line(model.params['Intercept'],
model.params['Distance'])
# Plot data points and the quantile regression line
ax.plot(Distance, y, color='black')
ax.scatter(Distance, Emission, alpha=.3)
ax.set_xlabel('Distance Traveled', fontsize=20)
ax.set_ylabel('Emission Generated', fontsize=20)
# Save the plot
fig.savefig('quantile_regression.png')
```

From the output of this program, we can derive the estimated regression equation as follows:

```
val = 39.5647 + 1.3042 * X (where X represents distance in kilometres)
```

This equation suggests that the 70th percentile of emissions for all cars travelling 'X' kilometres is expected to be val.

To gain deeper insights, we can visualise the quantile regression by overlaying it on a scatterplot of the data points. This approach provides a comprehensive view of how well the model captures the relationship between the variables.

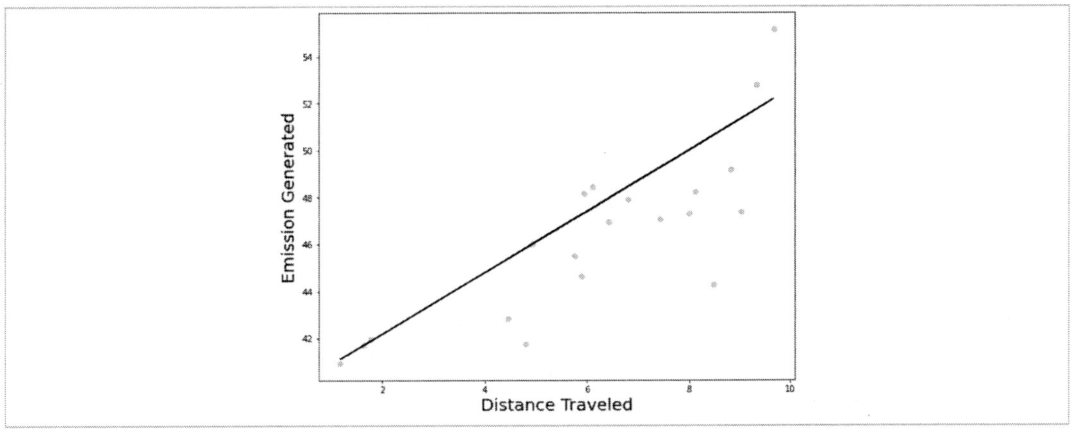

Isotonic Regression

Master said, "Isotonic regression is a powerful technique used to model relationships between predictor and target variables when the relationship is monotonic, meaning it consistently increases or decreases without oscillation. Mathematically, isotonic regression aims to find a monotonic function that minimises the sum of squared errors between predicted and observed target variable values."

The optimisation problem for isotonic regression can be expressed as:

Minimize $\sum_{i=1}^{n}(y_i - f(x_i)^2)$

subject to:

$$f(x_i) \leq f(x_{i+1})$$

where x_i and y_i represent the predictor and target variables, respectively, for the ith data point, and f is the monotonic function being fitted to the data. The constraint ensures that the function remains monotonic.

Isotonic regression finds applications in various domains:

- Calibration of Predicted Probabilities: It adjusts predicted probabilities from classifiers to improve calibration.
- Ordinal Regression: It models ordinal variables that can be ranked in order.
- Non-parametric Regression: Isotonic regression doesn't assume any specific functional form, making it useful in non-parametric regression.

- Imputing Missing Values: It predicts missing values based on surrounding non-missing values.
- Outlier Detection: It identifies outliers by detecting points significantly different from the overall trend.

In scikit-learn, the IsotonicRegression class is used to perform isotonic regression. This class fits a non-decreasing piecewise-constant function to the data.

Here's an example of how to use IsotonicRegression in scikit-learn:

Example P4 – U4 – D11

Isotonic Regression

```
import numpy as np
import matplotlib.pyplot as plt
from matplotlib.collections import LineCollection
from sklearn.isotonic import IsotonicRegression
from sklearn.linear_model import LinearRegression

# Sample dataset
n = 20
x = np.arange(n)
print('Input:\n', x)
y = np.random.randint(0, 20, size=n) + 10 * np.log1p(np.arange(n))
print("Target :\n", y)
# Isotonic Regression
ir = IsotonicRegression()
y_ir = ir.fit_transform(x, y)
print('Isotonic Regression Predictions  :\n', y_ir)
# Linear Regression
lr = LinearRegression()
lr.fit(x.reshape(-1, 1), y)
y_lr = lr.predict(x.reshape(-1, 1))
print('Linear Regression Prediction :\n', y_lr)

# Plotting
lines = [[[i, y[i]], [i, y_ir[i]]] for i in range(n)]
lc = LineCollection(lines)
plt.plot(x, y, '.', markersize=10, label='data')
plt.plot(x, y_ir, '-', markersize=10, label='isotonic regression')
plt.plot(x, y_lr, '-', label='linear regression')

plt.gca().add_collection(lc)
plt.legend()
plt.title("Isotonic Regression")
plt.show()
```

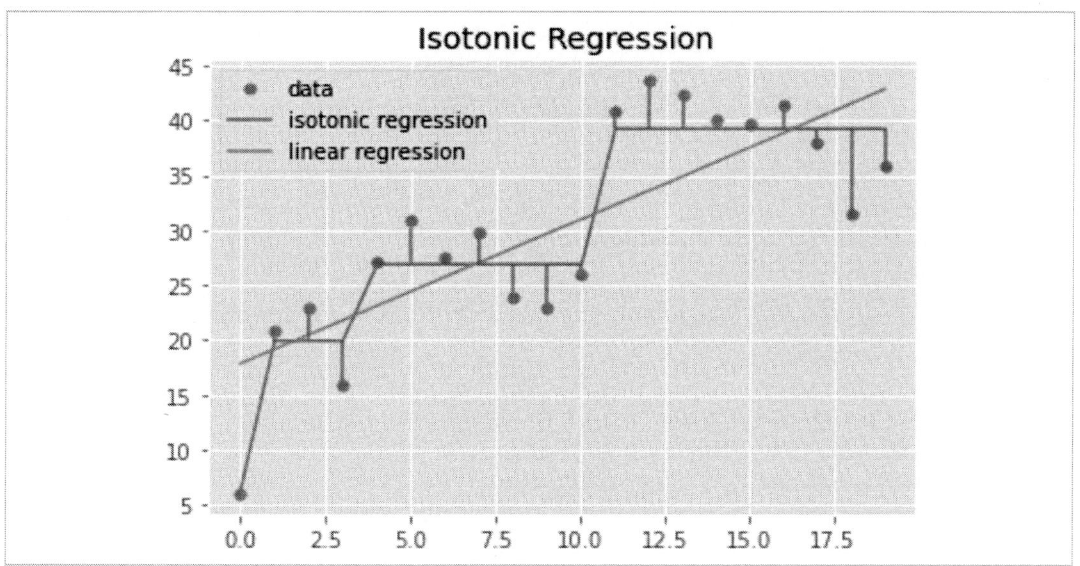

Stepwise Regression

John asked, "What is stepwise regression?"

Master said, "Stepwise regression is a method used to iteratively select variables for a regression model, aiming to find the smallest subset of variables that adequately explain the data. It can be categorised into two main types: forward selection and backward elimination."

Forward selection begins with an empty model and adds variables one by one until no further improvement is observed. On the other hand, backward elimination starts with a model containing all variables and removes them iteratively until no significant improvement remains.

The advantage of stepwise regression lies in its ability to automatically select essential variables, thus creating a parsimonious model. However, it's important to note that the selection process may not always yield the optimal model and could be sensitive to the order of variable inclusion or exclusion.

Stepwise regression finds utility in building regression models that balance accuracy with simplicity. By automatically selecting influential variables, it streamlines the model-building process and can enhance performance by eliminating irrelevant features, potentially mitigating overfitting issues.

Ultimately, stepwise regression serves as a valuable tool for constructing accurate and concise regression models capable of capturing complex relationships within the data. Its versatility makes it a popular choice across various domains for effective model selection and refinement.

Stepwise and other regression models:

Stepwise regression stands out from other regression techniques because of its automated selection of significant variables for model building. In contrast, methods like ordinary least squares (OLS) and least absolute shrinkage and selection operator (LASSO) require manual intervention from analysts to select variables.

The advantage of stepwise regression lies in its ability to streamline the modelling process, saving time and effort for analysts. Additionally, it enhances model performance by minimizing the number of variables, thus eliminating unnecessary or irrelevant ones. However, its reliance on iterative variable selection can lead to suboptimal model choices and sensitivity to the order of variable inclusion or exclusion.

While stepwise regression is a valuable tool for model selection, it's essential to use it judiciously and in conjunction with other regression techniques to ensure optimal model selection.

In comparison, linear regression is a statistical method that models the relationship between a dependent variable and one or more independent variables. It predicts the dependent variable based on the predictors' linear equation, making it a fundamental tool for predictive modelling.

On the other hand, stepwise regression is a process-driven approach to building regression models. It systematically adds or removes predictors to identify the subset that offers the best predictive performance for the response variable. This iterative procedure begins with an empty model and progresses by evaluating predictors' strength in relation to the response variable.

In summary, linear regression models the relationship between variables, while stepwise regression iteratively selects predictors to build an optimal regression model. Both techniques serve distinct purposes in the realm of regression analysis.

To implement Stepwise Regression in Python, follow these refined steps:

- Install mlxtend Library: Begin by installing the mlxtend library using pip. Run the command pip install mlxtend in your command prompt or terminal.
- Import Necessary Modules: Import the required modules from the mlxtend library, including SequentialFeatureSelector and linear_model.
- Define Features and Target: Define the features and target variables in your dataset.
- Initialize Stepwise Regression Model: Initialize the Stepwise Regression model using the SequentialFeatureSelector and specify the type of regression to be used, such as linear_model.LinearRegression for linear regression.
- Fit the Model: Fit the Stepwise Regression model to your dataset using the fit method.
- View Selected Features: Access the k_features attribute of the fitted model to see which features were selected by the Stepwise Regression.

Example P4 – U4 – D12	
Stepwise Regression	**Output**

import pandas as pd
import numpy as np
from sklearn.model_selection import train_test_split
from sklearn.linear_model import LogisticRegression
from mlxtend.feature_selection import SequentialFeatureSelector
 	
# Define the array of data 	
data = np.array([[1, 2, 3, 4],
              [5, 6, 7, 8],
              [9, 10, 11, 12]])
 	
# Convert the array into a dataframe 	
df = pd.DataFrame(data)
 	
# Select the features and target 	
X = df.iloc[:, :-1]
y = df.iloc[:, -1]
 	
# Build Stepwise Model 	
# Perform stepwise regression 	
sfs = SequentialFeatureSelector(LogisticRegression(),
                            k_features=3,
                            forward=True,
                            scoring='accuracy',
                            cv=None)
selected_features = sfs.fit(X, y)
 	
# Get the selected feature indices 	
selected_columns = list(selected_features.k_feature_idx_)
 	
# Create a dataframe with only the selected features 	
df_selected = df.iloc[:, selected_columns]
 	
# Split the data into train and test sets 	
X_train, X_test, y_train, y_test = train_test_split(
  df_selected, y, test_size=0.3, random_state=42)
 	
# Fit a logistic regression model using the selected features 	
logreg = LogisticRegression()
logreg.fit(X_train, y_train)
 	
# Make predictions using the test set 	
y_pred = logreg.predict(X_test)
 	
# Evaluate the model performance 	
	Predictions: [8]

```
print("Predictions:", y_pred)
```

Least Angel Regression

Master said, "Least Angle Regression (LARS) is a regression algorithm specifically designed for high-dimensional data, where the number of attributes is large. It operates similarly to forward stepwise regression but with some distinct characteristics."

Normalization:

Normalize all attribute values to have zero mean and unit variance. This standardization ensures that each attribute contributes equally to the model fitting process.

Selection of Attributes:

- LARS starts by identifying the attribute that is most highly correlated with the residual (the difference between observed and predicted values). This attribute is the most influential in predicting the target variable.
- It then adjusts the regression line in the direction of this attribute until another attribute with equal or higher correlation is encountered.

Handling Equal Correlation:

- If there are multiple attributes with the same correlation, LARS takes a unique approach. It moves the regression line in a direction that is at an angle equidistant between the two or more correlated attributes. This approach ensures fairness in incorporating highly correlated attributes into the model.

Iterative Process:

- LARS iteratively adds predictors to the model while adjusting the coefficients to minimize the residual error.
- At each step, it extends the current set of predictors in a direction that maintains an equal angle (least angle) with the attributes already in the model.

Model Generalization:

The algorithm continues adding predictors until all attributes are included or until the model is deemed sufficiently general.

Mathematical Procedure:

Initialization:

- All coefficients (B) are set to 0 initially.

Attribute Selection:

- Identify the predictor (x_j) that is most correlated with the target variable (y).

Coefficient Adjustment:

- Increase the coefficient (B_j) in the direction most correlated with y until another predictor (x_k) with equal or higher correlation is encountered.

Direction Adjustment:

- Extend the coefficient vector (B_j, B_k) in a direction that maintains the same angle between x_j and x_k.

Iteration:

- Repeat the process iteratively until all predictors are included in the model.

By following this algorithm, LARS effectively navigates through high-dimensional data, selecting influential attributes and building a model that generalizes well without overfitting.

LARS Lasso

Master explained that the Least Angle Regression (LARS) method, combined with Lasso regularization, known as LARS Lasso, is a powerful technique in linear regression. It merges the effectiveness of L1 regularization (Lasso) with the efficiency of forward selection.

Working Principle:

Efficient Feature Selection:

- LARS Lasso efficiently selects relevant features by gradually adding them to the model while moving in the direction of the target variable's highest correlation.
- It iteratively includes features until reaching a point where adding another feature would result in equal correlation with an existing feature.

Sparsity Induction:

- LARS Lasso induces sparsity in the model by shrinking unnecessary coefficients towards zero. This property is particularly beneficial for high-dimensional datasets where the underlying structure is believed to be sparse.

- The L1 penalty of Lasso regularisation encourages models with fewer non-zero coefficients, promoting a sparse subset of features.

Example P4 – U4 – D13

Least Angel Regression (LARS) and LARS Lasso

```
import numpy as np
from sklearn.linear_model import Lars, LassoLars
import matplotlib.pyplot as plt

# Example data generation
np.random.seed(123)
X = np.random.rand(100, 10)
y = 2 * X[:, 2] + 1.5 * X[:, 5] + np.random.normal(0, 0.5, 100)

# Apply LARS
lars = Lars()
lars.fit(X, y)

# Apply LARS Lasso with a different alpha value
alpha = 0.05  # Adjust alpha as needed
lars_lasso = LassoLars(alpha=alpha)
lars_lasso.fit(X, y)

# Plot the results
plt.figure(figsize=(10, 6))

plt.subplot(1, 2, 1)
plt.plot(lars.coef_, marker='o', label='LARS Coefficients')
plt.xlabel('Coefficient Index')
plt.ylabel('Coefficient Value')
plt.title('LARS Regression Coefficients')
plt.legend()

plt.subplot(1, 2, 2)
plt.plot(lars_lasso.coef_, marker='o', label='LARS Lasso Coefficients')
plt.xlabel('Coefficient Index')
plt.ylabel('Coefficient Value')
plt.title(f'LARS Lasso Regression with Alpha={alpha}')
plt.legend()
plt.tight_layout()
plt.show()
```

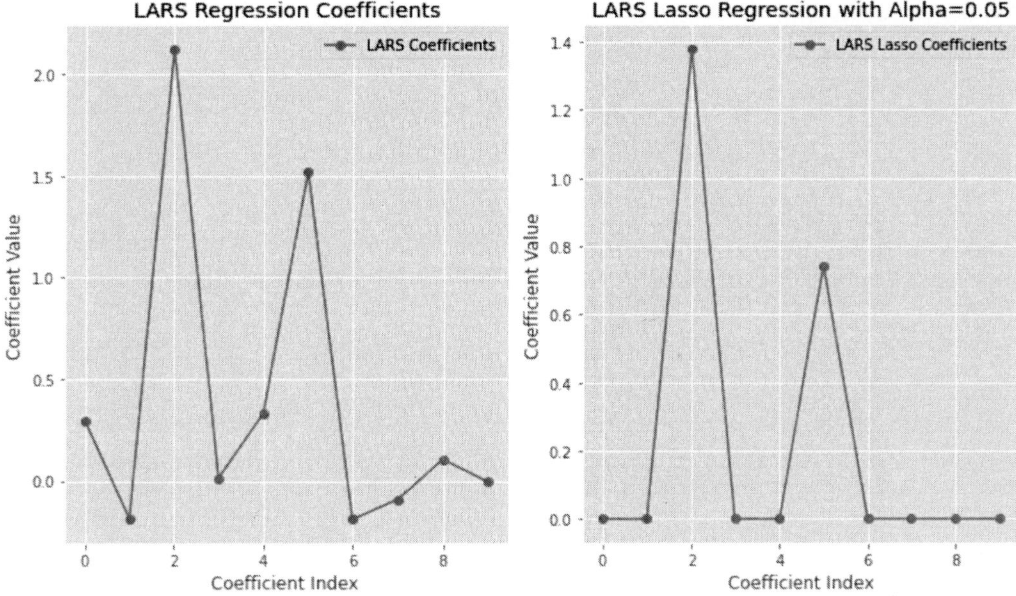

Summary:

In this unit, we delved into advanced regression techniques and Bayesian statistics. We explored Bayesian regression, Bayes' Theorem, Maximum Likelihood Estimation (MLE), Maximum A Posteriori (MAP) estimation, Likelihood Function, Precision, Prior, and Posterior Distribution. These concepts provided us with a deeper understanding of probabilistic modelling and parameter estimation in regression analysis.

Furthermore, we discussed regularization techniques such as Ridge, Lasso, and Elastic Net, which help mitigate overfitting by adding penalty terms to the regression coefficients. These methods promote simpler and more interpretable models while improving generalization performance.

We also addressed common challenges in regression modelling, including overfitting and underfitting, and explored solutions to these issues. Additionally, we introduced quantile regression, Isotonic regression, stepwise regression, Least Angle Regression (LARS), and LARS Lasso, which are powerful tools for building robust regression models and handling complex data patterns.

PART FOUR

DAY Twelve

Unit 4 - Lesson Three

Classification - Logistic

Logistic Regression: Classification

Master said, "Logistic regression is a statistical technique used to model the probability of a binary outcome based on one or more independent variables. It's commonly used when the dependent variable is categorical with two possible outcomes, such as 'yes' or 'no', 'pass' or 'fail', or 'spam' or 'not spam.'"

The logistic regression model applies a logistic function, also known as the sigmoid function, to the linear combination of the independent variables. The sigmoid function maps any real-valued number to the range [0, 1], which is suitable for representing probabilities.

$$P(y=1|X)= 1/1+e^{-(\beta 0+\beta 1x1+\beta 2x2+\cdots+\beta nxn)}$$

The above can be written in terms of the natural logarithm as:

$$\mathbf{1/1+e^{-z}, \text{ where } z = \beta_0 + \beta_1 x_1 + \beta_2 x_2 + \cdots + \beta_n x_n}$$

Where:

- $P(y=1|X)$ is the probability that the dependent variable y is equal to 1 given the independent variables X.
- e is the base of the natural logarithm.
- $\beta_0,\beta_1,\beta_2,\ldots,\beta_n$ are the coefficients associated with the independent variables.
- $x_1,x_2,\ldots,x_n$ are the values of the independent variables.

The logistic regression model estimates the values of the coefficients $\beta_0, \beta_1, \beta_2, \ldots, \beta_n$ that best fit the observed data. These coefficients are determined using optimization techniques such as maximum likelihood estimation.

The formula for logistic regression and the sigmoid function is closely related, but they serve different purposes in the context of machine learning.

Sigmoid Function Formula:

Master explained that the sigmoid function, denoted by σ(z), is a mathematical function that maps any real-valued number z to the range between 0 and 1. Its formula is:

$$\sigma(z) = \frac{1}{1+e^{-z}}$$

Where:

- z is the input to the sigmoid function.
- e is the base of the natural logarithm (approximately 2.71828).

$\sigma(z)$ tend towards 1 as $Z \rightarrow \infty$

$\sigma(z)$ tend towards 1 as $Z \rightarrow -\infty$

$\sigma(z)$ is always bounded between 0 and 1

Probability of being a class:

$P(y=1) = \sigma(z)$ $P(y=0) = 1 - \sigma(z)$

Exercise P4-U4 – D14	
Classification – Sigmoid function	**Output**

```
import numpy as np
import matplotlib.pyplot as plt
def sigmoid(x):
    return 1 / (1 + np.exp(-x))
# Generate x values
x_values = np.linspace(-10, 10, 100)
# Compute sigmoid function values
sigmoid_values = sigmoid(x_values)
# Plot the sigmoid function
plt.figure(figsize=(8, 6))
```

```
plt.plot(x_values, sigmoid_values, label='Sigmoid Function',
color='b')
plt.title('Sigmoid Function')
plt
```

The sigmoid function is used as an activation function in neural networks and logistic regression to introduce non-linearity and squash the output between 0 and 1.

Logistic Regression Formula:

Master said, "In logistic regression, the goal is to model the probability that a given input instance belongs to a particular class (e.g., positive or negative, 1 or 0). The logistic regression model uses the sigmoid function to model this probability. The formula for logistic regression involves a linear combination of input features, which is then passed through the sigmoid function."

$$P(y=1|X) = \sigma (\beta_0 + \beta_1 x_1 + \beta_2 x_2 + \cdots + \beta_n x_n)$$

Here, $P(y=1|X)$ represents the probability that the target variable y equals 1 given the input features σ is the sigmoid function, $\beta_0,\beta_1,\beta_2,\ldots,\beta_n$ are the coefficients, and $x_1,x_2,\ldots,x_n$ are the input features.

In summary, while the sigmoid function is a mathematical function used to map any real number to the range between 0 and 1, logistic regression uses the sigmoid function as part of its formula to model the probability of a binary outcome based on input features.

Key properties of the logistic regression equation include:

Dependent Variable Distribution: In logistic regression, the dependent variable follows a Bernoulli distribution, which is a probability distribution representing binary outcomes (e.g., success or failure, 1 or 0). The logistic regression model predicts the probability that an observation belongs to one of the two categories.

Maximum Likelihood Estimation: Estimation and prediction in logistic regression are typically based on the principle of maximum likelihood. This means that the parameters of the logistic regression model (coefficients) are estimated in such a way that the likelihood of observing the given data is maximized. The model finds the parameter values that make the observed outcomes most probable under the assumed logistic regression model.

These properties are fundamental to understanding how logistic regression models are formulated and how they make predictions based on input features.

Maximum Likelihood Estimation (MLE)

Maximum Likelihood for Binary Classification in Logistic Regression

Let's use an example of students applying to a top school. We want to predict whether a student will be accepted or rejected based on their grades.

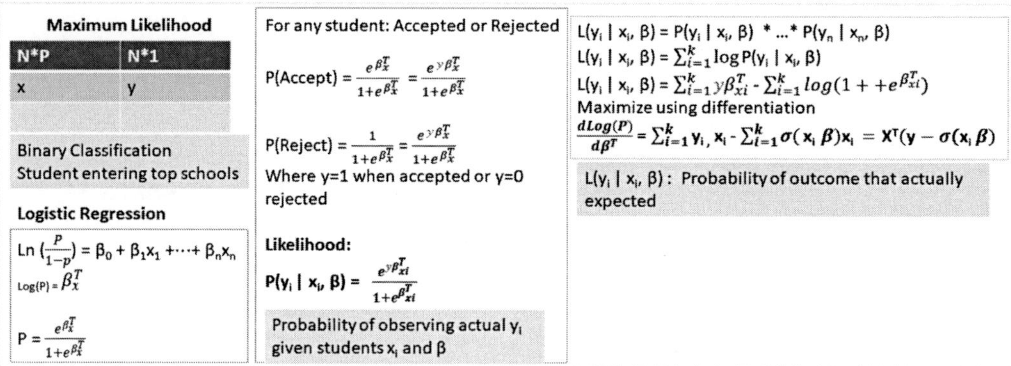

Probability of Acceptance and Rejection

In logistic regression, the probability of a binary outcome (e.g., acceptance or rejection) is modelled using the logistic function. For a given student with predictor variables x (e.g., grades):

Probability of Acceptance (P(Accept)):

$$\text{P(Accept)} = \frac{e^{\beta_x^T}}{1+e^{\beta_x^T}} = \frac{e^{y\beta_x^T}}{1+e^{\beta_x^T}}$$

Here, y = 1 if the student is accepted, and y = 0 if rejected.

Probability of Rejection (P(Reject)):

$$\text{P(Reject)} = \frac{1}{1+e^{\beta_x^T}} = \frac{e^{y\beta_x^T}}{1+e^{\beta_x^T}}$$

P(Reject) = 1−P(Accept)

Likelihood Function

The likelihood function represents the probability of observing the given outcomes (acceptances and rejections) for all students in the dataset:

$$P(y_i \mid x_i, \beta) = \frac{e^{y\beta^T_{xi}}}{1+e^{\beta^T_{xi}}}$$

Where:

- y_i is the observed outcome (1 if accepted, 0 if rejected) for the i-th student.
- x_i is the vector of predictor variables (e.g., grades) for the i-th student.
- β is the vector of parameters to be estimated.

Maximum Likelihood Estimation (MLE)

To estimate the parameters β, we use the method of maximum likelihood. This involves maximising the log-likelihood function. The log-likelihood for logistic regression is:

$$L(y_i \mid x_i, \beta) = \sum_{i=1}^{k} \log P(yi \mid xi, \beta)$$

$$L(y_i \mid x_i, \beta) = \sum_{i=1}^{k} yi \log P(Accept \mid xi, \beta) + (1 - yi) \log P(Reject \mid xi, \beta)$$

Gradient of the Log-Likelihood Function

The gradient of the log-likelihood function with respect to the parameter vector β is used to find the maximum likelihood estimates. The gradient is given by:

$$\frac{dLog(P)}{d\beta^T} = \sum_{i=1}^{k} y_i, xi - \sum_{i=1}^{k} \sigma(x_i\ \beta)x_i$$

Where:

- $\sigma(z) = \frac{1}{1+e^{-z}}$ is the sigmoid function.
- β is the vector of parameters to be estimated.

In matrix form, this can be written as:

$$X^T(y - \sigma(x_i\ \beta)$$

Where:

- X is the matrix of predictor variables.
- y is the vector of observed outcomes.
- $\sigma(X\beta)$ is the vector of predicted probabilities.

In summary, logistic regression models the probability of acceptance or rejection based on predictor variables (e.g., grades) using the logistic function. The parameters are estimated using maximum likelihood estimation, and the gradient of the log-likelihood function is used in optimisation algorithms to find the best-fitting model.

Types of Logistic Regression:

Logistic regression is a statistical method used for binary classification tasks, where the dependent variable is categorical with two possible outcomes. Here are some common types of logistic regression along with examples:

Binary or Binomial Logistic Regression:

Example: Predicting whether an email is spam (1) or not spam (0) based on features like email content, sender, and subject line.

Multinomial Logistic Regression:

Example: Predicting the type of fruit (e.g., apple, banana, orange) based on features like weight, color, and size.

Ordinal Logistic Regression:

Example: Predicting customer satisfaction levels (e.g., low, medium, high) based on factors like service quality, price, and location.

Regularized Logistic Regression:

Example: Predicting the likelihood of default on a loan based on borrower characteristics while mitigating overfitting using regularization techniques like L1 (Lasso) or L2 (Ridge) regularization.

Bayesian Logistic Regression:

Example: Predicting whether a customer will purchase a product (1) or not (0) based on demographic information, incorporating prior knowledge or beliefs about the relationships between features and outcomes.

Each type of logistic regression is suited for different scenarios and data distributions, allowing for flexible modelling of binary classification problems.

Exercise P4-U4 – D15	
Logistic Regression	**Output**
# import the necessary libraries from sklearn.datasets import load_breast_cancer from sklearn.linear_model import LogisticRegression from sklearn.model_selection import train_test_split	Logistic Regression model accuracy (in %): 98.24561403508771

```
from sklearn.metrics import accuracy_score
from sklearn.preprocessing import StandardScaler

def load_data():
    # Load the breast cancer dataset
    X, y = load_breast_cancer(return_X_y=True)
    # Split the dataset into train and test sets
    X_train, X_test, y_train, y_test = train_test_split(X, y,
test_size=0.20, random_state=23)
    return X_train, X_test, y_train, y_test

def preprocess_data(X_train, X_test):
    """
    Preprocess the data by scaling it using StandardScaler.
    Parameters:
    X_train: Features for training.
    X_test: Features for testing.
    Returns:
    X_train_scaled, X_test_scaled: Scaled train and test features.
    """
    scaler = StandardScaler()
    X_train_scaled = scaler.fit_transform(X_train)
    X_test_scaled = scaler.transform(X_test)
    return X_train_scaled, X_test_scaled

def train_logistic_regression(X_train, y_train, max_iter=1000):
    """
    Train a logistic regression model.
    Parameters:
    X_train: Features for training.
    y_train: Labels for training.
    max_iter: Maximum number of iterations for convergence.
    Returns:
    clf: Trained logistic regression model.
    """
    # Logistic Regression
    clf = LogisticRegression(random_state=0, max_iter=max_iter)
    clf.fit(X_train, y_train)
    return clf

def evaluate_model(clf, X_test, y_test):
    """
    Evaluate the trained logistic regression model.
    Parameters:
    clf: Trained logistic regression model.
    X_test: Features for testing.
    y_test: Labels for testing.
    """
```

``
    # Prediction
    y_pred = clf.predict(X_test)
 	
    # Calculate accuracy
    acc = accuracy_score(y_test, y_pred)
    print("Logistic Regression model accuracy (in %):", acc * 100)
 	
def main():
    # Load data
    X_train, X_test, y_train, y_test = load_data()
    # Preprocess data
    X_train_scaled, X_test_scaled = preprocess_data(X_train,
X_test)
    # Train model
    clf = train_logistic_regression(X_train_scaled, y_train)
    # Evaluate model
    evaluate_model(clf, X_test_scaled, y_test)
 	
if __name__ == "__main__":
    main()
``	

Multinomial Logistic Regression

Master explained that the Multinomial Logistic Regression is a powerful extension of binary logistic regression that accommodates scenarios where the target variable can have three or more distinct and unordered categories, such as "disease A," "disease B," and "disease C."

In this method, the softmax function is employed instead of the sigmoid function used in binary logistic regression. The softmax function computes the probabilities for each class, ensuring that the sum of the probabilities across all classes equals one. Mathematically, the softmax function for K classes is represented as:

$$\text{softmax}(z_i)=e^{z_i}/\ \sum_{j=1}^{k} e^{z_j}$$

Here, K represents the number of elements in the vector z, and i and j iterate over all the elements in the vector.

Multinomial Logistic Regression allows the output variable to have more than two possible discrete outputs, making it suitable for classification tasks with multiple classes.

Exercise P4-U4 – D16	
Multinomial Logistic Regression	**Output**
import numpy as np from sklearn.datasets import load_iris from sklearn.model_selection import train_test_split	Accuracy of Multinomial

Code	Output

from sklearn.preprocessing import StandardScaler
from sklearn.linear_model import LogisticRegression
from sklearn.metrics import accuracy_score
 	
# Load the iris dataset 	
X, y = load_iris(return_X_y=True)
# Split the dataset into train and test sets 	
X_train, X_test, y_train, y_test = train_test_split(X, y, test_size=0.2, random_state=42)
 	
# Scale the features 	
scaler = StandardScaler()
X_train_scaled = scaler.fit_transform(X_train)
X_test_scaled = scaler.transform(X_test)
 	
# Train Multinomial Logistic Regression model 	
model = LogisticRegression(multi_class='multinomial', solver='lbfgs', max_iter=1000)
model.fit(X_train_scaled, y_train)
 	
# Predictions 	
y_pred = model.predict(X_test_scaled)
 	
# Evaluate the model 	
accuracy = accuracy_score(y_test, y_pred)
print("Accuracy of Multinomial Logistic Regression: {:.2f}%".format(accuracy * 100))
	Logistic Regression: 100.00%

Multiclass vs Multilabel Classification

Nikash asked, "What is Multiclass and Multilabel classification?"

Master said, "Multiclass classification and multilabel classification are two distinct tasks in machine learning, each serving different purposes and requiring different approaches. In multiclass classification, the objective is to assign instances to one of multiple predefined classes or categories, with each instance belonging to exactly one class. On the other hand, multilabel classification allows instances to be associated with multiple labels simultaneously, enabling the assignment of multiple binary labels for each instance."

Understanding the differences between these two tasks, how they are evaluated, and how to choose the best method for your specific problem is crucial for successful model development and deployment.

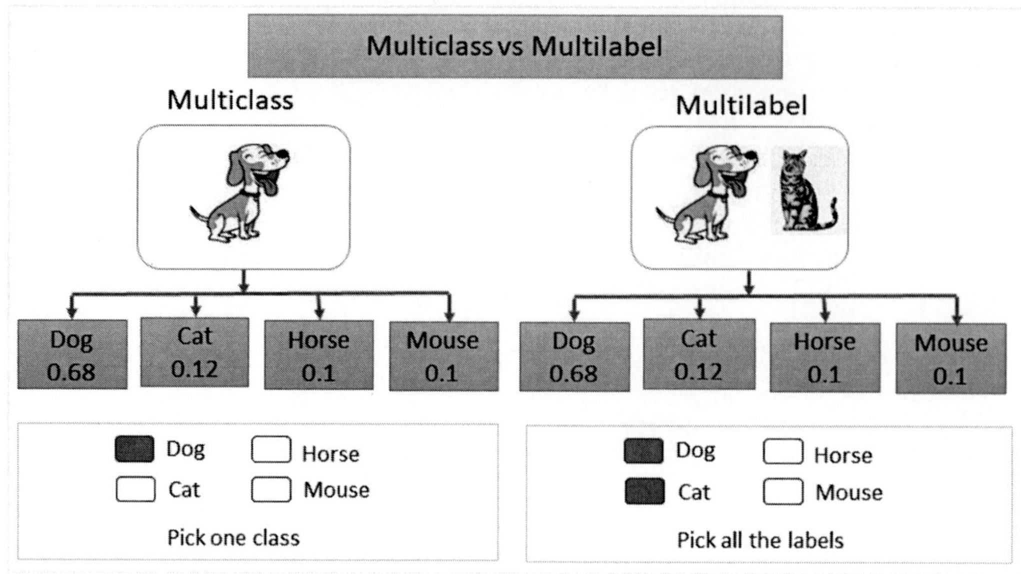

Multiclass Classification

In multiclass classification, the goal is to classify instances into one of several mutually exclusive categories. Each instance is assigned to exactly one class, and the model predicts the most likely class for each instance. Common algorithms for multiclass classification include logistic regression, decision trees, random forests, support vector machines, and neural networks.

Model training technique:

Training a multiclass classification model requires employing specific techniques to ensure accurate class assignment. One common approach is to utilise softmax activation in the output layer of the neural network. Softmax function transforms the raw model outputs into probabilities, assigning higher probabilities to the correct classes and providing a more interpretable prediction. Additionally, categorical cross-entropy loss is often employed as the objective function during training. This loss function measures the dissimilarity between the predicted probabilities and the actual class labels, guiding the model to minimize errors and improve accuracy by penalising deviations from the ground truth labels. By leveraging softmax activation and categorical cross-entropy loss, multiclass classification models can effectively learn to discriminate between multiple classes and make accurate predictions.

Evaluation Metrics:

Evaluation of multiclass classification models typically involves metrics, such as accuracy, precision, recall, F1-score, and confusion matrix. This metrics provide insights into the performance of the model across all classes and help assess its effectiveness in correctly predicting the class labels.

Multilabel Classification

In multilabel classification, each instance can be associated with multiple labels simultaneously, allowing for more nuanced and complex categorisation. This is particularly useful in scenarios where instances may belong to multiple categories simultaneously. For example, in text classification, a document may be relevant to multiple topics or themes.

Common approaches for multilabel classification include binary relevance, classifier chains, label powerset, and random k-labelsets. These approaches adapt traditional binary classification algorithms to handle multiple labels per instance.

Model Training techniques:

Sigmoid Activation: In the output layer of a neural network, sigmoid activation is commonly used. Unlike softmax, which is typical in multiclass scenarios, sigmoid independently activates each output node, generating a value between 0 and 1. This value represents the likelihood of the corresponding label being present or absent.

Binary Cross-Entropy Loss: During training, the binary cross-entropy loss function is often employed to quantify the dissimilarity between the predicted probabilities and the actual presence or absence of each label. By minimizing errors in its multi-label predictions, this loss function guides the model towards improved performance.

Evaluation Metrics:

Evaluation of multilabel classification models involves metrics such as precision, recall, F1-score, Hamming loss, and subset accuracy. Hamming Loss: This metric quantifies the fraction of labels that are incorrectly predicted by the model, offering a comprehensive measure of overall label accuracy.

- **Precision at k:** Precision at k evaluates the precision of the top-k predicted labels, acknowledging that only a subset of labels may be of interest. It provides insight into the relevance of the predicted labels, particularly when considering a limited number of top predictions.

- **Recall at k:** Similar to precision at k, recall at k assesses the recall of the top-k predicted labels. It emphasises the ability of the model to capture the relevant labels among the top predictions, which can be crucial in scenarios where retrieving relevant labels is prioritised.

These metrics assess the model's ability to predict each label accurately and capture the overall performance across all labels.

Choosing the Best Approach

The choice between multiclass and multilabel classification depends on the nature of the problem and the structure of the data. If instances belong to mutually exclusive categories and can only be assigned to one class, multiclass classification is appropriate. However, if instances can have multiple labels simultaneously, multilabel classification is more suitable.

Considerations such as the number of classes or labels, class imbalance, and the relationships between classes or labels can also influence the choice of approach. Experimentation with different algorithms and evaluation metrics can help identify the most effective solution for a given problem.

In summary, understanding the differences between multiclass and multilabel classification, their evaluation metrics, and the factors influencing their performance is essential for building accurate and effective classification models in machine learning.

Multi-class Classification Techniques

One vs. All (one-vs-rest):

- In this approach, the classification problem is decomposed into multiple binary classification subproblems.
- Each class is treated as a binary classification problem against all other classes combined.
- Separate classifiers are trained for each class, to distinguish that class from all other classes.

During prediction, the class with the highest confidence score from the individual classifiers is selected as the final prediction.

One vs. One:

- In this technique, a binary classifier is trained for each pair of classes.
- For N classes, N(N-1)/2 binary classifiers are trained.
- During prediction, each classifier gives a vote for one of the two classes, and the class with the most votes across all classifiers is chosen as the final prediction.

Both techniques have their advantages and are suitable for different scenarios. One vs. All is commonly used when dealing with a large number of classes, while One vs. One may be preferred when computational resources are not a limitation. Understanding the nature of the problem and the characteristics of the dataset can help in selecting the appropriate multi-class classification technique for optimal results.

Binary Classification vs. Multi-class Classification

Binary Classification

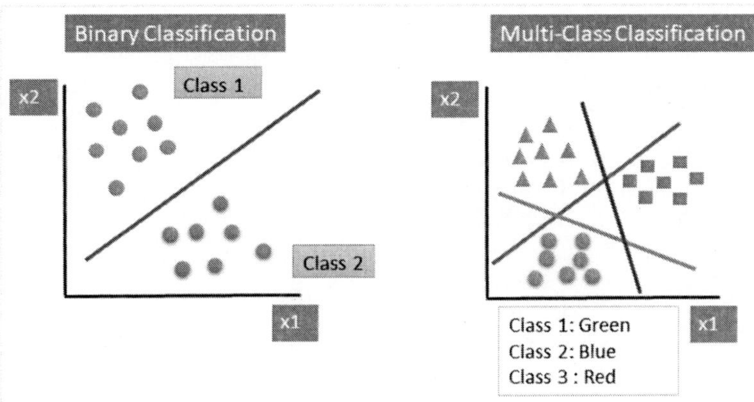

- Involves scenarios where there are only two class instances present in the dataset.
- Typically requires training a single classifier model to distinguish between the two classes.
- The confusion matrix generated from binary classification is straightforward to interpret and comprehend.
- Examples include determining if an email is spam or not, or predicting gender based on features like height and weight.

Multi-class Classification:

- Deals with datasets containing multiple class labels.
- The number of classifier models needed depends on the specific classification technique employed.
- While deriving the confusion matrix for multi-class classification is feasible, interpreting it can be more complex due to the presence of multiple classes.
- A common example is identifying the type of fruit as either an apple, banana, or orange based on various features.

Understanding the distinctions between binary and multi-class classification methods helps in selecting the appropriate approach based on the nature of the problem and the characteristics of the dataset.

One vs. All (one-vs-rest)

One-vs-All (One-vs-Rest) classification is a strategy employed when dealing with multi-class instances in a dataset. For an N-class dataset, N binary classifier models are generated, each aimed at distinguishing a single class from all other classes combined.

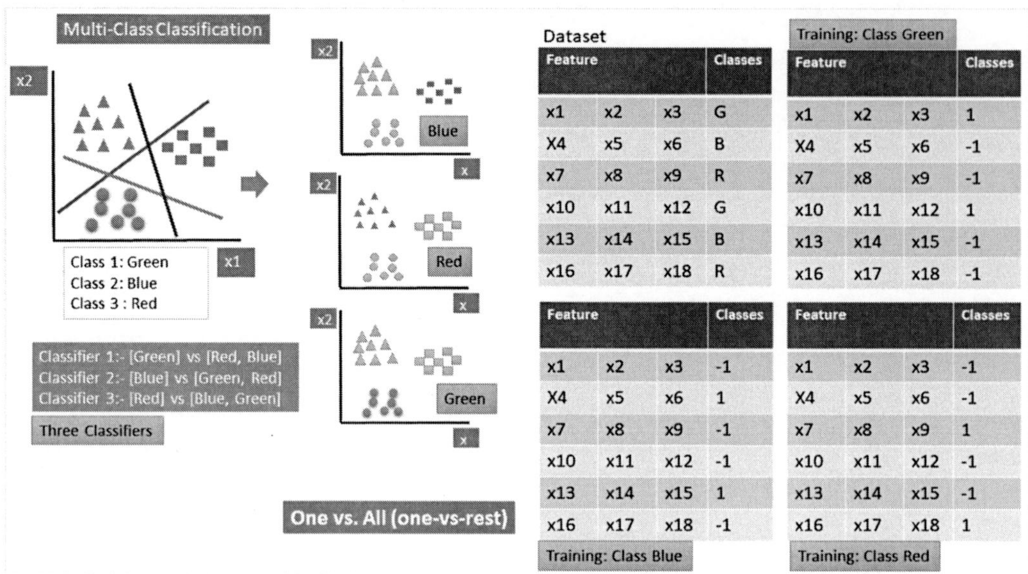

Dataset

Feature			Classes
x1	x2	x3	G
X4	x5	x6	B
x7	x8	x9	R
x10	x11	x12	G
x13	x14	x15	B
x16	x17	x18	R

Training: Class Green

Feature			Classes
x1	x2	x3	1
X4	x5	x6	-1
x7	x8	x9	-1
x10	x11	x12	1
x13	x14	x15	-1
x16	x17	x18	-1

Feature			Classes
x1	x2	x3	-1
X4	x5	x6	1
x7	x8	x9	-1
x10	x11	x12	-1
x13	x14	x15	1
x16	x17	x18	-1

Training: Class Blue

Feature			Classes
x1	x2	x3	-1
X4	x5	x6	-1
x7	x8	x9	1
x10	x11	x12	-1
x13	x14	x15	-1
x16	x17	x18	1

Training: Class Red

Let's illustrate this with an example where we have three classes: Green (type 1), Blue (type 2), and Red (type 3). To accommodate these classes, we create three binary classifiers:

- Classifier 1: Distinguishes Green from Red and Blue
- Classifier 2: Distinguishes Blue from Green and Red
- Classifier 3: Distinguishes Red from Blue and Green

To train these classifiers, we need to prepare three distinct training datasets. Each training dataset is created by assigning a '1 ' value to the class column for instances aligned with that particular class. For features not associated with the class, '-1' value is assigned in the class column.

For instance, in the primary dataset, if the first row corresponds to class G (Green) with feature values x1, x2, and x3, we assign a +1 value to the class column for the Green class. Similarly, for a different row with feature values x10, x11, and x12 associated with the Green class, a '1' value is assigned again. For features unrelated to the Green class, such as those associated with Blue or Red, a '-1' value is assigned in their respective class columns.

This process ensures that each binary classifier is trained to distinguish its associated class from all other classes combined, allowing for effective multi-class classification. After training each classifier with its respective dataset, we utilise them to classify input test data. When passing the test data to the model, it undergoes evaluation by all generated classifiers. If the input test data is likely to belong to a particular class, the corresponding classifier yields a positive response (1),

while the rest provide negative responses (-1). These responses are based on the binary classification models' predictions of the probability of correspondence with each class.
By analysing the probability scores generated by the classifiers, we determine the final predicted class. For instance, let's consider a scenario with three test features: y1, y2, and y3. Upon passing these features to the classifier models, we receive outcomes, such as a positive rating from the Green class classifier, with a probability score of 0.9. Similarly, we obtain a positive rating from the Blue class with a probability score of 0.4, along with a negative classification score from the Red classifier.
Based on the positive responses and the decisive probability scores, we conclude that our test input likely belongs to the Green class. This process of analysing probability scores allows us to make informed predictions about the class labels of the input test data.

One vs. One

In One-vs-One classification, we generate N * (N-1)/2 binary classifier models for an N-class instances dataset. With this approach, we decompose the classification problem into pairwise comparisons between each class and every other class.
For instance, consider a classification problem with three types: Green, Blue, and Red (N=3). We split this problem into N * (N-1)/2 = 3 binary classifier problems:

- Classifier 1: Green vs. Blue
- Classifier 2: Green vs. Red
- Classifier 3: Blue vs. Red

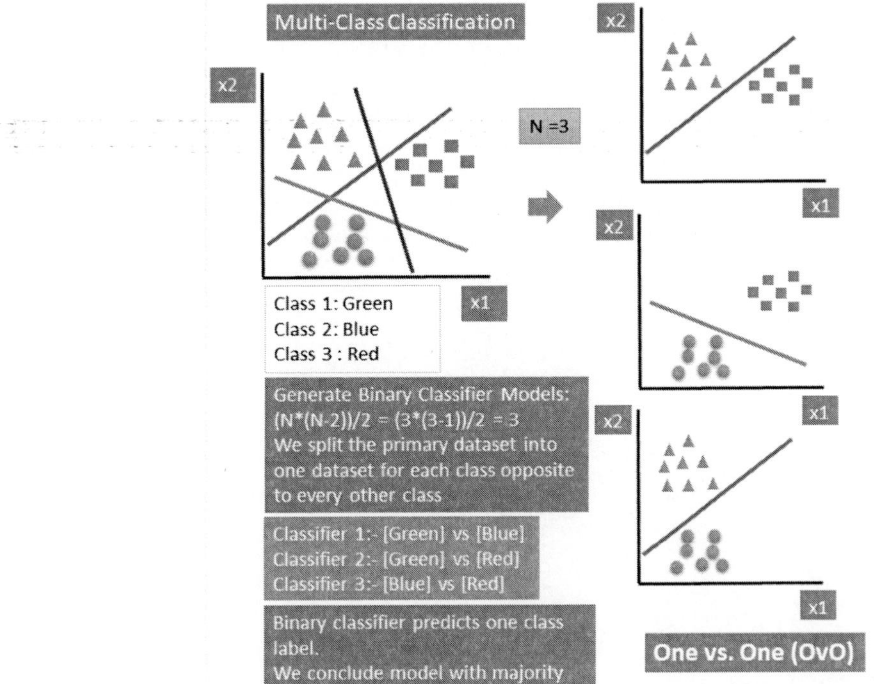

Each binary classifier is trained to distinguish between the two classes it represents. When we input test data to the classifiers, each model predicts a class label. The final result is determined by selecting the class label with the majority of votes among all classifiers. This voting mechanism allows for the determination of the most likely class label for the input data.

Demonstrating the application of a multi-class Logistic Regression model involves utilizing a built-in one-vs-rest (OvR) and one-vs-one (OvO) technique.

Exercise P4-U4 - D-17	
Multi-Class - One vs. All and One vs One	**Output**

from sklearn.linear_model import LogisticRegression
from sklearn.datasets import make_classification
from sklearn.model_selection import train_test_split
from sklearn.metrics import accuracy_score
 	
# Generate synthetic data for demonstration 	
X, y = make_classification(n_samples=1000, n_features=20, n_classes=2, n_clusters_per_class=2, random_state=42)
# Split the data into training and testing sets 	
X_train, X_test, y_train, y_test = train_test_split(X, y, test_size=0.2, random_state=42)
 	
# Train a Logistic Regression model using one-vs-rest strategy 	
multi_class_model_ovr = LogisticRegression(multi_class='ovr', solver='liblinear')
multi_class_model_ovr.fit(X_train, y_train)
# Train a Logistic Regression model using one-vs-one strategy 	
multi_class_model_ovo = LogisticRegression(multi_class='multinomial', solver='lbfgs')
multi_class_model_ovo.fit(X_train, y_train)
 	
# Predict the class labels for the test data using OvR 	
y_pred_ovr = multi_class_model_ovr.predict(X_test)
# Predict the class labels for the test data using OvO 	
y_pred_ovo = multi_class_model_ovo.predict(X_test)
 	
# Calculate accuracy scores for OvR and OvO 	
accuracy_ovr = accuracy_score(y_test, y_pred_ovr)
accuracy_ovo = accuracy_score(y_test, y_pred_ovo)
print("Accuracy (One-vs-Rest):", accuracy_ovr)
print("Accuracy (One-vs-One):", accuracy_ovo)
	Accuracy (One-vs-Rest): 0.855
	Accuracy (One-vs-One): 0.855

This code demonstrates the use of Logistic Regression models for multi-class classification using both One-vs-Rest (OvR) and One-vs-One (OvO) strategies. Here's a breakdown of the code:

Data Generation: Synthetic data is generated using the make_classification function from Scikit-learn. This data includes 1000 samples, 20 features, and 2 classes with 2 clusters per class.

Data Splitting: The generated data is split into training and testing sets using the train_test_split function.

Model Training (OvR): A Logistic Regression model is trained using the OvR strategy (multi_class='ovr'). This model is fitted to the training data using the fit method.

Model Training (OvO): Another Logistic Regression model is trained using the OvO strategy (multi_class='multinomial'). This model is also fitted to the training data using the fit method.

Prediction (OvR): The trained OvR model is used to predict the class labels for the test data using the predict method.

Prediction (OvO): Similarly, the trained OvO model is used to predict the class labels for the test data.

Accuracy Calculation: The accuracy scores for both OvR and OvO strategies are calculated using the accuracy_score function from Scikit-learn.

Output: Finally, the accuracy scores for both strategies are printed to compare the performance of the two multi-class classification approaches.

An example showcasing the use of the One-vs-Rest (OvR) classifier for both multiclass and multilabel classification tasks:

Exercise P4 - U4 - D-18	
Multi-Class and Multi-Label - One vs. All	**Output**

from sklearn.datasets import load_iris
from sklearn.model_selection import train_test_split
from sklearn.multiclass import OneVsRestClassifier
from sklearn.linear_model import LogisticRegression
from sklearn.metrics import accuracy_score, classification_report, hamming_loss
# Load the iris dataset 	
X, y = load_iris(return_X_y=True)
 	
# Split the data into training and testing sets 	
X_train, X_test, y_train, y_test = train_test_split(X, y, test_size=0.2, random_state=42)
 	
# Multiclass Classification with One-vs-Rest (OvR) Classifier 	
# Initialize the OvR classifier with Logistic Regression as the base estimator 	
ovr_clf = OneVsRestClassifier(LogisticRegression())
 	
# Train the OvR classifier 	
ovr_clf.fit(X_train, y_train)
	Multiclass Classification Results:
	Accuracy:
	0.9666666666666667
	
	Multilabel Classification Results:
	Hamming Loss:
	0.13333333333333333

# Predict the classes on the test set 	
y_pred_multiclass = ovr_clf.predict(X_test)
 	
# Evaluate the multiclass classification results 	
accuracy_multiclass = accuracy_score(y_test, y_pred_multiclass)
classification_report_multiclass = classification_report(y_test, y_pred_multiclass)
 	
print("Multiclass Classification Results:")
print("Accuracy:", accuracy_multiclass)
print("Classification Report:\n", classification_report_multiclass)
 	
# Multilabel Classification with One-vs-Rest (OvR) Classifier 	
# Create a multilabel dataset 	
y_multilabel = [[1, 0, 1] if label == 0 else [0, 1, 0] if label == 1 else [0, 0, 1] for label in y]
 	
# Split the multilabel data into training and testing sets 	
X_train_multi, X_test_multi, y_train_multi, y_test_multi = train_test_split(X, y_multilabel, test_size=0.2, random_state=42)
 	
# Initialize the OvR classifier with Logistic Regression as the base estimator 	
ovr_clf_multi = OneVsRestClassifier(LogisticRegression())
 	
# Train the OvR classifier for multilabel classification 	
ovr_clf_multi.fit(X_train_multi, y_train_multi)
 	
# Predict the labels on the test set for multilabel classification 	
y_pred_multilabel = ovr_clf_multi.predict(X_test_multi)
# Evaluate the multilabel classification results 	
hamming_loss_multilabel = hamming_loss(y_test_multi, y_pred_multilabel)
 	
print("\nMultilabel Classification Results:")
print("Hamming Loss:", hamming_loss_multilabel)	

```
Classification Report:
              precision    recall  f1-score   support
           0       1.00      1.00      1.00        10
           1       1.00      0.89      0.94         9
           2       0.92      1.00      0.96        11
    accuracy                           0.97        30
   macro avg       0.97      0.96      0.97        30
weighted avg       0.97      0.97      0.97        30
```

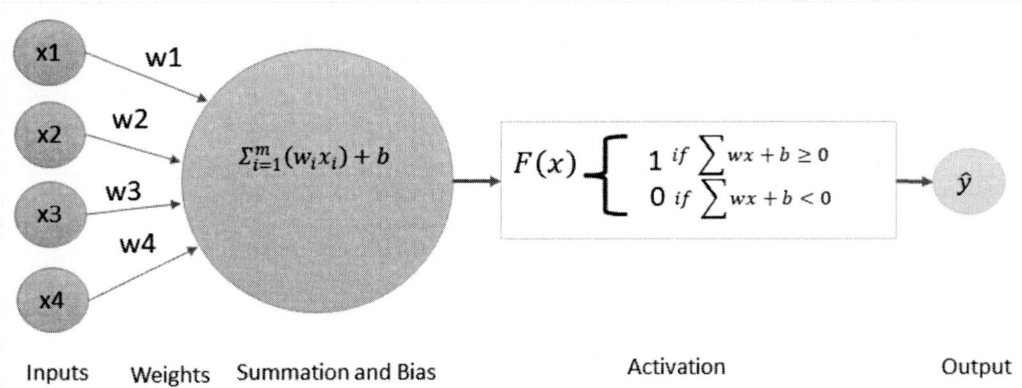

Understanding Activation Functions in Depth

Sam asked, "What is the activation function?"

Master said, "Activation functions are a crucial component of artificial neural networks, determining the output of individual neurons based on their input. They map the resulting values into a desired range, such as between 0 to 1 or -1 to 1, depending on the choice of the activation function. For instance, the logistic activation function maps inputs from the real number domain into the range of 0 to 1."

Consider a binary classification problem, where we aim to classify input data, such as images, into two categories: correct object (assigned label 1) or incorrect object (assigned label 0). This scenario exemplifies a binary classification problem.

Several important terms and mathematical concepts are associated with neural networks:

- Propagation: A procedure that adjusts weights iteratively to minimise the difference between the actual and desired output.
- Hidden Layers: Layers of neuron nodes situated between input and output layers, enabling neural networks to learn complex features, such as XOR logic.
- Backpropagation: An iterative procedure that adjusts weights to minimise the

difference between actual and desired output. It allows information to propagate backward through the network to compute gradients. Backpropagation involves iterating over nodes in reverse topological order to compute the derivative of the final node output, helping identify the most significant error contributors and adjust parameters accordingly.

- Gradient Descent: An optimisation algorithm employed during training to minimise a given function iteratively. It adjusts parameters to steer the model towards a local minimum of the cost function. A gradient measures how much the output of a function changes with slight changes in inputs. Ideally, during gradient descent, the cost function should decrease after each iteration, indicating model improvement.

Types of activation functions

Linear Activation Function:

1. Equation: $f(x) = x$f(x) = x
2. Range: $(-\infty,+\infty)$(−∞,+∞)

Non-linear Activation Functions:

Non-linear activation functions enable neural networks to generalise across a variety of data and differentiate between outputs. They are crucial for capturing complex patterns and relationships in data.

Non-linear activation functions are further categorised based on their range or curves:

Sigmoid:

Also known as the Binary Classifier or Logistic Activation function.

The sigmoid function produces values between 0 and 1, making it suitable for binary classification tasks.

Equation: $f(x) = \frac{1}{1+e^{-x}}$

ReLU (Rectified Linear Unit):

The most widely used activation function, especially in convolutional neural networks (CNNs).

ReLU is defined as f(x) = max(0,x), producing zero for negative inputs and retaining positive inputs.

It addresses the "dying ReLU" problem by allowing a small linear component for negative inputs in Leaky ReLU.

Tanh (Hyperbolic Tangent):

Squashes real-valued numbers to the range $[-1,1]$.

Tanh is similar to the sigmoid function but zero-centred, mapping negative inputs to strongly negative values and zero inputs to near zero.

Equation: $\tanh(x) = 2 \cdot \text{sigmoid}(2x) - 1$

Softmax:

Suited for multi-class classification tasks, softmax squashes the outputs of each unit to be between 0 and 1 and ensures the sum of all probabilities equals 1.

It provides a categorical probability distribution, indicating the probability of each class being true.

Equation: $\text{softmax}(z_i) = e^{z_i} / \sum_{j=1}^{k} e^{z_j}$

Here, K represents the number of elements in the vector z, and i and j iterate over all the elements in the vector.

Properties of Softmax Function:

- Calculated probabilities range from 0 to 1.
- The sum of all probabilities equals 1.

Usage of Softmax Function:

- Multiple classification logistic regression models.
- Neural networks, where softmax is used in different layers and multilayer perceptrons.

Exercise P4-U4 – D19

Activation Function

```
import numpy as np
import matplotlib.pyplot as plt
# Define the range of x values
x = np.linspace(-5, 5, 100)

# Linear Activation Function
def linear_activation(x):
    return x

# Sigmoid Activation Function
def sigmoid_activation(x):
    return 1 / (1 + np.exp(-x))

# ReLU (Rectified Linear Unit) Activation Function
```

```
def relu_activation(x):
    return np.maximum(0, x)

# Tanh (Hyperbolic Tangent) Activation Function
def tanh_activation(x):
    return np.tanh(x)

# Softmax Activation Function
def softmax_activation(x):
    exp_values = np.exp(x)
    return exp_values / np.sum(exp_values)

# Plotting the activation functions
plt.figure(figsize=(12, 8))

# Linear Activation Function
plt.subplot(2, 3, 1)
plt.plot(x, linear_activation(x))
plt.title('Linear Activation Function')
plt.xlabel('x')
plt.ylabel('f(x)')

# Sigmoid Activation Function
plt.subplot(2, 3, 2)
plt.plot(x, sigmoid_activation(x))
plt.title('Sigmoid Activation Function')
plt.xlabel('x')
plt.ylabel('f(x)')

# ReLU (Rectified Linear Unit) Activation Function
plt.subplot(2, 3, 3)
plt.plot(x, relu_activation(x))
plt.title('ReLU Activation Function')
plt.xlabel('x')
plt.ylabel('f(x)')

# Tanh (Hyperbolic Tangent) Activation Function
plt.subplot(2, 3, 4)
plt.plot(x, tanh_activation(x))
plt.title('Tanh Activation Function')
plt.xlabel('x')
plt.ylabel('f(x)')

# Softmax Activation Function
plt.subplot(2, 3, 5)
plt.plot(x, softmax_activation(x))
plt.title('Softmax Activation Function')
plt.xlabel('x')
```

```
plt.ylabel('f(x)')

plt.tight_layout()
plt.show()
```

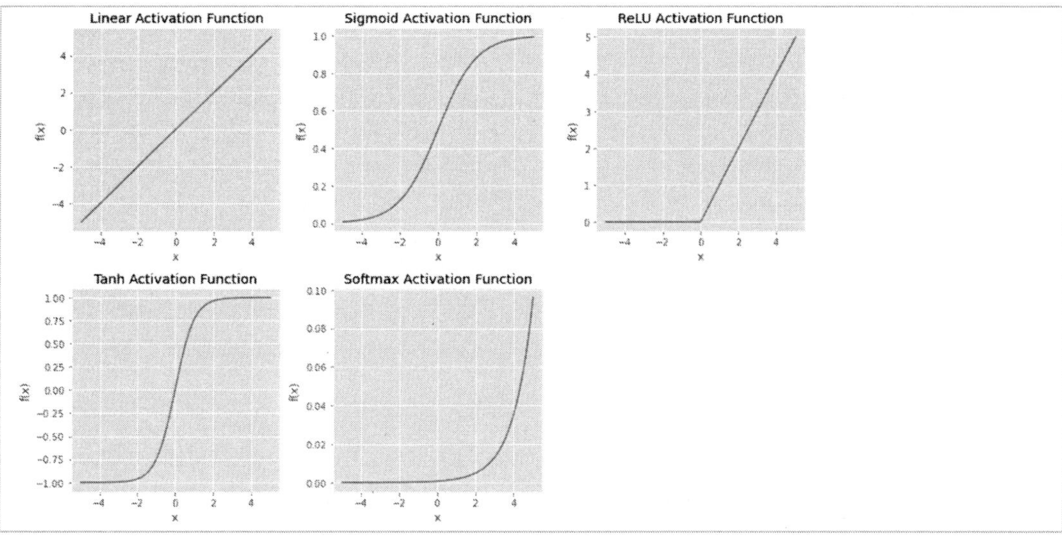

Summary:

In this unit, we extensively explored Logistic regression, a fundamental algorithm for binary and multi-class classification tasks. We delved into the sigmoid function, which is pivotal in Logistic regression for transforming linear outputs into probabilities, enabling classification decisions.

We also discussed various types of logistic regression, including Binary or Binomial logistic regression for two-class classification, Multinomial logistic regression for multi-class classification, and Ordinal logistic regression for ordered categorical outcomes. Additionally, we explored regularized and Bayesian logistic regression techniques, which enhance model robustness and interpretability.

Furthermore, we compared Multiclass vs Multilabel classification paradigms and discussed strategies such as One-vs-All and One-vs-One for handling multi-class classification tasks. Understanding activation functions, such as sigmoid, relu, tanh, and softmax, was a key aspect of our exploration, as these functions play a crucial role in determining the output of neural network models, enabling complex non-linear mappings between inputs and outputs.

PART FOUR

DAY THIRTEEN

Unit 4 - Lesson Four

Evaluation Metrics

Evaluation Metrics

Confusion Matrix

Apeksha asked, "What is a confusion matrix, and how do we use it?"

Master said, "Confusion matrices are vital tools in understanding and comparing the performance of machine learning models. By analysing a confusion matrix, you gain insights into a model's strengths and weaknesses, enabling informed decisions in model selection for specific applications. Traditionally, confusion matrices are derived from a model's predictions on a held-out test dataset."

The column labels, "Actually Positive" and "Actually Negative," correspond to the ground-truth labels in the dataset, representing whether an instance belongs to a certain class (e.g., 1 for positive or 0 for negative).

On the other hand, the row labels, "Predicted Positive" and "Predicted Negative," denote the model's predictions—what the model perceives the labels to be.

	Actually Positive (1)	Actually Negative (0)
Predicted Positive (1)	True Positives (TP)	False Positive (FP)
Predicted negative (0)	False Negative (FN)	True negative (TN)

Within the confusion matrix, the entries represent counts:

- True Positives (TP): Instances correctly classified as positive by the model.

- True Negatives (TN): Instances correctly classified as negative by the model.
- False Positives (FP – Type I Error): Instances incorrectly classified as positive by the model (False alarm).
- False Negatives (FN- Type II Error): Instances incorrectly classified as negative by the model (A miss).

From the confusion matrix, you can derive essential metrics like True Positive Rate (TPR) and False Positive Rate (FPR), crucial for calculating the Area Under the Receiver Operating Characteristic (AUROC) curve—a popular performance metric.

- TPR (True Positive Rate): Ratio of true positive predictions to all actual positive instances.
- FPR (False Positive Rate): Ratio of false positive predictions to all actual negative instances.

Precision, another critical metric, quantifies the accuracy of positive predictions made by the model:

- Precision: Ratio of true positive predictions to the total number of positive predictions (both true and false).

These metrics, derived from the confusion matrix, provide comprehensive insights into a model's performance, aiding in evaluation and comparison across different models and aiding in decision-making for model selection.

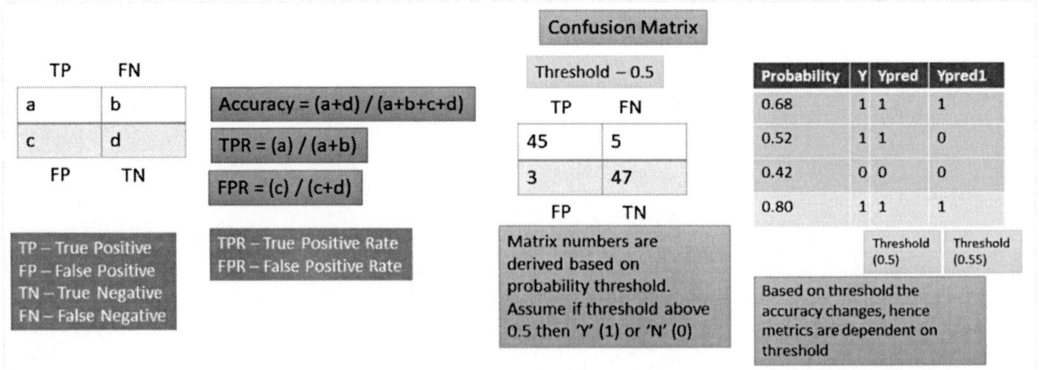

Example: Email Spam

In the context of email spam classification, a confusion matrix provides a breakdown of the model's performance in predicting whether an email is spam or not spam. Let's illustrate this with an example:

Suppose we have a dataset containing 100 emails, where 50 are spam emails and 50 are legitimate emails. After training our spam classification model, we use it to predict the labels for these emails.

Here's a hypothetical confusion matrix based on our model's predictions:

```
[[45 5] # 45 legitimate emails correctly predicted as not spam (true negatives)
[ 3 47]] # 47 spam emails correctly predicted as spam (true positives)
```

In this confusion matrix:

- The top-left cell (45) represents the number of legitimate emails that were correctly predicted as not spam. Out of the 50 legitimate emails, our model correctly identified 45 of them as not spam (true negatives).
- The bottom-right cell (47) represents the number of spam emails that were correctly predicted as spam. Out of the 50 spam emails, our model correctly identified 47 of them as spam (true positives).
- The top-right cell (5) represents the number of legitimate emails that were incorrectly predicted as spam. Out of the 50 legitimate emails, our model incorrectly classified 5 of them as spam (false positives).
- The bottom-left cell (3) represents the number of spam emails that were incorrectly predicted as not spam. Out of the 50 spam emails, our model incorrectly classified 3 of them as not spam (false negatives).

Accuracy, Precision and Sensitivity

Master said, "Performance metrics are measures used to evaluate the performance of machine learning models. They quantify how well a model is performing by comparing its predictions to the actual values in the dataset."

Here are some commonly used performance metrics along with their formulas and examples:

Accuracy:

Accuracy measures the proportion of correct predictions made by the model.

Formula:

Accuracy = Number of Correct Predictions/ Total Number of Predictions

Example:

- True Positives (TP) = 85
- True Negatives (TN) = 90
- False Positives (FP) = 10
- False Negatives (FN) = 15

Total Predictions = TP + TN + FP + FN

Accuracy = (TP+TN)/(Total Prediction)

Total Predictions = TP + TN + FP + FN = 85 + 90 + 10 + 15 = 200

Accuracy = (TP+TN)/(Total Prediction)

Accuracy = (85+90)/200 = 175/200 = 0.875 (or 87.5%)

Precision, Recall, F1 Measure, F-beta Measure, and Specificity are essential evaluation metrics in classification tasks. Here's an improved explanation of each:

Specificity:

Specificity, also referred to as the true negative rate, is a vital performance metric in binary classification tasks. It evaluates the model's capacity to accurately identify negative instances among all actual negative cases. Essentially, specificity quantifies the proportion of true negatives correctly classified by the model.

In scenarios like disease screening tests, where distinguishing true negatives is crucial, specificity plays a critical role. It complements sensitivity, which focuses on correctly identifying positive cases, by providing a comprehensive assessment of the model's performance across both positive and negative instances.

Precision = (True Negative) / (True Negative + False Positive)

Precision = (90) / (90 + 10) = 0.90 (or 90.0%)

Precision:

Precision measures the exactness of a model by calculating the proportion of correctly identified positive cases out of all cases labelled as positive. It's crucial when minimising false positives is a priority. For instance, in fraud detection, precision ensures that authentic transactions are not wrongly labelled as fraudulent.

Precision = (True Positives) / (True Positives + False Positive)

Precision = (85) / (85 + 10) = 0.894 (or 89.4%)

Recall (Sensitivity/TPR):

Recall, also known as sensitivity or true positive rate, assesses the ability of a model to identify all relevant positive cases. It quantifies the completeness of the model by calculating the proportion of correctly identified positive cases out of all actual positive cases. In scenarios where minimising false negatives is crucial, recall becomes vital. For example, in medical diagnosis, recall ensures that all actual cases of a disease are correctly identified.

Recall= (True Positives) / (True Positives + False Negatives)

Recall = (85)/(85+15) = 0.85 (or 85%)

F1 Score Measure:

The F1 measure is the harmonic mean of precision and recall, providing a balance between the two metrics. It ranges from 0 to 1, with 1 indicating perfect precision and recall. The F1 score reaches its optimal value at 1 and its worst value at 0. It is particularly useful when there is an uneven class distribution. It provides a single score that balances both precision and recall.

F1 = 2 × ((Precision×Recall) / (Precision+Recall))

F1 Score = 2×((0.894×0.85) / (0.894+0.85))

= 2×((0.7593)/ (1.744)) =1.52 (or 75.9%)

F-beta Measure:

The F-beta measure is a generalised form of the F1 measure, where beta controls the weight given to precision and recall. A beta of 0.5 emphasises precision, making it suitable for tasks where precision is of higher importance, while a beta of 2 prioritises recall, making it suitable for tasks where recall is critical.

These performance metrics are commonly used for evaluating classification models. Depending on the problem and the business requirements, different metrics may be prioritised. For example, in a medical diagnosis task, recall (sensitivity) may be more important to minimise false negatives (missing actual positive cases), even if it results in lower precision. Conversely, in a spam email detection task, precision may be more critical to minimise false positives (flagging legitimate emails as spam), even if it leads to lower recall.

Exercise P4-U4 – D20	
Confusion Matrix and Accuracy	**Output**

import numpy as np
import pandas as pd
import matplotlib.pyplot as plt
from sklearn.model_selection import train_test_split
from sklearn.metrics import confusion_matrix
import itertools
import scikitplot as skplt
 	
# Assuming the file is CSV 	
path = r'C:\Users\User\mraj4\Documents\Optimum\Py-lib\scikit\BankNote_Authentication.csv'
df = pd.read_csv(path)
# Check the distribution of target classes 	
print(df['class'].value_counts())
 	
# Defining features and target variables for X and y 	
y = df['class']
X = df.drop(columns=['class'])
# Splitting the data into train and test sets 	
X_train, X_test, y_train, y_test = train_test_split(X, y, test_size=0.25, random_state=42)
# Predicting using Logistic Regression for binary classification 	
from sklearn.linear_model import LogisticRegression
Log_Reg = LogisticRegression()
# Fitting the Model 	
Log_Reg.fit(X_train, y_train)
y_pred = Log_Reg.predict(X_test)
# Performance Evaluation using Confusion Matrix 	
def plot_confusion_matrix(cm, classes,
            normalize=False,
            title='Confusion matrix',
            cmap=plt.cm.Blues):
  # This function prints and plots the confusion matrix. Normalization can be applied by setting `normalize=True`.
  if normalize:
    cm = cm.astype('float') / cm.sum(axis=1)[:, np.newaxis]
    print("Normalized confusion matrix")
  else:
    print('Confusion matrix, without normalization')
  print(cm)
 	
  plt.imshow(cm, interpolation='nearest', cmap=cmap)
	class
	0 762
	1 610
	Name: count, dtype: int64
	Confusion matrix, without normalization
	[[189 2]
	 [2 150]]
	True Negatives: 189
	False Positives: 2
	False Negatives: 2
	True Positives: 150
	Accuracy 98.83%
	Specificity 0.99
	Precision 0.99
	Recall 0.99
	F1 Score 0.99
	F2 0.99
	
	F0.5 0.99

```
    plt.title(title)
    plt.colorbar()
    tick_marks = np.arange(len(classes))
    plt.xticks(tick_marks, classes, rotation=45)
    plt.yticks(tick_marks, classes)

    fmt = '.2f' if normalize else 'd'
    thresh = cm.max() / 2.
    for i, j in itertools.product(range(cm.shape[0]),
range(cm.shape[1])):
        plt.text(j, i, format(cm[i, j], fmt),
                 horizontalalignment="center",
                 color="white" if cm[i, j] > thresh else "black")

    plt.ylabel('True label')
    plt.xlabel('Predicted label')
    plt.tight_layout()

# Compute confusion matrix
cnf_matrix = confusion_matrix(y_test, y_pred)
np.set_printoptions(precision=2)
# Plot non-normalized confusion matrix
plt.figure()
plot_confusion_matrix(cnf_matrix, classes=['Forged',
'Authorized'],
                      title='Confusion matrix, without normalization')
# Extracting true positives, false positives, true negatives, false
negatives
tn, fp, fn, tp = confusion_matrix(y_test, y_pred).ravel()
print("True Negatives: ", tn)
print("False Positives: ", fp)
print("False Negatives: ", fn)
print("True Positives: ", tp)

# Accuracy (%)
accuracy = (tn + tp) * 100 / (tp + tn + fp + fn)
print("Accuracy {:0.2f}%".format(accuracy))

# Specificity
specificity = tn / (tn + fp)
print("Specificity {:0.2f}".format(specificity))

# Precision
precision = tp / (tp + fp)
print("Precision {:0.2f}".format(precision))

# Recall
recall = tp / (tp + fn)
```

```
print("Recall {:0.2f}".format(recall))

# F1 Score
f1_score = (2 * precision * recall) / (precision + recall)
print("F1 Score {:0.2f}".format(f1_score))

# F-beta score
def fbeta(precision, recall, beta):
    return ((1 + pow(beta, 2)) * precision * recall) / (pow(beta, 2) *
precision + recall)
f2 = fbeta(precision, recall, 2)
f0_5 = fbeta(precision, recall, 0.5)

print("F2 {:0.2f}".format(f2))
print("\nF0.5 {:0.2f}".format(f0_5))

# ROC curve
y_pred_proba = Log_Reg.predict_proba(X_test)
skplt.metrics.plot_roc_curve(y_test, y_pred_proba)
plt.show()
```

This code performs binary classification using logistic regression on a dataset named 'BankNote_Authentication.csv'. Here's a brief summary of what each part of the code does:

Imports: Import necessary libraries including NumPy, pandas, matplotlib, scikit-learn's train_test_split and confusion_matrix, itertools, and scikitplot.

Read Data: Load the dataset 'BankNote_Authentication.csv' into a pandas DataFrame.

Check Target Class Distribution: Print the count of unique values in the 'class' column to check the distribution of target classes.

Data Preparation: Separate the features (X) and target variable (y).

Train-Test Split: Split the dataset into training and testing sets using the train_test_split function from scikit-learn.

Model Training and Prediction: Fit a logistic regression model on the training data and make predictions on the test data.

Confusion Matrix: Define a function to plot the confusion matrix. Compute the confusion matrix and plot it using the defined function.

Performance Metrics: Calculate various performance metrics such as True Positives, False Positives, True Negatives, False Negatives, Accuracy, Specificity, Precision, Recall, F1 Score, F2 Score, and F0.5 Score.

ROC Curve: Plot the ROC curve using the predicted probabilities from the logistic regression model.

Overall, this code demonstrates how to train a logistic regression model for binary classification, evaluate its performance using various metrics, and visualise the performance using a ROC curve.

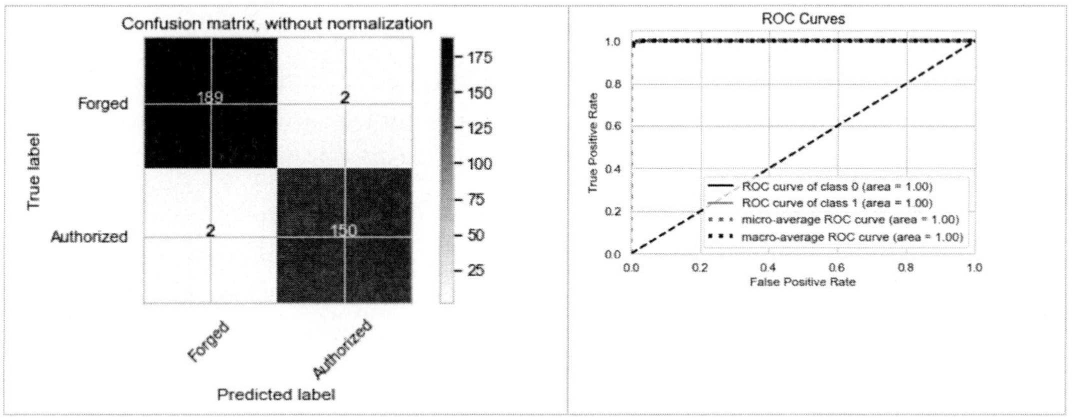

Decision Threshold

John asked, "What is the decision threshold?"

Master said, "Decision thresholds play a crucial role in converting predicted probabilities into predicted labels, which are essential for evaluating and interpreting machine learning model outputs. A decision threshold represents the cutoff point used to determine whether a probability indicates a positive or negative class prediction."

A commonly used decision threshold is 0.5, where probabilities greater than or equal to 0.5 are classified as positive, and those below 0.5 are classified as negative. However, the choice of decision threshold is flexible and can be adjusted based on specific requirements and the trade-offs between different evaluation metrics.

Extreme decision thresholds, such as 0 and 1, illustrate the impact of threshold selection on model performance metrics:

- Choosing a threshold of 0 classifies all examples as positive, resulting in a true positive rate (TPR) of 1 and a false positive rate (FPR) of 1. The precision depends on the data distribution, with a balanced dataset yielding a precision of 0.5.
- Conversely, selecting a threshold of 1 classifies all examples as negative, leading to a TPR of 0, an FPR of 0, and technically undefined precision due to zero true positives.

Understanding the implications of decision thresholds allows practitioners to tailor model evaluation and decision-making processes to their specific needs, considering factors like class imbalances and the relative importance of different performance metrics.

Roopa asked, "How to choose a decision threshold?"

Master said, "Choosing the appropriate decision threshold for your model hinges on the specific context and implications of your model's predictions in the real world."

For instance, in medical applications where detecting certain conditions is critical, such as identifying cases of melanoma in dermatology photos, minimising false negatives is paramount. In such cases, opting for a lower decision threshold to classify more instances as positive can help reduce false negatives, albeit potentially increasing false positives.

Conversely, in scenarios where false positives carry significant consequences, such as in a justice system where a model determines criminal convictions, prioritising precision becomes crucial. Avoiding false positives, which could lead to wrongful convictions, takes precedence over missing some true positives.

Visualising the trade-offs associated with different decision thresholds can be facilitated by plotting AUROC and AUPRC curves. These curves offer insights into how varying thresholds impact the true positive rate (sensitivity/recall/hit rate) and precision (positive predictive value), aiding in the selection of an optimal threshold for the model's intended application.

Understanding the implications of different decision thresholds and their trade-offs is essential for deploying models responsibly and effectively in real-world scenarios.

AUC and ROC Curve

This description provides a foundational understanding of the Receiver Operating Characteristic (ROC) curve, a fundamental tool in assessing classification model performance. The ROC curve visualises the model's performance across all potential classification thresholds, with its construction based on two key metrics:

- True Positive Rate (TPR): Representing the proportion of true positives correctly identified by the model, TPR is also known as sensitivity or recall.
- False Positive Rate (FPR): Reflecting the ratio of false positives to all actual negative instances, FPR serves as a measure of model specificity.

Understanding the interplay between sensitivity, specificity, FPR, and threshold values is crucial:

- Inverse Relationship: Sensitivity and specificity exhibit an inverse relationship, whereby an increase in one typically results in a decrease in the other. These dynamic underscores the trade-off between accurately identifying positive and negative instances.

- Threshold Adjustment: By adjusting the threshold value, practitioners can fine-tune the balance between sensitivity and specificity. Lower thresholds prioritise sensitivity, leading to higher true positive rates but increased false positives. Conversely, raising the threshold enhances specificity while potentially reducing sensitivity.

- FPR and Specificity Connection: The FPR is directly related to specificity, as FPR equals one minus specificity. Thus, higher specificity corresponds to lower FPR, and vice versa.

- TPR and FPR Relationship: Changes in TPR, representing true positive identification, are often mirrored by shifts in FPR. An increase in TPR typically coincides with a rise in FPR, reflecting more false positives. Conversely, decreases in TPR tend to result in lower FPR, indicating fewer false positives.

Understanding these relationships enables practitioners to interpret ROC curves effectively and make informed decisions when assessing classification model performance.

AUC and ROC

Index	Class	Probability
P1	1	0.95
P2	1	0.90
P3	0	0.85
P4	0	0.81
P5	1	0.78
P6	0	0.70

We have 6 points where P1, P2, and P5 belong to class 1 and P3, P4, and P6 belong to class 0

9 Pairs

Pair	isCorrect
(P1,P3)	Yes
(P1,P4)	Yes
(P1,P6)	Yes
(P2,P3)	Yes
(P2,P4)	Yes
(P2,P6)	Yes
(P3,P5)	No
(P4,P5)	No
(P5,P6)	Yes

We will take all possible pairs such that one point belongs to class 1 and the other belongs to class 0

Let's delve into how the Area Under the Curve of the Receiver Operating Characteristic (AUC-ROC) works from a probabilistic perspective. AUC quantifies a model's ability to differentiate between classes, with a higher value indicating better performance. For instance, an AUC of

0.75 suggests a 75% likelihood that the model can correctly rank or segregate two data points from different classes based on their predicted probabilities. In simpler terms, if a point is predicted to belong to the positive class with a higher probability, it ideally should indeed belong to the positive class.

Consider a scenario with six points, where P1, P2, and P5 belong to class 1, while P3, P4, and P6 belong to class 0. Each point's predicted probability is noted in the "Probability" column. To determine the model's ability to rank these points correctly, we assess all possible pairs, totalling nine pairs, consisting of one point from class 1 and another from class 0.

Examining the "Correct" column, we observe whether each pair is accurately rank-ordered based on predicted probability, i.e., whether the class 1 point has a higher probability than the class 0 point. Among the nine pairs, class 1 is ranked higher than class 0 in seven instances. This implies a 77% probability that if we select a pair of points from different classes, the model would correctly distinguish between them.

This intuitive understanding of the AUC number provides clarity on its significance. To further validate this concept, we can utilise Scikit-learn's AUC-ROC implementation, ensuring alignment between theoretical understanding and practical implementation.

Exercise P4-U4 – D21	
AUC_ROC	**Output**

import numpy as np
from sklearn.metrics import roc_auc_score
# True labels 	
y_true = [1, 1, 0, 0, 1, 0]
# Predicted probabilities 	
y_pred = [0.95, 0.90, 0.85, 0.81, 0.78, 0.70]
# Calculate AUC 	
auc = np.round(roc_auc_score(y_true, y_pred), 3)
# Print AUC 	
print("AUC for the sample data is: {}".format(auc))
	AUC for the sample data is: 0.778

Akshaya asked, "When should we use the AUC-ROC evaluation metric?"

Master said, "When considering the AUC-ROC evaluation metric, it's important to understand its strengths and limitations. AUC-ROC is particularly useful in scenarios where the dataset is balanced, and the cost of False Positives and False Negatives is balanced as well. It provides a comprehensive assessment of a model's ability to discriminate between positive and negative classes across various decision thresholds."

However, in highly imbalanced datasets, the ROC curve may yield overly optimistic results. This is because the False Positive Rate (FPR) becomes insensitive to changes in predictions related to the minority class due to the dominance of True Negatives in the denominator of the FPR formula. In such cases, Precision-Recall Curves offer a more suitable evaluation metric, especially for assessing the classifier's performance concerning the positive (minority) class.

Analysing the AUC-ROC curve can provide insights into the model's performance. A high AUC value close to 1 indicates excellent discriminative power, suggesting that the model effectively distinguishes between classes and produces reliable predictions. Conversely, a low AUC value near 0 implies poor performance, indicating the model's inability to differentiate between classes accurately. An AUC value around 0.5 suggests that the model is essentially making random guesses, indicating a lack of meaningful patterns learned from the data.

Understanding AUC and ROC curve (AUROC)

Understanding the ROC curve involves grasping the relationship between the False Positive Rate (FPR) and the True Positive Rate (TPR), commonly known as Sensitivity or Recall. Typically, the x-axis of an ROC curve represents the FPR, while the y-axis represents the TPR. A higher value on the x-axis (towards the right) indicates a higher FPR, and a higher value on the y-axis (towards the top) indicates a higher TPR.

The ROC curve serves as a graphical illustration of the trade-off between the TPR and FPR at various classification thresholds. It depicts how a classification model performs across different thresholds. The AUC (Area Under the Curve) quantifies the overall performance of the ROC curve, providing a summary measure of the model's performance.

The choice of threshold depends on the specific objectives of the problem and the acceptable trade-off between false positives and false negatives. For instance, if reducing false positives is a priority, a threshold resulting in a lower false positive rate might be preferred. Conversely, if maximizing true positives is the goal, a threshold leading to a higher true positive rate could be chosen.

To illustrate how ROC curves are generated for different thresholds and how a specific threshold relates to a confusion matrix, consider a binary classification scenario of identifying spam emails:

```
True Labels: [1, 0, 1, 0, 1, 1, 0, 0, 1, 0]

Predicted Probabilities: [0.85, 0.35, 0.65, 0.25, 0.7, 0.9, 0.4, 0.1, 0.75, 0.55]
```

These hypothetical data points represent the true labels and predicted probabilities for spam classification. By varying the threshold, different TPR and FPR values can be obtained, allowing us to construct the ROC curve and understand the model's performance across various classification scenarios.

By varying the threshold and observing the changes in True Positive Rate (TPR) and False Positive Rate (FPR), you can construct the ROC curve. Each point on the ROC curve corresponds to a specific threshold value.

Case 1: Threshold (0.5)

True Labels	Predicted Probabilities	Predicted Labels (Threshold = 0.5)
1	0.85	1
0	0.35	0
1	0.65	1
0	0.25	0
1	0.7	1
1	0.9	1
0	0.4	0
0	0.1	0
1	0.75	1
0	0.55	1

Confusion Matrix

	Prediction = 0	Prediction = 1
Actual = 0	TP=4	FN=1
Actual = 1	FP=0	TN=5

TPR = (TP)/(TP+FN) =(4)/(4+1) = 0.8	FPR = (FP)/(FP+TN) =(0)/(0+5) = 0.0

Case 2: Threshold (0.7)

True Labels	Predicted Probabilities	Predicted Labels (Threshold = 0.7)
1	0.85	1
0	0.35	0
1	0.65	0
0	0.25	0
1	0.7	0
1	0.9	1
0	0.4	0
0	0.1	0
1	0.75	1
0	0.55	0

	Prediction = 0	Prediction = 1
Actual = 0	TP=5	FN=0
Actual = 1	FP=2	TN=3

TPR = (TP)/(TP+FN) =(5)/(5+0) = 1.0	FPR = (FP)/(FP+TN) =(2)/(2+3) = 0.4

Case 3: Threshold (0.4)

True Labels	Predicted Probabilities	Predicted Labels (Threshold = 0.4)
1	0.8	1
0	0.3	0
1	0.6	1
0	0.2	0
1	0.7	1
1	0.9	1
0	0.4	0
0	0.1	0
1	0.75	1
0	0.55	1

	Prediction = 0	Prediction = 1
Actual = 0	TP=4	FN=1
Actual = 1	FP=0	TN=5

TPR = (TP)/(TP+FN) =(4)/(4+1) = 0.8	FPR = (FP)/(FP+TN) =(0)/(0+5) = 0

Case 4: Threshold (0.2)

True Labels	Predicted Probabilities	Predicted Labels (Threshold = 0.2)
1	0.8	1
0	0.3	1
1	0.6	1
0	0.2	0
1	0.7	1
1	0.9	1
0	0.4	1
0	0.1	0
1	0.75	1
0	0.55	1

	Prediction = 0	Prediction = 1
Actual = 0	TP=2	FN=3
Actual = 1	FP=0	TN=5

TPR = (TP)/(TP+FN) =(2)/(2+3) = 0.4	FPR = (FP)/(FP+TN) =(0)/(0+5) = 0

Here's how you can interpret the results:

At a threshold of 0.5:

- TPR (Sensitivity) = 0.8
- FPR = 0

This indicates that the model correctly identifies 80% of actual positives (TPR) without incorrectly classifying any actual negatives as positives (FPR).

For different thresholds:

- Threshold = 0.7: TPR = 1.0 and FPR = 0.4
- Threshold = 0.4: TPR = 0.8 and FPR = 0
- Threshold = 0.2: TPR = 0.4 and FPR = 0
- Threshold = 0.85 TPR = 1.0 and FPR = 0.8

These results show how TPR and FPR change as the threshold varies.

Based on these results, you can plot the ROC curve, where each point on the curve represents TPR vs. FPR for a specific threshold value. This curve provides valuable insights into the trade-off between true positive and false positive rates at different classification thresholds, helping you assess the model's performance across various scenarios.

Exercise P4-U4 – D22	
AUC_ROC	**Output**

import matplotlib.pyplot as plt
# True Positive Rate (Sensitivity) 	
true_positive_rate = [0.8, 1, 0.8, 0.4]
# False Positive Rate 	
false_positive_rate = [0, 0.4, 0, 0]
# Plot the ROC curve 	
plt.figure(figsize=(8, 6)) # Set the figure size for better visualization
plt.plot(false_positive_rate, true_positive_rate, marker='o', linestyle='-',
color='blue', linewidth=2, markersize=8, label='ROC Curve')
 	
# Plot the diagonal line (worst case scenario) 	
plt.plot([0, 1], [0, 1], linestyle='--', color='grey', label='Random Guessing')
# Set labels and title 	
plt.xlabel('False Positive Rate (FPR)')
plt.ylabel('True Positive Rate (TPR) or Sensitivity')
plt.title('Receiver Operating Characteristic (ROC) Curve')
plt.legend()
# Set x and y axis limits 	
plt.xlim([0, 1])
plt.ylim([0, 1])
# Add grid for better readability 	
plt.grid(True)
# Show plot 	
plt.show()	

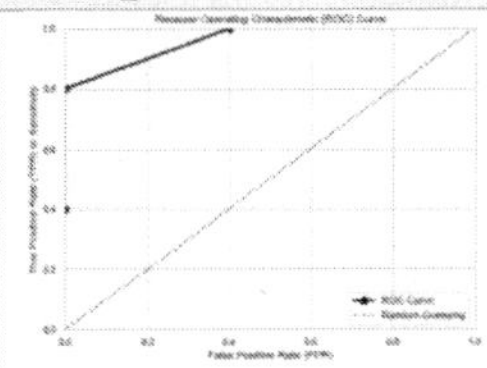

Key Insights from the ROC Curve

Worst-case Scenario: The gray dashed line represents the "Worst case" scenario, where the model's True Positive Rate (TPR) equals the False Positive Rate (FPR). This diagonal line signifies an equal likelihood of false positives and false negatives, which is the least desirable outcome.

Model Performance Improvement: Points deviating from the random guess line towards the upper-left corner indicate an improvement in the model's performance. As the curve moves closer to the top-left corner, the model achieves higher TPR (sensitivity) while maintaining a lower FPR.

Area Under the Curve (AUC): The Area Under the Curve (AUC) quantifies the model's discriminative ability. A higher AUC value, closer to 1.0, indicates superior performance. A perfect model would achieve an AUC of 1.0, representing 100% sensitivity and 100% specificity.

Conclusion:

The Receiver Operating Characteristic (ROC) curve visually depicts the trade-off between a binary classification model's True Positive Rate (sensitivity) and False Positive Rate at different decision thresholds. As the curve ascends towards the upper-left corner, it reflects the model's commendable ability to discriminate between positive and negative instances across various confidence thresholds. This upward trajectory signifies an enhanced performance, with higher sensitivity attained while minimising false positives, ultimately indicating the model's effectiveness in classification tasks.

Exercise P4-U4 – D23	
AUC_ROC	**Output**

import numpy as np
import pandas as pd
import matplotlib.pyplot as plt
from sklearn.datasets import make_classification
from sklearn.model_selection import train_test_split
from sklearn.linear_model import LogisticRegression
from sklearn.ensemble import RandomForestClassifier
from sklearn.metrics import roc_curve, auc
 	
# Generate synthetic data for demonstration 	
X, y = make_classification(
n_samples=1000, n_features=20, n_classes=2, random_state=42)
# Split the data into training and testing sets 	
X_train, X_test, y_train, y_test = train_test_split(
X, y, test_size=0.2, random_state=42)
 	
# Train two different models 	
logistic_model = LogisticRegression(random_state=42)
logistic_model.fit(X_train, y_train)
random_forest_model = RandomForestClassifier(n_estimators=100, random_state=42)
random_forest_model.fit(X_train, y_train)
 	
# Generate predictions 	
y_pred_logistic = logistic_model.predict_proba(X_test)[:, 1]
y_pred_rf = random_forest_model.predict_proba(X_test)[:, 1]
# Create a DataFrame 	
test_df = pd.DataFrame({'True': y_test, 'Logistic': y_pred_logistic, 'RandomForest': y_pred_rf})	

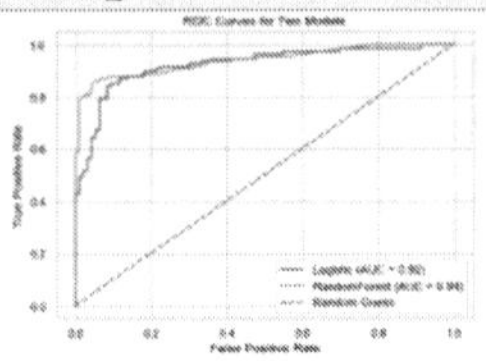

```
# Plot ROC curve for each model
plt.figure(figsize=(7, 5))
for model in ['Logistic', 'RandomForest']:
    fpr, tpr, _ = roc_curve(test_df['True'], test_df[model])
    roc_auc = auc(fpr, tpr)
    plt.plot(fpr, tpr, label=f'{model} (AUC = {roc_auc:.2f})')
# Plot random guess line
plt.plot([0, 1], [0, 1], 'r--', label='Random Guess')
# Set labels and title
plt.xlabel('False Positive Rate')
plt.ylabel('True Positive Rate')
plt.title('ROC Curves for Two Models')
plt.legend()
plt.show()
```

The provided code demonstrates the evaluation of two machine learning models, logistic regression, and random forest, using the Receiver Operating Characteristic (ROC) curve. Here's a brief overview:

- **Data Generation:** Synthetic data with 1000 samples and 20 features is generated using the make_classification function from sklearn.datasets.

- **Data Splitting:** The generated data is split into training and testing sets using the train_test_split function from sklearn.model_selection.

- **Model Training:** Two different models, logistic regression and random forest classifier, are trained on the training data using LogisticRegression and RandomForestClassifier from sklearn.linear_model and sklearn.ensemble, respectively.

- **Prediction:** The trained models are used to generate predictions for the testing data.

- **ROC Curve:** The ROC curve for each model is plotted using the roc_curve and auc functions from sklearn.metrics. The curve represents the trade-off between the true positive rate (sensitivity) and the false positive rate at various classification thresholds.

- **Random Guess Line:** A red dashed line representing the "Random Guess" scenario is plotted, indicating an equal likelihood of false positives and false negatives.

- **Visualization:** The ROC curves for both models are displayed in a single plot, with each curve labeled with the corresponding model name and its area under the curve (AUC) score.

Overall, the code provides a visual comparison of the performance of logistic regression and random forest classifiers using ROC curves, helping to assess the models' ability to distinguish between positive and negative instances across different decision thresholds.

Precision-Recall Curves

Exercise P4-U4 – D24	
PR curve	**Output**

```
import matplotlib.pyplot as plt
from sklearn.datasets import make_classification
from sklearn.model_selection import train_test_split
from sklearn.linear_model import LogisticRegression
from sklearn.ensemble import RandomForestClassifier
from sklearn.metrics import precision_recall_curve, auc

# Generate a synthetic dataset
X, y = make_classification(
    n_samples=1000, n_features=20, n_classes=2, random_state=42)

# Split the dataset into training and testing sets
X_train, X_test, y_train, y_test = train_test_split(X, y, test_size=0.2, random_state=42)

# Train a logistic regression model
logistic_model = LogisticRegression()
logistic_model.fit(X_train, y_train)

# Train a random forest classifier
rf_model = RandomForestClassifier(n_estimators=100, random_state=42)
rf_model.fit(X_train, y_train)

# Predict probabilities for the positive class
logistic_y_scores = logistic_model.predict_proba(X_test)[:, 1]
rf_y_scores = rf_model.predict_proba(X_test)[:, 1]

# Compute precision and recall values for logistic regression
logistic_precision, logistic_recall, _ = precision_recall_curve(y_test, logistic_y_scores)
logistic_auc_score = auc(logistic_recall, logistic_precision)

# Compute precision and recall values for random forest
rf_precision, rf_recall, _ = precision_recall_curve(y_test, rf_y_scores)
rf_auc_score = auc(rf_recall, rf_precision)
```

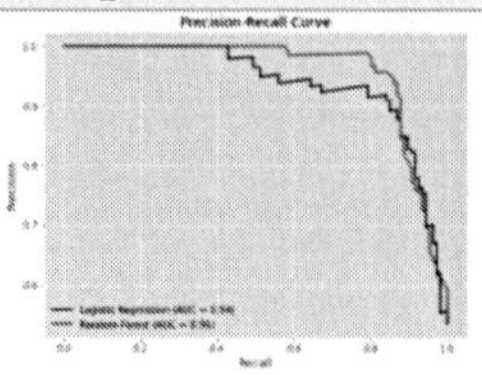

```
# Plot precision-recall curve
plt.figure(figsize=(8, 6))
plt.plot(logistic_recall, logistic_precision, label=f'Logistic Regression (AUC = {logistic_auc_score:.2f})', color='b', lw=2)
plt.plot(rf_recall, rf_precision, label=f'Random Forest (AUC = {rf_auc_score:.2f})', color='r', lw=2)
plt.xlabel('Recall')
plt.ylabel('Precision')
plt.title('Precision-Recall Curve')
plt.legend()
plt.grid(True)
plt.show()
```

Summary:

In this unit, we delved into various evaluation metrics crucial for assessing the performance of classification models. We began by exploring the confusion matrix, a tabular representation that summarises the model's predictions against actual class labels. From there, we examined essential metrics derived from the confusion matrix, including Accuracy, Precision, Sensitivity (Recall), and Specificity. These metrics offer insights into different aspects of model performance, such as overall correctness, the ability to identify positive instances correctly, and the ability to avoid misclassifying negative instances.

We then discussed the F1 score, a harmonic mean of Precision and Recall, which provides a balanced measure of a classifier's performance. Additionally, we explored F-beta score, which allows us to adjust the importance of Precision and Recall based on specific requirements.

Next, we delved into the concept of decision thresholds and their impact on classification outcomes. Adjusting the decision threshold can trade off between Precision and Recall, depending on the application's goals.

Moving forward, we explored more advanced evaluation techniques, such as the Area Under the Curve (AUC) and Receiver Operating Characteristic (ROC) curve. This metrics offer a comprehensive view of a classifier's performance across various decision thresholds and are particularly useful for assessing binary classifiers.

Finally, we discussed Precision-Recall curves, which visualise the trade-off between Precision and Recall for different decision thresholds. This curve provides valuable insights, especially in scenarios with imbalanced datasets or when one class is of particular interest.

By understanding and leveraging this evaluation metrics, one can make informed decisions about model performance and fine-tune their classification algorithms to meet specific requirements and goals.

What Next:

The study encompasses four major machine learning techniques: K-Nearest Neighbors (KNN), Support Vector Machines (SVM), Decision Trees, and Naive Bayes. KNN is elucidated for its reliance on distance metrics and intuitive "nearest neighbor" approach, laying a foundation for classification and regression tasks. SVM's versatility in handling diverse problems through various kernels and decision boundaries was highlighted, offering a comprehensive understanding of its capabilities. Decision trees are explored for their construction, optimal split determination, and strategies to mitigate overfitting, emphasising the importance of cross-validation techniques. Naive Bayes' simplicity and efficiency in classification tasks, rooted in Bayes' theorem, are discussed alongside its variants tailored for different data types, providing insights into probabilistic approaches in machine learning.

P4-U4-L1-4 - Practice Question

1. What are the fundamental techniques covered in this unit?
2. How do backward elimination and forward selection contribute to refining models?
3. What is polynomial regression, and how does it improve prediction accuracy?
4. Explain the concept of Bayesian regression and its importance in regression analysis.
5. How do regularization techniques like Ridge, Lasso, and Elastic Net help in regression modelling?
6. What are the common challenges addressed in regression modelling?
7. What are the different types of logistic regression discussed in this unit?
8. How do activation functions like sigmoid, relu, and tanh contribute to logistic regression?
9. What strategies are used for handling multi-class classification tasks in logistic regression?
10. What evaluation metrics are crucial for assessing classification model performance?
11. Explain the concept of decision thresholds in classification outcomes.
12. How do AUC-ROC curve and Precision-Recall curve offer insights into classifier performance?
13. What is the significance of Precision-Recall curves in classification scenarios?
14. How does F1 score provide a balanced measure of classifier performance?
15. What are the advantages of using Bayesian regression techniques in regression analysis?
16. Explain the concept of feature selection and its importance in model refinement.
17. How do activation functions like relu and tanh enable non-linear mappings in neural network models?
18. What role do regularization techniques play in mitigating overfitting in regression models?
19. What are the benefits of using polynomial regression over linear regression?
20. How do One-vs-All and One-vs-One strategies help in handling multi-class classification tasks?

Assignment: P4-A1

Assignment 1: Iris Dataset Analysis

Problem Statement: You are tasked with analyzing the famous Iris dataset to gain insights into the characteristics of different iris flower species. Using both supervised and unsupervised learning techniques, you need to build models to classify iris flowers and identify patterns in the data.

Background: The Iris dataset is a classic dataset in machine learning, containing measurements of iris flowers' sepal and petal dimensions. This dataset is often used for classification tasks, where the goal is to predict the species of iris flowers based on their attributes.

Objective: The objective of this assignment is to explore various machine learning techniques, including linear regression, logistic regression, clustering methods, and evaluation metrics, to analyze the Iris dataset. By building and evaluating classification models, we aim to classify iris flowers accurately and gain insights into their characteristics.

Data Description: The Iris dataset contains the following variables:

- Sepal length
- Sepal width
- Petal length
- Petal width
- Species (target variable): Setosa, Versicolor, or Virginica

Task:

Perform exploratory data analysis (EDA) to understand the distribution of variables and identify potential correlations.

Preprocess the data by handling missing values, encoding categorical variables, and scaling numerical features.

Split the dataset into training and testing sets.

Build classification models using logistic regression, K-nearest neighbors, and other supervised learning techniques.

Evaluate the performance of each model using appropriate evaluation metrics such as accuracy, precision, recall, and F1-score.

Implement clustering algorithms such as K-means clustering to identify natural groupings within the data.

Compare the performance of different models and clustering techniques and draw conclusions about the iris flowers' characteristics.

PART FIVE

Machine Learning Models

KNN | SVM

Decision Tree | Naïve Bayes

"Machine learning models are not just tools—they are seekers of order in chaos, finding silent patterns in the noise we overlook."

– Shree Shambav

PART FIVE

DAY FOURTEEN

Unit 5 - Lesson One

KNN

K Nearest Neighbour (KNN):

Task: Classification and Regression

- Description: Classifies data points based on the majority class of their k-nearest neighbors; for regression, it predicts the average of the target variable of k-nearest neighbors.
- Algorithm: KNN is a simple and effective classification and regression algorithm.
- Application: Handwriting recognition, credit card fraud detection, and recommendation systems.

K-Nearest Neighbor (K-NN) is a straightforward Supervised Learning algorithm that operates on the principle of similarity between data points. It categorises new data by comparing it to existing data and assigning it to the most similar category.

Key points about K-NN algorithm:

- Classification Technique: K-NN is primarily used for classification tasks, where it assigns new data points to categories based on their similarity to existing data.
- Storage of Data: K-NN stores all available data during the training phase and utilises it to classify new data points when they appear.
- Non-Parametric Algorithm: K-NN doesn't make assumptions about the underlying data distribution, making it flexible for various datasets.

- Lazy Learning Approach: K-NN is considered a lazy learner algorithm because it defers learning from the training set until classification time, storing the dataset instead.
- Usage: K-NN can be applied to both regression and classification problems, although it's predominantly used for classification tasks due to its simplicity and effectiveness.

Consider an example where we need to distinguish between images of cats and dogs. In such a scenario, the K-Nearest Neighbors (KNN) algorithm proves useful. Operating on the principle of similarity, KNN identifies the most similar features between the new image and existing cat and dog images.

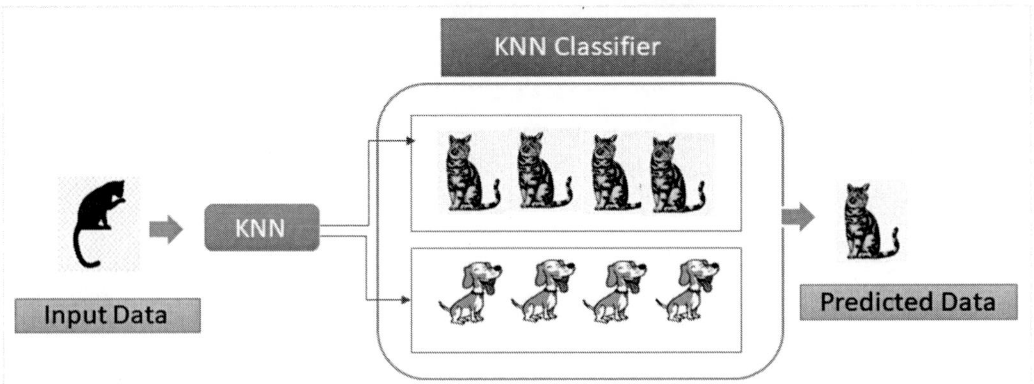

Upon receiving a new image, the KNN model evaluates its features and compares them with those of known cat and dog images. Based on the closest matches, determined by the "K" nearest neighbors, the algorithm categorizes the new image as either a cat or a dog.

When distinguishing between K-Nearest Neighbors (KNN) and K-Means:

The K-Nearest Neighbors (KNN) algorithm operates by identifying the K closest neighbors to a given data point, typically based on a distance metric as Euclidean distance. Subsequently, the class or value of the data point is determined through a majority vote or averaging of the K neighbors' classes or values. This methodology enables the algorithm to adapt to various patterns and make predictions based on the local data structure.

Distance Metrics Utilised in KNN Algorithm:

To identify the nearest points or groups for a query point in the KNN algorithm, appropriate distance metrics are essential. Here are some commonly used distance metrics:

Euclidean Distance: This metric calculates the Cartesian distance between two points in a plane or hyperplane. Visualised as the straight-line length joining the two points, it aids in measuring the net displacement between the two states of an object.

Euclidean Distance = $\sqrt{(x_2 - x_1)^2 + (y_2 - y_1)^2}$

For n-dimensional space: $\sqrt{\sum_{i=1}^{n}(x_{2i} - x_{1i})^2}$

Manhattan Distance: Manhattan Distance is preferred when the focus is on the total distance travelled by an object rather than just its displacement. It is computed by summing the absolute differences between the coordinates of the points across multiple dimensions.

Manhattan Distance = |x2−x1|+|y2−y1|

For n-dimensional space: $\sum_{i=1}^{n} 1\, |x_{2i} - x_{1i}|$

Minkowski Distance: The Minkowski distance encompasses both Euclidean and Manhattan distances as special cases. When the parameter 'p' is set to 2, it mirrors the formula for Euclidean distance, while 'p' set to 1 yields the formula for Manhattan distance.

Minkowski Distance = $(\sum_{i=1}^{n}(|x_{2i} - x_{1i}|)^p)^{\frac{1}{p}}$

Akshatha asked, "How does KNN work?"

Master explained that the operation of the K-Nearest Neighbors (KNN) algorithm can be elucidated through the following steps:

- Select the Number of Neighbors (K): Determine the value of K, which represents the number of nearest neighbors to consider during classification.
- Calculate Euclidean Distance: Compute the Euclidean distance between the new data point and each existing data point in the dataset.
- Identify K Nearest Neighbors: Select the K data points with the shortest Euclidean distances to the new data point.
- Determine Majority Category: Among the K nearest neighbors, tally the number of data points belonging to each category.
- Assign Category to New Data Point: Assign the new data point to the category that has the highest count among its K nearest neighbors.
- Model Finalization: Conclude the classification process, and the KNN model is now prepared for making predictions.

This systematic approach of the KNN algorithm enables it to classify new data points based on the categories of their nearest neighbors, making it a versatile and intuitive classification method.

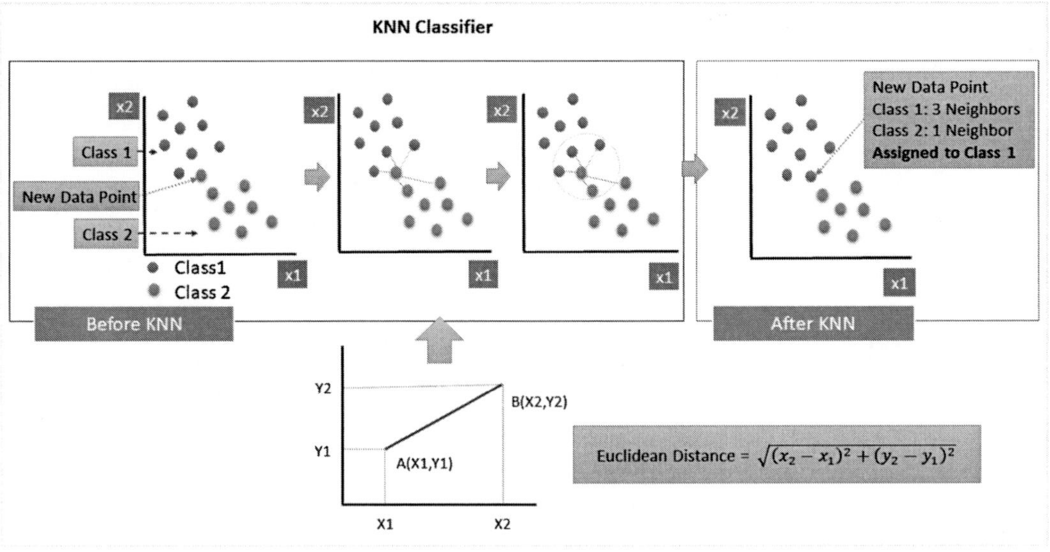

Determining the optimal value of k is pivotal for maximising the effectiveness of the KNN Algorithm. Proper selection of k directly impacts the algorithm's ability to accurately classify data points. To choose the right k value:

- Understand the Data: Gain insights into the characteristics of your dataset, such as the presence of outliers, noise, and the distribution of classes.
- Consider Odd Values: Opt for odd values of k to avoid tie situations during classification, ensuring clear decision-making.
- Evaluate Performance: Utilize cross-validation techniques to assess the performance of the algorithm with different k values. This helps identify the k value that yields the best classification accuracy.
- Balance Bias and Variance: Strike a balance between bias and variance by selecting a suitable k value. A smaller k value reduces bias but increases variance, while a larger k value decreases variance but may introduce bias.
- Iterate and Refine: Experiment with different k values iteratively, refining your selection based on the performance metrics obtained through validation techniques.

By following these guidelines, you can effectively choose the optimal k value for your KNN Algorithm, enhancing its accuracy and robustness in classifying data points.

Exercise P5 - U5 – D1	
ML Models - KNN	**Output**

from sklearn.datasets import load_iris
from sklearn.model_selection import train_test_split
from sklearn.neighbors import KNeighborsClassifier
from sklearn.metrics import confusion_matrix, accuracy_score
import seaborn as sns
import matplotlib.pyplot as plt
 	
# Load the iris dataset. 	
iris = load_iris()
X = iris.data
y = iris.target
# Split the data into training and testing sets with a 70-30 split and a fixed random state for reproducibility. 	
X_train, X_test, y_train, y_test = train_test_split(X, y, test_size=0.3, random_state=1)
 	
# Create a KNN classifier object with 3 neighbors. 	
classifier_knn = KNeighborsClassifier(n_neighbors=3)
# Train the classifier with the training data. 	
classifier_knn.fit(X_train, y_train)
# Make predictions using the testing data. 	
y_pred = classifier_knn.predict(X_test)
# Evaluate the model's accuracy. 	
accuracy = accuracy_score(y_test, y_pred)
print("Accuracy:", accuracy)
 	
# Provide sample data and make predictions. 	
sample = [[5, 5, 3, 3], [3, 4, 3, 5]]
preds = classifier_knn.predict(sample)
pred_species = [iris.target_names[p] for p in preds]
print("Predictions:", pred_species)
	Accuracy:
	0.9777777777777777
	Predictions:
	['versicolor', 'virginica']

This code snippet demonstrates the use of the K-Nearest Neighbors (KNN) classifier for classification tasks using the Iris dataset. Here's a brief overview:

Importing Libraries: Necessary libraries are imported, including load_iris from sklearn.datasets to load the Iris dataset, train_test_split from sklearn.model_selection to split the dataset into training and testing sets, KNeighborsClassifier from sklearn.neighbors for KNN classification, confusion_matrix and accuracy_score from sklearn.metrics for model evaluation, and seaborn and matplotlib.pyplot for visualization.

- Loading and Preparing Dataset: The Iris dataset is loaded using load_iris(), and the feature matrix (X) and target vector (y) are extracted from the dataset.

- Splitting Dataset: The dataset is split into training and testing sets using train_test_split(), with a 70-30 split ratio and a fixed random state for reproducibility.
- Creating and Training KNN Classifier: A KNN classifier object is created with 3 neighbors using KNeighborsClassifier(n_neighbors=3). The classifier is trained with the training data using classifier_knn.fit(X_train, y_train).
- Making Predictions: Predictions are made using the testing data (X_test) with classifier_knn.predict(X_test).
- Evaluating Model Accuracy: The accuracy of the model is evaluated using accuracy_score(y_test, y_pred) and printed to the console.
- Making Predictions with Sample Data: Sample data is provided, and predictions are made using the trained classifier. The predicted species names are printed on the console.

Overall, this code snippet showcases the complete workflow of training a KNN classifier on the Iris dataset, evaluating its performance, and making predictions on new data samples.

Brute Force Algorithm:

Akanksh asked, "What is the Brute Force Algorithm?"

Master said, "The brute force algorithm is a straightforward and exhaustive search strategy used to systematically explore all possible options until the solution to a problem is found. While effective for small-scale problems, its high temporal complexity renders it inefficient for larger issues."

Features of the brute force algorithm:

- Intuitive and Direct: It systematically examines all potential solutions to a problem.
- Widely Applicable: Used in daily tasks like finding the shortest path to a market or optimizing rack space.
- Commonplace: Despite its simplicity, it's frequently used in daily life activities.
- Versatile: Not restricted to specific problem domains, making it suitable for various scenarios.

Advantages:

- Guaranteed Solution: Ensures finding the correct solution by exhaustively listing all possible candidates.
- Generic Method: Applicable across diverse problem types.
- Ideal for Small Problems: Effective for simpler, small-scale issues.
- Benchmarking: Serves as a benchmark for comparing other algorithms' efficiency.

Disadvantages:

- Inefficiency: Inefficient for real-time problems, often exhibiting exponential growth (O(N!)).
- Reliance on Computational Power: Prioritises computational power over algorithmic efficiency.
- Slowness: Generally slower compared to other algorithms.
- Lack of Creativity: Lacks the constructive and creative aspects seen in alternative design paradigms.

Exercise P5-U5 – D2	
ML Model – KNN Regression	**Output**

# Step 1: Import necessary libraries 	
import numpy as np
import pandas as pd
import matplotlib.pyplot as plt
from sklearn.neighbors import KNeighborsRegressor
from sklearn.metrics import mean_squared_error, r2_score
from sklearn.model_selection import train_test_split
 	
# Ensure plots are displayed inline 	
%matplotlib inline
 	
# Step 2: Loading the data 	
file_path = r'C:\Users\User\mraj4\Documents\Optimum\Py-lib\scikit\Advertising.csv'
df = pd.read_csv(file_path)
 	
# Display the first 5 rows of the dataset 	
print(df.head())
 	
# Step 3: Select variables and draw a scatter Plot 	
# Select x Predictor 	
x = df[['TV']].values
	Mean Squared Error: 17.031634994391922
	R-squared Error: 0.4327118634644913

```
# Select y Predictor or output
y = df['Sales'].values
plt.scatter(x, y)
plt.xlabel('TV budget in 1000$', fontsize=20)
plt.ylabel('Sales in 1000$', fontsize=20)
plt.title('Scatter Plot', fontsize=25)

# Step 4: Split Data set
x_train, x_test, y_train, y_test = train_test_split(x, y, train_size=0.7)

# Step 5: Get the optimal value of k for our model
fig, ax = plt.subplots(figsize=(10, 10))
k_list = np.arange(1, 80, 1)
knn_dict = {}  # To store k and mse pairs
for i in k_list:
    # Knn Model Creation
    knn = KNeighborsRegressor(n_neighbors=int(i))
    model_knn = knn.fit(x_train, y_train)
    y_knn_pred = model_knn.predict(x_test)
    # Storing MSE
    mse = mean_squared_error(y_test, y_knn_pred)
    knn_dict[i] = mse

# Plotting the results
ax.plot(knn_dict.keys(), knn_dict.values())
ax.set_xlabel('K-VALUE', fontsize=20)
ax.set_ylabel('MSE', fontsize=20)
ax.set_title('ELBOW PLOT', fontsize=28)

# Step 6: Calculate MSE and R-squared error
mse = mean_squared_error(y_test, y_knn_pred)
r2 = r2_score(y_test, y_knn_pred)
print("Mean Squared Error:", mse)
print("R-squared Error:", r2)
```

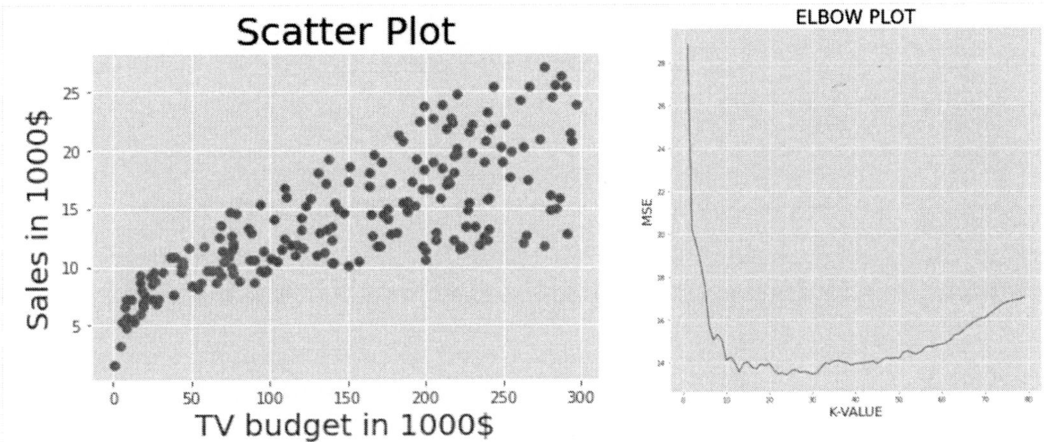

We aim to find the optimal value of k for our K-nearest neighbors model. We plot a graph between mean squared error (MSE) and k values to identify the point where the MSE is the lowest. This graph is known as an "elbow plot" due to its characteristic shape resembling an elbow.

Upon examining the elbow plot, we observe that the MSE is minimised when k=12. This choice of k yields the most accurate predictions for our model.

After building the model with k=12, the mean squared error (MSE) is calculated to be 17.03, indicating the average squared difference between predicted and actual values. Additionally, the R-squared (R2) value, which measures the proportion of the variance in the dependent variable that is predictable from the independent variable, is found to be 0.43. This indicates that approximately 43% of the variability in the sales data can be explained by our model.

Summary:

In this unit, we delved into the fundamentals of K-Nearest Neighbors (KNN) classification and regression techniques. We explored the underlying principles of KNN, including its reliance on distance metrics such as Euclidean, Manhattan, and Minkowski distances. Additionally, we discussed the mechanics of KNN, highlighting its intuitive "nearest neighbor" approach to classification and regression tasks. Furthermore, we examined the Brute Force algorithm, a straightforward yet effective strategy employed in KNN. Overall, this unit provided a comprehensive understanding of KNN and its application in both classification and regression scenarios, laying the groundwork for further exploration in machine learning methodologies.

PART FIVE

DAY FOURTEEN

Unit 5 - Lesson Two

SVM

Support Vector Machines (SVM)

Task: Classification and Regression

- Description: Classifies data points by finding the hyperplane that best separates different classes in feature space.
- Algorithm: SVM is a powerful classification algorithm that finds a hyperplane in an N-dimensional space.
- Application: Text classification, image recognition, and bioinformatics.

Support Vector Machine (SVM) is a versatile machine learning algorithm utilized for various tasks including linear or nonlinear classification, regression, and outlier detection. It finds applications in text classification, image classification, spam detection, handwriting identification, gene expression analysis, face detection, and anomaly detection due to its adaptability and efficiency in handling high-dimensional data and nonlinear relationships.

The main objective of the SVM algorithm is to construct the optimal decision boundary, known as a hyperplane, that effectively separates the n-dimensional space into distinct classes. Support vectors, which are the extreme points aiding in defining this hyperplane, are crucial in the SVM algorithm. The dimensionality of the hyperplane is determined by the number of features, such that for two input features, the hyperplane is a line, for three input features, it's a 2-D plane, and for higher-dimensional feature spaces, it's more complex.

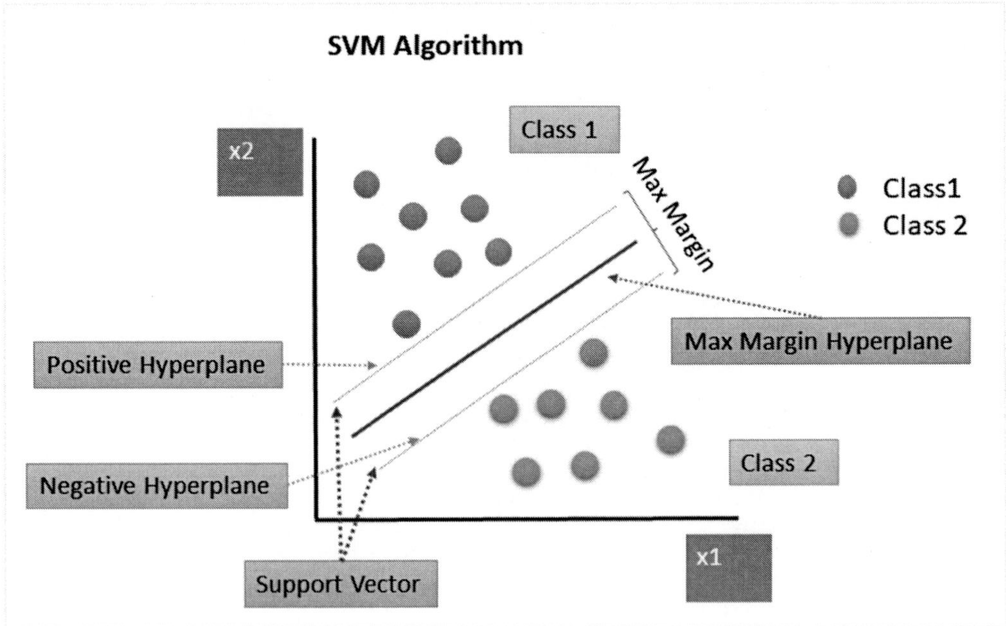

SVM, illustrated through a familiar example akin to our understanding of the KNN classifier, elucidates its functionality effectively. Imagine encountering a peculiar creature bearing resemblances to both a cat and a dog. To discern its identity accurately, we employ an SVM model trained on a plethora of cat and dog images. Through this training, the model familiarises itself with distinctive features of both species.

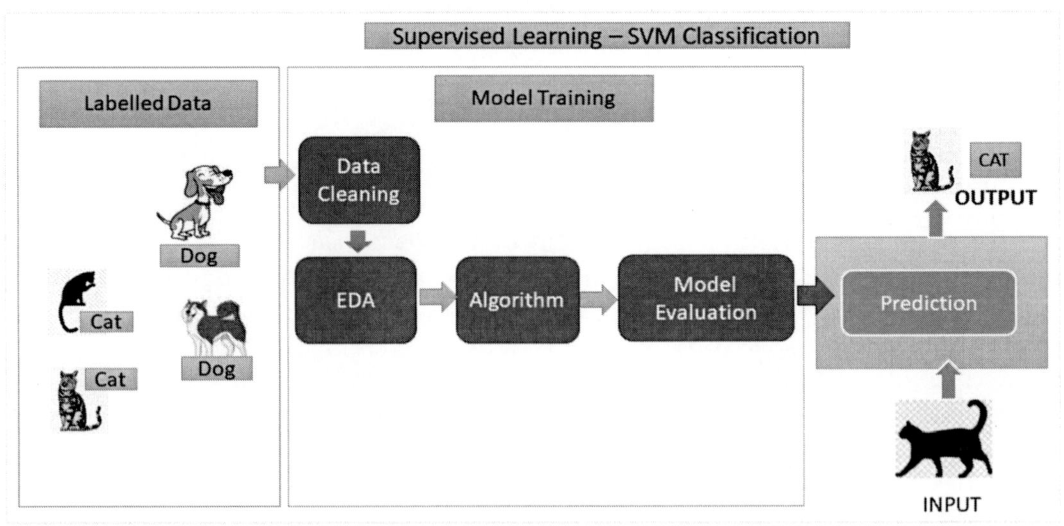

During testing, when confronted with the enigmatic creature, the SVM algorithm delineates a decision boundary, facilitated by support vectors, between the cat and dog data. By analysing these extreme cases, the SVM model determines the creature's classification. In this instance, if the support vectors highlight cat-like attributes predominantly, the creature would be classified as a cat.

In essence, SVM constructs a discerning boundary in the feature space, enabling precise classification even amidst ambiguous instances, thereby showcasing its efficacy in complex classification tasks.

Types of SVM

Master explained that the Support Vector Machines (SVM) encompass two primary types distinguished by the nature of their decision boundaries:

Linear SVM: Linear SVMs employ a linear decision boundary to segregate data points belonging to different classes. Ideally suited for situations where data can be precisely separated by a straight line (in 2D) or a hyperplane (in higher dimensions), linear SVMs maximize the margin between classes to define the decision boundary effectively.

The process of using SVM for classification in a 2-dimensional space:

- Dataset Preparation: Start with a dataset containing data points labelled with two classes, such as "green" and "blue," each represented by two features, x1 and x2.
- Understanding the Data: Analyse the dataset to understand its distribution and characteristics. Visualise the data to observe class separation.
- Linear Separability: Determine if the data points can be separated by a straight line. While a single line can often separate the classes, multiple lines may also achieve separation.
- SVM Algorithm: Utilise the SVM algorithm to find the optimal decision boundary, or hyperplane, that effectively separates the classes. The algorithm selects the hyperplane that maximises the margin between classes, ensuring robust classification.
- Finding the Hyperplane: Identify the hyperplane by considering support vectors, which are data points closest to the decision boundary. These vectors determine the hyperplane's position and orientation.
- Optimising the Hyperplane: SVM aims to maximise the margin between classes while minimising classification errors. Through optimisation techniques, SVM ensures the chosen hyperplane generalises well to unseen data.

- Final Classification: Once the hyperplane is determined, it serves as the decision boundary for classifying new data points. Any new point falling on one side of the hyperplane is assigned to the corresponding class.

Following these steps, SVM effectively classifies data points in 2-dimensional space, using hyperplanes to achieve accurate and robust classification results.

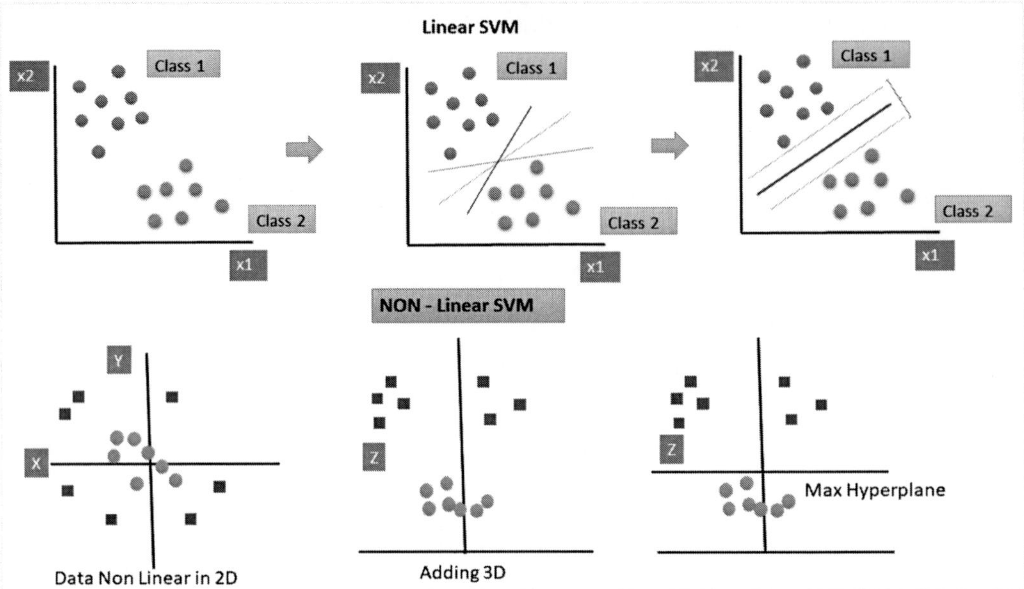

Non-Linear SVM: Non-Linear SVMs step in when data cannot be distinctly divided by a straight line (in 2D). Leveraging kernel functions, these SVMs transform the original input data into a higher-dimensional feature space, facilitating linear separation of data points. Despite their nonlinear separability, these SVMs utilize a linear SVM in the transformed space to identify a nonlinear decision boundary.

Popular kernel functions in SVM

Nikash asked, "What are the popular kernel functions in SVM?"

Master said, "Popular kernel functions in SVM play a crucial role in transforming low-dimensional input space into higher-dimensional space, making them particularly useful for tackling non-linear separation problems. These kernels execute complex data transformations to enable the segregation of data based on predefined labels or outputs."

Here are some commonly used kernel functions:

Linear Kernel: The linear kernel is straightforward, computing the dot product of the input vectors, which essentially results in a linear decision boundary in the original feature space:

$$K(w,x)=w^Tx+b$$

Polynomial Kernel: The polynomial kernel introduces non-linearity by raising the dot product of input vectors to a certain power N, allowing for curved decision boundaries:

$$K(w,x)=(\gamma \; w^Tx+b)^N$$

Gaussian Radial Basis Function (RBF) Kernel: The Gaussian RBF kernel is highly effective in capturing complex relationships between data points by measuring the similarity between them using the Euclidean distance. It transforms the data into an infinite-dimensional space, where data points are separated by non-linear decision boundaries:

$$K(w,x)=\exp(-\gamma||x_i-x_j||^2)$$

Sigmoid Kernel: The sigmoid kernel operates similarly to a two-layer perceptron neural network, mapping the input data into a higher-dimensional space using a hyperbolic tangent function:

$$K(xi,xj)=\tanh(\alpha x_i^T x_j+b)$$

Each kernel function offers distinct advantages and is suited for different types of data and problem scenarios in SVM classification.

Decision Boundary

Support Vector Machine (SVM) is a powerful algorithm used for classification tasks, making it ideal for predicting whether cancer is benign or malignant based on historical patient data. SVM works by finding the optimal hyperplane that best separates the data points into different classes.

To implement SVM in Python for this task, follow these steps:

Exercise P5-U5- D3

SVM - Classifier - Decision Boundary and Predictions

```
# Load the necessary libraries
from sklearn.datasets import load_breast_cancer
from sklearn.svm import SVC
import matplotlib.pyplot as plt
import numpy as np

# Load the dataset
cancer = load_breast_cancer()
X = cancer.data[:, :2]  # Considering only the first two features for visualization
```

```
y = cancer.target

# Build and train the SVM model
svm = SVC(kernel="rbf", gamma=0.5, C=1.0)
svm.fit(X, y)

# Plot Decision Boundary
def plot_decision_boundary(model, X, y):
    # Define step size in the mesh
    h = 0.02
    # Define boundaries for the plot
    x_min, x_max = X[:, 0].min() - 1, X[:, 0].max() + 1
    y_min, y_max = X[:, 1].min() - 1, X[:, 1].max() + 1
    # Generate a mesh grid
    xx, yy = np.meshgrid(np.arange(x_min, x_max, h), np.arange(y_min, y_max, h))
    # Predict the class for each mesh point
    Z = model.predict(np.c_[xx.ravel(), yy.ravel()])
    Z = Z.reshape(xx.shape)
    # Plot decision boundary and scatter plot
    plt.contourf(xx, yy, Z, alpha=0.8, cmap=plt.cm.Spectral)
    plt.xlabel(cancer.feature_names[0])
    plt.ylabel(cancer.feature_names[1])
    plt.scatter(X[:, 0], X[:, 1], c=y, s=20, edgecolors="k")

# Plot Decision Boundary and Scatter plot
plt.figure(figsize=(10, 6))
plot_decision_boundary(svm, X, y)
plt.title('SVM Decision Boundary for Breast Cancer Classification')
plt.show()

# Let's make predictions
X_new = [[120, 990], [85, 550]]  # New data points for prediction
predictions = svm.predict(X_new)

# Display predictions
print("Predictions for the new data points:")
for i, prediction in enumerate(predictions):
    print(f"Data point {i+1}: Predicted class - {cancer.target_names[prediction]}")
```

This Python code demonstrates the implementation of Support Vector Machine (SVM) for breast cancer classification using the Breast Cancer Wisconsin dataset. Here's a brief overview of the code:

Loading the Dataset: The code imports the necessary libraries and loads the Breast Cancer Wisconsin dataset using load_breast_cancer from sklearn.datasets. It extracts the first two features for visualization purposes.

Building and Training the SVM Model: An SVM model with a radial basis function (RBF) kernel is instantiated and trained using the dataset.

Plotting Decision Boundary: The plot_decision_boundary function is defined to plot the decision boundary of the SVM model along with the data points. It generates a mesh grid of points, predicts the class for each point, and visualizes the decision boundary using contourf from matplotlib.pyplot.

Visualization: The decision boundary and the data points are plotted using plot_decision_boundary, providing a visual representation of how the SVM model separates the two classes of breast cancer data.

Making Predictions: The code makes predictions on two new data points ([[120, 990], [85, 550]]) using the trained SVM model. The predicted classes are displayed, indicating whether the breast cancer is predicted to be benign or malignant.

Overall, the code showcases the implementation of SVM for binary classification of breast cancer data and provides insights into how the model separates the classes based on the selected features.

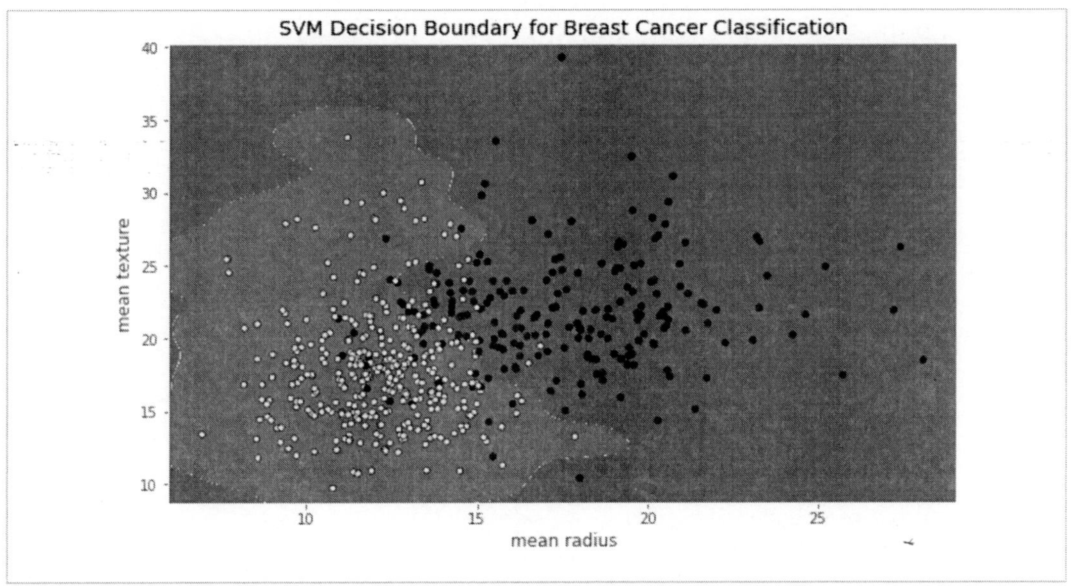

Predictions:

```
Predictions for the new data points:
```

```
Data point 1: Predicted class - malignant

Data point 2: Predicted class - malignant
```

Support Vector Regression (SVR) using Linear and Non-Linear Kernels

Support Vector Regression (SVR) is a powerful tool for regression tasks, capable of utilising both linear and non-linear kernels. Understanding key concepts associated with SVR is crucial for its effective usage:

Support Vector Machines (SVMs): SVR is a type of SVM, a supervised learning algorithm used for classification or regression. SVMs aim to find the hyperplane in a high-dimensional space that maximises the separation between different classes or output values.

Kernels: SVR employs various kernels to measure the similarity between input vectors. A linear kernel computes a simple dot product between vectors, while non-linear kernels capture intricate data patterns. The choice of kernel depends on the data's characteristics and the complexity of the task.

Hyperparameters: SVR offers several hyperparameters for adjusting the model's behaviour. For instance, the 'C' parameter regulates the balance between insensitive and sensitive loss. A higher 'C' value emphasizes minimizing insensitive loss, while a lower 'C' value allows for larger errors.

Model Evaluation: Evaluating SVR performance is essential. Typically, data is split into training and test sets, with the training set used for model fitting and the test set for evaluation. Metrics like mean squared error (MSE) or mean absolute error (MAE) quantify the disparity between predicted and true output values.

To illustrate SVR application, fitting models on sine curve data using different kernels can be insightful:

- Fitting an SVR model on the sine curve data using a Linear Kernel.
- Fitting an SVR model on the sine curve data using a Polynomial Kernel.
- Fitting an SVR model on the sine curve data using an RBF Kernel.

These examples showcase SVR's versatility in handling diverse data patterns and demonstrate how different kernels impact regression results.

Exercise P5-U5- D4

SVM - Regression

```
# Import necessary libraries
import numpy as np
import matplotlib.pyplot as plt
from sklearn.svm import SVR

# Generate sine wave data
X = np.sort(5 * np.random.rand(100, 1), axis=0)
y = np.sin(X).ravel()

# Fit SVR model with Linear Kernel
svr_linear = SVR(kernel='linear')
svr_linear.fit(X, y)

# Fit SVR model with Polynomial Kernel
svr_poly = SVR(kernel='poly', degree=3)
svr_poly.fit(X, y)

# Fit SVR model with RBF Kernel
svr_rbf = SVR(kernel='rbf', gamma=0.1)
svr_rbf.fit(X, y)

# Plot results
plt.figure(figsize=(10, 6))

# Plot original sine curve
plt.scatter(X, y, color='darkorange', label='Data')

# Plot SVR with Linear Kernel
plt.plot(X, svr_linear.predict(X), color='navy', lw=2, label='Linear Kernel model')

# Plot SVR with Polynomial Kernel
plt.plot(X, svr_poly.predict(X), color='c', lw=2, label='Polynomial Kernel model')

# Plot SVR with RBF Kernel
plt.plot(X, svr_rbf.predict(X), color='cornflowerblue', lw=2, label='RBF Kernel model')

plt.xlabel('Data')
plt.ylabel('Target')
plt.title('Support Vector Regression')
plt.legend()
plt.show()
```

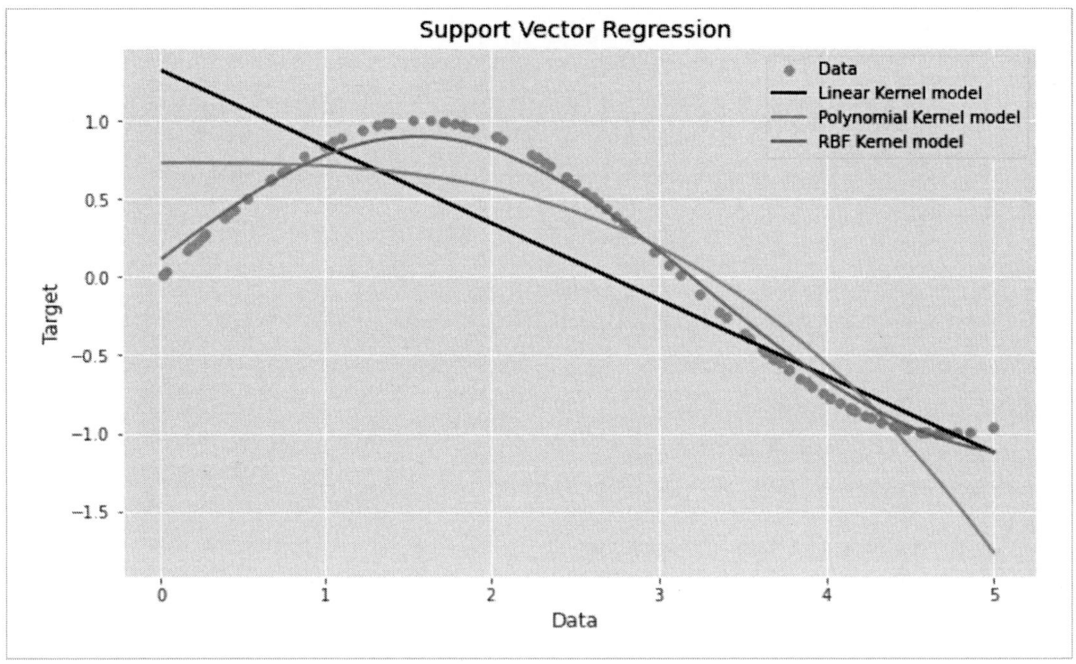

Major Kernel Functions in Support Vector Machine

Master said, “Kernel Functions play a crucial role in Support Vector Machines (SVM), facilitating the transformation of data into a suitable format for processing. These mathematical functions provide the means to manipulate data effectively, enabling SVMs to create decision boundaries in complex spaces.”

Here are some of the key kernel functions used in SVM:

Gaussian Kernel:

Purpose: Used when there’s no prior knowledge about the data distribution.

Function: It transforms the input data into a higher-dimensional space, allowing SVMs to find nonlinear decision boundaries.

Linear Kernel:

Purpose: Applied when the data is linearly separable.

Function: This kernel computes the inner product between two input data points, effectively creating a linear decision boundary.

Polynomial Kernel:

Purpose: Represents the similarity of vectors in the feature space over polynomials of the original variables.

Function: It calculates the similarity between data points based on polynomial transformations, enabling SVMs to capture complex patterns.

Gaussian Kernel Radial Basis Function (RBF):

Purpose: Enhances transformation by incorporating radial basis methods.

Function: Similar to the Gaussian kernel, this function adds radial basis elements to improve the transformation process.

Sigmoid Kernel:

Purpose: Equivalent to a two-layer perceptron model in neural networks.

Function: It acts as an activation function for artificial neurons, transforming input data into a format suitable for SVMs.

Exercise P5-U5- D5

SVM – Kernel Functions

```
# Importing necessary libraries
import numpy as np
import matplotlib.pyplot as plt

# Sample input data
X = np.linspace(-5, 5, 100)[:, np.newaxis]

# Define kernel functions
def gaussian_kernel(x1, x2, sigma=1):
    return np.exp(-np.linalg.norm(x1 - x2) ** 2 / (2 * (sigma ** 2)))

def linear_kernel(x1, x2):
    return np.dot(x1, x2.T)

def polynomial_kernel(x1, x2, degree=3, coef0=1):
    return (np.dot(x1, x2.T) + coef0) ** degree

def rbf_kernel(x1, x2, gamma=0.1):
    return np.exp(-gamma * np.linalg.norm(x1 - x2) ** 2)

def sigmoid_kernel(x1, x2, coef0=0.1):
    return np.tanh(np.dot(x1, x2.T) + coef0)

# Compute kernel matrices
```

```
gaussian_result = np.zeros((X.shape[0], X.shape[0]))
linear_result = np.zeros((X.shape[0], X.shape[0]))
polynomial_result = np.zeros((X.shape[0], X.shape[0]))
rbf_result = np.zeros((X.shape[0], X.shape[0]))
sigmoid_result = np.zeros((X.shape[0], X.shape[0]))

for i in range(X.shape[0]):
    for j in range(X.shape[0]):
        gaussian_result[i, j] = gaussian_kernel(X[i], X[j])
        linear_result[i, j] = linear_kernel(X[i], X[j])
        polynomial_result[i, j] = polynomial_kernel(X[i], X[j])
        rbf_result[i, j] = rbf_kernel(X[i], X[j])
        sigmoid_result[i, j] = sigmoid_kernel(X[i], X[j])

# Plot kernel matrices
plt.figure(figsize=(20, 10))

plt.subplot(231)
plt.imshow(gaussian_result, cmap='hot', interpolation='nearest')
plt.title('Gaussian Kernel')
plt.colorbar()

plt.subplot(232)
plt.imshow(linear_result, cmap='hot', interpolation='nearest')
plt.title('Linear Kernel')
plt.colorbar()

plt.subplot(233)
plt.imshow(polynomial_result, cmap='hot', interpolation='nearest')
plt.title('Polynomial Kernel')
plt.colorbar()

plt.subplot(234)
plt.imshow(rbf_result, cmap='hot', interpolation='nearest')
plt.title('RBF Kernel')
plt.colorbar()

plt.subplot(235)
plt.imshow(sigmoid_result, cmap='hot', interpolation='nearest')
plt.title('Sigmoid Kernel')
plt.colorbar()

plt.tight_layout()
plt.show()
```

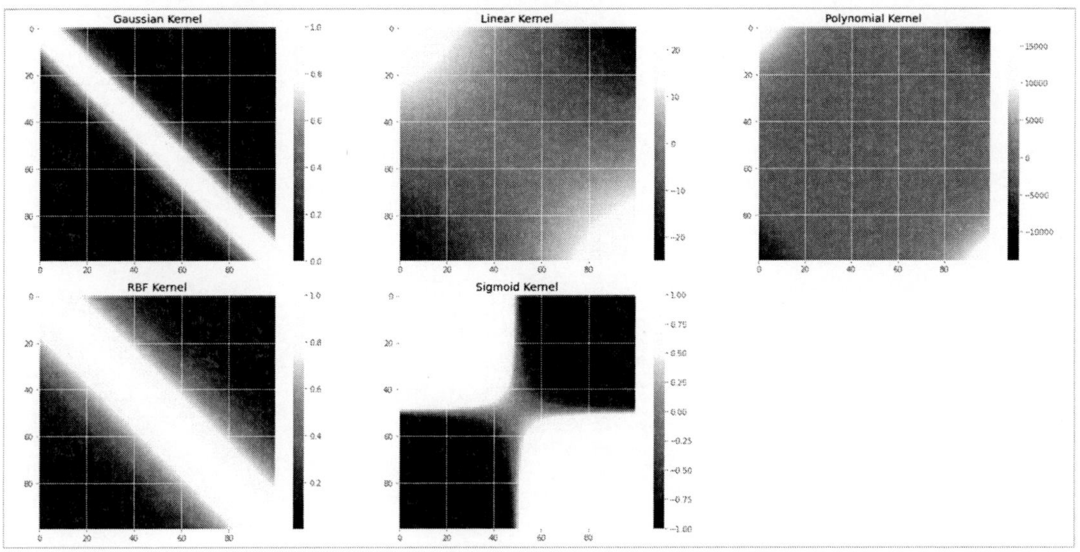

In summary, darker regions in each plot indicate higher similarity or kernel values between points, while lighter regions represent lower similarity or kernel values. These plots help visualize how different kernel functions measure similarity or distance between data points in different ways.

Understanding the characteristics and applicability of these kernel functions is essential for effectively utilizing SVMs in various machine learning tasks.

Summary:

In this unit, we delved into Support Vector Machine (SVM) classifiers and regression techniques, exploring their versatility and applicability in various machine learning tasks. We covered the different types of SVMs, including linear and nonlinear variants, which enable SVMs to handle a wide range of classification and regression problems. Furthermore, we discussed the role of kernel functions in SVMs, such as linear, polynomial, radial basis function (RBF), and sigmoid kernels, which allow SVMs to operate in high-dimensional spaces and capture complex relationships within the data. Additionally, we examined decision boundaries and how SVMs use them to separate different classes or predict continuous values in regression tasks. Overall, this unit provided a comprehensive overview of SVMs, their capabilities, and the essential concepts necessary for understanding and applying them effectively in real-world scenarios.

PART FIVE

DAY FIFTEEN

Unit 5 - Lesson Three

Decision Tree - I

Decision Trees

Task: Classification and Regression

- Description: Uses a tree-like model of decisions to make predictions; splits the dataset into subsets based on the most significant attribute.
- Algorithm: Decision trees are tree-like structures used for both classification and regression.
- Application: Customer churn prediction, fraud detection, and medical diagnosis.

Decision tree is a powerful supervised machine learning algorithm used for both classification and regression tasks. It resembles an inverted tree structure where each internal node represents a predictor variable (feature), the branches represent decision rules, and each leaf node represents an outcome (response variable). Here's an improved explanation along with an example and the basic formula:

Decision trees recursively partition the feature space into regions, with each split based on the feature that best separates the data according to a certain criterion (e.g., Gini impurity or information gain). This process continues until a stopping criterion is met, resulting in a tree structure that can be used to make predictions.

Example:

Consider a decision tree for predicting whether a passenger survived or not in the Titanic dataset. The features might include variables such as age, gender, ticket class, and fare paid. The decision tree would split the data based on these features, with each branch representing a decision rule (e.g., age <= 30), and each leaf node indicating the predicted outcome (survived or not survived).

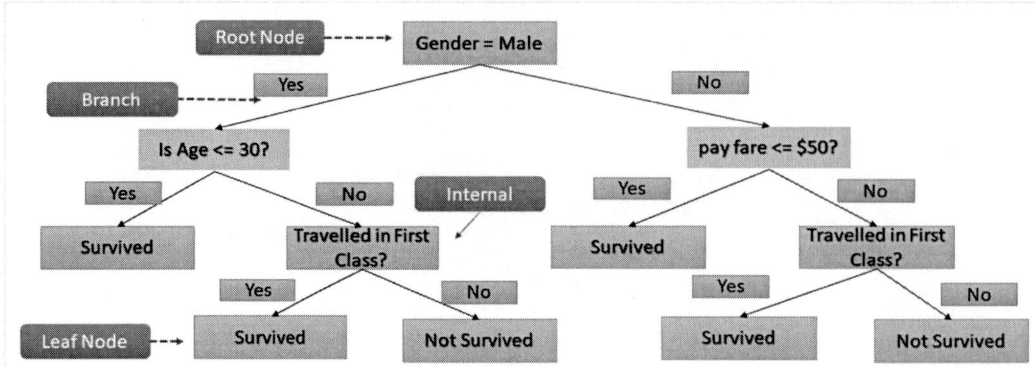

- The first split is based on gender. If the passenger is male, the tree goes left; otherwise, it goes right.
- If the passenger is male, the next split is based on age.
- If the passenger is female, the next split is based on whether they travelled in first class. If they did, they are predicted to have survived; otherwise, the prediction depends on whether they paid a fare less than or equal to $50.

Key components

Root Node: The topmost node in the tree, from which the tree starts growing. It represents the entire dataset and is split into two or more branches based on the feature that best separates the data.

Branch: A path along the tree from one node to another. Each branch represents a decision based on a feature's value. For example, if the age is less than or equal to 30, the branch might lead to a different node than if the age is greater than 30.

Internal Node: A node in the decision tree that has two or more child nodes. It represents a decision based on the value of a feature. Internal nodes split the data into subsets based on the feature's value.

Leaf Node (Terminal Node): A node in the decision tree that does not have any child nodes. It represents the final outcome or decision. Each leaf node corresponds to a specific class label or target value that the model predicts. For example, a leaf node might represent "Survived" or "Not Survived" in a Titanic survival prediction model.

In summary, the root node represents the entire dataset, internal nodes represent decisions based on feature values, branches represent possible outcomes of those decisions, and leaf nodes represent final predictions or outcomes.

Decision Rules are the guiding principles that determine how data is divided at each branch node within a decision tree. These rules dictate the conditions under which the data is partitioned, ultimately leading to the creation of distinct subsets at each level of the tree.

Attribute Selection is the pivotal process of identifying the most informative attribute to split the data at each node. It involves evaluating the attributes' relevance and discriminatory power to effectively segregate the dataset into homogeneous groups.

Splitting Criteria refers to the metrics employed to determine the optimal attribute for partitioning the data. Common criteria include Information Gain, Entropy, and the Gini Index, which quantify the purity or impurity of subsets resulting from a split. These metrics guide the decision-making process by assessing the effectiveness of potential splits in enhancing the homogeneity of the resulting subsets.

Decision trees offer interpretability, flexibility, and ease of visualisation, making them valuable tools for various machine learning tasks.

Assumptions made when using Decision Trees

Initial Root Selection: The entire training set is initially treated as the root of the decision tree.

Attribute Type: For calculating Information Gain, attributes are assumed to be categorical, while for Gini Index, attributes are considered continuous.

Recursive Data Distribution: Records are recursively distributed based on the values of attributes, leading to the creation of internal nodes and branches.

Attribute Ordering: Statistical methods are employed to determine the order of attributes as the root or internal nodes, prioritizing those attributes that contribute most to classification purity.

Pseudocode for Decision Tree Construction

1. **Select Best Attribute:** Identify the attribute that best splits the dataset, maximizing information gain or minimizing impurity.
2. **Place Attribute on Root:** Assign the selected attribute to the root node of the tree.
3. **Split Dataset:** Divide the training dataset into subsets based on the values of the selected attribute.
4. **Recurse on Subsets:** For each subset, repeat steps 1-3 recursively until certain termination conditions are met:
    - If a subset is homogeneous (contains only one class), designate it as a leaf node.

- If maximum depth is reached or minimum number of samples per leaf is satisfied, designate it as a leaf node.
- Otherwise, continue splitting the subset by selecting the best attribute and repeating the process.

5. **Leaf Node Creation:** Once termination conditions are met, create leaf nodes for each subset, representing the predicted class label.

Key Concepts in Decision Trees

Gini Index and Information Gain:

Master explained that the Gini index and information gain are methods used to select the attribute for the root or internal nodes of the decision tree.

- **Gini Index:** Measures how often a randomly chosen element would be incorrectly identified. A lower Gini index indicates better attribute selection.
- **Information Gain:** Measures the reduction in entropy or uncertainty after splitting the dataset based on an attribute. Higher information gain implies better attribute selection.

Entropy:

Entropy is a measure of uncertainty or impurity of a random variable. It characterises the randomness or disorder in a dataset. Higher entropy signifies greater uncertainty.

Information Gain Calculation:

Given a set of instances S and an attribute A with subset Sv when $A=v$, and $Values(A)$ as the set of all possible values of A, the information gain is calculated as the difference in entropy before and after the split.

Criterion in Scikit-Learn:

- Scikit-learn supports both "gini" and "entropy" criteria for splitting nodes based on Gini index and information gain, respectively.
- By default, Scikit-learn uses "gini" criterion. If "entropy" method is preferred, it needs to be specified explicitly.

Gini Index:

Master said, "The Gini Index, also known as Gini impurity, serves as a metric to gauge the purity or impurity of a dataset. Ranging between 0 and 1, the Gini impurity indicates how mixed or homogeneous the dataset is. A Gini impurity of 0 signifies an entirely pure dataset, where all samples belong to the same class. Conversely, a Gini impurity of 1 denotes a dataset that is completely impure, containing a diverse mix of different classes."

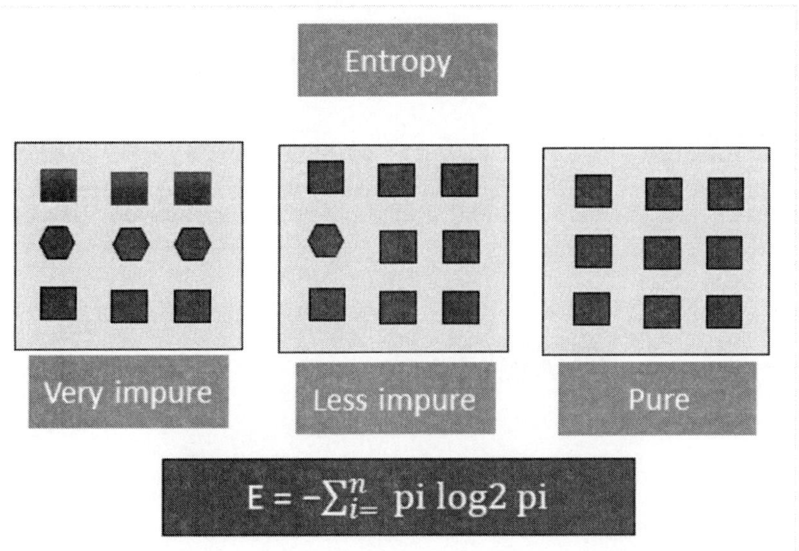

In decision tree algorithms, the objective is to split the dataset into subsets based on features such that the resulting subsets are as pure as possible. Therefore, features with lower Gini impurity are preferred for splitting, as they facilitate the creation of more homogeneous subsets. Essentially, the lower the Gini impurity associated with an attribute, the more suitable it is for dividing the dataset into subsets that predominantly consist of samples from the same class.

The basic formula for decision trees involves calculating impurity measures such as Gini impurity or entropy. For example, the Gini impurity at a node can be calculated as follows:

$$\text{Gini}(p) = 1 - \sum_{i=1}^{n} p_i^2$$

where pi represents the probability of each class 'I' in the node. The goal is to minimise the impurity at each node to create effective splits in the data.

Example:

Consider an example where we are constructing a decision tree to forecast whether a loan granted to an individual would lead to a write-off or not. Our dataset comprises 30 instances, with 16 falling into the write-off category and the remaining 14 into the non-write-off category.

We have two features: "Balance," which can be categorised as "< 75K" or "> 75K," and "Residence," which can be classified as "OWN," "RENT," or "Others".

Feature 1: Balance

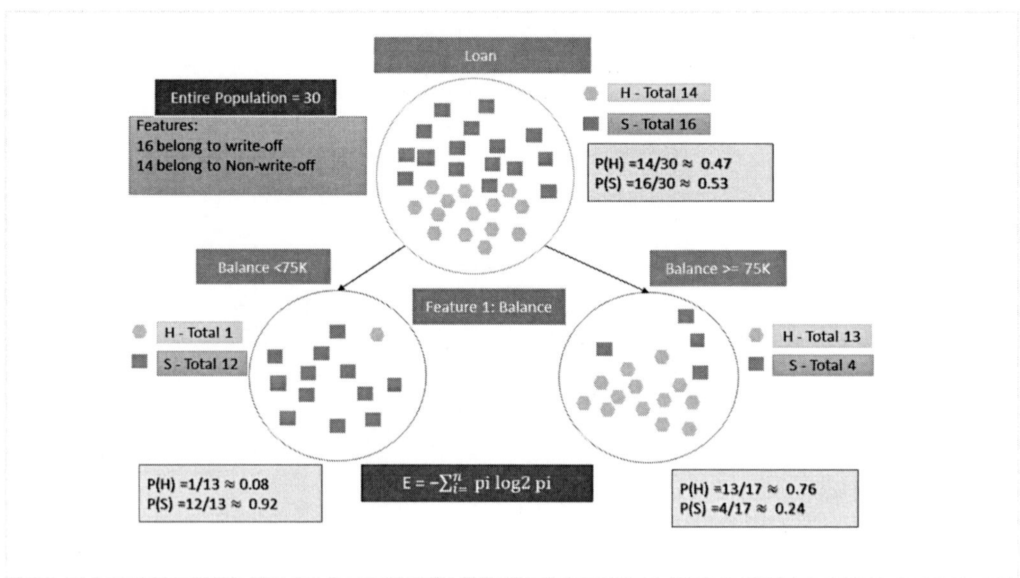

$$E(Parent) = -(16/30)\ \log_2 (16/30) - (14/30)\ \log_2 (14/30) \approx 0.99$$

Entropy Calculation Using Math and Scipy Libraries

Master explained that this code demonstrates two methods for calculating the entropy of a binary distribution representing the probabilities of two outcomes: "Write Off" (p_wo) and "Not Write Off" (p_Nwo). Entropy is a measure of the unpredictability or information content within a probability distribution.

Exercise P5-U11 – D6 – Entropy	
E(Parent) – Using Math and scipy stats	**Output**

import math
from scipy.stats import entropy
# Define the probabilities for "Write Off" and "Not Write Off" 	
p_wo = 0.47
p_Nwo = 0.53
 	
# Store probabilities in a list 	
probabilities = [p_wo, p_Nwo]
	Entropy calculated using the math library:
	0.9974015885677396
	Entropy calculated using the scipy.stats library:

# Calculate entropy using the math library 	
manual_entropy = -(p_wo * math.log2(p_wo) + p_Nwo * math.log2(p_Nwo))
print("Entropy calculated using the math library:", manual_entropy)
 	
# Calculate entropy using the scipy.stats library 	
scipy_entropy = entropy(probabilities, base=2)
print("Entropy calculated using the scipy.stats library:", scipy_entropy)
	0.9974015885677396

Reduce by splitting on Balance:

$$E(\text{Balance} <75K) = -(12/13) \log_2 (12/13) - (1/13) \log_2 (1/13) \approx 0.39$$

$$E(\text{Balance} >75K) = -(4/17) \log_2 (4/17) - (13/17) \log_2 (13/17) \approx 0.79$$

Weighted Average of entropy of each node:

$$E(\text{Balance}) = ((13/30)*0.39 + (17/30)*0.79) = 0.62$$

Information Gain:

Information Gain = Entropy(Parent) – [Weighted Average]*Entropy(Children)

IG(Parent, Balance) = E(Parent) – E(Balance) =0.99 – 0.62 = **0.37**

Feature 2: Residence

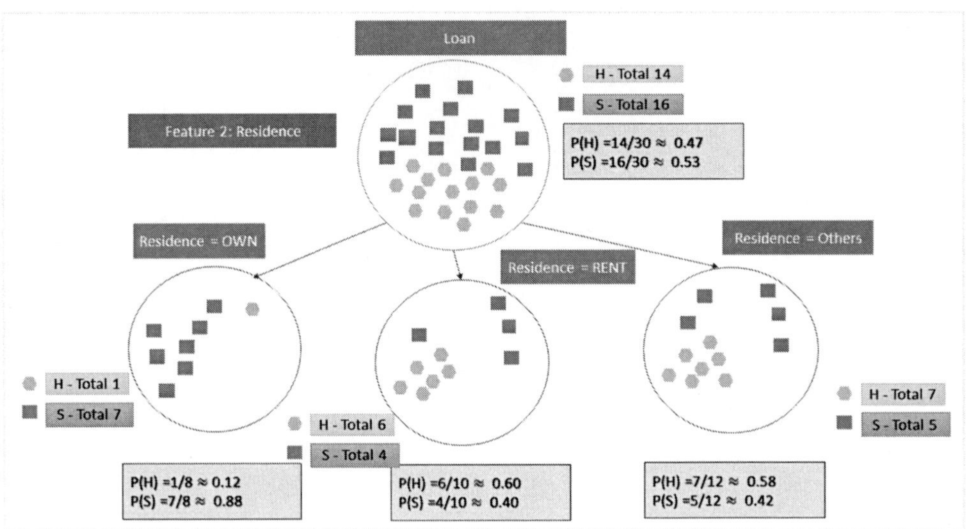

$$E(\text{Parent}) = -(16/30) \log_2 (16/30) - (14/30) \log_2 (14/30) \approx 0.99$$

$$E(\text{Residence} = \text{OWN}) = -(7/8) \log_2 (7/8) - (1/8) \log_2 (1/8) \approx 0.54$$

$$E(\text{Residence} = \text{RENT}) = -(4/10) \log_2 (4/10) - (6/10) \log_2 (6/10) \approx 0.97$$

$$E(\text{Residence} = \text{Others}) = -(5/12) \log_2 (5/12) - (7/12) \log_2 (7/12) \approx 0.98$$

Weighted Average of entropy of each node:

$$E(\text{Balance}) = ((8/30)*0.54 + (10/30)*0.97 + (12/30)*0.98) = 0.86$$

Information Gain:

$$IG(\text{Parent, Balance}) = E(\text{Parent}) - E(\text{Balance}) = 0.99 - 0.86 = \mathbf{0.13}$$

The feature "Balance," which exhibits a higher information gain of 0.37, is deemed more informative and hence should be employed to partition the data at the subsequent internal node.

We may also opt to utilize Gini impurity as an alternative to Entropy. Although the outcomes may not significantly differ regardless of which metric you choose, Gini impurity typically offers a slight computational advantage over entropy. While entropy tends to produce more balanced trees, Gini impurity has a tendency to isolate the majority class into its own branch.

Decision Tree Classifier: Gini and Entropy

The purpose of this code is to identify the best feature in the Iris dataset based on two criteria: Gini impurity and entropy. These metrics help determine how well a feature can split the data into distinct classes, which is important for constructing effective decision trees.

Exercise P5-U5 – D7

Decision Tree Classifier – Gini Impurities and Entropy

```
# Import necessary libraries
from sklearn import datasets
from sklearn.tree import DecisionTreeClassifier
import numpy as np

# Load the Iris dataset
iris = datasets.load_iris()
X = iris.data
y = iris.target

# Initialize dictionaries to hold Gini impurities and entropies for each feature
gini_impurities = {}
entropies = {}

# Function to calculate entropy
def calculate_entropy(probs):
    return -np.sum(probs * np.log2(probs + 1e-9))

# Loop through each feature
for i in range(X.shape[1]):
    # Select only the current feature for the classifier
    X_feature = X[:, i].reshape(-1, 1)

    # Train Decision Tree Classifier Using Gini Criterion
    # Create the decision tree classifier for Gini criterion
    clf_gini = DecisionTreeClassifier(criterion='gini')
    clf_gini.fit(X_feature, y)
    prob_gini = clf_gini.predict_proba(X_feature)

    # Calculate the Gini impurity for the current feature
    gini_impurity = 1 - np.sum(prob_gini**2, axis=1).mean()
    gini_impurities[i] = gini_impurity

    # Train Decision Tree Classifier Using Entropy Criterion
    # Create the decision tree classifier for Entropy criterion
```

```
    clf_entropy = DecisionTreeClassifier(criterion='entropy')
    clf_entropy.fit(X_feature, y)
    prob_entropy = clf_entropy.predict_proba(X_feature)

    # Calculate the entropy for the current feature
    entropy = np.apply_along_axis(calculate_entropy, 1, prob_entropy).mean()
    entropies[i] = entropy

# Identify the Best Feature
# Find the feature with the lowest Gini impurity and entropy
best_feature_gini = min(gini_impurities, key=gini_impurities.get)
best_feature_entropy = min(entropies, key=entropies.get)

# Print the results
print(f"Best Feature Index by Gini: {best_feature_gini}")
print(f"Gini Impurities for each feature: {gini_impurities}")
print(f"Best Feature Index by Entropy: {best_feature_entropy}")
print(f"Entropies for each feature: {entropies}")
```

Output:

Best Feature Index by Gini: 2

Gini Impurities for each feature: {0: 0.31940740740740736, 1: 0.46767491767491753, 2: 0.06266666666666676, 3: 0.06277777777777793}

Best Feature Index by Entropy: 2

Entropies for each feature: {0: 0.7080248770505059, 1: 1.0683196215878084, 2: 0.13864597535373993, 3: 0.14906466023753653}

Decision Tree Classifier - Prediction

The provided code demonstrates the construction and visualization of a decision tree classifier using the Iris dataset.

Exercise P5-U5 – D8

Decision Tree Classifier

```
# Import required libraries
from sklearn.datasets import load_iris
from sklearn.tree import DecisionTreeClassifier, plot_tree
import numpy as np
import matplotlib.pyplot as plt

# Load the Iris dataset
iris = load_iris()
X = iris.data
y = iris.target
```

```
# Initialize dictionaries to hold Gini impurities and entropies for each feature
gini_impurities = {}
entropies = {}

# Function to calculate entropy
def calculate_entropy(probs):
    return -np.sum(probs * np.log2(probs + 1e-9))

# Loop through each feature
for i in range(X.shape[1]):
    X_feature = X[:, i].reshape(-1, 1)

    # Create the decision tree classifier for Gini criterion
    clf_gini = DecisionTreeClassifier(criterion='gini')
    clf_gini.fit(X_feature, y)
    prob_gini = clf_gini.predict_proba(X_feature)

    # Calculate the Gini impurity for the current feature
    gini_impurity = 1 - np.sum(prob_gini**2, axis=1).mean()
    gini_impurities[i] = gini_impurity

    # Create the decision tree classifier for Entropy criterion
    clf_entropy = DecisionTreeClassifier(criterion='entropy')
    clf_entropy.fit(X_feature, y)
    prob_entropy = clf_entropy.predict_proba(X_feature)

    # Calculate the entropy for the current feature
    entropy = np.apply_along_axis(calculate_entropy, 1, prob_entropy).mean()
    entropies[i] = entropy

# Find the feature with the lowest Gini impurity and entropy
best_feature_gini = min(gini_impurities, key=gini_impurities.get)
best_feature_entropy = min(entropies, key=entropies.get)

# Print the results
print(f"Best Feature Index by Gini: {best_feature_gini}")
print(f"Gini Impurities for each feature: {gini_impurities}")

print(f"Best Feature Index by Entropy: {best_feature_entropy}")
print(f"Entropies for each feature: {entropies}")

# Plot the decision tree using all features and the Gini criterion
clf_gini_all = DecisionTreeClassifier(criterion='gini', max_depth=4, min_samples_leaf=4)
clf_gini_all.fit(X, y)

fig, ax = plt.subplots(figsize=(12, 8))
plot_tree(clf_gini_all, ax=ax, feature_names=iris.feature_names,
class_names=iris.target_names, filled=True)
```

```
plt.title("Decision Tree using Gini Impurity")
plt.show()

# Plot the decision tree using all features and the Entropy criterion
clf_entropy_all = DecisionTreeClassifier(criterion='entropy', max_depth=4,
min_samples_leaf=4)
clf_entropy_all.fit(X, y)

fig, ax = plt.subplots(figsize=(12, 8))
plot_tree(clf_entropy_all, ax=ax, feature_names=iris.feature_names,
class_names=iris.target_names, filled=True)
plt.title("Decision Tree using Entropy")
plt.show()

# Make predictions
sample_data = [[5, 3.5, 1.3, 0.3]]
predictions_gini = clf_gini_all.predict(sample_data)
predictions_entropy = clf_entropy_all.predict(sample_data)

print("Prediction for sample data using Gini:", predictions_gini)
print("Predicted class name using Gini:", iris.target_names[predictions_gini[0]])
print("Prediction for sample data using Entropy:", predictions_entropy)
print("Predicted class name using Entropy:", iris.target_names[predictions_entropy[0]])
```

Output:

Best Feature Index by Gini: 2
Gini Impurities for each feature: {0: 0.31940740740740736, 1: 0.46767491767491753, 2: 0.06266666666666676, 3: 0.06277777777777793}
Best Feature Index by Entropy: 2
Entropies for each feature: {0: 0.7080248770505059, 1: 1.0683196215878084, 2: 0.13864597535373993, 3: 0.14906466023753653}
Prediction for sample data using Gini: [0]
Predicted class name using Gini: setosa
Prediction for sample data using Entropy: [0]
Predicted class name using Entropy: setosa

This indicates that according to the decision tree's prediction, the input sample is classified as belonging to class 0, which corresponds to the Setosa species, based on the information learned from the training data.

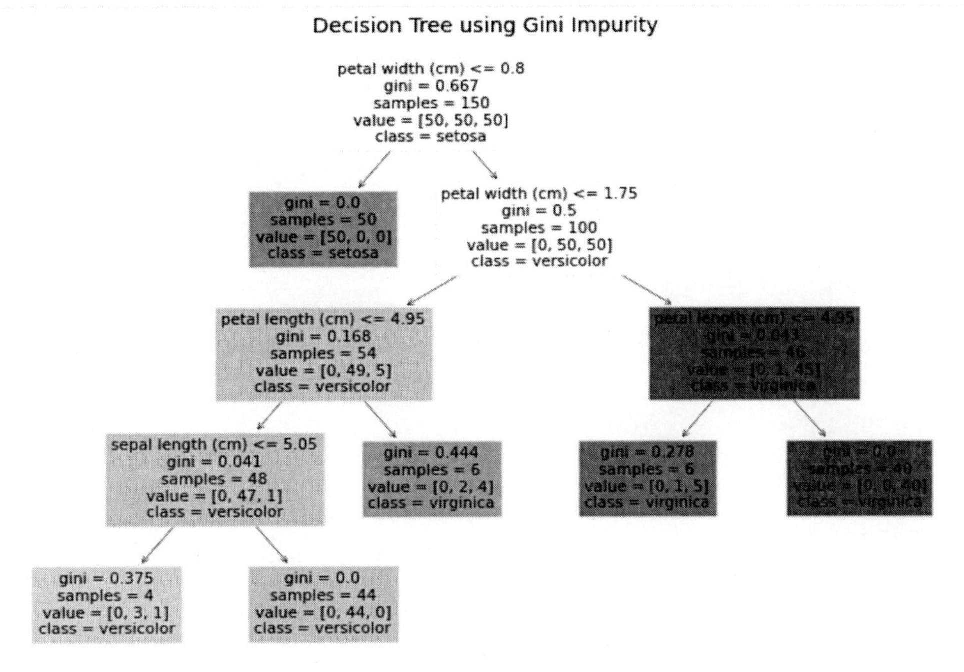

The code demonstrates how to build and visualise decision trees using both Gini impurity and entropy criteria. Additionally, it calculates Gini impurities and entropies for each feature in the Iris dataset and identifies the best features based on these criteria.

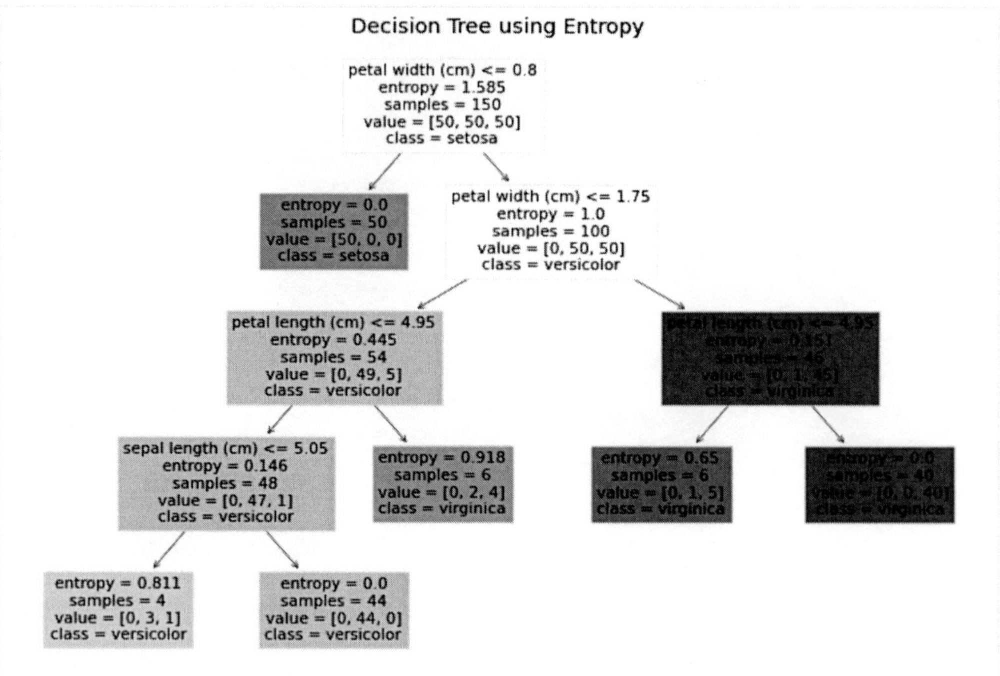

Types of algorithms in Decision Tree

Master said, "There are several types of decision tree algorithms, each with its own characteristics and advantages."

Some of the most commonly used decision tree algorithms include:

- ID3 (Iterative Dichotomiser 3): ID3 is one of the earliest decision tree algorithms developed by Ross Quinlan. It uses entropy and information gain to select the best split at each node. However, ID3 only works with categorical attributes and cannot handle continuous-valued attributes.

- C4.5 (Successor of ID3): C4.5 is an extension of ID3 that addresses some of its limitations. It can handle both categorical and continuous-valued attributes, and it uses gain ratio instead of information gain to handle bias towards attributes with many values.

- C5.0: An enhancement of the C4.5 algorithm, C5.0 uses less memory and builds smaller rulesets while maintaining higher accuracy compared to C4.5.

- CART (Classification and Regression Trees): CART is a versatile decision tree algorithm that can be used for both classification and regression tasks. It uses Gini impurity (for classification) or mean squared error (for regression) to measure impurity and select the best split at each node. CART also supports binary splits, making it more efficient than ID3 and C4.5.

- CHAID (Chi-squared Automatic Interaction Detection): CHAID is a decision tree algorithm specifically designed for classification tasks. It uses chi-squared tests to determine the significance of splits and selects the split that maximises the association between the target variable and the input attributes.

- Random Forest: Random Forest is an ensemble learning method that uses multiple decision trees to improve predictive accuracy. Each tree is trained on a random subset of the training data and makes a prediction. The final prediction is then determined by averaging the predictions of all trees (for regression) or using a voting mechanism (for classification).

- Gradient Boosting Machines (GBM): GBM is another ensemble learning method that builds decision trees sequentially, with each tree correcting the errors from the previous ones. It combines the predictions of multiple weak learners (shallow decision trees) to create a strong learner with high predictive accuracy.

These are some of the most used decision tree algorithms, each with its own strengths and weaknesses. The choice of algorithm depends on the specific characteristics of the dataset and the requirements of the task at hand.

CART:

Master explained that the CART works by recursively partitioning the input space into subsets, with the goal of minimising impurity within each subset.

Here's how the CART algorithm works:

Binary Splitting: At each node of the tree, the algorithm considers all possible splits of the data into two groups based on the values of a single input feature (attribute). It selects the split that minimises impurity in the resulting subsets.

Splitting Criterion: The impurity measure used in CART depends on the type of task:

- For classification tasks, the Gini impurity or entropy measures are commonly used.

- For regression tasks, the mean squared error (MSE) is typically used.

Recursive Partitioning: After selecting the best split, the algorithm recursively applies the splitting process to each subset, continuing until a stopping criterion is met. This may involve reaching a maximum tree depth, having nodes with fewer than a minimum number of samples, or other criteria.

Pruning (Optional): After the tree is fully grown, it may be pruned to prevent overfitting. Pruning involves removing nodes that do not significantly improve predictive accuracy on a separate validation dataset.

Prediction: Once the tree is built, it can be used to make predictions for new data points by traversing the tree from the root node to a leaf node, where each leaf node corresponds to a class label (for classification) or a predicted numerical value (for regression).

CART for Classification

A classification tree is an algorithm where the target variable is categorical. This algorithm is used to identify the "class" within which the target variable is most likely to fall. Classification trees are useful when the dataset needs to be split into classes corresponding to the response variable (such as yes or no).

In a decision tree learning algorithm for classification, the tree-like structure predicts class labels. The tree consists of nodes representing different decision points and branches representing the possible outcomes of those decisions. The predicted class labels are found at each leaf node of the tree.

How does CART for Classification work?

CART (Classification and Regression Trees) for classification works by recursively splitting the training data into smaller subsets based on certain criteria. The goal is to split the data in a way that minimizes the impurity within each subset. Impurity measures how mixed the data is in a particular subset. For classification tasks, CART uses Gini impurity.

Gini Impurity

- **Definition:** Gini impurity measures the probability of misclassifying a random instance from a subset labelled according to the majority class.
- **Purpose:** Lower Gini impurity indicates a higher purity of the subset.

Splitting Criteria

- **Evaluation:** The CART algorithm evaluates all potential splits at each node and chooses the one that best decreases the Gini impurity of the resultant subsets.
- **Process:** This process continues recursively until a stopping criterion is reached, such as a maximum tree depth or a minimum number of instances in a leaf node.

Exercise P5-U5 – D9

CART for Classification

```
# Import necessary libraries
from sklearn import datasets
from sklearn.tree import DecisionTreeClassifier, plot_tree
from sklearn.model_selection import train_test_split
from sklearn.metrics import accuracy_score
import numpy as np
import matplotlib.pyplot as plt

# Load the Iris dataset
iris = datasets.load_iris()
X = iris.data
y = iris.target

# Split the dataset into training and testing sets
X_train, X_test, y_train, y_test = train_test_split(X, y, test_size=0.3, random_state=42)

# Create and train the decision tree classifier using Gini impurity
clf_gini = DecisionTreeClassifier(criterion='gini', max_depth=4, min_samples_leaf=4)
clf_gini.fit(X_train, y_train)

# Predict the class labels for the test set
y_pred_gini = clf_gini.predict(X_test)

# Calculate and print the accuracy of the Gini classifier
accuracy_gini = accuracy_score(y_test, y_pred_gini)
print(f"Accuracy (Gini): {accuracy_gini:.2f}")

# Create and train the decision tree classifier using Entropy
clf_entropy = DecisionTreeClassifier(criterion='entropy', max_depth=4,
min_samples_leaf=4)
clf_entropy.fit(X_train, y_train)

# Predict the class labels for the test set
y_pred_entropy = clf_entropy.predict(X_test)

# Calculate and print the accuracy of the Entropy classifier
accuracy_entropy = accuracy_score(y_test, y_pred_entropy)
print(f"Accuracy (Entropy): {accuracy_entropy:.2f}")

# Function to plot the decision tree
def plot_decision_tree(clf, title):
    plt.figure(figsize=(12, 8))
    plot_tree(clf, feature_names=iris.feature_names, class_names=iris.target_names,
filled=True)
    plt.title(title)
```

```
    plt.show()

# Plot the decision trees
plot_decision_tree(clf_gini, "Decision Tree (Gini Impurity)")
plot_decision_tree(clf_entropy, "Decision Tree (Entropy)")
```

The code provides a complete implementation of CART for classification, comparing the Gini impurity and entropy criteria, and visualising the decision trees.

Output:
Accuracy (Gini): 1.00 *Accuracy (Entropy): 1.00*

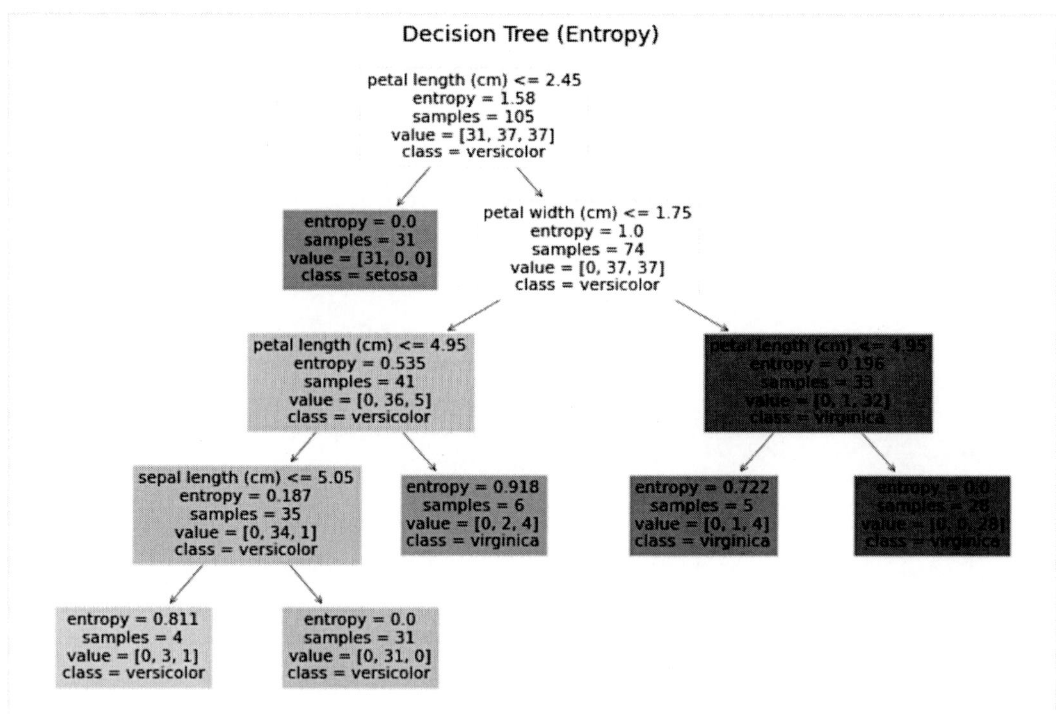

CART for Regression

Master explained that a Regression tree is an algorithm where the target variable is continuous, and the tree is used to predict its value. Regression trees are employed when the response variable is continuous, such as predicting the temperature of the day.

How Does CART Work for Regression?

CART for regression is a decision tree learning method that creates a tree-like structure to predict continuous target variables. The tree consists of nodes representing different decision points and branches, indicating the possible outcomes of those decisions. Predicted values for the target variable are stored in each leaf node of the tree.

Key Concepts:

- Residual Reduction: It measures how much the average squared difference between the predicted values and the actual values for the target variable is reduced by splitting the subset. Lower residual reduction implies a better model fit to the data.

- Splitting Criteria: CART evaluates all possible splits at each node and selects the one resulting in the greatest reduction of residual error in the resulting subsets. This process repeats until a stopping criterion is met, such as reaching the maximum tree depth or having too few instances in a leaf node.

This approach enables the creation of decision trees tailored to regression tasks, providing insights into how different features influence continuous target variables.

Overall, the CART algorithm is a powerful and versatile tool for building decision trees that can be applied to a wide range of machine learning tasks.

Advantages of CART

- **Simplicity of Results:** CART produces straightforward and easy-to-interpret results, making it accessible to users without extensive statistical knowledge.

- **Nonparametric and Nonlinear:** Classification and regression trees are flexible and can capture complex relationships in the data without assuming a specific functional form.

- **Implicit Feature Selection:** CART inherently performs feature selection by identifying the most informative attributes for partitioning the data, reducing the need for manual feature engineering.

- **Robust to Outliers:** Outliers in the data have minimal impact on CART's performance, as the algorithm focuses on splitting data based on relative patterns rather than absolute values.

- **Minimal Supervision:** CART requires minimal supervision during model building, making it suitable for scenarios where extensive labeled data or domain expertise may be lacking.

Limitations of CART

- **Overfitting:** CART models are prone to overfitting, especially when the tree grows deep and captures noise in the data, leading to poor generalization performance on unseen data.

- **High Variance:** Due to their recursive partitioning nature, CART trees tend to have high variance, meaning small changes in the training data can lead to significantly different tree structures.

- **Low Bias:** While low bias allows CART to capture complex relationships, it can also result in overly flexible models that fit the training data too closely, leading to poor performance on new data.

- **Instability of Tree Structure:** Small changes in the training data or input features can lead to large changes in the tree structure, making the resulting models unstable and difficult to interpret.

Despite these limitations, CART remains a popular and widely used machine learning algorithm, especially in domains where interpretability and ease of use are paramount.

ID3 (Iterative Dichotomiser 3) algorithm

The ID3 (Iterative Dichotomiser 3) algorithm is a classic decision tree learning algorithm used for classification tasks

Here's an overview of how the ID3 algorithm works:

Entropy Calculation: The algorithm begins by calculating the entropy of the target variable (class labels) in the dataset. Entropy measures the impurity or randomness of a set of examples. A set with low entropy contains mostly examples from a single class, while a set with high entropy contains examples from multiple classes.

Attribute Selection: Next, the algorithm evaluates each attribute in the dataset to determine which attribute would be the best choice for splitting the data. This is done by calculating the information gain for each attribute. Information gain measures the reduction in entropy achieved by splitting the dataset on a particular attribute. The attribute with the highest information gain is selected as the splitting attribute.

Splitting the Dataset: Once the attribute with the highest information gain is identified, the dataset is partitioned into subsets based on the different values of that attribute.

Recursive Tree Building: The splitting process is applied recursively to each subset of the data until one of the stopping criteria is met. Stopping criteria may include reaching a maximum tree depth, having no further attributes to split on, or reaching a minimum number of samples in a node.

Creating Leaf Nodes: Once the splitting process is complete, leaf nodes are created at the end of each branch. Each leaf node corresponds to a class label, and the majority class label in the leaf node is assigned as the predicted class for instances that reach that node.

Pruning (Optional): Pruning techniques may be applied to remove unnecessary branches or nodes from the tree to prevent overfitting and improve the model's generalisation ability.

The ID3 algorithm is simple, interpretable, and efficient, making it suitable for small to medium-sized datasets with categorical attributes. However, it may not perform well with continuous attributes or datasets with missing values. Additionally, ID3 tends to create deep trees that can lead to overfitting, so techniques like pruning are often employed to address this issue.

Decision Tree Regression

Exercise P5-U5 – D10

Decision Tree - Regression

```
# Step 1: Import necessary libraries
import numpy as np
import pandas as pd
import matplotlib.pyplot as plt
from sklearn.tree import DecisionTreeRegressor
from sklearn.model_selection import GridSearchCV, RandomizedSearchCV

# Step 2: Loading the data
file_path = r'C:\Users\User\mraj4\Documents\Optimum\Py-lib\scikit\Position_Salaries.csv'
df = pd.read_csv(file_path)

# Extracting independent and dependent variables
x = df.iloc[:, 1:-1].values
y = df.iloc[:, -1].values

# Step 3: Create and train the Decision Tree Regressor model
regressor = DecisionTreeRegressor(random_state=21)
regressor.fit(x, y)

# Predicting a new result
predicted_salary = regressor.predict([[6.5]])

# Step 4: Visualize the Decision Tree Regression results
# Creating a smoother curve for the visualization
x_grid = np.arange(min(x), max(x), 0.01).reshape(-1, 1)

# Scatter plot of the actual data points
plt.scatter(x, y, color='red', label='Actual')

# Plotting the regression line
```

```
plt.plot(x_grid, regressor.predict(x_grid), color='blue', label='Predicted')

# Adding title and labels
plt.title('Actual vs Predicted Salary (Decision Tree Regression)')
plt.xlabel('Position Level')
plt.ylabel('Salary')

# Save the plot as an image
plt.savefig('decision_tree_regression.png', bbox_inches='tight')

# Display the plot
plt.legend()
plt.show()

# Hyperparameter Tuning using GridSearchCV
param_grid = {
   'max_depth': [None, 5, 10],
   'min_samples_split': [2, 5, 10],
   'min_samples_leaf': [1, 2, 4]
}

grid_search = GridSearchCV(DecisionTreeRegressor(), param_grid, cv=5)
grid_search.fit(x, y)
best_params_grid = grid_search.best_params_
print("Best Hyperparameters (GridSearchCV):", best_params_grid)

# Hyperparameter Tuning using RandomizedSearchCV
param_random = {
   'max_depth': [None, 5, 10],
   'min_samples_split': [2, 5, 10],
   'min_samples_leaf': [1, 2, 4]
}

random_search = RandomizedSearchCV(DecisionTreeRegressor(random_state=25),
param_random, n_iter=10, cv=5)
random_search.fit(x, y)
best_params_random = random_search.best_params_
print("Best Hyperparameters (RandomizedSearchCV):", best_params_random)
```

Output:

Best Hyperparameters (GridSearchCV): {'max_depth': None, 'min_samples_leaf': 1, 'min_samples_split': 2}
Best Hyperparameters (RandomizedSearchCV): {'min_samples_split': 2, 'min_samples_leaf': 1, 'max_depth': 10}

This code showcases the application of Decision Tree Regression to predict salary based on position levels. It includes:

Model_Implementation: The code builds a Decision Tree Regressor model using scikit-learn's DecisionTreeRegressor class and trains it on the provided dataset.

Hyperparameter Tuning: Utilizes GridSearchCV and RandomizedSearchCV techniques to fine-tune the model's hyperparameters, optimizing its performance.

Best Parameters Identification: The best hyperparameters obtained from both GridSearchCV and RandomizedSearchCV methods are printed for reference.

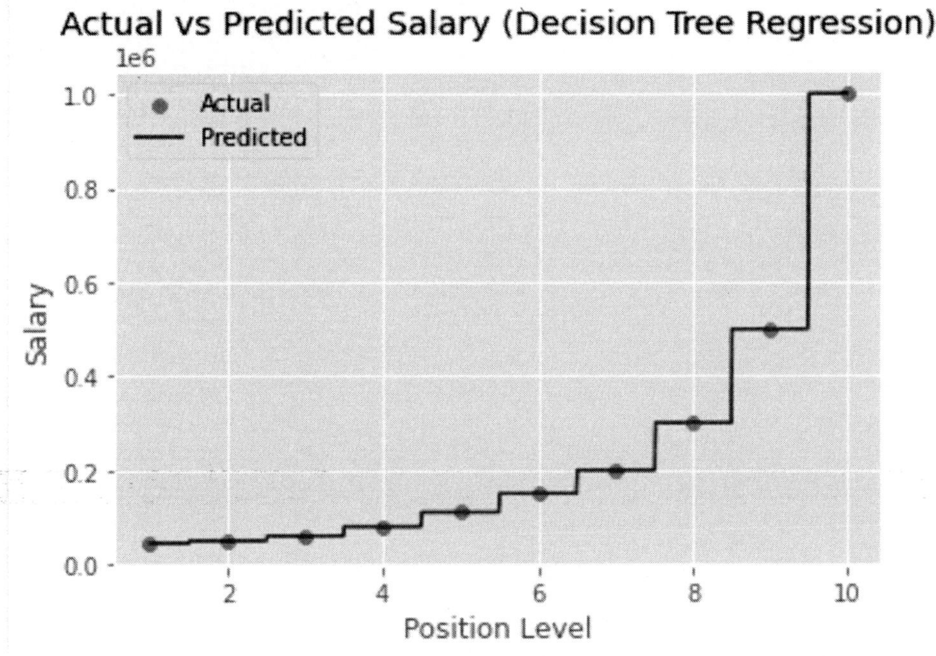

Overall, this code offers a holistic demonstration of Decision Tree Regression, covering model training, prediction, visualization, and hyperparameter tuning, providing insights into its implementation and optimization.

PART FIVE

DAY SIXTEEN

Unit 5 - Lesson Four

Decision Tree - II

Overfitting

Master said, "Decision Trees are susceptible to overfitting, especially when allowed to grow to their maximum depth. Overfitting happens when the tree becomes overly complex and captures noise from the training data rather than the underlying patterns, leading to poor generalisation on new, unseen data."

To mitigate overfitting in decision trees, several strategies can be employed:

Pruning: Limiting the maximum depth of the tree or the minimum number of samples required to split a node can prevent the tree from growing too large and complex.

Minimum Samples per Leaf: Setting a minimum threshold for the number of samples required to be at a leaf node can prevent the tree from splitting unnecessarily and capturing noise.

Cross-Validation: Using techniques like k-fold cross-validation to assess the model's performance on multiple subsets of the data can help identify and prevent overfitting.

Feature Selection: Selecting only the most informative features or performing feature engineering to reduce the dimensionality of the input data can help simplify the decision tree and reduce overfitting.

Ensemble Methods: Combining multiple decision trees through techniques like Random Forest or Gradient Boosting can help mitigate overfitting by averaging out the predictions of individual trees.

Cross Validation

Master explained that the Cross-validation is a technique used to assess the performance of machine learning models by splitting the dataset into multiple subsets, called folds. The model is trained on a portion of the data (training set) and then evaluated on the remaining portion (validation set or test set). This process is repeated multiple times, with different subsets used for training and validation in each iteration.

The main goal of cross-validation is to estimate the model's performance on unseen data. It helps to evaluate how well the model generalises to new data and provides a more reliable estimate of its performance compared to simply splitting the dataset into a training set and a separate test set.

Here's how cross-validation typically works:

- **Partitioning the Dataset:** The dataset is divided into k equal-sized folds. The value of k is usually chosen based on factors like the size of the dataset and computational resources. Common choices for k include 5 and 10.

- **Training and Validation:** The model is trained on k-1 folds (training set) and evaluated on the remaining fold (validation set) in each iteration. This process is repeated k times, with each fold used exactly once as the validation set.

- **Performance Metric Calculation:** After each iteration, the performance metric (such as accuracy, precision, recall, F1 score, or others) is computed on the validation set. These performance metrics are then aggregated across all iterations to obtain an overall estimate of the model's performance.

- **Model Selection and Tuning:** Cross-validation can also be used for model selection and hyperparameter tuning. Different models or sets of hyperparameters can be compared based on their average performance across multiple cross-validation folds.

- **Final Model Evaluation:** Once the best model or set of hyperparameters is selected based on cross-validation results, it can be trained on the entire dataset (using all folds) to obtain the final model. This final model can then be evaluated on a separate test set, which was not used during training or cross-validation, to assess its performance on unseen data.

Overall, cross-validation provides a more robust and reliable estimate of a model's performance compared to a single train-test split, especially when the dataset is small or the model's performance is sensitive to the choice of training data. It helps to detect overfitting and provides a more accurate assessment of how well the model will generalize to new, unseen data.

Methods used for Cross-Validation

Cross-validation techniques are pivotal in evaluating machine learning models for robustness and generalization. Here's a detailed overview of common methods:

Validation Set Approach: In the Validation Set Approach, the dataset is split into two subsets: a training set and a validation (or test) set, typically each comprising 50% of the data. However, this approach has a significant drawback. By using only half of the dataset for training, the model may not capture crucial information, potentially leading to underfitting.

Leave-P-Out Cross-Validation: Leave-P-Out Cross-Validation involves leaving out P data points for validation, repeating this process for all possible subsets. While effective, this method can be computationally demanding, especially for large values of P.

Leave-One-Out Cross-Validation (LOOCV): LOOCV, a variant of Leave-P-Out, reserves a single data point for validation while training on the remaining samples. This process is repeated for each data point, resulting in N training and testing iterations for N data points. While offering minimal bias, LOOCV is computationally intensive and prone to high variance due to the iterative testing against single data points.

K-Fold Cross-Validation: K-Fold Cross-Validation partitions the dataset into K equally sized folds. The model is trained K times, each time using a different fold as the validation set and the remaining folds for training. This method is popular due to its lower bias compared to the Validation Set Approach and its ease of implementation.

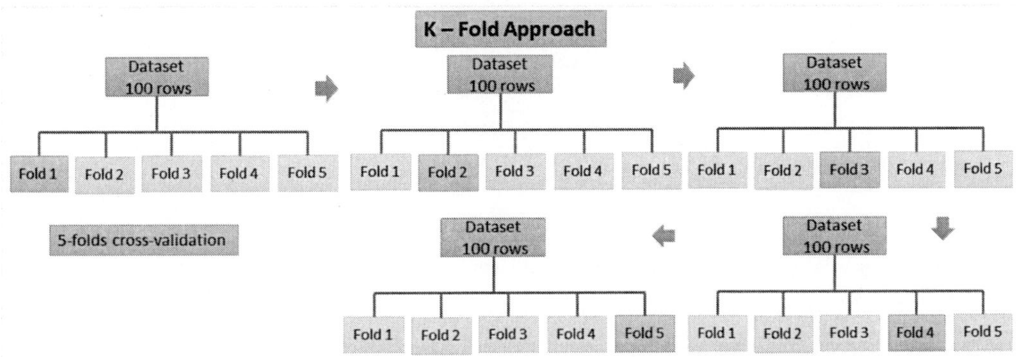

Stratified K-Fold Cross-Validation: Stratified K-Fold Cross-Validation is akin to K-Fold Cross-Validation but includes additional steps to ensure that each fold represents the dataset's distribution. This technique is particularly useful for addressing bias and variance issues, especially in datasets with uneven class distributions.

Holdout Method: The Holdout Method is the simplest cross-validation technique. It involves dividing the data into training and validation subsets, training the model on the training set, and evaluating its performance on the validation set. However, this method suffers from high variance and may produce misleading results.

Each cross-validation method has its advantages and limitations, and the choice depends on factors such as dataset size, computational resources, and the desired balance between bias and variance in model evaluation.

The comparison between cross-validation and train/test split in machine learning hinges on their respective methodologies and outcomes:

Train/Test Split:

Methodology: The dataset is partitioned into two segments: a training set and a test set, typically on ratios like 70:30 or 80:20.

Advantages: Provides a straightforward approach to model evaluation, with clear separation between training and testing data.

Disadvantages: High variance due to dependency on a single split. It can lead to overfitting or underfitting, depending on the data distribution.

Cross-Validation:

- Methodology: The dataset is divided into multiple subsets, with each subset serving as both training and testing data, iteratively.
- Advantages: Overcomes the limitations of train/test split by averaging results across multiple splits, reducing variance. Every observation is utilized for training and testing, enhancing efficiency.
- Disadvantages: More computationally intensive compared to train/test split, especially for larger datasets. However, it provides a more accurate assessment of model performance.

In summary, while train/test split offers simplicity, cross-validation provides a more robust evaluation of model performance by mitigating the variance associated with a single split. Cross-validation is particularly useful for optimizing model performance and ensuring generalization to unseen data.

GridSearchCV:

Sam asked, "What is GridSearchCV?"

Master said, "GridSearchCV is a method used for hyperparameter tuning in machine learning, particularly for optimizing the performance of models by finding the best combination of hyperparameters. It is part of the scikit-learn library in Python."

Here's how GridSearchCV works:

- **Grid Search:** GridSearchCV exhaustively considers all parameter combinations specified in a grid of values.
- **Cross-Validation:** It employs cross-validation techniques to assess the performance of each parameter combination. Typically, k-fold cross-validation is used, where the dataset is split into k subsets, and the model is trained and evaluated k times, each time using a different subset as the test set and the remaining data as the training set.
- **Evaluation:** GridSearchCV evaluates each parameter combination using a scoring metric, such as accuracy, precision, recall, or F1-score. The scoring metric is specified by the user.
- **Best Parameters:** After evaluating all parameter combinations, GridSearchCV identifies the combination that produces the highest score according to the specified metric.
- **Best Estimator:** It returns the best estimator, which is the model trained with the optimal hyperparameters found during the grid search.

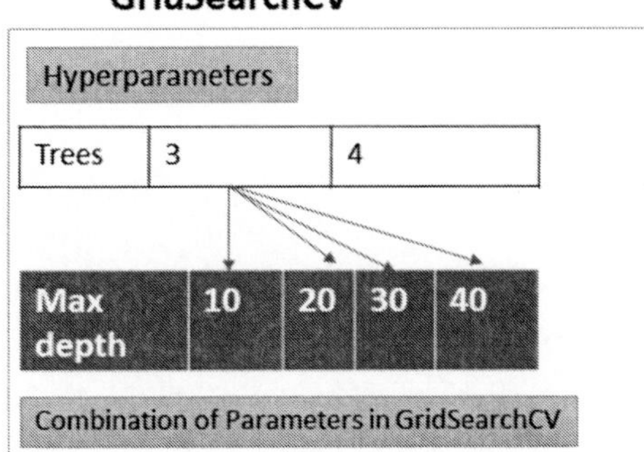

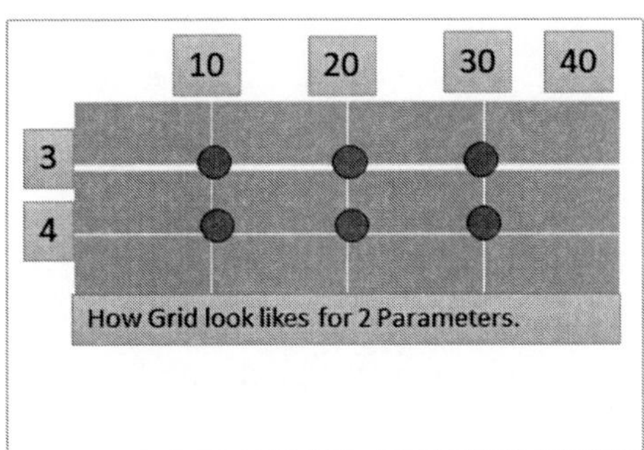

GridSearchCV simplifies the process of hyperparameter tuning by systematically searching through a predefined set of hyperparameters and evaluating their performance, allowing data scientists to find the best model configuration for their specific task.

When conducting a grid search with two hyperparameters, such as trees and max_depth, the grid represents a two-dimensional space where each point corresponds to a unique combination of the two parameters being tested.

Tree/Max depth	10	20	30	40
3				
4				

Here's what each part signifies:

- The rows represent the possible values of the trees parameter.
- The columns depict the possible values of the max_depth parameter.
- Each cell in the grid signifies a unique combination of trees and max_depth, with - indicating that the evaluation metric for that combination hasn't been computed yet.

During the grid search process, GridSearchCV evaluates every combination of parameter values (each cell in the grid) using cross-validation. Once all combinations have been assessed, it identifies the combination that yields the best performance based on the specified evaluation metric.

It's important to note that with a grid of size 3x4 (12 combinations), the computational complexity increases. For larger datasets or more complex models, this can lead to longer computation times. Therefore, it's crucial to consider computational resources and time constraints when performing grid search on extensive datasets with multiple hyperparameters.

RandowmSearchCV:

John asked, "What is RandomizedSearchCV?"

Master said, "RandomizedSearchCV is another hyperparameter optimisation technique provided by scikit-learn, similar to GridSearchCV. While GridSearchCV exhaustively searches through a specified grid of hyperparameter values, RandomizedSearchCV samples a fixed number of parameter settings from specified probability distributions. This sampling is done iteratively, and each sampled combination of hyperparameters is evaluated using cross-validation."

RandomizedSearchCV is particularly useful when the hyperparameter search space is large and exhaustive search using GridSearchCV becomes computationally expensive or impractical. By sampling from the search space, RandomizedSearchCV efficiently explores a broader range of hyperparameter values in a shorter amount of time. However, it does not guarantee that all possible combinations of hyperparameters will be evaluated, as it depends on random sampling. Nonetheless, it often provides good results in practice and is widely used for hyperparameter tuning.

Limitations of Cross-Validation:

While cross-validation is a powerful technique for model evaluation, it does have certain limitations:

Ideal Conditions Dependency: Cross-validation assumes ideal conditions for optimal performance. Inconsistent or noisy data may lead to unpredictable outcomes, undermining its reliability.

Data Evolution: Predictive modeling often deals with evolving datasets. Over time, the data distribution may change, leading to discrepancies between the training and validation sets. This dynamic nature poses challenges for cross-validation's effectiveness.

Applications of Cross-Validation:

Despite its limitations, cross-validation remains widely used in various domains:

Model Selection: Cross-validation helps in comparing and selecting the best-performing model among multiple candidates by assessing their performance across different datasets.

Hyperparameter Tuning: It aids in fine-tuning model parameters, such as regularization strength or tree depth, by iteratively evaluating the model's performance on different subsets of data.

Generalization Assessment: Cross-validation provides insights into a model's ability to generalize to unseen data, enhancing confidence in its predictive capabilities.

Feature Selection: It assists in identifying the most relevant features for predictive modeling by evaluating the model's performance with different subsets of features.

Model Validation: Cross-validation serves as a robust validation technique, especially in scenarios where traditional train/test splits may not provide reliable estimates of model performance.

Summary:

In this unit, we embarked on a comprehensive exploration of decision trees, versatile structures employed in both classification and regression tasks. We delved into the fundamental components of decision trees, elucidating their construction and operation. Key concepts such as Gini index, Information Gain, and Entropy were meticulously dissected, offering insight into the metrics used for determining optimal splits in decision trees. Additionally, we examined prominent algorithms like CART and ID3, which underpin decision tree learning. Moreover, we scrutinised the challenge of overfitting and elucidated strategies to mitigate it, including the indispensable technique of cross-validation. Various cross-validation methods were elucidated, ranging from the Validation Set Approach to sophisticated techniques like Leave-One-Out Cross-Validation (LOOCV) and K-Fold Cross-Validation. We further explored advanced techniques, such as Stratified K-Fold Cross-Validation and the Holdout Method, each offering unique advantages in model evaluation. Finally, we delved into the practical application of cross-validation using GridSearchCV and RandomSearchCV, powerful tools for hyperparameter tuning and model optimisation. This unit provided a robust foundation in decision tree methodologies and comprehensive insights into the intricacies of cross-validation, empowering practitioners to build robust and accurate predictive models.

What Next:

In this unit, we will explore various unsupervised learning techniques, focusing on clustering algorithms and dimensionality reduction methods. We will begin with clustering, covering algorithms like K-Means, the elbow method for determining the optimal number of clusters, and Mini-batch K-Means for large datasets. Hierarchical clustering and BIRCH will also be discussed. Dimensionality reduction techniques, including Principal Component Analysis (PCA), its variants, and Singular Value Decomposition (SVD), will be covered. We will explore advanced methods such as Incremental PCA and Randomized SVD. Additionally, we will examine t-SNE for visualization, DBSCAN for density-based clustering, and evaluation metrics like the Silhouette Score and Adjusted Rand Index (ARI), as well as advanced clustering methods like OPTICS, Spectral Clustering, Gaussian Mixture Models (GMM), and Mean-shift clustering.

P5-U5-L1-5 - Practice Question

1. What is the fundamental principle behind the K-Nearest Neighbors (KNN) algorithm?
2. Describe the concept of KNN in both classification and regression tasks.
3. Explain the role of distance metrics in KNN.
4. What is the Brute Force algorithm in the context of KNN?
5. How does the choice of k affect the KNN algorithm's performance?
6. Can KNN handle datasets with missing values? Explain.
7. What happens when there is a tie vote in the KNN classification algorithm?
8. How does KNN handle categorical features in the dataset?
9. Discuss the concept of "curse of dimensionality" in the context of KNN.
10. What are some strategies to improve the efficiency of KNN?
11. What distinguishes Support Vector Machines (SVMs) from other classification algorithms?
12. Explain the concept of a kernel in SVMs.
13. What are the advantages of using SVMs in classification tasks?
14. How does the choice of kernel affect SVM performance?
15. What is the role of the regularization parameter (C) in SVMs?
16. How do SVMs handle multi-class classification problems?
17. Discuss the concept of a decision boundary in SVMs.
18. What are some common kernel functions used in SVMs?
19. How does SVM regression differ from SVM classification?
20. What is the significance of support vectors in SVMs?
21. Explain the fundamental principle behind decision trees in machine learning.
22. What are the key components of a decision tree?
23. How does the Gini index measure impurity in decision trees?
24. Discuss the concept of entropy in decision trees.
25. What is the role of information gain in decision tree learning?
26. Explain the concept of overfitting in decision trees.
27. What are some techniques to prevent overfitting in decision trees?
28. Describe the CART algorithm used in decision trees.
29. How does cross-validation help in building robust decision tree models?
30. Discuss the use of GridSearchCV in decision tree hyperparameter tuning.

Assignment: P5-A1

K-Nearest Neighbors (KNN) and Support Vector Machines (SVM)

Problem Statement

In this assignment, you will explore and compare the performance of K-Nearest Neighbors (KNN) and Support Vector Machines (SVM) in classifying a dataset. You will evaluate the effectiveness of both algorithms and understand the impact of various parameters on their performance.

Background

K-Nearest Neighbors (KNN) is a simple, intuitive algorithm used for both classification and regression tasks. It relies on the distance between data points to make predictions. Support Vector Machines (SVM) is a powerful, flexible algorithm that constructs a hyperplane in a high-dimensional space to separate different classes. Both algorithms are widely used in machine learning for their effectiveness and simplicity.

Objective

- To implement and understand KNN and SVM algorithms.
- To compare the performance of KNN and SVM on a given dataset.
- To tune the parameters of both algorithms for optimal performance.

Data Description

You will use the "Iris" dataset, a famous dataset for classification tasks. It consists of 150 samples of iris flowers, each described by four features: sepal length, sepal width, petal length, and petal width. The dataset contains three classes: Iris-setosa, Iris-versicolor, and Iris-virginica.

Feature	Description
Sepal Length	Length of the sepal in cm
Sepal Width	Width of the sepal in cm
Petal Length	Length of the petal in cm
Petal Width	Width of the petal in cm
Class	Species of the iris flower

Tasks

Data Preprocessing

- Load the Iris dataset.
- Explore the dataset and visualize the features using scatter plots and pair plots.
- Split the dataset into training and testing sets.

K-Nearest Neighbors (KNN)

- Implement the KNN algorithm using scikit-learn.
- Tune the value of k using cross-validation.
- Evaluate the performance of KNN using accuracy, precision, recall, and F1-score.

Support Vector Machines (SVM)

- Implement the SVM algorithm using scikit-learn.
- Experiment with different kernel functions (linear, polynomial, RBF).
- Tune the hyperparameters (C, gamma) using GridSearchCV.
- Evaluate the performance of SVM using accuracy, precision, recall, and F1-score.

Comparison and Analysis

- Compare the performance of KNN and SVM.
- Analyze the impact of different parameters on the performance of both algorithms.
- Discuss the advantages and disadvantages of each algorithm based on your findings.

PART SIX

Machine Learning Models - Unsupervised

Clustering

"In unsupervised learning, there is no teacher—only terrain. Clustering becomes the instinctive cartographer, sketching maps where no path has been defined."

– Shree Shambav

PART SIX

DAY SEVENTEEN

Unit 6 - Lesson One

K-MEANS

"Clustering is the craft of discerning natural groupings within chaos, revealing underlying structures where objects within a cluster resonate in similarity, while distinctly diverging from those in other clusters, thus uncovering the hidden order in complexity." – Shree Shambav.

Machine Learning Algorithm: Unsupervised Learning

K – Means:

"It embodies an iterative approach, methodically partitioning an unlabeled dataset into k distinct clusters, ensuring that each data point finds its place in a group sharing similar characteristics. This process seeks to uncover underlying patterns and structures within the data, facilitating more insightful analysis and decision-making." – Shree Shambav

What does the K-Means Algorithm entail?

Master said, "K-means clustering is an unsupervised learning algorithm widely used in machine learning and data science for solving clustering problems. It operates iteratively, partitioning an unlabelled dataset into k distinct clusters, each containing data points with similar properties."

In this approach, the value of k defines the number of clusters to be formed. For instance, if k=2, the algorithm will create two clusters, and for k=3, there will be three clusters, and so forth. By autonomously grouping the data into different clusters, K-Means enables the discovery of inherent categories within the dataset without prior training.

This algorithm is centroid-based, meaning each cluster is represented by a centroid, which is the mean position of all the data points within that cluster. The primary objective of K-Means is to minimize the total distance between each data point and its corresponding centroid, ensuring a compact and well-separated cluster formation.

To execute the algorithm, an unlabelled dataset is provided as input, and the algorithm iteratively refines the clusters until the optimal configuration is achieved. It's crucial to predefine the value of k beforehand, as this parameter dictates the number of clusters to be created.

The k-means clustering algorithm is central to two primary tasks:

- Determining Optimal Centroids: Through an iterative process, the algorithm identifies the most suitable positions for K centre points or centroids within the dataset. These centroids serve as the focal points around which clusters will be formed.
- Assigning Data Points: Each data point is then assigned to its nearest centroid, effectively grouping them based on proximity. This assignment creates clusters wherein data points exhibit similarities with one another and distinguish themselves from points in other clusters.

As a result, each cluster encapsulates data points that share common traits, forming cohesive groupings while maintaining distinct boundaries from other clusters.

What is the operational mechanism of the K-Means Algorithm?

The K-Means algorithm operates through the following steps:

Step 1: Determine the Number of Clusters (K) - Define the desired number of clusters, denoted as K, which represents the total groups into which the data will be partitioned.

Step 2: Initialise Centroids - Randomly select K points or centroids within the dataset. These initial centroids serve as the starting points for cluster formation.

Step 3: Assign Data Points - Each data point is assigned to the nearest centroid, forming K initial clusters based on proximity to the centroids.

Step 4: Update Centroids - Calculate the mean of the data points within each cluster, establishing new centroids for each group.

Step 5: Reassign Data Points - Reassign each data point to the closest centroid based on the updated centroid positions.

Step 6: Iterative Refinement - Iterate between steps 4 and 5 until there is minimal or no change in centroid positions or data point assignments.

Step 7: Finalisation - Once convergence is achieved, indicating stable centroids and cluster assignments, the algorithm concludes, and the model is ready for use.

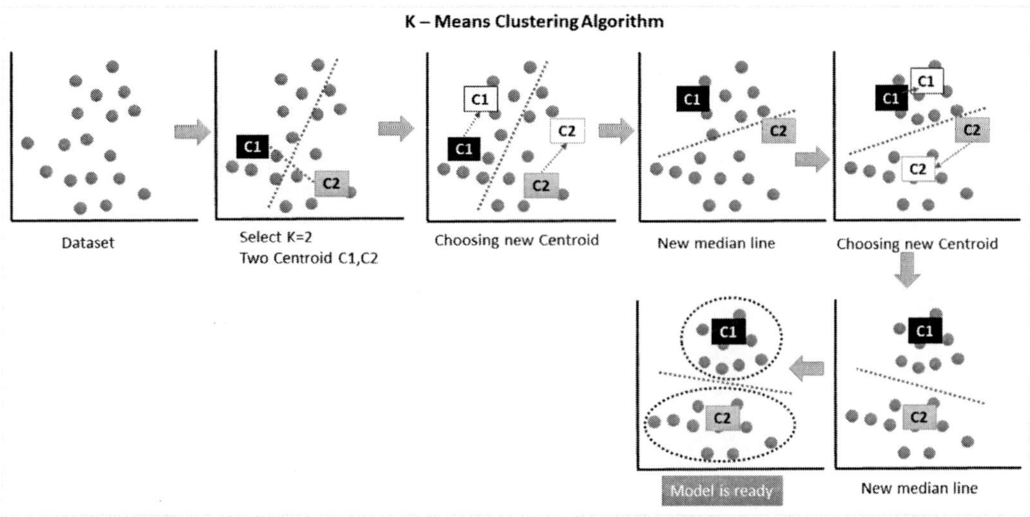

Let's visualise the steps with the help of a scatter plot of two variables, M1 and M2:

- Select the Number of Clusters (K) suppose we choose K=2, indicating our aim to partition the dataset into two distinct clusters.
- Initialise centroids randomly: Select two points as initial centroids, denoted as C1 and C2. These centroids serve as the starting points for cluster formation.
- Assign data points: Each data point in the scatterplot is assigned to the nearest centroid. Based on proximity, the data points are grouped into two initial clusters around centroids C1 and C2.
- Update centroids: Calculate the mean position of data points within each cluster, determining new centroid positions. These updated centroids represent the centre of each cluster.
- Reassign data points: Reassign each data point to the closest centroid based on the updated centroid positions. Data points are reallocated to clusters based on their proximity to the new centroids.
- Iterative Refinement: Iterate the process of centroid recalculation and data point reassignment until convergence is achieved. This iterative refinement aims to minimise the variance within clusters and maximise the separation between them.
- Finalization: Upon convergence, indicating stable centroids and cluster assignments,

the K-Means algorithm concludes, and the dataset is effectively partitioned into two distinct clusters.

Example: Optimal locations for pizza parlours to best serve customers.

The K-Means clustering algorithm can be effectively used to determine the optimal locations for pizza parlours to best serve customers. Here's how you can apply K-Means clustering to achieve this:

Data Collection:

Gather data on customer locations, which could be represented by coordinates (latitude and longitude) of delivery addresses or order points.

Choosing the Number of Clusters (K):

Decide on the number of pizza parlours (clusters) you want to set up. This number is the *K* in K-Means. This can be determined based on business constraints, budget, or by using methods like the Elbow Method to identify the optimal number of clusters.

Applying K-Means Algorithm:

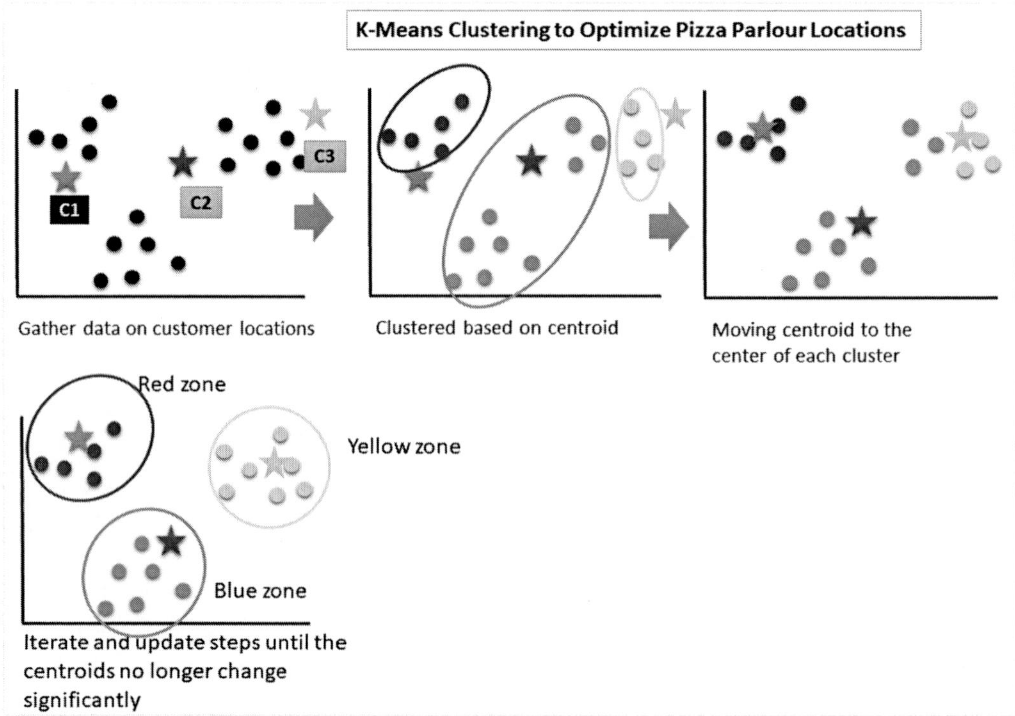

Use the K-Means algorithm to partition the customer data into *K clusters*. Each cluster will represent a zone that a pizza parlour will serve.

Algorithm Steps:

- **Initialisation**: Randomly initialise *K* cluster centroids.
- **Assignment Step**: Assign each data point (customer location) to the nearest centroid, creating *K* clusters.
- **Update Step**: Recalculate the centroids as the mean of all data points assigned to each cluster.
- **Repeat**: Iterate the assignment and update steps until the centroids no longer change significantly (convergence).

Interpretation of Results:

- After the algorithm converges, the *K* centroids represent the optimal locations for the pizza parlours.
- Each customer is assigned to the nearest centroid, indicating which pizza parlour should serve which zone.

Visualising Clusters:

- Plot the customer locations and the final centroids on a map.
- Use different colours to represent different clusters. For example, red points for the red zone, blue points for the blue zone, and yellow points for the yellow zone. Each color-coded region shows the area served by a particular pizza parlour.

Elbow Method:

Akshaya asked, "What is an elbow method?"

Master said, "The elbow method is a technique used to determine the optimal number of clusters (K) in a dataset for clustering algorithms, such as K-means. It involves plotting the within-cluster sum of squares (WCSS) against the number of clusters and identifying the point where the rate of decrease in WCSS slows down abruptly, resembling an 'elbow' in the plot."

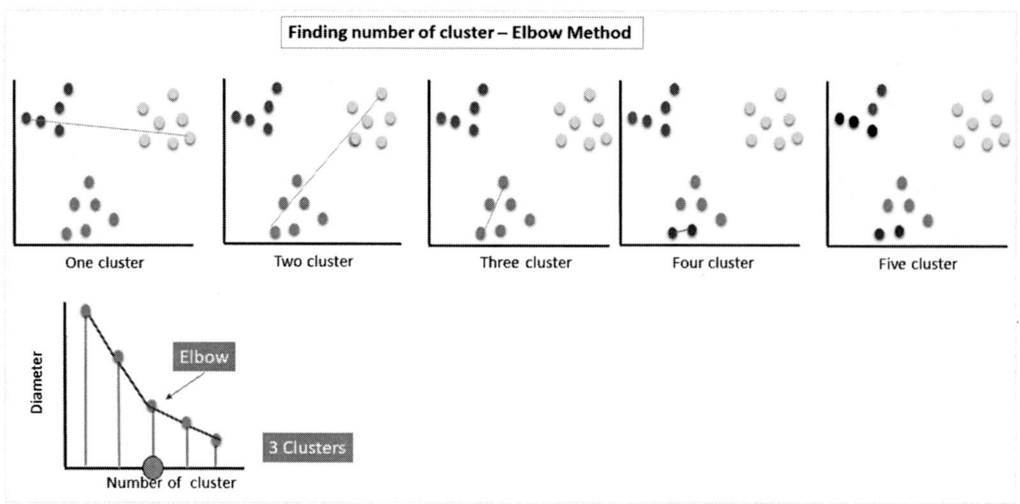

AThe number of clusters at this "elbow" point is considered the optimal value of K.

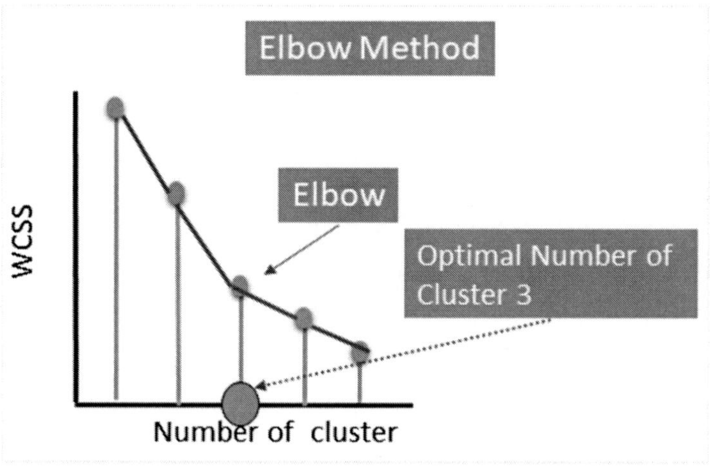

The formula for calculating WCSS is as follows:

$$\text{WCSS} = \Sigma_{i=1}^{k} \sum_{x \in C} \|x - \mu_i\|^2$$

Where:

- K is the number of clusters.
- Ci represents the ith cluster.
- μi is the centroid of the ith cluster.
- x represents each data point within the cluster Ci.

- $||x-\mu_i||^2$ denotes the squared Euclidean distance between the data point x and the centroid μ_i.

By plotting the number of clusters (K) against the corresponding WCSS values and identifying the "elbow" point in the plot, one can determine the optimal number of clusters for the dataset.

Mini-batch K-Means:

Master said, "Mini-batch K-means is an optimised version of the conventional K-means clustering algorithm, specifically tailored for handling massive datasets. While traditional K-means processes the entire dataset in each iteration, which can be resource-intensive for large datasets, Mini-batch K-means mitigates this challenge by operating on smaller, randomly sampled subsets known as mini-batches."

Instead of updating cluster centroids based on the entire dataset, Mini-batch K-means updates centroids using the data within the mini-batch, significantly reducing computational overhead and memory usage. This approach enables Mini-batch K-means to converge more swiftly while conserving computational resources compared to its traditional counterpart.

Exercise P6-U6 – D1

K-Means

```
# Importing the required libraries
import matplotlib.pyplot as plt
from sklearn.datasets import make_blobs
from sklearn.cluster import KMeans
# Creating the cluster dataset, independent and dependent features
X, Y = make_blobs(
    n_samples=200, n_features=2,
    centers=4, cluster_std=1,
    shuffle=True, random_state=10
)

# Plotting the original clusters
plt.scatter(
    X[:, 0], X[:, 1],
    c='lightpink',
    marker='o', s=50
)
plt.title("Original Clusters")
plt.show()

# Applying KMeans clustering
K_Means = KMeans(
    n_clusters=3, init="k-means++",
    n_init=15, max_iter=350,
    tol=1e-04, random_state=10
```

```
)
y_kmeans = K_Means.fit_predict(X)

# Plotting the 3 clusters created by KMeans
plt.scatter(
    X[y_kmeans == 0, 0], X[y_kmeans == 0, 1],
    s=50, c='red',
    marker='o', label='Cluster 1'
)

plt.scatter(
    X[y_kmeans == 1, 0], X[y_kmeans == 1, 1],
    s=50, c='blue',
    marker='s', label='Cluster 2'
)

plt.scatter(
    X[y_kmeans == 2, 0], X[y_kmeans == 2, 1],
    s=50, c='green',
    marker='s', label='Cluster 3'
)

# Plotting the centroids of the clusters
plt.scatter(
    K_Means.cluster_centers_[:, 0], K_Means.cluster_centers_[:, 1],
    s=250, marker='*',
    c='black',
    label='Centroids'
)
plt.title("KMeans Clustering with 3 clusters")
plt.legend(scatterpoints=1)
plt.grid()
plt.show()
```

Output

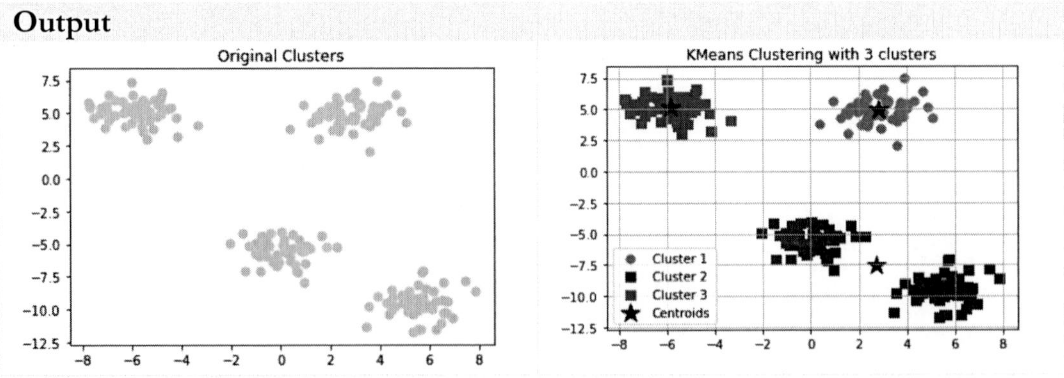

This code demonstrates the application of K-Means clustering algorithm using the scikit-learn library. Here's a brief explanation:

- Importing Libraries: The required libraries, including matplotlib.pyplot for plotting and make_blobs from sklearn.datasets to create sample data, and KMeans from sklearn.cluster, are imported.

- Creating Dataset: A synthetic dataset with 200 samples and 2 features is created using the make_blobs function. This dataset consists of 4 clusters (centers=4) with a standard deviation of 1 for each cluster (cluster_std=1).

- Plotting Original Clusters: The original clusters are visualized using a scatter plot with different colors for each cluster.

- Applying KMeans Clustering: The KMeans clustering algorithm is instantiated with n_clusters=3 to create 3 clusters. The algorithm's parameters, such as initialization method (init), maximum number of iterations (max_iter), and convergence tolerance (tol), are specified.

- Fitting and Predicting: The KMeans algorithm is fitted to the dataset, and cluster labels are predicted using the fit_predict method.

- Plotting KMeans Clusters: The predicted clusters are visualised using a scatter plot, where data points belonging to each cluster are plotted with different colours. Additionally, the centroids of the clusters are plotted with asterisks.

- Displaying the Plot: Finally, the plot is displayed to visualise the KMeans clustering results with 3 clusters.

The purpose of this code is to explore and evaluate the performance of the KMeans clustering algorithm on the Iris dataset. The Iris dataset is a well-known dataset in the machine learning community, used for both classification and clustering tasks. The code aims to:

- Determine the optimal number of clusters using the Elbow Method.

- Implement and train a KMeans clustering model.

- Evaluate the model using silhouette scores.

- Visualize the clustering results.

Exercise P6-U6 – D2

K-Means – Elbow Plot and Prediction

```
# Importing the required libraries
import pandas as pd
import numpy as np
import seaborn as sns
import matplotlib.pyplot as plt
import matplotlib.cm as cm
from sklearn.datasets import load_iris
from sklearn.cluster import KMeans
from sklearn.model_selection import train_test_split
from sklearn.metrics import silhouette_score, accuracy_score

# Load the Iris dataset
X, y = load_iris(return_X_y=True)

# Elbow Method to find the optimum number of clusters
# Initialize a list to store the sum of squared errors (SSE) for each k
sse = []
for k in range(1, 11):
    km = KMeans(n_clusters=k, random_state=2)
    km.fit(X)
    sse.append(km.inertia_)

# Plot the Elbow graph to find the optimum number of clusters
sns.set_style("whitegrid")
plt.figure(figsize=(10, 6))
elbow_plot = sns.lineplot(x=range(1, 11), y=sse)
elbow_plot.set(xlabel="Number of clusters (k)", ylabel="Sum of Squared Errors (SSE)",
title="Elbow Method")
plt.show()

# Split the dataset into training and testing sets
X_train, X_test, y_train, y_test = train_test_split(X, y, test_size=0.2, random_state=42)

# Build the KMeans clustering model with the optimum number of clusters (k=3) using
the training set
kmeans = KMeans(n_clusters=3, random_state=2)
kmeans.fit(X_train)

# Find the cluster centers
cluster_centers = kmeans.cluster_centers_

# Predict the cluster group for each data point in the training set
train_pred = kmeans.predict(X_train)
print("Predicted cluster labels for training set:", train_pred)
```

```
# Predict the cluster group for each data point in the test set
test_pred = kmeans.predict(X_test)
print("Predicted cluster labels for test set:", test_pred)

# Evaluate the model performance using silhouette score
silhouette_avg_train = silhouette_score(X_train, train_pred)
silhouette_avg_test = silhouette_score(X_test, test_pred)

print("Silhouette Score for training set:", silhouette_avg_train)
print("Silhouette Score for test set:", silhouette_avg_test)

# Plot the cluster centers with data points for the training set
plt.figure(figsize=(12, 6))

# Plot for the first two features (sepal length and sepal width)
plt.subplot(1, 2, 1)
plt.scatter(X_train[:, 0], X_train[:, 1], c=train_pred, cmap=cm.Accent, edgecolor='k')
for center in cluster_centers:
   plt.scatter(center[0], center[1], marker='^', c='red', s=100, edgecolor='k')
plt.xlabel("Sepal Length (cm)")
plt.ylabel("Sepal Width (cm)")
plt.title("KMeans Clustering (Sepal) - Training Set")

# Plot for the next two features (petal length and petal width)
plt.subplot(1, 2, 2)
plt.scatter(X_train[:, 2], X_train[:, 3], c=train_pred, cmap=cm.Accent, edgecolor='k')
for center in cluster_centers:
   plt.scatter(center[2], center[3], marker='^', c='red', s=100, edgecolor='k')
plt.xlabel("Petal Length (cm)")
plt.ylabel("Petal Width (cm)")
plt.title("KMeans Clustering (Petal) - Training Set")
plt.tight_layout()
plt.show()

# Plot the cluster centers with data points for the test set
plt.figure(figsize=(12, 6))

# Plot for the first two features (sepal length and sepal width)
plt.subplot(1, 2, 1)
plt.scatter(X_test[:, 0], X_test[:, 1], c=test_pred, cmap=cm.Accent, edgecolor='k')
for center in cluster_centers:
   plt.scatter(center[0], center[1], marker='^', c='red', s=100, edgecolor='k')
plt.xlabel("Sepal Length (cm)")
plt.ylabel("Sepal Width (cm)")
plt.title("KMeans Clustering (Sepal) - Test Set")

# Plot for the next two features (petal length and petal width)
plt.subplot(1, 2, 2)
```

```
plt.scatter(X_test[:, 2], X_test[:, 3], c=test_pred, cmap=cm.Accent, edgecolor='k')
for center in cluster_centers:
    plt.scatter(center[2], center[3], marker='^', c='red', s=100, edgecolor='k')
plt.xlabel("Petal Length (cm)")
plt.ylabel("Petal Width (cm)")
plt.title("KMeans Clustering (Petal) - Test Set")
plt.tight_layout()
plt.show()
```

Elbow Method:

The Elbow Method is used to determining the optimal number of clusters by plotting the sum of squared errors (SSE) against the number of clusters (k).

A range of k values from 1 to 10 is tested, and the SSE for each k is calculated and stored.

The Elbow Graph is plotted using seaborn to visually identify the optimal number of clusters. The “elbow” point in the graph indicates the optimal k value.

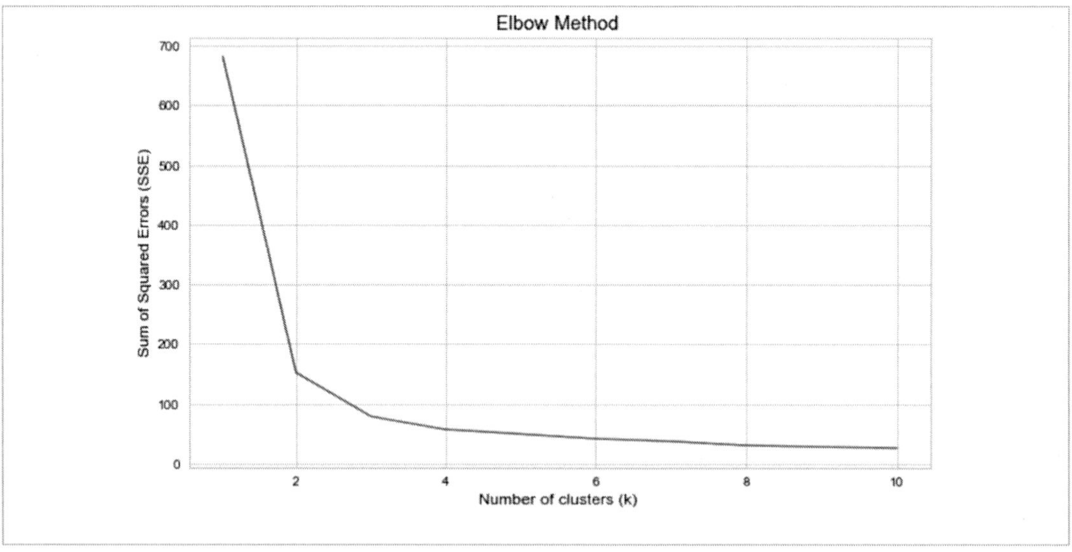

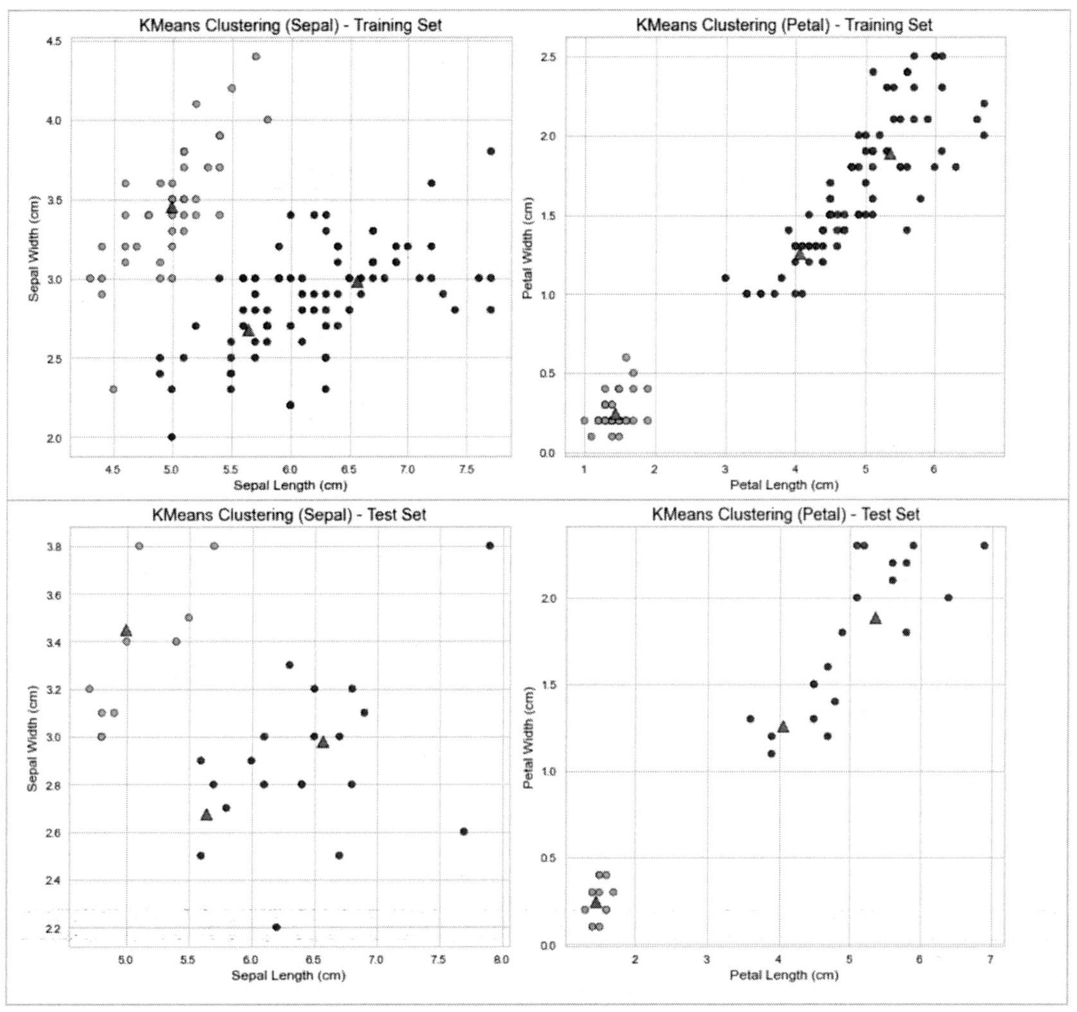
KMeans Clustering (Sepal) - Training Set
Sepal Width (cm)
Sepal Length (cm)
KMeans Clustering (Petal) - Training Set
Petal Width (cm)
Petal Length (cm)
KMeans Clustering (Sepal) - Test Set
Sepal Width (cm)
Sepal Length (cm)
KMeans Clustering (Petal) - Test Set
Petal Width (cm)
Petal Length (cm)

PART SIX

DAY SEVENTEEN

Unit 6 - Lesson Two

Hierarchical Clustering

An Overview

Master said, "Hierarchical clustering is a method of cluster analysis that builds a hierarchy of clusters in a tree-like structure, often represented by a dendrogram. This technique is particularly useful for visualizing the relationships and similarities between data points."

Types of Clustering Algorithms in Machine Learning

Clustering algorithms can be categorized into several types based on their approach to forming clusters:

Connectivity-Based Clustering:

- Builds clusters based on the connectivity between data points.
- Example: Hierarchical clustering.

Centroid-Based Clustering:

- Forms clusters around the centroids (central points) of data points.
- Examples: K-Means clustering, K-Mode clustering.

Distribution-Based Clustering:

- Uses statistical distributions to model the data points within a cluster.

- Example: Gaussian Mixture Models (GMM).

Density-Based Clustering:

- Groups together data points that are in high-density regions and separates points in low-density regions.
- Example: DBSCAN (Density-Based Spatial Clustering of Applications with Noise).

Hierarchical Clustering

Hierarchical clustering is a connectivity-based clustering model that groups data points based on their similarity or distance. The underlying assumption is that data points closer to each other are more similar than those farther apart.

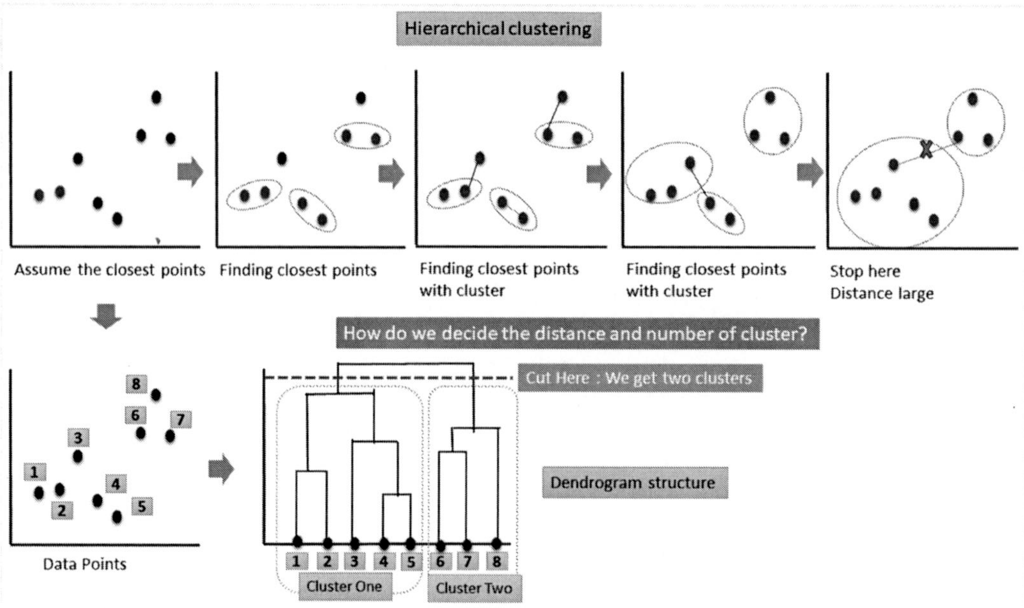

A dendrogram, a tree-like structure produced by hierarchical clustering, visually represents the hierarchical relationships between groups. The individual data points are located at the bottom of the dendrogram, while the largest clusters, which include all data points, are at the top. Different numbers of clusters can be generated by cutting the dendrogram at various heights.

The dendrogram is created through iterative merging or splitting of clusters based on a similarity or distance measure between data points. Clusters are repeatedly merged or divided until all data points are in a single cluster, or until the desired number of clusters is achieved.

To determine the optimal number of clusters, one can examine the dendrogram and identify the height at which distinct clusters form. The dendrogram can be cut at this height to define the number of clusters.

Types of Hierarchical Clustering

Hierarchical clustering can be divided into two main types:

Agglomerative Clustering:

- Also known as the bottom-up approach or Hierarchical Agglomerative Clustering (HAC).
- This method treats each data point as a singleton cluster at the start and successively merges pairs of clusters until all clusters have been combined into a single cluster containing all data points.
- This approach does not require pre-specifying the number of clusters.

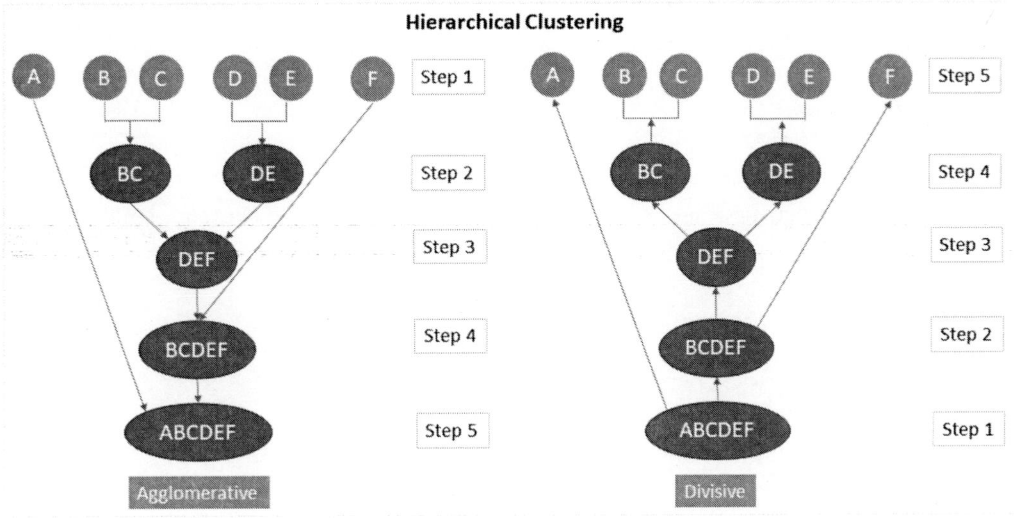

Divisive Clustering:

- Known as the top-down approach.
- This method starts with a single cluster containing all data points and recursively splits clusters until each data point is its own cluster or the desired number of clusters is reached.

Steps for Hierarchical Agglomerative Clustering

Hierarchical clustering involves a sequence of steps where clusters are iteratively merged or split based on their similarity or distance. Here's a detailed process using an example of alphabets:

Initialisation:

Start with each alphabet (data point) as its cluster. For example, we have clusters [A], [B], [C], [D], [E], and [F].

Calculate Distances:

Calculate the distance (or similarity) between each pair of clusters. This results in a distance matrix.

First Merge:

- Identify the two clusters that are most similar (i.e., have the smallest distance). Merge these clusters to form a new cluster.
- For example, if clusters [B] and [C] are the most similar, merge them to get clusters [A], [BC], [D], [E], [F].

Recalculate Proximity:

- Update the distance matrix to reflect the newly formed cluster. The distance between clusters is recalculated according to the chosen linkage criterion (e.g., single linkage, complete linkage, average linkage).

Second Merge:

- Again, find the two clusters with the smallest distance and merge them.
- For example, if clusters [D] and [E] are the most similar, merge them to get clusters [A], [BC], [DE], [F].

Repeat Merging:

- Continue this process of finding the closest clusters and merging them.
- For instance, merge [DE] and [F] to form clusters [A], [BC], [DEF].

Further Merges:

- Keep merging the closest clusters.
- If clusters [DEF] and [BC] are the closest, merge them to form clusters [A], [BCDEF].

Final Merge:

- Continue until all clusters are merged into a single cluster.
- Finally, merge [A] and [BCDEF] to get the single cluster [ABCDEF].

Hierarchical Agglomerative Clustering (HAC)

Nikash asked, "What is HAC?"

Master said, "Hierarchical Agglomerative Clustering (HAC) is a widely used method in hierarchical clustering. It begins with each data point as an individual cluster and merges the most similar pairs of clusters step by step until only one cluster remains or the desired clustering structure is achieved. This method provides a detailed hierarchical structure of clusters, which is more informative than the flat clustering methods."

Steps in HAC:

- **Start** with each data point as a separate cluster.
- **Compute** the distance (or similarity) between all pairs of clusters.
- **Merge** the two closest clusters.
- **Repeat** steps 2 and 3 until only a single cluster remains or a predefined condition (such as a specific number of clusters) is met.

Hierarchical clustering, particularly the agglomerative approach, is valuable for its ability to provide a detailed hierarchical relationship among data points, offering insights that are not easily obtained through other clustering methods.

Computing Distance Matrix in Hierarchical Clustering

When merging clusters in hierarchical clustering, we need to determine the distance between clusters to decide which clusters to merge next. There are several methods to define the inter-cluster distance (or similarity). Here are the commonly used methods:

Minimum Distance (Single Linkage):

This method calculates the distance between the closest points in each cluster.

Formula:

$$D(Ci,Cj) = \min\{d(x,y) \mid x \in Ci, y \in Cj\}$$

- Advantages: It can handle non-elliptical shapes.
- Disadvantages: It can result in "chaining", where clusters can form long, snake-like structures.

Maximum Distance (Complete Linkage):

This method calculates the distance between the farthest points in each cluster.

Formula:

$$D(C_i,C_j) = \max\{d(x,y) \mid x \in C_i, y \in C_j\}$$

- Advantages: Tends to create more compact clusters.
- Disadvantages: Sensitive to outliers.

Group Average (Average Linkage):

This method calculates the average distance between all pairs of points in the two clusters.

Formula:

$$D(C_i,C_j) = 1 / (|C_i|\cdot|C_j|) \sum_{x \in C_i} \sum_{y \in C_j} d(x,y)$$

- Advantages: Provides a balance between single and complete linkage.
- Disadvantages: Can be computationally intensive for large datasets.

Ward's Method:

This method merges clusters based on the increase in the total within-cluster variance after merging. It aims to minimise the increase in the total within-cluster variance.

Formula:

$$D(C_i,C_j) = \sum_{x\in(C_i \cup C_j)} \| x - \mu_{C_i \cup C_j} \|^2 - (\sum_{x \in C_i} \|x-\mu_{C_i}\|^2 + \sum_{x \in C_j} \|x-\mu_{C_j}\|^2)$$

- Advantages: Tends to create clusters of similar size and shape.
- Disadvantages: Assumes spherical clusters, sensitive to outliers.

The purpose of this code is to demonstrate two methods of hierarchical clustering using a small, randomly chosen dataset. It showcases how to perform agglomerative clustering and visualize the hierarchical clustering process with a dendrogram.

Example P6 – U6 – D3

Hierarchical clustering and Agglomerative Clustering

```
# Import necessary libraries
from sklearn.cluster import AgglomerativeClustering
import numpy as np
# Define the dataset
X = np.array([[1, 2], [1, 4], [1, 0],
          [4, 2], [4, 4], [4, 0]])

# Initialize the Agglomerative Clustering model with the number of clusters specified
# If n_clusters is not specified, the result will be a single cluster containing all data points
clustering = AgglomerativeClustering(n_clusters=2).fit(X)

# Print the cluster labels for each data point
print("Agglomerative Clustering labels:")
print(clustering.labels_)

# Import necessary libraries for dendrogram
from scipy.cluster.hierarchy import dendrogram, linkage
import matplotlib.pyplot as plt
# Perform hierarchical clustering using the Ward method
# 'ward' minimizes the variance of the clusters being merged
Z = linkage(X, 'ward')

# Plot the dendrogram to visualize the hierarchical clustering
plt.figure()
dendrogram(Z)

# Add titles and labels to the dendrogram plot
plt.title('Hierarchical Clustering Dendrogram')
plt.xlabel('Data point index')
plt.ylabel('Distance')
# Show the plot
plt.show()
```

Output
Agglomerative Clustering labels: [1 1 1 0 0 0]

Agglomerative Clustering:

- This part of the code uses the AgglomerativeClustering class from sklearn.cluster to perform agglomerative (bottom-up) hierarchical clustering.
- The number of clusters (n_clusters=2) is specified, and the algorithm groups the data points into the specified number of clusters.
- The resulting cluster labels for each data point are printed.

Hierarchical Clustering Dendrogram:

- This part uses the linkage function from scipy.cluster.hierarchy to perform hierarchical clustering using the Ward method, which minimizes the variance within each cluster.
- The dendrogram function is then used to plot a dendrogram, which visually represents the hierarchical clustering process, showing how clusters are formed at each step based on distance.
- The dendrogram helps to understand the clustering structure and the distances at which clusters are merged.

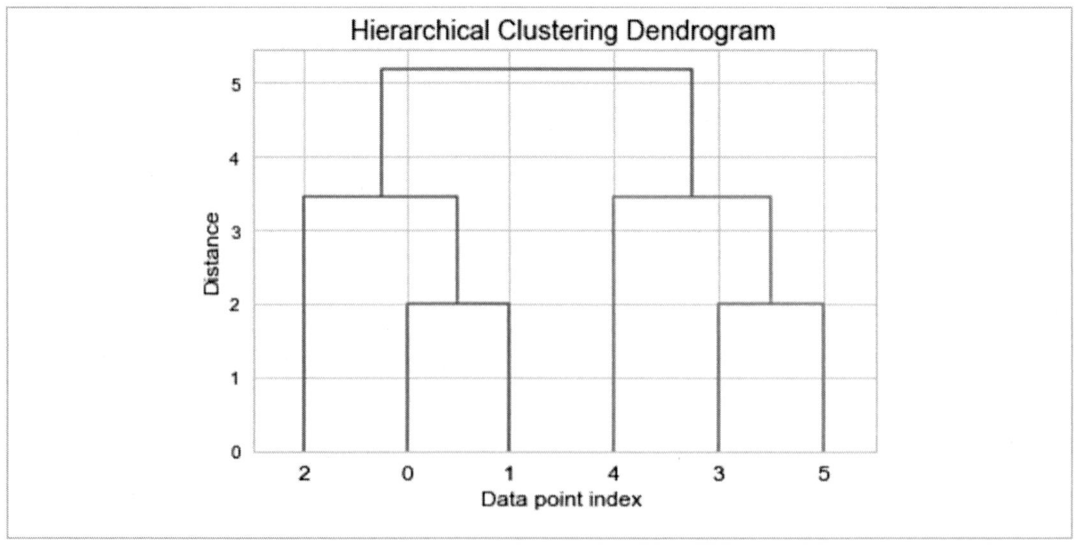

Overall, the code illustrates the process of hierarchical clustering and how to visualize the clustering hierarchy using a dendrogram. This is useful for understanding the relationships between data points and the structure of the data in a hierarchical manner.

BIRCH

Master said, "The BIRCH (Balanced Iterative Reducing and Clustering using Hierarchies) algorithm is designed for performing hierarchical clustering on large datasets. It constructs a tree structure called the CF Tree (Clustering Feature Tree) to represent the data."

The CF Tree is advantageous because it allows for efficient clustering by storing compact and summarised information about the data in the CF (Clustering Feature) nodes. This feature reduces the need to store the entire input data in memory, making BIRCH suitable for handling large datasets.

The BIRCH algorithm performs clustering in a two-step process. In the first step, it builds the CF Tree by recursively partitioning the data and creating CF nodes to represent each partition. In the second step, it applies a clustering algorithm to the CF nodes to obtain the final clusters.

In Scikit-learn, you can use the sklearn.cluster.Birch module to perform BIRCH clustering. This module enables you to apply the BIRCH algorithm to your data, taking advantage of its memory-efficient nature. By utilising the sklearn.cluster.Birch module, you can perform hierarchical clustering on large datasets and get compact representations of clusters using the CF Tree structure.

PART SIX

DAY SEVENTEEN

Unit 6 - Lesson Three

Dimensionality Reduction Technique

Principal Component Analysis (PCA)

John asked, "What is PCA?"

Master said, "Principal Component Analysis (PCA) is a fundamental unsupervised learning algorithm utilised for dimensionality reduction in machine learning. By statistically transforming correlated features into linearly uncorrelated ones through orthogonal transformation, PCA generates a set of new features known as Principal Components (PCs). Widely acclaimed for its efficacy in exploratory data analysis and predictive modelling, PCA is instrumental in extracting robust patterns from datasets by reducing variances."

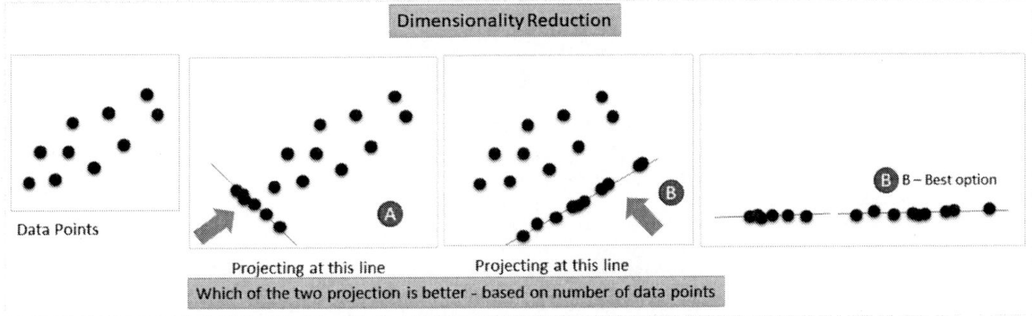

PCA endeavours to identify a lower-dimensional surface to represent high-dimensional data effectively. This is achieved by evaluating the variance of each attribute, with higher variance attributes contributing significantly to class differentiation, thereby guiding the dimensionality reduction process. Real-world applications of PCA span diverse domains including image processing, movie recommendation systems, and optimising power allocation in communication channels. As a feature extraction technique, PCA retains essential variables while discarding less relevant ones.

Dimensionality reduction is a technique used to reduce the number of features in a dataset while retaining as much information as possible. This can be particularly useful for visualization, noise reduction, and reducing computational complexity. Here, we will discuss two methods: reducing 5-dimensional housing data to 2-dimensional data as illustrated, and projecting two features related to house size into one-dimensional space.

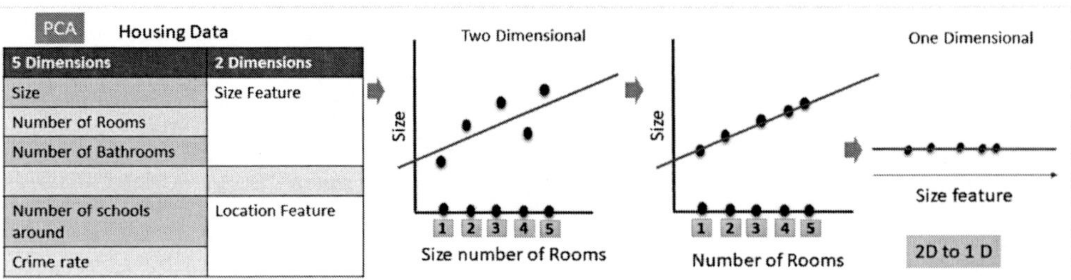

The PCA algorithm relies on key mathematical concepts such as variance, covariance, eigenvalues, and eigenvectors. By leveraging these mathematical principles, PCA enables efficient dimensionality reduction and data analysis across various machine-learning tasks.

Calculating Mean, Variance, and the Impact of Data Projection

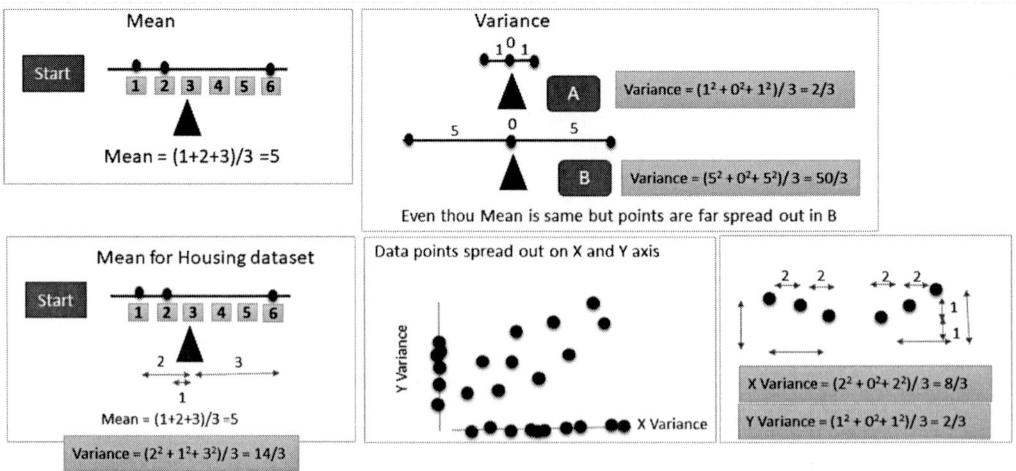

Dimensionality reduction techniques help in simplifying complex datasets by reducing the number of features while preserving essential information. Here, we illustrate the calculation of mean, variance, and the impact of data projection on variance using an example dataset.

Example based on given dataset in the code:

Example P6 – U6 – D4
Mean and Variance

```
import numpy as np
import pandas as pd
data = np.array([
    [2, 3],
    [3, 5],
    [4, 7],
    [5, 9],
    [6, 11]
])
df = pd.DataFrame(data, columns=['X', 'Y'])
# Calculating Mean: The mean (average) of the dataset provides a central value.
mean_x = df['X'].mean()
mean_y = df['Y'].mean()
print(f"Mean of X: {mean_x}")
print(f"Mean of Y: {mean_y}")

# Calculating Variance: Variance measures the spread of data points around the mean.
variance_x = df['X'].var()
variance_y = df['Y'].var()
print(f"Variance of X: {variance_x}")
print(f"Variance of Y: {variance_y}")
```

Output:

```
Mean of X: 4.0
Mean of Y: 7.0
Variance of X: 2.5
Variance of Y: 10.0
```

Here, the means of X and Y are 4.0 and 7.0 respectively, and their variances indicate the spread of the data points around these means.

We will also cover covariance, covariance matrix, linear transformation, and finding eigenvalues and eigenvectors.

Understanding Covariance

Covariance indicates the direction of the linear relationship between two variables.

- Positive Covariance: Both variables increase together.

- Negative Covariance: One variable increase while the other decreases.
- Zero Covariance: No linear relationship between the variables.

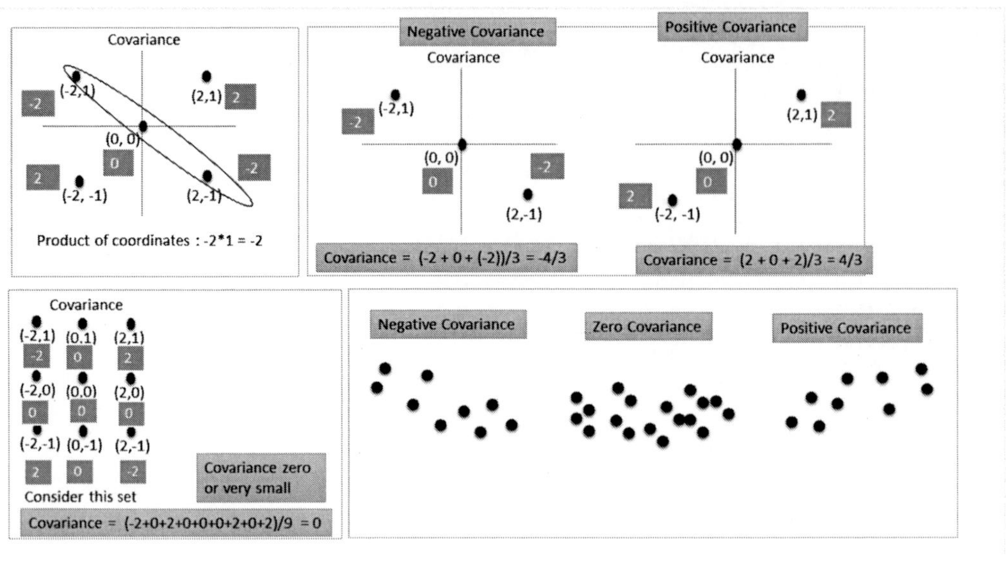

Covariance Matrix and Linear Transformatio

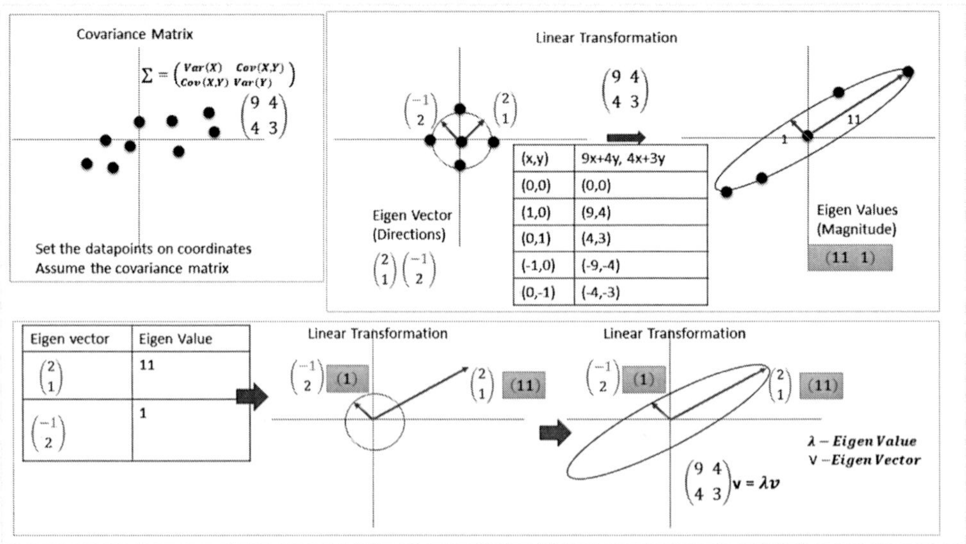


```
# Calculating Covariance
covariance_matrix = np.cov(data, rowvar=False)
print("Covariance Matrix:")
print(covariance_matrix)
```

Output:
```
Covariance Matrix:
[[ 2.5  5. ]
 [ 5.  10. ]]
```

The covariance matrix shows the covariances between each pair of variables.

Linear Transformation and Eigenvalues/Eigenvectors

Principal Component Analysis (PCA) transforms data into a new coordinate system using eigenvalues and eigenvectors.

Eigen Values (Magnitude)

Characteristic Polynomial

$$\begin{pmatrix} 9 & 4 \\ 4 & 3 \end{pmatrix} \Rightarrow \begin{vmatrix} X-9 & -4 \\ -4 & X-3 \end{vmatrix} = (X-9)(X-3)-(-4)(-4) = (X^2 - 12X = 11) = (X-11)(X-1)$$

Eigen Vector (Directions)

$$\begin{pmatrix} 9 & 4 \\ 4 & 3 \end{pmatrix}\begin{pmatrix} u \\ v \end{pmatrix} = 11 \begin{pmatrix} u \\ v \end{pmatrix} \qquad \begin{pmatrix} 9 & 4 \\ 4 & 3 \end{pmatrix}\begin{pmatrix} u \\ v \end{pmatrix} = 1 \begin{pmatrix} u \\ v \end{pmatrix}$$

$$\begin{pmatrix} u \\ v \end{pmatrix} = \begin{pmatrix} 2 \\ 1 \end{pmatrix} \qquad \begin{pmatrix} u \\ v \end{pmatrix} = \begin{pmatrix} -1 \\ 2 \end{pmatrix}$$

Eigenvalues and eigenvectors are critical in understanding the directions of maximum variance.

```
import matplotlib.pyplot as plt
# Getting eigenvalues and eigenvectors from the covariance matrix
eigenvalues, eigenvectors = np.linalg.eig(covariance_matrix)

print("Eigenvalues:", eigenvalues)
print("Eigenvectors:", eigenvectors)
# Plot original data points
plt.scatter(data[:, 0], data[:, 1], c='blue', label='Data points')

# Plot eigenvectors
for i in range(len(eigenvalues)):
   plt.quiver(mean_x, mean_y, eigenvectors[0, i], eigenvectors[1, i], angles='xy', scale_units='xy', scale=1, color=['r', 'g'][i], label=f'Eigenvector {i+1}')

plt.xlabel('X')
```

```
plt.ylabel('Y')
plt.legend()
plt.title('Data Points and Eigenvectors')
plt.show()
```

```
Output:
Eigenvalues: [ 0.  12.5]
Eigenvectors: [[-0.89442719 -0.4472136 ]
 [ 0.4472136  -0.89442719]]
```

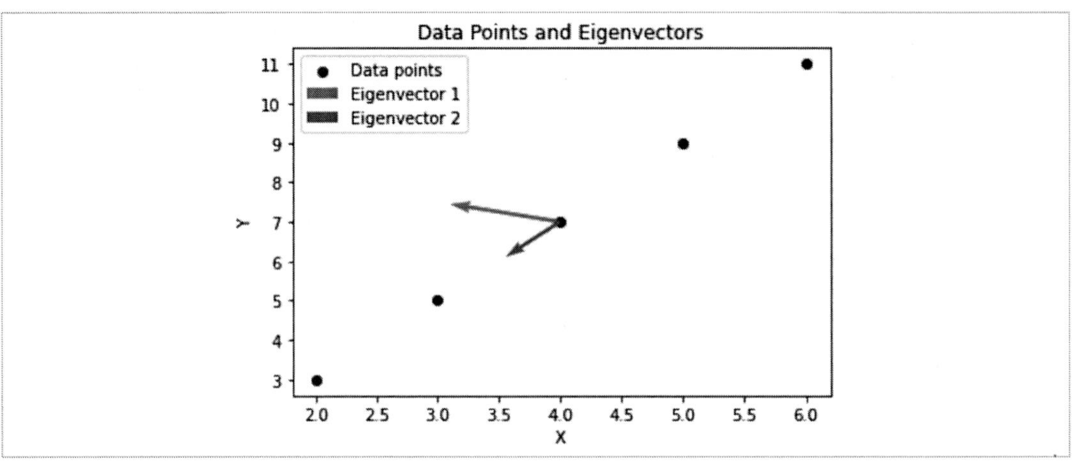

PCA – Dimension reduction

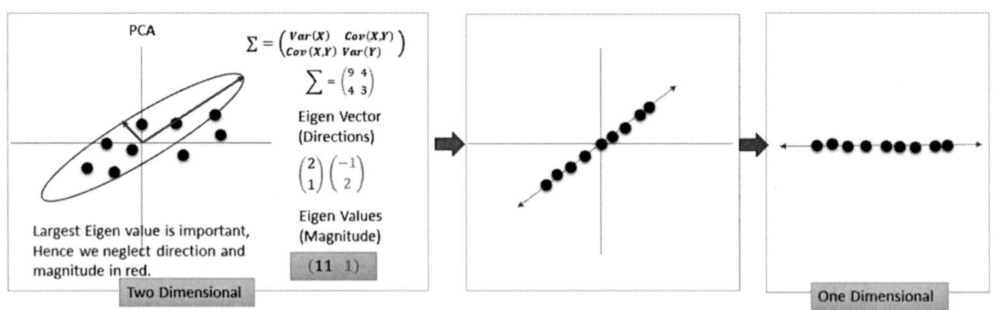


```
from sklearn.decomposition import PCA
import matplotlib.pyplot as plt
pca = PCA(n_components=2)
principal_components = pca.fit_transform(data)

# Create a DataFrame with principal components
```

```
principal_df = pd.DataFrame(data=principal_components, columns=['PC1', 'PC2'])

# Plotting the 2-dimensional data
plt.figure(figsize=(8, 6))
plt.scatter(principal_df['PC1'], principal_df['PC2'], c='blue', edgecolor='k')
plt.xlabel('Principal Component 1')
plt.ylabel('Principal Component 2')
plt.title('2D Projection of Dataset using PCA')
plt.show()

# Variance explained by each principal component
explained_variance = pca.explained_variance_
print(f"Variance by PC1: {explained_variance[0]}")
print(f"Variance by PC2: {explained_variance[1]}")
```

Output:

```
Variance by PC1: 12.500000000000004
Variance by PC2: 5.768050627259039e-32
```

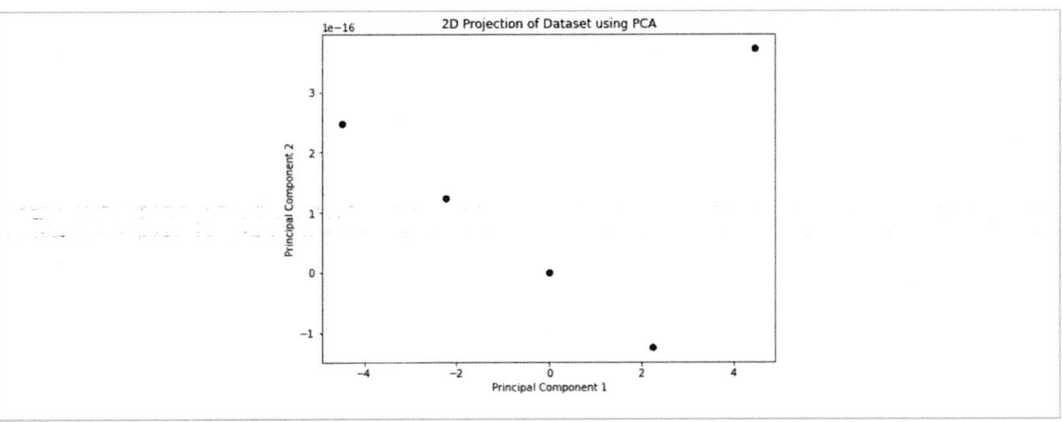

Summary:

- Mean and Variance: Calculated to understand the central tendency and spread of data.
- Covariance: Measures the linear relationship between variables.
- PCA: Used for dimensionality reduction by projecting data into principal components.
- Eigenvalues and Eigenvectors: Provide the directions and magnitudes of maximum variance.

By using these techniques, we can reduce the complexity of high-dimensional data while retaining essential information, making it easier to analyze and visualize.

Principal Component Analysis (PCA) is a widely used algorithm for linear dimensionality reduction. It leverages Singular Value Decomposition (SVD) to transform high-dimensional data into a lower-dimensional space while retaining the maximum variance. PCA is beneficial for simplifying data analysis, improving computational performance, and visualizing high-dimensional data.

Variants of PCA

Incremental Principal Component Analysis (IPCA):

- Purpose: IPCA is designed to handle large datasets that cannot be processed in a single batch.
- Advantage: It processes data in mini-batches, making it suitable for online learning and large-scale applications.

Kernel Principal Component Analysis (Kernel PCA):

- Purpose: Kernel PCA extends PCA to enable non-linear dimensionality reduction.
- Advantage: By using kernel functions, it maps the original data into a higher-dimensional space where linear separation is possible, thus capturing complex structures in the data.

Principal Component Analysis (PCA) with Randomized SVD:

- Purpose: This variant uses a randomized algorithm to approximate the singular value decomposition.
- Advantage: It efficiently reduces the dimensionality of large datasets by focusing on the most significant singular vectors, thereby speeding up the computation without sacrificing much accuracy.

Common Terms in PCA Algorithm:

Dimensionality: Refers to the number of features or variables present in the dataset. Simply put, it corresponds to the number of columns in the dataset.

Correlation: Describes the strength of the relationship between the two variables. A correlation value ranges from -1 to +1, where -1 signifies an inverse relationship (as one variable increases, the other decreases), and +1 indicates a direct proportional relationship (both variables increase or decrease together).

Orthogonal: Denotes that variables are uncorrelated, resulting in a correlation of zero between the pair of variables.

Eigenvectors: In a square matrix M, a non-zero vector v is considered an eigenvector if Av is a scalar multiple of v. Eigenvectors play a crucial role in PCA for determining the directions of maximum variance in the dataset.

Covariance Matrix: A matrix that contains the covariances between pairs of variables in the dataset. It provides insights into how variables change together and is a fundamental component in PCA for calculating the principal components.

Principal Components in PCA

Principal Components (PCs) are the transformed features generated by PCA, either equal to or fewer than the original features in the dataset. Below are some key properties of principal components:

Linear Combination: Principal components are formed as linear combinations of the original features present in the dataset.

Orthogonality: Each principal component is orthogonal to the others, meaning there is zero correlation between pairs of variables represented by different principal components.

Decreasing Importance: The significance of each principal component diminishes from the first (PC1) to the last (PCn), with PC1 capturing the maximum variance and subsequent components capturing decreasing amounts of variance. Thus, PC1 is the most important, while PCn holds the least importance.

Step by Step for PCA

Step 1: Getting the Dataset:

Divide the input dataset into two subsets: X (training set) and Y (validation set).

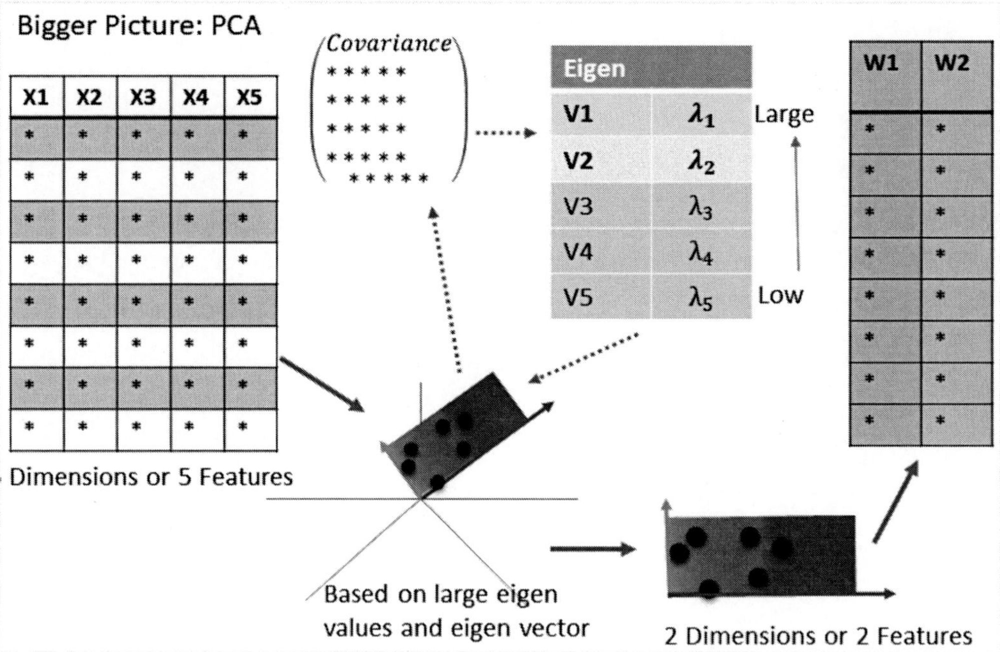

Step 2: Representing Data into a Structure:

Represent the dataset as a two-dimensional matrix, where each row corresponds to a data item and each column corresponds to a feature. The number of columns equals the dimensions of the dataset.

Step 3: Standardization:

Standardize the dataset to ensure that features with higher variance contribute more to the analysis. If feature importance is independent of variance, scale each data item in a column by the standard deviation of the column to obtain the matrix Z.

$$z = \frac{k - \mu}{\sigma}$$

Step 4: Calculating the Covariance of Z:

Calculate the covariance matrix of Z by taking the transpose of Z and multiplying it by Z.

Step 5A: Calculating the Eigenvalues and Eigenvectors:

- Compute the eigenvalues and eigenvectors for the covariance matrix Z. Eigenvectors represent directions of axes with high information, and eigenvalues are the coefficients associated with these eigenvectors.

Step 5B: Sorting the Eigenvectors:

- Sort the eigenvalues in decreasing order (from largest to smallest) and arrange the corresponding eigenvectors accordingly in matrix P*.

Step 6: Calculating the New Features or Principal Components:

Compute the new features by multiplying the matrix P* with Z. Each observation in the resulting matrix Z* is a linear combination of the original features, and the columns of Z* are independent of each other.

Step 7: Removing Less or Unimportant Features from the New Dataset:

Decide which features to keep and which to discard in the new dataset. Retain only the relevant or important features, discarding less important ones to create a refined feature set.

Applications of Principal Component Analysis (PCA)

Dimensionality Reduction in AI Applications:

- PCA serves as a powerful technique for reducing the dimensionality of datasets in various AI applications like computer vision, image compression, and signal processing. By reducing the number of features while retaining the most relevant information, PCA helps streamline computational processes and improve efficiency.

Pattern Discovery in High-Dimensional Data:

- PCA aids in uncovering hidden patterns within datasets characterized by high dimensions. It identifies underlying structures and relationships between variables, making it valuable in fields such as finance, data mining, psychology, and more. By extracting the most informative components, PCA simplifies complex datasets and facilitates insightful analysis.

How does Principal Component Analysis (PCA) work?

Master explained that the purpose of this code is to perform Principal Component Analysis (PCA) on the Breast Cancer dataset, which is included in the scikit-learn library. PCA is a dimensionality reduction technique used to transform a large set of variables into a smaller one that still contains most of the information in the large set. The specific goals of this code include:

Example P6 – U6 – D5	
PCA	**Output**

# Importing necessary libraries 	
import pandas as pd
import numpy as np
import matplotlib.pyplot as plt
import seaborn as sns
from sklearn.datasets import load_breast_cancer
 	
# Load the breast cancer dataset 	
cancer = load_breast_cancer(as_frame=True)
 	
# Create a dataframe from the dataset 	
df = cancer.frame
 	
# Print the shape of the original dataframe 	
print('Original Dataframe shape:', df.shape)
 	
# Extract input features 	
X = df[cancer['feature_names']]
print('Inputs Dataframe shape   :', X.shape)
 	
# Calculate Mean and Standard Deviation for Standardization 	
X_mean = X.mean()
X_std = X.std()
 	
# Standardize the data (Z-score normalization) 	
Z = (X - X_mean) / X_std
 	
# Compute the covariance matrix of the standardized data 	
cov_matrix = Z.cov()
 	
# Plot the covariance matrix 	
plt.figure(figsize=(12, 8))
sns.heatmap(cov_matrix, cmap='coolwarm', annot=False)
plt.title('Covariance Matrix')
plt.show()
 	
# Compute the eigenvalues and eigenvectors of the covariance matrix 	
eigenvalues, eigenvectors = np.linalg.eig(cov_matrix)
print('Eigenvalues:\n', eigenvalues)
print('Eigenvalues Shape:', eigenvalues.shape)
	Original Dataframe shape:
	(569, 31)
	Inputs Dataframe shape :
	(569, 30)
	Eigenvalues:
	 [1.33e+01 5.69e+00
	2.82e+00 1.98e+00 1.65e+00
	1.21e+00 6.75e-01 4.77e-01
	……
	Eigenvalues Shape: (30,)
	Eigenvectors Shape: (30, 30)
	Explained Variance: [0.44
	0.63 0.73 0.79 0.85 0.89 0.91
	0.93 0.94 0.95 0.96 0.97 0.98
	0.98
	 0.99 0.99 0.99 0.99 0.99 1. 1.
	1. 1. 1. 1. 1. 1. 1.
	 1. 1.]
	Number of Principal Components: 2
	Principal Component Values:
	      PCA1 PCA2
	0 9.184755 1.946870
	1 2.385703 -3.764859
	2 5.728855 -1.074229
	3 7.116691 10.266556
	4 3.931842 -1.946359

```
print('Eigenvectors Shape:', eigenvectors.shape)

# Sort eigenvalues and corresponding eigenvectors in
descending order
idx = eigenvalues.argsort()[::-1]
eigenvalues = eigenvalues[idx]
eigenvectors = eigenvectors[:, idx]

# Calculate the explained variance
explained_var = np.cumsum(eigenvalues) /
np.sum(eigenvalues)
print('Explained Variance:', explained_var)

# Determine the number of principal components to
retain 50% variance
n_components = np.argmax(explained_var >= 0.50) + 1
print('Number of Principal Components:',
n_components)

# Extract the eigenvectors corresponding to the selected
principal components
u = eigenvectors[:, :n_components]

# Create a dataframe for the principal components
pca_component = pd.DataFrame(u,
index=cancer['feature_names'], columns=[f'PC{i+1}' for
i in range(n_components)])

# Plot the heatmap for the principal components
plt.figure(figsize=(10, 6))
sns.heatmap(pca_component, cmap='viridis',
annot=True)
plt.title('PCA Components')
plt.show()

# Project the data onto the selected principal
components
Z_pca = Z @ pca_component

# Rename the columns for clarity
Z_pca.columns = [f'PCA{i+1}' for i in
range(n_components)]

# Print the principal component values
print('Principal Component Values:')
print(Z_pca.head())
```

Loading and Preparing the Data:

- Load the Breast Cancer dataset.
- Create a DataFrame to work with the data and print the shapes of the original and input feature datasets.

Standardizing the Data:

- Calculate the mean and standard deviation of the input features.
- Standardize the dataset to have zero mean and unit variance, which is crucial for PCA.

Computing the Covariance Matrix:

- Calculate the covariance matrix of the standardized data to understand how the variables vary with respect to each other.
- Visualize the covariance matrix using a heatmap.

Performing PCA:

- Compute the eigenvalues and eigenvectors of the covariance matrix, which are the foundation of PCA.
- Sort the eigenvalues and corresponding eigenvectors in descending order to prioritize the components that explain the most variance.

Explained Variance:

- Calculate the cumulative explained variance to determine how much information (variance) is retained by the principal components.
- Determine the number of principal components needed to retain at least 50% of the total variance.

Projecting Data onto Principal Components:

- Extract the principal components based on the sorted eigenvectors.
- Project the standardized data onto these principal components to reduce its dimensionality.
- Visualize and print the principal components and the resulting transformed dataset.

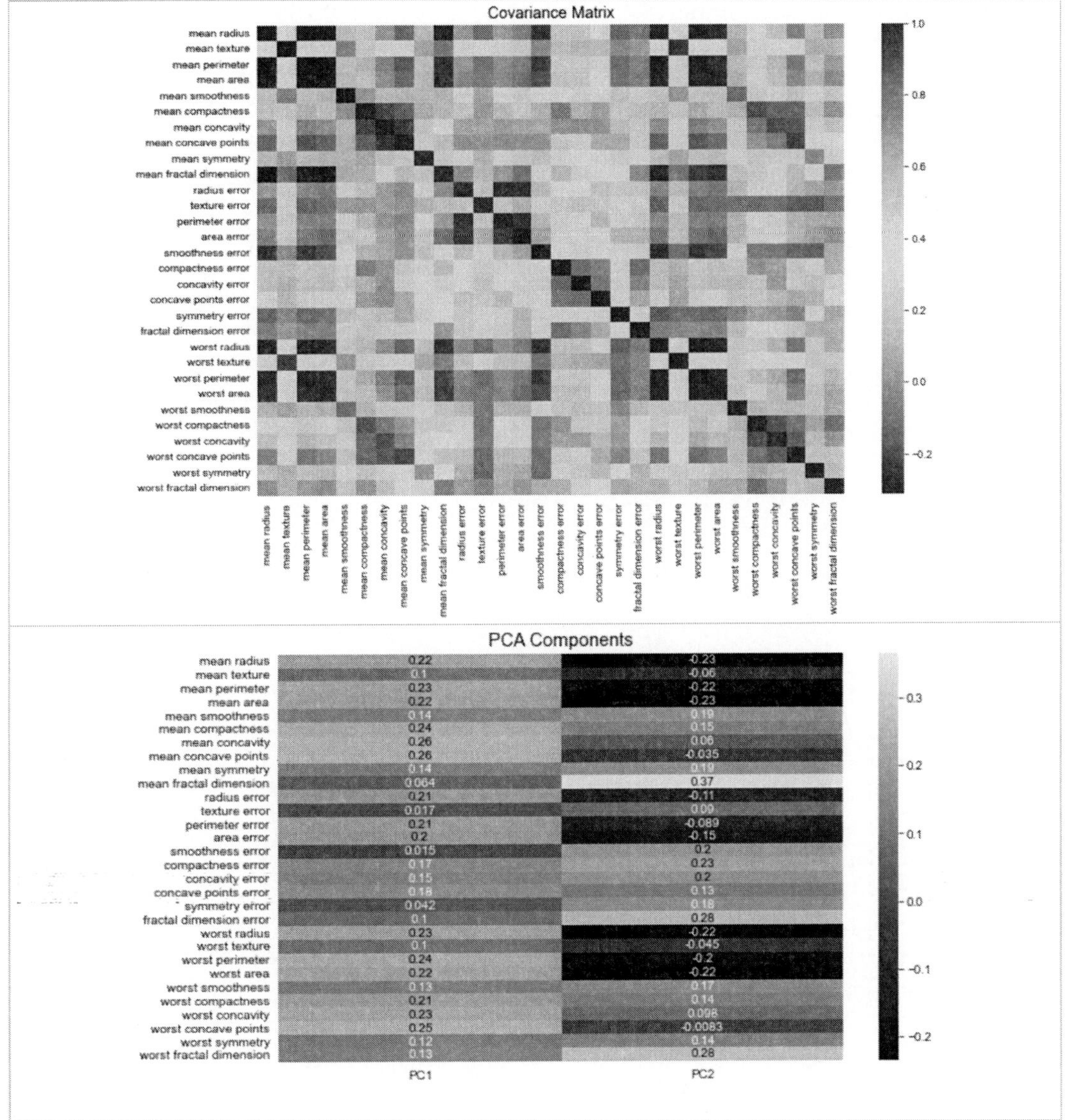

Using SKLEARN

Example P6 – U6 – D6	
PCA – Using SKLEARN	**Output**
# Importing necessary libraries import pandas as pd import numpy as np import matplotlib.pyplot as plt import seaborn as sns from sklearn.datasets import load_breast_cancer	Original Dataframe shape: (569, 31) Inputs Dataframe shape: (569, 30) PC1 PC2

from sklearn.decomposition import PCA
 	
# Load the Breast Cancer dataset from sklearn 	
cancer = load_breast_cancer(as_frame=True)
 	
# Creating a DataFrame from the dataset 	
df = cancer.frame
 	
# Display the shape of the original DataFrame 	
print('Original Dataframe shape:', df.shape)
 	
# Input features (all columns except the target) 	
X = df[cancer['feature_names']]
print('Inputs Dataframe shape:', X.shape)
 	
# Calculate the mean and standard deviation of the features 	
X_mean = X.mean()
X_std = X.std()
 	
# Standardize the features (mean=0, variance=1) 	
Z = (X - X_mean) / X_std
 	
# Calculate the covariance matrix 	
cov_matrix = Z.cov()
 	
# Plot the covariance matrix as a heatmap 	
plt.figure(figsize=(10, 8))
sns.heatmap(cov_matrix, annot=True, fmt=".2f", cmap='coolwarm')
plt.title('Covariance Matrix')
plt.show()
 	
# Perform PCA, reducing the dataset to 2 principal components 	
n_components = 2
pca = PCA(n_components=n_components)
pca.fit(Z)
x_pca = pca.transform(Z)
 	
# Create a DataFrame containing the principal components 	
df_pca = pd.DataFrame(x_pca, columns=['PC{}'.format(i+1) for i in range(n_components)])
print(df_pca.head())
 	
# Plot the first two principal components 	
	0 9.184755 1.946870
	1 2.385703 -3.764859
	2 5.728855 -1.074229
	3 7.116691 10.266556
	4 3.931842 -1.946359
	
	PCA Components (Eigenvectors):
	[[0.22 0.1 0.23 0.22 0.14 0.24 0.26 0.26 0.14 0.06 0.21 0.02
	....

```
plt.figure(figsize=(8, 6))
plt.scatter(x_pca[:, 0], x_pca[:, 1], c=cancer['target'],
cmap='plasma')
plt.xlabel('First Principal Component')
plt.ylabel('Second Principal Component')
plt.title('PCA of Breast Cancer Dataset')
plt.colorbar(label='Cancer Target')
plt.show()

# Display the components (eigenvectors)
print("PCA Components (Eigenvectors):\n",
pca.components_)
```

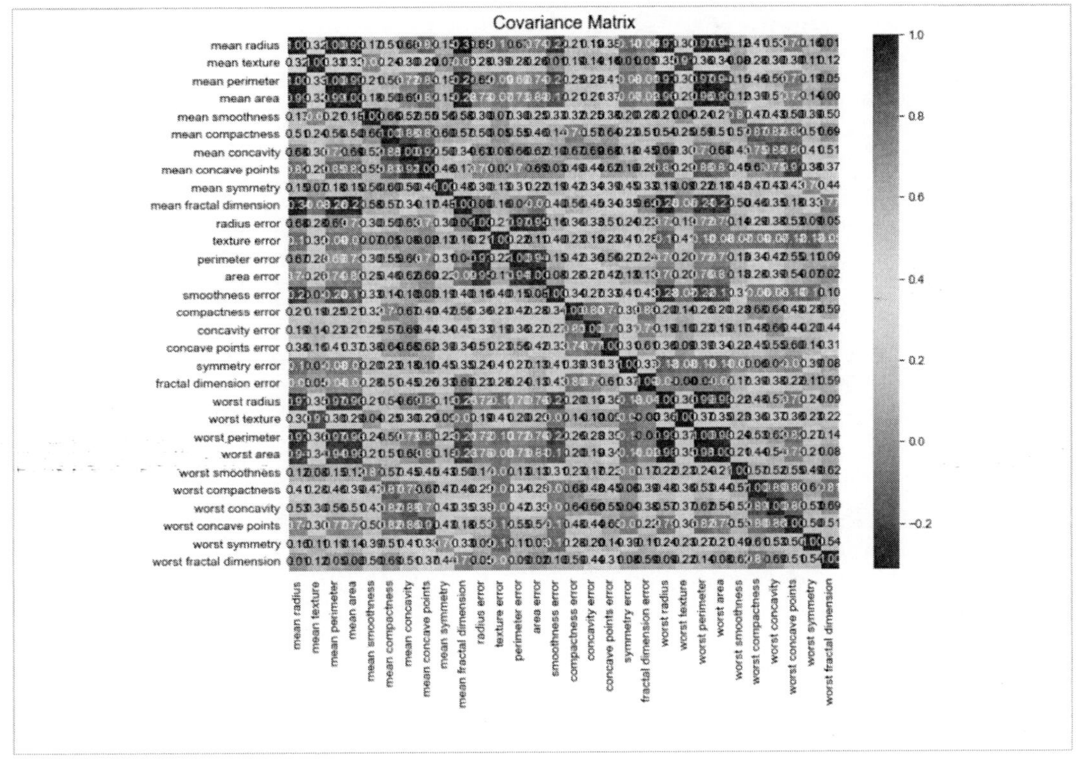

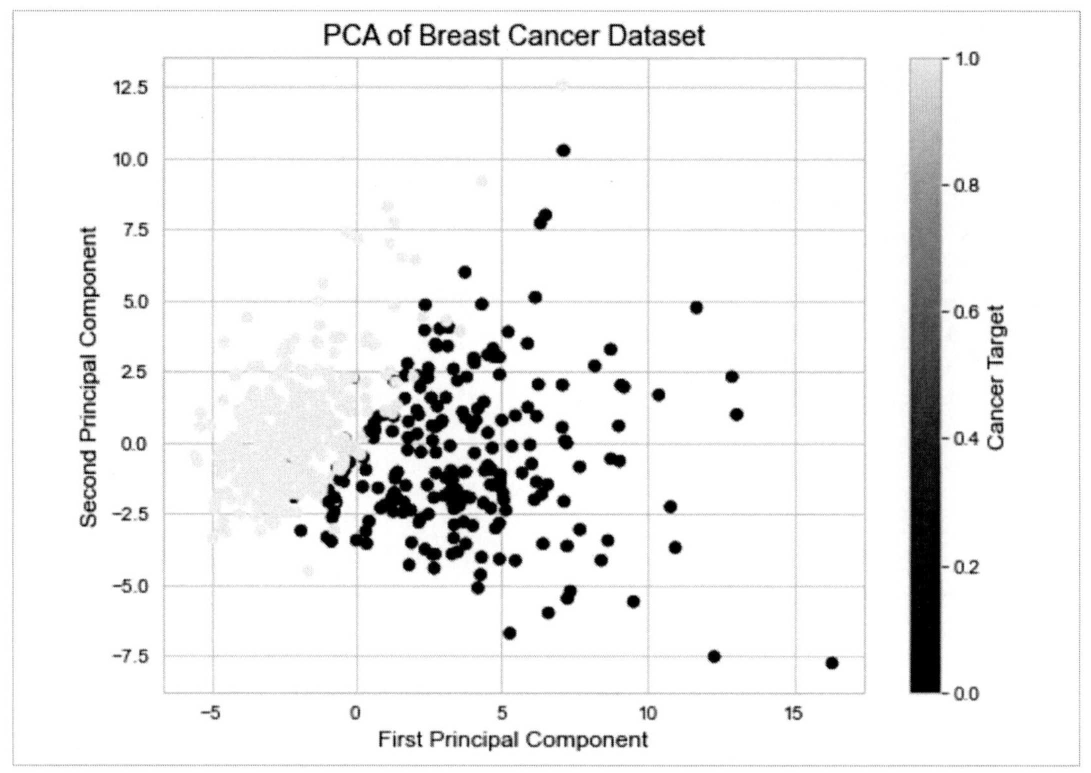

Singular Value Decomposition (SVD)

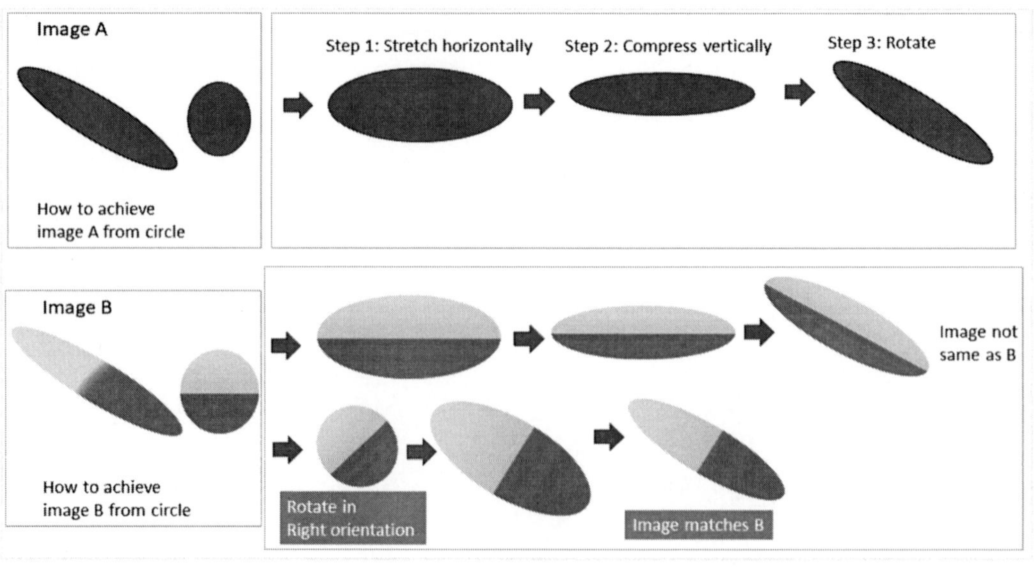

Master said, "An image can undergo various transformations such as stretching, compressing horizontally or vertically, and rotating. These transformations can be effectively described and performed using linear transformations, which are mathematically represented by matrices."

Combining Transformations:

Complex transformations can be achieved by combining simple transformations through matrix multiplication. For example, to apply a rotation followed by a scaling, you multiply the rotation matrix by the scaling matrix.

Example: Image Transformation Consider an image represented as a matrix of pixel values. Applying a linear transformation to this image can stretch, compress, or rotate it.

Linear Transformations and Matrices

Linear Transformation: A linear transformation is a function that maps vectors from one vector space to another while preserving the operations of vector addition and scalar multiplication.

Matrix Representation: Every linear transformation can be represented by a matrix. When we apply a linear transformation to a vector, it is equivalent to multiplying that vector by a matrix. This is a powerful way to handle geometric transformations in various applications, including computer graphics and image processing.

Geometric Transformations Using Matrices

Stretching/Compressing Horizontally, Stretching/Compressing Vertically, Rotation, Scaling, Shearing

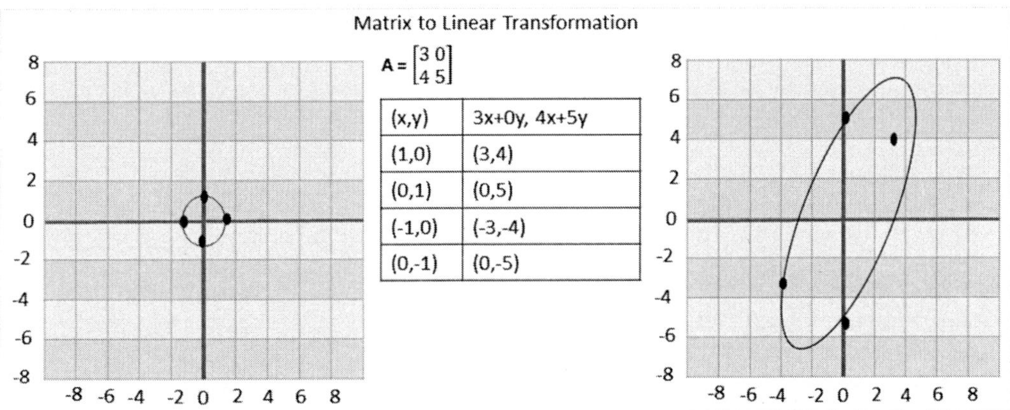

Linear transformations, represented by matrices, allow us to perform geometric transformations such as stretching, compressing, rotating, and shearing on vectors and images. By understanding how to use matrices for these transformations, we can efficiently manipulate data in various fields, enhancing our ability to analyse and visualize complex datasets.

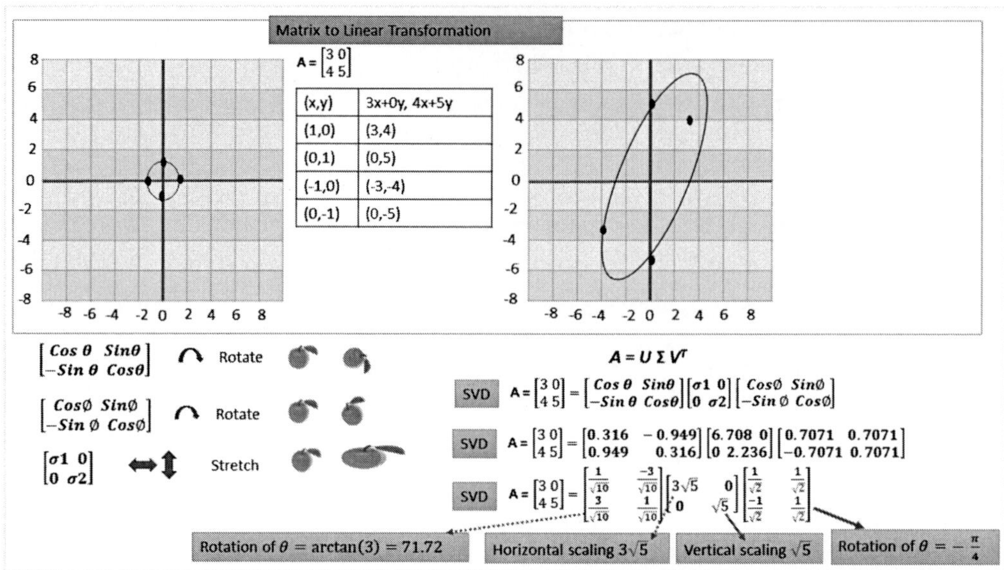

In this example, we'll use Python to demonstrate linear transformations such as stretching, compressing, and rotating an image using matrices.

Example P6 – U6 – D7

Linear Transformation

```
# Step 1: Import Necessary Libraries
import numpy as np
import matplotlib.pyplot as plt
from skimage import data
from skimage.transform import warp
# Step 2: Define Transformation Matrices
# Horizontal stretch by a factor of 2
horizontal_stretch_matrix = np.array([
    [2, 0],
    [0, 1]
])

# Vertical compress by a factor of 0.5
vertical_compress_matrix = np.array([
    [1, 0],
    [0, 0.5]
])

# Rotate by 45 degrees
theta = np.deg2rad(45)
rotation_matrix = np.array([
    [np.cos(theta), -np.sin(theta)],
    [np.sin(theta), np.cos(theta)]
```

```
])

# Step 3: Load and Transform an Image
def apply_transformation(image, transformation_matrix):
    def transform_coords(coords):
        return np.dot(transformation_matrix, coords.T).T
    return warp(image, transform_coords)

# Load sample image
image = data.astronaut()

# Step 4: Apply transformations
stretched_image = apply_transformation(image, horizontal_stretch_matrix)
compressed_image = apply_transformation(image, vertical_compress_matrix)
rotated_image = apply_transformation(image, rotation_matrix)

# Plot original and transformed images
fig, axes = plt.subplots(1, 4, figsize=(15, 5))
axes[0].imshow(image)
axes[0].set_title('Original Image')
axes[1].imshow(stretched_image)
axes[1].set_title('Stretched Horizontally')
axes[2].imshow(compressed_image)
axes[2].set_title('Compressed Vertically')
axes[3].imshow(rotated_image)
axes[3].set_title('Rotated 45 Degrees')
for ax in axes:
    ax.axis('off')
plt.show()
```

Original Image

Stretched Horizontally

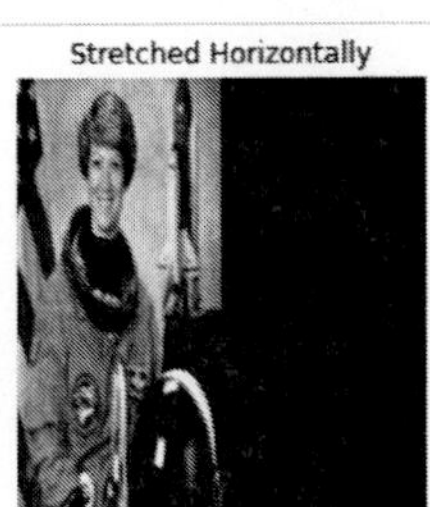

Compressed Vertically

Rotated 45 Degrees

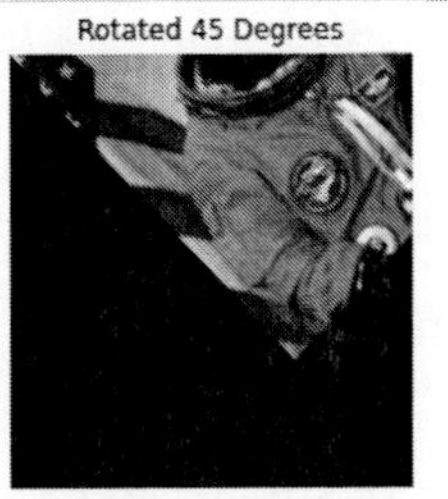

SVD:

Singular Value Decomposition (SVD) is a mathematical technique used in linear algebra to decompose a matrix into three simpler matrices. It has numerous applications in fields, such as data compression, noise reduction, and principal component analysis. The formula for SVD is as follows:

Given a matrix A of dimensions $m \times n$, the SVD of A is:

$$A = U\Sigma V^T$$

Where:

- U is an $m \times m$ orthogonal matrix.
- Σ is an $m \times n$ diagonal matrix with non-negative real numbers on the diagonal.
- V is an $n \times n$ orthogonal matrix.
- V^T is the transpose of V.

Components Explained

Matrix U:

- The columns of U are called the left singular vectors of A.
- U is an orthogonal matrix, meaning $U^TU=I$, where I is the identity matrix.

Matrix Σ:

- Σ is a diagonal matrix containing the singular values of A, which are the square roots of the eigenvalues of A^TA (or AA^T).
- The singular values are typically arranged in descending order along the diagonal of Σ.

Matrix V:

- The columns of V are called the right singular vectors of A.
- V is also an orthogonal matrix, meaning $V^TV=I$

Example P6 – U6 – D8

SVD

```
import numpy as np
from numpy.linalg import svd

# Define the matrix A
A = np.array([[3, 0], [4, 5]])

try:
    # Perform Singular Value Decomposition
    U, S, VT = svd(A)

    # Display the results
    print("Matrix A:")
    print(A)
    print("\nU matrix:")
    print(U)
```

```
    print("\nSingular values:")
    print(S)
    print("\nVT matrix:")
    print(VT)
except Exception as e:
    print(f"An error occurred: {e}")
```

Output:

Matrix A:

[[3 0]
 [4 5]]

U matrix:

[[-0.31622777 -0.9486833]
 [-0.9486833 0.31622777]]

Singular values:

[6.70820393 2.23606798]

VT matrix:

[[-0.70710678 -0.70710678]
 [-0.70710678 0.70710678]]

Steps to Compute SVD

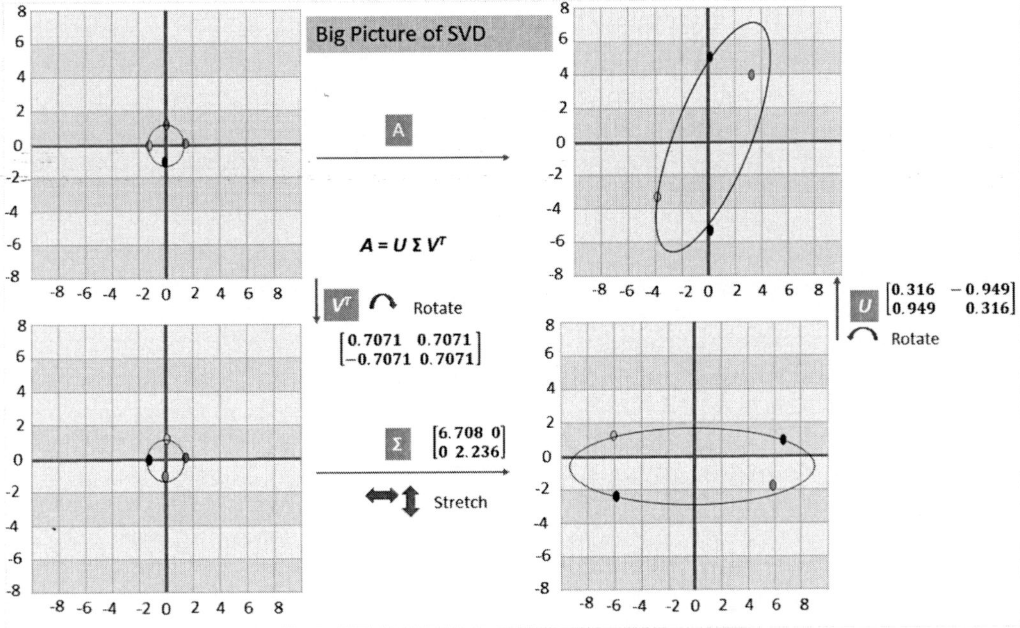

- Compute $A^T A$ and find its eigenvalues and eigenvectors. The eigenvalues are the squares of the singular values.

- Compute AA^T and find its eigenvalues and eigenvectors. These eigenvectors form the columns of U.
- Form the diagonal matrix Σ using the square roots of the eigenvalues obtained from A^TA or AA^T.
- Form the orthogonal matrix V using the eigenvectors obtained from A^TA.

Dimensionality Reduction Using Singular Value Decomposition (SVD) and Ranking

Dimensionality reduction is a crucial technique in data science and machine learning for simplifying datasets while preserving their essential structure and information. Singular Value Decomposition (SVD) is a powerful method for dimensionality reduction.

Additionally, ranking techniques can be applied to the reduced dimensions to extract the most significant features or components.

Dimensionality reduction using SVD is a robust technique for simplifying complex datasets. By combining SVD with ranking methods, we can effectively identify and retain the most critical components, making it easier to analyse and visualise high-dimensional data.

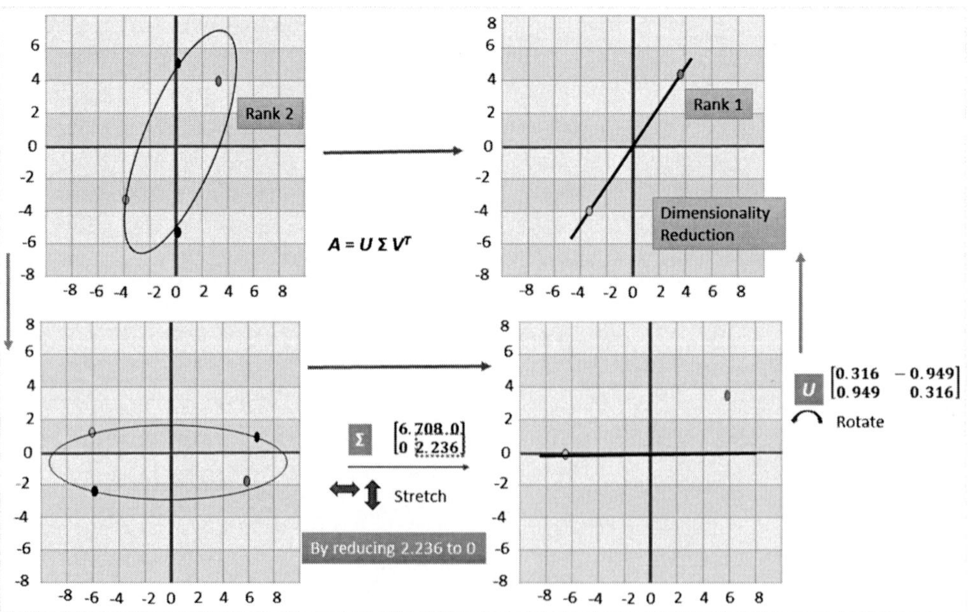

Example P6 – U6 – D9	
Incremental PCA	**Output**

# Step 1: Import Necessary Libraries 	
import numpy as np
from sklearn.decomposition import TruncatedSVD
import matplotlib.pyplot as plt
import pandas as pd
# Step 2: Generate or Load a Dataset 	
# Create a sample dataset 	
np.random.seed(0)
X = np.random.rand(100, 10) # 100 samples, 10 features
# Step 3: Apply SVD for Dimensionality Reduction 	
# Perform SVD 	
svd = TruncatedSVD(n_components=2) # Reduce to 2 dimensions
X_reduced = svd.fit_transform(X)
 	
# Print the singular values to understand the explained variance 	
print("Singular Values:", svd.singular_values_)
 	
# Step 4: Visualize the Reduced Dimensions 	
# Plot the reduced dimensions 	
plt.scatter(X_reduced[:, 0], X_reduced[:, 1], c='blue', edgecolor='k', s=50)
plt.xlabel('Component 1')
plt.ylabel('Component 2')
plt.title('2D Representation of Data after SVD')
plt.show()
# Step 5: Ranking Features Based on SVD Components 	
# Get the components (loadings) of SVD 	
components = svd.components_
 	
# Create a DataFrame for better visualization 	
df_components = pd.DataFrame(components.T, columns=['Component 1', 'Component 2'])
df_components['Feature'] = [f'Feature {i+1}' for i in range(X.shape[1])]
df_components.set_index('Feature', inplace=True)
 	
# Ranking features based on their contribution to the first component 	
df_components['Component 1'].abs().sort_values(ascending=False)
# Step 6: Example Output and Interpretation 	
# Print ranked features for the first component 	
	Singular Values:
	[16.06993052 3.56733291]
	Features ranked by their contribution to Component 1:
	Feature
	Feature 9 0.354099
	Feature 10 0.345040
	Feature 5 0.329292
	Feature 7 0.313910
	Feature 6 0.312313
	Feature 1 0.311413
	Feature 2 0.307896
	Feature 4 0.296497
	Feature 8 0.293094
	Feature 3 0.292331

print("Features ranked by their contribution to Component 1:") print(df_components['Component 1'].abs().sort_values(ascending=False))	

Incremental PCA and Randomized Singular Value Decomposition

Master explained that the purpose of this code is to demonstrate the application of two advanced Principal Component Analysis (PCA) techniques—Incremental Principal Component Analysis (IPCA) and PCA with Randomized Singular Value Decomposition (Randomized SVD)—on the Breast Cancer dataset. The code aims to reduce the dimensionality of the dataset, visualise the principal components, and interpret the underlying structure of the data.

Example P6 – U6 – D10	
Incremental PCA	**Output**

# Importing necessary libraries 	
import pandas as pd
import numpy as np
import matplotlib.pyplot as plt
import seaborn as sns
from sklearn.datasets import load_breast_cancer
from sklearn.decomposition import IncrementalPCA, PCA
 	
# Load the Breast Cancer dataset from sklearn 	
cancer = load_breast_cancer(as_frame=True)
 	
# Creating a DataFrame from the dataset 	
df = cancer.frame
 	
# Display the shape of the original DataFrame 	
print('Original Dataframe shape:', df.shape)
 	
# Input features (all columns except the target) 	
X = df[cancer['feature_names']]
print('Inputs Dataframe shape:', X.shape)
 	
# Calculate the mean and standard deviation of the features 	
X_mean = X.mean()
X_std = X.std()
 	
# Standardize the features (mean=0, variance=1) 	
Z = (X - X_mean) / X_std
	Original Dataframe shape:
	(569, 31)
	Inputs Dataframe shape:
	(569, 30)
	Incremental PCA
	DataFrame:
	PC1 PC2
	0 9.205571 1.895872
	1 2.347733 -3.732546
	2 5.719009 -1.083997
	3 7.191001 10.449775
	4 3.926427 -2.156872
	Incremental PCA
	Components (Eigenvectors):
	[[0.22 0.1 0.23 0.22 0.14 0.24 0.26 0.26 0.14 0.07 0.21 0.02……
	
	PCA with Randomized SVD
	DataFrame:
	PC1 PC2
	0 9.184755 1.946870
	1 2.385703 -3.764859
	2 5.728855 -1.074229
	3 7.116691 10.266556
	4 3.931842 -1.946359
	PCA with Randomized SVD
	Components (Eigenvectors):

``
# Calculate the covariance matrix 	
cov_matrix = Z.cov()
 	
# Plot the covariance matrix as a heatmap 	
plt.figure(figsize=(10, 8))
sns.heatmap(cov_matrix, annot=True, fmt=".2f",
cmap='coolwarm')
plt.title('Covariance Matrix')
plt.show()
 	
# Perform Incremental PCA, reducing the dataset to 2 	
principal components
n_components = 2
ipca = IncrementalPCA(n_components=n_components,
batch_size=10)
ipca.fit(Z)
x_ipca = ipca.transform(Z)
 	
# Create a DataFrame containing the principal 	
components from IPCA
df_ipca = pd.DataFrame(x_ipca,
columns=['PC{}'.format(i+1) for i in
range(n_components)])
print("Incremental PCA DataFrame:\n", df_ipca.head())
 	
# Plot the first two principal components from IPCA 	
plt.figure(figsize=(8, 6))
plt.scatter(x_ipca[:, 0], x_ipca[:, 1], c=cancer['target'],
cmap='plasma')
plt.xlabel('First Principal Component')
plt.ylabel('Second Principal Component')
plt.title('Incremental PCA of Breast Cancer Dataset')
plt.colorbar(label='Cancer Target')
plt.show()
 	
# Display the components (eigenvectors) from IPCA 	
print("Incremental PCA Components (Eigenvectors):\n",
ipca.components_)
 	
# Perform PCA with Randomized SVD, reducing the 	
dataset to 2 principal components
pca_randomized = PCA(n_components=n_components,
svd_solver='randomized')
pca_randomized.fit(Z)
x_pca_randomized = pca_randomized.transform(Z)
 	
# Create a DataFrame containing the principal 	
components from PCA with Randomized SVD
``
	[[0.22 0.1 0.23 0.22 0.14
	0.24 0.26 0.26 0.14 0.06
	0.21 0.02….

```
df_pca_randomized = pd.DataFrame(x_pca_randomized,
columns=['PC{}'.format(i+1) for i in
range(n_components)])
print("PCA with Randomized SVD DataFrame:\n",
df_pca_randomized.head())

# Plot the first two principal components from PCA with
Randomized SVD
plt.figure(figsize=(8, 6))
plt.scatter(x_pca_randomized[:, 0], x_pca_randomized[:,
1], c=cancer['target'], cmap='plasma')
plt.xlabel('First Principal Component')
plt.ylabel('Second Principal Component')
plt.title('PCA with Randomized SVD of Breast Cancer
Dataset')
plt.colorbar(label='Cancer Target')
plt.show()

# Display the components (eigenvectors) from PCA with
Randomized SVD
print("PCA with Randomized SVD Components
(Eigenvectors):\n", pca_randomized.components_)
```

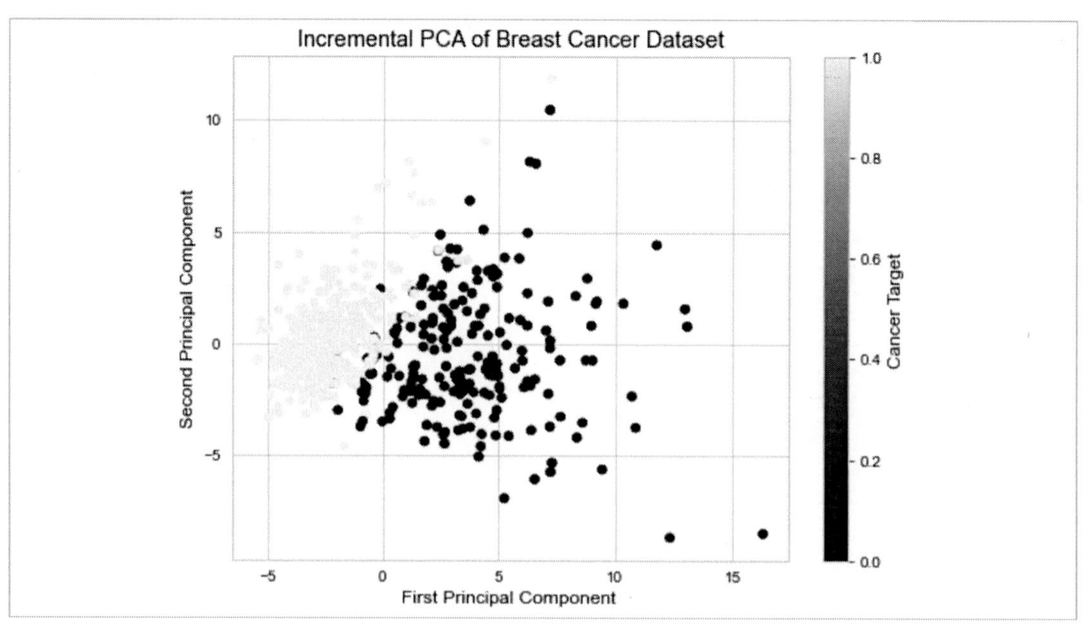

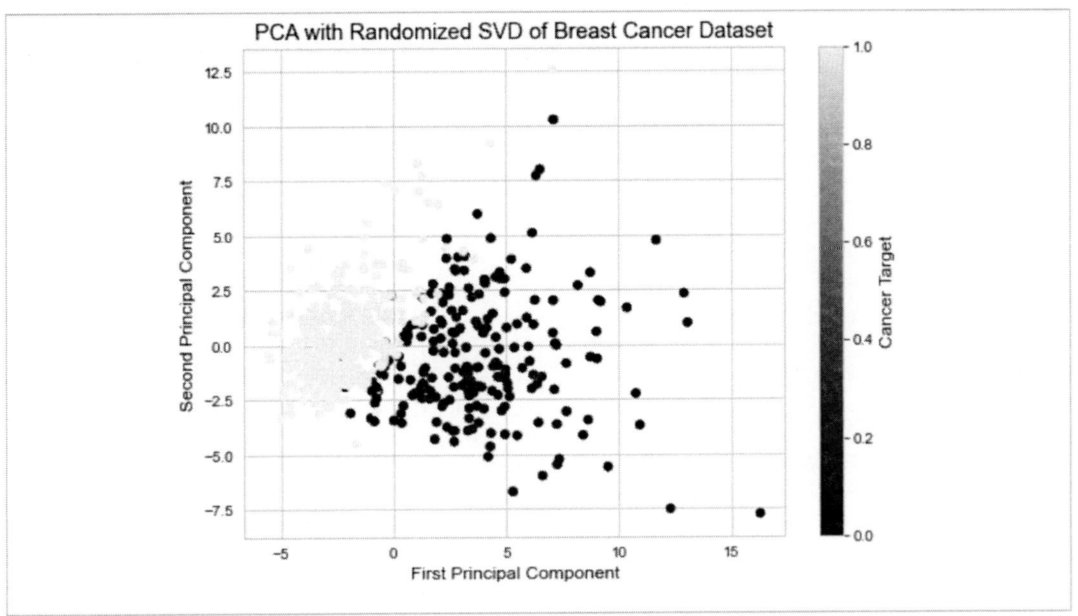

Applications and Benefits

- **Dimensionality Reduction**: PCA simplifies the dataset by reducing the number of features while preserving essential information, making it easier to analyze and visualize.
- **Feature Selection**: PCA helps identify and select the most important features, which is crucial in machine learning tasks with high-dimensional data.
- **Multicollinearity**: PCA addresses multicollinearity by transforming correlated variables into a set of linearly uncorrelated principal components.
- **Noise Reduction**: PCA improves the signal-to-noise ratio by discarding components with low variance, which are assumed to represent noise.
- **Data Compression**: PCA compresses data by representing it with fewer principal components, reducing storage requirements and enhancing processing speed.
- **Outlier Detection**: PCA can identify outliers by detecting data points that deviate significantly from the principal component space.

By leveraging these PCA techniques, one can effectively reduce the complexity of data, facilitate better visualization, and enhance the performance of machine learning algorithms.

PART SIX

DAY EIGHTEEN

Unit 6 - Lesson Four

t-SNE and Dimensionality Reduction

t-SNE and Dimensionality Reduction

T-distributed Stochastic Neighbor Embedding (t-SNE) is a nonlinear dimensionality reduction technique well-suited for embedding high-dimensional data into a low-dimensional space, typically two or three dimensions, for visualization purposes.

Apeksha asked, "What is Dimensionality Reduction?"

Master said, "Dimensionality reduction is the process of reducing the number of features (variables) in a dataset while retaining as much of the relevant information as possible. This is often done to simplify data analysis, improve computational efficiency, and facilitate data visualization."

For example, consider a classification problem where we want to predict if a student will play football based on temperature and humidity. Since temperature and humidity are highly correlated, we can reduce the number of features by collapsing them into a single underlying feature. This simplifies the problem and can make it easier to visualize. In general, reducing a 3-D problem to 2-D or 1-D makes it more manageable and interpretable.

Nikash asked, "What is the t-SNE Algorithm?"

Master said, "**t-Distributed Stochastic Neighbor Embedding (t-SNE)** is a technique specifically designed for dimensionality reduction. It uses a probabilistic approach to map high-dimensional data to a lower-dimensional space while preserving the local structure of the data. This means that points that are close in the high-dimensional space remain close in the lower-dimensional representation."

t-SNE focuses on retaining the local structures, making it particularly useful for visualizing the data by plotting it in 2D or 3D, allowing us to explore and understand high-dimensional data better.

Benefits of t-SNE:

- **Visualization**: t-SNE excels at visualizing high-dimensional data in 2D or 3D, making complex data more interpretable.
- **Local Structure Preservation**: By focusing on retaining local relationships, t-SNE helps in identifying clusters and patterns in the data that may not be apparent in higher dimensions.
- **Nonlinear Mapping**: Unlike linear methods like PCA, t-SNE can capture nonlinear relationships between features, providing a more meaningful representation of the data in many cases.

Difference between PCA and t-SNE Algorithms

Even though both PCA (Principal Component Analysis) and t-SNE (t-distributed Stochastic Neighbor Embedding) are unsupervised algorithms used for dimensionality reduction, they differ significantly in their methodologies, applications, and outcomes.

PCA:

Deterministic Method: PCA is a deterministic algorithm that reduces dimensionality by identifying the principal components (directions of maximum variance) in the data.

Linear Transformation: It uses linear transformations to map high-dimensional data to a lower-dimensional space.

Preserves Variance: PCA aims to preserve the global structure by maintaining the maximum variance in the data.

Affected by Outliers: PCA is sensitive to outliers, as it focuses on capturing the variance which can be disproportionately influenced by extreme values.

Applications: PCA is often used for feature extraction, noise reduction, and preparing data for other machine learning algorithms.

t-SNE:

Randomized Non-Linear Method: t-SNE is a non-linear, probabilistic algorithm that uses a random approach to map high-dimensional data to a lower-dimensional space.

Local Structure Preservation: t-SNE focuses on preserving the local structure of the data, meaning it retains the relative distances between nearby points more accurately.

Robust to Outliers: t-SNE is less affected by outliers compared to PCA because it emphasises local rather than global relationships.

Visualization: The primary use of t-SNE is for data visualization, making high-dimensional data interpretable by plotting it in 2D or 3D spaces.

Computationally Intensive: t-SNE has a higher computational cost with quadratic time and space complexity, making it slower and more resource-intensive for large datasets.

t-SNE Works:

Apeksha asked, "How t-SNE Works?"

Master said, "t-SNE is a non-linear dimensionality reduction algorithm that discovers patterns in data based on the similarities between data points."

Here's a brief overview of its working mechanism:

- **Similarity Computation:** t-SNE calculates the similarity of data points by determining the conditional probability that point A would choose point B as its neighbor, based on their distance.
- **Probability Minimization:** It aims to minimize the difference between these conditional probabilities (or similarities) in the high-dimensional space and the lower-dimensional space. This process ensures that similar points in the high-dimensional space remain close in the lower-dimensional representation.
- **Optimization:** The algorithm iteratively optimizes the placement of points in the lower-dimensional space to best preserve these local similarities, often using gradient descent techniques.

Space and Time Complexity

t-SNE's complexity arises from the need to compute pairwise conditional probabilities and minimize their differences across dimensions, leading to:

Time Complexity: Quadratic in the number of data points, making it slow for large datasets.

Space Complexity: Also quadratic, requiring significant memory for large datasets.

The purpose of the code is to perform dimensionality reduction and visualize high-dimensional data using the t-distributed Stochastic Neighbor Embedding (t-SNE) algorithm.

Example P6 – U6 – D11	
t-SNE	**Output**

# Importing necessary modules 	
import numpy as np
import pandas as pd
import matplotlib.pyplot as plt
import seaborn as sns
from sklearn.manifold import TSNE
from sklearn.preprocessing import StandardScaler
 	
# Load the dataset 	
path =
r'C:\Users\User\mraj4\Documents\Optimum\Py-lib\scikit\mnist\mnist_train.csv'
df = pd.read_csv(path)
 	
# Print the first five rows of the dataframe 	
print(df.head())
 	
# Save the labels into a variable 'labels' 	
labels = df['label']
 	
# Drop the label column and store the pixel data in 'data' 	
data = df.drop("label", axis=1)
 	
# Standardize the data 	
scaler = StandardScaler()
standardized_data = scaler.fit_transform(data)
print(f'Standardized data shape:
{standardized_data.shape}')
 	
# Pick the top 1000 points as t-SNE takes a lot of time for larger datasets 	
data_1000 = standardized_data[0:1000, :]
labels_1000 = labels[0:1000]
 	
# Initialize and fit t-SNE 	
model = TSNE(n_components=2, random_state=0)
tsne_data = model.fit_transform(data_1000)
 	
# Create a new dataframe for plotting 	
tsne_data = np.vstack((tsne_data.T, labels_1000)).T
tsne_df = pd.DataFrame(data=tsne_data,
columns=["Dim_1", "Dim_2", "label"])
	label 1x1 1x2 1x3 1x4 1x5
	... 28x23 28x24 28x25
	28x26 28x27 28x28
	0 5 0 0 0 0 0 ...
	0 ……
	
	Standardized data shape:
	(60000, 784)

```
# Plot the t-SNE result
plt.figure(figsize=(10, 8))
sns.scatterplot(data=tsne_df, x='Dim_1', y='Dim_2',
hue='label', palette="bright")
plt.title('t-SNE Visualization of MNIST Dataset')
plt.show()
```

Here's a breakdown of the main steps and objectives:

Loading Data: The code loads the MNIST dataset, which contains handwritten digits represented as images.

Preprocessing: It preprocesses the dataset by standardizing the pixel values using StandardScaler. Standardization ensures that each feature (pixel) has a mean of 0 and a standard deviation of 1, which is a common practice in machine learning algorithms.

Dimensionality Reduction: It applies t-SNE to reduce the dimensionality of the dataset from a high-dimensional space to a lower-dimensional space (usually 2D or 3D) while preserving the local structure of the data points.

Visualization: It visualizes the reduced-dimensional data using a scatter plot, where each data point is represented by its coordinates in the reduced space. The color of each point represents its corresponding label (digit from 0 to 9).

Output: The code produces a scatter plot that visualizes the relationships between data points in the reduced-dimensional space, providing insights into the underlying structure of the dataset.

Overall, the code serves as a demonstration of how t-SNE can be used for visualizing high-dimensional data in a lower-dimensional space, making it easier to understand and interpret complex datasets such as the MNIST dataset.

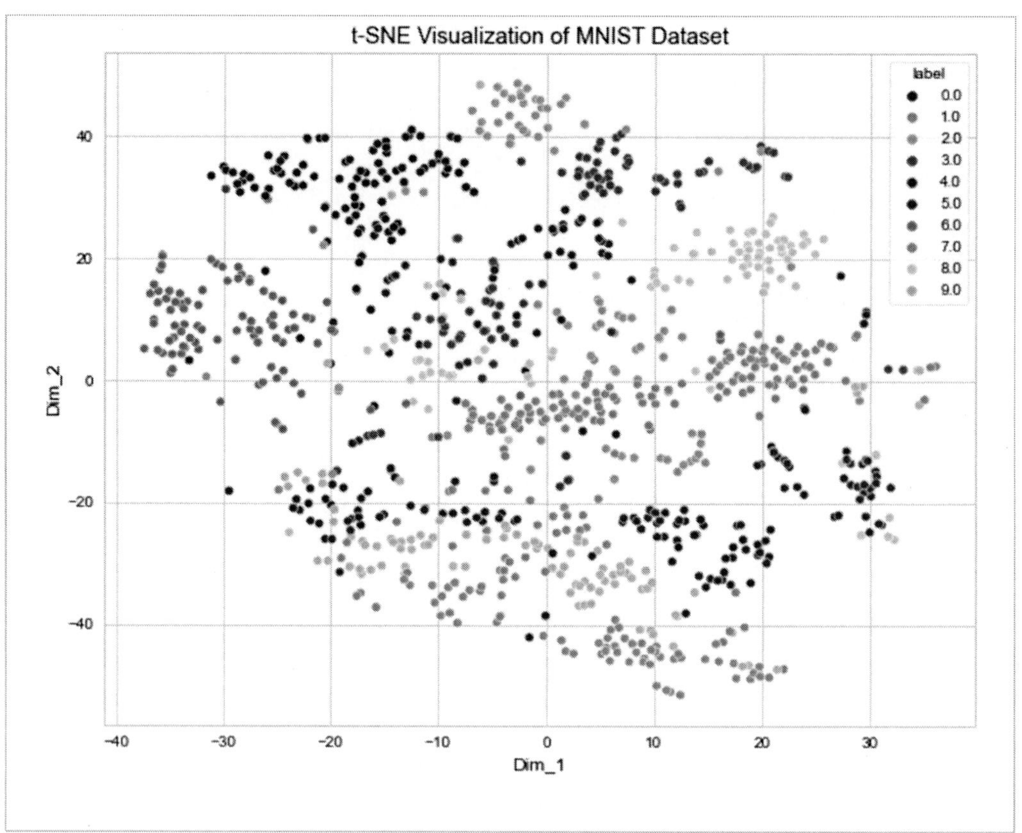
t-SNE Visualization of MNIST Dataset
label
0.0
1.0
2.0
3.0
4.0
5.0
6.0
7.0
8.0
9.0
Dim_2
Dim_1
40
20
0
−20
−40
−40
−30
−20
−10
0
10
20
30

PART SIX

DAY EIGHTEEN

Unit 6 - Lesson Five

DBSCAN

Clustering analysis, or simply clustering, is an unsupervised learning method that divides data points into specific groups or clusters. The goal is to ensure that data points within the same cluster are more similar to each other than to those in different clusters. This method does not rely on pre-labeled data and instead finds structure in the data itself. Various clustering algorithms employ different techniques to measure and maximise this similarity.

DBSCAN is a clustering algorithm that identifies dense regions in the data space, separated by areas of lower density. It works by expanding clusters from points that meet the density criteria, considering points in high-density regions as cluster points and points in low-density regions as noise or outliers.

John asked, "Why DBSCAN?"

Master said, "The DBSCAN (Density-Based Spatial Clustering of Applications with Noise) algorithm is a density-based clustering method. It operates based on the intuitive notion of clusters and noise, where clusters are considered as dense regions of data points separated by regions of lower density."

Handling Arbitrary Shapes: Unlike partitioning methods like K-means and hierarchical clustering which are limited to finding spherical or convex clusters, DBSCAN can find clusters of arbitrary shapes. This makes it versatile for real-life data which often has irregular cluster shapes.

Robust to Noise: DBSCAN can effectively handle noise and outliers. It classifies points in low-density regions as noise, which makes it more robust compared to algorithms that can be severely affected by such irregularities.

Key Parameters for DBSCAN

eps (epsilon): This parameter defines the radius of the neighborhood around a data point. Two points are considered neighbors if the distance between them is less than or equal to eps.

- **Choosing eps:** If eps is too small, many points will be classified as noise. If it's too large, clusters will merge, resulting in fewer, larger clusters. A common approach to determine eps is using the k-distance graph, plotting the distance to the k-th nearest neighbor for each point and finding the "elbow" point in the graph.

MinPts (Minimum Points): This is the minimum number of points required to form a dense region (i.e., a cluster).

- **Choosing MinPts:** The appropriate value for MinPts depends on the dataset size and dimensionality. As a rule of thumb, MinPts should be at least D + 1, where D is the number of dimensions. Generally, MinPts is set to a minimum of 3.

How DBSCAN Works

- **Core Points:** A point is a core point if it has at least MinPts points within its eps neighborhood.
- **Border Points:** A point that is not a core point, but falls within the eps neighborhood of a core point.
- **Noise Points:** Points that are neither core points nor border points.

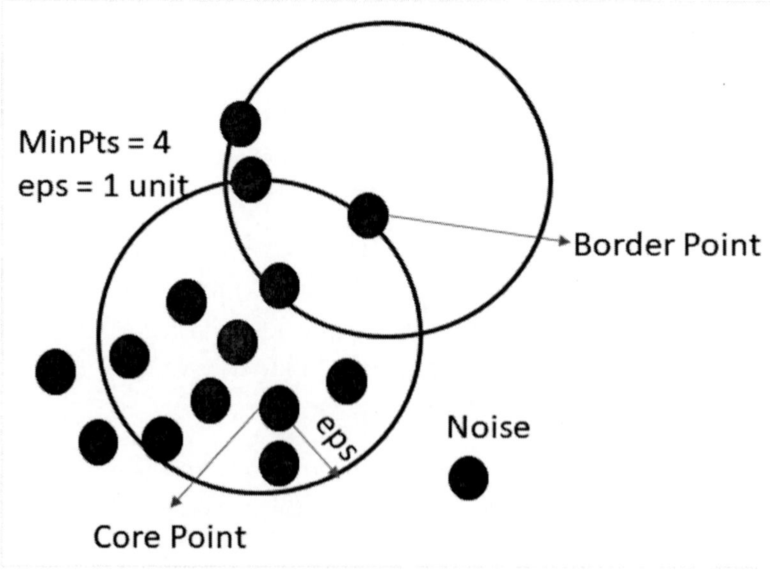

The algorithm starts by selecting an arbitrary point and checks if it is a core point. If it is, a cluster is formed. The algorithm then iteratively expands the cluster by including all points that are density-reachable from the core point. This process continues until all points have been processed.

DBSCAN is particularly useful for discovering clusters in data with noise and for identifying clusters of varying shapes and sizes, making it a powerful tool in exploratory data analysis and anomaly detection.

Steps used in DBSCAN Algorithm

Identify Core Points and Neighbors:

- For each data point, compute its neighbors (points within the eps radius).
- If the number of neighbors is greater than or equal to MinPts, mark the point as a core point.

Form Clusters from Core Points:

- If a core point is not yet part of any cluster, initiate a new cluster and assign the core point to it.

Expand Clusters:

- For each core point in the cluster, find its neighbors.
- For each neighbor, if it is also a core point and not yet part of any cluster, recursively expand the cluster to include all its neighbors.
- Continue this process until all points density-reachable from the initial core point are assigned to the cluster.

Identify Noise Points:

- Any point that is not a core point and not density-reachable from any core point is labelled as noise.

Example:

Consider points a, b, c, d, and e:

- If b is a neighbor of c, c is a neighbor of d, and d is a neighbor of e, which is a neighbor of a, then b and a are density-connected through the chain b -> c -> d -> e -> a.
- These density-connected points are assigned to the same cluster.

In Scikit-learn, you can use the sklearn.cluster.DBSCAN module to perform DBSCAN clustering. This module allows you to apply DBSCAN to your data, specifying parameters such as eps and min_samples. The eps parameter determines the maximum distance between two points for them to be considered neighbors, while the min_samples parameter defines the minimum number of data points required to form a dense region or cluster.

The purpose of this code is to demonstrate the implementation of the Density-Based Spatial Clustering of Applications with Noise (DBSCAN) algorithm using Python's scikit-learn library.

Example P6 – U6 – D12

DBSCAN – with Noise

```
import numpy as np
import matplotlib.pyplot as plt
from sklearn.cluster import DBSCAN
from sklearn import metrics
from sklearn.datasets import make_blobs
from sklearn.metrics import adjusted_rand_score

# Generate sample data
# Create a dataset with 300 samples, 4 centers, and a standard deviation of 0.50
X, y_true = make_blobs(n_samples=300, centers=4, cluster_std=0.50, random_state=0)

# Apply DBSCAN clustering algorithm
# eps: The maximum distance between two samples for one to be considered as in the
neighborhood of the other
# min_samples: The number of samples (or total weight) in a neighborhood for a point to
be considered as a core point.
db = DBSCAN(eps=0.3, min_samples=10).fit(X)

# Identify core samples
# Create a boolean mask for core samples (True if core sample, False otherwise)
core_samples_mask = np.zeros_like(db.labels_, dtype=bool)
core_samples_mask[db.core_sample_indices_] = True

# Extract labels for each point
# -1 indicates noise points
labels = db.labels_

# Number of clusters in labels, ignoring noise (-1 label)
n_clusters_ = len(set(labels)) - (1 if -1 in labels else 0)
```

```
# Plot the clusters
unique_labels = set(labels)
colors = ['y', 'b', 'g', 'r', 'c', 'm']  # Define colors for different clusters

for k, col in zip(unique_labels, colors):
    if k == -1:
        # Use black for noise points
        col = 'k'

    # Plot core samples for the current cluster
    class_member_mask = (labels == k)
    xy = X[class_member_mask & core_samples_mask]
    plt.plot(xy[:, 0], xy[:, 1], 'o', markerfacecolor=col, markeredgecolor='k', markersize=6)

    # Plot non-core samples for the current cluster
    xy = X[class_member_mask & ~core_samples_mask]
    plt.plot(xy[:, 0], xy[:, 1], 'o', markerfacecolor=col, markeredgecolor='k', markersize=6)

# Set the plot title
plt.title('Number of clusters: %d' % n_clusters_)
plt.show()

# Evaluate clustering performance using Silhouette Coefficient
# The Silhouette Coefficient is calculated using the mean intra-cluster distance and the
mean nearest-cluster distance for each sample
sc_score = metrics.silhouette_score(X, labels)
print("Silhouette Coefficient: %0.2f" % sc_score)

# Evaluate clustering performance using Adjusted Rand Index
# The Adjusted Rand Index is a function that measures the similarity of the two
assignments, ignoring permutations and with chance normalization
ari_score = adjusted_rand_score(y_true, labels)
print("Adjusted Rand Index: %0.2f" % ari_score)
```

Clustering Evaluation:

```
Silhouette Coefficient: 0.13

Adjusted Rand Index: 0.31
```

- Compute the Silhouette Coefficient to evaluate the quality of the clustering results. The Silhouette Coefficient measures the compactness and separation of the clusters.

- Compute the Adjusted Rand Index (ARI) to evaluate the similarity between the true cluster labels (ground truth) and the labels assigned by DBSCAN. A higher ARI indicates better clustering performance.

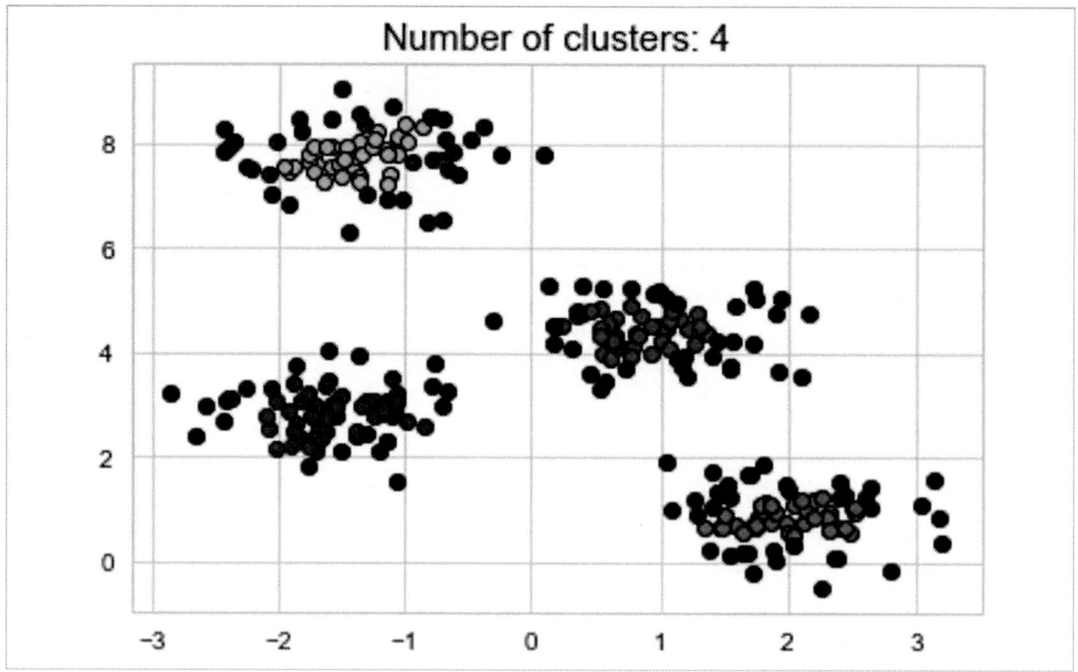

Overall, the code serves to demonstrate how to use DBSCAN for clustering and evaluate its performance using relevant metrics.

Evaluation Metrics

Silhouette Score: Range: -1 to 1

Interpretation:

- A score near 1 indicates dense, well-separated clusters with data points tightly grouped within their own clusters and well-separated from other clusters.
- A score around 0 suggests overlapping clusters, where data points may be close to the boundary between clusters.
- A score near -1 indicates that data points may have been assigned to the wrong clusters.

Adjusted Rand Score (ARI): Range: 0 to 1

Interpretation:

- A score close to 1 indicates excellent cluster recovery, meaning the clustering results agree almost perfectly with the ground truth labels.

- A score above 0.8 suggests a good recovery, indicating strong agreement between the clustering and true labels.
- A score below 0.5 suggests poor recovery, indicating little agreement between the clustering and true labels.

These evaluation metrics provide insight into the quality of clustering results obtained from the DBSCAN algorithm. The Silhouette Score assesses the compactness and separation of clusters, while the Adjusted Rand Score measures the agreement between the clustering and true labels. By considering both metrics, we can better understand the performance of DBSCAN in grouping similar data points together while keeping them separate from dissimilar points.

Example:

This code performs DBSCAN clustering on a dataset, evaluates the clustering using two metrics (Silhouette Score and Adjusted Rand Index), and visualizes the clustering results before and after parameter tuning.

Example P6 – U6 – D13

DBSCAN – with Noise

```
import numpy as np
import pandas as pd
import matplotlib.pyplot as plt

from sklearn.cluster import DBSCAN
from sklearn.preprocessing import StandardScaler
from sklearn.preprocessing import normalize
from sklearn.decomposition import PCA
from sklearn.metrics import silhouette_score, adjusted_rand_score

# Step 1: Loading the data
input_path = r'C:\Users\User\mraj4\Documents\Optimum\Py-lib\scikit\CC_GENERAL.csv'
X = pd.read_csv(input_path)

# Dropping the 'CUST_ID' column from the data
X = X.drop('CUST_ID', axis=1)

# Handling missing values
X.ffill(inplace=True)

# Step 2: Preprocessing the data
# Scaling the data to bring all the attributes to a comparable level
scaler = StandardScaler()
X_scaled = scaler.fit_transform(X)
```

```
# Normalizing the data to approximate a Gaussian distribution
X_normalized = normalize(X_scaled)

# Step 3: Dimensionality reduction for visualization
pca = PCA(n_components=2)
X_principal = pca.fit_transform(X_normalized)
X_principal = pd.DataFrame(X_principal, columns=['P1', 'P2'])

# Step 4: Building the clustering model
# Fit DBSCAN with default parameters
db_default = DBSCAN(eps=0.0375, min_samples=3).fit(X_principal)
labels = db_default.labels_

# Step 5: Visualizing the clustering
# Define color mapping for each cluster label
colours = {0: 'r', 1: 'g', 2: 'b', -1: 'k'}
cvec = [colours[label] for label in labels]

# Plot clustered data points
plt.figure(figsize=(9, 9))
plt.scatter(X_principal['P1'], X_principal['P2'], c=cvec)
plt.legend(colours.keys(), title='Cluster Label')
plt.show()

# Step 6: Tuning the parameters of the model
db_tuned = DBSCAN(eps=0.0375, min_samples=50).fit(X_principal)
labels1 = db_tuned.labels_

# Step 7: Visualizing the changes
# Update color mapping for each cluster label
colours1 = {0: 'r', 1: 'g', 2: 'b', 3: 'c', 4: 'y', 5: 'm', -1: 'k'}
cvec = [colours1[label] for label in labels1]

# Plot clustered data points with updated colors
plt.figure(figsize=(9, 9))
plt.scatter(X_principal['P1'], X_principal['P2'], c=cvec)
plt.legend(colours1.keys(), title='Cluster Label')
plt.show()

# Step 8: Evaluate clustering using Silhouette Score
silhouette_avg = silhouette_score(X_principal, labels)
print("Silhouette Score:", silhouette_avg)

# Step 9: Evaluate clustering using Adjusted Rand Index
# Generating ground truth labels (for demonstration purposes)
y_true = np.random.randint(0, 2, size=len(labels))

ari_score = adjusted_rand_score(y_true, labels)
```

```
print("Adjusted Rand Index:", ari_score)
```

```
Silhouette Score: -0.16145319831701732
Adjusted Rand Index: 5.201419235710847e-06
```

Output:

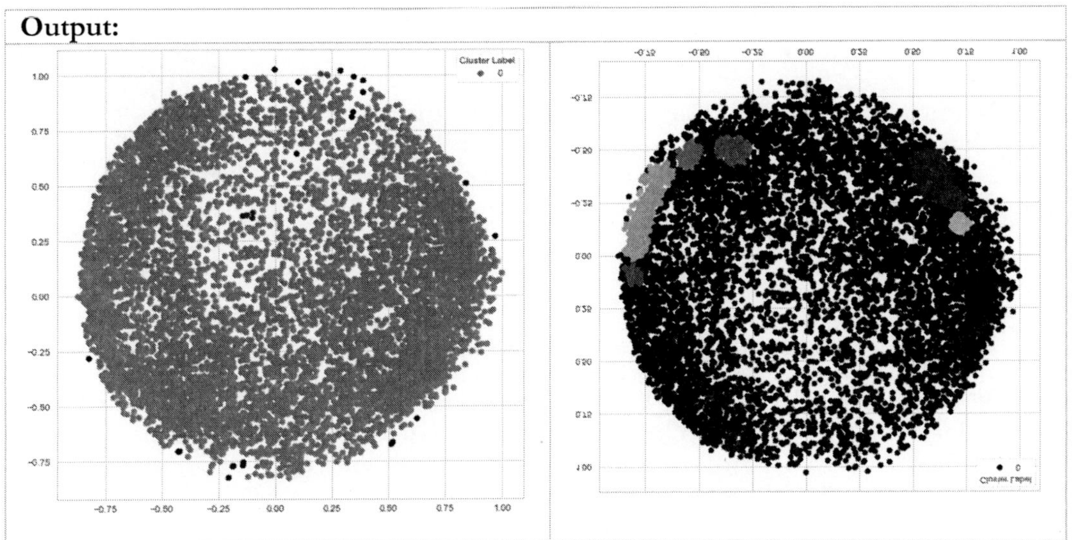

Here's the breakdown of the code's purpose:

Loading Data: It loads a dataset from a CSV file, drops unnecessary columns (in this case, the 'CUST_ID' column), and handles missing values by forward filling.

Preprocessing Data: The data is standardized using StandardScaler and then normalised to approximate a Gaussian distribution using normalize.

Dimensionality Reduction: PCA (Principal Component Analysis) is applied to reduce the dimensionality of the data to 2 dimensions for visualization purposes.

Building Clustering Model: DBSCAN (Density-Based Spatial Clustering of Applications with Noise) is applied to cluster the data. The model is first fitted with default parameters, and then it is refitted after tuning the parameters (eps and min_samples).

Visualizing Clustering: The clustering results are visualized using scatter plots. Each cluster is represented by a different colour, and noise points are labelled as black.

Evaluating Clustering: Two evaluation metrics are calculated

Benefits of DBSCAN:

- Handles arbitrary shapes: Unlike K-means and hierarchical clustering, DBSCAN can find clusters of any shape.
- Robust to Noise: Effectively identifies and handles outliers by marking them as noise.
- No need to specify the number of clusters: Automatically determines the number of clusters based on the density of points.

DBSCAN is a versatile clustering algorithm, well-suited for datasets with clusters of varying shapes and densities, especially in the presence of noise and outliers.

OPTICS

Akshaya asked, "What is OPTICS?"

Master said, "The OPTICS (Ordering Points To Identify the Clustering Structure) algorithm is another density-based clustering method that aims to address a limitation of the DBSCAN algorithm. Like DBSCAN, OPTICS identifies density-based clusters in spatial data."

The key idea behind OPTICS is to order the points in the dataset so that neighbouring points in the ordering are spatially close to each other. This ordering allows for a more flexible exploration of the density-based clustering structure, especially where the density of the data varies.

By ordering the points, OPTICS provides a hierarchical view of the clustering structure, revealing dense regions and their relationships. The algorithm does not require the number of clusters to be specified in advance, and it can handle datasets with varying density and irregular cluster shapes.

In Scikit-learn, you can use the sklearn.cluster.OPTICS module to perform OPTICS clustering. This module allows you to apply the OPTICS algorithm to your data, providing insights into the density-based clustering structure. It enables you to explore the hierarchical nature of clusters and extract meaningful information from datasets with varying density.

Sam asked, "When to use DBSCAN over K-Means?"

Master said, "DBSCAN (Density-Based Spatial Clustering of Applications with Noise) and K-Means are both popular clustering algorithms, but they have different strengths and are suited to different types of data."

Here's when you might prefer to use DBSCAN over K-Means:

- **Non-Spherical Data:** DBSCAN is more robust to non-spherical clusters compared to K-Means. It can identify clusters of arbitrary shapes, whereas K-Means assumes clusters to be spherical. If your data contains irregularly shaped clusters or clusters of varying densities, DBSCAN is a better choice.

- **Variable Cluster Density:** DBSCAN can handle clusters with varying densities, which is a limitation of K-Means. In K-Means, each cluster is assumed to have roughly the same density, which might not hold true for all datasets. DBSCAN adapts to the local density of data points, making it suitable for datasets with varying cluster densities.

- **Unknown Number of Clusters:** DBSCAN does not require you to specify the number of clusters beforehand, unlike K-Means. It automatically detects the number of clusters based on the density of the data points. This makes DBSCAN more flexible and applicable in scenarios where the number of clusters is unknown or variable.

- **Handling Noise:** DBSCAN explicitly identifies noise points as outliers, whereas K-Means assigns all data points to clusters, even if they do not belong to any discernible cluster. If your data contains noise or outliers that need to be handled separately, DBSCAN is more suitable.

In summary, you should consider using DBSCAN over K-Means when dealing with non-spherical data, variable cluster densities, an unknown number of clusters, or when noise handling is important. It offers greater flexibility and robustness in clustering analysis for such scenarios.

Clustering Performance Evaluation

Master said, "Scikit-learn provides several evaluation metrics and functions to assess the performance of clustering algorithms."

Some of the commonly used functions for evaluating clustering performance are:

Adjusted Rand Index (ARI):

Function: sklearn.metrics.adjusted_rand_score

Description: Measures the similarity between the predicted clustering labels and the ground truth labels, accounting for chance agreement.

Mutual Information (MI):

Function: sklearn.metrics.adjusted_mutual_info_score

Description: Measures the amount of shared information between the predicted clustering labels and the ground truth labels.

Homogeneity, Completeness, and V-measure:

Functions:

sklearn.metrics.homogeneity_score, sklearn.metrics.completeness_score, sklearn.metrics.v_measure_score

Description:

- Homogeneity: Measures the extent to which each cluster contains only samples from a single class.
- Completeness: Measures the extent to which all samples from the same class are assigned to the same cluster.
- V-measure: Harmonic mean of homogeneity and completeness.

Silhouette Coefficient:

Function: sklearn.metrics.silhouette_score

Description: Measures how close each sample in one cluster is to the samples in the neighboring clusters, providing an indication of cluster cohesion and separation.

Calinski-Harabasz Index:

Function: sklearn.metrics.calinski_harabasz_score

Description: Evaluates the ratio of between-cluster dispersion to within-cluster dispersion, indicating compact and well-separated clusters.

Contingency Matrix:

Function: sklearn.metrics.cluster.contingency_matrix

Description: Creates a contingency matrix that summarizes the agreement between the true labels and the predicted labels.

Fowlkes-Mallows Score:

Function: sklearn.metrics.fowlkes_mallows_score

Description: Computes a geometric mean of the pairwise precision and recall to evaluate the similarity between two clusterings.

Adjusted Mutual Information (AMI):

Function: sklearn.metrics.adjusted_mutual_info_score

Description: Measures the amount of shared information between two clusterings, adjusted for chance agreement.

Normalized Mutual Information (NMI):

Function: sklearn.metrics.normalized_mutual_info_score

Description: Measures the amount of shared information between two clusterings, normalized by the entropy of the cluster assignments.

These functions can assess the quality and performance of clustering algorithms by comparing different clustering results or evaluating them against ground truth labels (if available).

PART SIX

DAY EIGHTEEN

Unit 6 - Lesson Six

Spectral Clustering

Spectral Clustering is a powerful technique used for clustering data by leveraging the connectivity between data points. It operates by utilising the eigenvalues and eigenvectors of the data matrix to project the data into a lower-dimensional space, where clustering can be performed effectively. The process involves several key steps:

Building the Similarity Graph of the Data: This step involves constructing a similarity graph, represented as an adjacency matrix. The graph captures the relationships between data points, where nodes represent data points, and edges represent the similarity or affinity between them. There are different approaches to building the similarity graph, such as using an Epsilon-neighbourhood graph, K-Nearest Neighbors, or a Fully-Connected Graph.

Projecting the Data onto a Lower-Dimensional Space: After constructing the similarity graph, the data is projected onto a lower-dimensional space to facilitate clustering. This is crucial as it helps to overcome the limitations of the original high-dimensional space, where members of the same cluster may be far apart. The projection is typically achieved by computing the Graph Laplacian Matrix, which captures the relationships between data points in the graph.

By performing these steps, Spectral Clustering effectively identifies clusters in the data based on their connectivity and relationships, making it suitable for datasets with complex structures and non-linear separations. It offers a powerful tool for clustering analysis in various applications, including image segmentation, community detection in networks, and pattern recognition.

The code demonstrates the computation of the Graph Laplacian Matrix, a crucial step in spectral clustering algorithms. Spectral clustering utilizes the eigenvalues and eigenvectors of this matrix to partition data into clusters.

Example P6 – U6 – D14	
Spectral clustering	**Output**

import numpy as np
# Defining the adjacency matrix 	
A = np.array([
  [0, 1, 1, 0, 0, 0, 0, 0, 1, 1],
  [1, 0, 1, 0, 0, 0, 0, 0, 0, 0],
  [1, 1, 0, 0, 0, 0, 0, 0, 0, 0],
  [0, 0, 0, 0, 1, 1, 0, 0, 0, 0],
  [0, 0, 0, 1, 0, 1, 0, 0, 0, 0],
  [0, 0, 0, 1, 1, 0, 1, 1, 0, 0],
  [0, 0, 0, 0, 0, 1, 0, 1, 0, 0],
  [0, 0, 0, 0, 0, 1, 1, 0, 0, 0],
  [1, 0, 0, 0, 0, 0, 0, 0, 0, 1],
  [1, 0, 0, 0, 0, 0, 0, 0, 1, 0]
])
 	
# Degree matrix is defined 	
D = np.diag(A.sum(axis=1))
print("Degree Matrix (D):\n", D)
 	
# Graph Laplacian Matrix is defined as: L = D - A 	
L = D - A
print("\nGraph Laplacian Matrix (L):\n", L)
 	
# Matrix is then normalized for mathematical efficiency - Calculating eigenvalues and eigenvectors 	
# Find eigenvalues and eigenvectors 	
vals, vecs = np.linalg.eig(A)
	Degree Matrix (D):
	[[4 0 0 0 0 0 0 0 0 0]
	[0 2 0 0 0 0 0 0 0 0]
	[0 0 2 0 0 0 0 0 0 0]
	[0 0 0 2 0 0 0 0 0 0]
	[0 0 0 0 2 0 0 0 0 0]
	[0 0 0 0 0 4 0 0 0 0]
	[0 0 0 0 0 0 2 0 0 0]
	[0 0 0 0 0 0 0 2 0 0]
	[0 0 0 0 0 0 0 0 2 0]
	[0 0 0 0 0 0 0 0 0 2]]
	
	Graph Laplacian Matrix (L):
	[[4 -1 -1 0 0 0 0 0 -1 -1]
	[-1 2 -1 0 0 0 0 0 0 0]
	[-1 -1 2 0 0 0 0 0 0 0]
	[0 0 0 2 -1 -1 0 0 0 0]
	[0 0 0 -1 2 -1 0 0 0 0]
	[0 0 0 -1 -1 4 -1 -1 0 0]
	[0 0 0 0 0 -1 2 -1 0 0]
	[0 0 0 0 0 -1 -1 2 0 0]
	[-1 0 0 0 0 0 0 0 2 -1]
	[-1 0 0 0 0 0 0 0 -1 2]]

Here's a breakdown of the purpose of each part of the code:

Defining the Adjacency Matrix (A): The adjacency matrix represents the connectivity between data points. It is a binary matrix where each element indicates whether there is an edge (connection) between two nodes (data points).

Calculating the Degree Matrix (D): The degree matrix is a diagonal matrix where each diagonal element represents the degree (number of connections) of a corresponding node in the graph. This step computes the sum of connections for each node and creates the degree matrix accordingly.

Defining the Graph Laplacian Matrix (L): The Graph Laplacian Matrix is calculated as the difference between the degree matrix (D) and the adjacency matrix (A). It captures the structure of the graph and is used in spectral clustering algorithms.

Normalization (Optional): In some cases, the Graph Laplacian Matrix is normalized for mathematical efficiency. However, in this code, normalization is not performed.

Calculating Eigenvalues and Eigenvectors: The eigenvalues and eigenvectors of the adjacency matrix (A) are computed. These eigenvalues and eigenvectors play a crucial role in spectral clustering algorithms, as they are used to determine the optimal number of clusters and to partition the data into clusters.

Overall, this code provides a foundational understanding of the Graph Laplacian Matrix and its computation, which is essential for implementing spectral clustering algorithms in machine learning.

Clustering the Data

This process primarily entails clustering the reduced data using a traditional clustering technique, typically K-Means Clustering. Initially, each node is assigned a row of the normalised Graph Laplacian Matrix. Subsequently, this data undergoes clustering using any traditional technique. To interpret the clustering result, the node identifier is preserved.

Properties:

- Assumption-Less: Unlike other traditional techniques, this clustering method does not presume the data to adhere to specific properties. Consequently, it can address a broader range of clustering problems.
- Ease of Implementation and Speed: This algorithm is simpler to implement compared to other clustering algorithms and demonstrates high computational speed, primarily involving mathematical computations.
- Not Scalable: Due to the matrix building and eigenvalue/eigenvector computations involved, it becomes time-intensive for dense datasets.
- Dimensionality Reduction: By utilising eigenvalue decomposition, the algorithm effectively reduces the dimensionality of the data, facilitating easier visualization and analysis.
- Cluster Shape: Spectral clustering can accommodate non-linear cluster shapes,

rendering it suitable for diverse applications.

- Noise Sensitivity: The algorithm is sensitive to noise and outliers, potentially impacting the quality of resultant clusters.
- Number of Clusters: Users must specify the number of clusters in advance, which can pose a challenge in certain scenarios.
- Memory Requirements: Significant memory is necessary to store the similarity matrix, posing limitations for large datasets.

Example:

The purpose of this code is to perform Spectral Clustering on a dataset and evaluate its performance using different affinity settings. Spectral Clustering is a technique that uses the connectivity between data points to form clusters.

Example P6 – U6 – D15
Spectral clustering

```
# Step 1: Importing required libraries
import pandas as pd
import matplotlib.pyplot as plt
from sklearn.cluster import SpectralClustering
from sklearn.preprocessing import StandardScaler, normalize
from sklearn.decomposition import PCA
from sklearn.metrics import silhouette_score

# Step 2: Loading the data
input_path = r'C:\Users\User\mraj4\Documents\Optimum\Py-
lib\scikit\CC_GENERAL.csv'
X = pd.read_csv(input_path)

# Step 3: Cleaning the data
# Dropping the 'CUST_ID' column from the data
X = X.drop('CUST_ID', axis=1)

# Handling the missing values using forward fill
X.ffill(inplace=True)

# Step 4: Preprocessing the data
# Scaling the data to bring all features to a comparable level
scaler = StandardScaler()
X_scaled = scaler.fit_transform(X)

# Normalizing the data to have a Gaussian distribution
X_normalized = normalize(X_scaled)
```

```
# Converting the numpy array into a pandas DataFrame
X_normalized = pd.DataFrame(X_normalized)

# Reducing the dimensions of the data using PCA
pca = PCA(n_components=2)
X_principal = pca.fit_transform(X_normalized)
X_principal = pd.DataFrame(X_principal, columns=['P1', 'P2'])

# Step 5A: Building and visualizing the clustering model with 'rbf' affinity
# Creating the Spectral Clustering model with 'rbf' affinity
spectral_model_rbf = SpectralClustering(n_clusters=2, affinity='rbf')

# Training the model and storing the predicted cluster labels
labels_rbf = spectral_model_rbf.fit_predict(X_principal)

# Building the label to color mapping
colours = {0: 'b', 1: 'y'}

# Building the color vector for each data point
cvec = [colours[label] for label in labels_rbf]

# Plotting the clustered scatter plot
plt.figure(figsize=(9, 9))
plt.scatter(X_principal['P1'], X_principal['P2'], c=cvec)
plt.title('Spectral Clustering with rbf Affinity')
plt.xlabel('P1')
plt.ylabel('P2')
plt.show()

# Step 5B: Building and visualizing the clustering model with 'nearest_neighbors' affinity
# Creating the Spectral Clustering model with 'nearest_neighbors' affinity
spectral_model_nn = SpectralClustering(n_clusters=2, affinity='nearest_neighbors')

# Training the model and storing the predicted cluster labels
labels_nn = spectral_model_nn.fit_predict(X_principal)

# Building the label to color mapping
colours = {0: 'b', 1: 'y'}

# Building the color vector for each data point
cvec = [colours[label] for label in labels_nn]

# Plotting the clustered scatter plot
plt.figure(figsize=(9, 9))
plt.scatter(X_principal['P1'], X_principal['P2'], c=cvec)
plt.title('Spectral Clustering with nearest_neighbors Affinity')
plt.xlabel('P1')
plt.ylabel('P2')
```

```
plt.show()

# Step 6: Evaluating the performance
# List of different values of affinity
affinity = ['rbf', 'nearest_neighbors']

# List of Silhouette Scores
s_scores = []

# Evaluating the performance
s_scores.append(silhouette_score(X_principal, labels_rbf))
s_scores.append(silhouette_score(X_principal, labels_nn))

# Printing silhouette scores
print("Silhouette Scores:", s_scores)

# Step 7: Comparing the performances
# Plotting a bar graph to compare the models
plt.figure(figsize=(9, 6))
plt.bar(affinity, s_scores, color=['blue', 'yellow'])
plt.xlabel('Affinity')
plt.ylabel('Silhouette Score')
plt.title('Comparison of different Clustering Models')
plt.show()
```

```
Silhouette Scores: [0.4473160266062024, 0.44672635820102524]
```

This code specifically:

Loads and Preprocesses the Data:

- It loads a dataset from a CSV file.
- Drops unnecessary columns and handles missing values.
- Scales and normalizes the data to prepare it for clustering.
- Reduces the dimensionality of the data using Principal Component Analysis (PCA) for better visualization.

Applies Spectral Clustering:

- It applies Spectral Clustering with two different affinity settings: 'rbf' and 'nearest_neighbors'.

- The clustering results are visualized using scatter plots, with different colors representing different clusters.

Evaluate the Clustering Performance:

- The quality of the clustering is evaluated using the silhouette score, which measures how similar an object is to its cluster compared to other clusters.
- The performance of the clustering models with different affinity settings is compared using a bar graph.

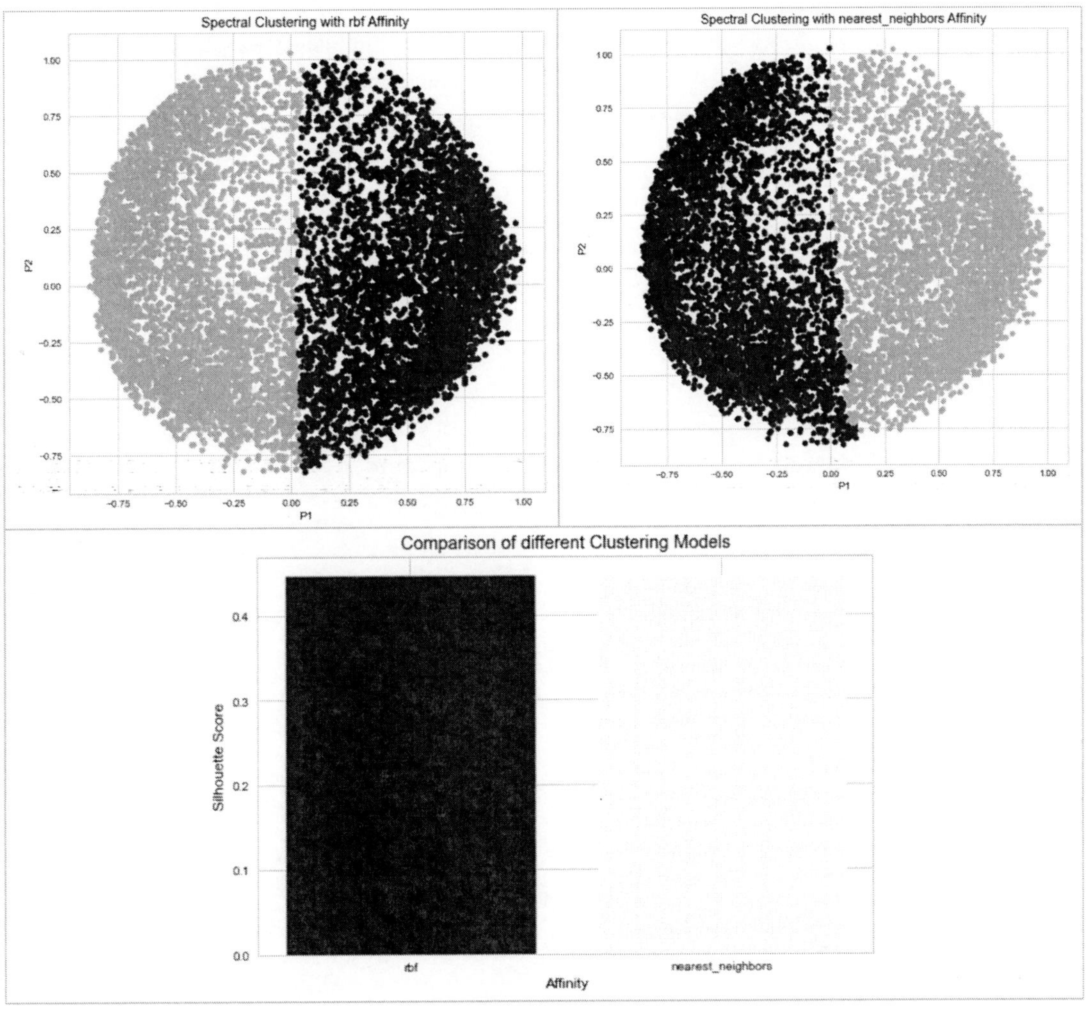

Advantages of Spectral Clustering:

- Scalability: Spectral clustering can efficiently handle large datasets and high-dimensional data. It achieves this by reducing the dimensionality of the data before applying the clustering algorithm, making the process more manageable and less computationally intensive.

- Flexibility: Spectral clustering is effective for non-linearly separable data. Unlike traditional distance-based clustering methods, it leverages the connectivity between data points and can identify clusters of arbitrary shapes, making it versatile for various types of data distributions.

- Robustness: Spectral clustering can be more robust to noise and outliers. By considering the global structure of the data and forming clusters based on eigenvalues and eigenvectors, it is less influenced by local anomalies compared to traditional clustering methods that focus on local distances.

Disadvantages of Spectral Clustering:

- Complexity: Spectral clustering can be computationally expensive, especially for large datasets. This is due to the need to compute eigenvalues and eigenvectors of the similarity matrix, which can be time-consuming and resource-intensive.

- Model Selection: Choosing the appropriate number of clusters and the correct similarity matrix can be challenging. This process often requires expert knowledge or extensive trial and error, which can be a significant drawback for users without sufficient experience or resources to fine-tune these parameters.

PART SIX

DAY NINETEEN

Unit 6 - Lesson Seven

Gaussian Mixture

Master said, "The Gaussian Mixture Model (GMM) is a versatile probabilistic model used for clustering and density estimation. GMM assumes that the data is generated from a mixture of several Gaussian distributions, each representing a distinct cluster. This allows GMM to assign probabilities to data points, permitting them to belong to multiple clusters simultaneously. This flexibility makes GMM widely used in machine learning and pattern recognition applications."

Normal or Gaussian Distribution

In real life, many datasets can be modelled by the Gaussian (or Normal) distribution, which can be univariate or multivariate. It is quite natural and intuitive to assume that clusters within these datasets originate from different Gaussian distributions. This assumption leads to the concept of modelling the dataset as a mixture of several Gaussian distributions, which is the core idea behind the Gaussian Mixture Model (GMM).

Probability Density Function (PDF) of a Gaussian Distribution

In one dimension, the probability density function (PDF) of a Gaussian distribution is given by:

$$f(x|\mu,\sigma^2) = \frac{1}{\sqrt{2\pi\sigma^2}}\exp(-(x-\mu)^2/2\sigma^2)$$

$$f(x|\mu,\sigma^2) = \frac{1}{\sqrt{2\pi\sigma^2}}\exp(-(x-\mu)^2/2\sigma^2)$$

where:

- x is the variable,
- μ is the mean of the distribution,
- $\sigma 2$ is the variance of the distribution,
- σ is the standard deviation of the distribution.

This function describes the likelihood of a variable taking on a particular value given the parameters of the distribution.

Gaussian Mixture Models (GMM)

A Gaussian Mixture Model (GMM) extends the concept of the Gaussian distribution to multiple dimensions and multiple clusters. A GMM is a probabilistic model that assumes all the data points are generated from a mixture of a finite number of Gaussian distributions with unknown parameters. Each Gaussian distribution within the mixture can have its mean and variance, and the overall probability distribution is a weighted sum of these individual Gaussian distributions.

Multivariate Gaussian Distribution

For higher dimensions, the multivariate Gaussian distribution is used, where the probability density function is defined as:

$$f(x|\mu,\Sigma) = 1/(2\pi)^{k/2}|\Sigma|^{1/2}\exp(-1/2(x-\mu)^T\Sigma^{-1}(x-\mu))$$

where:

- x is a k-dimensional vector,
- μ is the mean vector,
- Σ is the covariance matrix,
- k is the number of dimensions.

This function generalises the Gaussian distribution to multiple dimensions, capturing the relationship between different variables in the data.

Concept of Gaussian Mixture Models

GMMs assume that there are a certain number of Gaussian distributions within the dataset, and each of these distributions represents a cluster. Consequently, a Gaussian Mixture Model tends to group data points belonging to the same distribution together.

Consider three Gaussian distributions – GD1, GD2, and GD3. Each distribution has a specific mean ($\mu1$, $\mu2$, $\mu3$) and variance ($\sigma1$, $\sigma2$, $\sigma3$). For any given set of data points, GMM calculates the probability of each data point belonging to each of these distributions.

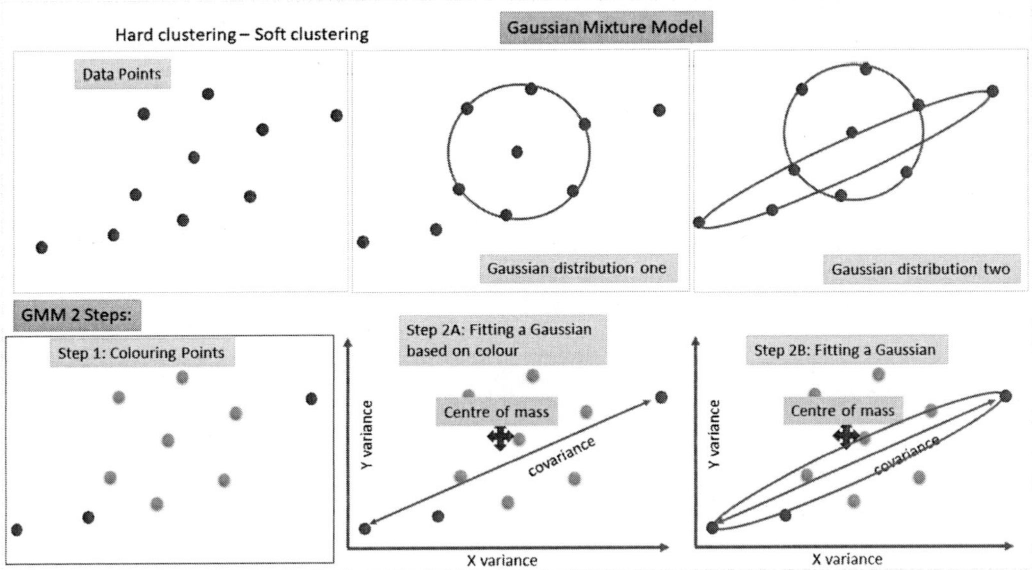

The Gaussian Mixture Model (GMM) algorithm involves two primary steps: colouring data points based on cluster assignment and fitting Gaussian distributions to these clusters. The fitting process involves calculating the centre of mass (mean), x-variance, y-variance, and covariance for each cluster. The model iteratively adjusts these parameters, creating different Gaussian mixtures until convergence is achieved or the best model is found.

Detailed Steps

Colouring Data Points: The algorithm initially assigns data points to clusters, each represented by a different colour. These assignments are based on the probability of each point belonging to each cluster.

Fitting Gaussian Distributions: For each cluster, a Gaussian distribution is fitted by calculating the following:

- Centre of Mass (Mean): The average position of data points in the cluster.
- X-Variance and Y-Variance: Measures of how spread out the data points are along the x and y axes, respectively.

- Covariance: A measure of how changes in one variable are associated with changes in another.

Iterative Process: The GMM algorithm iteratively refines the parameters of the Gaussian distributions. In each iteration, the algorithm:

- Reassigns data points to clusters based on updated probabilities.
- Recalculates the parameters of the Gaussian distributions based on the new assignments.

Convergence: The process continues until the log-likelihood (a measure of model fit) converges, meaning further iterations result in negligible changes, indicating the best model has been found.

GMMs are probabilistic models that use a soft clustering approach, allowing data points to be associated with multiple clusters based on probability scores.

Example:

The purpose of this code is to perform clustering on a dataset using the Gaussian Mixture Model (GMM) algorithm and visualise the resulting clusters.

Example P6 – U6 – D16

Gaussian Mixture

```
# Step 1: Importing required libraries
import pandas as pd
import matplotlib.pyplot as plt
from sklearn.mixture import GaussianMixture

# Step 2: Loading the data
input_path = r'C:\Users\User\mraj4\Documents\Optimum\Py-
lib\scikit\Clustering_gmm.csv'
data = pd.read_csv(input_path)

# Step 3: Training Gaussian Mixture Model
gmm = GaussianMixture(n_components=4, random_state=42)
gmm.fit(data)

# Step 4: Predictions from GMM
labels = gmm.predict(data)
data['cluster'] = labels

# Step 5: Plotting the clustered data
colors = ['blue', 'green', 'cyan', 'black']
plt.figure(figsize=(10, 6))
```

```
for k in range(4):
    cluster_data = data[data['cluster'] == k]
    plt.scatter(cluster_data.iloc[:, 0], cluster_data.iloc[:, 1],
                c=colors[k], label=f'Cluster {k}')

plt.xlabel('Weight')
plt.ylabel('Height')
plt.title('Clusters formed by GMM')
plt.legend()
plt.grid(True)
plt.show()
```

Here's a breakdown of the steps and their purposes:

Import Libraries:

Import necessary libraries for data manipulation (pandas), visualization (matplotlib.pyplot), and clustering (sklearn.mixture.GaussianMixture).

Load Data:

Load the dataset from a CSV file into a pandas DataFrame for further analysis.

Train Gaussian Mixture Model:

Initialise and fit a Gaussian Mixture Model (GMM) with a specified number of components (clusters) to the data. The GMM algorithm identifies the clusters by modelling the data as a mixture of several Gaussian distributions.

Predict Clusters:

Use the trained GMM to predict the cluster labels for each data point. These labels indicate to which cluster each data point belongs.

Visualise Clusters:

Create a scatter plot to visualise the clusters formed by the GMM. Different colours are used to represent different clusters, and the plot includes labels for the axes, a title, and a legend for clarity.

The overall goal is to use the GMM algorithm to identify distinct groups within the data and to visualise these groups to understand the structure and distribution of the data points. This approach is commonly used in data analysis to uncover hidden patterns and relationships within datasets.

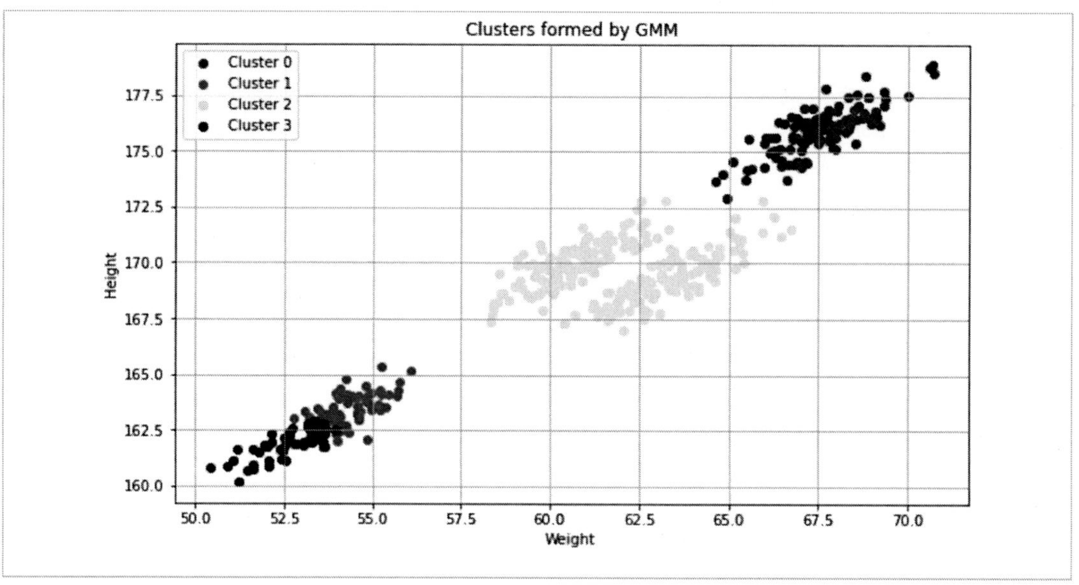

Expectation-Maximization (EM) Algorithm

Master explained that the Expectation-Maximization (EM) algorithm is a powerful iterative method used to find maximum-likelihood estimates of model parameters in scenarios where the data is incomplete, has missing values or includes hidden variables.

EM starts by assigning random values to the missing data points and then uses these values to generate a new dataset. These updated values are recursively used to improve the dataset until the estimates stabilise.

Expectation- Maximization (EM) Algorithm for GMM

Expectation Step (E-step): In this step, the algorithm estimates the missing data points using the current parameters of the model. This step involves calculating the expected value of the log-likelihood function with respect to the current parameter estimates.

Key steps:

Initialisation:

Initialise the model parameters: mean (μ_k), covariance matrix (Σ_k), and mixing coefficients (π_k).

Expectation Step (E-step):

Compute the posterior probabilities (responsibilities) for each data point belonging to each cluster using the current parameter values. These responsibilities are represented by the latent variables γ_{ik}, where i indexes the data points and k indexes the clusters.

Formally, the responsibility γ_{ik} is calculated as:

$$\gamma_{ik} = \pi_k N(x_i|\mu_k,\Sigma_k) \;/\; \sum_{j=1}^{K} \pi_j \; N(x_i|\mu_j,\Sigma_j)$$

where $N(x_i|\mu_k,\Sigma_k)$ is the probability density function of the multivariate Gaussian distribution for the i-th data point in the k-th cluster.

Maximization Step (M-step):

Maximization Step (M-step): In this step, the algorithm updates the model parameters to maximize the expected log-likelihood found in the E-step. This step effectively improves the parameter estimates based on the new complete data.

Update the parameter values using the responsibilities calculated in the E-step:

Update the means (μ_k):

$$\mu_k = \sum_{i=1}^{N} \gamma_{ik}\, x_i \;/\; \sum_{i=1}^{N} \gamma_{ik}$$

Update the covariance matrices (Σ_k):

$$\Sigma_k = \sum_{i=1}^{N} \gamma_{ik}\, (x_i-\mu_k)(x_i-\mu_k)^T \;/\; \sum_{i=1}^{N} \gamma_{ik}$$

Update the mixing coefficients (π_k):

$$\pi_k = \sum_{i=1}^{N} \gamma_{ik} / N$$

where N is the total number of data points.

Convergence:

Repeat the E-step and M-step until convergence, which typically occurs when the change in the log-likelihood or the parameters falls below a predefined threshold, or after a maximum number of iterations.

The log-likelihood is given by:

$$\text{Log}\, L = \sum_{i=1}^{N} log\; (\sum_{i=1}^{N} \pi_k\, N(x_i \mid \mu_k,\Sigma_k))$$

Intuitive Explanation

E-step: Calculate the probabilities that each data point belongs to each cluster (i.e., how much each data point "belongs" to each Gaussian distribution).

M-step: Update the parameters of the Gaussian distributions to maximise the likelihood of the data, given the current assignment probabilities.

Applications of EM Algorithm

The EM algorithm is a general framework that can be applied to various models, including GMMs. Beyond GMMs, the EM algorithm is used in other contexts, such as:

- Hidden Markov Models (HMMs) for speech recognition.
- Missing data problems in statistics.
- Image reconstruction.

These two steps are iteratively performed until the model parameters converge, leading to a stable solution.

Example:

The Gaussian Mixture class in the sklearn.mixture module to implement Gaussian Mixture Models (GMM). In this example, we will load the Iris dataset from the datasets package. To keep things simple, we will use only the first two columns (i.e., sepal length and sepal width).

Example P6 – U6 – D17

GMM

```
import numpy as np
import pandas as pd
import matplotlib.pyplot as plt
from sklearn import datasets
from sklearn.mixture import GaussianMixture

# Step 1: Load the iris dataset
iris = datasets.load_iris()

# Step 2: Select the first two columns (sepal length and sepal width)
X = iris.data[:, :2]

# Step 3: Convert the data to a pandas DataFrame
d = pd.DataFrame(X, columns=['Sepal Length', 'Sepal Width'])

# Step 4: Plot the initial data
plt.scatter(d['Sepal Length'], d['Sepal Width'])
```

```
plt.xlabel('Sepal Length')
plt.ylabel('Sepal Width')
plt.title('Iris Data: Sepal Length vs Sepal Width')
plt.show()

# Step 5: Initialize the Gaussian Mixture Model with 3 components
gmm = GaussianMixture(n_components=3)

# Step 6: Fit the GMM model to the data
gmm.fit(d)

# Step 7: Assign a label to each observation (clustering)
labels = gmm.predict(d)
d['Cluster'] = labels

# Step 8: Plot the clustered data
colors = ['r', 'yellow', 'g']
for i in range(3):
    cluster_data = d[d['Cluster'] == i]
    plt.scatter(cluster_data['Sepal Length'], cluster_data['Sepal Width'], c=colors[i],
label=f'Cluster {i}')
plt.xlabel('Sepal Length')
plt.ylabel('Sepal Width')
plt.title('GMM Clustering of Iris Data')
plt.legend()
plt.show()

# Step 9: Print the converged log-likelihood value and the number of iterations
print(f'Converged log-likelihood value: {gmm.lower_bound_}')
print(f'Number of iterations for convergence: {gmm.n_iter_}')
```

We will fit the data as a mixture of 3 Gaussians. After fitting the model, we will perform clustering by assigning a label to each observation. Additionally, we will find the number of iterations needed for the log-likelihood function to converge and the converged log-likelihood value. These values will be printed to provide insight into the model's performance. Specifically, it took 7 iterations for the log-likelihood to converge. Performing more iterations results in no significant change in the log-likelihood value.

```
Converged log-likelihood: -1.4987505566235169

Number of iterations: 8
```

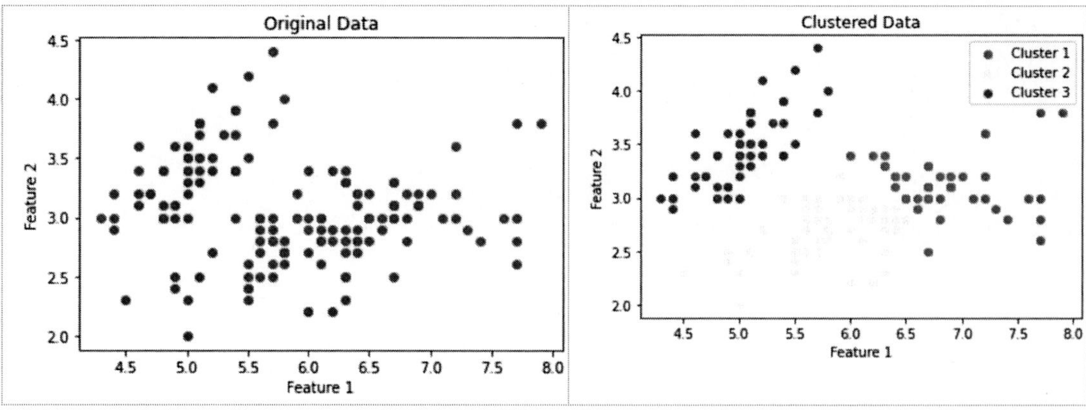

GMMs and the EM algorithm together form a robust framework for clustering and density estimation. GMM's ability to handle overlapping clusters through soft clustering, combined with the EM algorithm's iterative parameter optimisation, makes this approach particularly powerful for analysing complex datasets.

PART SIX

DAY NINETEEN

Unit 6 - Lesson Eight

Mean-Shift Clustering

Mean-shift clustering is one such algorithm that has gained popularity due to its ability to discover clusters without the need for prior knowledge of the number of clusters.

Akshaya asked, "What is Mean-Shift Clustering?"

Master said, "Mean-shift clustering is an unsupervised machine learning algorithm used to identify clusters within a dataset. It is a density-based clustering method that focuses on finding regions of high data point density and iteratively shifting data points towards the areas with the highest density. This process continues until convergence, meaning that the points move to the densest part of the cluster, hence the name 'mean-shift.'"

The key advantage of mean-shift clustering is that it does not require any prior information about the number of clusters in the data. This characteristic makes it particularly useful for exploratory data analysis, where the inherent structure of the data is unknown. By automatically discovering the number of clusters, mean-shift clustering can reveal insights and patterns in the data that might not be apparent with methods requiring predefined cluster numbers.

How Does Mean-Shift Clustering Work?

Mean-shift clustering operates through three main steps:

Kernel Density Estimation:

The first step involves estimating the underlying probability density function (PDF) of the data points using kernel density estimation. In this method, each data point is represented by a kernel function, such as a Gaussian kernel, centred at that point. The kernel function determines the weight assigned to each data point in the density estimation process, thereby creating a smooth estimate of the data's density distribution.

Shifting Data Points:

In the second step, the algorithm iteratively shifts each data point towards regions of higher density. This shift is directed by the mean shift vector, which is calculated for each data point. The mean shift vector indicates the direction and magnitude of the shift and is computed as the weighted average of the differences between the data point and its neighbouring points. The weights are determined by the kernel function.

Convergence and Cluster Identification:

The algorithm continues to shift the data points until convergence is reached, which occurs when the mean shift vectors become very small or negligible. At this stage, data points have moved to the points of maximum density, indicating the cluster centres. Once convergence is achieved, each data point is assigned to the nearest cluster centre, thereby identifying and forming clusters within the dataset. This process allows mean-shift clustering to effectively discover the intrinsic cluster structure in the data without prior knowledge of the number of clusters, making it a powerful tool for exploratory data analysis.

Example:

The code clusters the Iris dataset using the MeanShift algorithm and visualizes the resulting clusters through 2D and 3D plots, highlighting the clusters and their centers.

Example P6 – U6 – D18

Mean-Shift Clustering

```
# Importing the necessary libraries
from sklearn.cluster import MeanShift
from sklearn.datasets import load_iris
import matplotlib.pyplot as plt
import numpy as np
from mpl_toolkits.mplot3d import Axes3D
from scipy.stats import kde

# Loading the Iris dataset
iris = load_iris()
X = iris.data

# Creating an instance of MeanShift clustering
ms = MeanShift()
# Fitting the model to the data
ms.fit(X)
```

```
# Extracting the cluster labels and cluster centers
labels = ms.labels_
centers = ms.cluster_centers_

# Visualizing the clusters with scatter plot
plt.figure(figsize=(12, 5))

# 2D Contour Plot
plt.subplot(1, 2, 1)
x = X[:, 0]
y = X[:, 1]

# Perform kernel density estimation
k = kde.gaussian_kde([x, y])
xi, yi = np.mgrid[x.min():x.max():100j, y.min():y.max():100j]
zi = k(np.vstack([xi.flatten(), yi.flatten()]))

plt.scatter(x, y, c=labels, cmap='viridis')
plt.contour(xi, yi, zi.reshape(xi.shape), colors='k', linewidths=0.5)
plt.scatter(centers[:, 0], centers[:, 1], marker='x', color='red', s=200)
plt.xlabel('Sepal Length')
plt.ylabel('Sepal Width')
plt.title('Mean-Shift Clustering on Iris Dataset (2D Contour Plot)')

# 3D Surface Plot
ax = plt.subplot(1, 2, 2, projection='3d')
x = X[:, 0]
y = X[:, 1]
z = X[:, 2]

# Perform kernel density estimation in 3D
k = kde.gaussian_kde([x, y, z])
xi, yi, zi = np.mgrid[x.min():x.max():30j, y.min():y.max():30j, z.min():z.max():30j]
positions = np.vstack([xi.ravel(), yi.ravel(), zi.ravel()])
values = k(positions).reshape(xi.shape)

# Using plot_trisurf for 3D plotting
ax.plot_trisurf(x, y, z, cmap='viridis', alpha=0.6)
ax.scatter(X[:, 0], X[:, 1], X[:, 2], c=labels, cmap='viridis')
ax.scatter(centers[:, 0], centers[:, 1], centers[:, 2], marker='x', color='red', s=200)
ax.set_xlabel('Sepal Length')
ax.set_ylabel('Sepal Width')
ax.set_zlabel('Petal Length')
ax.set_title('Mean-Shift Clustering on Iris Dataset (3D Surface Plot)')

plt.tight_layout()
plt.show()
```

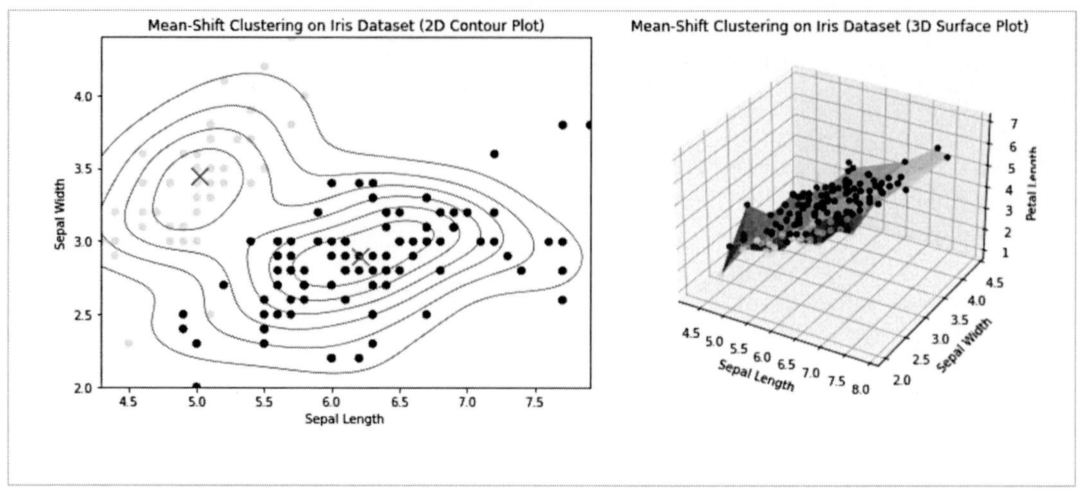

Summary:

In this unit, we explored various unsupervised learning techniques, focusing primarily on clustering algorithms and dimensionality reduction methods. We began with clustering, covering algorithms like K-Means, the elbow method for determining the optimal number of clusters, and Mini-batch K-Means for large datasets. We also delved into hierarchical clustering, discussing its types, including Hierarchical Agglomerative Clustering and BIRCH.

Dimensionality reduction techniques were another key focus. We covered Principal Component Analysis (PCA), its variants, and Singular Value Decomposition (SVD). We explored how these techniques help in reducing the dimensionality of data while retaining essential features and discussed advanced methods like Incremental PCA and Randomized Singular Value Decomposition.

Additionally, we examined t-SNE for visualization, DBSCAN for density-based clustering, and evaluation metrics, such as the Silhouette Score and Adjusted Rand Index (ARI) for assessing clustering performance. We also introduced advanced clustering methods like OPTICS, Spectral Clustering, Gaussian Mixture Models (GMM), and Mean-shift clustering.

These topics provide a comprehensive understanding of unsupervised learning techniques, equipping us with the tools to analyse and interpret complex datasets effectively.

What Next:

This unit delves into essential data mining techniques, focusing on association rule learning and matrix factorization. We will begin with association rule learning, which uncovers relationships and patterns within datasets using metrics like support, confidence, and lift. Key algorithms such as Apriori and ECLAT will be discussed, along with their limitations and the introduction of the FP-Growth algorithm as an improvement. The unit will then shift to matrix factorization techniques, which help uncover latent features in data. This includes an introduction to recommender systems, explaining collaborative filtering, content-based filtering, and hybrid methods. We will also focus on using matrix factorization techniques such as SVD and NMF to enhance recommendation accuracy in recommender systems.

P6-U6-L1-8 - Practice Question

1. What is the main objective of clustering in unsupervised learning?
2. Which method is used to determine the optimal number of clusters in K-Means clustering?
3. What is Mini-batch K-Means?
4. What are the two main types of hierarchical clustering?
5. What does BIRCH stand for in clustering?
6. What is the purpose of Principal Component Analysis (PCA)?
7. What does Singular Value Decomposition (SVD) do?
8. What is t-SNE commonly used for?
9. How does DBSCAN differ from K-Means?
10. What is the Silhouette Score used for?
11. What does the Adjusted Rand Index (ARI) measure?
12. What is the main advantage of OPTICS over DBSCAN?
13. What is Spectral Clustering based on?
14. What does a Gaussian Mixture Model (GMM) assume about the data?
15. What is the key idea behind Mean-shift clustering?

PART SEVEN

Machine Learning Models - Unsupervised

Association

"Association rule mining doesn't speak in absolutes—it listens to the quiet rhythms of co-occurrence, revealing truths not by logic, but by likelihood woven through repetition."

– Shree Shambav

PART SEVEN

DAY TWENTY

Unit 7 - Lesson One

Association rule

"Association is the art of unveiling hidden patterns within vast expanses of data, transforming the mundane into insights that illuminate the intricate web of relationships, driving informed decisions and innovations."
– Shree Shambav

Association Rule Mining

Master said, "Association Rule Mining is an unsupervised, non-linear algorithm used to uncover relationships between items in a dataset. It is particularly useful for identifying items that frequently appear together in transactions or relations. This technique is widely employed by retailers, grocery stores, and online marketplaces that maintain large transactional databases. For example, recommendation engines on e-commerce and social media platforms use association rule mining to predict what items you might buy next based on past customer data. When you see product recommendations at checkout, it's often the result of association rule mining applied to historical transaction data."

Key Metrics in Association Rule Mining:

Support:

Definition: Measures the popularity of an itemset by calculating the proportion of transactions in which the itemset appears.

Formula:

Support = Number of transactions containing X / Total number of transactions

Confidence:

Definition: Indicates the likelihood of item Y being purchased when item X is purchased, expressed as {X -> Y}.

Formula:

$$\text{Confidence}(X \rightarrow Y) = \text{Support}(X \cup Y) \ / \ \text{Support}(X)$$

Lift:

Definition: Measures how likely item Y is purchased when item X is purchased, while controlling for the overall popularity of item Y.

Formula:

$$\text{Lift}(X \rightarrow Y) = \text{Confidence}(X \rightarrow Y) \ / \ \text{Support}(Y)$$

Interpretation: A lift value greater than 1 indicates a positive association between X and Y, while a value less than 1 indicates a negative association.

Sam asked, "How Does Association Rule Learning Work?"

Master said, "Association rule learning is a machine learning method that identifies interesting relationships or associations between items within large datasets. This approach is primarily used in data mining and business intelligence to uncover relationships, associations, and dependencies between different sets of items."

Here's a comprehensive explanation of how association rule learning works:

Input Data:

Association rule learning starts with a dataset comprising various transactions or instances and items. Each transaction can be likened to a supermarket basket containing a set of items. The algorithm seeks to identify rules about how these items are arranged or co-occur within the transactions.

Association Rule Mining:

In association rule mining, Support, Confidence, and Lift are essential metrics for measuring the strength and importance of associations between items.

- Support: Shows how frequently an itemset appears in the dataset.
- Confidence: Reflect the likelihood of one item being present when another item is present.
- Lift: Evaluate the strength of an association by considering the co-occurrence of items relative to their frequencies.

Apriori Algorithm:

Master said, "One of the most popular algorithms used for association rule learning is the Apriori algorithm. It operates in several iterative steps, starting with finding frequently occurring items and progressively building more complex patterns from these frequent items."

Frequent Itemset Generation:

- Initial Detection: The algorithm first identifies frequent itemsets that meet a specified minimum support threshold. It discards infrequent itemsets and focuses only on those that appear frequently in the dataset.
- Iteration: In subsequent iterations, the algorithm generates larger itemsets from the frequent itemsets of the previous step, ensuring they meet the support threshold.

Rule Generation:

From the frequent itemsets, the algorithm then generates association rules. These rules are typically expressed in an "If-Then" format, revealing relationships between itemsets. For example, if a certain item appears in a transaction, the rule might state that another specific item is also likely to appear.

Evaluation and Pruning:

- Evaluation: The generated rules are evaluated using the confidence metric. Rules with confidence below a specified threshold are considered less reliable.
- Pruning: This process eliminates less meaningful rules, ensuring that only the most significant and beneficial associations are retained.

Interpretation and Application:

After the rules are generated and pruned, they are analysed by data analysts or domain experts. These rules provide valuable insights into the interactions between items, aiding in decision-making processes across various domains, such as market basket analysis, inventory management, and recommendation systems.

Summary:

Association rule learning efficiently discovers interesting associations within large datasets by utilising metrics like support and confidence. The Apriori algorithm plays a crucial role in identifying frequent itemsets and generating meaningful rules, which are then evaluated, pruned, and interpreted to provide actionable insights.

Types of Association Rules in Data Mining

Master explained that in data mining, association rules are essential for discovering relationships and patterns within large datasets.

There are typically four different types of association rules:

- Multi-Relational Association Rules
- Generalized Association Rules
- Interval Information Association Rules
- Quantitative Association Rules

Multi-Relational Association Rules

Also known as MRAR, multi-relational association rules represent a new class of association rules derived from multi-relational databases. These rules involve multiple entities with different relationships, highlighting indirect relationships between entities. This approach is particularly useful when data spans multiple tables or sources, allowing for more complex pattern discovery that incorporates multiple types of relationships.

Generalized Association Rules

Generalized association rules are used to uncover interesting patterns that are often hidden within the data. Unlike standard association rules, these rules can generalize over multiple levels of a hierarchy or taxonomy. For example, in a supermarket dataset, a generalized rule might discover that “dairy products” are frequently bought with “bakery items,” without specifying particular items like “milk” or “bread.” This provides a higher-level understanding of associations.

Interval Information Association Rules

Interval information association rules focus on discovering relationships involving interval-based data. These rules are particularly useful in scenarios where data attributes are continuous and can be divided into intervals. For instance, they might reveal that customers aged 35-45 frequently buy certain products, providing insights that are not visible when data is considered in its raw, continuous form.

Quantitative Association Rules

Quantitative association rules differ from other types by incorporating numeric attributes. Unlike generalised association rules, which deal with categorical attributes, quantitative association rules involve at least one numeric attribute on either the left or right side of the rule. This allows for more detailed and specific insights, such as "customers who purchase more than 15 units of product A also tend to spend more than $120 on product B."

These different types of association rules provide a range of methods for uncovering patterns and relationships in data. By applying the appropriate type of association rule, data analysts can gain deeper insights into various kinds of data, whether it involves multiple relational databases, hierarchical structures, interval-based attributes, or numeric data. This flexibility makes association rule mining a powerful tool in data mining and business intelligence.

Association vs Clustering

Association rule learning and clustering are distinct data mining techniques with different objectives and methodologies.

Association Rule Learning

Purpose:

To find interesting relationships or associations among a set of items in large databases.

Methodology:

It identifies frequent itemsets (combinations of items) and generates rules from these itemsets that indicate the likelihood of co-occurrence.

Commonly used algorithms include Apriori, Eclat, and FP-Growth.

Output:

Association rules in the form of "If-Then" statements. For example, "If a customer buys bread, they are 80% likely to buy butter."

Measures of interest, such as support, confidence, and lift.

Applications:

Market basket analysis, recommendation systems, cross-selling strategies.

Clustering

Purpose:

To group a set of objects in such a way that objects in the same group (or cluster) are more similar to each other than to those in other groups.

Methodology:

It identifies the inherent groupings in the data based on distance or similarity measures.

Commonly used algorithms include K-Means, hierarchical clustering, DBSCAN, and Gaussian Mixture Models.

Output:

A set of clusters, each containing objects that are similar to each other.

Often visualized in plots or through cluster assignments for each data point.

Applications:

Customer segmentation, image segmentation, anomaly detection, document clustering.

Key Differences

- **Objective:** Association rule learning focuses on finding rules that predict the occurrence of an item based on the occurrences of other items, while clustering aims to find natural groupings in data.

- **Output Type:** Association rule learning outputs rules and their associated metrics, whereas clustering outputs clusters and their members.

- **Application:** Association rules are used to uncover patterns and relationships, while clustering is used to identify groups and structure within the data.

In summary, while both are data mining techniques, association rule learning and clustering serve different purposes and are used to uncover different types of patterns within data.

Algorithms for Association Rule Mining in Data Mining

Master said, "Association rule mining involves discovering interesting relationships between variables in large datasets."

Three main algorithms are commonly used for generating association rules:

- Apriori Algorithm
- Eclat Algorithm
- FP-Growth Algorithm

Apriori Algorithm

The Apriori algorithm is one of the most popular and foundational algorithms for association rule mining. It operates on the principle that any subset of a frequent itemset must also be frequent. Here's how it works:

- Identification of Frequent Items: The algorithm starts by identifying individual items that meet a minimum support threshold.
- Expansion to Larger Itemsets: It then expands these items into larger itemsets by combining them and checking if they appear frequently enough in the database.
- Pruning: Itemsets that do not meet the minimum support threshold are pruned, ensuring that only frequent itemsets are expanded in subsequent iterations.

Eclat Algorithm

The Eclat algorithm (Equivalence Class Clustering and bottom-up Lattice Traversal) is an alternative to the Apriori algorithm. It is known for being more efficient in certain contexts. Here's a brief overview:

- Tidsets (Transaction ID Sets): Instead of using a horizontal data layout like Apriori, Eclat uses a vertical data layout where each item is associated with a list of transaction IDs (tidsets) where it appears.
- Recursive Intersection: The algorithm recursively intersects these tidsets to generate frequent itemsets.
- Efficiency: By working with tidsets, Eclat can often be more efficient, especially in cases with a dense dataset, as it avoids the combinatorial explosion of candidate generation that occurs in Apriori.

FP-Growth Algorithm

The FP-Growth (Frequent Pattern Growth) algorithm is another powerful tool for association rule mining. It avoids the candidate generation process altogether, making it particularly efficient:

- FP-Tree Construction: The algorithm begins by constructing an FP-tree (Frequent Pattern tree) from the dataset, which compresses the data while maintaining the itemset association information.
- Pattern Extraction: It then recursively extracts frequent itemsets directly from the FP-tree.
- Efficiency: FP-Growth is highly efficient for large datasets and is particularly well-suited for scenarios where the dataset contains many frequent patterns.

Apriori, Eclat, and FP-Growth - each have their strengths and are suited to different types of data and scenarios:

- **Apriori:** Best for understanding the foundational principles of association rule mining, and it works well with smaller datasets or datasets where candidate generation is manageable.
- **Eclat:** More efficient than Apriori in dense datasets due to its vertical data layout and use of tidsets.
- **FP-Growth:** Highly efficient for large datasets and frequent pattern discovery, as it avoids candidate generation through its use of the FP-tree structure.

By choosing the appropriate algorithm, data analysts can efficiently uncover meaningful associations and patterns in large datasets, aiding in data-driven decision-making processes.

PART SEVEN

DAY TWENTY

Unit 7 - Lesson Two

APRIORI

Apriori Algorithm:

Impulsive buying is a common phenomenon, and retailers leverage machine learning techniques like the Apriori algorithm to capitalise on it. Understanding the workings of the Apriori algorithm involves delving into market basket analysis and association rule mining.

Market basket analysis is a crucial technique utilised by retailers to uncover associations between items frequently bought together. By identifying such associations, retailers can optimise product placement strategies, thereby boosting revenue. For instance, if customers often purchase bread and butter together, retailers may target them with offers on complementary items like eggs, incentivizing additional purchases.

Consider a pizza shop offering combos comprising pizza, soft drinks, and breadsticks, often accompanied by discounts. This strategy capitalises on the association between these items, assuming that customers purchasing pizza are likely to also buy soft drinks and breadsticks. By simplifying the purchasing process and incentivizing bundled purchases, the shop enhances its sales performance.

These examples exemplify association rules in data mining, providing valuable insights into the workings of the Apriori algorithm. Through market basket analysis and association rule mining, retailers can optimise their marketing strategies and enhance customer engagement, ultimately driving revenue growth.

John asked, "What is Apriori algorithm?"

Master said, "The Apriori algorithm is a powerful tool used in mining frequent item sets and deriving relevant association rules from large transactional databases, such as customer purchases at a supermarket."

The Apriori algorithm, introduced by R. Agrawal and R. Srikant in 1994, is designed for discovering frequent itemsets in datasets to derive boolean association rules. Its name, "Apriori," stems from its utilization of prior knowledge regarding frequent itemset properties. This algorithm employs an iterative approach, known as level-wise search, wherein k-frequent itemsets are leveraged to uncover k+1 itemsets.

To enhance the efficiency of generating frequent itemsets in a level-wise manner, the Apriori algorithm capitalises on an essential property known as the Apriori property, which aids in reducing the search space.

Apriori Property: The Apriori property dictates that all non-empty subsets of a frequent itemset must also be frequent. Central to the Apriori algorithm is the anti-monotonicity of the support measure. Apriori operates under the assumption that frequent itemsets are composed of subsets that are also frequent, thereby streamlining the process of identifying frequent itemsets.

Key Components of the Apriori Algorithm:

Support: Support measures the default popularity of a product. It is calculated as the ratio of the number of transactions containing a specific product to the total number of transactions in the dataset.

For instance, if there are 500 transactions containing bread out of 5000 total transactions, the support for bread would be 10%.

Support (Bread) = (Transactions relating Bread) / (Total transactions) = 500/5000 =10%

Confidence: Confidence represents the likelihood that customers purchase both bread and butter together. It is computed by dividing the number of transactions containing both items by the total number of transactions involving breads.

For example, if 250 out of 500 transactions containing breads also include butter, the confidence for this association would be 50%.

Confidence = (Transactions relating both Bread and Butter) / (Total transactions involving Bread) = 250/500=50%

Lift: Lift measures the increase in the ratio of butter sales when breads are sold. Mathematically, it is the ratio of the confidence of the association (breads and butter) to the support of the antecedent (bread).

A lift value greater than one indicates that the probability of customers buying both items together is higher than expected, making it a favourable combination. Conversely, a lift value below one suggests that the association is less likely.

Lift = (Confidence (Bread - Butter)/ (Support (Bread) = 50/10 = 5

For instance, if the lift value for the association between bread and butter is 5, it implies that customers are five times more likely to purchase butter when they buy bread compared to purchasing bread alone. Higher lift values indicate stronger associations between items.

Apeksha asked, "What is the operational mechanism of the Apriori Algorithm in Data Mining?"

Master said, "Association Mining, often referred to as Frequent Mining, involves identifying frequent items in a dataset to uncover associations and correlations between item sets in transactional and relational databases. Essentially, it reveals which items frequently co-occur in transactions or relationships."

The primary objective of Frequent Mining is to generate association rules from transactional datasets. For instance, if items X and Y are frequently purchased together, it suggests an opportunity to optimize store layouts or offer discounts to increase sales.

For example, if customers often buy milk and bread together, an association rule such as ['milk'] => ['bread'] implies that they are likely to purchase butter as well.

[Milk]^[Bread] -> [Butter]

Leveraging such associations, sellers can strategically recommend complementary items to customers, thereby boosting sales.

Support(A -> B) = Support_count(A ∪ B)

Confidence(A -> B) = Support_count(A ∪ B) / Support_count(A)

To comprehend the Apriori algorithm, let's walk through an example with mathematical calculations:

Example:

Consider a dataset comprising various transactions. Using the Apriori algorithm, we aim to identify frequent itemsets and generate association rules. Given Minimum Support = 2 and Minimum Confidence = 50%.

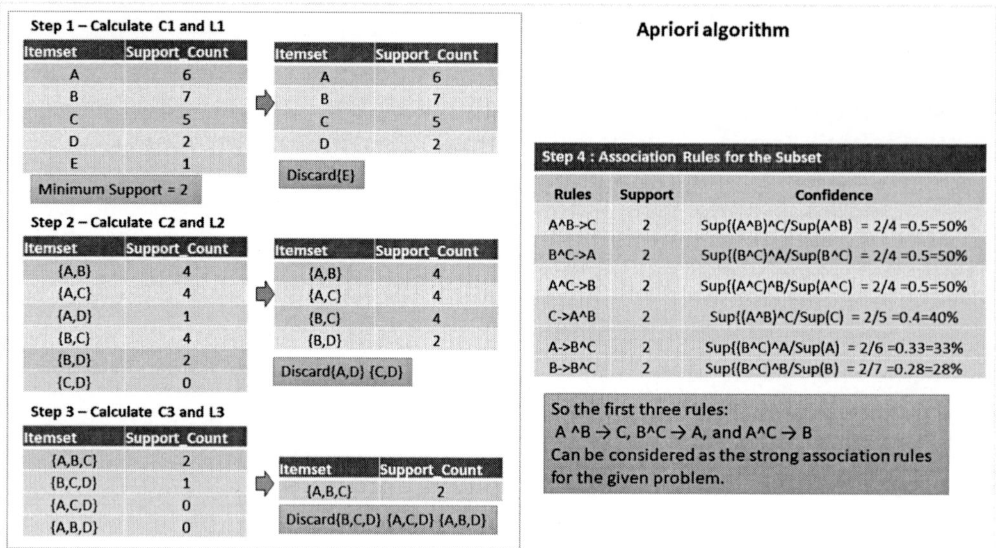

Apriori algorithm

Step 1 – Calculate C1 and L1

Itemset	Support_Count
A	6
B	7
C	5
D	2
E	1

Minimum Support = 2

Itemset	Support_Count
A	6
B	7
C	5
D	2

Discard{E}

Step 2 – Calculate C2 and L2

Itemset	Support_Count
{A,B}	4
{A,C}	4
{A,D}	1
{B,C}	4
{B,D}	2
{C,D}	0

Itemset	Support_Count
{A,B}	4
{A,C}	4
{B,C}	4
{B,D}	2

Discard{A,D} {C,D}

Step 3 – Calculate C3 and L3

Itemset	Support_Count
{A,B,C}	2
{B,C,D}	1
{A,C,D}	0
{A,B,D}	0

Itemset	Support_Count
{A,B,C}	2

Discard{B,C,D} {A,C,D} {A,B,D}

Step 4 : Association Rules for the Subset

Rules	Support	Confidence
A^B->C	2	Sup{(A^B)^C/Sup(A^B) = 2/4 =0.5=50%
B^C->A	2	Sup{(B^C)^A/Sup(B^C) = 2/4 =0.5=50%
A^C->B	2	Sup{(A^C)^B/Sup(A^C) = 2/4 =0.5=50%
C->A^B	2	Sup{(A^B)^C/Sup(C) = 2/5 =0.4=40%
A->B^C	2	Sup{(B^C)^A/Sup(A) = 2/6 =0.33=33%
B->B^C	2	Sup{(B^C)^B/Sup(B) = 2/7 =0.28=28%

So the first three rules:
A ^B → C, B^C → A, and A^C → B
Can be considered as the strong association rules for the given problem.

Step 1: Calculating C1 and L1:

Firstly, we construct a table, known as the Candidate set or C1, displaying the support count (frequency) of each itemset in the dataset. Next, we filter out itemsets with a support count greater than the Minimum Support (2), forming the table for frequent itemset L1. Since all itemsets meet or exceed the minimum support, except for E, the E itemset will be excluded or Discard{E}.

This process establishes the foundation for subsequent steps in the Apriori algorithm, where we iteratively generate candidate itemsets and prune those that do not meet the minimum support threshold.

Step 2: Candidate Generation C2 and L2:

In this step, we proceed to generate C2 using the frequent itemset L1. C2 consists of pairs of itemsets from L1 in the form of subsets.

Subsequently, we determine the support count of these pairs by examining the main transaction table of the dataset, indicating how frequently these pairs occur together.

Next, we compare the support count of C2 with the minimum support count, eliminating itemsets with insufficient support from the C2 table. This process yields the table for L2, containing itemsets that meet the minimum support threshold.

Step 3: Candidate Generation C3 and L3:

In this step, we extend the process to generate C3 by forming subsets of three itemsets from the frequent itemset L2. The support count of these triplets is calculated from the dataset.

Subsequently, we create the L3 table. From the generated C3 table, we observe that only one combination of itemsets meets the minimum support count requirement. Therefore, the L3 table contains only one combination, namely {A, B, C}.

Step 4: Finding Association Rules for the Subsets:

To generate association rules, we begin by creating a new table containing possible rules derived from the combination {A, B, C}. For each rule, we calculate the confidence using the formula sup(A ^ B) / sup(A). After computing the confidence value for each rule, we exclude those with confidence lower than the minimum threshold (50%).

Given the minimum confidence threshold of 50%, the following rules can be considered strong association rules for the problem at hand: **A ^ B → C, B ^ C → A, and A ^ C → B.**

Other Key Terminologies:

Association rule mining: Association rule mining is a data mining technique aimed at identifying associations or relationships between items in a dataset.

Frequent itemsets: Frequent itemsets are sets of items that co-occur together in a dataset with a frequency greater than or equal to a specified threshold.

Apriori principle: The Apriori principle is a fundamental property of frequent itemsets, stating that any subset of a frequent itemset must also be frequent.

Apriori algorithm: The Apriori algorithm is an iterative algorithm utilized for mining frequent itemsets and association rules from a dataset.

Candidate itemsets: Candidate itemsets are sets of items generated during the execution of the Apriori algorithm by combining frequent itemsets.

Pruning: Pruning is the process of removing infrequent itemsets or association rules to reduce the size of the search space and enhance the efficiency of the Apriori algorithm.

Minimum support threshold: The minimum support threshold is the minimum frequency of occurrence required for an itemset to be considered frequent in the context of the Apriori algorithm.

Improving the efficiency of the Apriori algorithm involves employing several techniques aimed at optimising its performance. Here are two key methods:

Hash-based Itemset Counting:

- This method involves the utilisation of hashing to efficiently count itemsets.
- By hashing itemsets and maintaining counts in corresponding buckets, the algorithm can quickly identify infrequent itemsets.
- In practice, if the count of a k-itemset's hashing bucket falls below a predefined threshold, it can be excluded from further consideration as it is deemed infrequent.
- This approach helps reduce the computational burden by eliminating the need to explore infrequent itemsets.

Transaction Reduction:

- Transaction reduction is a strategy to minimise the number of transactions that need to be scanned repeatedly.
- If a transaction does not contain any frequent itemset, it is considered non-valuable for subsequent scans.
- By removing such transactions from further consideration, the algorithm can focus its efforts on relevant transactions that contain potentially frequent itemsets.
- This reduces the overall computational complexity and speeds up the execution of the algorithm by avoiding unnecessary scans of irrelevant transactions.

Most Commonly Used Algorithms:

Apriori Algorithm: The Apriori algorithm is a foundational algorithm in association rule mining, utilised to discover frequent itemsets in a dataset.

FP-growth (Frequent Pattern Growth): FP-growth is an alternative to Apriori, employing a more efficient method for searching frequent itemsets. It constructs a compact data structure called a frequent pattern tree to expedite the mining process.

Eclat (Equivalence Class Transformation): Eclat, akin to Apriori, efficiently mines frequent itemsets but utilises a vertical database representation. This representation simplifies the process by focusing on the intersection of transactions containing individual items.

Mahout: Mahout is a machine-learning library featuring an implementation of the Apriori algorithm for frequent itemset mining. It provides scalable solutions for various machine-learning tasks, including association rule mining.

SPMF: SPMF is an open-source data mining library encompassing diverse implementations of frequent itemset mining algorithms. Alongside Apriori, it includes implementations of Eclat, FP-growth, and other algorithms, offering flexibility and choice to data miners and researchers.

PyFIM: Specifically designed for Python users, PyFIM offers implementations of several association rule mining algorithms, including Apriori, Eclat, and FP-growth. It facilitates efficient exploration and analysis of datasets within the Python ecosystem.

Weka: Renowned as a popular data mining software, Weka incorporates implementations of several association rule mining algorithms, including Apriori and FP-growth. It provides a user-friendly interface for seamless exploration and experimentation with association rule mining techniques.

Application across Industries:

Food Industry: In the food industry, the Apriori algorithm is employed to analyse customer purchase behaviour, enabling personalised product recommendations and menu suggestions.

Travel Industry: In the travel sector, the Apriori algorithm is utilised to examine customer booking histories, providing tailored recommendations for travel destinations, hotels, and flight options.

Social Media Industry: The Apriori algorithm finds application in social media platforms for analysing user behaviour, preferences, and interests, facilitating personalised content delivery and targeted advertisements.

Insurance Industry: Within the insurance domain, the Apriori algorithm is instrumental in identifying fraud patterns in insurance claims, thereby mitigating the risk of fraudulent activities.

Banking Industry: In banking, the Apriori algorithm is deployed to analyse transaction data and detect patterns indicative of fraudulent transactions, enhancing security measures.

Telecommunications Industry: The telecommunications sector utilises the Apriori algorithm to analyse call data records (CDRs), identifying usage patterns and optimising network performance.

Healthcare Industry: In healthcare, the Apriori algorithm is applied for disease analysis and pattern recognition in medical data, aiding in treatment effectiveness assessment and medical decision-making.

E-commerce Industry: Within e-commerce, the Apriori algorithm is leveraged to analyse customer purchase histories, recommend products, and deliver personalised product suggestions to customers.

Retail Industry: Retailers extensively use the Apriori algorithm for market basket analysis, gaining insights into customer purchasing behaviours and facilitating targeted product recommendations to enhance sales performance.

The purpose of this code is to perform association rule mining on a dataset of transactions using the Apriori algorithm. Association rule mining is a technique used to discover interesting relationships, patterns, or associations among a set of items in large databases. This method is widely used in market basket analysis to identify items that frequently co-occur in transactions.

<table>
<tr><th>Exercise P7-U7 - D1</th><th></th></tr>
<tr><td>Association Rule - Apriori Algorithm</td><td>Output</td></tr>
<tr><td>import numpy as np
import pandas as pd
from apyori import apriori

# Step 1: Loading the data
input_path = r'C:\Users\User\mraj4\Documents\Optimum\Py-lib\scikit\store_data.csv'
store_data = pd.read_csv(input_path, header=None)

# Displaying the first few rows of the dataset
print(store_data.head())
print("Shape of the dataset:", store_data.shape)

# Extracting transactions from the dataset
transactions = []
for i in range(len(store_data)):
   transactions.append([str(store_data.values[i, j]) for j in range(store_data.shape[1])])

# Applying Apriori algorithm
association_rules = apriori(transactions, min_support=0.0045, min_confidence=0.2, min_lift=3, min_length=2)
association_results = list(association_rules)

print("Number of association rules derived:", len(association_results))

# Displaying the association rules
for item in association_results:
   pair = item[0] # Base and add items
   items = [x for x in pair]</td><td>Shape of the dataset: (7501, 20)
Number of association rules derived: 48

Rule: light cream -> chicken
Support: 0.004532728969470737
Confidence: 0.29059829059829057
Lift: 4.84395061728395
****
Rule: escalope -> mushroom cream sauce
Support: 0.005732568990801226
Confidence: 0.3006993006993007
Lift: 3.790832696715049
****
Rule: escalope -> pasta
Support: 0.005865884548726837
Confidence: 0.3728813559322034
Lift: 4.700811850163794
******************</td></tr>
</table>

```
    print(f"Rule: {items[0]} -> {items[1]}")
    print(f"Support: {item[1]}")
    print(f"Confidence: {item[2][0][2]}")
    print(f"Lift: {item[2][0][3]}")
    print("****************************")
```

The provided Python code demonstrates the use of the Apriori algorithm to discover strong association rules from a given dataset. Here's a brief overview of the code:

Loading the Data: The code begins by loading the dataset from a specified file path using Pandas. The dataset is assumed to be in CSV format and is read into a Pandas DataFrame.

Data Preprocessing: Next, the code prepares the dataset for association rule mining. It extracts transactions from the DataFrame, where each transaction represents a set of items bought together.

Apriori Algorithm: The apriori function from the apyori library is applied to the transactions to generate association rules. Parameters such as minimum support, minimum confidence, minimum lift, and minimum length of itemsets are specified to filter out weak rules and focus on strong associations.

Printing Association Rules: The code iterates through the list of association rules generated by the Apriori algorithm. For each rule, it extracts the antecedent and consequent items, as well as their support, confidence, and lift values. Only rules with a length greater than 1 (i.e., containing both antecedent and consequent) are considered to be strong association rules.

Displaying Results: The code prints out the strong association rules along with their corresponding support, confidence, and lift values. Each rule is printed in a readable format, providing insights into the relationships between different items in the dataset.

The initial rule, "Light cream → chicken," indicates that light cream and chicken are frequently purchased together by a significant portion of customers. The support for this rule is 0.0045, suggesting that it occurs in approximately 0.45% of all transactions. Additionally, the confidence level associated with this rule is 29%, implying that if a customer buys light cream, there is a 29% likelihood that they will also purchase chicken. Thus, this association rule is indicative of a moderately strong relationship between these two items in the dataset.

Practical Applications

- Market Basket Analysis: Retailers can use this code to analyse transaction data to understand which products are often bought together, enabling them to optimise product placement, cross-sell, and up-sell strategies.
- Recommendation Systems: E-commerce platforms can use the discovered association

rules to recommend products to customers based on their purchase history.

- Customer Insights: Helps businesses understand customer behaviour and preferences, allowing for more targeted marketing and personalised experiences.

PART SEVEN

DAY TWENTY

Unit 7 - Lesson Three

ECLAT

Master said, "The ECLAT algorithm is a data mining algorithm specifically designed to discover frequent items. Unlike some association rule mining algorithms that operate on horizontal data formats, ECLAT exclusively utilises a vertical data format for generating frequent itemsets. This vertical approach contributes to its efficiency, making it faster compared to algorithms like Apriori."

In essence, ECLAT cannot directly handle horizontal databases. Thus, if the dataset is in a horizontal format, it needs to be transformed into a vertical format before applying the ECLAT algorithm. These characteristics underscore the importance of data preprocessing in ensuring compatibility with the algorithm's requirements.

Horizontal

TID	Items
T1	Bread, Butter, Jam
T2	Butter, Coke
T3	Butter, Milk
T4	Bread, Butter, Coke

Vertical

TID	Items
Bread	{T1, T4}
Butter	{T1, T2, T3, T4}
Milk	{T3}
Coke	{T2, T4}
Jam	{T1}

The ECLAT (Equivalence Class Clustering and bottom-up Lattice Traversal) algorithm is a popular method for association rule mining. It is recognized as a more efficient and scalable alternative to the Apriori algorithm. Unlike the Apriori algorithm, which operates in a horizontal manner similar to Breadth-First Search (BFS) in graph theory, the ECLAT algorithm adopts a vertical approach akin to Depth-First Search (DFS). This vertical methodology enhances the speed and performance of the ECLAT algorithm compared to the Apriori algorithm.

> Note: *For a comprehensive exploration of Breadth-First Search (BFS) and Depth-First Search (DFS), delve into the Shree Shambav series: "OPTIMUM - Python Series II - Exploring Data Structures and Algorithms."*

ECLAT Algorithm:

Akshatha asked, "How does the ECLAT algorithm work?"

Master said, "The fundamental concept of the ECLAT algorithm involves the use of Transaction ID Sets (tidsets) intersections to compute the support value of candidate itemsets, thereby eliminating the need to generate subsets that do not exist in the prefix tree."

Here is a step-by-step explanation of how the algorithm works:

Initial Setup:

In the initial step, the algorithm considers all single items in the dataset along with their corresponding tidsets (sets of transaction IDs where each item appears).

Recursive Function Calls:

The algorithm then enters a recursive process. In each recursive call, the current item-tidset pairs are examined and combined with other item-tidset pairs to form larger candidate itemsets.

Intersection of Tidsets:

For each combination of item-tidset pairs, the intersection of their tidsets is computed to determine the support value of the resulting candidate itemset.

Pruning:

Candidate itemsets that do not meet the minimum support threshold are pruned, meaning they are discarded from further consideration.

Continuation of Process:

This process of combining item-tidset pairs and computing intersections continues recursively until no further combinations are possible, indicating that no more frequent itemsets can be generated.

Example Illustration

To better understand the ECLAT algorithm, let's consider a simple example:

Initial Tidsets:

Suppose we have a dataset with transactions and items as follows

```
T1: {A, B, C}

T2: {A, B}

T3: {A, C}

T4: {B, C}

T5: {A, B, C}
```

The initial tidsets for each item are:

```
A: {T1, T2, T3, T5}

B: {T1, T2, T4, T5}

C: {T1, T3, T4, T5}
```

First Recursive Call:

Combine item A with items B and C

```
{A, B}: {T1, T2, T5} (Intersection of {T1, T2, T3, T5} and {T1, T2, T4, T5})
```

{A, C}: {T1, T3, T5} (Intersection of {T1, T2, T3, T5} and {T1, T3, T4, T5})

Second Recursive Call:

Combine item pairs {A, B} and {A, C} with item C

{A, B, C}: {T1, T5} (Intersection of {T1, T2, T5} and {T1, T3, T5})

Result:

The frequent itemsets are {A}, {B}, {C}, {A, B}, {A, C}, and {A, B, C}, with their respective support values computed from the intersections of tidsets.

Let's illustrate the ECLAT algorithm using an example:

Mining Association Rules from Transaction Data

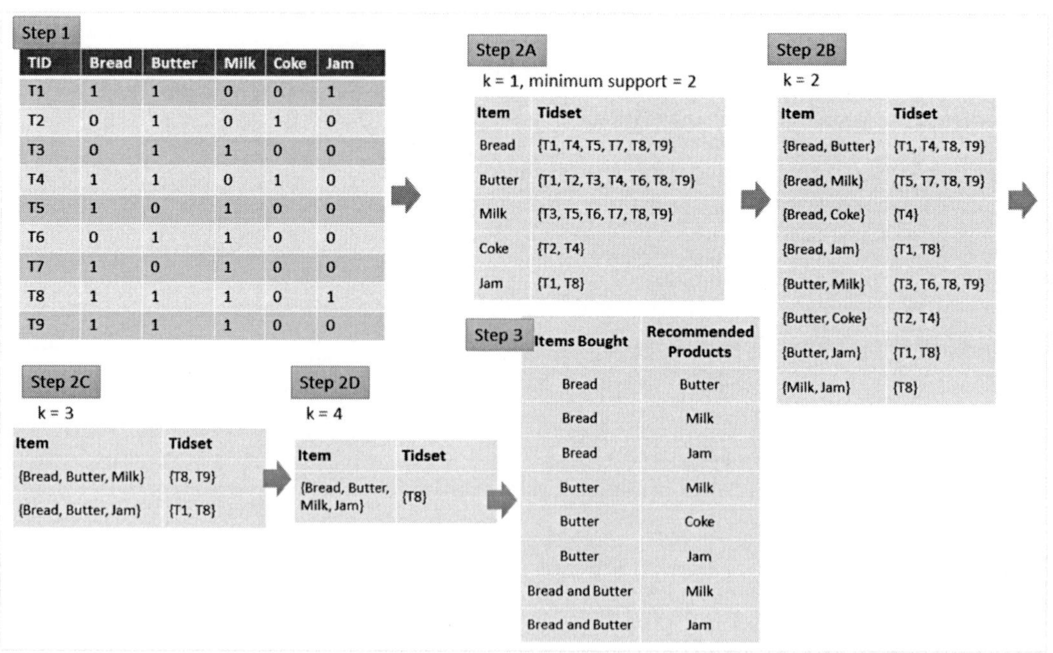

Step 1

TID	Bread	Butter	Milk	Coke	Jam
T1	1	1	0	0	1
T2	0	1	0	1	0
T3	0	1	1	0	0
T4	1	1	0	1	0
T5	1	0	1	0	0
T6	0	1	1	0	0
T7	1	0	1	0	0
T8	1	1	1	0	1
T9	1	1	1	0	0

Step 2A

k = 1, minimum support = 2

Item	Tidset
Bread	{T1, T4, T5, T7, T8, T9}
Butter	{T1, T2, T3, T4, T6, T8, T9}
Milk	{T3, T5, T6, T7, T8, T9}
Coke	{T2, T4}
Jam	{T1, T8}

Step 2B

k = 2

Item	Tidset
{Bread, Butter}	{T1, T4, T8, T9}
{Bread, Milk}	{T5, T7, T8, T9}
{Bread, Coke}	{T4}
{Bread, Jam}	{T1, T8}
{Butter, Milk}	{T3, T6, T8, T9}
{Butter, Coke}	{T2, T4}
{Butter, Jam}	{T1, T8}
{Milk, Jam}	{T8}

Step 2C

k = 3

Item	Tidset
{Bread, Butter, Milk}	{T8, T9}
{Bread, Butter, Jam}	{T1, T8}

Step 2D

k = 4

Item	Tidset
{Bread, Butter, Milk, Jam}	{T8}

Step 3

Items Bought	Recommended Products
Bread	Butter
Bread	Milk
Bread	Jam
Butter	Milk
Butter	Coke
Butter	Jam
Bread and Butter	Milk
Bread and Butter	Jam

Step 1: Data Representation

We have a dataset consisting of transactions and items, represented as a boolean matrix. Each cell (i, j) denotes whether the jth item is present in the ith transaction (1 for true, 0 for false).

Step 2A: Initial Setup

We start by organizing each item with its corresponding tidset (set of transaction IDs where the item appears) in a tabular format.

Step 2B: Recursive Function Calls

We recursively call the function to combine item-tidset pairs until no more pairs can be merged. We increment the value of k (the size of the itemset) at each recursive step.

Step 2C: Continuing Recursion

We continue the recursive process, gradually increasing the size of the itemsets (k), until no further combinations are possible.

Step 2D: Completion of Recursion

We stop the recursion process once we reach the specified maximum size of the itemset (e.g., k = 4) or when no more item-tidset pairs can be combined.

Step 3: Conclusion

Based on the minimum support threshold (e.g., support = 2), we derive association rules from the dataset.

This code implements the ECLAT (Equivalence Class Clustering and bottom-up Lattice Traversal) algorithm for mining frequent itemsets and generating association rules from a transactional dataset. The ECLAT algorithm is used for discovering patterns or associations between items in a dataset.

Example P7 – U7 – D2	
ECLAT	**Output**

import pandas as pd
 	
# Step 1: Loading the data 	
input_path =
r'C:\Users\User\mraj4\Documents\Optimum\Py-lib\scikit\store_data.csv'
store_data = pd.read_csv(input_path, header=None)
 	
# Displaying the first few rows of the dataset 	
print(store_data.head())
print("Shape of the dataset:", store_data.shape)
 	
# Extracting transactions from the dataset 	
transactions = []
for i in range(len(store_data)):
	Number of association rules derived: 28
	Rule: ['mushroom cream sauce'] -> ['escalope']
	Confidence:
	0.3006993006993007
	Lift: 3.790832696715049
	*****************************
	Rule: ['tomato sauce'] ->
	['ground beef']
	Confidence:
	0.37735849056603776
	Lift: 3.840659481324083 3

| ```
    transactions.append([str(store_data.values[i, j]) for j in range(store_data.shape[1])])

# Step 2: Convert transactions to vertical format (item -> transactions containing the item)
from collections import defaultdict

def create_vertical_format(transactions):
    vertical = defaultdict(set)
    for tid, transaction in enumerate(transactions):
        for item in transaction:
            if item != 'nan':  # Exclude NaN values
                vertical[item].add(tid)
    return vertical

vertical_format = create_vertical_format(transactions)

# Function to find frequent itemsets using ECLAT algorithm
def eclat(prefix, items, min_support):
    while items:
        item, tids = items.pop()
        support = len(tids)
        if support >= min_support:
            yield prefix + [item], support
            suffix = []
            for other_item, other_tids in items:
                new_tids = tids & other_tids
                if len(new_tids) >= min_support:
                    suffix.append((other_item, new_tids))
            yield from eclat(prefix + [item], suffix, min_support)

# Applying ECLAT algorithm
min_support_count = len(transactions) * 0.0045
frequent_itemsets = list(eclat([], list(vertical_format.items()), min_support_count))

# Displaying the frequent itemsets
print("Number of frequent itemsets derived:", len(frequent_itemsets))
for itemset, support in frequent_itemsets:
    print("Itemset:", itemset)
    print("Support:", support)
    print("****************************")

# Step 3: Generate association rules from frequent itemsets
``` | ```
****************************
Rule: ['herb & pepper'] -> ['ground beef']
Confidence: 0.32345013477088946
Lift: 3.291993841134928
****************************
Rule: ['herb & pepper', 'spaghetti'] -> ['ground beef']
Confidence: 0.39344262295081966
Lift: 4.004359721511666
****************************
``` |

```
def generate_association_rules(frequent_itemsets,
min_confidence, min_lift):
    rules = []
    for itemset, support in frequent_itemsets:
        if len(itemset) > 1:
            for i in range(len(itemset)):
                antecedent = itemset[:i] + itemset[i+1:]
                consequent = [itemset[i]]
                antecedent_support = next(sup for items, sup
in frequent_itemsets if items == antecedent)
                confidence = support / antecedent_support
                consequent_support = next(sup for items, sup
in frequent_itemsets if items == consequent)
                lift = confidence / (consequent_support /
len(transactions))
                if confidence >= min_confidence and lift >=
min_lift:
                    rules.append((antecedent, consequent,
confidence, lift))
    return rules

# Setting minimum confidence and lift
min_confidence = 0.2
min_lift = 3

association_rules =
generate_association_rules(frequent_itemsets,
min_confidence, min_lift)

# Displaying the association rules
print("Number of association rules derived:",
len(association_rules))
for antecedent, consequent, confidence, lift in
association_rules:
    print(f"Rule: {antecedent} -> {consequent}")
    print(f"Confidence: {confidence}")
    print(f"Lift: {lift}")
    print("******************************")
```

Advantages of the ECLAT Algorithm

- Efficiency: The vertical data representation and depth-first search approach make the ECLAT algorithm faster and more efficient than the Apriori algorithm, especially for dense datasets.
- Scalability: ECLAT can handle larger datasets more effectively by reducing the

number of candidates itemsets generated and evaluated.

- Simplified Pruning: By using tidset intersections, the algorithm can quickly prune non-frequent itemsets without generating unnecessary subsets.

The ECLAT algorithm's ability to efficiently mine frequent itemsets from large and complex datasets makes it a powerful tool in the field of association rule mining.

PART SEVEN

DAY TWENTY

Unit 7 - Lesson Four

FP-Growth

Akshaya asked, "What are the drawbacks of the Apriori algorithm, and how does the FP-Growth algorithm address them?"

Master explained that the Apriori algorithm, while foundational and widely used in association rule mining, has two primary drawbacks that affect its efficiency:

Frequent Candidate Set Generation:

- At each step, the algorithm generates candidate sets of frequent itemsets. This involves a combinatorial explosion of possibilities, especially as the size of the itemsets increases.
- Managing and processing these candidate sets requires significant computational resources.

Repeated Database Scans:

- To build and validate these candidate sets, the algorithm needs to repeatedly scan the entire database.
- This repeated scanning is time-consuming and adds to the computational burden, making the algorithm slower as the dataset grows larger.

Solution: Frequent Pattern Growth (FP-Growth) Algorithm

Master continued, "The FP-Growth algorithm was developed to address these inefficiencies. FP-Growth improves upon the Apriori algorithm by eliminating the need for candidate generation and reducing the number of database scans."

Here's how it works:

FP-Tree Construction:

- The FP-Growth algorithm starts by constructing an FP-tree (Frequent Pattern Tree) to store the database in a compressed form. The FP-tree is a Trie data structure that maintains the itemset association information.
- Each transaction in the database is mapped onto the FP-tree, where common prefixes are shared, leading to a more compact representation of the data.

Pattern Extraction:

- Instead of generating candidate sets, the FP-Growth algorithm directly mines the FP-tree to extract frequent itemsets.
- This is done through a recursive process that explores the tree to find frequent patterns, significantly reducing the computational overhead.

Let's understand the process using an example:

Step-by-Step Example

Step 1: Hypothetical Dataset

Assume we have a dataset of transactions, with each letter representing an item. For example:

- Transaction 1: {K, E, M, O, Y}
- Transaction 2: {K, E, O, Y}
- Transaction 3: {K, E, M}
- Transaction 4: {K, M, Y}
- Transaction 5: {K, E, O}

Step 2: Compute Frequency of Individual Items

Count the frequency of each item in all transactions:

- K: 5
- E: 4
- M: 3

- O: 3
- Y: 3

Step 3: Build a Frequent Pattern Set

Set a minimum support threshold of 3. Create a set containing items with frequencies ≥ 3, sorted in descending order of frequency:

L = {K, E, M, O, Y}

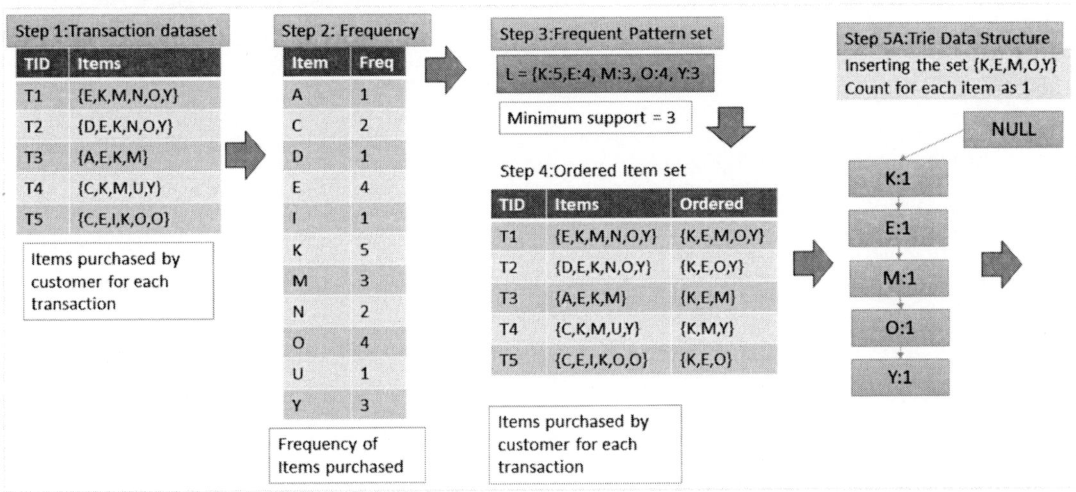

Step 4: Build Ordered-Item Sets

For each transaction, create an ordered-item set by retaining items that appear in the frequent pattern set, ordered by their frequency in L:

- Transaction 1: {K, E, M, O, Y}
- Transaction 2: {K, E, O, Y}
- Transaction 3: {K, E, M}
- Transaction 4: {K, M, Y}
- Transaction 5: {K, E, O}

Step 5: Insert Ordered-Item Sets into a Trie (FP-Tree)

Construct the FP-tree by inserting each ordered-item set:

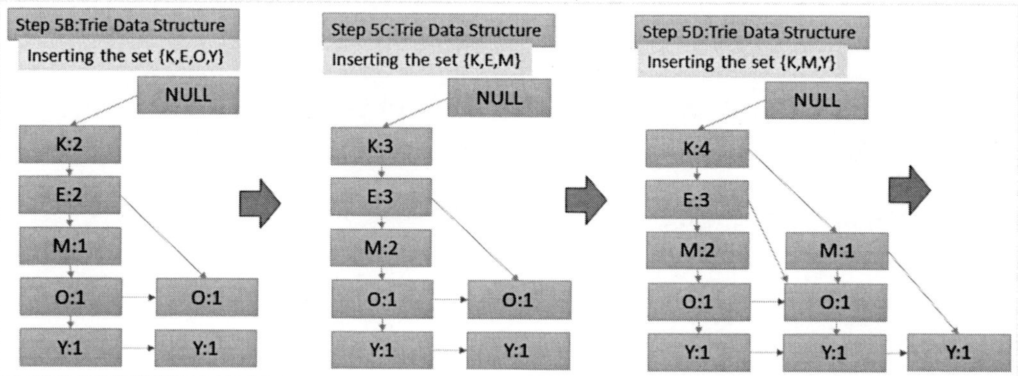

Insert {K, E, M, O, Y}:

- Link items in order: K → E → M → O → Y, with support count 1 for each.

Insert {K, E, O, Y}:

- Increase support count for K and E to 2.
- No direct link between E and O; create a new node for O and link to E.
- Add new node for Y and link to O.

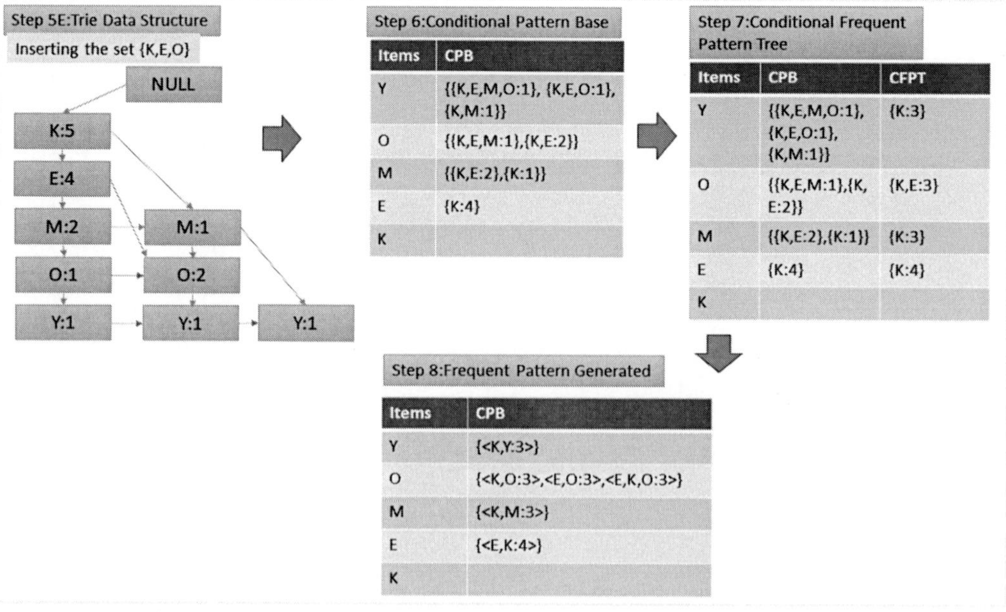

Step 6:Conditional Pattern Base

Items	CPB
Y	{{K,E,M,O:1}, {K,E,O:1}, {K,M:1}}
O	{{K,E,M:1},{K,E:2}}
M	{{K,E:2},{K:1}}
E	{K:4}
K	

Step 7:Conditional Frequent Pattern Tree

Items	CPB	CFPT
Y	{{K,E,M,O:1}, {K,E,O:1}, {K,M:1}}	{K:3}
O	{{K,E,M:1},{K, E:2}}	{K,E:3}
M	{{K,E:2},{K:1}}	{K:3}
E	{K:4}	{K:4}
K		

Step 8:Frequent Pattern Generated

Items	CPB
Y	{<K,Y:3>}
O	{<K,O:3>,<E,O:3>,<E,K,O:3>}
M	{<K,M:3>}
E	{<E,K:4>}
K	

Insert {K, E, M}:

- Increase support count for K, E, and M to 2 each.

Insert {K, M, Y}:

- Increase support count for K to 3.
- Create new nodes for M and Y, link accordingly.

Insert {K, E, O}:

- Increase support counts for K and E to 4.
- Increase support count for existing node O to 2.

Step 6: Compute Conditional Pattern Base

- For each item, identify the paths leading to its nodes in the FP-tree, sorted by ascending frequency.

Step 7: Build Conditional Frequent Pattern Trees

- For each item, build its Conditional Frequent Pattern Tree by identifying common elements in all paths from the Conditional Pattern Base and summing their support counts.

Step 8: Generate Frequent Pattern Rules

Generate rules from the Conditional Frequent Pattern Tree:

- Pair items in the tree with the corresponding item.
- For each itemset, create rules in the form of "If X, then Y" (e.g., K → Y and Y → K).
- Calculate the confidence for each rule and retain those with confidence ≥ minimum confidence value.

By following these steps, we efficiently mine frequent patterns and generate association rules using the FP-Growth algorithm, addressing the inefficiencies of the Apriori algorithm.

Summary

- FP-Growth Algorithm: Efficiently mines frequent patterns by constructing a compact FP-tree and avoids candidate generation.
- Improved Efficiency: Reduces computational overhead by minimising database scans

and leveraging a Trie data structure for data representation.

- Association Rule Generation: Extracts meaningful rules by analysing the structure and frequency of itemsets, aiding in decision-making processes across various domains.

The purpose of this code is to perform association rule mining on a dataset of transactions using the FP-Growth algorithm. Association rule mining is a technique used to uncover interesting relationships or associations between items in large datasets. This method is commonly applied in market basket analysis, where the goal is to find patterns of items that frequently co-occur in transactions.

Example P7 – U7 – D3	
FP - Growth	**Output**

import numpy as np
import pandas as pd
from mlxtend.frequent_patterns import fpgrowth, association_rules
from mlxtend.preprocessing import TransactionEncoder
 	
# Step 1: Loading the data 	
input_path = r'C:\Users\User\mraj4\Documents\Optimum\Py-lib\scikit\store_data.csv'
store_data = pd.read_csv(input_path, header=None)
 	
# Displaying the first few rows of the dataset 	
print(store_data.head())
print("Shape of the dataset:", store_data.shape)
 	
# Step 2: Data Preparation 	
transactions = []
for i in range(len(store_data)):
   transactions.append([str(store_data.values[i, j]) for j in range(store_data.shape[1]) if str(store_data.values[i, j]) != 'nan'])
 	
te = TransactionEncoder()
te_ary = te.fit(transactions).transform(transactions)
df = pd.DataFrame(te_ary, columns=te.columns_)
 	
# Step 3: Applying FP-Growth Algorithm 	
frequent_itemsets = fpgrowth(df, min_support=0.0045, use_colnames=True)
print(frequent_itemsets.head())
 	
# Step 4: Generating Association Rules 	
	Shape of the dataset: (7501, 20)
	  support itemsets
	0 0.238368 (mineral water)
	1 0.132116 (green tea)
	2 0.076523 (low fat yogurt)
	3 0.071457 (shrimp)
	4 0.065858 (olive oil)
	Number of association rules derived: 28
	Rule: frozenset({'mineral water', 'shrimp'}) -> frozenset({'frozen vegetables'})
	Support: 0.007199040127982935
	Confidence: 0.305084745762711 83
	Lift: 3.200616332819722
	************************
	Rule: frozenset({'frozen vegetables', 'spaghetti'}) -> frozenset({'shrimp'})
	Support: 0.005999200106652446
	Confidence: 0.215311004784688 98
	Lift: 3.0131489680782684
	************************

```
rules = association_rules(frequent_itemsets,
metric="confidence", min_threshold=0.2)
rules = rules[rules['lift'] >= 3]

# Step 5: Output
print("Number of association rules derived:", len(rules))

for index, rule in rules.iterrows():
    print("Rule: " + str(rule['antecedents']) + " -> " +
str(rule['consequents']))
    print("Support: " + str(rule['support']))
    print("Confidence: " + str(rule['confidence']))
    print("Lift: " + str(rule['lift']))
    print("*****************************")
```

Advantages of FP-Growth

Efficiency:

- By avoiding the generation of candidate sets and reducing database scans, FP-Growth is much faster and more scalable than the Apriori algorithm.
- The compact FP-tree structure efficiently captures the frequency of itemsets and their co-occurrences, enabling quick retrieval of frequent patterns.

Scalability:

- FP-Growth can handle large datasets more effectively due to its reduced computational complexity.
- It is particularly well-suited for datasets with many frequent patterns, where the Apriori algorithm would struggle with candidate set explosion and repeated scans.

In summary, while the Apriori algorithm laid the groundwork for association rule mining, its drawbacks in candidate set generation and repeated database scans limit its efficiency. The FP-Growth algorithm overcomes these issues by using an FP-tree to compress the data and directly mine frequent patterns, making it a more efficient and scalable solution for large datasets.

PART SEVEN

DAY TWENTY

Unit 7 - Lesson Five

Matrix Factorization

LU Decomposition and Recommender Systems

LU Decomposition

Master said, "LU decomposition, short for Lower-Upper decomposition, is a matrix factorization technique used to break down a square matrix into the product of a lower triangular matrix (L) and an upper triangular matrix (U). This method is widely utilised in numerical analysis and linear algebra to simplify solving systems of linear equations, inverting matrices, and calculating determinants."

Recommender Systems

Recommender systems are integral in various domains, providing personalised recommendations to users. Notable examples include platforms like Amazon, UberEats, Netflix, and YouTube.

Collaborative Filtering

Collaborative filtering is a technique used to predict a user's interests by collecting preferences from many users. The core idea is that if users agreed in the past, they will agree in the future. This method leverages user behaviour and preferences to recommend items. For instance, if two users have similar viewing histories on Netflix, the system can suggest shows watched by one user to the other.

Content-Based Filtering

Content-based filtering recommends items based on the items' characteristics rather than the user's behaviour. This approach uses item features (such as genre, actors, and directors in the case of movies) to recommend similar items. For example, if a user likes a particular action movie, the system may recommend other action movies with similar features.

Matrix Factorization in Recommender Systems

Master explained that the Matrix factorization is a key technique used to improve the accuracy of recommender systems. It involves decomposing the user-item interaction matrix into the product of lower-dimensional matrices, which helps in capturing latent features underlying the interactions.

Techniques for Matrix Factorization

- Singular Value Decomposition (SVD): This technique decomposes the user-item matrix into three matrices, capturing the latent structure of the data.
- Probabilistic Matrix Factorization (PMF): PMF models the rating matrix with probabilistic distributions to handle missing data and noise.
- Non-negative Matrix Factorization (NMF): NMF decomposes the matrix into factors containing only non-negative elements, making the factors more interpretable.
- Bayesian Probabilistic Matrix Factorization (BPMF): This method incorporates Bayesian inference into matrix factorization, providing a robust framework for handling uncertainty.
- Tensor Matrix Factorization: Extends matrix factorization to higher-order data representations, capturing more complex relationships among users and items.

These matrix factorization techniques are crucial for capturing the similarities between users and items, enhancing the performance and accuracy of recommender systems.

LU decomposition is a powerful tool in linear algebra for matrix factorization, aiding in various computational tasks. Recommender systems, essential in modern digital platforms, leverage techniques like collaborative filtering, content-based filtering, and matrix factorization to provide personalised recommendations. Understanding these methods helps in developing more accurate and efficient recommender systems, thereby improving user satisfaction and engagement.

Introduction to Matrix Factorization

Matrix factorization is a technique used to decompose a large matrix into the product of two or more matrices to uncover latent features. In the context of recommender systems, matrix factorization is applied to discover relationships between two different kinds of entities, such as users and items, by analyzing their interactions. This method is particularly useful in collaborative filtering, where the goal is to predict how users might rate items based on their past interactions.

Collaborative Filtering with Matrix Factorization

Collaborative filtering aims to make predictions about users' interests by collecting preferences from many users. When matrix factorization is applied to collaborative filtering, it helps in identifying latent factors from user-item interactions. These latent factors are essentially hidden features that explain the observed user-item preferences.

Given a matrix of user ratings for items (e.g., movies), matrix factorization breaks it down into two lower-dimensional matrices:

- User matrix (U): Represents the latent features of users.
- Item matrix (V): Represents the latent features of items.

The product of these two matrices approximates the original rating matrix.

Example Scenario

Consider a rating matrix where 5 users have rated 5 movies, with ratings ranging from 1 to 5. Not every user has rated every movie, resulting in a sparse matrix with missing values. To perform matrix factorization, we initially fill these missing values with zeros (or mean-centered values), making the matrix complete for the factorization process.

	Movie 1	Movie 2	Movie 3	Movie 4	Movie 5
User 1	5	3	4		1
User 2	4		5	2	3
User 3	3	4	2	1	
User 4	1		3	4	2
User 5		2	4	5	3

Discovering Latent Features

Matrix factorization reveals hidden patterns in the data. For example, if two users both rate action movies highly, this pattern is captured as a latent feature in the factorized matrices. These latent features help predict how users would rate items they have not yet rated.

For instance, if User 1 and User 3 both rate Movie 2 and Movie 3 highly, it suggests they have similar preferences. Matrix factorization can leverage this similarity to predict ratings for movies that User 1 and User 3 have not rated yet.

Predicting Missing Ratings

To predict whether User 4 would like Movie 4, we:

- Identify users with similar preferences to User 4 by analysing the latent features from the user matrix.
- Use the ratings provided by these similar users for Movie 4 to predict User 4's rating.

This prediction helps in recommending items (movies) to User 4 based on the inferred preferences from similar users.

Example: The code for implementing matrix factorization using gradient descent to discover latent features in a user-item ratings matrix. The code includes initialisation, the gradient descent method, and convergence criteria.

Explanation:

Users (U) and Items (D):

- Define a set of users and items.
- The matrix R ($|U| \times |D|$) includes all the ratings given by users to items.

Latent Features (K):

- The goal is to discover K latent features.

Matrices P and Q:

- Matrix P ($|U| \times K$) represents the association between users and features.
- Matrix Q ($|D| \times K$) represents the association between items and features.
- The product of P and Q generates the predicted ratings matrix $\hat{R}$.

Gradient Descent:

- Initialise matrices P and Q with random values.
- Calculate the error matrix M as the difference between R and $\hat{R}$.
- Minimise the error through gradient descent by iteratively updating P and Q until convergence.

Example P7 – U7 – D4	
Matrix Factorisation	**Output**

import numpy as np
def matrix_factorization(R, P, Q, K, steps=5000, alpha=0.0002, beta=0.02):
  """
  Perform matrix factorization to predict empty entries in a matrix.
  Parameters:
  R (ndarray): The user-item ratings matrix.
  P (ndarray): The user-feature matrix.
  Q (ndarray): The item-feature matrix.
  K (int): The number of latent features.
  steps (int): The maximum number of steps to perform the optimization.
  alpha (float): The learning rate.
  beta (float): The regularization parameter.
  Returns:
  tuple: The final matrices P and Q.
  """
  Q = Q.T
  for step in range(steps):
    for i in range(len(R)):
      for j in range(len(R[i])):
        if R[i][j] > 0:
          # Calculate the error of the prediction
          eij = R[i][j] - np.dot(P[i, :], Q[:, j])
          for k in range(K):
            P[i][k] += alpha * (2 * eij * Q[k][j] - beta * P[i][k])
            Q[k][j] += alpha * (2 * eij * P[i][k] - beta * Q[k][j])
 	
    # Calculate the total error
    eR = np.dot(P, Q)
    e = 0
    for i in range(len(R)):
      for j in range(len(R[i])):
        if R[i][j] > 0:
	Original Ratings Matrix (R):
	[[5 3 4 0 1]
	 [4 0 5 2 3]
	 [3 4 2 1 0]
	 [1 0 3 4 2]
	 [0 2 4 5 3]]
	
	User-Feature Matrix (P):
	[[0.16470762 0.43134307 2.22797118]
	 [1.24090944 1.07800149 1.50621665]
	 [1.7390881 0.05840868 0.84229844]
	 [0.50865923 1.64318201 -0.01738584]
	 [0.9041755 2.03865607 -0.02424196]]
	
	Item-Feature Matrix (Q):
	[[0.61336898 0.36084274 2.06670264]
	 [1.69765072 0.24560127 1.17783632]
	 [0.51864115 1.7450666 1.44541475]
	 [0.73321295 2.11115321 -0.6505809]
	 [1.30181805 0.88068546 0.2084279]]

```
            e += (R[i][j] - np.dot(P[i, :], Q[:, j])) ** 2
            for k in range(K):
                e += (beta / 2) * (P[i][k] ** 2 + Q[k][j] **
2)
    if e < 0.001:
        break
  return P, Q.T

# Example Usage:
# Number of users and items
num_users = 5
num_items = 5
# Number of latent features
K = 3

# User-Item ratings matrix (|U|*|D|)
R = np.array([
  [5, 3, 4, 0, 1],
  [4, 0, 5, 2, 3],
  [3, 4, 2, 1, 0],
  [1, 0, 3, 4, 2],
  [0, 2, 4, 5, 3]
])

# Initialize user-feature matrix P (|U|*K)
P = np.random.rand(num_users, K)
# Initialize item-feature matrix Q (|D|*K)
Q = np.random.rand(num_items, K)
# Apply matrix factorization
nP, nQ = matrix_factorization(R, P, Q, K)
# Generate the predicted ratings matrix R
nR = np.dot(nP, nQ.T)

# Print the resulting matrices
print("Original Ratings Matrix (R):")
print(R)
print("\nUser-Feature Matrix (P):")
print(nP)
print("\nItem-Feature Matrix (Q):")
print(nQ)
print("\nPredicted Ratings Matrix (R):")
print(nR)
```

Steps in the Code:

- Initialise: Import necessary libraries and initialise the ratings matrix R, and matrices P and Q with random values.

- Matrix Factorization: Define the matrix_factorization function to perform the optimisation using gradient descent.
- Fit the Model: Apply the matrix factorization function to fit the model and predict the ratings matrix $\hat{R}$.
- Print Results: Print the original ratings matrix, the final user-feature and item-feature matrices, and the predicted ratings matrix.

This code provides a comprehensive approach to understanding and implementing matrix factorization for collaborative filtering, focusing on discovering latent features and minimising prediction errors through gradient descent.

```
Predicted Ratings Matrix (R):
[[ 4.86122748  3.00973978  4.05848894 -0.41807843  1.05866829]
 [ 4.26302631  4.14546602  4.70187888  2.2057614   2.87875614]
 [ 2.82855944  3.9587991   2.22136029  0.85044832  2.49097446]
 [ 0.86899473  1.24661561  3.10614391  3.85327541  2.10568459]
 [ 1.24012653  2.00711764  3.99149357  4.98263985  2.96743406]]
```

As we can see, the predicted matrix $\hat{R}$ closely matches the true values in the original ratings matrix R. The zero ratings, which represent unknown or missing values in R, have been replaced with predictions based on the similar preferences of other users.

For the ratings that were already present, the predicted values are very close to the true values, showcasing the accuracy of the model. Additionally, the algorithm provides plausible predictions for the previously unknown ratings, giving us a complete matrix that can be used for further analysis or recommendations.

By using three latent features (K=3), the algorithm effectively associates users and items with these three underlying factors. This means that the users and items are grouped based on three distinct characteristics inferred from the data. The predictions follow these associations, reflecting the relationships captured by the model.

In summary, this approach fills in the missing ratings and retains the structure and patterns of the known ratings, making it a powerful tool for collaborative filtering and recommendation systems.

Example: The purpose of the provided code is twofold: first, it demonstrates basic data visualisation using the Iris dataset, and second, it illustrates how to perform dimensionality reduction using Truncated Singular Value Decomposition (SVD) on a user-item rating matrix, often used in recommendation systems.

Example P7 – U7 – D5	
Matrix Factorisation	**Output**

import numpy as np
import pandas as pd
import matplotlib.pyplot as plt
from sklearn.decomposition import TruncatedSVD
# Load the dataset (e.g., the Iris dataset for demonstration purposes) 	
from sklearn import datasets
iris = datasets.load_iris()
 	
# Select the first two columns (e.g., sepal length and sepal width) 	
X = iris.data[:, :2]
 	
# Convert the data into a DataFrame 	
df = pd.DataFrame(X, columns=['Sepal Length', 'Sepal Width'])
 	
# Plot the data 	
plt.scatter(df['Sepal Length'], df['Sepal Width'])
plt.xlabel('Sepal Length')
plt.ylabel('Sepal Width')
plt.title('Iris Dataset - Sepal Dimensions')
plt.show()
 	
# Assume the data is a user-item ratings matrix 	
# For demonstration, we'll create a user-item ratings matrix 	
# (In practice, this would be your actual ratings matrix) 	
R = np.array([
   [5, 3, 0, 1],
   [4, 0, 0, 1],
   [1, 1, 0, 5],
   [1, 0, 0, 4],
   [0, 1, 5, 4]
])
 	
# Number of latent features 	
K = 3
 	
# Apply TruncatedSVD 	
	Original Ratings Matrix (R):
	[[5 3 0 1]
	 [4 0 0 1]
	 [1 1 0 5]
	 [1 0 0 4]
	 [0 1 5 4]]
	
	User-Feature Matrix (P):
	[[3.94592157 4.16887476 1.11814254]
	 [2.68400116 2.76010383 0.18929134]
	 [4.65943967 -0.84914207 -2.07165283]
	 [3.61265495 -0.69003845 -1.82469149]
	 [4.90266747 -3.55087873 2.30987748]]
	
	Item-Feature Matrix (Q):
	[[0.47488998 0.78203025 0.17212379]
	 [0.26234348 0.20891356 0.25224247]
	 [0.3005118 -0.45754472 0.81089006]
	 [0.78444124 -0.36801718 -0.49920382]]
	
	Root Mean Squared Error (RMSE):
	0.3225210533787111

```
svd = TruncatedSVD(n_components=K)
P = svd.fit_transform(R)  # User-feature matrix
Q = svd.components_.T  # Item-feature matrix

# Generate the predicted ratings matrix R_hat
R_hat = np.dot(P, Q.T)

# Print the results
print("Original Ratings Matrix (R):")
print(R)
print("\nUser-Feature Matrix (P):")
print(P)
print("\nItem-Feature Matrix (Q):")
print(Q)
print("\nPredicted Ratings Matrix (R_hat):")
print(R_hat)

# Evaluate the performance (e.g., Root Mean Squared
Error)
def rmse(R, R_hat):
   mask = R != 0
   return np.sqrt(np.sum((R[mask] - R_hat[mask])**2) /
np.sum(mask))

print("\nRoot Mean Squared Error (RMSE):")
print(rmse(R, R_hat))
```

```
Predicted Ratings Matrix (R_hat):

[[ 5.32652372  2.18816428  0.18504005  1.00294508]

 [ 3.46567149  1.32850063 -0.30280243  0.99518063]

 [ 1.19208569  0.52241748  0.10885441  5.00173251]

 [ 0.86190988  0.34333338 -0.07825527  3.9987545 ]

 [-0.05108206  1.1270053   4.97105194  3.99953927]]
```

Summary:

In this unit, we explored essential data mining techniques, focusing on association rule learning and matrix factorization. We began with association rule learning, which identifies relationships and patterns within datasets using metrics like support, confidence, and lift. We detailed the Apriori algorithm, which finds frequent itemsets iteratively, and discussed various types of association rules. We compared association rule learning with clustering, highlighting their different focuses. We then covered the ECLAT algorithm as an alternative to Apriori, and addressed the limitations of Apriori by introducing the FP-Growth algorithm. Additionally, we provided an overview of matrix factorization techniques for uncovering latent features in data, and introduced recommender systems, explaining collaborative filtering, content-based filtering, and hybrid methods. Finally, we focused on using matrix factorization techniques as SVD and NMF in recommender systems to enhance recommendation accuracy.

What Next:

In this unit, we will cover ensemble methods and their various techniques and applications. We will explore the differences between stacking, bagging, and boosting. We will also cover Gradient Boosting, focusing on its optimization via the loss function, and examine XGBoost for its enhancements. Additionally, we will discuss CatBoost for handling categorical features and LightGBM for its speed and efficiency. Lastly, we will cover sampling techniques, evaluation metrics, and stacked generalization (stacking) for improved predictive accuracy.

P7-U7-L1-5 - Practice Question

1. What is the association rule learning?
2. What is the Apriori algorithm?
3. Name three types of association rules.
4. How does association rule learning differ from clustering?
5. What is the ECLAT algorithm?
6. What is a major drawback of the Apriori algorithm?
7. How does the FP-Growth algorithm address the limitations of the Apriori algorithm?
8. What is matrix factorization?
9. What is LU decomposition?
10. What are recommender systems?
11. What are the three types of recommender systems covered in this unit?
12. What is Singular Value Decomposition (SVD) used for in recommender systems?
13. What is Non-negative Matrix Factorization (NMF)?
14. How does collaborative filtering work in recommender systems?
15. What is the main advantage of using hybrid recommender systems?

PART EIGHT

Machine Learning Models

Ensemble Methods

"Just as no single perspective reveals the whole truth, no single model captures every pattern. Ensemble methods unite many minds of code to uncover deeper insights."

– Shree Shambav

PART EIGHT

DAY TWENTY-ONE

Unit 8 - Lesson One

Ensemble Methods - 1

Ensemble Methods:

Ensemble methods are techniques that combine the predictions of multiple machine learning models to improve overall performance.

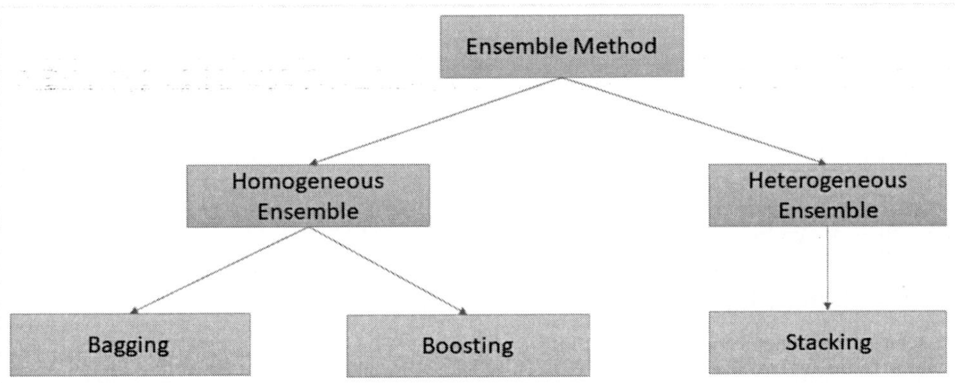

Difference between Stack, Bagging, and Boosting in Ensemble Methods:

Stacking (Stacked Generalisation):

- Stacking combines the predictions of multiple base models using a meta-learner, often a simple linear model or another machine learning algorithm.
- It leverages the diverse predictions of base models to make more accurate predictions than any individual model.

- Stacking is versatile and can be applied to various machine learning tasks.

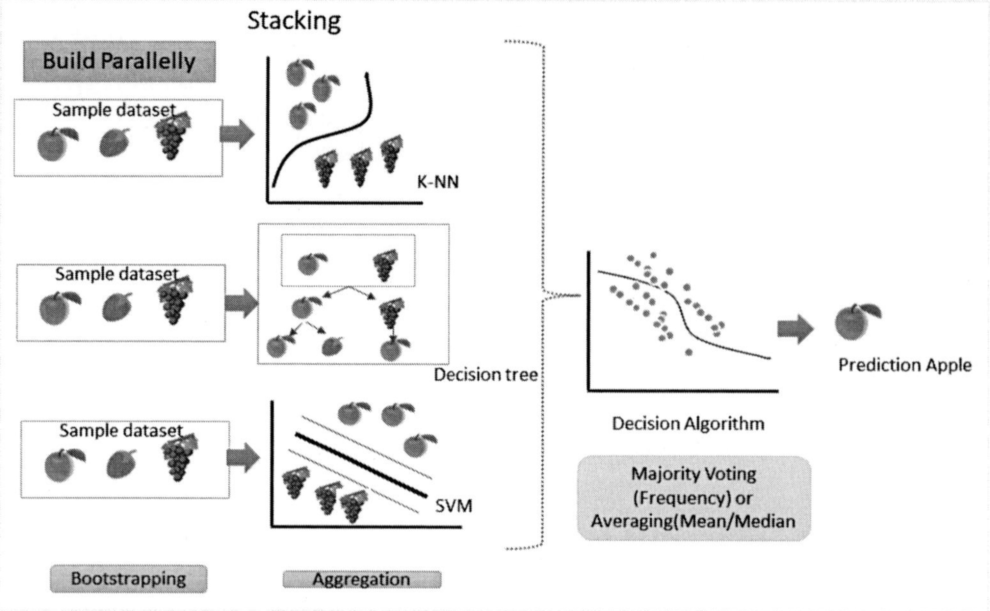

Example: In a Kaggle competition to predict housing prices, a stacking ensemble could combine predictions from different regression models, such as linear regression, decision trees, and support vector machines, to improve prediction accuracy.

Algorithm: The algorithm involves training several base models on the training data and then training a meta-learner using the predictions of these base models as features.

Bagging (Bootstrap Aggregating):

Apeksha asked, "What is bagging?"

Master said, "The bagging method is effective in reducing bias in models. By training multiple instances of the model on different subsets of the training data and then combining their predictions, bagging helps to mitigate bias by reducing the reliance on any single instance of the model."

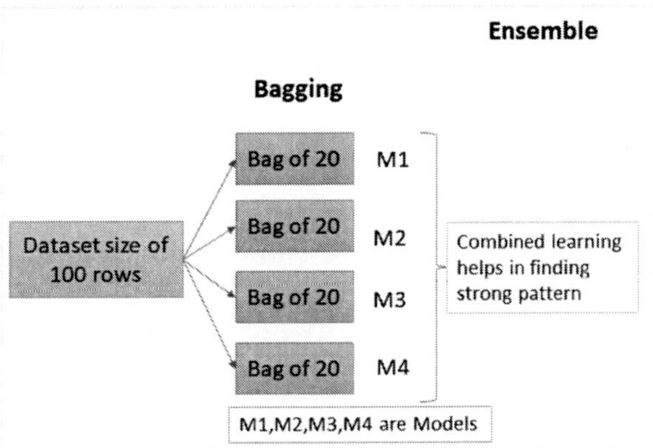

In the context of bagging (Bootstrap Aggregating), bias refers to the error introduced by the model's inability to capture the true relationship between the features and the target variable in the training data. This bias arises due to the simplifying assumptions made by the model or the limitations of the model architecture in representing complex relationships.

Mathematically, bias can be quantified as the difference between the average prediction of the model and the true value across all possible training datasets. Bagging (Bootstrap Aggregating) is a technique that helps reduce bias by combining the predictions of multiple base models trained on different subsets of the training data.

Here's how bagging helps in reducing bias:

Model Diversity: Bagging involves training multiple base models (often referred to as weak learners) on random subsets of the training data. Since these subsets are sampled with replacement, each base model sees a slightly different view of the data. As a result, the ensemble model benefits from the diversity of these base models, capturing different aspects of the underlying data relationships.

Averaging Predictions: In bagging, the final prediction of the ensemble model is typically obtained by averaging the predictions of all base models. This averaging process helps smooth out the individual biases present in each base model. By combining predictions from multiple models, the ensemble model tends to produce more stable and reliable predictions, thereby reducing bias.

Variance-Bias Tradeoff: While bagging primarily aims to reduce variance by improving the stability and robustness of the model, it often leads to a reduction in bias as well. This is because the averaging process in bagging tends to mitigate the impact of any systematic errors or biases present in individual base models.

Overfitting: It reduces overfitting and variance by averaging the predictions of multiple models trained on diverse subsets of the data.

Unstable Models: Bagging is particularly effective for unstable models or when the dataset is prone to noise.

Overall, bagging is a powerful technique for improving the performance of machine learning models by reducing both variance and bias, leading to more accurate and reliable predictions.

Example: In a random forest, which is an ensemble of decision trees trained using bagging, each tree is trained on a bootstrap sample of the training data, and the final prediction is obtained by averaging the predictions of all trees.

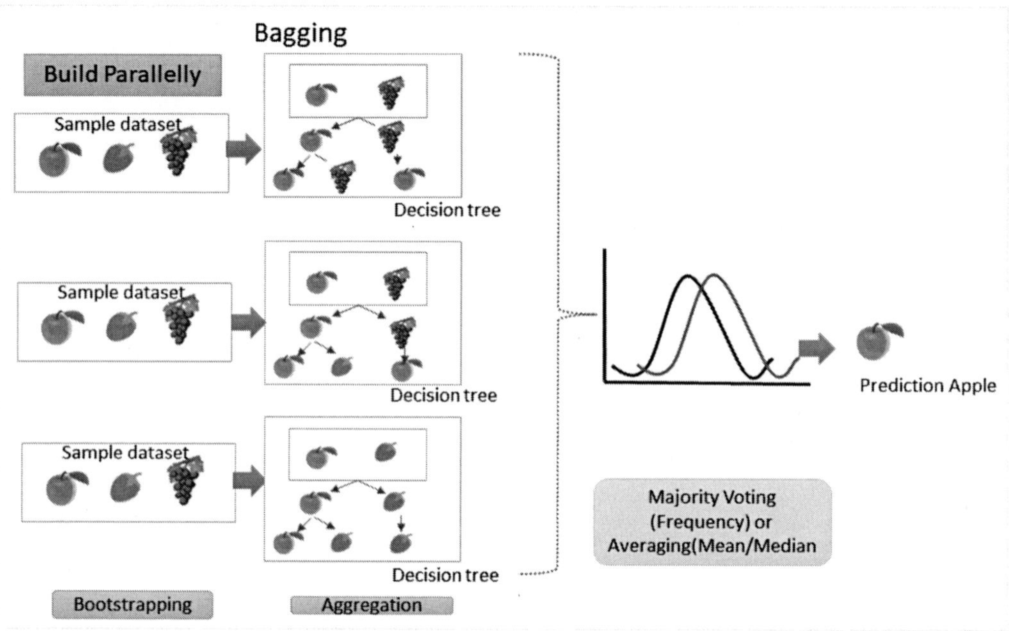

Algorithm: The algorithm involves randomly sampling subsets of the training data with replacement, training a base model on each subset, and aggregating the predictions of all models to obtain the final prediction.

Boosting:

- Boosting sequentially trains a series of weak learners, where each subsequent model focuses on the instances that the previous models misclassified.
- It improves model performance by iteratively correcting errors made by earlier models.

- Boosting is effective for reducing bias and improving accuracy, especially when used with weak base models.

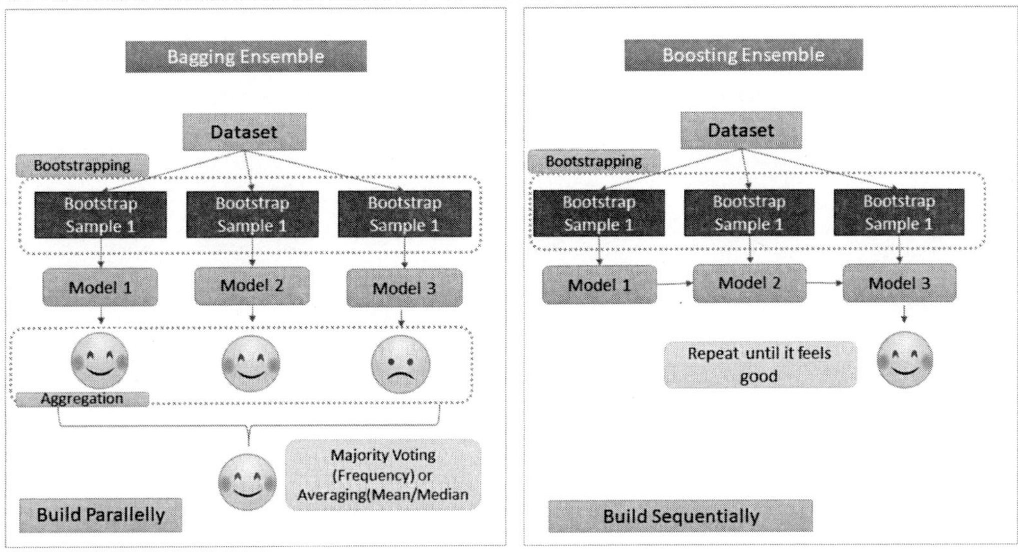

Example: AdaBoost (Adaptive Boosting) is a popular boosting algorithm that combines multiple weak classifiers, such as decision stumps, to create a strong classifier.

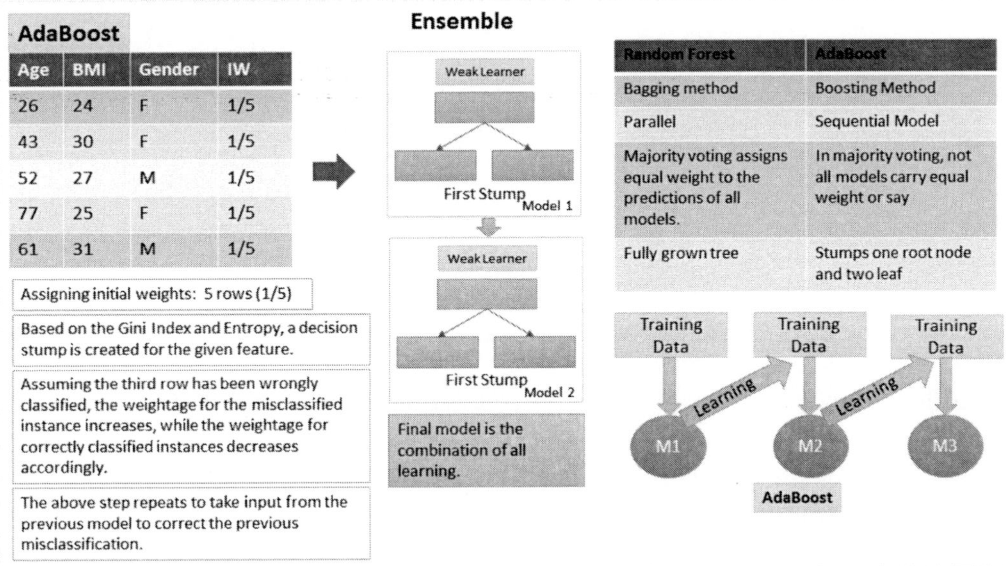

Algorithm: The algorithm involves training a base model on the entire training data, assigning higher weights to misclassified instances, and then training the next model to focus more on these misclassified instances. This process is repeated iteratively until a stopping criterion is met.

The popular tools for boosting in ensemble methods include:

AdaBoost (Adaptive Boosting):

- Classic boosting algorithm that sequentially trains weak learners.
- Assign higher weights to misclassified instances in each iteration.
- Widely used for binary classification tasks due to simplicity and effectiveness.

GBM (Gradient Boosting Machine) in Scikit-Learn:

- scikit-learn: GradientBoostingClassifier and GradientBoostingRegressor.
- User-friendly implementation integrated with other scikit-learn functionalities.

XGBoost (Extreme Gradient Boosting):

- Scalable and efficient implementation of gradient boosting machines.
- Offers support for various objective functions and evaluation metrics.
- Provides advanced features such as tree pruning and parallel computation.

CatBoost:

- Developed by Yandex, designed for efficient handling of categorical features.
- Automatically handles categorical variables without preprocessing.
- Incorporates novel techniques to improve model performance.

LightGBM (Light Gradient Boosting Machine):

- High-performance framework developed by Microsoft.
- Uses histogram-based approach for tree splitting, leading to faster training times.

- Supports categorical features and custom objective functions.

These tools offer a variety of features and optimizations, catering to different requirements and preferences in boosting-based ensemble learning tasks.

In summary, while stacking combines the predictions of diverse models using a meta-learner, bagging trains multiple instances of the same base model on different subsets of the data, and boosting sequentially trains a series of models, each focusing on correcting the errors made by the previous models. Each ensemble method has its strengths and applications, depending on the characteristics of the dataset and the problem at hand.

Data Structures:

Data structures play a crucial role in implementing machine learning algorithms efficiently. Some important data structures include:

- Arrays: Storing feature vectors, and dataset representation.
- Lists: Dynamic storage of data, flexible for various operations.
- Matrices: Representing datasets, and mathematical operations in linear algebra.
- Trees: Decision trees, binary trees for organising and searching data.
- Graphs: Representing complex relationships in data.
- Hash Tables: Efficient retrieval and storage of key-value pairs.
- Queues: Managing data in a first-in, first-out (FIFO) manner.
- Stacks: Managing data in a last-in, first-out (LIFO) manner.

Understanding both algorithms and data structures is fundamental for implementing machine learning solutions effectively.

These are just a few examples, and there are many other machine learning models and algorithms, each with its strengths and weaknesses. The choice of a model depends on the nature of the data and the specific problem at hand.

For instance, Predictive analytics models are crafted to assess historical data, unveil patterns, analyze trends, and use those insights to forecast future trends.

Predictive Problems

Classify	Predict Binary outcomes: Is there a likelihood that this loan will default?
Forecast	Forecast numeric value: What is the anticipated price for the product? How many years can we expect the machine to last?
Anomaly	Recognize Unusual Behavior Does this transaction exhibit signs of fraud? Does this claim display indications of fraud?
Cluster	Categorize into Segments Customer segmentation for targeted outreach Patient segmentation for enhanced care
Time Series	Predict for the Next 4 Months Forecasting sales for the upcoming 5 months

Bagging

Random Forest:

Master said, "Random forest is a powerful ensemble learning technique that combines the predictive strength of multiple decision trees, aptly called the forest, to produce more accurate and stable predictions."

Task: Classification and Regression

- Description: Ensemble method that constructs multiple decision trees during training and outputs the mode of the classes (classification) or mean prediction (regression) of the individual trees.
- Algorithm: Random Forest is an ensemble method that builds multiple decision trees and merges them.
- Application: Image classification, recommendation systems, and finance.

In Randon Forest, we create multiple subsets of the original dataset by randomly sampling rows and columns. These subsets, known as bags, are constructed independently, allowing for the possibility of data repetition. Typically, each bag contains a fraction of the original dataset, ensuring diversity among the samples. For instance, if we have a dataset of size M rows and N columns, only a portion of it, say 2/3, will be moved into bags, with rows and columns potentially repeating across bags.

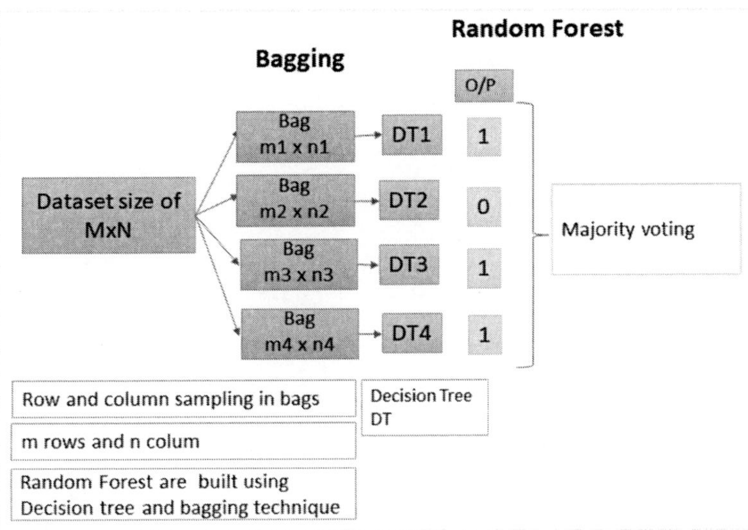

Once the bags are prepared, we train decision trees on each bag using binary classification (a two-class classifier). During prediction, the ensemble model combines the results from all individual trees using techniques like majority voting or averaging.

But why choose random forest over other models?

Enhanced Accuracy: By aggregating the predictions of numerous decision trees, random forest achieves a higher level of accuracy compared to individual trees. This is particularly beneficial in scenarios where precision is paramount, such as predicting whether a person has heart disease.

Prevention of Overfitting: Overfitting occurs when a model learns the training data too well, capturing noise rather than the underlying patterns. Random forest mitigates this risk by using bootstrapping, a resampling technique that creates multiple datasets from the original, thus reducing the likelihood of overfitting.

Bagging Technique: Random forest employs bagging aggregation, which involves creating diverse subsets of the data through random sampling with replacement. This diversity ensures that each decision tree in the forest learns from a slightly different perspective, reducing the variance and improving generalisation.

Here's how random forest works in predicting whether a person has heart disease:

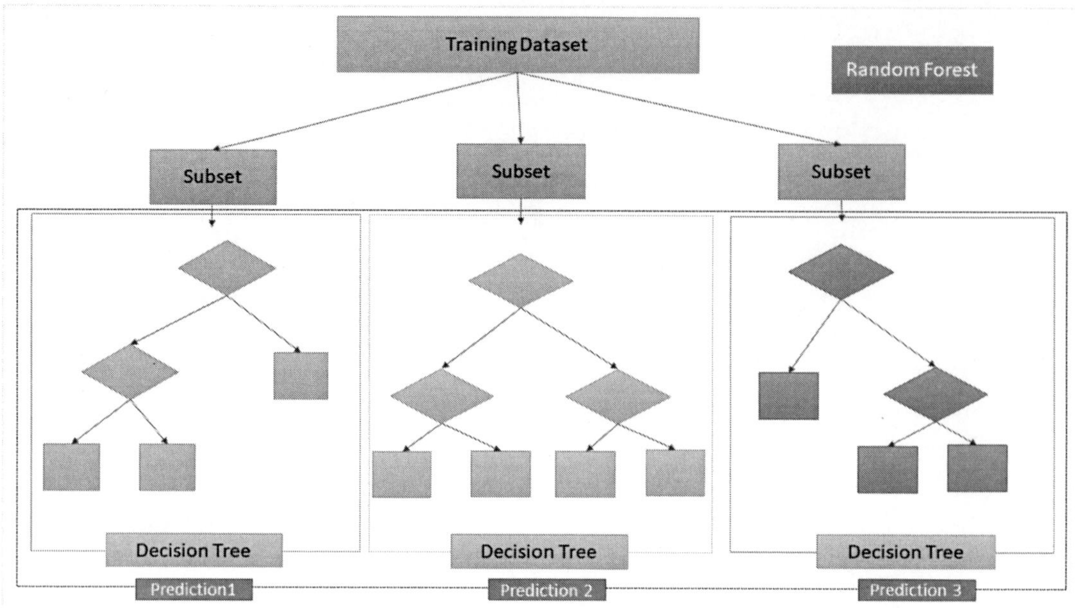

$$\text{Final Prediction} = \sum_{1}^{N} \frac{(Prediction)n}{N}$$

Sample Dataset: Just for understanding

Blood Flow	Blocked Arteries	Pain	Weight	Cardiac Disease
Normal	Yes	Yes	190	Yes
Abnormal	No	No	135	No
Abnormal	Yes	Yes	185	Yes
Abnormal	Yes	No	175	No

Step 1: Create a Bootstrapped Dataset

Bootstrapping involves generating multiple datasets by resampling from the original dataset. Each bootstrap sample contains a random subset of the original data, ensuring diversity in the training sets.

Step 2: Build Decision Trees

Decision trees are constructed using the bootstrapped datasets. Starting from the root node, the algorithm selects the best attribute to split the data and recursively partitions it into branches based on the chosen criteria.

Step 3: Repeat and Iterate

The process of creating bootstrapped datasets and building decision trees is repeated multiple times, creating an ensemble of diverse trees. Each tree predicts the output class based on a subset of predictor variables, adding to the collective wisdom of the forest.

Step 4: Predict Outcomes

To predict whether a new patient has heart disease, the data is passed down each decision tree in the forest. The final prediction is determined by aggregating the votes from all the trees, with the majority class being chosen as the final prediction.

Step 5: Evaluate the Model

The model's performance is evaluated using out-of-bag (OOB) samples, which are data points not included in the bootstrapped datasets. By assessing the accuracy of predictions on these unseen samples, we gain insight into the model's generalisation ability and robustness.

In summary, random forest offers a compelling solution for predicting heart disease by harnessing the collective intelligence of multiple decision trees, resulting in superior accuracy, reduced overfitting, and robustness to unseen data.

Exercise P8-U8 – D1	
Random Forest	**Output**

from sklearn.datasets import load_iris
from sklearn.ensemble import RandomForestClassifier
from sklearn.model_selection import GridSearchCV, train_test_split
 	
# Load the iris dataset 	
iris = load_iris()
X = iris.data
y = iris.target
 	
# Split the data into training and test sets 	
X_train, X_test, y_train, y_test = train_test_split(X, y, test_size=0.3, random_state=0)
 	
# Create a grid of hyperparameters to search over 	
param_grid = {
'n_estimators': [100, 150],
'max_features': ['sqrt'], # Updated to valid options only
'max_depth': [3, 6, 9, None],
'min_samples_split': [2, 4, 6, 7, 9],
'min_samples_leaf': [1, 2, 3, 4],
'criterion': ['gini', 'entropy'],
'oob_score': [True, False]
	Best parameters: {'criterion': 'gini', 'max_depth': 3, 'max_features': 'sqrt', 'min_samples_leaf': 1, 'min_samples_split': 2, 'n_estimators': 100, 'oob_score': True}
	OOB score: 0.9428571428571428

```
}

# Instantiate the RandomForestClassifier
rf = RandomForestClassifier(random_state=0)
# Instantiate the grid search
grid_search = GridSearchCV(estimator=rf,
param_grid=param_grid, cv=5)

# Fit the grid search to the data
grid_search.fit(X_train, y_train)

# Print the best hyperparameters
print("Best parameters:", grid_search.best_params_)
# Print the out-of-bag (OOB) score
print("OOB score:", grid_search.best_estimator_.oob_score_)
```

This code snippet demonstrates the use of GridSearchCV to find the best hyperparameters for a RandomForestClassifier model trained on the Iris dataset. Here's a brief overview:

- Loading the Iris Dataset: The Iris dataset is loaded using load_iris() from sklearn.datasets, and the feature matrix X and target vector y are extracted.
- Splitting Dataset: The dataset is split into training and testing sets using train_test_split() from sklearn.model_selection, with a 70-30 split ratio and a fixed random state for reproducibility.
- Defining Hyperparameter Grid: A grid of hyperparameters to search over is defined using a dictionary param_grid. It includes various hyperparameters such as the number of estimators, maximum depth, minimum samples split, etc.
- Instantiating RandomForestClassifier: A RandomForestClassifier object rf is instantiated with a specified random state.
- Instantiating Grid Search: GridSearchCV is instantiated with the RandomForestClassifier (rf) as the estimator and the hyperparameter grid (param_grid).
- Fitting Grid Search: The grid search is fitted to the training data using grid_search.fit(X_train, y_train).
- Printing Best Hyperparameters: The best hyperparameters found by grid search are printed using grid_search.best_params_.
- Printing Out-of-Bag Score: The out-of-bag (OOB) score of the best estimator found by grid search is printed using grid_search.best_estimator_.oob_score_.

Overall, this code efficiently tunes the hyperparameters of a RandomForestClassifier model using grid search and evaluates its performance on the Iris dataset.

The OOB score serves as a pivotal indicator of model accuracy. In this instance, the value of 0.9428571428571428 underscores the model's proficiency in correctly predicting the target variable approximately 94.29% of the time, solely utilising the out-of-bag samples. This metric encapsulates the random forest classifier's capacity to generalise effectively to fresh, unseen data points, thereby affirming its robustness and reliability in real-world scenarios.

Advantages:

- **High Accuracy:** Random Forest leverages multiple decision trees trained on different subsets of data to aggregate predictions, resulting in more accurate forecasts through averaging or voting. This ensemble approach typically yields higher accuracy compared to single decision tree models.

- **Robustness to Noise:** The combination of forecasts from multiple decision trees makes Random Forest resilient to noisy data. Outliers or noisy data points are less likely to significantly impact the overall model performance, enhancing its robustness, and reliability.

- **Non-Parametric Nature:** Random Forest is non-parametric, meaning it doesn't assume specific data distributions or correlations. This adaptability allows it to be applied to diverse datasets and identify complex patterns without imposing strict constraints.

- **Estimating Feature Importance:** Random Forest calculates feature importance based on their contributions to variance reduction (for regression) or impurity reduction (for classification) across all trees. This helps in feature selection and understanding the relevance of characteristics for prediction.

- **Handles Missing Data and Outliers:** Random Forest naturally handles missing data and outliers without requiring preprocessing methods like imputation or outlier removal. Each decision tree is trained on random subsets of input, making it robust against missing values and less susceptible to outlier influence.

- **Handles Both Numerical and Categorical Data:** Random Forest can handle both numerical and categorical data without bias, as it randomly selects feature subsets for each decision tree during training, eliminating the need for feature engineering strategies like one-hot encoding.

Disadvantages

- **Computational Complexity:** Training a Random Forest model with numerous trees or on large datasets can be computationally expensive due to the separate training of each tree, resulting in longer training times and higher memory utilisation, especially on resource-limited systems.

- **Memory Usage:** Random Forest models consume significant memory, particularly with large datasets or deeply rooted trees, as each decision tree in the forest stores training data, feature splits, and leaf node predictions, leading to potential memory limitations on certain hardware.

- **Prediction Time:** Random Forest models may have longer prediction times, especially with numerous trees or large datasets, as each observation must traverse multiple decision trees in the forest to obtain a final prediction, potentially impacting real-time or latency-sensitive applications.

- **Lack of Interpretability:** Understanding the logic behind each prediction in Random Forest models can be challenging due to their ensemble nature, often referred to as 'black-box' models. While feature importance measures can help identify important features, complex relationships between features and predictions may be difficult to interpret.

- **Overfitting:** Random Forest can overfit the training data, capturing noise and leading to poor generalisation on unseen data. This can reduce predictive accuracy in real-world scenarios where the model fails to generalise well beyond the training data.

Boosting:

ADA Boost:

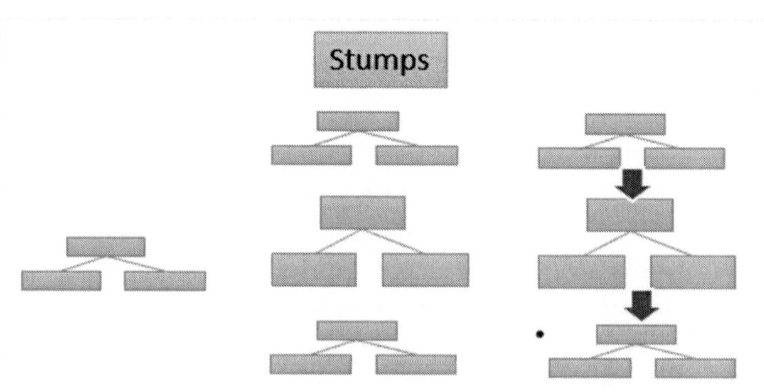

Master explained that the AdaBoost combines multiple weak learners to improve classification accuracy. Weak learners are typically simple models, often referred to as "stumps," which are decision trees with only one split. In AdaBoost, each weak learner receives a certain level of importance, known as "say," in the classification process. This importance is determined based on the learner's performance in correcting the mistakes made by previous learners.

In the first step, sample weights are calculated using the formula:

$W(x_i,y_i)=1/N$ where N denotes the total number of data points.

Chest Pain	Blocked arteries	Patient Weight	Heart Disease	Sample weight I1
Yes	Yes	200	Yes	1/8
No	Yes	178	Yes	1/8
Yes	No	205	Yes	1/8
Yes	Yes	165	Yes	1/8
No	Yes	165	No	1/8
No	Yes	125	No	1/8
Yes	No	165	No	1/8
Yes	Yes	173	No	1/8

Prediction: Based on Chest pain and Blocked arteries

Chest Pain	Blocked arteries	Patient Weight	Heart Disease	Sample weight I1
Yes	Yes	200	Yes	1/8
No	Yes	178	Yes	1/8
Yes	No	205	Yes	1/8
Yes	Yes	165	Yes	1/8
No	Yes	165	No	1/8
No	Yes	125	No	1/8
Yes	No	165	No	1/8
Yes	Yes	173	No	1/8

Step 1: Sample weight

Total Sample – 8
Initial weight: Same weight for all i.e 1/8

Chest Pain

Heart Disease - Yes		Heart Disease - No	
Correct	Incorrect	Correct	Incorrect
3	2	2	1

Blocked Heart

Heart Disease - Yes		Heart Disease - No	
Correct	Incorrect	Correct	Incorrect
3	2	2	1

Weight > 175

Heart Disease - Yes		Heart Disease - No	
Correct	Incorrect	Correct	Incorrect
3	0	4	1

Step 2: Create Stump for each feature

Create stump using feature Chest Pain

Create stump using feature Blocked arteries, Patient weight, Heart disease

Step 2: For each feature, a decision stump is created. This decision stump acts as a weak learner and makes predictions based on a single feature.

Step 3: The Gini index is calculated for each decision stump. The Gini index measures the impurity of the split created by the stump. The stump with the lowest Gini index is selected as the best split for the given feature.

Step 4: We will now calculate the "Amount of Say," which represents the importance or influence of this classifier in categorizing the data points:

Amount of Say = ½ log(1-Total Error)/Total Error

The total error is calculated as the sum of the sample weights of all misclassified data points. For instance, if there is one misclassified output in our dataset out of a total of five data points, then our total error would be 1/5. In such a scenario, the alpha value, which indicates the performance of the stump, can be calculated as follows:

$$\text{Performance of the stump} = \frac{1}{2} \log\left(\frac{1-\text{Total Error}}{\text{Total error}}\right)$$

$$\alpha = \frac{1}{2}log\left(\frac{1-Total\ Error}{Total\ error}\right) = \alpha = \frac{1}{2}log\left(\frac{1-1/8}{1/8}\right)$$

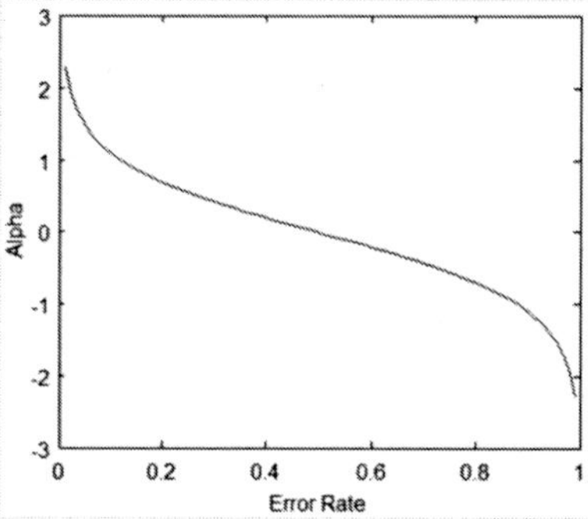

In the graph, '0' indicates a flawless stump, whereas '1' represents a poor stump.

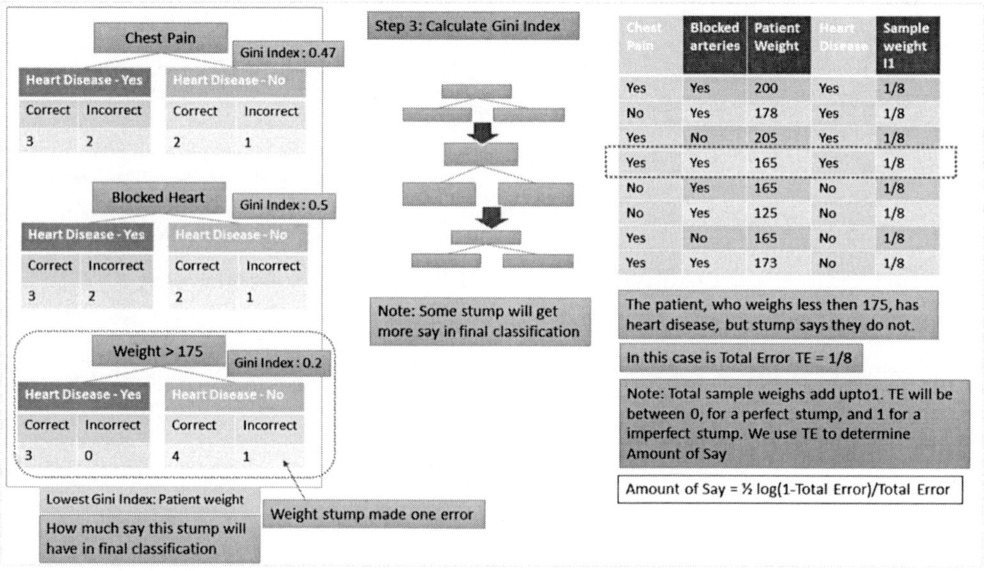

The graph illustrates that in situations where there are no misclassifications, and the total error is 0, the "amount of say" or alpha value is notably high. Conversely, when the classifier correctly predicts half of the samples and misclassifies the other half, resulting in a total error of 0.5, the alpha value decreases to 0, indicating minimal influence. However, if all samples are misclassified, resulting in a significant total error close to 1, the alpha value will be a negative integer.

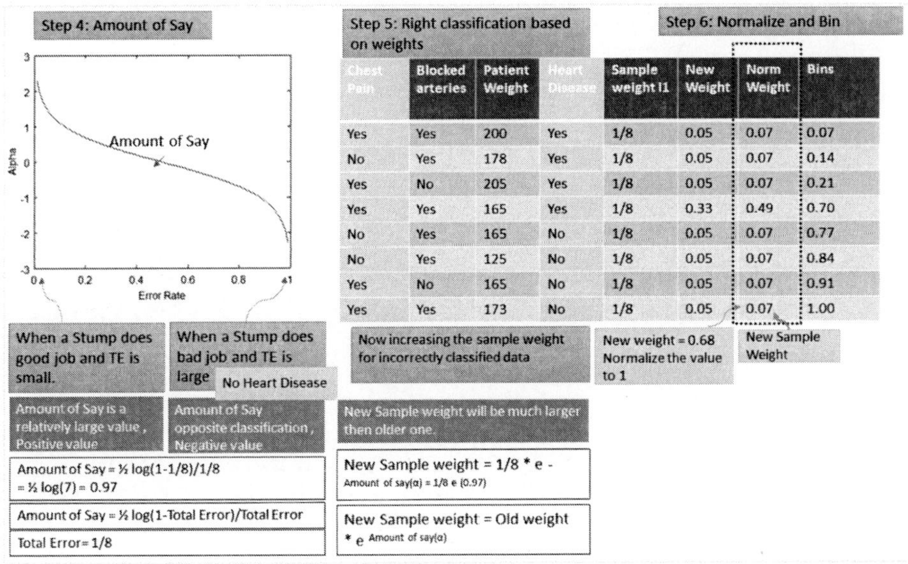

Chest Pain	Blocked arteries	Patient Weight	Heart Disease	Sample weight I1	New Weight	Norm Weight	Bins
Yes	Yes	200	Yes	1/8	0.05	0.07	0.07
No	Yes	178	Yes	1/8	0.05	0.07	0.14
Yes	No	205	Yes	1/8	0.05	0.07	0.21
Yes	Yes	165	Yes	1/8	0.33	0.49	0.70
No	Yes	165	No	1/8	0.05	0.07	0.77
No	Yes	125	No	1/8	0.05	0.07	0.84
Yes	No	165	No	1/8	0.05	0.07	0.91
Yes	Yes	173	No	1/8	0.05	0.07	1.00

Step 5:

Understanding the total error (TE) and performance of a stump is essential because it guides the adjustment of weights. Without this adjustment, subsequent models may yield similar results to the previous ones. To facilitate learning and adaptation, the weights of incorrectly predicted samples are increased, while those of correctly predicted ones are reduced. Consequently, when building the next model, greater emphasis is placed on samples with higher weights. After assessing the classifier's significance and total error, the weights are updated using the following formula:

> New Sample weight = Old weight * e $^{\text{Amount of say}(\alpha)}$

When a sample is correctly classified, the amount of say (alpha) will be positive, while for misclassified samples, it will be negative. Suppose we have four correctly categorized samples and one misclassified sample. In this scenario, the sample weight for each data point is 1/8, and the amount of say (or performance) for the Weight stump is determined to be 0.97. For the correctly classified samples, the new weights are calculated as follows:

New Sample Weight = (1/8) * exp(-0.97). As for the misclassified sample, its adjusted weight will be:

Chest Pain	Blocked arteries	Patient Weight	Heart Disease	Sample weight I1	New Weight
Yes	Yes	200	Yes	1/8	0.05
No	Yes	178	Yes	1/8	0.05
Yes	No	205	Yes	1/8	0.05
Yes	Yes	165	Yes	1/8	0.33
No	Yes	165	No	1/8	0.05
No	Yes	125	No	1/8	0.05
Yes	No	165	No	1/8	0.05
Yes	Yes	173	No	1/8	0.05

We understand that the sum of all sample weights must be equal to one. However, when we add up all the new sample weights, we obtain a total of 0.68. To rectify this and ensure that the sum equals 1, we normalise these weights by dividing each weight by the total sum of updated weights, which is 0.68. Consequently, after normalising the sample weights, the sum now equals 1, ensuring that our dataset is properly balanced.

Chest Pain	Blocked arteries	Patient Weight	Heart Disease	Sample weight I1	New Weight	Norm Weight
Yes	Yes	200	Yes	1/8	0.05	(0.05/0.68) =0.07
No	Yes	178	Yes	1/8	0.05	(0.05/0.68) =0.07
Yes	No	205	Yes	1/8	0.05	(0.05/0.68) =0.07
Yes	Yes	165	Yes	1/8	0.33	(0.33/0.68) =0.49
No	Yes	165	No	1/8	0.05	(0.05/0.68) =0.07
No	Yes	125	No	1/8	0.05	(0.05/0.68) =0.07
Yes	No	165	No	1/8	0.05	(0.05/0.68) =0.07

Yes	Yes	173	No	1/8	0.05	(0.05/0.68) =0.07

Step 6:

Now, we need to generate a new dataset to assess whether the errors have diminished. To accomplish this, we'll exclude the "sample weights" and "new sample weights" columns. Then, we'll partition our data points into bins according to the "new sample weights."

Step 7:

We're almost there. Now, the approach randomly selects values ranging from 0 to 1. Since misclassified records have higher sample weights, they have a higher chance of being selected. Let's suppose the five random floats chosen by our algorithm are 0.75, 0.45, 0.82, 0.45, 0.38,0.42, 0.56, 0.51. Next, we'll determine where these random numbers fall within the bins and construct our new dataset, as shown below.

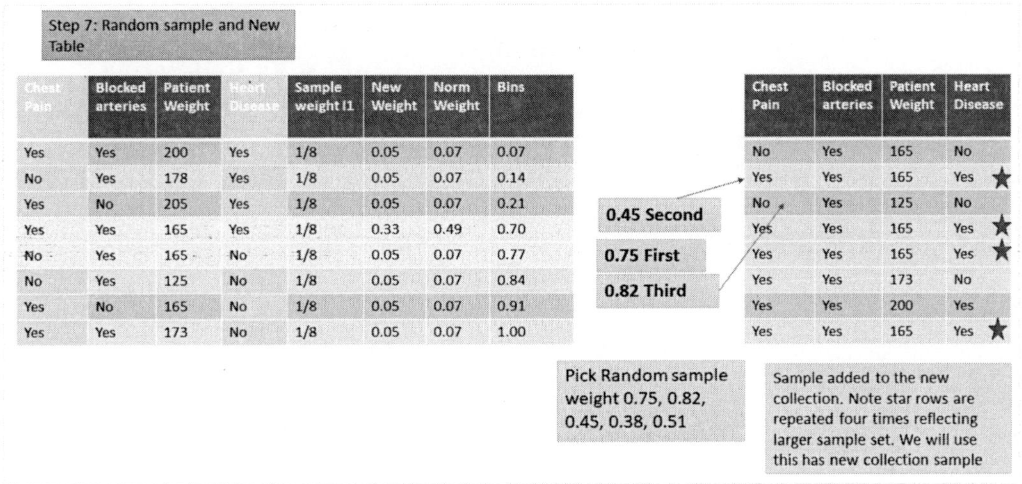

Step 7: Random sample and New Table

Chest Pain	Blocked arteries	Patient Weight	Heart Disease	Sample weight I1	New Weight	Norm Weight	Bins
Yes	Yes	200	Yes	1/8	0.05	0.07	0.07
No	Yes	178	Yes	1/8	0.05	0.07	0.14
Yes	No	205	Yes	1/8	0.05	0.07	0.21
Yes	Yes	165	Yes	1/8	0.33	0.49	0.70
No	Yes	165	No	1/8	0.05	0.07	0.77
No	Yes	125	No	1/8	0.05	0.07	0.84
Yes	No	165	No	1/8	0.05	0.07	0.91
Yes	Yes	173	No	1/8	0.05	0.07	1.00

Chest Pain	Blocked arteries	Patient Weight	Heart Disease
No	Yes	165	No
Yes	Yes	165	Yes ★
No	Yes	125	No
Yes	Yes	165	Yes ★
Yes	Yes	165	Yes ★
Yes	Yes	173	No
Yes	Yes	200	Yes
Yes	Yes	165	Yes ★

This is our new dataset, and we can see that the data point that was incorrectly categorised has been picked three times since it has a greater weight.

Step 8:

This new dataset now becomes our updated dataset, and we need to repeat all the previous steps. That is, assign equal weights to each data point, identify the stump that best separates the new set of samples by calculating their Gini index and selecting the one with the lowest value. Update the previous sample weights based on the "Amount of Say" and "Total Error."

Normalise the newly calculated sample weights. Repeat these steps iteratively until achieving a low training error.

Suppose we've constructed three decision trees (DT1, DT2, and DT3) sequentially based on our dataset. If we pass our test data through all these decision trees, we'll eventually determine the majority class, and we'll make predictions for our test dataset accordingly.

AdaBoost is a versatile and powerful machine learning algorithm used extensively for classification and regression tasks across various domains. It effectively combines multiple weak or base learners into a robust single strong learner, showcasing impressive generalisation performance. Its strength lies in its capability to assign weights to instances based on previous classifications, making it resilient to noisy and imbalanced datasets. AdaBoost is computationally efficient, less prone to overfitting, and relatively straightforward to implement. It excels particularly in binary classification tasks but can also handle multi-class classification problems. However, AdaBoost may not perform well with noisy data and is sensitive to outliers.

Exercise P8-U8 – D2	
Ensemble - Adaboost Algorithm	Output

# Importing necessary libraries 	
from sklearn.ensemble import AdaBoostClassifier
from sklearn import datasets
from sklearn.model_selection import train_test_split
from sklearn import metrics
from sklearn.svm import SVC
# Load the iris dataset. 	
iris = datasets.load_iris()
X = iris.data
y = iris.target
 	
# Split the dataset into training set and test set - 70% training and 30% test. 	
X_train, X_test, y_train, y_test = train_test_split(X, y, test_size=0.3)
# Create AdaBoost classifier object. 	
abc = AdaBoostClassifier(n_estimators=50, learning_rate=1)
# Train the AdaBoost classifier. 	
model = abc.fit(X_train, y_train)
# Predict the response for the test dataset. 	
y_pred = model.predict(X_test)
# Model Accuracy: how often is the classifier correct? 	
print("Accuracy:", metrics.accuracy_score(y_test, y_pred))
 	
# Using Different Base Learners 	
# Creating an AdaBoost classifier object with Support Vector Classifier as the base estimator 	
svc = SVC(probability=True, kernel='linear')
	Accuracy:
	0.9333333333333333
	Accuracy:
	0.9555555555555556

```
abc = AdaBoostClassifier(n_estimators=50, estimator=svc,
learning_rate=1)
# Training the AdaBoost classifier
model = abc.fit(X_train, y_train)
# Predicting the response for the test dataset
y_pred = model.predict(X_test)
# Model Accuracy: how often is the classifier correct?
print("Accuracy:", metrics.accuracy_score(y_test, y_pred))
```

Gradient Boosting Machines

Task: Classification and Regression

- Description: Ensemble technique that builds a series of weak learners (typically decision trees) and combines their predictions. Popular implementations of GBM include XGBoost, LightGBM, and CatBoost.

- Algorithm: The algorithm builds trees sequentially, with each tree correcting the errors of the previous ones. GBM is widely used for both regression and classification tasks and is known for its high predictive accuracy.

- Application: Anomaly Detection, Ranking and Recommendation Systems, Click-Through Rate Prediction, Customer Churn Prediction, Financial Fraud Detection, Energy Consumption Forecasting, and Time Series Forecasting.

Understanding Gradient Boosting

Gradient boosting is a powerful machine-learning algorithm used for both regression and classification tasks. It works by combining multiple weak learners, typically decision trees, to create a strong predictive model.

Key Concepts:

Tabular Data: Gradient boosting works with tabular data consisting of rows and columns, where each row represents an observation and each column represents a feature or target variable.

Features and Target: The algorithm learns from the relationship between the features (X) and the target variable (y). In the provided example, features like Employee age and Designation are used to predict the target variable, Salary.

Employee	Designation	Salary
2	Developer	50
4	Lead	70
6	Manager	80
7	Project Manager	100

Gradient Boosting, breaking down the steps:

Step 1: Compute the average of the target feature in a regression problem to establish the initial base model.

Step 2A: Create the base model.

Step 2B: Calculate the Residual 1 (Res1) by finding the difference between the actual and predicted values.

Step 2C: Build a new model or decision tree (Residual model) based on the Res1 residuals.

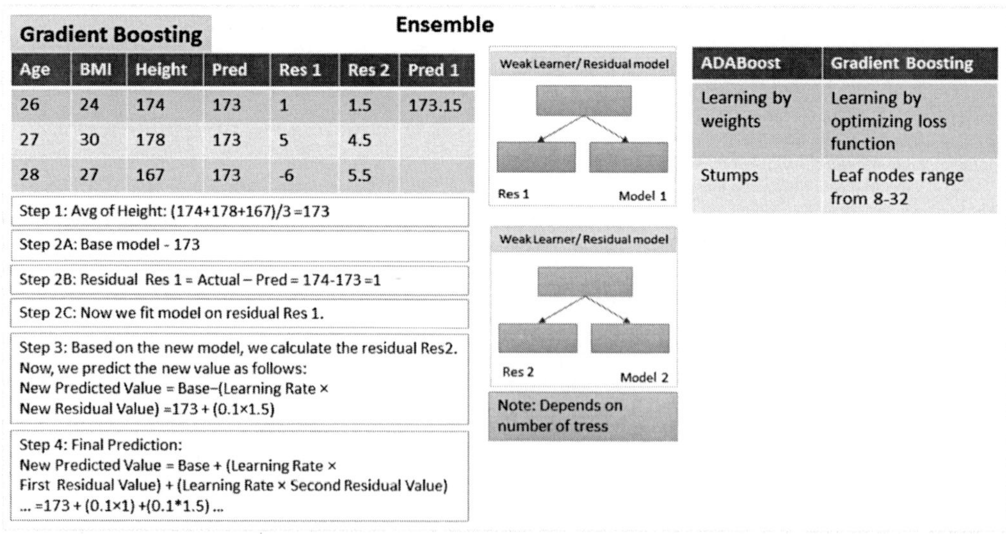

Step 3: Determine Residual 2 (Res2) using the new model. Then, predict the new value using the formula:

$$\textbf{New Predicted Value} = \textbf{Base} - (\textbf{Learning Rate} \times \textbf{New Residual Value})$$

Step 4: Step 2 to 3 process continues for subsequent trees,

Step 5: Final Prediction:

New Predicted Value = Base + (Learning Rate × First Residual Value) + (Learning Rate × Second Residual Value) ...

Finally, each contributes to the final prediction based on the number of trees.

Loss Functions:

Gradient boosting minimizes a loss function to iteratively improve the model's predictions. Two common loss functions used in gradient boosting are:

- **Mean Squared Error (MSE):** This loss function is commonly used for regression tasks. It measures the average squared difference between the predicted and actual values. The one-half multiplier simplifies the differentiation process, making it computationally efficient.

- **Cross-Entropy:** Cross-entropy is often used for classification tasks with discrete categories in the target variable. It measures the difference between the predicted probability distribution and the actual distribution of classes.

The Mean Squared Error (MSE) is a common loss function used in regression tasks to measure the average squared difference between the predicted and actual values. The formula for MSE is as follows:

$$\mathbf{MSE} = \frac{1}{n}\sum_{i=0}^{n}\left(\left(y_i - \hat{y}_j\right)^2\right)$$

Where:

- n is the number of observations in the dataset.
- y_i is the actual value of the target variable for the ith observation.
- $\hat{y}_j$ is the predicted value of the target variable for the ith observation.

To compute MSE:

- Calculate the squared difference between each actual (y_i) and predicted ($\hat{y}_j$) value.
- Sum up all the squared differences.
- Divide the sum by the total number of observations (n).

Other Loss Function:

Mean Absolute Error:

$$\text{MAE} = \frac{1}{n}\sum_{i=1}^{n}(|y_i - \hat{y}_i|)$$

Root Mean Squared Error (RMSE):

$$\text{RMSE} = \sqrt{MSE}$$

Mean Absolute Percentage Error (MAPE):

$$\text{MAE} = \frac{1}{n}\sum_{i=1}^{n}(|(y_i - \hat{y}_i)/y_i|) * 100\%$$

Example:

Suppose we have a simple employee dataset with employee age and designation as features and salary as the target variable. The gradient boosting algorithm learns from this data to predict salaries based on employee characteristics.

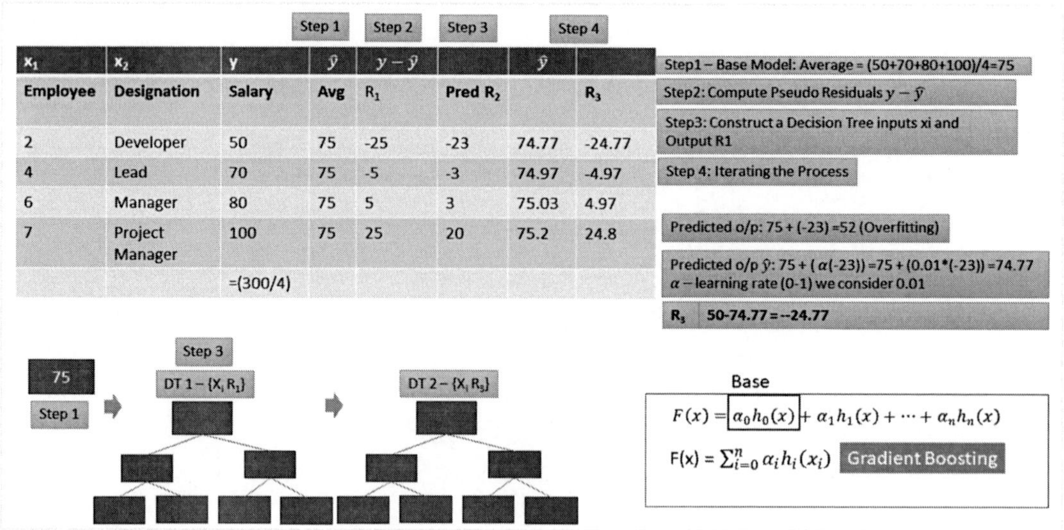

			Step 1	Step 2	Step 3		Step 4
x_1	x_2	y	$\hat{y}$	$y - \hat{y}$		$\hat{y}$	
Employee	**Designation**	**Salary**	**Avg**	R_1	**Pred R_2**		R_3
2	Developer	50	75	-25	-23	74.77	-24.77
4	Lead	70	75	-5	-3	74.97	-4.97
6	Manager	80	75	5	3	75.03	4.97
7	Project Manager	100	75	25	20	75.2	24.8
		=(300/4)					

Step1 – Base Model: Average = (50+70+80+100)/4=75

Step2: Compute Pseudo Residuals $y - \hat{y}$

Step3: Construct a Decision Tree inputs xi and Output R1

Step 4: Iterating the Process

Predicted o/p: 75 + (-23) =52 (Overfitting)

Predicted o/p $\hat{y}$: 75 + (α(-23)) =75 + (0.01*(-23)) =74.77
α – learning rate (0-1) we consider 0.01

R_3 50-74.77 = --24.77

75

Step 1

Step 3

DT 1 – {X, R_1}

DT 2 – {X, R_3}

Base

$F(x) = \alpha_0 h_0(x) + \alpha_1 h_1(x) + \cdots + \alpha_n h_n(x)$

$F(x) = \sum_{i=0}^{n} \alpha_i h_i(x_i)$ Gradient Boosting

Step 1: Establishing the Initial Prediction

Gradient boosting, an iterative algorithm known for refining prediction accuracy, begins with an initial estimation. This starting point is crucial for setting the groundwork. Typically, the initial prediction is set as the average of the target variable. In simpler terms, during the initial round, our model assumes uniformity, predicting that all outcomes are identical.

Step 2: Computing the Pseudo-Residuals

In the subsequent phase, we compute the deviations between each observed value and our initial prediction:

In traditional linear regression, these disparities between observed and predicted values are termed residuals. However, in the context of gradient boosting, we refer to them as pseudo-residuals.

Step 3: Constructing a Weak Learner

In this stage, we proceed to develop a decision tree, often referred to as a weak learner, tasked with predicting the pseudo-residuals. We utilise two features, namely Employee age and Designation, for this purpose. While we constrain the decision tree to only four leaves (terminal nodes) in this scenario, it's common practice to select a range of leaves between 8 and 32.

Once the tree is fitted to the data, predictions are generated for each observation in the dataset.

Now, you might wonder why we need multiple trees. The reason lies in our current state of overfitting to the training data. Our objective is to foster model generalisation. To address this issue, gradient boosting incorporates a parameter known as the learning rate.

The learning rate, ranging between 0 and 1, serves as a scaling factor for the predictions generated by each weak learner. By introducing an arbitrary learning rate of 0.01, our prediction is adjusted to 74.77, helping to combat overfitting and promote better generalisation of the model.

Step 4: Iterating the Process

Moving forward, we continue with the process outlined in Step 3 by constructing additional weak learners. The key point to note is that, with each iteration, we incorporate the residuals generated by the previous trees into our initial prediction. This cumulative approach ensures that each subsequent weak learner addresses the remaining discrepancies, progressively refining our model's predictive capabilities.

Mathematical Formula:

$$\boldsymbol{F(x) = \alpha_0 h_0(x) + \alpha_1 h_1(\alpha x) + \cdots + \alpha_n h_n(x)}$$

α - Learning rate 0-1

Gradient Boosting

$$\mathrm{F(x)} = \sum_{i=0}^{n} \alpha_i h_i(x_i)$$

For instance, suppose we're constructing a sequence of 10 trees, and the residuals from each tree are represented as r_i (where $1 \leq I \leq 10$). In this scenario, the prediction for the tenth round ($p10$) would be updated as follows:

$p_{10} = 175 + a \cdot (r_1 + r_2 + \ldots + r_{10})$

Here, p_{10} signifies the prediction in the tenth round, and α represents the learning rate.

Now, when employing early stopping, we opt for a substantial number of trees, such as 1000 or 10000. However, rather than awaiting the completion of all these trees, we continuously monitor the loss. If there's no improvement in the loss over a specified number of boosting rounds, say 50, we halt the training prematurely. This approach conserves time and computational resources, ensuring efficient model training.

Gradient boosting models, a powerful tool for tabular supervised learning tasks, offer various hyperparameters to fine-tune the model's behaviour. Here's a summary of key hyperparameters and their roles:

- Objective: Determines the direction and loss function of the algorithm, crucial for regression (MSE) or classification (Cross-Entropy) tasks.
- Learning Rate: Controls the contribution of each weak learner, influencing model strength and overfitting. Smaller values require more trees for training but yield stronger models.
- Number of Trees: Also known as the number of boosting rounds, it dictates the ensemble's strength and complexity. However, increasing the number of trees can lead to overfitting, mitigated by early stopping and a low learning rate.
- Max Depth: Sets the maximum levels in each decision tree, influencing model complexity. A value close to 3 is often chosen to prevent overfitting, with a maximum depth recommended at 10.
- Minimum Samples per Leaf: Controls branch splitting in decision trees, affecting the model's sensitivity to noise and overfitting.
- Subsampling Rate: Determines the proportion of data used to train each tree, useful for large datasets to prevent overfitting.
- Feature Sampling Rate: Similar to sub-sampling but applies to feature selection, reducing the risk of overfitting in datasets with numerous features.

Exercise P8-U8 - D3	
Ensemble – Gradient Boosting Algorithm	Output

import pandas as pd
import seaborn as sns
import numpy as np
from sklearn.compose import ColumnTransformer
from sklearn.ensemble import GradientBoostingClassifier
from sklearn.metrics import confusion_matrix, classification_report
from sklearn.model_selection import GridSearchCV, train_test_split
from sklearn.pipeline import Pipeline
from sklearn.preprocessing import OneHotEncoder, StandardScaler
# Step 1: Loading the data 	
input_path = r'C:\Users\User\mraj4\Documents\Optimum\Py-lib\scikit\diamonds.csv'
store_data = pd.read_csv(input_path, header=None)
 	
# Load the diamonds dataset from Seaborn 	
store_data = sns.load_dataset("diamonds")
# Step 2: Split data into features and target 	
X = store_data.drop("cut", axis=1)
y = store_data["cut"]
# Step 3: Split data into train and test sets 	
X_train, X_test, y_train, y_test = train_test_split(
   X, y, test_size=0.2, random_state=42
)
# Step 4: Define categorical and numerical features 	
categorical_features = X.select_dtypes(include=["object"]).columns.tolist()
numerical_features = X.select_dtypes(include=["float64", "int64"]).columns.tolist()
# Step 5: Define preprocessing steps for categorical and numerical features 	
preprocessor = ColumnTransformer(
   transformers=[
      ("cat", OneHotEncoder(), categorical_features),
      ("num", StandardScaler(), numerical_features),
   ]
)
# Step 6: Create a Gradient Boosting Classifier pipeline 	
pipeline = Pipeline(
   [
      ("preprocessor", preprocessor),
	Best Parameters: {'classifier__learning_rate': 0.1, 'classifier__max_depth': 6, 'classifier__n_estimators': 300}
	Train Score: 0.7963014460511679
	Test Score: 0.8027437893956247

```
        ("classifier",
GradientBoostingClassifier(random_state=42)),
    ]
)
# Step 7: Define the parameter grid
param_grid = {
    'classifier__learning_rate': [0.01, 0.05, 0.1],
    'classifier__n_estimators': np.arange(100, 500, 100),
    'classifier__max_depth': [2, 3, 4, 5, 6, 7]
}
# Step 8: Initialize the GridSearchCV object
gb_cv = GridSearchCV(pipeline, param_grid, cv=4)
# Step 9: Fit the GridSearchCV object to the training data
gb_cv.fit(X_train, y_train)
# Step 10: Display the best parameters, train score, and test
score
print("Best Parameters:", gb_cv.best_params_)
print("Train Score:", gb_cv.best_score_)
print("Test Score:", gb_cv.score(X_test, y_test))
# Step 11: Generate confusion matrix and classification report
y_pred = gb_cv.predict(X_test)
conf_matrix = confusion_matrix(y_test, y_pred)
report = classification_report(y_test, y_pred)

print("\nConfusion Matrix:")
print(conf_matrix)
print("\nClassification Report:")
print(report)
```

```
Confusion Matrix:
[[ 306   16    1    8    4]
 [  26  718   16   15  229]
 [   3    9 3914  171  195]
 [   4    4  304 2268  195]
 [   5  157  501  265 1454]]
```

```
Classification Report:
              precision    recall  f1-score   support

        Fair       0.89      0.91      0.90       335
        Good       0.79      0.72      0.75      1004
       Ideal       0.83      0.91      0.87      4292
     Premium       0.83      0.82      0.82      2775
   Very Good       0.70      0.61      0.65      2382

    accuracy                           0.80     10788
```

```
macro avg       0.81      0.79      0.80     10788
weighted avg    0.80      0.80      0.80     10788
```

This code performs the following tasks:

Data Loading: It loads the diamonds dataset from a CSV file using pandas and Seaborn libraries.

Data Preprocessing: It splits the data into features (X) and the target variable (y). Categorical features are identified and numerical features are scaled using a preprocessing pipeline.

Model Training: It sets up a Gradient Boosting Classifier pipeline, which includes preprocessing and the classifier itself. The classifier is configured to use default hyperparameters.

Hyperparameter Tuning: It defines a parameter grid for hyperparameter tuning, including learning_rate, n_estimators, and max_depth. It uses GridSearchCV to search through the parameter grid and find the best combination of hyperparameters using cross-validation.

Model Evaluation: It prints out the best parameters found by the grid search, along with the corresponding train score and test score. Additionally, it generates a confusion matrix and a classification report to evaluate the model's performance on the test set.

Overall, this code demonstrates the process of hyperparameter tuning for a Gradient Boosting Classifier using GridSearchCV and evaluates the performance of the tuned model on unseen data.

PART EIGHT

DAY TWENTY-ONE

Unit 8 - Lesson Two

Ensemble Methods - II

XGBoost

Master said, "Decision trees have been widely used for both classification and regression tasks, but they often suffer from overfitting issues because they tend to create complex, high-variance models. To address these issues, various ensemble methods have been developed."

One approach is bagging, where multiple decision trees are trained on different subsets of the data and their predictions are averaged. However, bagging can be computationally inefficient as trees are built independently.

To address this, boosting algorithms were introduced. These algorithms build trees sequentially, with each subsequent tree aiming to correct the errors of the previous ones. Gradient boosting is one such method that minimises the error in predictions by fitting each tree to the residuals of the previous ones.

To further enhance the performance of boosting, XGBoost was developed. XGBoost implements several optimizations, such as parallelisation and regularisation, making it faster and more accurate than traditional gradient boosting.

Another notable algorithm is CatBoost, which is designed to handle categorical features efficiently. It incorporates novel techniques for handling categorical data and achieves state-of-the-art performance.

LightGBM is another boosting algorithm that has gained popularity due to its efficiency and scalability. It uses a novel tree-building algorithm and is particularly well-suited for large datasets.

In summary, while decision trees are powerful models, ensemble methods like boosting have significantly improved their performance. XGBoost, CatBoost, and LightGBM are some of the most advanced algorithms that have emerged to address the limitations of traditional decision trees.

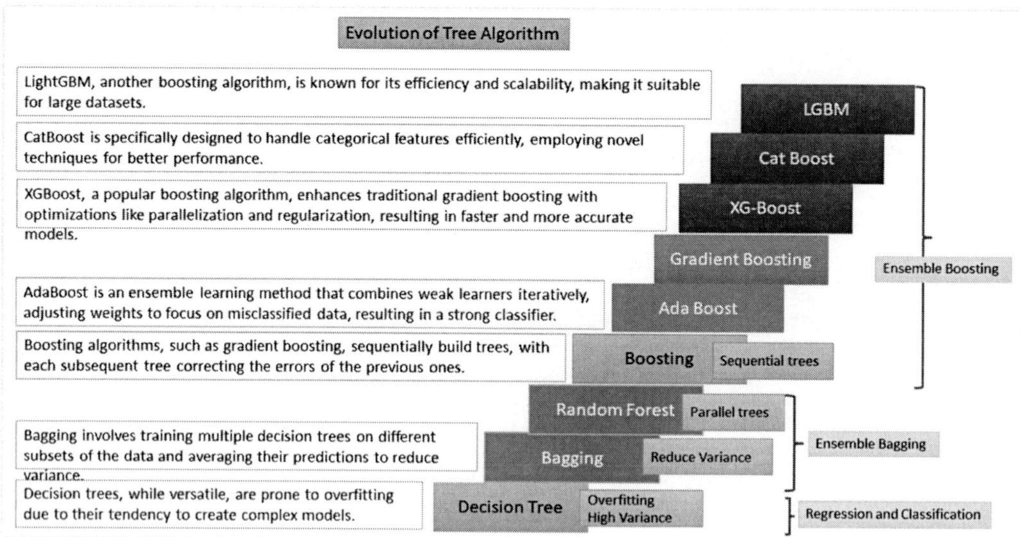

John asked, "What is XGBoost algorithm?"

Master said, "XGBoost, short for Extreme Gradient Boosting, is a distributed gradient boosting toolkit designed for efficient and scalable training of machine learning models. By combining predictions from multiple weak models, it achieves enhanced accuracy. Renowned for its ability to handle large datasets and deliver top-notch performance in tasks like classification and regression, XGBoost is widely utilised. Its strengths include efficient management of missing values without extensive preprocessing, parallel processing capabilities, and versatility in adjusting various model parameters for improved performance. With applications ranging from Kaggle competitions to recommendation systems, XGBoost stands out for its adaptability and effectiveness."

Let us try to understand with a simple example:

XGBoost operates on a simple dataset comprising features like Age and the predicted or dependent feature IQ. Initially, a base model, M0, is created by averaging the IQ values. Then, using this average, we calculate residuals and, subsequently, errors. The next model is then formulated based on error optimization.

In this process, three crucial parameters come into play: lambda for regularisation, gamma for automatic pruning of branches, and eta for rapid convergence. We build decision trees based on the Age feature and compute a similarity index using residuals and lambda. Initially, lambda is set to zero and progressively adjusted for subsequent models.

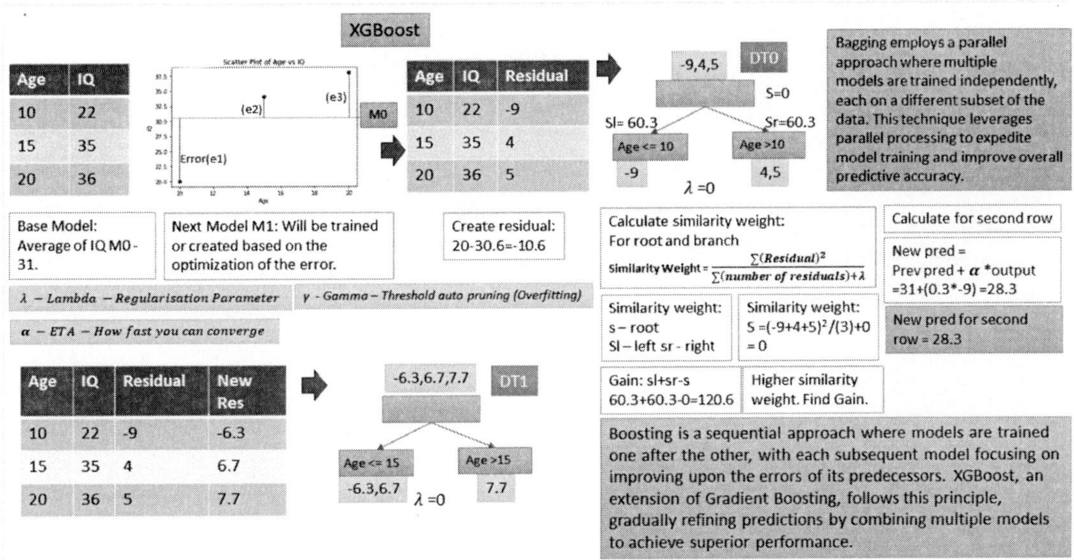

When the similarity index and branch values share the same sign, indicating higher values, we calculate the gain. If the gamma value surpasses the gain, the split halts, and automatic pruning is triggered.

For predicting new values, we utilise the previous predictions, assuming a learning rate of 0.3, and generate outputs. Based on these outcomes, we derive new residual values. This iterative process continues until we achieve an optimal model.

Example:

Let's consider a loan approval dataset with features like salary and credit score, and loan approval status as the target variable. Using XGBoost, we aim to predict loan approval based on salary and credit score attributes.

Step 1: Establishing Initial Prediction

XGBoost, renowned for refining prediction accuracy iteratively, begins with an initial estimation. This starting point, often the base model or average of loan approvals, sets the groundwork. In the initial round, the model assumes uniformity, predicting identical outcomes.

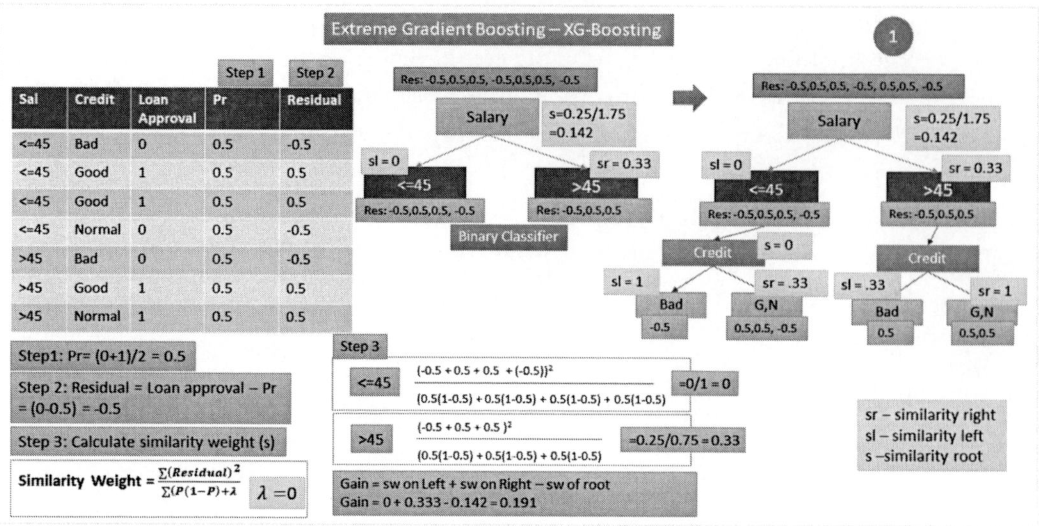

Step 2: Computing Residuals

In the subsequent phase, we compute deviations between each observed value and our initial prediction:

Residual = Loan approval - Initial prediction

Step 3: Constructing a Weak Learner

In this stage, we develop a decision tree, often referred to as a weak learner, tasked with predicting the residuals. Utilising features like Salary and Credit, we build the tree. Once fitted to the data, predictions are generated for each observation. We calculate similarity weight using the binary classifier tree formula. For root, left branch, and right branch, similarity weight is computed based on the residual. Finally, the Gain is determined, influencing the flow of the left or right branch:

$$\text{Similarity Weight} = \frac{\sum(\boldsymbol{Residual})^2}{\sum(\boldsymbol{P}(\mathbf{1}-\boldsymbol{P})+\boldsymbol{\lambda}}$$

- Residuals calculated
- Pr – Probability of 0 for no and 1 for yes
- $\lambda = 0$

Gain = (sl + sr - s)

- Sl – Similarity weight for left

- Sr – Similarity weight for right

> Similarity weight for <=45 = (-0.5 + 0.5 + 0.5 + (-0.5))^2 / (0.5(1-0.5) + 0.5(1-0.5) + 0.5(1-0.5) + 0.5(1-0.5)) = 0/1 = 0
>
> Gain = (sl + sr - s) = 0 + 0.33 - 0.142 = 0.191

We sum up the residuals before squaring to ensure that positive and negative residuals cancel each other out. This process helps balance the impact of outliers and ensures a more stable optimisation process.

Next, we introduce a regularization parameter, lambda, in the denominator. Boosting algorithms like XGBoost are susceptible to overfitting, and lambda helps mitigate this by constraining the model's learning capacity. Adding lambda reduces both the similarity score and gain, paving the way for tree pruning.

Step 4: Creating branches

We proceed by creating branches based on the credit feature, computing similarity weight, and determining the Gain. The decision on the flow is based on the Gain value. To prune the branch, we utilize Cover Pruning, calculated as Pr(1-Pr).

To mitigate overfitting, we implement pruning techniques for both leaves and nodes in the decision tree. In XGBoost, γ (gamma) represents the minimum acceptable gain for a node. Nodes with gains lower than γ are pruned, resulting in a shallower tree. By setting a high γ or introducing a large λ during similarity score computation, we constrain the tree's depth.

Pruning occurs in a bottom-up fashion. If a lower node exhibits higher gain than γ, pruning stops. However, even if the top node's gain is lower than γ, it remains unpruned.

> Cover pruning = Pr(1-Pr)

Step 5: Iterating the Process

Continuing the process, we repeat Step 4 to build the Decision Tree (DT).

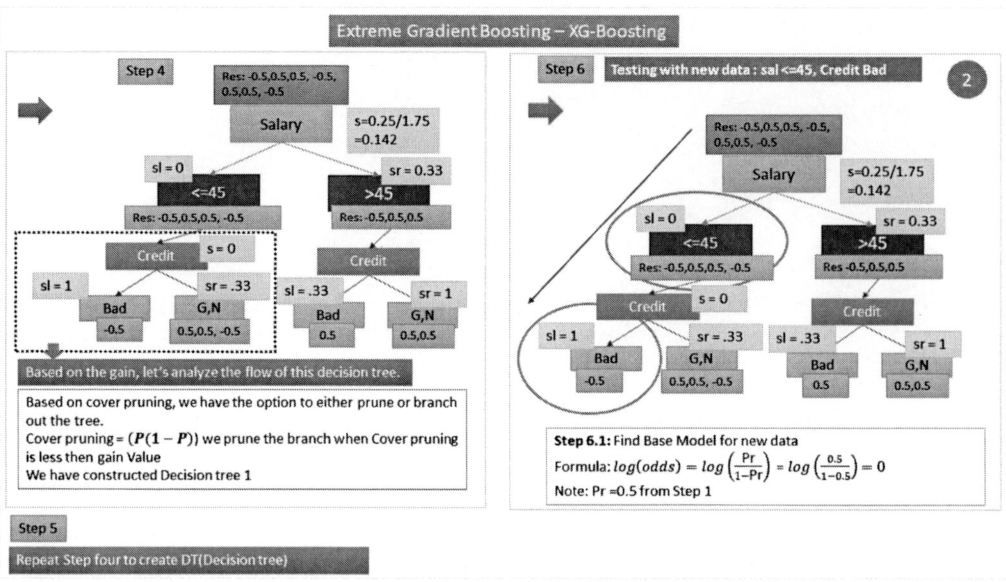

Step 6.1: Finding the Base Model for New Data

Compute the output value of each node in log-odds to ensure consistency with the model's predictions. Despite building the tree and leaves based on residuals of probabilities, the output values should be at log-odds. The conventional formula for this transformation is widely employed for this purpose.

Formula: $\mathbf{log(odds)} = \mathbf{log}\left(\frac{\text{Pr}}{\mathbf{1-}\text{Pr}}\right) = \mathbf{log}\left(\frac{\mathbf{0.5}}{\mathbf{1-0.5}}\right) = \mathbf{0}$

Note: Pr =0.5 from Step 1

Step 6.2:

Following the Path Based on the given Data

$\sigma(\text{Base}+\alpha(\text{sl})) = 0+(0.1\times1) = \sigma(0.1)$

The sigmoid function of 0.1 is approximately 0.524.

α (learning rate) = 0.1

The learning rate, often referred to as eta, plays a crucial role in the XGBoost algorithm. When eta is set to a high value, the new tree learns extensively from the previous tree, potentially leading to overfitting. Conversely, a low eta results in slower improvement, necessitating a larger number of trees to achieve high accuracy. Therefore, eta serves as a regularization parameter to mitigate overfitting and strike a balance between learning speed and accuracy.

The learning rate, ranging between 0 and 1, serves as a scaling factor for the predictions generated by each weak learner. By introducing an arbitrary learning rate of 0.1.

Based on the new probability Pr for the test data, we can calculate the residual.

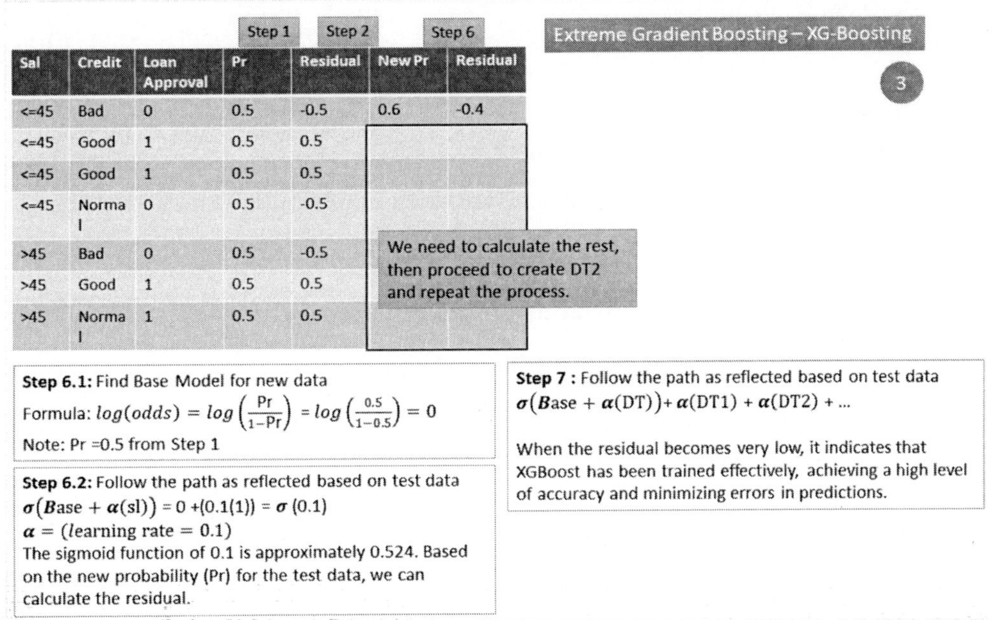

Sal	Credit	Loan Approval	Pr	Residual	New Pr	Residual
<=45	Bad	0	0.5	-0.5	0.6	-0.4
<=45	Good	1	0.5	0.5		
<=45	Good	1	0.5	0.5		
<=45	Normal	0	0.5	-0.5		
>45	Bad	0	0.5	-0.5		
>45	Good	1	0.5	0.5		
>45	Normal	1	0.5	0.5		

Now, you might wonder why we need multiple trees. The reason lies in our current state of overfitting to the training data. Our objective is to foster model generalisation. To address this issue, boosting incorporates a parameter known as the learning rate.

Step 7: Following the Path Based on Test Data

$$\sigma(\text{Base} + \alpha(\text{DT})) + \alpha(\text{DT1}) + \alpha(\text{DT2}) + \ldots$$

When the residual becomes very low, it indicates that XGBoost has been trained effectively, achieving a high level of accuracy and minimising errors in predictions.

Optimisation:

XGBoost employs several optimisation techniques to enhance its performance and efficiency:

- Regularisation: Utilises Lasso and Ridge Regression to penalise overly complex models, mitigating overfitting.
- Parallelisation and Cache Blocks: While training multiple trees cannot be parallelised, XGBoost accelerates the generation of tree nodes in parallel by sorting data into blocks, stored in compressed column format.
- Tree Pruning: Implements a depth-first approach for pruning trees backward, based on the max_depth parameter, enhancing computational efficiency.
- Cache-Awareness and Out-of-Core Computation: Efficiently utilises hardware resources by allocating internal buffers in each thread and optimising disk space for handling large datasets.
- Sparsity Awareness: Capable of handling sparse data with a specialised split finding algorithm that accommodates various sparsity patterns.
- Weighted Quantile Sketch: Employs a distributed weighted quantile sketch algorithm to facilitate the identification of optimal split points in weighted datasets.
- Cross-Validation: Provides a built-in cross-validation method to prevent overfitting, particularly beneficial for smaller datasets.

The Iris dataset, a staple in machine learning, consists of 150 samples of iris flowers characterised by four features: sepal length, sepal width, petal length, and petal width. Our objective is to classify the iris flowers into three species: setosa, versicolor, and virginica. To achieve this, we'll employ the XGBoost library for classification. Let's proceed with the demonstration.

Exercise P8-U8 – D4	
Ensemble – XG-Boost Algorithm	Output
import xgboost as xgb from sklearn.datasets import load_iris from sklearn.model_selection import train_test_split, GridSearchCV from sklearn.metrics import accuracy_score, classification_report, confusion_matrix	Best Hyperparameters: {'colsample_bytree': 0.6, 'gamma': 0.1, 'learning_rate': 0.05, 'max_depth': 3, 'min_child_weight': 1,

``
import time
 	
# Loading the Iris dataset 	
data = load_iris()
X, y = data.data, data.target
 	
# Splitting the data into training and test sets 	
X_train, X_test, y_train, y_test = train_test_split(X, y, test_size=0.2, random_state=42)
 	
# Defining parameter grid for hyperparameter tuning 	
param_grid = {
    'learning_rate': [0.01, 0.05, 0.1],
    'n_estimators': [100, 200, 300],
    'max_depth': [3, 5, 7],
    'subsample': [0.6, 0.8, 1.0],
    'gamma': [0, 0.1, 0.2],
    'reg_alpha': [0, 0.1, 0.5],
    'colsample_bytree': [0.6, 0.8, 1.0],
    'min_child_weight': [1, 3, 5]
}
 	
# Creating an XGBoost classifier 	
model = xgb.XGBClassifier()
 	
# Initialize GridSearchCV object 	
grid_search = GridSearchCV(model, param_grid, cv=5, scoring='accuracy', n_jobs=-1)
 	
# Training the model on the training data 	
start_training = time.time()
grid_search.fit(X_train, y_train)
end_training = time.time()
 	
# Extracting the best estimator 	
best_model = grid_search.best_estimator_
 	
# Making predictions on the test set 	
start_prediction = time.time()
predictions = best_model.predict(X_test)
end_prediction = time.time()
 	
# Calculating accuracy 	
accuracy = accuracy_score(y_test, predictions)
 	
# Classification report 	
report = classification_report(y_test, predictions, target_names=data.target_names)
``
	'n_estimators': 100, 'reg_alpha': 0.5, 'subsample': 0.6}
	
	Accuracy: 1.0
	
	Training Time (seconds): 593.2574729919434
	Prediction Time (seconds): 0.003039836883544922

```
# Confusion matrix
conf_matrix = confusion_matrix(y_test, predictions)

# Time consumed for training and prediction
training_time = end_training - start_training
prediction_time = end_prediction - start_prediction

print("Best Hyperparameters:", grid_search.best_params_)
print("\nAccuracy:", accuracy)
print("\nClassification Report:")
print(report)
print("\nConfusion Matrix:")
print(conf_matrix)
print("\nTraining Time (seconds):", training_time)
print("Prediction Time (seconds):", prediction_time)
```

The code utilises XGBoost, a machine learning algorithm, to train a classifier on the Iris dataset with optimal hyperparameters obtained through grid search. After training, the model's prediction accuracy is evaluated on a test set. The code also measures the time taken for training and prediction. In this case, the training process took approximately 593.26 seconds, while the prediction phase was completed in just 0.00304 seconds.

Classification and Confusion Matrix:

```
Classification Report:
              precision    recall  f1-score   support

      setosa       1.00      1.00      1.00        10
  versicolor       1.00      1.00      1.00         9
   virginica       1.00      1.00      1.00        11

    accuracy                           1.00        30
   macro avg       1.00      1.00      1.00        30
weighted avg       1.00      1.00      1.00        30

Confusion Matrix:
[[10  0  0]
 [ 0  9  0]
 [ 0  0 11]]
```

XGBoost Regression In-Depth Intuition

Example: Consider a dataset containing employee salary information with features such as experience and gap, and salary as the target variable. Employing XGBoost Regression, our objective is to predict salary based on experience and gap.

Step 1: Establishing Initial Prediction

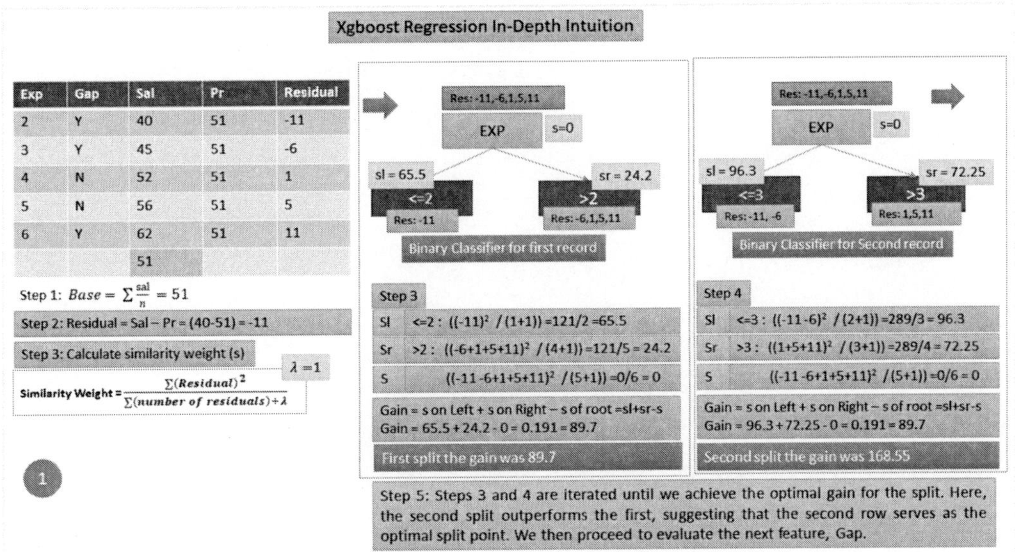

XGBoost, known for its iterative refinement of prediction accuracy, starts with an initial estimate. This starting point, typically the base model or average salary, lays the foundation. During the initial round, the model assumes uniformity, predicting identical outcomes.

Step 2: Computing Residuals

Next, we compute the deviations between each observed value and our initial prediction:

$$\text{Residual} = \text{salary} - \text{Initial prediction}$$

Step 3 and Step 4: Constructing a Weak Learner

In this stage, we develop a decision tree, often referred to as a weak learner, tasked with predicting the residuals. Utilising features like Experience and Gap, we build the tree. Once fitted to the data, predictions are generated for each observation. We calculate the similarity weight using the binary classifier tree formula. For the root, left branch, and right branch, the similarity weight is computed based on the residual. Finally, the Gain is determined, influencing the flow of the left or right branch: Note: The first split is based on the first record, and the second split is based on the second row.

Similarity Weight = $\frac{\sum(\boldsymbol{Residual})^2}{\sum(\boldsymbol{number\ of\ residuals})+\boldsymbol{\lambda}}$

- Residuals calculated
- Pr – Probability of 0 for no and 1 for yes
- $\lambda = 1$

Gain = (sl + sr - s)

- Sl – Similarity weight for left
- Sr – Similarity weight for right

Sl: <=2 : $((-11)^2 \ / \ (1+1)) = 121/2 = 65.5$

Sr: >2 : $((-6+1+5+11)^2 \ / \ (4+1)) = 121/5 = 24.2$

S: $\mathbf{((-11 -6+1+5+11)^2 \ / \ (5+1)) = 0/6 = 0}$

First split Gain = (sl + sr - s) = 65.5 + 24.2 - 0 = 0.191 = 89.7

Step 5: Creating Branches

We iterate Step 3 and Step 4 until we achieve the optimal gain for the split. In this instance, the second split outperforms the first, indicating that the second row serves as the optimal split point. We then proceed to evaluate the next feature, Gap.

We create branches based on the Gap feature, computing similarity weight, and determining the Gain. The decision on the flow is based on the Gain value.

To mitigate overfitting, we implement pruning techniques for both leaves and nodes in the decision tree. In XGBoost, γ (gamma) represents the minimum acceptable gain for a node. Nodes with gains lower than γ are pruned, resulting in a shallower tree. By setting a high γ or introducing a large λ during similarity score computation, we constrain the tree's depth.

Pruning occurs in a bottom-up fashion. If a lower node exhibits higher gain than γ, pruning stops. However, even if the top node's gain is lower than γ, it remains unpruned.

Step 6: Iterating the Process

We follow the path based on the second feature and its split. Additionally, we calculate the new residual value.

$(\mathbf{Base} + \boldsymbol{\alpha}(\mathbf{sl})) = 51 + (0.5(-8.5)) = (46.75)$

$\boldsymbol{\alpha} = (\boldsymbol{learning\ rate} = \mathbf{0.5})$

Step 7: Following the Path Based on the given Data

$(\mathbf{Base} + \boldsymbol{\alpha}(\mathbf{DT})) + \boldsymbol{\alpha}(\mathbf{DT1}) + \boldsymbol{\alpha}(\mathbf{DT2}) + \ldots$

When the residual becomes very low, it indicates that XGBoost has been trained effectively, achieving a high level of accuracy and minimising errors in predictions.

Exercise P8-U8 – D5	
Ensemble – XG-Boost Regression Algorithm	Output

import xgboost as xgb
from sklearn.datasets import fetch_california_housing
from sklearn.model_selection import train_test_split, GridSearchCV
from sklearn.metrics import mean_squared_error, r2_score
# Loading the California housing dataset 	
data = fetch_california_housing(as_frame=True)
X, y = data.data, data.target
# Splitting the data into training and test sets 	
X_train, X_test, y_train, y_test = train_test_split(X, y, test_size=0.2, random_state=42)
# Defining the parameter grid for Grid Search 	
param_grid = {
  'max_depth': [3, 5, 7],
  'learning_rate': [0.1, 0.01, 0.001],
  'subsample': [0.6, 0.8, 1.0],
  'colsample_bytree': [0.6, 0.8, 1.0],
  'n_estimators': [100, 200, 300]
}
# Creating an XGBoost regressor 	
model = xgb.XGBRegressor()
# Setting up Grid Search with cross-validation 	
grid_search = GridSearchCV(estimator=model, param_grid=param_grid, cv=5, scoring='neg_mean_squared_error', n_jobs=-1)
# Training the model on the training data 	
grid_search.fit(X_train, y_train)
# Getting the best parameters 	
best_params = grid_search.best_params_
	Best parameters: {'colsample_bytree': 0.8, 'learning_rate': 0.1, 'max_depth': 7, 'n_estimators': 300, 'subsample': 1.0}
	Mean Squared Error: 0.19749632976756834
	R-squared Score: 0.8492864952492247

```
# Creating the final model with the best parameters
model = xgb.XGBRegressor(**best_params)
# Training the final model on the full training data
model.fit(X_train, y_train)
# Making predictions on the test set
predictions = model.predict(X_test)
# Calculate the mean squared error and R-squared score
mse = mean_squared_error(y_test, predictions)
r2 = r2_score(y_test, predictions)
print("Best parameters:", best_params)
print("Mean Squared Error:", mse)
print("R-squared Score:", r2)
```

The provided code performs hyperparameter tuning for an XGBoost regressor using Grid Search and then evaluates the model's performance on the California housing dataset. Here's a brief overview:

Data Loading and Splitting: The code loads the California housing dataset using fetch_california_housing from sklearn.datasets. It splits the dataset into training and test sets with a ratio of 80:20.

Grid Search for Hyperparameter Tuning: It defines a parameter grid containing different values for max_depth, learning_rate, subsample, colsample_bytree, and n_estimators. Then, it uses GridSearchCV from sklearn.model_selection to perform an exhaustive search over the parameter grid with 5-fold cross-validation. The objective is to find the combination of hyperparameters that minimises the negative mean squared error.

Training the Final Model: After finding the best parameters using Grid Search, it creates the final XGBoost regressor model with those parameters.

Model Evaluation: The code trains the final model on the full training data and makes predictions on the test set. It calculates the mean squared error and R-squared score to evaluate the model's performance on the test set.

Output: Finally, it prints the best parameters found during Grid Search, along with the mean squared error and R-squared score of the final model on the test set.

Advantages:

- XGBoost excels in speed and efficiency, effortlessly managing large datasets and outperforming other algorithms in terms of processing time.
- Renowned for its exceptional accuracy, XGBoost consistently delivers superior results and can be fine-tuned to further enhance performance.

- Offering flexibility, XGBoost supports parallel and distributed computing across various platforms, ensuring adaptability to diverse computing environments.
- With an array of customisable features, such as regularization, cross-validation, and early stopping, XGBoost empowers users to tailor their models for optimal outcomes.

Cat Boost

Master said, "CatBoost, developed by Yandex in 2017, stands out as a versatile and efficient open-source machine learning algorithm. Yandex, often dubbed the "Russian Google," specializes in search and information services, making CatBoost a product of substantial expertise."

As its name suggests, CatBoost, short for "Categorical Boosting," shines in handling categorical variables without the need for conventional preprocessing techniques like one-hot encoding. This unique capability streamlines the training process, eliminating the cumbersome task of transforming non-numeric data into numeric values.

Moreover, CatBoost goes beyond its categorical prowess by seamlessly integrating various data types, including images, audio, and text features, into a unified framework. This flexibility empowers data scientists to work with diverse datasets efficiently, regardless of the data's format or nature.

One of CatBoost's notable advantages lies in its ability to handle categorical data effortlessly, a feat that many other machine learning algorithms struggle with. By automating the processing of categorical features, CatBoost simplifies feature engineering, eliminating the need for manual transformation and reducing the complexity of model development.

LightGBM leverages the symmetric weighted quantile sketch (SWQS) algorithm to effectively manage missing values within datasets. This approach not only mitigates the risk of overfitting but also enhances the dataset's overall performance. By automatically handling missing values, SWQS ensures that LightGBM can optimise its model without being adversely impacted by incomplete data, thereby improving the accuracy and reliability of the results.

In essence, CatBoost's innovative approach to handling categorical variables and its compatibility with a wide range of data types make it a powerful tool for data scientists and machine learning practitioners.

Features:

CatBoost presents a suite of built-in features that streamline the machine-learning process and enhance model performance. Firstly, it efficiently handles categorical features without preprocessing, eliminating the need for converting non-numeric factors into numerical values. This simplifies data preparation, saving time and effort.

Moreover, CatBoost delivers excellent results even without extensive parameter tuning, offering competitive performance with default parameters. It can also handle missing values in input data without requiring imputation, ensuring robustness in real-world datasets.

Additionally, CatBoost automatically scales all columns to the same scaling internally, reducing the need for extensive manual column conversions. This feature contributes to smoother model building and improves overall efficiency.

To prevent overfitting, CatBoost implements robust tree boosting, ordered boosting, and random permutations for feature combinations. These techniques promote model generalisation to unseen data, enhancing reliability and performance.

Furthermore, CatBoost internally applies built-in cross-validation methods to select the best hyperparameters for the model, optimising model performance.

Lastly, CatBoost offers a GPU-accelerated version of its algorithm, enabling fast and scalable model training on large datasets. The GPU implementation enhances scalability and performance, especially beneficial for multi-card configurations.

```
pip install catboost
```

Order and Target Encoding:

Order Encoding: CatBoost internally handles categorical variables by default, employing order encoding. It assigns unique numerical values to each category based on the ordering of the categories and the mean target value associated with them. This approach preserves the ordinal relationship between categories and the target variable.

Target Encoding: In addition to order encoding, CatBoost performs target encoding. It calculates the mean target value for each category and uses these values as numerical representations during model training. This technique leverages the relationship between categorical features and the target variable to enhance predictive accuracy.

Sampling Techniques

CatBoost builds upon the foundational principles of decision trees and gradient boosting, a technique aimed at sequentially combining multiple weak models to create a robust predictive model. By iteratively refining the model's predictions, gradient boosting enhances its performance, gradually minimising errors and improving accuracy.

Unlike traditional gradient boosting approaches, CatBoost takes a unique approach to growing decision trees. Instead of following the conventional method, which involves sequentially fitting decision trees and learning from their mistakes, CatBoost adopts an oblivious tree growing procedure. In this approach, all nodes at the same level of the tree test the same predictor with the same condition, facilitating efficient computation through bitwise operations.

The oblivious tree strategy offers several advantages. It simplifies the fitting process, making it more efficient, particularly on CPUs. Additionally, the uniformity in testing predictors and conditions across nodes helps regulate the model's complexity, reducing the risk of overfitting. As a result, CatBoost strikes a balance between model performance and generalisation, ultimately yielding competitive predictive accuracy while mitigating the risk of overfitting.

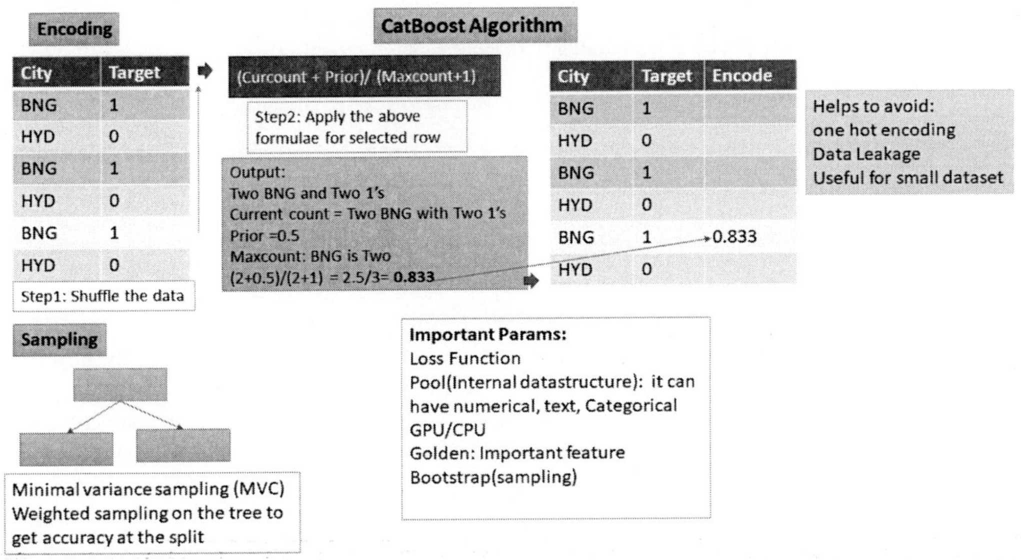

CatBoost implements various sampling techniques to improve model robustness and generalization:

- **Random Sampling:** Randomly selects subsets of data for training each tree in the ensemble.
- **Bootstrap Sampling:** Uses bootstrap sampling to create multiple datasets from the original data, enabling the model to learn from diverse perspectives.
- **Stratified Sampling:** Ensures balanced representation of target classes within each sampled subset, reducing bias and improving model performance on imbalanced datasets.

Types of Parameters

CatBoost offers a comprehensive set of parameters to fine-tune model behaviour and performance:

- **Core Parameters:** Define fundamental aspects of the model, such as learning rate, tree depth, and regularization.
- **Tree Parameters:** Control the structure and complexity of individual decision trees in the ensemble.
- **Boosting Parameters:** Influence the boosting process, including the number of trees and the learning rate schedule.
- **Regularization Parameters:** Prevent overfitting by applying L2 regularization, bagging, and other techniques.

SHAP Values and Usage

- **SHAP (SHapley Additive exPlanations)** values enable interpretation of CatBoost models by quantifying the contribution of each feature to individual predictions:
- **Calculation:** After training, SHAP values are computed for each instance in the dataset, revealing the impact of features on model predictions.
- **Interpretation:** Analyzing SHAP values helps understand feature importance and how they influence model outcomes.
- **Visualization:** Visualizing SHAP values provides intuitive insights into model behaviour and feature contributions, aiding in model explanation and validation.

In essence, CatBoost's unique capabilities in handling categorical features, coupled with its rich parameterisation and interpretability features like SHAP values, make it a powerful choice for a wide range of tabular data problems.

CatBoost Metrics:

Master explained that the CatBoost metrics encompass performance evaluation measures crucial for assessing the accuracy and effectiveness of CatBoost models. These metrics, spanning accuracy, precision, recall, F1-score, ROC-AUC, and RMSE, evaluate predictive capabilities across classification, regression, and ranking tasks. Analyzing these metrics aids in understanding model performance, identifying strengths and weaknesses, and guiding improvements for enhanced accuracy and reliability.

CatBoost employs parallelism and GPU training to expedite model training, enhancing speed and efficiency. Leveraging parallelism techniques optimizes CPU core utilization during training, significantly accelerating the process. Additionally, supporting GPU training harnesses the computing power of graphics processing units, further expediting training. These features facilitate faster model convergence and scalability, making CatBoost suitable for large datasets and complex machine learning challenges.

Training and Analysis:

CatBoost Model Training and Analysis involve optimising parameters and techniques to enhance model performance. Users manipulate parameters like tree parameters and optimisation techniques, leveraging methods such as grid search and Bayesian optimisation for hyperparameter tuning. Visualisation tools aid in analysing training parameters, feature importance, and overfitting. Cross-validation ensures robustness, while monitoring training progress and regularisation parameters promotes model stability and generalisation.

Key aspects include:

- Manipulating CatBoost parameters and hyperparameters
- Techniques like grid search and Bayesian optimisation for tuning
- Visualising training parameters and feature importance
- Monitoring overfitting and model stability
- Utilising cross-validation for robustness
- Analysing training progress and regularisation parameters

Exercise P8-U8 – D6	
Ensemble – Catboost Algorithm	Output

import pandas as pd
import numpy as np
from catboost import CatBoostRegressor, Pool, cv
from sklearn.metrics import mean_squared_error, mean_absolute_error, r2_score
from sklearn.model_selection import train_test_split, GridSearchCV
# Loading the data 	
input_path = r'C:\Users\User\mraj4\Documents\Optimum\Py-lib\scikit\Housing\train.csv'
store_data = pd.read_csv(input_path)
	Best Parameters: {'depth': 4, 'iterations': 150, 'l2_leaf_reg': 0.2, 'learning_rate': 0.1}
	
	Root Mean Squared Error: 27982.650601792684
	Mean Absolute Error: 17845.51248309017

<table>
<tr>
<td>

```
# Check if 'SalePrice' column exists in the DataFrame
if 'SalePrice' in store_data.columns:
    # Choose features and target variable
    features = store_data.columns.difference(['SalePrice'])  # All
columns except 'SalePrice'
    target = 'SalePrice'

    # Convert categorical features to strings
    categorical_features                                    =
store_data[features].select_dtypes(include=['object']).columns
    for feature in categorical_features:
        store_data[feature] = store_data[feature].astype(str)

    # Split data into features and target
    X = store_data[features]
    y = store_data[target]
    # Split the data into training and testing sets
    X_train,  X_test,  y_train,  y_test  =  train_test_split(X,  y,
test_size=0.2, random_state=42)
    # Find categorical features for CatBoost
    categorical_features_indices    =    np.where(X.dtypes    ==
'object')[0]

    # Define hyperparameters for grid search
    params_grid = {
        'iterations': [100, 150, 200],
        'learning_rate': [0.03, 0.1],
        'depth': [2, 4, 6, 8],
        'l2_leaf_reg': [0.2, 0.5, 1, 3]
    }

    # Create CatBoost Regressor
    model = CatBoostRegressor()

    # Perform grid search with cross-validation
    grid_search        =        GridSearchCV(estimator=model,
param_grid=params_grid,                                   cv=3,
scoring='neg_root_mean_squared_error')
    grid_search.fit(X_train,                            y_train,
cat_features=categorical_features_indices)

    # Get best parameters
    best_params = grid_search.best_params_
    print("Best Parameters:", best_params)

    # Train CatBoost model with best parameters
    best_model = CatBoostRegressor(**best_params)
```

</td>
<td>R-squared Score: 0.8979145458027186</td>
</tr>
</table>

```
    best_model.fit(X_train,                                        y_train,
cat_features=categorical_features_indices)

    # Make predictions on test set
    predictions = best_model.predict(X_test)

    # Calculate RMSE, MAE, and R-squared Score
    rmse = np.sqrt(mean_squared_error(y_test, predictions))
    mae = mean_absolute_error(y_test, predictions)
    r2 = r2_score(y_test, predictions)

    print("Root Mean Squared Error:", rmse)
    print("Mean Absolute Error:", mae)
    print("R-squared Score:", r2)

else:
    print("'SalePrice' column does not exist in the DataFrame.")
```

This Python code demonstrates the process of building and evaluating a CatBoostRegressor model for predicting house prices using a real estate dataset. Here's a brief overview:

Data Loading and Preprocessing:

- The code begins by loading the dataset from a CSV file and checking if the 'SalePrice' column exists.
- Categorical features are converted to strings, and the dataset is split into features (X) and the target variable (y).
- The data is further split into training and testing sets using a 80-20 ratio.

Grid Search for Hyperparameter Tuning:

- Hyperparameters for the CatBoostRegressor model are defined in a parameter grid.
- GridSearchCV is employed to perform a grid search for cross-validation (3 folds) to find the best combination of hyperparameters.
- The grid search is conducted using negative root mean squared error (RMSE) as the scoring metric.

Model Training with Best Parameters:

- The best parameters obtained from the grid search are used to instantiate a new

CatBoostRegressor model.

- The model is trained on the training data, including categorical features.

Model Evaluation:

- Predictions are made on the test set using the trained model.
- Root mean squared error (RMSE), mean absolute error (MAE), and R-squared score are calculated to evaluate the model's performance.
- The evaluation metrics are printed to the console.

Output Handling:

- If the 'SalePrice' column does not exist in the DataFrame, a message indicating this is displayed.

Overall, the code showcases the workflow of training a CatBoostRegressor model, tuning hyperparameters, and evaluating its performance on a real estate dataset.

CatBoost Applications:

CatBoost is a versatile gradient-boosting library widely applied across various domains and use cases requiring predictive modeling. Its applications include:

Classification Tasks:

- Binary classification with CatBoost
- Multiclass classification with CatBoost
- Multi-label classification with CatBoost

Examples:

- Sentiment analysis
- Email spam detection
- Breast cancer prediction

Regression Tasks:

- Regression with CatBoost
- Multiregression with CatBoost

Examples:

- House price prediction in real estate
- Fuel consumption prediction in vehicles
- Share price prediction in stock market
- Demand forecasting in retail

Ranking and Recommendation Systems:

CatBoost supports ranking tasks, making it suitable for personalised recommendations and search result ranking.

Examples:

- E-commerce product recommendations
- Movie recommendations
- Job or candidate recommendations in recruitment platforms

These applications demonstrate CatBoost's versatility and effectiveness in various predictive modelling scenarios, ranging from classification and regression to ranking and recommendation systems.

PART EIGHT

DAY TWENTY-ONE

Unit 8 - Lesson Three

Ensemble Methods - III

LightGBM

Master said, "LGBM, or LightGBM, is a gradient boosting framework developed by Microsoft that focuses on tree-based learning algorithms. It is known for its high efficiency, low memory usage, and fast training speed."

LightGBM tree:

A LightGBM tree, integral to the LightGBM gradient boosting framework, embodies decision tree structures, composed of nodes for feature splits and leaf nodes for predictions. Constructed recursively, LightGBM trees adopt a leaf-wise approach, prioritizing maximum loss reduction at each training step. Through optimization of specific objective functions, they support diverse splitting criteria and pruning techniques, crucial for enhancing model performance. These trees collectively form an ensemble model, culminating in accurate and efficient machine-learning predictions.

Key features of LightGBM's tree growth strategy include its leaf-wise approach, gradient-based optimization, and histogram-based learning techniques. Additionally, LightGBM excels in efficiently handling categorical features, further contributing to its effectiveness in various machine-learning tasks.

LightGBM Boosting Algorithms:

LightGBM Boosting Algorithms, including Gradient Boosting Decision Trees (GBDT), Gradient-based One-Side Sampling (GOSS), Exclusive Feature Bundling (EFB), and Dropouts meet Multiple Additive Regression Trees (DART), offer a comprehensive toolkit for efficient and accurate machine learning. GBDT sequentially builds decision trees to iteratively correct errors, while GOSS optimizes efficiency by sampling instances with large gradients. EFB reduces overfitting by bundling exclusive features, and DART enhances model robustness through dropout regularization, training an ensemble of diverse models. These algorithms strike a balance between speed, memory usage, and accuracy, making LightGBM a versatile and powerful choice for various machine learning tasks, including regression, classifications, and time series analysis.

Binning, also known as discretization, is a process of transforming continuous numerical features into discrete intervals or bins. This helps simplify the learning process for tree-based models like LightGBM by reducing the number of splits required during training.

EFB, or Exclusive Feature Bundling, is a technique used in LightGBM to further enhance efficiency and reduce memory usage. It involves grouping related features together into bundles based on their correlations, thus reducing the number of features the model needs to consider during training.

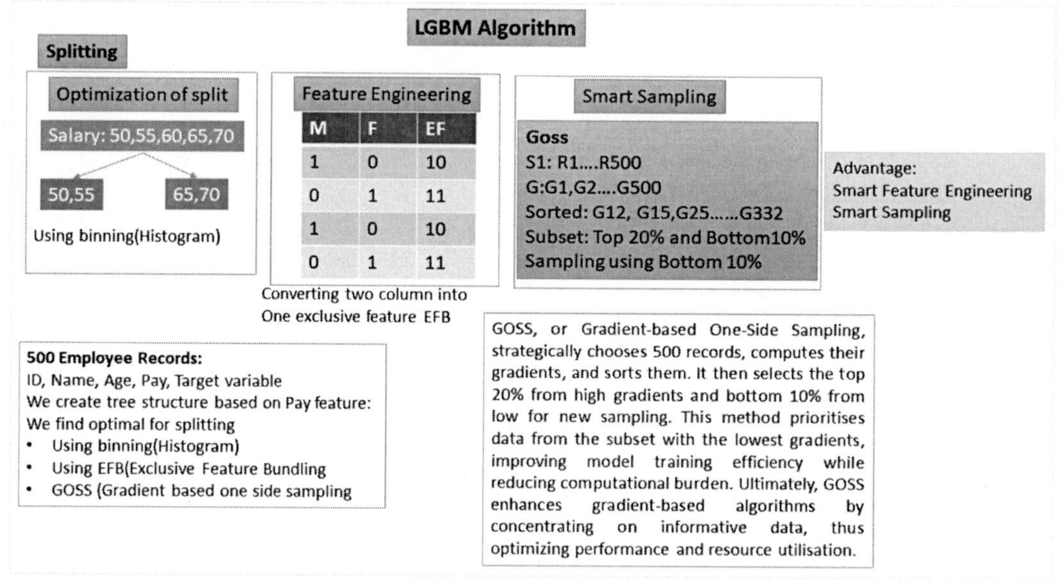

Baseline Model: Gradient-based One-Side Sampling (GOSS)

In the Gradient-based One-Side Sampling (GOSS) technique, a subset of data is selected based on the gradients computed during the training process. Here's how it works:

Data Selection: Initially, a sample of 500 records is randomly selected from the dataset.

Gradient Computation: Gradients (G1, G2, etc.) are calculated for each record in the sample.

Sorting Gradients: The computed gradients are sorted in descending order.

Selection Criteria: The top 20% and bottom 10% of the sorted gradient list are selected based on their values.

Subset Creation: Two subsets are created from the original sample:

- **Top 20% Subset:** Records with the highest gradients are included in this subset.
- **Bottom 10% Subset:** Records with the lowest gradients are included in this subset.

Sampling Strategy: Data is primarily sampled from the bottom 10% subset. This means that more emphasis is placed on records with lower gradients during the sampling process.

By using GOSS, the model focuses on training with the most informative data points while reducing the computational overhead associated with processing large datasets. This technique helps enhance the efficiency and effectiveness of gradient-based optimisation algorithms in machine learning models.

The LightGBM library offers two algorithms for multiclass classification: “multiclass” and “multiclassova” (One-vs-All).

- Multiclass Objective: Utilizes the softmax multiclass objective function to directly optimize the classification task across all classes simultaneously.
- Multiclassova Objective: Employs the One-vs-All binary objective function, where each class is treated as a separate binary classification problem against all other classes.

Both algorithms aim to optimize classification accuracy, with the choice between them typically not significantly impacting model performance.

LightGBM Ranker:

Master explained that the LightGBM Ranker is a specialized model within the LightGBM framework designed for ranking tasks, particularly suited for scenarios like search engine ranking and recommendation systems. By employing pairwise ranking objective functions, it optimizes the order of items within pairs to maximise ranking metrics such as NDCG (Normalized Discounted Cumulative Gain). LightGBM Ranker excels at learning the relative importance and relevance of items in ranked lists, enhancing user experience by delivering more accurate and personalised recommendations.

Training and evaluating:

Training and evaluating a LightGBM model involve iterative fitting of gradient boosting trees to minimize a specified loss function, with parameters adjusted to enhance performance. Evaluation metrics like mean squared error or accuracy gauge model effectiveness, often using cross-validation to prevent overfitting. Loading data, training, and evaluation form the core workflow, with hyperparameter tuning optimizing model behavior. Techniques like grid search and Bayesian optimization systematically explore hyperparameter space, aiming to improve performance based on specified metrics. Key hyperparameters include learning rate, number of leaves, and regularization terms, crucial for achieving optimal results. Early stopping strategies further refine model training, ensuring efficient convergence.

Core parameters:

LightGBM Core Parameters are crucial settings dictating the behaviour and performance of LightGBM models during training. These parameters influence various aspects, including model structure, optimisation process, and objective function, and are pivotal for fine-tuning model performance. Examples include learning rate, number of leaves, maximum depth, regularisation terms, and optimisation strategies. Understanding and adjusting these parameters is essential for achieving optimal model performance.

- **objective:** Defines the loss function to optimise during training, such as regression or classification.
- **task:** Specifies the task as either training or prediction.
- **num_leaves:** Determines the maximum number of leaves in each tree, influencing model complexity.
- **learning_rate:** Governs the step size during gradient descent, affecting learning speed and generalisation.
- **max_depth:** Sets the maximum depth of each tree, impacting model intricacy and potential overfitting.
- **min_data_in_leaf:** Specifies the minimum data points required for a leaf node, balancing between overfitting and underfitting.
- **num_iterations:** Determine the number of iterations for training.
- **feature_fraction:** Controls the fraction of features considered for each tree, enhancing model diversity.
- **bagging_fraction:** Specifies the fraction of data used for bagging during training, improving robustness.
- **lambda_l1 and lambda_l2:** Regularisation parameters penalising large coefficients to prevent overfitting.
- **min_split_gain:** Specifies the minimum gain needed to split a node, regulating tree

growth.

- **categorical_feature:** Identifies categorical features for training the model.

```
pip install lightbgm
```

LightGBM Parallel and GPU Training optimizes model training by leveraging parallel processing and GPU acceleration. Parallel training distributes computations across multiple CPU cores or machines, while GPU training accelerates mathematical operations. These features enhance training speed and efficiency, especially for large datasets and complex models.

Feature Importance and Visualization in LightGBM involve assessing input features' significance and visualizing their impact on model predictions. SHAP values offer a unified measure of feature importance, quantifying each feature's impact on individual predictions.

Exercise P8-U8 – D7	
Ensemble – LGBM Algorithm	**Output**

import pandas as pd
from sklearn.model_selection import train_test_split, GridSearchCV
from lightgbm import LGBMClassifier
from sklearn.metrics import accuracy_score, log_loss, classification_report
# Loading the data with the correct delimiter 	
input_path = r'C:\Users\User\mraj4\Documents\Optimum\Py-lib\scikit\wine\winequality-red.csv'
store_data = pd.read_csv(input_path, sep=';')
# Replace whitespace in column names with underscores 	
store_data.columns = store_data.columns.str.replace(' ', '_')
 	
# Verify the presence of the 'quality' column 	
if 'quality' in store_data.columns:
   # Split the data into features and target
   X = store_data.drop('quality', axis=1)
   y = store_data['quality']
 	
   # Split the data into training and testing sets
   X_train, X_test, y_train, y_test = train_test_split(X, y, test_size=0.2, random_state=42)
 	
   # Define hyperparameters for grid search
   param_grid = {
      'learning_rate': [0.05, 0.1, 0.2],
      'n_estimators': [50, 100, 150],
	Best Parameters: {'learning_rate': 0.05, 'max_depth': 5, 'n_estimators': 100, 'num_leaves': 30}
	Accuracy: 0.6375
	Log loss: 0.8779697471219483

```
    'num_leaves': [20, 30, 40],
    'max_depth': [5, 10, 15]
  }

  # Create the model
  model = LGBMClassifier(verbose=-100)

  # Perform grid search with cross-validation
  grid_search = GridSearchCV(estimator=model,
param_grid=param_grid, cv=3, scoring='accuracy')
  grid_search.fit(X_train, y_train)

  # Get best parameters
  best_params = grid_search.best_params_
  print("Best Parameters:", best_params)

  # Train the model with best parameters
  best_model = LGBMClassifier(**best_params, verbose=-
100)
  best_model.fit(X_train, y_train)

  # Make predictions
  y_pred = best_model.predict(X_test)
  y_prob = best_model.predict_proba(X_test)

  # Compute the accuracy and log loss
  accuracy = accuracy_score(y_test, y_pred)
  logloss = log_loss(y_test, y_prob)

  # Generate a classification report
  report = classification_report(y_test, y_pred,
zero_division='warn')

  # Print results
  print('Accuracy:', accuracy)
  print('Log loss:', logloss)
  print('Classification report:\n', report)
else:
  print("'quality' column not found in the DataFrame.")
```

Output

```
Classification report:
              precision    recall  f1-score   support
           3       0.00      0.00      0.00         1
           4       1.00      0.10      0.18        10
           5       0.70      0.75      0.72       130
           6       0.60      0.64      0.62       132
```

```
           7       0.60      0.50     0.55       42
           8       0.00      0.00     0.00        5

    accuracy                          0.64      320
   macro avg       0.48      0.33     0.34      320
weighted avg       0.64      0.64     0.62      320
```

The provided code performs model training and evaluation using LightGBM for a wine quality classification task. Here's a brief overview:

Data Loading and Preprocessing:

- Loads the dataset from a CSV file with a specific delimiter.
- Replaces whitespace in column names with underscores for consistency.

Model Training and Evaluation:

- Splits the data into features (X) and the target variable (y).
- Splits the dataset into training and testing sets using a 80-20 split ratio.
- Defines a grid of hyperparameters for grid search optimization.
- Initialises a LightGBM classifier model with verbose=-100 to suppress training information.
- Performs grid search with cross-validation to find the best combination of hyperparameters using accuracy as the evaluation metric.
- Trains the model with the best hyperparameters found from grid search.
- Makes predictions on the test set and computes accuracy and log loss metrics.
- Generates a classification report including precision, recall, F1-score, and support for each class.
- Prints the best parameters, accuracy, log loss, and classification report.

Output:

- Displays the best parameters selected by grid search.
- Prints the accuracy and log loss of the trained model on the test set.
- Shows the classification report containing precision, recall, F1-score, and support for

each class.

Overall, the code efficiently trains a LightGBM classifier for wine quality classification, optimises hyperparameters using grid search, and evaluates model performance using accuracy and log loss metrics. It provides valuable insights into the model's predictive capabilities through the classification report.

Advantages of LightGBM include faster speed and higher accuracy compared to other gradient boosting algorithms, lower memory usage for handling large datasets, and better accuracy due to innovative algorithms like leaf-wise tree growth. LightGBM also supports parallel and distributed GPU learning, making it efficient for large-scale data and various industries' big data applications.

It include its ability to handle large datasets efficiently, its fast-training speed compared to other gradient boosting frameworks, its low memory usage, and its support for parallel and distributed computing. Additionally, LightGBM often achieves competitive performance with minimal hyperparameter tuning.

Comparing and Contrasting Boosting Algorithms

When comparing different boosting algorithms, it's essential to consider various aspects to make an informed decision.

Here's a breakdown of key factors to evaluate:

- **Theoretical Foundations:** Examine the underlying principles and mathematical formulations of each boosting algorithm. Consider how they address the problem of ensemble learning and how they handle weak learners.
- **Implementation Details:** Explore the specific implementations of the algorithms, including optimisation techniques, tree-building strategies, and handling of categorical variables. Look for differences in computational complexity and memory efficiency.
- **Parameter Settings:** Investigate the available hyperparameters and their effects on model performance. Understand how tuning these parameters can impact the trade-off between bias and variance.
- **Empirical Results:** Analyse the performance of each algorithm on real-world datasets. Use a variety of evaluation metrics, such as accuracy, precision, recall, F1-score, and area under the ROC curve (AUC). Compare results across different datasets and scenarios to assess generalizability.
- **Interpretability and Explainability:** Consider the interpretability of the models produced by each algorithm. Evaluate how easily stakeholders can understand and trust the predictions made by the model.

- **Scalability:** Assess the scalability of each algorithm, particularly concerning large datasets and computational resources. Look for features such as parallelization and distributed computing support.
- **Robustness:** Examine the robustness of each algorithm to noisy or imbalanced data, as well as its ability to handle missing values and outliers.

Choosing the Best Algorithm

Selecting the best boosting algorithm depends on various factors tailored to your specific needs:

- Data Characteristics: Consider the size, complexity, and nature of your dataset. AdaBoost may be suitable for smaller or less complex datasets, while XGBoost or LightGBM may be more appropriate for larger or more complex datasets.
- Modelling Objectives: Clarify your modelling objectives, such as maximising accuracy, minimising computational resources, or achieving a balance between interpretability and performance.
- Computational Resources: Consider your available computational resources, including CPU/GPU power and memory constraints. Choose an algorithm that can efficiently utilise these resources.
- Personal Preferences: Factor in your personal preferences and familiarity with each algorithm. Choose an algorithm that aligns with your expertise and workflow.

Ultimately, the best choice of a boosting algorithm is a nuanced decision that requires careful consideration of these factors and potentially experimentation with multiple algorithms on your specific dataset.

Stacking (Stacked Generalisation):

Apeksha asked, "What is stacking?"

Master said, "Stacked Generalization, or "Stacking," is an ensemble machine learning technique that combines predictions from multiple models on the same dataset. Similar to bagging and boosting, stacking aims to enhance predictive performance by leveraging the strengths of different models. However, stacking focuses on addressing the question of how to determine which model to trust when faced with multiple skilful models that excel in different ways."

In stacking, diverse models, often referred to as base models or level-0 models, are trained on the same dataset. These base models generate predictions, which are then combined by a meta-model, also known as a level-1 model. The meta-model learns how to best merge the predictions from the base models to produce the final output.

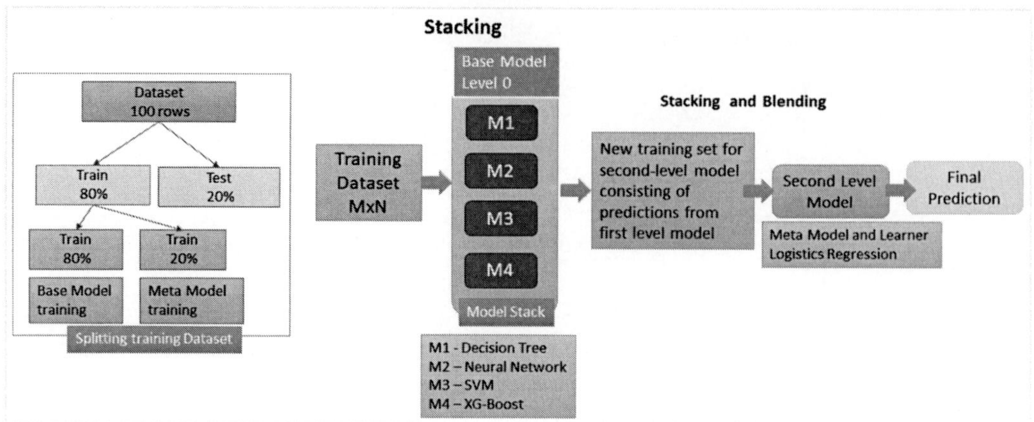

The training process for the meta-model involves using the predictions from the base models, along with the corresponding true outputs, as input-output pairs. Typically, k-fold cross-validation is employed to prepare the training dataset for the meta-model, using out-of-fold predictions from the base models. The meta-model may also consider additional input features used by the base models.

Base models in stacking are often complex and diverse, spanning different machine learning algorithms and assumptions about the underlying data distribution. This diversity helps ensure that the predictions made by the base models are uncorrelated or have low correlation, a crucial requirement for successful stacking.

On the other hand, the meta-model is typically simpler, providing an interpretable combination of the base model predictions. Linear regression is a common choice for regression tasks, while logistic regression is often used for classification tasks. This simplicity gives stacking its colloquial name "blending," as the final prediction is essentially a weighted average of the base model predictions.

Although stacking is designed to improve predictive performance, its success depends on various factors such as the complexity of the problem, the quality and diversity of the base models, and the correlation between their predictions. If a single base model performs as well as or better than the stacking ensemble, it may be preferred due to its simplicity and ease of interpretation.

Process:

Here's a breakdown of the stacking process:

- Data Preparation: The data is prepared by selecting relevant features, cleaning the dataset, and splitting it into training and validation sets.
- Model Selection: A diverse set of base models is chosen to ensure that they generate different types of errors and complement each other.
- Training the Base Models: Each selected base model is trained on the training set using various algorithms or hyperparameters to ensure diversity.
- Predictions on the Validation Set: The trained base models make predictions on the validation set.
- Developing a Meta Model: A meta-model, also known as a meta learner, is created to combine the predictions of the base models and generate the final prediction. This meta-model can be any algorithm like linear regression, logistic regression, or a neural network.
- Training the Meta Model: The meta-model is trained using the predictions made by the base models on the validation set. These predictions serve as features for the meta-model.
- Making Test Set Predictions: The meta-model is then used to make predictions on the test set. The predictions of the base models on the test set are fed into the meta-model, which generates the final prediction.
- Model Evaluation: Finally, the performance of the stacking ensemble is evaluated by comparing its predictions to the actual values on the test set using evaluation metrics such as accuracy, precision, recall, or F1 score.

Overall, the stacking process aims to leverage the strengths of multiple base models by feeding their predictions into a meta-model, which learns how to weigh and combine them effectively to produce the final prediction. This often results in improved performance compared to using a single model alone.

Stacking Ensemble Family

Master explained that the Stacking Ensemble Family encompasses various techniques for combining predictions from multiple base models to improve overall predictive performance. One such method is Voting Ensembles, which employs basic statistics to aggregate predictions from diverse models. It is useful for both regression tasks, where it can predict the mean or median of base model outputs, and classification tasks, where it employs hard or soft voting based on total votes received.

Another approach is the Weighted Average Ensemble, which assigns weights to each model based on its performance on training or hold-out datasets. This method offers more sophistication than simple voting, as it considers the relative skill levels of individual models and adjusts their influence accordingly during prediction aggregation.

Blending Ensembles utilize k-fold cross-validation to prepare out-of-sample predictions for the meta-model. Learner models are trained on distinct training sets, and predictions on validation sets are utilized as features for the meta-model. This method ensures that the meta-model can effectively combine predictions from base models without overfitting to the training data.

Additionally, the Super Learner Ensemble is akin to blending but focuses specifically on out-of-fold predictions from learner models. It builds a meta-model using predictions from base models on out-of-sample data, providing an alternative approach to combining model outputs.

While these are some of the prominent methods within the Stacking Ensemble Family, other variations and adaptations exist, each with its own strengths and suitability for different datasets and modelling tasks. Techniques such as Stacked Autoencoders and Deep Stacking Networks are examples of more advanced stacking methods that leverage deep learning architectures for improved performance in specific domains. These methods continue to evolve, offering researchers and practitioners a diverse toolkit for ensemble learning and predictive modelling.

Exercise P8-U8 – D8	
Ensemble – Stacking Algorithm	Output

from sklearn.tree import DecisionTreeClassifier
from sklearn.ensemble import RandomForestClassifier, StackingClassifier, GradientBoostingClassifier, AdaBoostClassifier
from sklearn.linear_model import LogisticRegression
import xgboost
import lightgbm as lgb
from catboost import CatBoostClassifier
import pandas as pd
from sklearn.model_selection import cross_val_score
from sklearn.datasets import load_breast_cancer
 	
# Load the breast cancer dataset 	
store_data = load_breast_cancer()
 	
# Separate features and target variable 	
X = pd.DataFrame(columns=store_data.feature_names, data=store_data.data)
y = store_data.target
 	
# Create a DataFrame for target variable 	
target = {'target': store_data.target}
y = pd.DataFrame(data=target)
	Decision Tree: 0.9174
	Random Forest: 0.9631
	XGBoost: 0.9701
	Gradient Boosting: 0.9579
	LightGBM: 0.9701
	ADABoost: 0.9701
	CATBoost: 0.9719
	Stacking Ensemble: 0.9684

```
y = y['target']

# Define classifiers
classifiers = {
    'Decision Tree': DecisionTreeClassifier(),
    'Random Forest': RandomForestClassifier(),
    'XGBoost': xgboost.XGBClassifier(),
    'Gradient Boosting': GradientBoostingClassifier(),
    'LightGBM': lgb.LGBMClassifier(),
    'ADABoost': AdaBoostClassifier(),
    'CATBoost': CatBoostClassifier()
}

# Perform cross-validation for each classifier and store accuracy
score
accuracy_scores = {}
for clf_name, clf in classifiers.items():
    scores = cross_val_score(clf, X, y, cv=5, scoring='accuracy')
    accuracy_scores[clf_name] = scores.mean()

# Define meta-model
meta_model = LogisticRegression()

# Create stacking classifier
stack_model                                                    =
StackingClassifier(estimators=list(classifiers.items()),
final_estimator=meta_model)

# Perform cross-validation for stacking classifier and store
accuracy score
stack_score = cross_val_score(stack_model, X, y, cv=5,
scoring='accuracy')
accuracy_scores['Stacking Ensemble'] = stack_score.mean()

# Write accuracy scores to file
input_path                                                     =
r'C:\Users\User\mraj4\Documents\Optimum\Py-
lib\datafiles\classifier_accuracy.txt'
with open(input_path, 'w') as file:
    for clf_name, accuracy in accuracy_scores.items():
        file.write(f'{clf_name}: {accuracy:.4f}\n')

print("Accuracy scores written to classifier_accuracy.txt file.")
```

This code performs a comparative analysis of multiple machine learning classifiers and a stacking ensemble using cross-validation, and stores the accuracy scores in a text file.

Dataset Loading and Preparation: It loads the breast cancer dataset using scikit-learn's load_breast_cancer() function and separates the features and target variables.

Defining Classifiers: Several classifiers are defined, including Decision Tree, Random Forest, XGBoost, Gradient Boosting, LightGBM, ADABoost, and CATBoost.

Cross-validation for Individual Classifiers: The code performs cross-validation for each classifier using a 5-fold cross-validation strategy. It calculates the mean accuracy score for each classifier and stores it in a dictionary named accuracy_scores.

Defining Meta-Model: Logistic Regression is chosen as the meta-model for the stacking ensemble.

Creating Stacking Classifier: A stacking classifier is created using scikit-learn's StackingClassifier. It uses the previously defined classifiers as base estimators and Logistic Regression as the final estimator.

Cross-validation for Stacking Classifier: Similar to individual classifiers, cross-validation is performed for the stacking classifier using a 5-fold cross-validation strategy. The mean accuracy score is calculated and stored in the accuracy_scores dictionary under the key 'Stacking Ensemble'.

Writing Accuracy Scores to File: Finally, the accuracy scores for all classifiers, including the stacking ensemble, are written to a text file named classifier_accuracy.txt. Each line in the file contains the classifier name, followed by its accuracy score.

Overall, this code provides a systematic approach to evaluating the performance of various classifiers and a stacking ensemble on the breast cancer dataset and saves the results for further analysis or comparison.

Summary:

In this unit, we covered ensemble methods and their various techniques and applications. We began by exploring the differences between stacking, bagging, and boosting in ensemble methods. Bagging, exemplified by models like Random Forest, reduces variance by combining the predictions of multiple models trained on different subsets of the data. Boosting, including methods like AdaBoost and Gradient Boosting, sequentially trains models to correct the errors of their predecessors, improving overall performance.

We delved into the details of Gradient Boosting, explaining its reliance on the loss function to guide the optimization process. We examined XGBoost, a powerful and efficient implementation of gradient boosting for regression and classification tasks, highlighting its enhancements over traditional boosting techniques.

Additionally, we explored CatBoost, which handles categorical features using techniques like order and target encoding, and LightGBM, a gradient-boosting framework known for its speed and efficiency. LightGBM's innovations, such as Gradient-based One-Side Sampling (GOSS) and the LightGBM Ranker, were also discussed.

We covered various sampling techniques and evaluation metrics essential for assessing model performance. Finally, we looked at stacked generalization (stacking), a technique that combines multiple models to improve predictive accuracy by training a meta-model on their predictions.

These topics provide a comprehensive understanding of ensemble methods and their applications, equipping us with the knowledge to implement advanced machine learning models effectively.

What Next:

In this unit, we cover a range of probabilistic models essential for machine learning tasks. We start with Naive Bayes, discussing its core concepts and variants for different data types. Then, we explore Multinomial Naive Bayes for text classification in NLP. Gaussian Process Classification is introduced for probabilistic modelling. We contrast Discriminant Analysis methods like LDA and QDA with PCA for dimensionality reduction. Finally, we delve into Bayesian Belief Networks, offering insights into their application in real-world scenarios.

P8-U8-L1-3 - Practice Question

1. What is the primary goal of ensemble methods in machine learning?
2. What does bagging stand for?
3. Which ensemble method involves training multiple models sequentially, each focusing on correcting the errors of its predecessor?
4. Name a popular bagging algorithm.
5. What is the main difference between bagging and boosting?
6. What does AdaBoost stand for?
7. In Gradient Boosting, what role does the loss function play?
8. What are the key features of XGBoost that enhance its performance?
9. How does CatBoost handle categorical features?
10. What does LightGBM stand for?
11. What is Gradient-based One-Side Sampling (GOSS) in LightGBM?
12. What is the primary use of the LightGBM Ranker?
13. What is the purpose of stacked generalization (stacking) in ensemble methods?
14. Which metric is commonly used to evaluate the performance of classification models?
15. What is the main advantage of using ensemble methods in machine learning?

PART NINE

APPENDIX

"Data is the ink of intelligence, and machine learning is the quill that writes the future—each algorithm, a brushstroke shaping the canvas of tomorrow."

– Shree Shambav

APPENDIX A

Online Resources

Online resources:

The supplementary materials for the book can be accessed online at:

Setup instructions:

The setup instructions provided here are the same as those in the book but include clickable links to all the components. If you encounter any difficulties during the setup process, please consult this resource.

Updates:

Python, like any other language, undergoes continuous updates and changes. We maintain a comprehensive collection of updates, so if you encounter any issues, please check this resource to see if the instructions have been changed.

Data:

The book provides some sample raw data for running the programs, but you can also create your samples using various file formats such as Excel, CSV, or JSON.

Practice questions:

You are encouraged to allocate ample time to work on the exercises independently. If you encounter any challenges and cannot proceed, consult this reference link.

Exercises and assignments:

While it's important to try the exercises on your own, you might encounter difficulties that prevent you from making progress. If that happens, you can find solutions to most of the exercises online. We encourage you to dedicate sufficient time to working on the exercises independently before seeking help.

Cheat sheets:

You can also find a wide range of cheat sheets online covering major concepts, which you can download and use for quick reference.

Errata

Despite our efforts to ensure the accuracy of our content, errors may still occur. If you come across any errors in the book, whether in the text or the code, please report them to us. Your feedback will not only aid in enhancing future editions of this book, but also assist other readers in avoiding potential frustrations.

Advance material:

Advanced material is provided for those seeking further insights into the subject. Beginners may choose to skip the advanced section at the outset.

Reference links:

Activities	Sheets	Links
Login	Signup/Login page	https://www.shambav.org/artifacts/signup.php
Practice question	With answer sheet	https://www.shambav.org/artifacts/optimum-python-series-4
Exercises, Assignments	With answers	
Quiz	Quiz answers	
Data	Data Sheet	
Supplementary	Advanced material	
Instruction	Setup instruction	
Advance materials	Programs, tricks, assignments, mini projects, issues	
Cheat sheets	Major concepts	

APPENDIX B

Practice Question

Answers to the Practice question

Introduction and Type ML

P1-U1-L1-2 - Practice Question

1. What are the core categories of machine learning discussed in this unit?

The core categories of machine learning discussed are supervised, unsupervised, semi-supervised, and reinforcement learning.

2. Define supervised learning and provide an example.

Supervised learning involves training a model on a labeled dataset, where the algorithm learns from both input data and corresponding output labels. An example is predicting house prices based on features like size, location, and number of bedrooms using historical data.

3. Explain unsupervised learning and give an example.

Unsupervised learning involves training a model on an unlabelled dataset, where the algorithm discovers patterns and relationships within the data. An example is clustering customer segments based on their purchasing behaviour without prior labels.

4. What is semi-supervised learning, and when is it used.

Semi-supervised learning combines elements of both supervised and unsupervised learning by training models on partially labelled data. It is used when labelled data is scarce or expensive to obtain.

5. Describe reinforcement learning and provide a real-world application.

Reinforcement learning involves training an agent to make sequential decisions by interacting with an environment and receiving feedback in the form of rewards. An example is training an AI to play video games by maximising the score through trial and error.

6. What are the main types of learning tasks in machine learning?

The main types of learning tasks include Classification, Regression, Clustering, Dimensionality Reduction, and Association Rule Mining.

7. Give an example of a Classification task.

Classifying emails as spam or non-spam based on their content is an example of a Classification task.

8. Explain Regression and provide a real-world scenario?

Regression involves predicting a continuous output variable based on input features. An example is predicting the price of a house based on its features such as size, location, and number of rooms.

9. What is Clustering, and when is it used?

Clustering involves grouping similar data points together based on their features. It is used for tasks such as customer segmentation, anomaly detection, and image compression.

10. Describe Dimensionality Reduction and its significance?

Dimensionality Reduction involves reducing the number of input variables while preserving the essential information. It helps in visualisation, computational efficiency, and removing redundant features.

11. What is Association Rule Mining, and give an example.

Association Rule Mining involves discovering interesting relationships between variables in large datasets. An example is identifying patterns in customer purchasing behavior to recommend products.

12. Name some traditional machine learning algorithms?

Traditional machine learning algorithms include Decision Trees, Logistic Regression, Support Vector Machines, Naive Bayes, and k-Nearest Neighbors.

13. Mention some advanced machine learning techniques.

Advanced machine learning techniques include Deep Learning, Ensemble Methods (such as Random Forest and Gradient Boosting), Neural Networks, and Reinforcement Learning.

14. Explain the Data Collection and Integration stage of the machine learning pipeline.

Data Collection and Integration involve gathering raw data from various sources and harmonising it into a unified dataset suitable for analysis.

15. What is Feature Identification, and why is it important?

Feature Identification involves identifying relevant attributes or features from the dataset to inform subsequent analysis. It is important, as it determines the input variables used for model training.

16. Describe Exploratory Data Analysis (EDA) and its role in machine learning.

Exploratory Data Analysis involves exploring and summarising the main characteristics of the dataset using statistical methods and visualisation techniques. It helps in understanding the data distribution, identifying patterns, and detecting anomalies.

17. What is Feature Selection, and how does it contribute to model performance?

Feature Selection involves choosing the most relevant features from the dataset while discarding irrelevant or redundant ones. It contributes to model performance by reducing overfitting, improving computational efficiency, and enhancing interpretability.

18. Explain the Model Training phase of the machine learning pipeline.

Model Training involves using labelled data to train machine learning algorithms to recognise patterns and make predictions. It is a crucial step in building predictive models.

19. What is Model Evaluation, and why is it necessary?

Model Evaluation involves assessing the performance of trained models using appropriate evaluation metrics. It is necessary to ensure that the models generalise well to unseen data and perform optimally in real-world scenarios.

20. Define Prediction and its significance in machine learning.

Prediction involves deploying well-trained models to make informed predictions or decisions on new, unseen data. It is significant as it enables businesses and organizations to leverage insights from data for decision-making and problem-solving purposes.

Part 2 – Machine Learning Basics

P2-U2-L1-6 - Practice Question

1. What is the range of the dataset [1,3,5,7,9]?

$9-1 = 8$

2. How is the standard deviation different from variance?

Standard deviation is the square root of the variance and provides a measure of dispersion in the same units as the data.

3. What is the derivative of $f(x)=x^2$?

> $f'(x)=2x$

4. Define conditional probability.

> Conditional probability is the probability of an event occurring given that another event has already occurred, denoted as $P(A|B)$.

5. What does a P-value represent in hypothesis testing?

> The P-value represents the probability of obtaining test results at least as extreme as the results actually observed, under the assumption that the null hypothesis is correct.

6. What is the main difference between parametric and non-parametric tests?

> Parametric tests assume underlying statistical distributions, while non-parametric tests do not.

7. What is a moving average in time series analysis?

> A moving average is a statistical technique used to smooth out short-term fluctuations and highlight longer-term trends in time series data.

8. What is the key characteristic of a normal distribution?

> A normal distribution is symmetric, bell-shaped, and characterized by its mean and standard deviation.

9. Describe the binomial distribution.

> The binomial distribution models the number of successes in a fixed number of independent Bernoulli trials, each with the same probability of success.

10. What is the purpose of Recursive Feature Elimination (RFE)?

RFE aims to select the most significant features by recursively removing the least important features and building models with the remaining ones.

11. What does the binary cross-entropy loss measure?

Binary cross-entropy loss measures the performance of a classification model whose output is a probability value between 0 and 1.

12. What is the difference between probability and non-probability sampling?

Probability sampling involves random selection, allowing each member of the population an equal chance of being selected, while non-probability sampling does not involve random selection.

13. What does the R-squared value indicate in linear regression?

The R-squared value indicates the proportion of the variance in the dependent variable that is predictable from the independent variables.

14. What is a Type I error in hypothesis testing?

A Type I error occurs when the null hypothesis is rejected when it is true (false positive).

15. What is autocorrelation in a time series?

Autocorrelation measures the correlation of a time series with its past values.

16. What is the difference between a stationary and a non-stationary time series?

A stationary time series has constant mean and variance over time, while a non-stationary time series does not.

17. How do you determine if a data set follows a normal distribution?

You can use graphical methods like Q-Q plots, or statistical tests like the Shapiro-Wilk test.

18. What is the purpose of Principal Component Analysis (PCA)?

PCA reduces the dimensionality of the data by transforming it into a set of orthogonal (uncorrelated) components while preserving as much variance as possible.

19. What is stratified sampling?

Stratified sampling involves dividing the population into homogeneous subgroups (strata) and then randomly sampling from each subgroup.

20. What does multicollinearity refer to in regression analysis?

Multicollinearity occurs when independent variables in a regression model are highly correlated, making it difficult to isolate the effect of each variable.

21. What is the purpose of cross-validation in model training?

Cross-validation assesses the model's ability to generalise to new data by partitioning the data into training and validation sets multiple times.

22. How do you interpret an adjusted R-squared value?

Adjusted R-squared accounts for the number of predictors in the model, providing a more accurate measure of model fit, particularly for models with multiple predictors. It adjusts the R-squared value based on the number of predictors and sample size, decreasing if unnecessary predictors are added.

Part 3 - Data Processing

P3-U3-L1-7 - Practice Question

1. What is data processing, and why is it essential in data analysis?

Data processing involves transforming raw data into a usable format for analysis, including cleaning, transformation, integration, and interpretation. It's crucial for extracting meaningful insights from data.

2. How can test datasets be created for binary classification tasks?

Test datasets for binary classification tasks involve generating datasets with features and labels, balancing class distributions, and ensuring data quality.

3. What techniques are used for handling missing values in data cleaning?

Techniques for handling missing values include imputation methods such as mean imputation, median imputation, or using predictive models to estimate missing values.

4. Explain the concept of one-hot encoding and its role in data preprocessing.

One-hot encoding converts categorical variables into binary vectors, where each category becomes a binary feature. It's used to represent categorical data numerically for machine learning algorithms.

5. What is Exploratory Data Analysis (EDA), and why is it important in data analysis?

EDA involves exploring and analyzing data to uncover patterns, trends, and relationships. It's crucial for gaining insights into the data before building models or making decisions.

6. How can outliers be handled in data cleaning?

Outliers can be handled by identifying them using statistical methods and then either removing them or transforming them using techniques such as winsorization or log transformation.

7. What are the common techniques for feature scaling and normalization?

Common techniques for feature scaling and normalization include Min-Max Scaling (Normalization), Mean Normalization, Standardization (Z-score Scaling), Robust Scaling, and Log Transformation.

8. What is the Dummy Variable Trap, and how can it be avoided?

The Dummy Variable Trap occurs when dummy variables are highly correlated with each other. It can be avoided by using one-hot encoding and dropping one of the dummy variables.

9. What is Feature Engineering, and why is it important in machine learning?

Feature Engineering involves creating new features or transforming existing ones to improve model performance. It's essential for selecting relevant features and enhancing the predictive power of machine learning models.

10. What are some resampling techniques used for handling imbalanced datasets?

Resampling techniques for handling imbalanced datasets include Random Under-Sampling, Random Over-Sampling, SMOTE (Synthetic Minority Over-sampling Technique), and NearMiss Algorithm.

11. How does Random Over-Sampling address class imbalance in datasets?

Random Over-Sampling duplicates instances from the minority class to increase its representation in the dataset, balancing the class distribution.

12. What is the goal of Exploratory Data Analysis (EDA)?

The goal of EDA is to gain insights into the data by exploring and visualizing its properties, patterns, and relationships.

13. What are some techniques used in multivariate analysis?

Techniques used in multivariate analysis include correlation matrix plots, factor analysis, and cluster analysis to identify patterns and relationships among multiple variables.

14. Why is it important to change the performance metric when evaluating models on imbalanced datasets?

It's important to change the performance metric because accuracy can be misleading on imbalanced datasets. Metrics like precision, recall, F1 score, and AUROC provide a more nuanced assessment of model performance.

15. How does Feature Scaling improve the performance of machine learning algorithms?

Feature Scaling ensures that features are on a similar scale, which helps optimisation algorithms to converge faster and improve the overall performance of machine learning algorithms.

16. What are some techniques for handling outliers in data cleaning?

Techniques for handling outliers include removing them, transforming them using techniques like winsorization or log transformation, or treating them as special cases in the analysis.

17. How can the Dummy Variable Trap be avoided?

The Dummy Variable Trap can be avoided by dropping one of the dummy variables created during one-hot encoding.

18. What is the purpose of Feature Engineering?

Feature Engineering aims to create new features or transform existing ones to improve the performance of machine learning models by selecting relevant features and enhancing predictive power.

19. How does SMOTE address class imbalance in datasets?

SMOTE generates synthetic instances for the minority class based on feature interpolation, increasing its representation in the dataset and balancing the class distribution.

20. What is the significance of Exploratory Data Analysis (EDA) in data analysis?

> EDA is significant in data analysis as it helps uncover patterns, trends, and relationships within the data, providing insights that inform further analysis and decision-making.

21. Why is it important to handle missing values in data cleaning?

> Handling missing values is important to ensure the quality and reliability of the data used in machine learning and data analysis tasks, preventing biases and inaccuracies in the results.

22. How can imbalanced datasets affect model training and evaluation?

> Imbalanced datasets can lead to biased models that prioritize the majority class, resulting in poor performance in minority class instances and misleading evaluation metrics.

23. What role does Feature Scaling play in machine learning?

> Feature Scaling ensures that features are on a similar scale, preventing attributes with larger magnitudes from dominating the learning process and improving the convergence of optimisation algorithms.

24. What are some common techniques for encoding categorical variables?

> Common techniques for encoding categorical variables include one-hot encoding, label encoding, binary encoding, and frequency encoding.

25. How does Random Under-Sampling address class imbalance in datasets?

> Random Under-Sampling involves randomly removing instances from the majority class to balance the class distribution, ensuring equal representation of both classes in the dataset.

Part 4 – Classification and Regression

P4-U4-L1-4 - Practice Question

1. What are the fundamental techniques covered in this unit?

The fundamental techniques covered in this unit include supervised learning techniques such as linear regression, logistic regression, and unsupervised learning techniques like clustering methods.

2. How do backward elimination and forward selection contribute to refining models?

Backward elimination and forward selection are feature selection techniques that help in selecting the most relevant features for model optimization, thus refining the models.

3. What is polynomial regression, and how does it improve prediction accuracy?

Polynomial regression is an extension of linear regression that allows modeling nonlinear relationships between variables, thus capturing complex data patterns and improving prediction accuracy.

4. Explain the concept of Bayesian regression and its importance in regression analysis.

Bayesian regression involves using Bayes' Theorem to estimate model parameters, providing a probabilistic approach to regression analysis, which enhances our understanding of parameter estimation and uncertainty.

5. How do regularization techniques like Ridge, Lasso, and Elastic Net help in regression modelling?

Regularization techniques mitigate overfitting in regression models by adding penalty terms to the regression coefficients, promoting simpler models and improving generalization performance.

6. What are the common challenges addressed in regression modelling?

Common challenges in regression modelling include overfitting, underfitting, and handling complex data patterns, which can be addressed using techniques like regularization and feature selection.

7. What are the different types of logistic regression discussed in this unit?

The different types of logistic regression discussed include Binary or Binomial logistic regression, Multinomial logistic regression, and Ordinal logistic regression, each suited for specific classification tasks.

8. How do activation functions like sigmoid, relu, and tanh contribute to logistic regression?

Activation functions transform linear outputs into probabilities in logistic regression, enabling classification decisions by mapping inputs to outputs through non-linear functions.

9. What strategies are used for handling multi-class classification tasks in logistic regression?

Strategies such as One-vs-All and One-vs-One are used for handling multi-class classification tasks, enabling the classification of instances into multiple classes.

10. What evaluation metrics are crucial for assessing classification model performance?

Answer: Important evaluation metrics include Accuracy, Precision, Recall, F1 score, and advanced techniques like AUC-ROC curve and Precision-Recall curve.

11. Explain the concept of decision thresholds in classification outcomes.

Decision thresholds determine the trade-off between Precision and Recall in classification outcomes, allowing adjustments based on the application's goals.

12. How do AUC-ROC curve and Precision-Recall curve offer insights into classifier performance?

AUC-ROC curve and Precision-Recall curve provide comprehensive views of classifier performance across various decision thresholds, particularly useful for assessing binary classifiers and imbalanced datasets.

13. What is the significance of Precision-Recall curves in classification scenarios?

Precision-Recall curves visualize the trade-off between Precision and Recall for different decision thresholds, offering valuable insights, especially in scenarios with imbalanced datasets or specific class interests.

14. How does F1 score provide a balanced measure of classifier performance?

F1 score, being the harmonic mean of Precision and Recall, provides a balanced measure of classifier performance by considering both false positives and false negatives.

15. What are the advantages of using Bayesian regression techniques in regression analysis?

Bayesian regression offers a probabilistic approach to regression analysis, providing insights into parameter estimation, uncertainty, and model robustness.

16. Explain the concept of feature selection and its importance in model refinement.

Feature selection techniques like backward elimination and forward selection aid in selecting the most relevant features, thus refining models and optimizing their performance.

17. How do activation functions like relu and tanh enable non-linear mappings in neural network models?

Activation functions like relu and tanh transform inputs into non-linear outputs, enabling neural network models to capture complex relationships between inputs and outputs.

18. What role do regularization techniques play in mitigating overfitting in regression models?

> Regularization techniques like Ridge, Lasso, and Elastic Net add penalty terms to regression coefficients, promoting simpler models and preventing overfitting by reducing the model's complexity.

19. What are the benefits of using polynomial regression over linear regression?

> Polynomial regression allows modelling of nonlinear relationships between variables, capturing complex data patterns and improving prediction accuracy compared to linear regression.

20. How do One-vs-All and One-vs-One strategies help in handling multi-class classification tasks?

> One-vs-All and One-vs-One strategies enable the classification of instances into multiple classes by breaking down the multi-class problem into binary classification sub-problems.

Part 5 - Learning Models

P5-U5-L1-4 - Practice Question

KNN

1. What is the fundamental principle behind the K-Nearest Neighbors (KNN) algorithm?

> KNN relies on the idea that similar instances are likely to have similar target values.

2. Describe the concept of KNN in both classification and regression tasks.

> In classification, KNN assigns the most common class among the k nearest neighbors of a query point. In regression, it predicts the target value by averaging the target values of the k nearest neighbors.

3. Explain the role of distance metrics in KNN?

Distance metrics determine how "closeness" or "similarity" between instances is measured, influencing neighbor selection in KNN. Common distance metrics include Euclidean, Manhattan, and Minkowski distances.

4. What is the Brute Force algorithm in the context of KNN?

The Brute Force algorithm in KNN involves computing distances between the query point and all other points in the dataset, selecting the k nearest neighbors without employing data structures for efficiency.

5. How does the choice of k affect the KNN algorithm's performance?

Smaller values of k may lead to more flexible decision boundaries but are prone to noise, while larger values of k may lead to smoother decision boundaries but could miss local patterns.

6. Can KNN handle datasets with missing values? Explain.?

No, KNN requires complete datasets because it relies on calculating distances between points, which is not possible if there are missing values.

7. What happens when there is a tie vote in the KNN classification algorithm?

In case of a tie, the algorithm may randomly select one of the classes or use a weighted approach based on distance to break the tie.

8. How does KNN handle categorical features in the dataset?

KNN requires converting categorical features into numerical representations, often through techniques like one-hot encoding, before computing distances.

9. Discuss the concept of "curse of dimensionality" in the context of KNN?

The curse of dimensionality refers to the phenomenon where the effectiveness of KNN decreases as the number of dimensions (features) increases, due to the increased sparsity of data points in higher-dimensional spaces.

10. What are some strategies to improve the efficiency of KNN?

> Strategies to improve efficiency include using dimensionality reduction techniques like PCA, employing approximate nearest neighbor algorithms, and implementing data structures like KD-trees or Ball trees.

SVM

11. What distinguishes Support Vector Machines (SVMs) from other classification algorithms?

> SVMs aim to find the optimal hyperplane that best separates classes in the feature space, maximizing the margin between different classes.

12. Explain the concept of a kernel in SVMs.

> A kernel in SVMs allows the algorithm to operate in higher-dimensional spaces by implicitly mapping the input data into a higher-dimensional feature space, where nonlinear relationships can be captured.

13. What are the advantages of using SVMs in classification tasks?

> SVMs are effective in high-dimensional spaces, robust against overfitting in high-dimensional data, and versatile due to the ability to use different kernel functions.

14. How does the choice of kernel affect SVM performance?

> The choice of kernel influences the decision boundary's flexibility and the model's ability to capture nonlinear relationships in the data.

15. What is the role of the regularization parameter (C) in SVMs?

> The regularization parameter (C) balances the trade-off between maximising the margin and minimising the classification error. Higher values of C result in a smaller margin but fewer classification errors, while lower values prioritise maximising the margin.

16. How do SVMs handle multi-class classification problems?

SVMs can handle multi-class classification through techniques like one-vs-one or one-vs-rest, where multiple binary classifiers are trained and combined to make predictions.

17. Discuss the concept of a decision boundary in SVMs.

The decision boundary in SVMs is the hyperplane that separates different classes in the feature space. It is determined by support vectors, which are data points closest to the decision boundary.

18. What are some common kernel functions used in SVMs?

Common kernel functions include linear, polynomial, radial basis function (RBF), and sigmoid kernels, each suitable for capturing different types of data distributions.

19. How does SVM regression differ from SVM classification?

SVM regression aims to predict continuous target variables by finding the hyperplane that best fits the data, while SVM classification focuses on separating classes using a decision boundary.

20. What is the significance of support vectors in SVMs?

Support vectors are data points that lie closest to the decision boundary and play a crucial role in defining the decision boundary and margin in SVMs.

Decision Tree

21. Explain the fundamental principle behind decision trees in machine learning.

Decision trees are hierarchical structures that use a sequence of if-else conditions to make decisions based on features' values, ultimately leading to a predicted outcome.

22. What are the key components of a decision tree?

Key components include root node, decision nodes, leaf nodes, branches (edges), and decision rules associated with each node.

23. How does the Gini index measure impurity in decision trees?

The Gini index measures the probability of misclassifying a randomly chosen element in a dataset, with lower values indicating purer nodes.

24. Discuss the concept of entropy in decision trees.

Entropy is a measure of impurity or disorder in a dataset, with higher entropy values indicating greater disorder.

25. What is the role of information gain in decision tree learning?

Information gain measures the effectiveness of a feature in reducing entropy or impurity in the dataset when used for splitting, helping to determine the best feature for node splitting.

26. Explain the concept of overfitting in decision trees.

Overfitting occurs when a decision tree captures noise or irrelevant patterns in the training data, resulting in poor generalization to unseen data.

27. What are some techniques to prevent overfitting in decision trees?

Techniques include setting maximum tree depth, pruning, using minimum samples per leaf, and cross-validation.

28. Describe the CART algorithm used in decision trees.

CART (Classification and Regression Trees) is an algorithm that creates binary trees by splitting nodes based on the feature that provides the maximum information gain or reduction in impurity.

29. How does cross-validation help in building robust decision tree models?

Cross-validation helps assess the model's performance on different subsets of the data, providing insights into its generalization ability and reducing the risk of overfitting.

30. Discuss the use of GridSearchCV in decision tree hyperparameter tuning?

GridSearchCV systematically searches through a predefined set of hyperparameters, evaluating model performance through cross-validation to identify the best hyperparameters for optimal model performance.

Part 6 – Unsupervised Clustering

P6-U6-L1-8 - Practice Question

1. What is the main objective of clustering in unsupervised learning?

To group similar data points together based on their features.

2. Which method is used to determine the optimal number of clusters in K-Means clustering?

The elbow method.

3. What is Mini-batch K-Means?

An extension of K-Means that uses small, random samples of the data to perform clustering, making it faster and more efficient for large datasets.

4. What are the two main types of hierarchical clustering?

Agglomerative and divisive clustering.

5. What does BIRCH stand for in clustering?

Balanced Iterative Reducing and Clustering using Hierarchies.

6. What is the purpose of Principal Component Analysis (PCA)?

To reduce the dimensionality of data while retaining most of the variance in the dataset.

7. What does Singular Value Decomposition (SVD) do?

It decomposes a matrix into three other matrices, revealing the latent structure of the data

8. What is t-SNE commonly used for?

For visualizing high-dimensional data in a low-dimensional space.

9. How does DBSCAN differ from K-Means?

DBSCAN is a density-based clustering algorithm that can identify clusters of varying shapes and sizes, including outliers, whereas K-Means assumes spherical clusters

10. What is the Silhouette Score used for?

To measure how similar a data point is to its own cluster compared to other clusters, thereby evaluating clustering performance.

11. What does the Adjusted Rand Index (ARI) measure?

The similarity between two different clusterings by considering all pairs of samples and counting pairs that are assigned in the same or different clusters in the predicted and true clusterings.

12. What is the main advantage of OPTICS over DBSCAN?

OPTICS can identify clusters with varying densities without requiring a fixed distance threshold.

13. What is Spectral Clustering based on?

Graph theory and the eigenvalues of similarity matrices.

14. What does a Gaussian Mixture Model (GMM) assume about the data?

> That the data is generated from a mixture of several Gaussian distributions with unknown parameters.

15. What is the key idea behind Mean-shift clustering?

> To shift data points towards the mode (highest density area) iteratively until convergence, allowing the identification of clusters based on density.

Association

P7-U7-L1-5 - Practice Question

1. What is association rule learning?

> Association rule learning is a data mining technique used to identify interesting relationships and patterns within datasets using metrics like support, confidence, and lift

2. What is the Apriori algorithm?

> The Apriori algorithm is a method for finding frequent itemsets in a dataset through an iterative approach that leverages the principle that all subsets of a frequent itemset must also be frequent.

3. Name three types of association rules.

> Multilevel association rules, multidimensional association rules, and quantitative association rules.

4. How does association rule learning differ from clustering?

> Association rule learning focuses on finding relationships between items in a dataset, while clustering groups similar data points based on their attributes.

5. What is the ECLAT algorithm?

The ECLAT algorithm is an alternative to the Apriori algorithm that uses a depth-first search approach and vertical data format to mine frequent itemsets

6. What is a major drawback of the Apriori algorithm?

The Apriori algorithm has high computational intensity and can result in the exponential growth of candidate itemsets.

7. How does the FP-Growth algorithm address the limitations of the Apriori algorithm?

The FP-Growth algorithm uses an FP-tree data structure and a divide-and-conquer approach to efficiently mine frequent itemsets, reducing computational costs.

8. What is matrix factorization?

Matrix factorization is a technique for decomposing a matrix into multiple matrices to uncover latent features, often used in applications like image processing and recommender systems.

9. What is LU decomposition?

LU decomposition is a mathematical method that decomposes a matrix into a lower triangular matrix (L) and an upper triangular matrix (U), useful for solving linear equations and matrix inversion.

10. What are recommender systems?

Recommender systems are algorithms designed to suggest relevant items to users based on their preferences and past behavior.

11. What are the three types of recommender systems covered in this unit?

Collaborative filtering, content-based filtering, and hybrid methods.

12. What is Singular Value Decomposition (SVD) used for in recommender systems?

SVD is used to decompose the user-item interaction matrix to discover latent factors, which helps in making accurate recommendations.

13. What is Non-negative Matrix Factorization (NMF)?

NMF is a matrix factorization technique where the factorized matrices have no negative elements, often used to uncover hidden features in datasets.

14. How does collaborative filtering work in recommender systems?

Collaborative filtering recommends items based on the preferences of similar users or items, leveraging user-item interactions.

15. What is the main advantage of using hybrid recommender systems?

Hybrid recommender systems combine multiple recommendation techniques to improve accuracy and overcome the limitations of individual methods.

Part 8 - Ensemble Models

P8-U8-L1-3 - Practice Question

1. What is the primary goal of ensemble methods in machine learning?

To improve model performance by combining the predictions of multiple models.

2. What does bagging stand for?

Bootstrap Aggregating.

3. Which ensemble method involves training multiple models sequentially, each focusing on correcting the errors of its predecessor?

Boosting

4. Name a popular bagging algorithm?

Random Forest.

5. What is the main difference between bagging and boosting?

Bagging reduces variance by training models on different subsets of data simultaneously, while boosting reduces bias by training models sequentially

6. What does AdaBoost stand for?

Adaptive Boosting

7. In Gradient Boosting, what role does the loss function play?

It guides the optimization process by measuring the error of the model and helping to update the model to reduce this error.

8. What are the key features of XGBoost that enhance its performance?

Regularization, parallel processing, handling missing values, and tree pruning.

9. How does CatBoost handle categorical features?

Using techniques like order and target encoding.

10. What does LightGBM stand for?

Light Gradient Boosting Machine

11. What is Gradient-based One-Side Sampling (GOSS) in LightGBM?

A technique to reduce the number of data points considered for splitting, focusing on those with larger gradients to speed up training.

12. What is the primary use of the LightGBM Ranker?

For ranking tasks, where the goal is to predict the order of items rather than their exact values

13. What is the purpose of stacked generalization (stacking) in ensemble methods?

To improve predictive accuracy by combining the predictions of multiple models using a meta-model.

14. Which metric is commonly used to evaluate the performance of classification models?

Accuracy, precision, recall, F1-score, and AUC-ROC.

15. What is the main advantage of using ensemble methods in machine learning?

They typically yield better performance and more robust models by combining the strengths of multiple algorithms.

APPENDIX C

ASSIGNMENT

Code Snippet

Data Processing

ASSIGNMENT: P3 – A1

Problem Statement: Exploratory Data Analysis of Used Car Dataset

Dataset: Use dataset – Used Cars.

Data Processing

EDA

```
# Step 1: Import libraries
import pandas as pd
import numpy as np
import matplotlib.pyplot as plt
import seaborn as sns

# To ignore warnings
import warnings
warnings.filterwarnings('ignore')

# Step 2: Reading Dataset
path = r'C:\Users\User\mraj4\Documents\Optimum\Py-
lib\scikit\UsedCars\used_cars_data.csv'
data = pd.read_csv(path)

# Analyzing the Data
data.head()  # Display the first few rows
data.tail()  # Display the last few rows
data.info()  # Display information about the dataset

# Check for Duplication
data.nunique()  # Check for unique values in each column

# Missing Values Calculation
data.isnull().sum()  # Count missing values in each column

# Calculate the percentage of missing values in each column
```

```
missing_percentage = (data.isnull().sum() / len(data)) * 100
print(missing_percentage)

# Step 3: Data Reduction
# Remove 'S.No.' column from data
data = data.drop(['S.No.'], axis=1)
data.info()  # Display information about the modified dataset

# Step 4: Feature Engineering
# Step 5: Creating Features
# Introducing a new column, 'Car_Age' to know the age of the car
from datetime import date
data['Car_Age'] = date.today().year - data['Year']
data.head()  # Display the modified dataset

# Let's split the name and introduce new variables 'Brand' and 'Model'
data['Brand'] = data.Name.str.split().str.get(0)
data['Model'] = data.Name.str.split().str[1:].str.join(' ')
data[['Name', 'Brand', 'Model']]  # Display the Name, Brand, and Model columns

# Step 6: Data Cleaning/Wrangling
print(data.Brand.unique())  # Display unique values in the 'Brand' column
print(data.Brand.nunique())  # Display the number of unique values in the 'Brand' column

# Correcting brand names
searchfor = ['ISUZU', 'Mini', 'Land']
data['Brand'] = data['Brand'].replace({"ISUZU": "Isuzu", "Mini": "Mini Cooper", "Land": "Land
Rover"})

# Step 7: EDA Exploratory Data Analysis
# Step 8: Statistics Summary
data.describe().T  # Generate summary statistics for numerical columns
data.describe(include='all').T  # Generate summary statistics for all columns

# Separate Numerical and categorical variables for easy analysis
cat_cols = data.select_dtypes(include=['object']).columns
num_cols = data.select_dtypes(include=np.number).columns.tolist()
print("Categorical Variables:")
print(cat_cols)
print("Numerical Variables:")
print(num_cols)

# Step 9: EDA Univariate Analysis
for col in num_cols:
    print(col)
    print('Skew:', round(data[col].skew(), 2))
    plt.figure(figsize=(15, 4))
    plt.subplot(1, 2, 1)
    data[col].hist(grid=False)
    plt.ylabel('Count')
    plt.subplot(1, 2, 2)
    sns.boxplot(x=data[col])
    plt.show()
```

```
fig, axes = plt.subplots(3, 2, figsize=(18, 18))
fig.suptitle('Bar plot for all categorical variables in the dataset')
for i, ax in enumerate(axes.flatten()):
    if i < len(cat_cols):
        sns.countplot(ax=ax, x=cat_cols[i], data=data, color='blue',
order=data[cat_cols[i]].value_counts().index)
        ax.tick_params(labelrotation=45)
plt.tight_layout()

# Step 10: Data Transformation
# Function for log transformation of the column
def log_transform(data, col):
    for colname in col:
        if (data[colname] == 1.0).all():
            data[colname + '_log'] = np.log(data[colname] + 1)
        else:
            data[colname + '_log'] = np.log(data[colname])
    data.info()
log_transform(data, ['Kilometers_Driven', 'Price'])
# Log transformation of the feature 'Kilometers_Driven'
sns.distplot(data["Kilometers_Driven_log"], axlabel="Kilometers_Driven_log")

# Step 12: EDA Bivariate Analysis
plt.figure(figsize=(13, 17))
sns.pairplot(data=data.drop(['Kilometers_Driven', 'Price'], axis=1))
plt.show()

fig, axarr = plt.subplots(4, 2, figsize=(12, 18))
price_log_mean = data['Price_log'].mean()
for i, (col, ax) in enumerate(zip(['Location', 'Transmission', 'Fuel_Type', 'Owner_Type', 'Brand',
'Model', 'Seats', 'Car_Age'], axarr.flatten())):
    if col not in ['Brand', 'Model']:
        data.groupby(col)['Price_log'].mean().sort_values(ascending=False).plot.bar(ax=ax,
fontsize=12)
        ax.axhline(price_log_mean, color='r', linestyle='--')
        ax.set_title(f"{col} Vs Price", fontsize=18)
        ax.set_xlabel(col)
        ax.set_ylabel('Price_log')
        ax.tick_params(axis='x', rotation=90)
plt.tight_layout()
plt.show()
```

Classification and Regression

ASSIGNMENT: P4– A1

Problem Statement: You are tasked with analyzing the famous Iris dataset to gain insights into the characteristics of different iris flower species. Using both supervised and unsupervised learning techniques, you need to build models to classify iris flowers and identify patterns in the data.

Dataset: **Iris Dataset Analysis**: Use dataset The Iris dataset contains the following variables:

- Sepal length
- Sepal width
- Petal length
- Petal width
- Species (target variable): Setosa, Versicolor, or Virginica

.

Supervised and Unsupervised
Classification

```
# Importing necessary libraries
import pandas as pd
import numpy as np
import seaborn as sns
import matplotlib.pyplot as plt
from sklearn.model_selection import train_test_split
from sklearn.preprocessing import StandardScaler, LabelEncoder
from sklearn.linear_model import LogisticRegression
from sklearn.neighbors import KNeighborsClassifier
from sklearn.cluster import KMeans
from sklearn.metrics import accuracy_score, precision_score, recall_score, f1_score,
confusion_matrix

# Load the Iris dataset
iris_df = sns.load_dataset('iris')

# Exploratory Data Analysis (EDA)
print(iris_df.head())  # Display first few rows of the dataset
print(iris_df.info())  # Summary of the dataset
print(iris_df.describe())  # Statistical summary of numerical variables
print(iris_df['species'].value_counts())  # Frequency distribution of target variable
```

```
# Data Preprocessing
# Handling missing values (if any)
print(iris_df.isnull().sum())

# Encoding categorical variable 'species'
label_encoder = LabelEncoder()
iris_df['species'] = label_encoder.fit_transform(iris_df['species'])

# Splitting the dataset into features (X) and target variable (y)
X = iris_df.drop('species', axis=1)
y = iris_df['species']

# Splitting the dataset into training and testing sets
X_train, X_test, y_train, y_test = train_test_split(X, y, test_size=0.2, random_state=42)

# Scaling numerical features
scaler = StandardScaler()
X_train_scaled = scaler.fit_transform(X_train)
X_test_scaled = scaler.transform(X_test)

# Building Classification Models
# Logistic Regression
log_reg_model = LogisticRegression()
log_reg_model.fit(X_train_scaled, y_train)

# K-Nearest Neighbors
knn_model = KNeighborsClassifier()
knn_model.fit(X_train_scaled, y_train)

# Evaluating Model Performance
# Logistic Regression
log_reg_pred = log_reg_model.predict(X_test_scaled)
print("Logistic Regression - Accuracy:", accuracy_score(y_test, log_reg_pred))
print("Logistic Regression - Precision:", precision_score(y_test, log_reg_pred,
average='weighted'))
print("Logistic Regression - Recall:", recall_score(y_test, log_reg_pred,
average='weighted'))
print("Logistic Regression - F1 Score:", f1_score(y_test, log_reg_pred,
average='weighted'))

# K-Nearest Neighbors
knn_pred = knn_model.predict(X_test_scaled)
print("K-Nearest Neighbors - Accuracy:", accuracy_score(y_test, knn_pred))
print("K-Nearest Neighbors - Precision:", precision_score(y_test, knn_pred,
average='weighted'))
print("K-Nearest Neighbors - Recall:", recall_score(y_test, knn_pred, average='weighted'))
print("K-Nearest Neighbors - F1 Score:", f1_score(y_test, knn_pred, average='weighted'))
```

```
# Implementing K-Means Clustering
kmeans = KMeans(n_clusters=3, random_state=42)
kmeans.fit(X_train_scaled)
clusters = kmeans.predict(X_test_scaled)

# Visualizing Clusters
plt.scatter(X_test_scaled[:, 0], X_test_scaled[:, 1], c=clusters, cmap='viridis')
plt.xlabel('Sepal Length (scaled)')
plt.ylabel('Sepal Width (scaled)')
plt.title('K-Means Clustering')
plt.show()

# Comparing Model Performance
# Further analysis and comparison of logistic regression, K-nearest neighbors, and K-means clustering can be done here.
# Conclusion
# Conclude the analysis and draw insights about iris flowers' characteristics based on the models and clustering results.
```

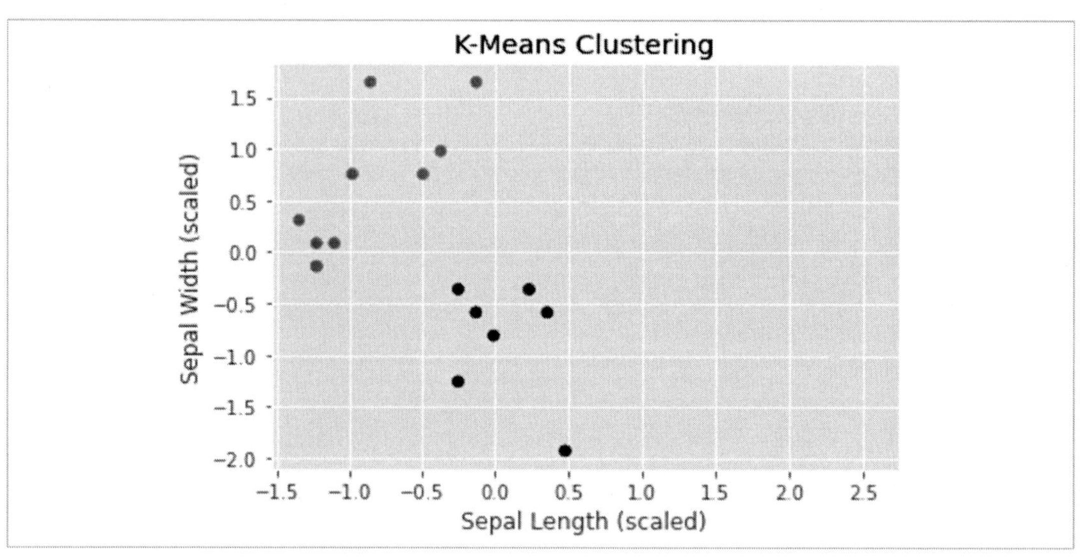

Machine Learning Models

ASSIGNMENT: P5– A1

In this assignment, you will explore and compare the performance of K-Nearest Neighbors (KNN) and Support Vector Machines (SVM) in classifying a dataset. You will evaluate the effectiveness of both algorithms and understand the impact of various parameters on their performance.

Dataset: Use dataset – IRIS

You will use the "Iris" dataset, a famous dataset for classification tasks. It consists of 150 samples of iris flowers, each described by four features: sepal length, sepal width, petal length, and petal width. The dataset contains three classes: Iris-setosa, Iris-versicolor, and Iris-virginica.

Machine Learning Models
KNN and SVM

```
# Importing necessary libraries
import numpy as np
import pandas as pd
import matplotlib.pyplot as plt
from sklearn.datasets import load_iris
from sklearn.model_selection import train_test_split
from sklearn.neighbors import KNeighborsClassifier
from sklearn.svm import SVC
from sklearn.metrics import accuracy_score, precision_score, recall_score, f1_score
from sklearn.model_selection import cross_val_score, GridSearchCV

# Load the Iris dataset
iris = load_iris()
X = iris.data
y = iris.target

# Data Preprocessing
# Visualize the dataset
plt.figure(figsize=(12, 6))
for i in range(4):
    plt.subplot(2, 2, i+1)
    plt.scatter(X[:, i], y, c=y, cmap='viridis', edgecolor='k')
    plt.xlabel(iris.feature_names[i])
    plt.ylabel('Species')
    plt.colorbar(ticks=[0, 1, 2], label='Species')
plt.tight_layout()
plt.show()

# Split the dataset into training and testing sets
```

```
X_train, X_test, y_train, y_test = train_test_split(X, y, test_size=0.2, random_state=42)

# K-Nearest Neighbors (KNN)
# Implement the KNN algorithm
knn = KNeighborsClassifier()

# Tune the value of k using cross-validation
k_range = range(1, 31)
k_scores = []
for k in k_range:
    knn = KNeighborsClassifier(n_neighbors=k)
    scores = cross_val_score(knn, X_train, y_train, cv=5, scoring='accuracy')
    k_scores.append(scores.mean())

# Find the optimal value of k
optimal_k = k_range[np.argmax(k_scores)]
print("Optimal value of k:", optimal_k)

# Evaluate the performance of KNN
knn = KNeighborsClassifier(n_neighbors=optimal_k)
knn.fit(X_train, y_train)
y_pred_knn = knn.predict(X_test)
accuracy_knn = accuracy_score(y_test, y_pred_knn)
precision_knn = precision_score(y_test, y_pred_knn, average='weighted')
recall_knn = recall_score(y_test, y_pred_knn, average='weighted')
f1_score_knn = f1_score(y_test, y_pred_knn, average='weighted')

print("KNN Performance Metrics:")
print("Accuracy:", accuracy_knn)
print("Precision:", precision_knn)
print("Recall:", recall_knn)
print("F1 Score:", f1_score_knn)

# Support Vector Machines (SVM)
# Implement the SVM algorithm
svm = SVC()

# Experiment with different kernel functions
kernel_functions = ['linear', 'poly', 'rbf']
for kernel in kernel_functions:
    svm = SVC(kernel=kernel)
    svm.fit(X_train, y_train)
    y_pred_svm = svm.predict(X_test)
    accuracy_svm = accuracy_score(y_test, y_pred_svm)
    precision_svm = precision_score(y_test, y_pred_svm, average='weighted')
    recall_svm = recall_score(y_test, y_pred_svm, average='weighted')
    f1_score_svm = f1_score(y_test, y_pred_svm, average='weighted')
    print(f"\nSVM Performance Metrics (Kernel: {kernel}):")
```

```
    print("Accuracy:", accuracy_svm)
    print("Precision:", precision_svm)
    print("Recall:", recall_svm)
    print("F1 Score:", f1_score_svm)

# Tune the hyperparameters (C, gamma) using GridSearchCV
param_grid = {'C': [0.1, 1, 10, 100], 'gamma': [1, 0.1, 0.01, 0.001], 'kernel': ['rbf']}
grid = GridSearchCV(SVC(), param_grid, refit=True, verbose=2)
grid.fit(X_train, y_train)

# Evaluate the performance of SVM
best_svm = grid.best_estimator_
y_pred_svm_grid = best_svm.predict(X_test)
accuracy_svm_grid = accuracy_score(y_test, y_pred_svm_grid)
precision_svm_grid = precision_score(y_test, y_pred_svm_grid, average='weighted')
recall_svm_grid = recall_score(y_test, y_pred_svm_grid, average='weighted')
f1_score_svm_grid = f1_score(y_test, y_pred_svm_grid, average='weighted')

print("\nBest SVM Performance Metrics:")
print("Accuracy:", accuracy_svm_grid)
print("Precision:", precision_svm_grid)
print("Recall:", recall_svm_grid)
print("F1 Score:", f1_score_svm_grid)

# Comparison and Analysis
# Compare the performance of KNN and SVM
print("\nComparison:")
print("KNN Accuracy:", accuracy_knn)
print("SVM Accuracy (GridSearchCV):", accuracy_svm_grid)
```

Best SVM Performance Metrics: Accuracy: 1.0 Precision: 1.0 Recall: 1.0 F1 Score: 1.0 **Comparison:** KNN Accuracy: 1.0 SVM Accuracy (GridSearchCV): 1.0	**Optimal value of k: 3** KNN Performance Metrics: Accuracy: 1.0 Precision: 1.0 Recall: 1.0 F1 Score: 1.0

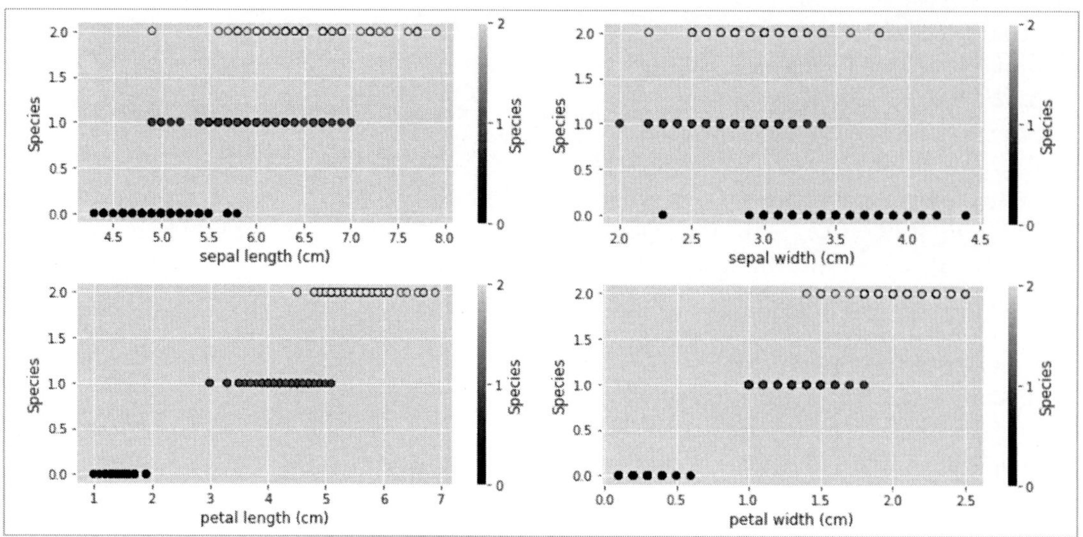
Species
sepal length (cm)
sepal width (cm)
petal length (cm)
petal width (cm)

APPENDIX D

QUIZ

Part 1 – Introduction and Type ML

1. What are the core categories of machine learning?
A. Supervised, Unsupervised, Semi-Supervised, Reinforcement B. Descriptive, Predictive, Prescriptive, Diagnostic C. Linear, Non-linear, Logistic, Ridge D. None of the above

2. Which type of learning involves training a model on labelled data?
A. Unsupervised learning B. Semi-supervised learning C. Supervised learning D. Reinforcement learning

3. What is the main goal of unsupervised learning?
A. Predicting a continuous output variable B. Discovering patterns and relationships in unlabelled data C. Maximising rewards through trial and error D. Classifying data into predefined categories

4. Semi-supervised learning is used when:
A. Labelled data is abundant B. Unlabelled data is abundant C. Both labelled and unlabelled data are scarce **D.** None of the above

5. Which learning approach involves training an agent to make sequential decisions based on rewards?
A. Supervised learning B. Unsupervised learning C. Semi-supervised learning D. Reinforcement learning

6. Which task involves predicting a categorical outcome?
A. Regression B. Clustering C. Classification D. Association Rule Mining

7. Regression is used for:
A. Predicting a continuous output variable B. Grouping similar data points together C. Discovering patterns in unlabelled data D. None of the above

8. What is the primary objective of Clustering?
A. Predicting future outcomes B. Reducing the number of input variables C. Grouping similar data points together D. Identifying association rules

9. Dimensionality Reduction helps in:
A. Increasing computational complexity B. Visualisation and computational efficiency C. Adding redundant features to the dataset D. None of the above

10. Association Rule Mining involves:

A. Grouping similar data points together
B. Predicting a continuous output variable
C. Discovering interesting relationships between variables
D. Classifying data into predefined categories

11. Traditional machine learning algorithms include:

A. Deep Learning, Neural Networks
B. Decision Trees, Logistic Regression
C. Gradient Boosting, Random Forest
D. All of the above

12. Advanced machine learning techniques encompass:

A. Linear Regression, Naive Bayes
B. Deep Learning, Ensemble Methods
C. K-Means Clustering, PCA
D. None of the above

13. What is the initial stage of the machine learning pipeline?

A. Model Evaluation
B. Feature Engineering
C. Data Collection and Integration
D. Model Training

14. Feature Selection contributes to model performance by:

E. Increasing overfitting
F. Reducing computational efficiency
G. Enhancing interpretability and reducing overfitting
H. None of the above

15. Model Evaluation is necessary to:
A. Ensure models generalize well to unseen data B. Overfit the training data C. Speed up the training process D. None of the above

Part 3 - Data Pre-Processing

1. What is the primary goal of data processing in the context of data analysis?
E. Generating random datasets F. Transforming raw data into a usable format G. Deleting all missing values H. Ignoring outliers

2. Which of the following is NOT a step involved in data processing?
A. Data cleaning B. Data transformation C. Data visualization D. Data interpretation

3. How can test datasets be created for binary classification tasks?
A. By excluding class labels B. By ignoring feature engineering C. By balancing class distributions D. By omitting data cleaning

4. What technique is commonly used for handling missing values in data cleaning?
A. Deleting rows with missing values B. Ignoring missing values C. Imputing missing values D. Adding random values

5. Which of the following is a technique used for handling outliers?
A. Ignoring outliers B. Transforming outliers into missing values C. Identifying and removing outliers D. Only using outliers for analysis

6. What is the purpose of Feature Engineering?
A. Removing features from the dataset B. Transforming features to improve model performance C. Adding irrelevant features to the dataset D. Only selecting features with high correlation

7. How does Random Over-Sampling address class imbalance in datasets?
A. By removing instances from the majority class B. By duplicating instances from the minority class C. By converting categorical variables into numerical values D. By performing feature scaling on the dataset

8. What is the main goal of Exploratory Data Analysis (EDA)?
A. Building predictive models B. Understanding the data C. Deleting outliers D. Ignoring missing values

9. Which technique can be used for Feature Scaling and normalization?

A. Deleting features
B. Imputing missing values
C. Standardization (Z-score Scaling)
D. Removing outliers

10. What is the purpose of SMOTE in handling imbalanced datasets?

A. Removing outliers
B. Generating synthetic instances for the minority class
C. Balancing class distributions
D. Deleting features

11. What is the significance of changing the performance metric when evaluating models on imbalanced datasets?

A. To increase computation time
B. To decrease model accuracy
C. To address limitations of accuracy
D. To ignore minority class

12. Which technique is used to handle the Dummy Variable Trap?

E. Label Encoding
F. One-Hot Encoding
G. Binary Encoding
H. Dropping one of the dummy variables

13. What is the primary objective of Random Under-Sampling?

A. Balancing class distributions
B. Increasing class imbalance
C. Removing instances from the minority class
D. Generating synthetic instances for the minority class

14. What is the role of Feature Scaling in machine learning?
A. To ignore features with low variance B. To ensure features are on a similar scale C. To increase model complexity D. To decrease model accuracy

15. Which technique is used to transform categorical variables into numerical representations?
A. Standardization B. Min-Max Scaling C. One-Hot Encoding D. Mean Normalization

16. What is the primary goal of data cleaning?
A. Adding noise to the data B. Transforming features C. Ensuring data quality and consistency D. Removing all features

17. How can outliers be handled in data cleaning?
A. By converting them into missing values B. By increasing their impact on the analysis C. By ignoring them completely D. By identifying and removing them

18. What technique can be used to balance class distributions in imbalanced datasets?
A. One-Hot Encoding B. Feature Scaling C. Random Over-Sampling D. Data Cleaning

19. What is the primary objective of EDA?

A. Building predictive models
B. Understanding the data
C. Deleting missing values
D. Removing outliers

20. What is the purpose of Feature Transformation?

A. To remove features with low variance
B. To ensure features are on a different scale
C. To convert features into a different representation
D. To increase model accuracy

21. Which technique is used to impute missing values?

A. Deleting rows with missing values
B. Ignoring missing values
C. Filling missing values with statistical measures
D. Increasing the number of missing values

22. How does SMOTE address class imbalance in datasets?

A. By removing instances from the majority class
B. By generating synthetic instances for the minority class
C. By ignoring class distributions
D. By performing feature selection

23. What is the primary purpose of Feature Engineering?

A. To increase computation time
B. To remove features with low variance
C. To transform and select relevant features
D. To decrease model accuracy

24. What technique is used to handle the Dummy Variable Trap?
A. Label Encoding B. One-Hot Encoding C. Binary Encoding D. Dropping one of the dummy variables

25. What is the significance of changing the performance metric when evaluating models on imbalanced datasets?
E. To increase computation time F. To address limitations of accuracy G. To decrease model accuracy H. To ignore minority class

Part 4 – Classification and Regression

1. Which type of regression allows modelling of nonlinear relationships between variables?
A. Linear Regression B. Polynomial Regression C. Logistic Regression D. Bayesian Regression

2. What technique is used for selecting the most relevant features in model refinement?
A. Regularization B. Backward Elimination C. Gradient Descent D. Cross-Validation

3. Which activation function transforms linear outputs into probabilities in logistic regression?

    A. Sigmoid
    B. ReLU
    C. Tanh
    D. Softmax

4. What technique is used to mitigate overfitting in regression models by adding penalty terms to regression coefficients?

    A. Feature Selection
    B. Dimensionality Reduction
    C. Regularization
    D. Clustering

5. Which type of logistic regression is suitable for multi-class classification tasks?

    A. Binary Logistic Regression
    B. Multinomial Logistic Regression
    C. Ordinal Logistic Regression
    D. Bayesian Logistic Regression

6. What metric provides a balanced measure of a classifier's performance by considering both Precision and Recall?

    A. Accuracy
    B. F1 Score
    C. AUC-ROC Curve
    D. Specificity

7. Which curve provides insights into the trade-off between Precision and Recall for different decision thresholds?
A. Precision-Recall Curve B. ROC Curve C. Cumulative Gain Curve D. Lift Curve

8. What is the primary purpose of Bayesian regression in regression analysis?
A. To estimate model parameters B. To select relevant features C. To handle non-linear relationships D. To visualize data patterns

9. Which technique involves breaking down a multi-class classification problem into multiple binary classification sub-problems?
A. One-vs-All B. One-vs-One C. All-vs-One D. All-vs-All

10. What is the range of values for the linear activation function?
E. (0, 1) F. $(-\infty, \infty)$ G. (-1, 1) H. [0, 1]

11. What technique helps in selecting the most relevant features and optimizing model performance?

A. Dimensionality Reduction
B. Regularization
C. Feature Scaling
D. Backward Elimination

12. Which type of logistic regression is used when the target variable is ordinal?

A. Binary Logistic Regression
B. Multinomial Logistic Regression
C. Ordinal Logistic Regression
D. Bayesian Logistic Regression

13. What metric measures the fraction of labels that are incorrectly predicted?

A. Accuracy
B. Precision
C. Sensitivity
D. Hamming Loss

14. Which regularization technique adds both L1 and L2 penalties to the regression coefficients?

A. Ridge Regression
B. Lasso Regression
C. Elastic Net
D. Logistic Regression

15. Which function is pivotal in transforming linear outputs into probabilities in logistic regression?

A. Tanh
B. ReLU
C. Sigmoid
D. Softmax

16. What is the primary objective of using regularization techniques in regression modelling?
A. To increase overfitting B. To decrease model complexity C. To introduce noise in the data D. To improve model performance

17. Which curve provides a comprehensive view of a classifier's performance across various decision thresholds?
A. ROC Curve B. Precision-Recall Curve C. Cumulative Gain Curve D. Lift Curve

18. What metric adjusts the importance of Precision and Recall based on specific requirements?
A. F1 Score B. Accuracy C. AUC-ROC D. F-beta Score

19. What technique is used to handle multi-class classification tasks by comparing each class with every other class?
A. One-vs-All B. One-vs-One C. All-vs-One D. All-vs-All

20. Which function divides each output such that the total sum of the outputs is equal to 1?

    A. Sigmoid
    B. Tanh
    C. ReLU
    D. Softmax

Part 5 – Machine Learning Models

1. What is the primary principle behind KNN?

    A. Finding the mean of all data points
    B. Finding the nearest neighbors to a given point
    C. Using a decision tree structure
    D. Using a probabilistic approach

2. Which distance metric is most commonly used in KNN?

    A. Manhattan distance
    B. Cosine similarity
    C. Euclidean distance
    D. Hamming distance

3. How does KNN classify a new data point?

    A. By calculating the mean value of the target variable
    B. By finding the majority class among the nearest neighbors
    C. By building a decision tree
    D. By using a probabilistic model

4. What is the "k" in KNN?
A. The number of classes B. The number of features C. The number of nearest neighbors considered D. The number of iterations

5. Which technique can be used to handle large datasets efficiently in KNN?
A. Linear Regression B. Decision Trees C. KD-Trees D. PCA

6. What is the main goal of an SVM classifier?
A. To maximize the distance between data points B. To find the hyperplane that best separates classes C. To create a decision tree D. To reduce the dimensionality of data

7. What does the kernel function in SVM do?
A. It normalizes the data B. It transforms data into higher dimensions C. It reduces overfitting D. It prunes the decision tree

8. Which of the following is not a common SVM kernel?
A. Linear B. Polynomial C. Radial Basis Function (RBF) D. Gaussian Naive Bayes

9. What does the regularization parameter (C) in SVM control?

E. The number of features
F. The margin width
G. The learning rate
H. The depth of the tree

10. How can SVM handle multi-class classification problems?

A. By using multiple binary classifiers
B. By averaging all classes
C. By combining KNN and SVM
D. By using a single classifier for all classes

11. What is the Gini index used for in decision trees?

A. To measure the accuracy of the model
B. To measure the impurity of a node
C. To reduce the dimensionality of data
D. To handle missing values

12. What does a leaf node in a decision tree represent?

A. A decision points
B. A branch in the tree
C. A class label or a predicted value
D. A root node

13. Which algorithm is commonly used for constructing decision trees?

A. KNN
B. CART
C. SVM
D. Naive Bayes

14. What is overfitting in the context of decision trees?
A. When the tree is too simple B. When the tree is too complex and captures noise in the data C. When the tree does not capture the data well D. When the tree has too few nodes

15. Which method is not used for cross-validation in decision trees?
A. K-Fold Cross-Validation B. Holdout Method C. Bootstrap Aggregation D. Random Search

16. What is the key assumption behind Naive Bayes?
A. All features are independent of each other B. All features are dependent on each other C. Features have a linear relationship D. Features follow a normal distribution

17. What type of data is Gaussian Naive Bayes best suited for?
A. Categorical data B. Binary data C. Continuous data D. Text data

18. Which variant of Naive Bayes is commonly used for text classification?
E. Gaussian Naive Bayes F. Multinomial Naive Bayes G. Bernoulli Naive Bayes H. Decision Tree Naive Bayes

19. What does the prior probability represent in Naive Bayes?

A. The probability of the data given the class
B. The initial probability of each class
C. The conditional probability of the features
D. The likelihood of the data

20. How does Naive Bayes handle missing values?

A. By removing the instances with missing values
B. By ignoring the missing values during probability computation
C. By filling in missing values with mean
D. By using a different model for missing values

21. Which algorithm is known for its simplicity and efficiency, especially in high-dimensional spaces?

A. KNN
B. SVM
C. Decision Trees
D. Naive Bayes

22. Which algorithm is particularly effective in finding the optimal hyperplane for classification tasks?

A. KNN
B. SVM
C. Decision Trees
D. Naive Bayes

23. Which technique helps mitigate overfitting in decision trees?

E. Increasing tree depth
F. Pruning
G. Adding more features
H. Reducing the number of training samples

24. What is the primary use of the Brute Force algorithm in KNN

A. To efficiently find the nearest neighbors
B. To simplify the decision boundary
C. To reduce dimensionality
D. To handle missing values

25. What is one advantage of using GridSearchCV in model tuning?

A. It automatically handles missing values
B. It systematically searches for the best hyperparameters
C. It simplifies the model
D. It reduces the dataset size

APPENDIX E

PROJECTS

Project One

EDA and Feature Engineering with Visualization

Introduction

The Zomato dataset provides a comprehensive look at the restaurant landscape in Bengaluru City. With over 50,000 entries and 17 attributes, it serves as an excellent source for performing Exploratory Data Analysis (EDA) and feature engineering, aimed at uncovering patterns, trends, and insights within the data. This project will leverage visualizations to enhance the understanding of the data and derive meaningful conclusions.

Dataset Description

The dataset, sourced from Kaggle, includes detailed information about restaurants registered on the Zomato platform in Bengaluru. The key attributes are:

- Online Delivery: Indicates whether a restaurant offers online delivery services.
- Table Booking: Specifies if a restaurant provides the option for table reservations.
- Table Booking Rate vs Rate: Explores the correlation between table booking availability and overall restaurant ratings.
- Best Location: Highlights are the most favourable locations based on various factors.
- Relation between Location and Rating: Investigate the relationship between restaurant locations and their ratings.
- Restaurant Type: Categorises restaurants based on their types.
- Gaussian Restaurant Type and Rating: Examines the distribution of restaurant types and their ratings.

- Types of Services: Identifies the various services offered by restaurants.
- Relation between Type and Rating: Analyses the correlation between restaurant types and their ratings.
- Cost of Restaurant: Provides insights into the cost associated with dining at different restaurants.
- Number of Restaurants in a Location: Quantifies the concentration of restaurants in specific locations.
- Restaurant Type: Further details on the types of restaurants available.
- Most Famous Restaurant Chains in Bengaluru: Spotlights renowned restaurant chains contributing to the city's culinary landscape.

Objectives

- Data Cleaning and Preparation: Ensure the dataset is clean and ready for analysis, handling missing values, and correcting any inconsistencies.
- Exploratory Data Analysis (EDA): Perform an in-depth analysis to uncover trends and patterns within the data.
- Feature Engineering: Create new features that can help in deriving more insights and improving the analysis.
- Visualization: Use visualizations to effectively communicate findings and insights from the data.

Methodology

Data Cleaning:

- Identify and handle missing values.
- Standardize data formats for consistency.
- Remove or correct any anomalies.

Exploratory Data Analysis (EDA):

- Descriptive Statistics: Summarise the basic features of the dataset.
- Correlation Analysis: Identify relationships between different attributes.

- Distribution Analysis: Explore the distribution of key attributes, such as ratings, cost, and services.

Feature Engineering:

- New Features: Create new features based on existing data to provide more insights (e.g., average cost per location, delivery popularity score).
- Interaction Features: Develop features that capture interactions between different attributes (e.g., interaction between type of service and rating).

Visualization:

- Bar Charts and Histograms: Display the distribution of categorical and numerical data.
- Heatmaps: Visualize correlation matrices to identify relationships between variables.
- Scatter Plots: Analyse relationships between numerical attributes.
- Geographical Plots: Map restaurant locations to visualize the spatial distribution.

Expected Outcomes

- Comprehensive Insights: Detailed understanding of the restaurant landscape in Bengaluru, including trends and patterns related to services, ratings, and locations.
- Enhanced Features: Development of new features that provide deeper insights and can be used for further analysis or predictive modelling.
- Visual Storytelling: Effective visualizations that communicate the findings clearly and concisely, making the data more accessible and understandable.

Conclusion

This project aims to leverage the rich dataset provided by Zomato to gain valuable insights into the restaurant industry in Bengaluru. Through meticulous EDA, thoughtful feature engineering, and impactful visualizations, we will uncover trends and patterns that can inform decision-making and enhance the overall culinary experience in the city.

Project Two

Customer Churn Prediction and Analysis

Introduction

The Kaggle dataset "Customer Churn" provides a comprehensive look into the factors influencing customer churn within a financial institution. The dataset consists of 1,000 rows and 14 attributes, offering a robust foundation for identifying and visualizing the factors contributing to customer churn. Our primary objectives are to build predictive models to classify whether a customer is likely to churn and to select a model that assigns a probability to churn. This approach will enable targeted preventive measures by customer service to retain at-risk customers.

Dataset Description

The dataset comprises detailed customer information, including demographic, account, and transactional attributes.

Objectives

Data Review and Preparation:

- Understand the input space of the dataset.
- Prepare the dataset for exploratory and predictive tasks.

Exploratory Data Analysis (EDA): Identify relationships between attributes and customer churn.

Feature Engineering: Develop new features that might influence the probability of churn.

Model Fitting and Selection: Build and evaluate different models to classify and predict customer churn probability.

Data Review & Preparation

In this section, we will explore the structure of the dataset to:

- Gain an understanding of the input space.
- Determine essential attributes and necessary data manipulations before conducting EDA and predictive modeling.

Key questions to address during this phase:

- The dataset appears to be a snapshot at a specific point in time. Understanding the significance of the snapshot date and exploring the possibility of obtaining balances over time.
- Some customers who have exited still maintain a balance. Investigate whether these customers have exited a specific product rather than the bank itself.
- Clarify the definition of an "active member" and explore the degree of activity by providing transaction counts for both credits and debits.
- Analyze the breakdown of products purchased by each customer for deeper insights.

Exploratory Data Analysis (EDA)

The primary focus here is to understand how the given attributes relate to the 'Exited' status:

- Approximately 20% of customers have churned, setting a baseline for prediction.

Notable observations include:

- The majority of customers are from France, but regions with fewer clients have higher churn rates.
- Female customers exhibit a higher churn rate compared to male customers.
- Most churned customers possess credit cards, warranting further investigation.
- Inactive members show higher churn rates, indicating that increasing activity could reduce churn.
- No significant difference in credit score distribution between retained and churned customers.
- Older customers are more likely to churn, suggesting different service preferences across age groups.
- Customers with extreme tenures (short or long) are more likely to churn.
- The bank is losing customers with significant bank balances, potentially impacting loan capital.

Feature Engineering

Our goal is to introduce features likely to influence the probability of churning. Initial observations suggest that the ratio of bank balance to estimated salary correlates with increased churn, impacting the bank's loan capital. We will split the dataset into train and test sets and develop additional features as needed.

Data Preparation for Model Fitting

Model Fitting and Selection

We will experiment with various modelling approaches to identify the best-performing model:

- Logistic Regression: In the primal space and with multiple kernels.
- Support Vector Machines (SVM): In the primal space and with different kernels.
- Ensemble Models: Combining multiple models to improve predictive performance.

Expected Outcomes

- Comprehensive Insights: A detailed understanding of the factors contributing to customer churn.
- Accurate Prediction Models: Models that can classify and predict customer churn probability.
- Targeted Preventive Measures: Insights that enable customer service to implement targeted strategies to retain at-risk customers.
- Effective Visualizations: Visual representations of the findings to facilitate better understanding and communication.

Conclusion

This project aims to leverage the Kaggle "Customer Churn" dataset to identify and visualize factors contributing to customer churn. Through rigorous EDA, thoughtful feature engineering, and effective modelling, we seek to develop predictive models that enable the financial institution to retain at-risk customers and enhance overall customer satisfaction.

APPENDIX F

Machine Learning Cheat Sheet

A Quick Overview

PART ONE: Fundamentals of Machine Learning

- Learning Types: Supervised, Unsupervised, Reinforcement
- Key Terms: Features, Labels, Training/Testing Data, Metrics
- Tasks: Classification, Regression, Clustering, Dimensionality Reduction
- Pipeline Stages: Data Collection → EDA → Feature Engineering → Training → Evaluation → Deployment

PART TWO: Mathematical Foundations

- Linear Algebra: Vectors, Matrices, Matrix Operations
- Statistics: Mean, Median, Variance, Standard Deviation
- Calculus: Derivatives & Integrals in Optimization
- Probability: Bayes' Theorem, Hypothesis Testing, Distributions (Normal, Binomial, Poisson)
- Regression & Sampling: Linear Regression, R^2, Cross-Validation, Sampling Types

PART THREE: Data Processing & EDA

- Data Types/Quality: Handling Categorical Data, Missing Values, Outliers
- EDA: Univariate, Bivariate, Multivariate Analysis
- Feature Engineering: Encoding, Scaling (Normalization/Standardization)
- Imbalanced Data: SMOTE, NearMiss, Undersampling, Oversampling

- Model Metrics: Choose appropriate metrics for imbalance

PART FOUR: Core Algorithms & Evaluation

- Regression: OLS, Bayesian, Regularization
- Logistic Regression: Sigmoid, ReLU, Softmax, Multiclass & Multilabel
- Metrics: Confusion Matrix, Precision, Recall, F1, ROC-AUC, PR Curve

PART FIVE: Classical Algorithms

- KNN: Distance-based, Lazy Learner
- SVM: Kernel Trick, Margin Maximization
- Decision Trees: Splitting, Pruning, Overfitting Mitigation
- Naive Bayes: Probabilistic Classifier, Bayes' Rule, Variants

PART SIX: Unsupervised Learning

- Clustering: K-Means, Hierarchical (Agglomerative, BIRCH), DBSCAN, OPTICS
- Dimensionality Reduction: PCA, SVD, t-SNE, Incremental PCA
- Evaluation Metrics: Silhouette Score, ARI

PART SEVEN: Data Mining & Recommendations

- Association Rules: Apriori, ECLAT, FP-Growth
- Key Metrics: Support, Confidence, Lift
- Recommender Systems: Collaborative, Content-Based, Hybrid
- Matrix Factorization: SVD, NMF

PART EIGHT: Ensemble Learning

- Bagging: Random Forests – reduce variance
- Boosting: AdaBoost, Gradient Boosting, XGBoost, CatBoost, LightGBM – reduce bias
- Stacking: Combine different models to improve performance
- Evaluation & Sampling: Advanced metrics, ensemble-level validation

TESTIMONIALS

Optimum – Python – Ultimate Guide for Beginners – Series 1

“Optimum - Python Series I” provides readers with a roadmap to Python mastery, thanks to Shree Shambav's expertise and guidance. The book's structured learning path, clear explanations, and practical examples make it easy to grasp even the most complex concepts. Whether you're a beginner looking to learn the basics or an experienced coder seeking to expand your skill set, this book has something for everyone. I highly recommend it to anyone interested in Python programming!

Optimum – Exploring Data Structures and Algorithms – Series II

As a Python programmer looking to deepen one’s understanding of data structures and algorithms, I can confidently say that Optimum – Exploring Data Structures and Algorithms – Series II is one of the best resources I’ve come across. Whether you’re just starting or you’re already experienced with Python, this book is an indispensable guide for anyone who wants to master both the fundamentals and the more advanced aspects of programming.

ACKNOWLEDGEMENTS

To my grandfathers, grandmothers, mothers, fathers, aunts, uncles, neighbours, sisters, brothers, friends, and teachers, they poured in endless moral stories, retellings of Ramayana, Mahabharata, Puranas, Upanishads, and so on.

My teachers, neighbours, and kindred souls. Who provided us with a stage to perform wonderful Puranic stories and were gracious enough to acknowledge our efforts.

The artists and translators of epics have served as a source of inspiration, invigorating our spirits, making these works accessible, and enabling us to grasp the profound depths and deeper dimensions they contain.

I also cherish the stimulating conversations; I had with my wonderful mothers, Punitha Muniswamy and Uma Devi.

Our family's youngest member, Aadhya, who always overwhelmed me with questions, inspired this book.

I would likewise prefer to express gratitude to Mr Sivakumar, Mrs Roopa Sivakumar, Mr Akshaya Rajesh, Ms Akshatha Rajesh, Ms Apeksha Prabhu, Mr Akanksh Prabhu, Mr Nikash Sarasambi, Mrs Spoorthi Nikash for their valuable inputs.

I must thank Mr Rajesh, Mr Savan Prabhu, Mrs Revathi Rajesh, Mrs Rajani Sarasambi, and Mrs Manju Reshma, who encouraged me and often suggested writing a book. Their unwavering belief that I had something valuable to offer kept me going during my writing sessions.

Love you all,

Shree Shambav

www.shambav.org

shreeshambav@gmail.com

BOOKS BY – AUTHOR

Optimum - Python Series I: Ultimate Guide for Beginners

"Optimum - Python Series I" is the perfect starting point for anyone eager to learn Python. This book offers a step-by-step approach to mastering the language, making even the most complex concepts easy to understand. Through clear explanations, practical examples, and real-world projects, Shambav helps readers build a solid foundation in Python programming.

Designed for both beginners and aspiring professionals, the guide covers Python's versatile applications across industries, enhancing problem-solving skills through coding challenges. With supplementary online resources, learners gain hands-on experience and a deeper understanding of Python's real-world impact.

Whether you're looking to develop software applications, analyze data, or improve logical thinking, Optimum equips you with the essential tools to succeed. Shambav's passion for making Python accessible and empowering shines through every chapter, helping readers unlock Python's full potential.

Embark on your coding adventure with Optimum and take your first step toward Python mastery!

OPTIMUM Python Series II - Exploring Data Structures and Algorithms

Take a deep dive into the world of data structures and algorithms with OPTIMUM Python Series II, a comprehensive guide designed to enhance your problem-solving skills through Python. Whether you're a beginner or an experienced coder, this book provides step-by-step explanations, real-world examples, and hands-on exercises to reinforce your understanding.

The book covers a wide range of topics, from fundamental concepts like stacks, queues, and hash tables to advanced techniques such as graph-based structures, dynamic programming, and multiprocessing in Python. You'll explore searching and sorting algorithms, complexity analysis, tree structures, greedy algorithms, and even practical applications like task scheduling and multithreading.

Designed as a complete learning experience, OPTIMUM Python Series II equips you with the knowledge and tools needed to tackle complex coding challenges with confidence. Whether you're preparing for technical interviews or looking to sharpen your skills, this book is your essential companion on the path to Python mastery.

## TWENTY ONE

Optimum – Python Power – Series III - Unleashing the Potential of Data Science with Libraries

Optimum – Python Power Series III is your essential guide to mastering the most powerful Python libraries that are shaping the future of data science. Whether you're just starting out or refining your skills, this book offers a clear, practical path through the core tools of the trade—NumPy, Pandas, Matplotlib, Seaborn, SciPy, and Scikit-learn.

Begin with foundational data science principles using the Python Standard Library, then dive into numerical computing, data manipulation, visualization, scientific analysis, and machine learning. Each chapter is crafted to not only teach the technical how-to but also develop critical thinking and real-world problem-solving.

Perfect for analysts, developers, and aspiring data scientists, Optimum – Python Power Series III transforms complex concepts into digestible, actionable knowledge. Empower yourself with the skills to analyze, interpret, and visualize data with confidence—and take your data science journey to the next level with the unmatched versatility of Python.

9 789334 300697

Printed at Repro India Ltd.